TAKING↻SIDES

Clashing Views on Controversial

Issues in American History, Volume I, The Colonial Period to Reconstruction

NINTH EDITION

TAKING SIDES

Clashing Views on Controversial

Issues in American History, Volume I, The Colonial Period to Reconstruction

NINTH EDITION

Selected, Edited, and with Introductions by

Larry Madaras
Howard Community College

and

James M. SoRelle
Baylor University

McGraw-Hill/Dushkin
A Division of The McGraw-Hill Companies

To Maggie and Cindy

Photo Acknowledgment
Cover image: © 2001 by PhotoDisc, Inc.

Cover Art Acknowledgment
Charles Vitelli

Manufactured in the United States of America

Ninth Edition

3456789BAHBAH4321

Library of Congress Cataloging-in-Publication Data
Main entry under title:
Taking sides: clashing views on controversial issues in American history, volume i, the colonial period to reconstruction/selected, edited, and with introductions by Larry Madaras and James M. SoRelle.—9th ed.
Includes bibliographical references and index.
1. United States—History. I. Madaras, Larry, comp. II. SoRelle, James M., comp.
973
0-07-243095-8
ISSN: 1091-8833

Printed on Recycled Paper

Preface

T he success of the past eight editions of *Taking Sides: Clashing Views on Controversial Issues in American History* has encouraged us to remain faithful to its original objectives, methods, and format. Our aim has been to create an effective instrument to enhance classroom learning and to foster critical thinking. Historical facts presented in a vacuum are of little value to the educational process. For students, whose search for historical truth often concentrates on *when* something happened rather than on *why*, and on specific events rather than on the *significance* of those events, *Taking Sides* is designed to offer an interesting and valuable departure. The understanding that the reader arrives at based on the evidence that emerges from the clash of views encourages the reader to view history as an *interpretive* discipline, not one of rote memorization.

As in previous editions, the issues are arranged in chronological order and can be easily incorporated into any American history survey course. Each issue has an issue *introduction*, which sets the stage for the debate that follows in the pro and con selections and provides historical and methodological background to the problem that the issue examines. Each issue concludes with a *postscript*, which ties the readings together, briefly mentions alternative interpretations, and supplies detailed *suggestions for further reading* for the student who wishes to pursue the topics raised in the issue. Also, Internet site addresses (URLs) have been provided on the *On the Internet* page that accompanies each part opener, which should prove useful as starting points for further research. At the back of the book is a listing of all the *contributors to this volume* with a brief biographical sketch of each of the prominent figures whose views are debated here.

Changes to this edition In this edition we have continued our efforts to maintain a balance between the traditional political, diplomatic, and cultural issues and the new social history, which depicts a society that benefited from the presence of Native Americans, African Americans, women, and workers of various racial and ethnic backgrounds. With this in mind, we present seven entirely new issues: *Were Socioeconomic Tensions Responsible for the Witchcraft Hysteria in Salem?* (Issue 3); *Did Capitalist Values Motivate the American Colonists?* (Issue 4); *Was the American Revolution a Conservative Movement?* (Issue 6); *Was Thomas Jefferson Committed to Bringing an End to Chattel Slavery?* (Issue 8); *Was Slavery Profitable?* (Issue 11); *Is Robert E. Lee Overrated as a General?* (Issue 15); and *Was Reconstruction a "Splendid Failure"?* (Issue 17). In all, there are 14 new selections.

A word to the instructor   An *Instructor's Manual With Test Questions* (multiple-choice and essay) is available through the publisher for the instructor using *Taking Sides* in the classroom. A general guidebook, *Using Taking Sides in the Classroom,* which discusses methods and techniques for integrating the pro-con approach into any classroom setting, is also available. An online version of *Using Taking Sides in the Classroom* and a correspondence service for Taking Sides adopters can be found at http://www.dushkin.com/usingts/.

   Taking Sides: Clashing Views on Controversial Issues in American History is only one title in the Taking Sides series. If you are interested in seeing the table of contents for any of the other titles, please visit the Taking Sides Web site at http://www.dushkin.com/takingsides/.

Acknowledgments   Many individuals have contributed to the successful completion of this edition. We appreciate the evaluations submitted to McGraw-Hill/Dushkin by those who have used *Taking Sides* in the classroom. Special thanks to those who responded with specific suggestions for the ninth edition:

Gary Best
University of Hawaii–Hilo

James D. Bolton
Coastline Community College

Mary Borg
University of Northern Colorado

John Whitney Evans
College of St. Scholastica

Maryann Irwin
Diablo Valley College

Mark Hickerson
Chaffey College

Gordon Lam
Sierra College

Jon Nielson
Columbia College

Andrew O'Shaugnessy
University of Wisconsin-Oshkosh

Manian Padma
DeAnza College

Robert M. Paterson
Armstrong State College

Charles Piehl
Mankato State University

Ethan S. Rafuse
University of Missouri–Kansas City

John Reid
Ohio State University–Lima

Murray Rubinstein
CUNY Baruch College

Neil Sapper
Amarillo College

Preston Shea
Plymouth State College

Jack Traylor
William Jennings Bryan College

   We are particularly indebted to Maggie Cullen, Cindy SoRelle, Barry A. Crouch, Virginia Kirk, Joseph and Helen Mitchell, and Jean Soto, who shared their ideas for changes, pointed us toward potentially useful historical works, and provided significant editorial assistance. Megan Arnold performed indispensable typing duties connected with this project. Susan E. Myers and Elu Ciborowski in the library at Howard Community College provided essential help in acquiring books and articles on interlibrary loan. Finally, we are sincerely grateful for the commitment, encouragement, and patience provided over the years by David Dean, former list manager for the Taking Sides series; David Brackley, senior developmental editor; and the entire staff of McGraw-Hill/ Dushkin. Indispensible to this project is Ted Knight, the current list manager.

Larry Madaras
Howard Community College

James M. SoRelle
Baylor University

Contents In Brief

PART 1   Colonial Society   1

Issue 1.   Was Columbus an Imperialist?   2
Issue 2.   Was the Colonial Period a "Golden Age" for Women in
           America?   24
Issue 3.   Were Socioeconomic Tensions Responsible for the Witchcraft
           Hysteria in Salem?   44
Issue 4.   Did Capitalist Values Motivate the American Colonists?   66
Issue 5.   Was There a Great Awakening in Mid-Eighteenth-Century
           America?   90

PART 2   Revolution and the New Nation   115

Issue 6.   Was the American Revolution a Conservative Movement?
           116
Issue 7.   Were the Founding Fathers Democratic Reformers?   138
Issue 8.   Was Thomas Jefferson Committed to Bringing an End to
           Chattel Slavery?   162
Issue 9.   Was Andrew Jackson's Indian Removal Policy Motivated by
           Humanitarian Impulses?   182

PART 3   Antebellum America   205

Issue 10.   Were the Abolitionists "Unrestrained Fanatics"?   206
Issue 11.   Was Slavery Profitable?   232
Issue 12.   Was the Mexican War an Exercise in American Imperialism?
            254
Issue 13.   Did the Westward Movement Transform the Traditional Roles
            of Women in the Mid-Nineteenth Century?   280

PART 4   Conflict and Resolution   307

Issue 14.   Have Historians Overemphasized the Slavery Issue as a Cause
            of the Civil War?   308
Issue 15.   Is Robert E. Lee Overrated as a General?   328
Issue 16.   Did Abraham Lincoln Free the Slaves?   352
Issue 17.   Was Reconstruction a "Splendid Failure"?   374

Contents

Preface   i

Introduction: The Study of History   xii

PART 1   COLONIAL SOCIETY   1

Issue 1.   Was Columbus an Imperialist?   2

YES: **Kirkpatrick Sale**, from *The Conquest of Paradise: Christopher Columbus and the Columbian Legacy* (Alfred A. Knopf, 1990)   *4*

NO: **Robert Royal**, from *1492 and All That: Political Manipulations of History* (Ethics and Public Policy Center, 1992)   *13*

Kirkpatrick Sale, a contributing editor of *The Nation*, characterizes Christopher Columbus as an imperialist who was determined to conquer both the land and the people he encountered during his first voyage to the Americas in 1492. Robert Royal, vice president for research at the Ethics and Public Policy Center, objects to Columbus's modern-day critics and insists that Columbus should be admired for his courage, his willingness to take a risk, and his success in advancing knowledge about other parts of the world.

Issue 2.   Was the Colonial Period a "Golden Age" for Women in America?   24

YES: **Lois Green Carr and Lorena S. Walsh**, from "The Planter's Wife: The Experience of White Women in Seventeenth-Century Maryland," *William and Mary Quarterly* (January 1977)   *26*

NO: **Mary Beth Norton**, from "The Myth of the Golden Age," in Carol Ruth Berkin and Mary Beth Norton, eds., *Women of America: A History* (Houghton Mifflin, 1979)   *34*

Adjunct professor of history Lois Green Carr and historian Lorena S. Walsh identify several factors that coalesced to afford women in seventeenth-century Maryland a higher status with fewer restraints on their social conduct than those experienced by women in England. Professor of American history Mary Beth Norton challenges the "golden age" theory, insisting that women in colonial America, whether white, black, or Native American, typically occupied a domestic sphere that was lacking in status, physically debilitating over time, and a barrier to educational opportunity and political power.

Issue 3.   Were Socioeconomic Tensions Responsible for the Witchcraft Hysteria in Salem?   44

YES: **Paul Boyer and Stephen Nissenbaum**, from *Salem Possessed: The Social Origins of Witchcraft* (Harvard University Press, 1974)   *46*

NO: Laurie Winn Carlson, from *A Fever in Salem* (Ivan R. Dee, 1999)
     55

Historians Paul Boyer and Stephen Nissenbaum argue that the Salem witchcraft hysteria of 1692 was prompted by economic and social tensions that occurred against the backdrop of an emergent commercial capitalism, conflicts between ministers and their congregations, and the loss of family lands, which divided the residents of Salem Town and Salem Village. Author Laurie Winn Carlson contends that the witchcraft hysteria in Salem was the product of people's responses to physical and neurological behaviors resulting from an unrecognized epidemic of encephalitis.

Issue 4.   Did Capitalist Values Motivate the American
           Colonists?   66

     YES: James T. Lemon, from *The Best Poor Man's Country: A Geographical Study of Early Southeastern Pennsylvania* (Johns Hopkins University Press, 1972)   *68*

     NO: James A. Henretta, from "Families and Farms: *Mentalité* in Pre-Industrial America," *William and Mary Quarterly* (January 1978)   *78*

Professor of geography James T. Lemon argues that the liberal, middle-class, white settlers of southeastern Pennsylvania placed individual freedom and material gain at a higher priority than that of the public interest. Professor of American history James A. Henretta contends that the colonial family determined the character of agrarian life because it was the primary economic and social unit.

Issue 5.   Was There a Great Awakening in
           Mid-Eighteenth-Century America?   90

     YES: Patricia U. Bonomi, from *Under the Cope of Heaven: Religion, Society, and Politics in Colonial America* (Oxford University Press, 1986)   *92*

     NO: Jon Butler, from "Enthusiasm Described and Decried: The Great Awakening as Interpretative Fiction," *The Journal of American History* (September 1982)   *103*

Professor of history Patricia U. Bonomi defines the Great Awakening as a period of intense revivalistic fervor that laid the foundation for socioreligious and political reform by spawning an age of contentiousness in the British mainland colonies. Professor of American history Jon Butler argues that to describe the colonial revivalistic activities of the eighteenth century as the "Great Awakening" is to seriously exaggerate their extent, nature, and impact on pre-Revolutionary American society and politics.

PART 2   REVOLUTION AND THE NEW NATION   115

Issue 6.   Was the American Revolution a Conservative
           Movement?   116

     YES: Carl N. Degler, from *Out of Our Past: The Forces That Shaped Modern America*, rev. ed. (Harper & Row, 1970)   *118*

NO: **Gordon S. Wood,** from *The Radicalism of the American Revolution* (Alfred A. Knopf, 1991) *126*

Pulitzer Prize–winning author Carl N. Degler argues that upper-middle-class colonists led a conservative American Revolution that left untouched the prewar economic and social class structure of an upwardly mobile people. Prize-winning historian Gordon S. Wood argues that the American Revolution was a far-reaching, radical event that produced a unique democratic society in which ordinary people could make money, pursue happiness, and be self-governing.

Issue 7. **Were the Founding Fathers Democratic Reformers?** 138

YES: **John P. Roche,** from "The Founding Fathers: A Reform Caucus in Action," *American Political Science Review* (December 1961) *140*

NO: **Alfred F. Young,** from "The Framers of the Constitution and the 'Genius' of the People," *Radical History Review* (vol. 42, 1988) *152*

Political scientist John P. Roche asserts that the Founding Fathers were not only revolutionaries but also superb democratic politicians who created a Constitution that supported the needs of the nation and at the same time was acceptable to the people. Historian Alfred F. Young argues that the Founding Fathers were an elite group of college-educated lawyers, merchants, slaveholding planters, and "monied men" who strengthened the power of the central government yet, at the same time, were forced to make some democratic accommodations in writing the Constitution in order to ensure its acceptance in the democratically controlled ratifying conventions.

Issue 8. **Was Thomas Jefferson Committed to Bringing an End to Chattel Slavery?** 162

YES: **Dumas Malone,** from *Jefferson and His Time, vol. 6: The Sage of Monticello* (Little, Brown, 1981) *164*

NO: **William Cohen,** from "Thomas Jefferson and the Problem of Slavery," *The Journal of American History* (December 1969) *172*

American historian Dumas Malone (1892–1986) asserts that, although he did not live to see slavery abolished, Thomas Jefferson sincerely deplored the slave system as unjust to its victims and injurious to the masters. Malone maintains that Jefferson was one of the first Americans to propose a specific plan for emancipation. American historian William Cohen contends that libertarian views had virtually no impact on Jefferson's actions after 1784 and that his behavior as a slave owner differed little from that of Virginia planters who opposed his antislavery speculations and who were committed to protecting their chattel property.

Issue 9. **Was Andrew Jackson's Indian Removal Policy Motivated by Humanitarian Impulses?** 182

YES: **Robert V. Remini,** from *Andrew Jackson and the Course of American Freedom, 1822–1832, vol. 2* (Harper & Row, 1981) *184*

NO: Anthony F. C. Wallace, from *The Long, Bitter Trail: Andrew Jackson and the Indians* (Hill & Wang, 1993) *194*

Historical biographer Robert V. Remini argues that Andrew Jackson did not seek to destroy Native American life and culture. He portrays Jackson as a national leader who sincerely believed that the Indian Removal Act of 1830 was the only way to protect Native Americans from annihilation at the hands of white settlers. Historian and anthropologist Anthony F. C. Wallace contends that Andrew Jackson oversaw a harsh policy with regard to Native Americans. This policy resulted in the usurpation of land, attempts to destroy tribal culture, and the forcible removal of Native Americans from the southeastern United States to a designated territory west of the Mississippi River.

PART 3 ANTEBELLUM AMERICA 205

Issue 10. Were the Abolitionists "Unrestrained Fanatics"? 206

YES: Avery Craven, from *The Coming of the Civil War,* 2d ed. (University of Chicago Press, 1957) *208*

NO: Irving H. Bartlett, from "The Persistence of Wendell Phillips," in Martin Duberman, ed., *The Antislavery Vanguard: New Essays on the Abolitionists* (Princeton University Press, 1965) *218*

Historian Avery Craven asserts that the fanaticism of the abolitionist crusade created an atmosphere of crisis that resulted in the outbreak of the Civil War. Irving H. Bartlett, a retired professor of American civilization, differentiates between agitation and fanaticism and states that abolitionists like Wendell Phillips were deeply committed to improving the quality of life for all Americans, including African Americans held as slaves.

Issue 11. Was Slavery Profitable? 232

YES: Kenneth M. Stampp, from *The Peculiar Institution: Slavery in the Ante-Bellum South* (Alfred A. Knopf, 1956) *234*

NO: Eugene D. Genovese, from *The Political Economy of Slavery: Studies in the Economy and Society of the Slave South* (Vintage Books, 1965) *243*

Kenneth M. Stampp, a professor emeritus of history, contends that although slaveholding did not guarantee affluence, slave labor held a competitive advantage over free white labor. He finds ample evidence that the average slaveholder earned a reasonably satisfactory return from his investment in slaves. Historian Eugene D. Genovese maintains that poorly fed and inadequately trained slaves lacked the versatility and incentive to be particularly productive agricultural laborers and, consequently, contributed to the backwardness of the antebellum southern economy.

Issue 12. Was the Mexican War an Exercise in American Imperialism? 254

YES: Rodolfo Acuña, from *Occupied America: A History of Chicanos,* 3rd ed. (Harper & Row, 1988) *256*

NO: **Norman A. Graebner,** from "The Mexican War: A Study in Causation," *Pacific Historical Review* (August 1980) *269*

Professor of history Rodolfo Acuña argues that Euroamericans took advantage of the young, independent, and unstable government of Mexico and waged unjust and aggressive wars against the Mexican government in the 1830s and 1840s in order to take away half of Mexico's original soil. Professor of diplomatic history Norman A. Graebner argues that President James Polk pursued an aggressive policy that he believed would force Mexico to sell New Mexico and California to the United States and to recognize the annexation of Texas without starting a war.

Issue 13. Did the Westward Movement Transform the Traditional Roles of Women in the Mid-Nineteenth Century? 280

YES: **Sandra L. Myres,** from *Westering Women and the Frontier Experience, 1800–1915* (University of New Mexico Press, 1982) *282*

NO: **John Mack Faragher,** from *Women and Men on the Overland Trail* (Yale University Press, 1979) *294*

Professor of history Sandra L. Myres (1933–1991) argues that first- and second-generation American women often worked outside the home as teachers, missionaries, doctors, lawyers, ranchers, miners, and businesspeople instead of simply assuming the traditional roles of wife and mother. According to professor John Mack Faragher, women were reluctant pioneers because they were unwilling to break away from their close networks of female relatives and friends. However, nineteenth-century marital laws gave their husbands the sole authority to make the decision to move west.

PART 4 CONFLICT AND RESOLUTION 307

Issue 14. Have Historians Overemphasized the Slavery Issue as a Cause of the Civil War? 308

YES: **Joel H. Silbey,** from *The Partisan Imperative: The Dynamics of American Politics Before the Civil War* (Oxford University Press, 1985) *310*

NO: **Michael F. Holt,** from *The Political Crisis of the 1850s* (John Wiley & Sons, 1978) *318*

Professor of history Joel H. Silbey argues that historians have overemphasized the sectional conflict over slavery and have neglected to analyze local enthnocultural issues among the events leading to the Civil War. Professor of history Michael F. Holt maintains that both Northern Republicans and Southern Democrats seized the slavery issue to sharply distinguish party differences and thus reinvigorate the loyalty of party voters.

Issue 15. Is Robert E. Lee Overrated as a General? 328

YES: **Alan T. Nolan,** from *"Rally, Once Again!" Selected Civil War Writings of Alan T. Nolan* (Madison House, 2000) *330*

NO: Gary W. Gallagher, from "Another Look at the Generalship of R. E. Lee," in Gary W. Gallagher, ed., *Lee the Soldier* (University of Nebraska Press, 1996)   *340*

Attorney Alan T. Nolan argues that General Robert E. Lee was a flawed grand strategist whose offensive operations produced heavy casualties in an unnecessarily prolonged war that the South could not win. According to professor of American history Gary W. Gallagher, General Lee was the most revered and unifying figure in the Confederacy, and he "formulated a national strategy predicated on the probability of success in Virginia and the value of battlefield victories."

Issue 16.   Did Abraham Lincoln Free the Slaves?   352

YES: James M. McPherson, from *Drawn With the Sword: Reflections on the American Civil War* (Oxford University Press, 1996)   *354*

NO: Vincent Harding, from *There Is a River: The Black Struggle for Freedom in America* (Vintage Books, 1981)   *364*

Historian James M. McPherson maintains that Abraham Lincoln was the indispensable agent in emancipating the slaves through his condemnation of slavery as a moral evil, his refusal to compromise on the question of slavery's expansion, his skillful political leadership, and his implementation and direction of Union troops as an army of liberation. Professor of religion and social transformation Vincent Harding credits slaves themselves for engaging in a dramatic movement of self-liberation. He argues that Lincoln initially refused to declare the destruction of slavery as a war aim and then issued the Emancipation Proclamation, which failed to free any slaves in areas over which he had any authority.

Issue 17.   Was Reconstruction a "Splendid Failure"?   374

YES: Eric Foner, from "The New View of Reconstruction," *American Heritage* (October/November 1983)   *376*

NO: Thomas Holt, from *Black Over White: Negro Political Leadership in South Carolina During Reconstruction* (University of Illinois Press, 1977)   *386*

Professor of history Eric Foner asserts that although Reconstruction did not achieve radical goals, it was a "splendid failure" because it offered African Americans in the South a temporary vision of a free society. Thomas Holt, a professor of American and African American history, contends that in South Carolina, where African Americans wielded significant political clout, Reconstruction failed to produce critical economic reforms for working-class blacks because of social and cultural divisions within the black community.

Contributors   398
Index   404

Introduction

The Study of History

Larry Madaras

James M. SoRelle

In a pluralistic society such as ours, the study of history is bound to be a complex process. How an event is interpreted depends not only on the existing evidence but also on the perspective of the interpreter. Consequently, understanding history presupposes the evaluation of information, a task that often leads to conflicting conclusions. An understanding of history, then, requires the acceptance of the idea of historical relativism. Relativism means that redefinition of our past is always possible and desirable. History shifts, changes, and grows with new and different evidence and interpretations. As is the case with the law and even with medicine, beliefs that were unquestioned 100 or 200 years ago have been discredited or discarded since.

Relativism, then, encourages revisionism. There is a maxim that "the past must remain useful to the present." Historian Carl Becker argued that every generation should examine history for itself, thus ensuring constant scrutiny of our collective experience through new perspectives. History, consequently, does not remain static, in part because historians cannot avoid being influenced by the times in which they live. Almost all historians commit themselves to revising the views of other historians, synthesizing theories into macrointerpretations, or revising the revisionists.

Schools of Thought

Three predominant schools of thought have emerged in American history since the first graduate seminars in history were given at the Johns Hopkins University in Baltimore in the 1870s. The *progressive* school dominated the professional field in the first half of the twentieth century. Influenced by the reform currents of Populism, progressivism, and the New Deal, these historians explored the social and economic forces that energized America. The progressive scholars tended to view the past in terms of conflicts between groups, and they sympathized with the underdog.

The post–World War II period witnessed the emergence of a new group of historians who viewed the conflict thesis as overly simplistic. Writing against the backdrop of the cold war, these *neoconservative* or *consensus* historians argued that Americans possess a shared set of values and that the areas of agreement within the nation's basic democratic and capitalistic framework were more important than the areas of disagreement.

In the 1960s, however, the civil rights movement, women's liberation, and the student rebellion (with its condemnation of the war in Vietnam) fragmented the consensus of values upon which historians and social scientists of the 1950s had centered their interpretations. This turmoil set the stage for the emergence of another group of scholars. *New Left* historians began to reinterpret the past once again. They emphasized the significance of conflict in American history, and they resurrected interest in those groups ignored by the consensus school. In addition, New Left historians critiqued the expansionist policies of the United States and emphasized the difficulties confronted by Native Americans, African Americans, women, and urban workers in gaining full citizenship status.

Progressive, consensus, and New Left history is still being written. The most recent generation of scholars, however, focuses upon social history. Their primary concern is to discover what the lives of "ordinary Americans" were really like. These new social historians employ previously overlooked court and church documents, house deeds and tax records, letters and diaries, photographs, and census data to reconstruct the everyday lives of average Americans. Some employ new methodologies, such as quantification (enhanced by advancing computer technology) and oral history, while others borrow from the disciplines of political science, economics, sociology, anthropology, and psychology for their historical investigations.

The proliferation of historical approaches, which are reflected in the issues debated in this book, has had mixed results. On the one hand, historians have become so specialized in their respective time periods and methodological styles that it is difficult to synthesize the recent scholarship into a comprehensive text for the general reader. On the other hand, historians know more about the American past than at any other time in history. They dare to ask new questions or ones that previously were considered to be germane only to scholars in other social sciences. Although there is little agreement about the answers to these questions, the methods employed and issues explored make the "new history" a very exciting field to study.

The topics that follow represent a variety of perspectives and approaches. Each of these controversial issues can be studied for its individual importance to our nation's history. Taken as a group, they interact with one another to illustrate larger historical themes. When grouped thematically, the issues reveal continuing motifs in the development of American history.

Comparative History: America in a Global Perspective

The role of American history within the larger framework of world history is central to the discussion presented in Issue 1. Kirkpatrick Sale places the "discovery" of America by Christopher Columbus within the context of European imperialism of the late fifteenth century. Robert Royal takes Sale and other Columbus denigrators to task for failing to recognize Columbus's courage and the many benefits derived from his and other European explorers' voyages to the New World.

A discussion of early-nineteenth-century foreign policy in Issue 12 concerns both U.S. diplomatic relations with the rest of the world and America's self-perception within the world of nations. Did the U.S. government conceive of its power as continental, hemispheric, or worldwide? And what were the consequences of these attitudes? Rodolfo Acuña argues that the United States waged a racist and imperialistic war against Mexico for the purpose of conquering what became the American Southwest. Norman A. Graebner contends that President James K. Polk pursued an aggressive (but not imperialistic) policy that would force Mexico to recognize the U.S. annexation of Texas and to sell New Mexico and California to its northern neighbor without starting a war.

The New Social History

Some of the most innovative historical research over the last 30 years reflects the interests of the new social historians. The work of several representatives of this group who treat the issues of gender, race, and class appears in this volume.

Two issues explore the field of women's history. One question frequently asked is whether or not the colonial period was a "golden age" for women in America. In Issue 2, Lois Green Carr and Lorena S. Walsh argue that "immigrant predominance, early death, late marriage and sexual imbalance" gave women in early Maryland power in the household that English women did not enjoy. Mary Beth Norton, however, challenges the "golden age" theory by emphasizing the subordinate status occupied by colonial women in virtually every aspect of their daily lives.

Issue 13 examines women as participants in the westward movement of the mid-nineteenth century. Sandra L. Myres portrays the frontier as a liberating environment for both men and women. Westering women did not just stay at home and raise a family; they often worked as teachers and nurses as well as in nontraditional occupations as physicians, lawyers, ranchers, shopkeepers, and salespersons. John Mack Faragher reminds us that men were largely responsible for the decision to move their families west even when the women in those families preferred to maintain their existing female networks.

Study of the Salem witch trials has produced several imaginative scholarly explanations for this episode in New England's history. In Issue 3, Paul Boyer and Stephen Nissenbaum explore the social, economic, and geographical dynamics of Salem, Massachusetts, in an effort to explain the pattern of accusations that occurred in 1692. Laurie Winn Carlson discusses the witchcraft hysteria in biological and medical terms, concluding that the physical symptoms that were mistaken for evidence of sorcery were, in fact, the products of an epidemic of encephalitis.

In Issue 4, James T. Lemon and James A. Henretta discuss the socioeconomic values of the colonists who populated the Atlantic seaboard in the seventeenth and eighteenth centuries. Lemon identifies the settlers of south-eastern Pennsylvania as liberal, middle-class whites whose primary motivation was material gain for themselves and their families. Henretta, however, asserts that these colonists were guided by a preindustrial/precapitalistic worldview that focused upon communal, not individual, interests.

Religion, Revolution, Reform, and Reconstruction

Beyond suggesting that much of the colonizing experiment in British North America was motivated by a search for religious freedom, many textbooks avoid extended discussions of religion as a force in history. In the last half century, however, professional historians have assumed that the religious revivals of the mid-eighteenth century, known as the "Great Awakening," sparked intercolonial unity, and some have described this event as a direct precursor to the political upheaval of the American Revolution. In Issue 5, Patricia U. Bonomi offers a traditional view of the Great Awakening as a series of revivals occurring throughout the American colonies from 1739 to 1745, which generated a divisiveness that affected a number of religious, social, and political institutions. Jon Butler denies that any great unified revival movement emerged in the eighteenth century, and he suggests that historians should abandon altogether the label "Great Awakening."

The nature of the American Revolution is considered in Issue 6. Carl N. Degler depicts the Revolution as a conservative movement that produced few economic changes. Gordon S. Wood, in contrast, views the American Revolution as a truly radical event that led to the adoption of a republican form of government in the newly established nation.

During the 1830s and 1840s, a wave of reformism swept across the United States. Various individuals and groups sought to strengthen the democratic experiment in the nation by ridding the society of its imperfections. Issue 9 is framed within the context of the role of humanitarianism in the formulation of public policy with regard to Native Americans. Robert V. Remini argues that President Andrew Jackson's support for the Indian Removal Act of 1830 was predicated on Jackson's desire to protect Native Americans from almost certain annihilation at the hands of white settlers in the southeastern United States. Anthony F. C. Wallace depicts Jackson as a key initiator of the brutal program of forced removal of several tribes from their longtime homeland.

The major and most controversial reform effort in the pre–Civil War period was the movement to abolish slavery. Issue 10 deals with the motivations of those who became abolitionists. Avery Craven states that the Civil War was caused unnecessarily by extremists in both the North and the South. In particular, Craven denounces the abolitionists as irresponsible fanatics who filled their propagandistic literature and speeches with lies about lazy, aristocratic plantation owners who constantly brutalized their slaves. Irving H. Bartlett's sympathetic portrayal of Wendell Phillips reflects a revisionist approach to the abolitionists.

The Civil War is one of the most frequently studied episodes in American history. The military leadership of Confederate general Robert E. Lee is the focus of the selections in Issue 15. Alan T. Nolan argues that Lee was a flawed strategist whose offensive operations produced heavy casualties in a war that the South could not win. Gary W. Gallagher, however, seeks to restore Lee's reputation as the most revered and unifying figure in the Confederacy.

Perhaps no other period of American history has been subjected to more myths than the era of Reconstruction. Only within the past 25 years has the traditional, pro-southern interpretation been revised in high school and college texts. In Issue 17, Eric Foner concedes that Reconstruction was not very radical, much less revolutionary. However, he argues that it was nevertheless a "splendid failure" because it offered the former slaves a vision of what a free society should look like. Thomas Holt agrees that Reconstruction did not produce many of the goals of its architects, but he sees nothing positive in the fact that in South Carolina, where African Americans constituted a majority of the population and wielded significant political clout, social and cultural divisions within the black community undermined the potential effectiveness of critical economic reforms for the freedmen.

Politics in America

The American people gave legitimacy to their revolution through the establishment of a republican form of government. The United States has operated under two constitutions: The first established the short-lived confederation from 1781 to 1789; the second was written in 1787 and remains in effect over 200 years later. In Issue 7, John P. Roche contends that the drafters of the Constitution of the United States were democratic reformers. Alfred F. Young argues that the Founding Fathers were an elitist group who made some democratic accommodations in framing the Constitution to make sure it was acceptable to the democratically controlled ratifying conventions.

The remaining four issues concern the politics of slavery. Was slavery essential to the political economy of the nation? In Issue 11, Kenneth M. Stampp argues that southern slave owners realized a reasonably satisfactory return on their investment in slaves. Eugene D. Genovese, on the other hand, attributes low productivity at that time to slave labor.

Most historians have argued that Abraham Lincoln became president in 1860 because sectional conflicts over the slavery issue divided the nation and destroyed the second political party system, which was composed of Whigs and Democrats, in the late 1850s. Political historians, employing a statistical analysis of election issues, voter behavior, and legislative patterns on the local, state, and national levels, however, have rejected or significantly modified the traditional emphasis on sectionalism in the 1850s. In Issue 14, Joel H. Silbey argues that historians have paid too much attention to the sectional conflict over slavery and have neglected to analyze local ethnocultural issues as keys to the Civil War. Michael F. Holt maintains that both Northern Republicans and Southern Democrats seized the slavery issue to highlight the sharp differences existing between them and thus to reinvigorate the loyalty of their traditional partisans.

Finally, two issues debate the roles played by Thomas Jefferson and Lincoln, respectively, in bringing an end to the institution of slavery. In Issue 8, Dumas Malone argues that Jefferson was deeply committed to ending slavery. William Cohen, however, contends that Jefferson's behavior as a slave owner differed very little from that of his planter peers, who were committed to preserving the master-slave relationship.

Lincoln's image as "the Great Emancipator" is the focus of the essays in Issue 16. James M. McPherson supports the view that Lincoln's leadership was essential to ending slavery. Vincent Harding, however, defends the position that slaves were the agents of their own freedom, while Lincoln was reluctant to make emancipation a war issue.

Conclusion

The process of historical study should rely more on thinking than on memorizing data. Once the basics of who, what, when, and where are determined, historical thinking shifts to a higher gear. Analysis, comparison and contrast, evaluation, and explanation take command. These skills not only increase our knowledge of the past but they also provide general tools for the comprehension of all the topics about which human beings think.

The diversity of a pluralistic society, however, creates some obstacles to comprehending the past. The spectrum of differing opinions on any particular subject eliminates the possibility of quick and easy answers. In the final analysis, conclusions are often built through a synthesis of several different interpretations, but, even then, they may be partial and tentative.

The study of history in a pluralistic society allows each citizen the opportunity to reach independent conclusions about the past. Since most, if not all, historical issues affect the present and future, understanding the past becomes essential to social progress. Many of today's problems have a direct connection with the past. Additionally, other contemporary issues may lack obvious direct antecedents, but historical investigation can provide illuminating analogies. At first, it may appear confusing to read and to think about opposing historical views, but the survival of our democratic society depends on such critical thinking by acute and discerning minds.

On the Internet . . .

The Columbus Navigation Homepage

This noted site by Keith A. Pickering examines the history, navigation, and landfall of Christopher Columbus. Click on "Links to other sites about Columbus and his times" to find dozens of sites on Columbus, including scholarly papers on Columbus's treatment of the American Indians.

http://www1.minn.net/~keithp/

Women in American History

This Women in American History site was created by Encyclopedia Britannica and contains a section on early America (1600–1820). Included in this section are a timeline of events, biographies of influential women of the time, and a recommended reading list.

http://women.eb.com/women/earlyamerica01.html

The Salem Witch Trials

This comprehensive site on the Salem witch trials includes an essay that outlines the causes of the 1692 trials. Also on this site are trial transcripts, a timeline, and a list of books on the subject. Visitors to this site are encouraged to participate in the forum in order to express their thoughts and opinions.

http://www.salemwitchtrials.com/index.html

Spiritual Leaders During the Great Awakening

This site is devoted to some spiritual leaders of the Great Awakening.

http://dylee.keel.econ.ship.edu/ubf/leaders/leaders.htm

PART 1

Colonial Society

*C*olonial settlement took place in the context of conditions that were unique to that time and place. The ethnic identity of the colonists affected their relations with Native Americans and Africans, as well as with each other. Many of the attitudes, ideals, and institutions that emerged from the colonial experience served the early settlers well and are still emulated today. Others, such as slavery and racism, have left a less positive legacy.

- Was Columbus an Imperialist?

- Was the Colonial Period a "Golden Age" for Women in America?

- Were Socioeconomic Tensions Responsible for the Witchcraft Hysteria in Salem?

- Did Capitalist Values Motivate the American Colonists?

- Was There a Great Awakening in Mid-Eighteenth-Century America?

ISSUE 1

Was Columbus an Imperialist?

YES: Kirkpatrick Sale, from *The Conquest of Paradise: Christopher Columbus and the Columbian Legacy* (Alfred A. Knopf, 1990)

NO: Robert Royal, from *1492 and All That: Political Manipulations of History* (Ethics and Public Policy Center, 1992)

ISSUE SUMMARY

YES: Kirkpatrick Sale, a contributing editor of *The Nation*, characterizes Christopher Columbus as an imperialist who was determined to conquer both the land and the people he encountered during his first voyage to the Americas in 1492.

NO: Robert Royal, vice president for research at the Ethics and Public Policy Center, objects to Columbus's modern-day critics and insists that Columbus should be admired for his courage, his willingness to take a risk, and his success in advancing knowledge about other parts of the world.

On October 12, 1492, Christopher Columbus, a Genoese mariner sailing under the flag and patronage of the Spanish monarchy, made landfall on a tropical Caribbean island, which he subsequently named San Salvador. This action established for Columbus the fame of having discovered the New World and, by extension, America. Of course, this "discovery" was ironic since Columbus and his crew members were not looking for a new world but, instead, a very old one —the much-fabled Orient. By sailing westward instead of eastward, Columbus was certain that he would find a shorter route to China. He did not anticipate that the land mass of the Americas would prevent him from reaching this goal or that his "failure" would guarantee his fame for centuries thereafter.

Columbus's encounter with indigenous peoples, whom he named "Indians" (*los indios*), presented further proof that Europeans had not discovered America. These "Indians" were descendants of the first people who migrated from Asia at least 30,000 years earlier and fanned out in a southeasterly direction until they populated much of North and South America. By the time Columbus arrived, Native Americans numbered approximately 40 million, 3 million of whom resided in the continental region north of Mexico.

None of this, however, should dilute the significance of Columbus's explorations, which were representative of a wave of Atlantic voyages emanating from Europe in the fifteenth, sixteenth, and seventeenth centuries. Spawned by the intellectual ferment of the Renaissance in combination with the rise of the European nation-state, these voyages of exploration were made possible by advances in shipbuilding, improved navigational instruments and cartography, the desirability of long-distance commerce, support from ruling monarchs, and the courage and ambition of the explorers themselves.

Columbus's arrival (and return on three separate occasions between 1494 and 1502) possessed enormous implications not only for the future development of the United States but for the Western Hemisphere as a whole, as well as for Europe and Africa. These consequences attracted a significant amount of scholarly and media attention in 1992 in connection with the quincentennial celebration of Columbus's first arrival on American shores and sparked often acrimonious debate over the true meaning of Columbus's legacy. Many wished to use the occasion to emphasize the positive accomplishments of Europe's contact with the New World. Others sought to clarify some of the negative results of Columbus's voyages, particularly as they related to European confrontations with Native Americans.

This debate provides the context for the selections that follow. To what extent should we applaud Columbus's exploits? Are there reasons that we should question the purity of Columbus's motivations? Did the European "discovery" of America do more harm than good?

Kirkpatrick Sale treats Columbus's arrival as an invasion of the land and the indigenous peoples that he encountered. By assigning European names to virtually everything he observed, Columbus, according to Sale, was taking possession on behalf of the Spanish monarchy. Similarly, one of Columbus's major goals was to build and arm a fortress by which he could carry out the subjugation and enslavement of the native population. Columbus's policies of conquest, religious conversion, settlement, and exploitation of natural resources were an example of European imperialism.

Robert Royal rejects the argument that Columbus was motivated by European arrogance and avarice. He also disputes the notion that Columbus was driven by a desire for gold or by racist assumptions of Native American inferiority. Royal asserts that Columbus exhibited genuine concern for justice in his contacts with the Native Americans and concludes that Columbus, though not without his faults, merits the admiration traditionally accorded his accomplishments.

1492–93

Admiral [Cristóbal] Colón [Christopher Columbus] spent a total of ninety-six days exploring the lands he encountered on the far side of the Ocean Sea—four rather small coralline islands in the Bahamian chain and two substantial coastlines of what he finally acknowledged were larger islands—every one of which he "took possession of" in the name of his Sovereigns.

The first he named San Salvador, no doubt as much in thanksgiving for its welcome presence after more than a month at sea as for the Son of God whom it honored; the second he called Santa María de la Concepcíon, after the Virgin whose name his flagship bore; and the third and fourth he called Fernandina and Isabela, for his patrons, honoring Aragon before Castile for reasons never explained (possibly protocol, possibly in recognition of the chief sources of backing for the voyage). The first of the two large and very fertile islands he called Juana, which Fernando says was done in honor of Prince Juan, heir to the Castilian throne, but just as plausibly might have been done in recognition of Princess Juana, the unstable child who eventually carried on the line; the second he named la Ysla Española, the "Spanish Island," because it resembled (though he felt it surpassed in beauty) the lands of Castile.

It was not that the islands were in need of names, mind you, nor indeed that Colón was ignorant of the names the native peoples had already given them, for he frequently used those original names before endowing them with his own. Rather, the process of bestowing new names went along with "taking possession of" those parts of the world he deemed suitable for Spanish ownership, showing the royal banners, erecting various crosses and pronouncing certain oaths and pledges. If this was presumption, it had an honored heritage: it was Adam who was charged by his Creator with the task of naming "every living creature," including the product of his own rib, in the course of establishing "dominion over" them.

Colón went on to assign no fewer than sixty-two other names on the geography of the islands—capes, points, mountains, ports—with a blithe assurance suggesting that in his (and Europe's) perception the act of name-giving was in some sense a talisman of conquest, a rite that changed raw neutral stretches of far-off earth into extensions of Europe. The process began slowly, even haltingly—he forgot to record, for example, until four days afterward that he named

From Kirkpatrick Sale, *The Conquest of Paradise: Christopher Columbus and the Columbian Legacy* (Alfred A. Knopf, 1990). Copyright © 1990 by Kirkpatrick Sale. Reprinted by permission of Alfred A. Knopf, a division of Random House, Inc. Notes omitted.

the landfall island San Salvador—but by the time he came to Española at the end he went on a naming spree, using more than two-thirds of all the titles he concocted on that one coastline. On certain days it became almost a frenzy: on December 6 he named six places, on the nineteenth six more, and on January 11 no fewer than ten—eight capes, a point, and a mountain. It is almost as if, as he sailed along the last of the islands, he was determined to leave his mark on it the only way he knew how, and thus to establish his authority—and by extension Spain's—even, as with baptism, to make it thus sanctified, and real, and official. (One should note that it was only his *own* naming that conveyed legitimacy: when Colón thought Martín Alonso Pinzón had named a river after himself, he immediately renamed it Río de Gracia instead.)

This business of naming and "possessing" foreign islands was by no means casual. The Admiral took it very seriously, pointing out that "it was my wish to bypass no island without taking possession" (October 15) and that "in all regions [I] always left a cross standing" (November 16) as a mark of Christian dominance. There even seem to have been certain prescriptions for it (the instructions from the Sovereigns speak of "the administering of the oath and the performing of the rites prescribed in such cases"), and Rodrigo de Escobedo was sent along as secretary of the fleet explicitly to witness and record these events in detail.

But consider the implications of this act and the questions it raises again about what was in the Sovereigns' minds, what in Colón's. Why would the Admiral assume that these territories were in some way *un*possessed—even by those clearly inhabiting them—and thus available for Spain to claim? Why would he not think twice about the possibility that some considerable potentate—the Grand Khan of China, for example, whom he later acknowledged (November 6) "must be" the ruler of Española—might descend upon him at any moment with a greater military force than his three vessels commanded and punish him for his territorial presumption? Why would he make the ceremony of possession his very first act on shore, even before meeting the inhabitants or exploring the environs, or finding out if anybody there objected to being thus possessed— particularly if they actually owned the great treasures he hoped would be there? No European would have imagined that anyone—three small boatloads of Indians, say—could come up to a European shore or island and "take possession" of it, nor would a European imagine marching up to some part of North Africa or the Middle East and claiming sovereignty there with impunity. Why were these lands thought to be different?

Could there be any reason for the Admiral to assume he had reached "unclaimed" shores, new lands that lay far from the domains of any of the potentates of the East? Can that really have been in his mind—or can it all be explained as simple Eurocentrism, or Eurosuperiority, mixed with cupidity and naiveté?

In any case, it is quite curious how casually and calmly the Admiral took to this task of possession, so much so that he gave only the most meager description of the initial ceremony on San Salvador, despite its having been a signal event in his career. He recorded merely that he went ashore in his long-boat, armed, followed by the captains of the two caravels, accompanied by royal standards and banners and two representatives of the court to "witness how he before them all was taking, as in fact he took, possession of the said island for the King and Queen." He added that he made "the declarations that are required, as is contained at greater length in the testimonies which were there taken down in writing," but he unfortunately didn't specify what these were and no such documents survive; we are left only with the image of a party of fully dressed and armored Europeans standing there on the white sand in the blazing morning heat while Escobedo, with his parchment and inkpot and quill, painstakingly writes down the Admiral's oaths.

Fernando Colón did enlarge on this scene, presumably on the authority of his imagination alone, describing how the little party then "rendered thanks to Our Lord, kneeling on the ground and kissing it with tears of joy for His great favor to them," after which the crew members "swore obedience" to the Admiral "with such a show of pleasure and joy" and "begged his pardon for the injuries that through fear and little faith they had done him." He added that these goings-on were performed in the presence of the "many natives assembled there," whose reactions are not described and whose opinions are not recorded. . . .

Once safely "possessed," San Salvador was open for inspection. Now the Admiral turned his attention for the first time to the "naked people" staring at him on the beach—he did not automatically give them a name, interestingly enough, and it would be another six days before he decided what he might call them—and tried to win their favor with his trinkets.

> They all go around as naked as their mothers bore them; and also the women, although I didn't see more than one really young girl. All that I saw were young people [*mancebos*], none of them more than 30 years old. They are very well built, with very handsome bodies and very good faces; their hair [is] coarse, almost like the silk of a horse's tail, and short. They wear their hair over their eyebrows, except for a little in the back that they wear long and never cut. Some of them paint themselves black (and they are of the color of the Canary Islanders, neither black nor white), and some paint themselves white, and some red, and some with what they find. And some paint their faces, and some of them the whole body, and some the eyes only, and some of them only the nose.

It may fairly be called the birth of American anthropology.

A crude anthropology, of course, as superficial as Colón's descriptions always were when his interest was limited, but simple and straightforward enough, with none of the fable and fantasy that characterized many earlier (and even some later) accounts of new-found peoples. There was no pretense to objectivity, or any sense that these people might be representatives of a culture equal to, or in any way a model for, Europe's. Colón immediately presumed the inferiority of the natives, not merely because (a sure enough sign) they were naked, but because (his society could have no surer measure) they seemed so technologically backward. "It appeared to me that these people were very poor in everything," he wrote on that first day, and, worse still, "they have no iron." And they went on to prove their inferiority to the Admiral by being ignorant of even such a basic artifact of European life as a sword: "They bear no arms, nor are they acquainted with them," he wrote, "for I showed them swords and they grasped them by the blade and cut themselves through ignorance." Thus did European arms spill the first drops of native blood on the sands of the New World, accompanied not with a gasp of compassion but with a smirk of superiority.

Then, just six sentences further on, Colón clarified what this inferiority meant in his eyes:

> They ought to be good servants and of good intelligence [*ingenio*]. . . . I believe that they would easily be made Christians, because it seemed to me that they had no religion. Our Lord pleasing, I will carry off six of them at my departure to Your Highnesses, in order that they may learn to speak.

No clothes, no arms, no possessions, no iron, and now no religion—not even speech: hence they were fit to be servants, and captives. It may fairly be called the birth of American slavery.

Whether or not the idea of slavery was in Colón's mind all along is uncertain, although he did suggest he had had experience as a slave trader in Africa (November 12) and he certainly knew of Portuguese plantation slavery in the Madeiras and Spanish slavery of Guanches in the Canaries. But it seems to have taken shape early and grown ever firmer as the weeks went on and as he captured more and more of the helpless natives. At one point he even sent his crew ashore to kidnap "seven head of women, young ones and adults, and three small children"; the expression of such callousness led the Spanish historian Salvador de Madariaga to remark, "It would be difficult to find a starker utterance of utilitarian subjection of man by man than this passage [whose] form is no less devoid of human feeling than its substance."

To be sure, Colón knew nothing about these people he encountered and considered enslaving, and he was hardly trained to find out very much, even if he was moved to care. But they were in fact members of an extensive, populous, and successful people whom Europe, using its own peculiar taxonomy, subsequently called "Taino" (or "Taíno"), their own word for "good" or "noble," and their response when asked who they were. They were related distantly by both language and culture to the Arawak people of the South American mainland, but it is misleading (and needlessly imprecise) to call them Arawaks, as historians are wont to do, when the term "Taino" better establishes their ethnic and historical distinctiveness. They had migrated to the islands from the mainland at about the time of the birth of Christ, occupying the three large islands we now call the Greater Antilles and arriving at Guanahani (Colón's San Salvador) and the end of the Bahamian chain probably sometime around A.D. 900. There they displaced an earlier people, the Guanahacabibes (sometimes called Guanahatabeys), who by the time of the European discovery occupied only the western third of Cuba and possibly remote corners of Española; and there, probably in the early fifteenth century, they eventually confronted another people moving up the islands from the mainland, the Caribs, whose culture eventually occupied a dozen small islands of what are called the Lesser Antilles.

The Tainos were not nearly so backward as Colón assumed from their lack of dress. (It might be said that it was the Europeans, who generally kept clothed head to foot during the day despite temperatures regularly in the eighties, who were the more unsophisticated in garmenture—especially since the Tainos, as Colón later noted, also used their body paint to prevent sunburn.) Indeed, they had achieved a means of living in a balanced and fruitful harmony with their natural surroundings that any society might well have envied. They had, to begin with, a not unsophisticated technology that made exact use of their available resources, two parts of which were so impressive that they were picked up and adopted by the European invaders: *canoa* (canoes) that were carved and fire-burned from large silk-cotton trees, "all in one piece, and wonderfully made" (October 13), some of which were capable of carrying up to 150 passengers; and *hamaca* (hammocks) that were "like nets of cotton" (October 17) and may have been a staple item of trade with Indian tribes as far away as the Florida mainland. Their houses were not only spacious and clean—as the Europeans noted with surprise and appreciation, used as they were to the generally crowded and slovenly hovels and huts of south European peasantry—but more apropos, remarkably resistant to hurricanes; the circular walls were made of strong cane poles set deep and close together ("as close as the fingers of a hand," Colón noted), the conical roofs of branches and vines tightly interwoven on a frame of smaller poles and covered with heavy palm leaves. Their artifacts and jewelry, with the exception of a few gold trinkets and ornaments, were based largely on renewable materials, including bracelets and necklaces of coral, shells, bone, and stone, embroidered cotton belts, woven baskets, carved statues and chairs, wooden and shell utensils, and pottery of variously intricate decoration depending on period and place.

Perhaps the most sophisticated, and most carefully integrated, part of their technology was their agricultural system, extraordinarily productive and perfectly adapted to the conditions of the island environment. It was based primarily on fields of knee-high mounds, called *conucos*, planted with *yuca* (sometimes called manioc), *batata* (sweet potato), and various squashes and beans grown all together in multicrop harmony: the root crops were excellent in resisting erosion and producing minerals and potash, the leaf crops effective in providing shade and moisture, and the mound configurations largely resistant to erosion and flooding and adaptable to almost all topographic conditions including steep hillsides. Not only was the *conuco* system environmentally appropriate—"conuco agriculture seems to have provided an exceptionally ecologically well-balanced and protective form of land use," according to David Watts's recent and authoritative *West Indies*—but it was also highly productive, surpassing in yields anything known in Europe at the time, with labor that amounted to hardly more than two or three hours a week, and in continuous yearlong harvest. The pioneering American geographical scholar Carl Sauer calls Taino agriculture "productive as few parts of the world," giving the "highest returns of food in continuous supply by the simplest methods and modest labor," and adds, with a touch of regret, "The white man never fully appreciated the excellent combination of plants that were grown in conucos."

In their arts of government the Tainos seem to have achieved a parallel sort of harmony. Most villages were small (ten to fifteen families) and autonomous, although many apparently recognized loose allegiances with neighboring villages, and they were governed by a hereditary official called a *kaseke* (*cacique*, in the Spanish form), something of a cross between an arbiter and a prolocutor, supported by advisers and elders. So little a part did violence play in their system that they seem, remarkably, to have been a society without war (at least we know of no war music or signals or artifacts, and no evidence of intertribal combats) and even without overt conflict (Las Casas reports that no Spaniard ever saw two Tainos fighting). And here we come to what was obviously the Tainos' outstanding cultural achievement, a proficiency in the social arts that led those who first met them to comment unfailingly on their friendliness, their warmth, their openness, and above all—so striking to those of an acquisitive culture— their generosity.

"They are the best people in the world and above all the gentlest," Colón recorded in his *Journal* (December 16), and from first to last he was astonished at their kindness:

> They became so much our friends that it was a marvel.... They traded and gave everything they had, with good will [October 12].
>
> I sent the ship's boat ashore for water, and they very willingly showed my people where the water was, and they themselves carried the full barrels to the boat, and took great delight in pleasing us [October 16].
>
> They are very gentle and without knowledge of what is evil; nor do they murder or steal [November 12].
>
> Your Highnesses may believe that in all the world there can be no better or gentler people ... for neither better people nor land can there be.... All the people show the most singular loving behavior and they speak pleasantly [December 24].
>
> I assure Your Highnesses that I believe that in all the world there is no better people nor better country. They love their neighbors as themselves, and they have the sweetest talk in the world, and are gentle and always laughing [December 25].

Even if one allows for some exaggeration—Colón was clearly trying to convince Ferdinand and Isabella that his Indians could be easily conquered and converted, should that be the Sovereigns' wish—it is obvious that the Tainos exhibited a manner of social discourse that quite impressed the rough Europeans. But that was not high among the traits of "civilized" nations, as Colón and Europe understood it, and it counted for little in the Admiral's assessment of these people. However struck he was with such behavior, he would not have thought that it was the mark of a benign and harmonious society, or that from it another culture might learn. For him it was something like the wondrous behavior of children, the naive guilelessness of prelapsarian creatures who knew no better how to bargain and chaffer and cheat than they did to dress themselves: "For a lace-point they gave good pieces of gold the size of two fingers" (January 6), and "They even took pieces of the broken hoops of the wine casks and, like beasts [*como besti*], gave what they had" (Santangel Letter). Like beasts; such innocence was not human.

It is to be regretted that the Admiral, unable to see past their nakedness, as it were, knew not the real virtues of the people he confronted. For the Tainos' lives were in many ways as idyllic as their surroundings, into which they fit with such skill and comfort. They were well fed and well housed, without poverty or serious disease. They enjoyed considerable leisure, given over to dancing, singing, ballgames, and sex, and expressed themselves artistically in basketry, woodworking, pottery, and jewelry. They lived in general harmony and peace, without greed or covetousness or theft. In short, as Sauer says, "the tropical idyll of the accounts of Columbus and Peter Martyr was largely true." . . .

One of the alternative possibilities for future Spanish glory in these none too promising islands suggested itself to Colón almost from the first. On his third day of exploration—a Sunday at that—he had set out to see "where there might be a fortress [built]" and in no time at all found a spit of land on which "there might be a fortress"—and from which "with fifty men they [the Tainos] could all be subjected and made to do all that one might wish" (October 14). Now, during the second leg of exploration along the north coast of Cuba, this grew into a full-blown fantasy of a colonial outpost, complete with a rich trade and merchants. And so Colón went on, rather like a young boy playing soldiers, turning various pieces of landscape into military sites: Puerto de Mares on November 5, a harbor for "a store and a fortress" on November 12, another harbor where "a fortress could be erected" on November 16, a placed where "a town or city and fortress" could be built on November 27—until finally, as we shall see, misfortune enabled him to translate his fancy into reality.

Now there was no particular reason to go about constructing fortresses—"I don't see that it would be necessary, because these people are very unskilled in arms" (October 14)—but that was the way his architectural imagination, suffused with his vision of colonial destiny, seemed to work: a spit of land, a promontory, a protected harbor, and right away he saw a fort. Such was the deeply ingrained militarism of fifteenth-century Europe, in which fortresses represent edifices more essential to civilization even than churches or castles.

It may have been that Colón began his explorations with nothing more than an idea of establishing some sort of entrepôt in these islands, a fortress-protected trading post rather like the one the Portuguese had established, and Colón had perhaps visited, on the Gold Coast of Africa, at El Mina. But as he sailed along the coast of Cuba he seems to have contrived something even grander, not just a trading port but an outright colonial settlement, an outpost of empire where Spaniards would settle and prosper, living off the labor of the natives ("Command them to do what you will," December 16) and the trade of the Europeans.

On November 27, toward the end of his sojourn along Cuba, Colón put into a large "very singular harbor" which he named Puerto Santo (today known as Puerto Baracoa, about a hundred miles from the eastern tip of the island) and was nearly speechless at its tropical splendor: "Truly, I was so astounded at the sight of so much beauty that I know not how to express myself." The vision of conquest, however, loosened his tongue, and at great length, too:

> And Your Highnesses will command a city and fortress to be built in these
> parts, and these lands converted; and I assure Your Highnesses that it seems
> to me that there could never be under the sun [lands] superior in fertility,
> in mildness of cold and heat, in abundance of good and healthy water....
> So may it please God that Your Highnesses will send here, or that there will

come, learned men and they will see the truth of all. And although before I have spoken of the site of a town and fortress on the Rio de Mares... yet there is no comparing that place with this here or with the Mar de Nuestra Señora; for inland here must be great settlements and innumerable people and things of great profit; for here, and in all else that I have discovered and have hopes of discovering before I return to Castile, I say that all Christendom will do business [*dad negociaçion*] with them, but most of all Spain, to which all this should be subject. And I say that Your Highnesses ought not to consent that any foreigner trade or set foot here except Catholic Christians, since this was the end and the beginning of the enterprise [*proposito*], that it was for the enhancement and glory of the Christian religion, nor should anyone who is not a good Christian come to these parts.

It may fairly be called the birth of European colonialism.

Here, for the first time that we know, are the outlines of the policy that not only Spain but other European countries would indeed adopt in the years to come, complete with conquest, religious conversion, city settlements, fortresses, exploitation, international trade, and exclusive domain. And that colonial policy would be very largely responsible for endowing those countries with the pelf, power, patronage, and prestige that allowed them to become the nation-states they did.

Again, one is at a loss to explain quite why Colón would so casually assume a right to the conquest and colonialization, even the displacement and enslavement, of these peaceful and inoffensive people 3,000 miles across the ocean. Except, of course, insofar as might, in European eyes, made that right, and after all "they bear no arms, and are all naked and of no skill in arms, and so very cowardly that a thousand would not stand against [*aguardariá*] three" (December 16). But assume it he did, and even Morison suggests that "every man in the fleet from servant boy to Admiral was convinced that no Christian need do a hand's turn of work in the Indies; and before them opened the delightful vision of growing rich by exploiting the labor of docile natives." The Admiral at least had no difficulty in seeing the Tainos in this light: "They are fit to be ordered about and made to work, to sow and do everything else that may be needed" (December 16); "nothing was lacking but to know the language and to give them orders, because all that they are ordered to do they will do without opposition" (December 21).

Missed in the dynamics of the assumed right of colonialism was an extraordinary opportunity, had it only been possible for the Christian intruders to know it, an opportunity for a dispirited and melancholy Europe to have learned something about fecundity and regeneration, about social comeliness and amity, about harmony with the natural world. The appropriate architecture for Colón to have envisioned along these shores might have been a forum, or an amphitheater, or an academy, perhaps an auditorium or a tabernacle; instead, a fortress....

Originally, so he tells us (October 19), Colón had planned to return to Castile sometime in April, when, he presumably knew from his earlier travels, the North Atlantic would be past its winter storm season. But now, after the wreck of the *Santa María* and with news that the *Pinta* was not far away, he apparently decided to sail back immediately. It was a risky decision and most unseamanlike—as he would soon discover, when he was blown off course and almost capsized by two fierce storms in February and March—that leads one to assume that the Admiral's need was dire. Yet all he ever said, a few days later, was that he intended to head back home "without detaining himself further," because "he had found that which he was seeking" (January 9) and intended "to come at full speed to carry the news" (January 8)....

Whatever the reasons for his haste, the Admiral certainly made his way along the remainder of the island's coast with great alacrity, and little more than a week after he met up with Pinzón, the two caravels were off on the homeward leg. Only one notable stop was made, at a narrow bay some 200 miles east of La Navidad, where a party Colón sent ashore discovered, for the first time, some Indians with bows and arrows.

The Admiral having given standing orders that his men should buy or barter away the weaponry of the Indians—they had done so on at least two previous occasions, presumably without causing enmity—these men in the longboat began to dicker with the bowmen with the plumes. After just two bows were sold, the Indians turned and ran back to the cover of the trees where they kept their remaining weapons and, so the sailors assumed, "prepared... to attack the Christians and capture them." When they came toward the Spaniards again brandishing ropes—almost certainly meaning to trade these rather than give up their precious bows—the sailors panicked and, "being prepared as always the Admiral advised them to be," attacked the Indians with swords and halberds, gave one "a great slash on the buttocks" and shot another in the breast with a crossbow. The Tainos grabbed their fallen comrades and fled in fright, and the sailors would have chased them and "killed many of them" but for the pilot in charge of the party, who somehow "prevented it." It may fairly be called the first pitched battle between Europeans and Indians in the New World—the first display of the armed power, and the will to use it, of the white invaders.

And did the Admiral object to this, transgressing as it did his previous idea of trying to maintain good relations with the natives so as to make them willing trading partners, if not docile servants? Hardly at all: now, he said, "they would have fear of the Christians," and he celebrated the skirmish by naming the cape and the harbor de las Flechas—of the Arrows.

It was not the first time (or the last) that Colón was able to delude himself—it may indeed have been a European assumption—that violence can buy obedience. Twice before, he had used a display of European arms to frighten the Tainos, to no purpose other than instilling more fear and awe than they already felt: once on December 26, when he had a Turkish longbow, a gun [*espingarda*], and a lombard demonstrated, at which occasion the people "all fell to earth" in terror and the *kaseke* "was astonished"; then again on the eve of his departure from La Navidad, when he ordered a lombard fired from the new fortress out at the remains of the *Santa María* so that Guacanagarí, when he saw "how it pierced the side of the ship and how the ball went far out to sea," would then "hold the Christians whom [Colón] left behind as friends" and be so scared "that he might fear them." Strange behavior at any time; toward this softhearted *kaseke* and his kindly people, almost inexplicable.

NO

Robert Royal

El Almirante

Let us hear what their comments are now—those who are so ready with accusations and quick to find fault, saying from their safe berths there in Spain, "Why didn't you do this or that when you were over there." I'd like to see their sort on this adventure. Verily I believe, there's another journey, of quite a different order, for them to make, or all our faith is vain.

— Columbus
Lettera Rarissima

After centuries of controversies, the life of Columbus lies beneath mountains of interpretation and misinterpretation. Sharp criticism of *El Almirante* (the admiral)—and sharp reaction to it—go back to the very beginnings of his explorations, as the passage cited above, written at a particularly threatening moment during Columbus's fourth and final voyage to the New World, graphically shows. Then, as now, it was easy for people who had never dared comparable feats to suggest how the whole business might have been done better. And in truth, Columbus's manifest errors and downright incapacities as a leader of men, anywhere but on the sea, played into the hands of his critics and properly made him the target of protests. His failures in leadership provoked atrocities against the Caribbean natives and harsh punishment, including executions, of Spaniards as well. Stubbornness, obsessiveness, and paranoia often dominated his psyche. Even many of his closest allies in the initial ventures clashed with him over one thing or another. In the wake of the titanic passions his epochal voyages unleashed, it is no wonder that almost every individual and event connected with his story has been praised or damned by someone during the past five hundred years....

Fact and Imagination

The temptation to project modern categories back upon earlier historical periods is always strong. Reviewing these first late-fifteenth-century contacts now, with knowledge of what befell indigenous peoples later, we are particularly inclined to read large-scale portents into small events. If Columbus mentions how

From Robert Royal, *1492 and All That: Political Manipulations of History* (Ethics and Public Policy Center, 1992). Copyright © 1992 by The Ethics and Public Policy Center, Washington, D.C. Reprinted by permission. Notes omitted.

easy it would be to subdue the natives, or expresses impatience with his failure to find the high and rich civilization of Asia, many historians readily fall into the error of seeing his attitudes as a combination of careless imperialism and greed, or even as a symbol of all that was to follow. We would do well to recall, however, that the Spanish record after Columbus is complex and not wholly bad, particularly in its gradual elaboration of native rights.

In Columbus the man, several conflicting currents existed side by side. [Bartolomé de] Las Casas is an important witness here because of both his passionate commitment to justice for Indians and his personal association with Columbus for several years. In a telling remark, Las Casas notes that while Christopher's brother, Bartolomé, was a resolute leader, he lacked the "sweetness and benignity" of the admiral. Columbus's noble bearing and gentle manners are confirmed in many other sources. Nevertheless, Las Casas can be harsh in his criticism. Chapter 119 of *History of the Indies* concludes with the judgment that both brothers mistakenly began to occupy land and exact tribute owing to "the most culpable ignorance, which has no excuse, of natural and divine law."

After five hundred years it may seem impossible to reconcile the contradictory traits Las Casas mentions. He attempted an explanation of his own:

> Truly, I would not dare blame the admiral's intentions, for I knew him well and I know his intentions were good. But ... the road he paved and the things he did of his own free will, as well as sometimes under constraint, stemmed from his ignorance of the law. There is much to ponder here and one can see the guiding principle of this whole Indian enterprise, namely, as is clear from the previous chapters, that the admiral and his Christians, as well as all those who followed after him in this land, worked on the assumption that the way to achieve their desires was first and foremost to instill fear in these people, to the extent of making the name Christian synonymous with terror. And to do this, they performed outstanding feats never before invented or dreamed of, as, God willing, I will show later. And this is contrary and inimical to the way that those who profess Christian benignity, gentleness and peace ought to negotiate the conversion of infidels.

As this excerpt shows, Las Casas's style of writing and mode of reasoning do not always yield great clarity, and his assessment here begs several questions. Columbus's policies, and official Spanish policy generally, were much more given to gentleness and kindness in the beginning than Las Casas, who only witnessed later troubled times, allows to appear. There is no question that conflicts with natives and factional infighting among Spaniards drove the admiral to more onerous measures, including enslavement of Indians captured in military actions.

While Las Casas's condemnation is cast in terms of absolute justice and as such has permanent relevance to evaluating Columbus's role in the New World, we should remember that Columbus was placed in unprecedented circumstances and should not be judged in the same way as we would a modern trained anthropologist. Paolo Emilio Taviani, an admiring but not uncritical recent biographer of Columbus, demonstrates the difficulty attending every particular of the first contact:

> The European scale of values was different from that of the natives. "They give everything for a trifle"; obviously what was a trifle on the European scale was not so for the natives. For them "a potsherd or a broken glass cup" was worth "sixteen skeins of cotton." Columbus warned that would never do, because from unrestricted trade between the two mentalities, the two conceptions of value, grave injustices would result, and so he immediately prohibited the cotton trade, allowing no one to take any and reserving the acquisition entirely for the king of Spain. A just prohibition, not easy to impose on ninety men—what strength could it have when nine hundred, nine thousand, or ninety thousand Europeans would arrive? Such were the first troubles in an encounter between two worlds that did not understand one another.

If we wish to task Columbus for all the asymmetries that ensued, we should credit him as well for this initial attempt, later repeated by many Spanish governors and theologians, to find some just route through the thicket of massive cultural difference. He failed and permitted far more wicked practices than unequal trade, but we should not let subsequent events blind us to his authentic concern for justice in the first contacts.

Some Brighter Moments

In spite of the cultural gulf, mutual affections and understanding did, at times, appear. After over two months of exploration in the Caribbean, Columbus's ship, the *Santa Maria*, went aground on Christmas 1492 in what is now Haiti. There Columbus encountered a people and a chief so helpful that his log entries for the following days view the entire episode as providential. He would never have chosen, as he admits, to come ashore or build the settlement of La Navidad (Christmas) there. He did not like the harbor at all. Yet he concluded that his relations with the Taínos and their chief Guacanagarí must be part of a divine plan in light of the friendship that sprung up between the two peoples.

Some Columbus scholars, perhaps a bit jaded from staring overlong at the historical lacunae and inconsistencies of the man, see in these log entries only an attempt to cover up the disastrous loss of the ship or a propaganda ploy to make the Spanish monarchs think well of the discoveries. Robert H. Fuson, a modern translator of the log, is a marine historian rather than a Columbus specialist. He is sometimes rightly criticized for his rather naive historical interpretations. But it is precisely because he is not predisposed to suspicion that he notices something overlooked by scholars occupied with weighing too many contradictory theories about the Haiti episode:

> Affection for the young chief in Haiti, and vice versa, is one of the most touching stories of love, trust, and understanding between men of different races and cultures to come out of this period in history. His [Columbus's] instructions to the men he left behind at La Navidad, for January 2, clearly illustrate his sincere fondness and respect for the Indians.

The January 2 entry, as we shall see below, indicates that Columbus had some ulterior motives in placating the natives. But that does not negate his genuine good feeling toward them or his gratitude for their generosity. Even if we assume that Columbus is putting the best interpretation on events for Ferdinand and Isabella, some sort of fellow feeling undeniably had arisen, at least temporarily, across the vast cultural divide separating the Taínos and the Europeans. Despite the great evils that would come later, this altruism was not without its own modest legacies.

An extreme but common form of the over-simple charges often leveled against the Europeans in general and Columbus in particular has come from the pen of the novelist Hans Koning. Writing in the *Washington Post* to influence public sentiments about the quincentenary, Koning insisted that from 1492 to 1500,

> there is not one recorded moment of awe, of joy, of love, of a smile. There is only anger, cruelty, greed, terror, and death. That is the record. Nothing else, I hold, is relevant when we discuss our commemoration of its 500th anniversary.

Riding the wave of revisionism about American history now sweeping over education, Koning made these claims under the title "Teach the Truth About Columbus."

The only problem with his assessment is that every particular in his catalog of what constitutes the truth is false. To take them in order: Columbus certainly records awe at his discoveries throughout his four voyages. His praise of the land's beauty was partly meant, of course, to convince the king and queen of the value of the properties Columbus had discovered for them. But some of it is simply awe; Columbus's enthusiasm for many of the new lands reaches a climax when he describes the sheer loveliness of the Venezuelan coast, which he believed to be the site of the original Garden of Eden, the earthly paradise. If that is not a record of awe, it is difficult to imagine what would be.

The relations between natives and Spaniards before 1500 are not, *pace* Koning, unrelieved darkness either. If anything, they are a frustrating reminder of a road not taken. Smiles there were—recorded smiles—at least on the native Taíno side: "They love their neighbors as themselves, and they have the softest and gentlest voices in the world and are always smiling" (*Log*, Tuesday, 25 December 1492). Columbus had reason to appreciate these people since they had just helped him salvage what was salvageable from the wreck of the *Santa María*. In the feast natives and Spaniards held after the rescue, the cacique Guacanagarí placed a crown on Columbus's head. The admiral reciprocated by giving him a scarlet cloak and a pair of colored boots, "and I placed upon his finger a large silver ring. I had been told that he had seen a silver ring on one of my sailors and desired it very much. The King was joyful and overwhelmed." Guacanagarí grew so close to Columbus that he asked if he and his brother might return with him to Castile.

When it came time to leave for Spain, Columbus placed thirty-nine men "under the command of three officers, all of whom are very friendly to King Guacanagarí," and furthermore ordered that "they should avoid *as they would death* annoying or tormenting the Indians, bearing in mind how much they owe these people." The emphasis added to this last quotation has a double purpose. Clearly, Columbus recognized the temptations his men would have; just as clearly he was determined, to the best of his ability, to anticipate and block those temptations. This is the entry of January 2 that Fuson reads as expressing sincere kindness and affection. That reading may be a little too simple, but it is not entirely mistaken.

What this incident and the founding of the settlement definitely are *not*, however, are instances of simple European arrogance and imperialism, or what John Noble Wilford, a recent biographer of Columbus, has called "a personal transition from discoverer to imperialist." Even when full-scale war between some Indians and Spaniards broke out during Columbus's second voyage, Guacanagarí remained loyal to Columbus in spite of—or perhaps in opposition to—commands from another local chief, Caonabó, for a cacique alliance. No source denies this loyalty between the Taíno and the admiral, even under trying cultural tensions and warfare. Though we are right to abhor many far-less-happy subsequent events between the inhabitants of the two worlds, the record of the early interaction is richer and more diverse than most people, blinded by contemporary polemics, think. Hans Koning might do well to calm down and read some of these passages.

The List of Charges

The principal moral questions about Columbus arise essentially from three of his actions:

1. He immediately kidnapped some Taínos during his first voyage for questioning and use as interpreters. In that act he showed not only his contempt for Indian life but his belief that Spanish language, culture, and religion were superior and rightly to be imposed on native peoples.

2. After the destruction of La Navidad and the turmoil that ensued during the second voyage, Columbus foolishly ordered exploratory missions without adequate safeguards to restrain outrageously violent men like Mosen Pedro Margarit and Alonso de Ojeda. He then punished the natives who objected to Spaniards living off the land or who resisted their commands. In addition to setting this evil precedent, he shipped home some natives to become slaves with a very poor excuse:

> Since of all the islands those of the cannibals are much the largest and much more fully populated, it is thought here that to take some of the men and women and to send them home to Castile would not be anything but well, for they may one day be led to abandon that inhuman custom that they have of eating men, and there in Castile, learning the language, they will much more readily receive baptism and secure the welfare of their souls.

3. Columbus instituted a system of gold tribute from the natives that was heavy—nearly impossible, in fact, given the small quantity of gold on the island of Hispaniola—and that was harshly enforced.

Each of these charges is true and no amount of admiration for Christopher Columbus can excuse what is simply inexcusable. Even the argument by Felipe Fernández-Armesto, one of the fairest Columbus historians, that "Columbus and his successors were guilty only of applying the best standards of their time" makes two false assumptions. First, that such behavior represents the best contemporary standards.... Second, that individuals should not be criticized for acting like the majority of their contemporaries because they are bound by culture and history. The latter argument draws strength from current philosophical schools that hold there are no privileged or absolute positions outside of historically conditioned views. But if we think we should condemn Aztec human sacrifice as wrong—not simply a different cultural form, but wrong— then we must admit there are universal principles that also allow us to criticize improper European use of force, enslavement, and exploitation.

Yet just as we try to understand the reasons behind Aztec human sacrifice or Carib cannibalism, and both tribes' imperialism toward other native peoples, we should also try to see what led to Columbus's behavior. Columbus, as Las Casas testified above, was not by nature a brutal man like Ojeda or Cortés. The first sign of harshness by him, in fact, seems to have been his acquiescence, during the second voyage, in a death sentence against some Indians on Hispaniola who had been caught stealing. Significantly, the pleading of another Indian moved him to remit the sentence in that case (the wavering too is characteristic of the uncertainty in handling questions of governance). Though he apparently regarded the Indians as inferior and always approached them with much the same assumption of superiority that Spaniards approached the Guanches of the Canary Islands and African tribes, he seemed at least partly—and when circumstances allowed—aware that good treatment was both morally called for and favorable to Spanish interests.

A fairer reading of the record reveals some mitigating factors, though these by no means add up to an exoneration.

1. Though Columbus did kidnap some Indians, two interpreters among them, he set one of them free immediately upon returning to Hispaniola during the second voyage. He hoped that the Indian set at liberty would tell others of Spain's wonders and of Columbus's good intentions. This was naive, crude, and manipulative on his part, but shows some perspicacity and good will.

2. Slavery was always a bone of contention between Columbus and the Spanish monarchs—they vehemently opposed this way of "civilizing" their subjects in the Indies. Columbus was not clear in his own mind about the issue. As late as the third voyage, the last in which he would be permitted to visit the growing colony on Hispaniola, Columbus ordered that slaves could only be taken during just war. His thinking was muddled, as was the thinking of the world for at least another half century until several crucial questions about Indian rights and just claims were sorted out.

3. The imposition of gold tribute for Spanish services stemmed from the belief that much gold existed on Hispaniola. And Indian failures to meet what seemed to the Spaniards modest levies were mistakenly attributed to laziness. Indians loved the tiny hawk's bells that the Spaniards brought as trinkets; asking them to fill a bell with gold every two months seemed a reasonable request.

Since all governments tax in some fashion, Spain was doing only what caciques and Carib conquerors had been doing for time immemorial. The Spanish system did not "introduce" a new evil to an idyllic people without politics, but it proved peculiarly burdensome because it was imposed from the outside and in ignorance of the realities on Hispaniola. Furthermore, contrary to many wild charges, the Spaniards never intended to commit "genocide." A ready supply of native workers served Spanish self-interest. European and African diseases, however, soon laid waste whole tribes.

Fernández-Armesto argues that Columbus's recourse to violence on Hispaniola resulted mostly from his basic inability to rule well, from "misjudgment rather than wickedness." Gonzalo Fernandez de Oviedo, who became the official Spanish historian of the New World, said that to govern the Hispaniola colony correctly a person would have to be "angelic indeed superhuman." Columbus was far from either; in fact, he was far from possessing even normal political acumen. During his second and third voyages he clearly tried to avoid facing political difficulties on Hispaniola by exploring further. The problem was not merely lack of political skill. As a foreigner, he felt that he could trust only family members and close personal friends. (In fact, recent research has revealed that the Columbus family belonged to an anti-Spanish faction in Genoa, a political embarrassment that may help account for some of Columbus's reticence about his early life.) The resentments arising from difficult conditions, moreover, served to reinforce his tendencies toward paranoia. His rule of both Indians and Spanish oscillated between being too indecisive and too harsh.

We should also understand the kinds of Indians and colonists he had to govern. Columbus had trouble enough with the natives and complained:

> At home they judge me as a governor sent to Sicily or to a city or two under settled government and where the laws can be fully maintained, without fear of all being lost.... I ought to be judged as a captain who went from Spain to the Indies to conquer a people, warlike and numerous, and with customs and beliefs very different from ours.

Even the Taínos were probably far less gentle than Columbus earlier reported and "not so innocent as Las Casas tried to show." The Caribs, their fierce, cannibalistic enemies, seem to have been as terrified of the supposedly pacific Taínos as vice versa. And recent archeological investigations suggest that the Taínos, contrary to Columbus's impression of them as being without religion, had a complex system of belief and ritual akin to those in Central America and Mexico. They appear to have played a ritual ball game re-enacting the cosmic struggle between light and darkness and ending with the religious sacrifice of one or more human victims. An early Spanish conquistador estimated that twenty thousand people were sacrificed yearly on Hispaniola alone, though that figure may be wildly exaggerated. In any event, native tribes were profoundly *other* to the unsophisticated sailors and explorers in Columbus's day— and remain profoundly other to us today.

The Spaniards with whom Columbus had to deal were not much better. After the second voyage he asked the monarchs to think carefully about whom they were sending on the voyages and to choose "such persons that there be no suspicion of them and that they consider the purpose for which they have been sent rather than their personal interests." Not only were some of the colonists unusually violent, but many Spanish gentlemen who had come expecting easy wealth resented Columbus, the need to work, and the unhealthy conditions on the island. In dealing with these settlers, as Las Casas observed, "The Admiral had to use violence, threats, and constraint to have the work done at all." ...

Bad in Any Case

... In Kirkpatrick Sale [*The Conquest of Paradise: Christopher Columbus and the Columbian Legacy*], Columbus is uniquely and doubly condemned for being medieval *and* for being of the Renaissance. His medieval side reflects superstitions, and his Renaissance side shows the destructive force of naked instrumental and mathematical reason, which Sale largely identifies with Renaissance Europe. Nevertheless, Sale also feels free to castigate Columbus for his lack of interest in numbers, that is, for not giving us the exact mathematical coordinates of the island where he made first landfall. Poor Columbus is merely the product of various opposing evil traditions that define Europe and Europeans—of which we are all the heirs, save, of course, the Kirkpatrick Sales who transcend cultural determinism.

All these attempts at neat categorizations assume that we can define a man, as well as a historical period, with far sharper boundaries than is ever the case. The mixture of human weakness and human greatness in even a key figure is never easy to calculate. The novelist Anthony Burgess has recently created a Mozart who says, "My desire and my hope is to gain honor, fame, and money." That sentence plausibly formulates a great deal of truth about Mozart's life. Yet few music lovers would deduce from this that Mozart's work is, therefore, solely the product of ambition and cupidity, or try to explain the man and his music by sociological analysis of the late eighteenth century. Columbus similarly spoke of "God, gold, and glory," and many of the Europeans who followed him were driven by multiple motives, not all of which were, by any means, merely self-serving.

Kirkpatrick Sale, as usual, well formulates the ultimate issue behind much of the public controversy over 1992:

> In the final analysis, it is not so important whether Columbus was a good man. What matters is that he brought over a culture centered on its own superiority. The failings of the man were and remain the failures of the culture.

This is a strained argument. It certainly does matter, if only for the sake of historical justice, that we try to discern the mix of good and evil in Columbus *per se*. Furthermore, no one can simply be identified with a whole culture. Every individual both draws on and opposes elements in his surroundings. If the preceding pages show anything, they show that Columbus, like the rest of us, was not simply good or bad. As a great human spirit, both his virtues and faults appear larger and more vivid than they do in most people. And his historical influence reflects the dimensions of what he was. The argument about the European sense of superiority, however, can be engaged quite well without dragging in Columbus, as if he were a mere conduit for European culture.

One reason that freedom arose in the West is the traditional Western separation of the City of Man from the City of God.... [M]any of the early missionaries and theologians showed, in the very face of state power and financial interests, that Christian principles pointed toward other paths than those most often taken by settlers in the New World. Columbus and Las Casas were sometimes at odds over specifics, but were not fundamentally opposed on these matters. Las Casas is the greater figure for his moral passion and courage, but Columbus, in spite of his faults, deserves no little admiration. Emblematic, perhaps, of their relationship is the suggestion of Simón Bolívar in 1819 that a newly liberated area of South America be named Colombia and its capital Las Casas: "Thus will we prove to the world that we not only have the right to be free, but we will demonstrate that we know how to honor the friends and benefactors of mankind."

POSTSCRIPT

Was Columbus an Imperialist?

Whether or not Christopher Columbus's actions in the Americas are viewed as the work of an imperialist, there is no doubt that the impact of his arrival in the Western Hemisphere carried with it enormous consequences, not the least of which was the so-called "Columbian Exchange," which involved a reciprocal trade in plants and animals, human beings, diseases, and ideas. For example, the introduction of destructive microorganisms produced epidemic outbreaks of smallpox, tuberculosis, measles, typhoid, and syphilis that decimated human populations on both sides of the Atlantic. On a more positive note, Europeans brought food items such as wheat and potatoes to the New World and brought home maize, beans, and manioc. Native Americans benefited from horses and other farm animals introduced from Europe, but these benefits were offset by the efforts of the Europeans to enslave and kill the indigenous peoples whom they encountered. The best study of these various by-products of European exploration is Alfred W. Crosby, *The Columbian Exchange: Biological and Cultural Consequences of 1492* (Greenwood Press, 1973).

The effects of the encounters between Europeans and Native Americans is explored in Gary B. Nash, *Red, White and Black: The Peoples of Early North America,* 3rd ed. (Prentice Hall, 1992) and in two works by James Axtell: *The European and the Indian: Essays in the Ethnohistory of Colonial North America* (Oxford University Press, 1981) and *The Invasion Within: The Contest of Cultures in Colonial North America* (Oxford University Press, 1985). Alvin M. Josephy, Jr., examines the pre-Columbian Native Americans in *1492: The World of the Indian Peoples Before the Arrival of Columbus* (Alfred A. Knopf, 1992).

Samuel Eliot Morison, *The European Discovery of America: The Northern Voyages* (Oxford University Press, 1971); David Beers Quinn, *England and the Discovery of America, 1481-1620* (Harper & Row, 1974); Wallace Notestein, *The English People on the Eve of Colonization, 1603-1630* (Harper & Brothers, 1954); Charles Gibson, *Spain in America* (Harper & Row, 1966); and W. J. Eccles, *France in America* (Harper & Row, 1972), discuss European contacts in North America.

Perhaps the best biographical treatment of Columbus is Samuel Eliot Morison's generally sympathetic *Admiral of the Ocean Sea: A Life of Christopher Columbus,* 2 vols. (Little, Brown, 1942). For a more recent objective and scholarly study, see Felipe Fernandez-Armesto, *Columbus* (Oxford University Press, 1991).

ISSUE 2

Was the Colonial Period a "Golden Age" for Women in America?

YES: Lois Green Carr and Lorena S. Walsh, from "The Planter's Wife: The Experience of White Women in Seventeenth-Century Maryland," *William and Mary Quarterly* (January 1977)

NO: Mary Beth Norton, from "The Myth of the Golden Age," in Carol Ruth Berkin and Mary Beth Norton, eds., *Women of America: A History* (Houghton Mifflin, 1979)

ISSUE SUMMARY

YES: Adjunct professor of history Lois Green Carr and historian Lorena S. Walsh identify several factors that coalesced to afford women in seventeenth-century Maryland a higher status with fewer restraints on their social conduct than those experienced by women in England.

NO: Professor of American history Mary Beth Norton challenges the "golden age" theory, insisting that women in colonial America, whether white, black, or Native American, typically occupied a domestic sphere that was lacking in status, physically debilitating over time, and a barrier to educational opportunity and political power.

$\mathbf{F}$or generations students in American history classes have read of the founding of the colonies in British North America, their political and economic development, and the colonists' struggles for independence, without ever being confronted by a female protagonist in this magnificent historical drama. The terms *Sons of Liberty* and *Founding Fathers* reflect the end result of a long tradition of gender-specific myopia. In fact, only in the last generation have discussions of the role of women in the development of American society made their appearance in standard textbooks. Consequently, it is useful to explore the status of women in colonial America.

The topic is complex. The status of colonial women was determined by cultural attitudes that were exported to the New World from Europe, by the specific conditions confronting successive waves of settlers—male and female—

in terms of labor requirements, and by changes produced by colonial maturation over time. It would be impossible to pinpoint a single, static condition in which *all* colonial women existed.

What was the status of women in the British North American colonies? To what degree did the legal status of women differ from their *de facto* status? A half century of scholarship has produced the notion that colonial women enjoyed a more privileged status than either their European contemporaries or their nineteenth-century descendants. This view, developed in the writings of Richard B. Morris, Elizabeth Dexter, and Mary Beard, was reinforced in the 1970s by John Demos and Roger Thompson. For example, Demos contends that despite the fact that Plymouth Colony was based on a patriarchal model in which women were expected to subordinate themselves to men, women still shared certain responsibilities with their husbands in some business activities and in matters relating to their children. They not only performed all household duties but also assisted the men with agricultural duties outside the home when the necessity arose. However, women were closed off from any formal public power in the colony even when they performed essential economic functions within the community. Society as a whole viewed them as "weaker vessels," physically, intellectually, and morally.

The following selections explore the status of women in seventeenth-century America. Lois Green Carr and Lorena S. Walsh assess this issue against the backdrop of four factors in colonial Maryland: the predominance of an immigrant population; the early death of male inhabitants; the late marriages of women due to their indentured servitude; and the sexual imbalance in which men greatly outnumbered women. As a result of these conditions, argue Carr and Walsh, Maryland women experienced fewer restraints on their social conduct and enjoyed more power than did their English counterparts. Most became planter's wives, enjoyed considerable freedom in choosing their husbands, and benefited from a substantial right to inherit property.

Mary Beth Norton's selection is broader in scope, giving consideration to women's status in both the sixteenth and seventeenth centuries and including women of various socioeconomic backgrounds. While noting that more research needs to be done on the conditions of African American and Native American women in the colonies, she provides evidence suggesting that, regardless of race, women shared a subordinate status in colonial America. According to Norton, women's lives were circumscribed by their general confinement to domestic responsibilities, social isolation from other women, and the absence of significant educational and political opportunities.

Lois Green Carr and
Lorena S. Walsh

 YES

The Planter's Wife: The Experience of White Women in Seventeenth-Century Maryland

$\mathbf{F}$our facts were basic to all human experience in seventeenth-century Maryland. First, for most of the period the great majority of inhabitants had been born in what we now call Britain. Population increase in Maryland did not result primarily from births in the colony before the late 1680s and did not produce a predominantly native population of adults before the first decade of the eighteenth century. Second, immigrant men could not expect to live beyond age forty-three, and 70 percent would die before age fifty. Women may have had even shorter lives. Third, perhaps 85 percent of the immigrants, and practically all the unmarried immigrant women, arrived as indentured servants and consequently married late. Family groups were never predominant in the immigration to Maryland and were a significant part for only a brief time at mid-century. Fourth, many more men than women immigrated during the whole period. These facts—immigrant predominance, early death, late marriage, and sexual imbalance—created circumstances of social and demographic disruption that deeply affected family and community life.

We need to assess the effects of this disruption on the experience of women in seventeenth-century Maryland. Were women degraded by the hazards of servitude in a society in which everyone had left community and kin behind and in which women were in short supply? Were traditional restraints on social conduct weakened? If so, were women more exploited or more independent and powerful than women who remained in England? Did any differences from English experience which we can observe in the experience of Maryland women survive the transformation from an immigrant to a predominantly native-born society with its own kinship networks and community traditions? The tentative argument put forward here is that the answer to all these questions is Yes. There were degrading aspects of servitude, although these probably did not characterize the lot of most women; there were fewer restraints on social conduct, especially in courtship, than in England; women were less protected but also more powerful than those who remained at home;

From Lois Green Carr and Lorena S. Walsh, "The Planter's Wife: The Experience of White Women in Seventeenth-Century Maryland," *William and Mary Quarterly*, 3rd ser., vol. 24 (October 1977). Copyright © 1977 by The Omohundro Institute of Early American History and Culture. Reprinted by permission. Notes omitted.

and at least some of these changes survived the appearance in Maryland of New World creole communities. . . .

Maryland was settled in 1634, but in 1650 there were probably no more than six hundred persons and fewer than two hundred adult women in the province. After that time population growth was steady; in 1704 a census listed 30,437 white persons, of whom 7,163 were adult women. Thus in discussing the experience of white women in seventeenth-century Maryland we are dealing basically with the second half of the century. . . .

Whatever their status, one fact about immigrant women is certain: many fewer came than men. Immigrant lists, head-right lists, and itemizations of servants in inventories show severe imbalance. On a London immigrant list of 1634–1635 men outnumbered women six to one. From the 1650s at least until the 1680s most sources show a ratio of three to one. From then on, all sources show some, but not great, improvement. Among immigrants from Liverpool over the years 1697–1707 the ratio was just under two and one half to one.

Why did not more women come? Presumably, fewer wished to leave family and community and venture into a wilderness. But perhaps more important, women were not as desirable as men to merchants and planters who were making fortunes raising and marketing tobacco, a crop that requires large amounts of labor. The gradual improvement in the sex ratio among servants toward the end of the century may have been the result of a change in recruiting the needed labor. In the late 1660s the supply of young men willing to emigrate stopped increasing sufficiently to meet the labor demands of a growing Chesapeake population. Merchants who recruited servants for planters turned to other sources, and among these sources were women. They did not crowd the ships arriving in the Chesapeake, but their numbers did increase.

To ask the question another way, why did women come? Doubtless, most came to get a husband, an objective virtually certain of success in a land where women were so far outnumbered. The promotional literature, furthermore, painted bright pictures of the life that awaited men and women once out of their time; and various studies suggest that for a while, at least, the promoters were not being entirely fanciful. Until the 1660s, and to a less degree the 1680s, the expanding economy of Maryland and Virginia offered opportunities well beyond those available in England to men without capital and to the women who became their wives.

Nevertheless, the hazards were also great, and the greatest was untimely death. Newcomers promptly became ill, probably with malaria, and many died. What proportion survived is unclear; so far no one has devised a way of measuring it. Recurrent malaria made the woman who survived seasoning less able to withstand other diseases, especially dysentery and influenza. She was especially vulnerable when pregnant. Expectation of life for everyone was low in the Chesapeake, but especially so for women. A woman who had immigrated to Maryland took an extra risk, though perhaps a risk not greater than she might have suffered by moving from her village to London instead.

The majority of women who survived seasoning paid their transportation costs by working for a four- or five-year term of service. The kind of work depended on the status of the family they served. A female servant of a small planter—who through about the 1670s might have had a servant—probably worked at the hoe. Such a man could not afford to buy labor that would not help with the cash crop. In wealthy families women probably were household servants, although some are occasionally listed in inventories of well-to-do planters as living on the quarters—that is, on plantations other than the dwelling plantation. Such women saved men the jobs of preparing food and washing linen but doubtless also worked in the fields. In middling households experience must have varied. Where the number of people to feed and wash for was large, female servants would have had little time to tend the crops.

Tracts that promoted immigration to the Chesapeake region asserted that female servants did not labor in the fields, except "nasty" wenches not fit for other tasks. This implies that most immigrant women expected, or at least hoped, to avoid heavy field work, which English women—at least those above the cottager's status—did not do. What proportion of female servants in Maryland found themselves demeaned by this unaccustomed labor is impossible to say, but this must have been the fate of some. . . .

The woman who immigrated to Maryland, survived seasoning and service, and gained her freedom became a planter's wife. She had considerable liberty in making her choice. There were men aplenty and no fathers or brothers were hovering to monitor her behavior or disapprove her preference. This is the modern way of looking at her situation, of course. Perhaps she missed the protection of a father, a guardian, or kinfolk, and the participation in her decision of a community to which she felt ties. There is some evidence that the absence of kin and the pressures of the sex ratio created conditions of sexual freedom in courtship that were not customary in England. A register of marriages and births for seventeenth-century Somerset County shows that about one-third of the immigrant women whose marriages are recorded were pregnant at the time of the ceremony—nearly twice the rate in English parishes. There is no indication of community objection to this freedom so long as marriage took place. No presentments for bridal pregnancy were made in any of the Maryland courts.

The planter's wife was likely to be in her mid-twenties at marriage. An estimate of minimum age at marriage for servant women can be made from lists of indentured servants who left London over the years 1683–1684 and from age judgments in Maryland county court records. If we assume that the 112 female indentured servants going to Maryland and Virginia whose ages are given in the London lists served full four-year terms, then only 1.8 percent married before age twenty but 68 percent after age twenty-four. Similarly, if the 141 women whose ages were judged in Charles County between 1666 and 1705 served out their terms according to the custom of the country, none married before age twenty-two, and half were twenty-five or over. When adjustments are made for the ages at which wives may have been purchased, the figures drop, but even so the majority of women waited until at least age twenty-four to marry. Actual age at marriage in Maryland can be found for few seventeenth-century female immigrants, but observations for Charles and Somerset counties place the mean age at about twenty-five.

Because of the age at which an immigrant woman married, the number of children she would bear her husband was small. She had lost up to ten years of her childbearing life—the possibility of perhaps four or five children, given the usual rhythm of childbearing. At the same time, high mortality would reduce both the number of children she would bear over the rest of her life and the number who would live. One partner to a marriage was likely to die within seven years, and the chances were only one in three that a marriage would last ten years. In these circumstances, most women would not bear more than three or four children—not counting those stillborn—to any one husband, plus a posthumous child were she the survivor. The best estimates suggest that nearly a quarter, perhaps more, of the children born alive died during their first year and that 40 to 55 percent would not live to see age twenty. Consequently, one of her children would probably die in infancy, and another one or two would fail to reach adulthood. Wills left in St. Mary's County during the seventeenth century show the results. In 105 families over the years 1660 to 1680 only twelve parents left more than three children behind them, including those conceived but not yet born. The average number was 2.3, nearly always minors, some of whom might die before reaching adulthood.

For the immigrant woman, then, one of the major facts of life was that although she might bear a child about every two years, nearly half would not reach maturity. The social implications of this fact are far-reaching. Because she married late in her childbearing years and because so many of her children would die young, the number who would reach marriageable age might not replace, or might only barely replace, her and her husband or husbands as child-producing members of the society. Consequently, so long as immigrants were heavily predominant in the adult female population, Maryland could not grow much by natural increase. It remained a land of newcomers. . . .

A hazard of marriage for seventeenth-century women everywhere was death in childbirth, but this hazard may have been greater than usual in the Chesapeake. Whereas in most societies women tend to outlive men, in this malaria-ridden area it is probable that men outlived women. Hazards of childbirth provide the likely reason that Chesapeake women died so young. Once a woman in the Chesapeake reached forty-five, she tended to outlive men who reached the same age. . . .

However long they lived, immigrant women in Maryland tended to outlive their husbands—in Charles County, for example, by a ratio of two to one. This was possible, despite the fact that women were younger than men at death, because women were also younger than men at marriage. Some women were widowed with no living children, but most were left responsible for two or three. These were often tiny, and nearly always not yet sixteen.

This fact had drastic consequences, given the physical circumstances of life. People lived at a distance from one another, not even in villages, must less towns. The widow had left her kin 3,000 miles across an ocean, and her husband's family was also there. She would have to feed her children and make her own tobacco crop. Though neighbors might help, heavy labor would be required of her if she had no servants, until—what admittedly was usually not difficult—she acquired a new husband.

In this situation dying husbands were understandably anxious about the welfare of their families. Their wills reflected their feelings and tell something of how they regarded their wives. In St. Mary's and Charles counties during the seventeenth century, little more than one-quarter of the men left their widows with no more than the dower the law required—one-third of his land for her life, plus outright ownership of one-third of his personal property. If there were no children, a man almost always left his widow his whole estate. Otherwise there were a variety of arrangements.

During the 1660s, when testators begin to appear in quantity, nearly a fifth of the men who had children left all to their wives, trusting them to see that the children received fair portions. Thus in 1663 John Shircliffe willed his whole estate to his wife "towards the maintenance of herself and my children into whose tender care I do Commend them Desireing to see them brought up in the fear of God and the Catholick Religion and Chargeing them to be Dutiful and obedient to her." As the century progressed, husbands tended instead to give the wife all or a major part of the estate for her life, and to designate how it should be distributed after her death. Either way, the husband put great trust in his widow, considering that he knew she was bound to remarry. Only a handful of men left estates to their wives only for their term of widowhood or until the children came of age. When a man did not leave his wife a life estate, he often gave her land outright or more than her dower third of his movable property. Such bequests were at the expense of his children and showed his concern that his widow should have a maintenance which young children could not supply.

A husband usually made his wife his executor and thus responsible for paying his debts and preserving the estate. Only 11 percent deprived their wives of such powers. In many instances, however, men also appointed overseers to assist their wives and to see that their children were not abused or their property embezzled. Danger lay in the fact that a second husband acquired control of all his wife's property, including her life estate in the property of his predecessor. Over half of the husbands who died in the 1650s and 1660s appointed overseers to ensure that their wills were followed. Some trusted to the overseers' "Care and good Conscience for the good of my widow and fatherless children." Others more explicit made overseers responsible for seeing that "my said child . . . and the other [expected child] (when pleases God to send it) may have their right Proportion of my Said Estate and that the said Children may be bred up Chiefly in the fear of God." A few men—but remarkably few—authorized overseers to remove children from households of stepfathers who abused them or wasted their property. On the whole, the absence of such provisions for the protection of the children points to the husband's overriding concern for the welfare of his widow and to his confidence in her management, regardless of the certainty of her remarriage. Evidently, in the politics of family life women enjoyed great respect.

We have implied that this respect was a product of the experience of immigrants in the Chesapeake. Might it have been instead a reflection of the English culture? Little work is yet in print that allows comparison of the provisions for Maryland widows with those made for the widows of English farmers. Possibly Maryland husbands were making traditional wills which could have been written in the communities they left behind. However, Margaret Spufford's recent study of three Cambridgeshire villages in the late sixteenth century and early seventeenth century suggests a different pattern. In one of these villages, Chippenham, women usually did receive a life interest in the property but in the other two they did not. If the children were all minors, the widow controlled the property until the oldest son came of age, and then only if she did not remarry. In the majority of cases adult sons were given control of the property with instructions for the support of their mothers. Spufford suggests that the pattern found in Chippenham must have been very exceptional. On the basis of village censuses in six other counties, dating from 1624 to 1724, which show only 3 percent of widowed people heading households that included a married child, she argues that if widows commonly controlled the farm, a higher proportion should have headed such households. However, she also argues that widows with an interest in land would not long remain unmarried. If so, the low percentage may be deceptive. . . .

Remarriage was the usual and often the immediate solution for a woman who had lost her husband. The shortage of women made any woman eligible to marry again, and the difficulties of raising a family while running a plantation must have made remarriage necessary for widows who had no son old enough to make tobacco. One indication of the high incidence of remarriage is the fact that there were only sixty women, almost all of them widows, among the 1,735 people who left probate inventories in four southern Maryland counties over the second half of the century. Most other women must have died while married and therefore legally without property to put through probate.

One result of remarriage was the development of complex family structures. Men found themselves responsible for stepchildren as well as their own offspring, and children acquired half-sisters and half-brothers. Sometimes a woman married a second husband who himself had been previously married, and both brought children of former spouses to the new marriage. They then produced children of their own. The possibilities for conflict over the upbringing of children are evident, and crowded living conditions, found even in the households of the wealthy, must have added to family tensions. Luckily, the children of the family very often had the same mother. In Charles County at least, widows took new husbands three times more often than widowers took new wives. The role of the mother in managing the relationships of half-brothers and half-sisters or stepfathers and stepchildren must have been critical to family harmony.

Early death in this immigrant population thus had broad effects on Maryland society in the seventeenth century. It produced what we might call a pattern of serial polyandry, which enabled more men to marry and to father families than the sex ratios otherwise would have permitted. It produced thousands of orphaned children who had no kin to maintain them or preserve their property, and thus gave rise to an institution almost unknown in England, the orphans' court, which was charged with their protection. And early death, by creating families in which the mother was the unifying element, may have increased her authority within the household.

When the immigrant woman married her first husband, there was usually no property settlement involved, since she was unlikely to have any dowry. But her remarriage was another matter. At the very least, she owned or had a life interest in a third of her former husband's estate. She needed also to think of her children's interests. If she remarried, she would lose control of the property. Consequently, property settlements occasionally appear in the seventeenth-century court records between widows and their future husbands. Sometimes she and her intended signed an agreement whereby he relinquished his rights to the use of her children's portions. Sometimes he deeded to her property which she could dispose of at her pleasure. Whether any of these agreements or gifts would have survived a test in court is unknown. We have not yet found any challenged. Generally speaking, the formal marriage settlements of English law, which bypassed the legal difficulties of the married woman's inability to make a contract with her husband, were not adopted by immigrants, most of whom probably came from levels of English society that did not use these legal formalities.

The wife's dower rights in her husband's estate were a recognition of her role in contributing to his prosperity, whether by the property she had brought to the marriage or by the labor she performed in his household. A woman newly freed from servitude would not bring property, but the benefits of her labor would be great. A man not yet prosperous enough to own a servant might need his wife's help in the fields as well as in the house, especially if he were paying rent or still paying for land. Moreover, food preparation was so time-consuming that even if she worked only at household duties, she saved him time he needed for making tobacco and corn. The corn, for example, had to be pounded in the mortar or ground in a handmill before it could be used to make bread, for there were very few water mills in seventeenth-century Maryland. The wife probably raised vegetables in a kitchen garden; she also milked the cows and made butter and cheese, which might produce a salable surplus. She washed the clothes and made them if she had the skill. When there were servants to do field work, the wife undoubtedly spent her time entirely in such household tasks. A contract of 1681 expressed such a division of labor. Nicholas Maniere agreed to live on a plantation with his wife and child and a servant. Nicholas and the servant were to work the land; his wife was to "Dresse the Vitualls milk the Cowes wash for the servants and Doe allthings necessary for a woman to doe upon the s[ai]d plantation." ...

Historians have only recently begun to explore the consequences of the shift from an immigrant to a predominantly native population. We would like to suggest some changes in the position of women that may have resulted from this transition. It is already known that as sexual imbalance disappeared, age at first marriage rose, but it remained lower than it had been for immigrants over the second half of the seventeenth century. At the same time, life expectancy improved, at least for men. The results were longer marriages and more children who reached maturity. In St. Mary's County after 1700, dying men far more often than earlier left children of age to maintain their widows, and widows may have felt less inclination and had less opportunity to remarry.

We may speculate on the social consequences of such changes. More fathers were still alive when their daughters married, and hence would have been able to exercise control over the selection of their sons-in-law. What in the seventeenth century may have been a period of comparative independence for women, both immigrant and native, may have given way to a return to more traditional European social controls over the creation of new families. . . .

We may also find the wife losing ground in the household polity, although her economic importance probably remained unimpaired. Indeed, she must have been far more likely than a seventeenth-century immigrant woman to bring property to her marriage. But several changes may have caused women to play a smaller role than before in household decision-making. Women became proportionately more numerous and may have lost bargaining power. Furthermore, as marriages lasted longer, the proportion of households full of stepchildren and half-brothers and half-sisters united primarily by the mother must have dimished. Finally, when husbands died, more widows would have had children old enough to maintain them and any minor brothers and sisters. There would be less need for women to play a controlling role, as well as less incentive for their husbands to grant it. The provincial marriage of the eighteenth century may have more closely resembled that of England than did the immigrant marriage of the seventeenth century.

If this change occurred, we should find symptoms to measure. There should be fewer gifts from husbands to wives of property put at the wife's disposal. Husbands should less frequently make bequests to wives that provided them with property beyond their dower. A wife might even be restricted to less than her dower, although the law allowed her to choose her dower instead of a bequest. At the same time, children should be commanded to maintain their mothers.

St. Mary's County wills show some of these symptoms. Wives occasionally were willed less than their dower, an arrangement that was rare in the wills examined for the period before 1710. More important, there was some decrease in bequests to wives of property beyond their dower, and a tendency to confine the wife's interest to the term of her widowhood or the minority of the oldest son. On the other hand, children were not exhorted to help their mothers or give them living space. Widows evidently received at least enough property to maintain themselves, and husbands saw no need to ensure the help of children in managing it. Still, St. Mary's County women lost some ground, within the family polity. Evidently, as demographic conditions became more normal, St. Mary's County widows began to lose ground to their children, a phenomenon that deserves further study.

The Myth of the Golden Age

Household Patterns

When discussing colonial women, we must focus on the household, for that was where most of their lives were spent. As daughters as well as wives and mothers, white women were expected to devote their chief energies to housekeeping and to the care of children, just as their husbands were expected to support them by raising crops or working for wages. Household tasks were not easily or lightly accomplished, although their exact nature varied according to the wealth and size of the family and its place of residence. In addition to the common chores still done today—cooking, cleaning, and washing—colonial women had the primary responsibility for food preservation and cloth production.

On farms women raised chickens, tended vegetable gardens, and ran the dairy, making cheese and butter for family use. When hogs and cattle were butchered in the fall, women supervised the salting and smoking of the meat so that the family would have an adequate supply for the winter. They also gathered and dried fruits, vegetables, and berries and occasionally oversaw the making of hard cider, the standard drink in the colonies. In towns and cities women also performed many of these chores, though on a lesser scale: They raised a few chickens and a cow or two, cultivated a kitchen garden, and preserved the beef and pork purchased at the local market. Only the wealthiest women with numerous servants could escape tiring physical labor, and as mistresses of the household they too had to understand the processes involved, for otherwise they could not ensure that the jobs were done correctly.

The task of making cloth by hand was tedious and time consuming. If women lived in towns and could afford to do so, they would usually purchase English cloth rather than manufacture their own. On remote farms or in poorer households, however, females had no choice: If the family was to have clothes, they had to spin the wool or flax threads, then weave those threads into material that could be used for dresses, shirts, and trousers. Usually girls were taught to spin at the early age of 7 or 8 so that they could relieve their mothers of that chore. Weaving demanded more technical skill, not to mention a large, bulky loom, and so not all women in an area would learn to weave. Instead neighbors

From Mary Beth Norton, "The Myth of the Golden Age," in Carol Ruth Berkin and Mary Beth Norton, eds., *Women of America: A History* (Houghton Mifflin, 1979). Copyright © 1979 by Houghton Mifflin Company. Reprinted by permission.

would cooperate, "changing work," and the woman who wove the cloth for her friends would be paid in cash or by barter.

Native American women had similar work roles. They did not spin or weave, but they did make clothing for the family by tanning and processing the hides of animals killed by their husbands and fathers. They had greater responsibilities for the cultivation of plants than did their white counterparts; the men of many tribes devoted most of their time to hunting, leaving their wives with the major share of the burden of raising the corn, squash, and beans that formed the staples of their diet. But like the whites, Native American cultures drew a division between the domestic labors of women and the public realm of men. Only in rare instances—as when the older women of the matrilineal Iroquois society named the chief of the tribe—did Indian women intrude upon that male realm.

The patterns for African women were somewhat more complex, but their lives too were largely determined by the type of household in which they lived. A female slave in a northern urban home—and there were many such by the mid-eighteenth century—would probably have been a cook or a maid. On small farms slave women would have been expected to work in both field and house. On large southern tobacco or rice plantations, however, black women might specialize in certain tasks, devoting themselves exclusively to spinning, cooking, childcare, dairy work, or poultry keeping, or they might be assigned to the fields. Black women were therefore more likely than whites to engage in labor out of doors. Significantly, the household in which they lived was not theirs: Their interests and wishes, and those of their husbands and children, always had to be subordinated to the interests of their white masters and mistresses. White women's lives, we might say, were governed by the whims of men, legally and in reality; but black women's lives were governed by white men and white women, and perhaps even by white children.

Women's Lives Outside the Home

For female whites or blacks living on isolated farms or plantations, opportunities for contacts with persons outside their immediate families were extremely rare. Thus, farm and plantation women took advantage of every excuse they could to see friends and neighbors: Quilting bees and spinning frolics were common in the North, barbecues were prevalent in the South. Church attendance provided a rural woman not only with the solace of religion, but also with a chance to greet acquaintances and exchange news. Literate women kept in touch with each other by writing letters, many of them carried not by the rudimentary colonial mail service but by passing travelers, usually men.

Because there were few colonial newspapers, and those were published exclusively in cities like Boston or Philadelphia, most farm areas were a part of what has been termed an *oral culture*. Much of the important information about local and regional developments was passed on by person-to-person contact, which generally occurred at the local tavern or the county courthouse, both of which were male bastions. As a result, white farm women tended to be excluded from men's communication networks and to rely for news on exchanges with each other or with their husbands.

Urban women were not nearly so isolated. Close to their friends, they could visit every day. Their attendance at church was not limited to infrequent occasions, and so they could become more active in religious affairs than their rural sisters. They had greater opportunities to receive an education, since the few girls' schools were located in or near colonial cities. For the most part their education consisted of elementary reading, writing, and arithmetic, with perhaps some needlework or musical training thrown in for good measure. Once women knew how to read, they had newspapers and books at their disposal. Moreover, because their household tasks were less demanding than those of their rural counterparts, they had more time to take advantage of all these amenities of the urban setting.

If this account makes it seem as though colonial women's lives lacked variety, that impression is correct. Their environment was both limited and limiting: limited, because of the small sphere of activity open to them; limiting, because they could not realistically aspire to leave that sphere. Faced with a paucity of alternatives, colonial women made the best of their situation. What evidence is available suggests that both white and black women often married for love, and that they cared a great deal for their children. Their female friends provided support in moments of crisis—such as childbirth or the death of a family member—and women could take some satisfaction from knowing that they were active contributors to their families' well-being.

The Myth Analyzed

Historians of American women have traditionally regarded the seventeenth and eighteenth centuries as a "golden age" in which women were better off than their English female contemporaries or their descendants of the succeeding Victorian era. Elisabeth Anthony Dexter explicitly asserted as much; other authors have accepted the same argument implicitly by contending that female Americans "lost status" in the nineteenth century. But even leaving aside the troublesome (and infrequently addressed) issue of how status is measured, there are a number of difficulties with the standard interpretation. Evaluation of women's position depends on what aspects of their experience are relevant to an understanding of their social and economic position, for no one would claim that colonial females exerted much political power.

Three basic assertions support the traditional interpretation. First, historians have noted the imbalanced sex ratio in all the colonies before 1700 and in some parts thereof during later years. Hypothesizing that the absence of sufficient numbers of women to provide wives for all male colonists would lead men to compete vigorously for mates, they have concluded that women would wield a good deal of power through their choice of a spouse. Second, scholars have commonly pointed to the economic contributions women made to the colonial household through their work in food processing and cloth production. They have correctly noted that it was practically impossible for a man to run a colonial household properly without a wife, for a woman's labor was essential to the survival of the family. They presume, then, that husbands recognized their wives' vital contributions to the household by according them a voice in decision making, and that a woman's economic role translated itself into a position of power within the home. Third and finally, historians argue that sex roles in early America were far more fluid and less well defined than they were in the nineteenth and twentieth centuries. They quote both foreign travelers' accounts and newspaper advertisements to show that in many instances women labored at tasks later considered masculine and frequently ran their own businesses.

In assessing these common contentions, we must look closely at their component parts in light of recent scholarship. When we do so, all are rendered suspect. The first argument asserts that a scarcity of women works to their advantage in the marriage market and assumes that the choice of a husband was entirely within a seventeenth-century colonial woman's discretion. Yet demographic studies have clearly demonstrated that, when women are scarce, the average female age at first marriage drops, sometimes precipitously. Even in New England, where the sex ratio was closer to being balanced than anywhere else in the early settlements, the average marriage age for women seems to have fallen into the high teens during the first years of colonization, in sharp contrast to England, where the nuptial age for women remained near the mid-20s.

These figures have several implications. Initially, they suggest that first marriages were not long delayed by women's searches for spouses who met exacting criteria. Furthermore, since seventeenth-century brides were often teenagers, even more frequently so in the Chesapeake Bay area than in New England, one wonders just how much power they could have wielded. Immature themselves, legally the wards of their parents, it is highly unlikely that they had much to say about the choice of a spouse.

A possible counter-argument might assert that the advantages of the imbalanced sex ratio are more applicable to a woman's second or third marriage than to her first, because then she would be older and in addition would have control of her first husband's property. Although studies of remarriage patterns in the early years of the colonies are not completely satisfactory, they nevertheless appear to challenge even this claim. In New England, life expectancy in the seventeenth century was sufficiently great that few marriages seem to have been broken early by death. Therefore, relatively few persons married more than once. In the Chesapeake area, where mortality was much higher, the frequency of remarriage was similarly high, but analyses of wills demonstrate that widows were rarely given much control over their dead husbands' estates. The property was usually held in trust for the decedent's minor children, with the widow receiving only a life interest in part of it. Sometimes even that income was to cease upon her remarriage.

Taken as a whole, then, the evidence indicates that seventeenth-century English women transplanted to American shores might not find the imbalanced sex ratio to be beneficial. After all, a scarce resource can be as easily exploited as it is cherished. . . . Also, by approximately 1720 the sex ratio had evened out in the Chesapeake, having already reached that point to the northward, so that whatever advantages women may have derived from the situation were negated and cannot be used to characterize the entire colonial period.

Turning next to the assertion that women's economic role gave them a powerful position in the household, we can discern problems with both the evidence and the reasoning that support it. Historians have not systematically examined the conditions under which women wield familial power, assuming instead that an essential economic contribution would almost automatically lead to such a result. Anthropologists who have investigated the question, however, have discovered that the mere fact that a woman's economic contribution to the household is significant is not sufficient to give her a voice in matters that might otherwise be deemed to fall within the masculine sphere. Rather, what is important is a woman's ability to control the distribution of familial resources. Thus, African women who not only cultivate crops but also sell that produce to others are more likely to wield power in their households than are their counterparts in other tribes whose husbands take on the trading role, or who live in a subsistence economy that does not allow for the sale of surplus goods.

That this analogy is indeed appropriate, despite the wide difference in time and space between twentieth-century Africa and colonial America, is suggested by a recent study of female Loyalist exiles in England after the American Revolution. In order to win compensation from the British government for the losses their families suffered as a result of their political sympathies, the women had to submit descriptions of the property confiscated from them by the rebels. In the process, they revealed their basic ignorance of family landholdings and income, in turn demonstrating that their husbands had not regularly discussed financial affairs with them. If the Loyalist women refugees, who were drawn from all ranks of society, had actively participated in economic decision making, then they would have been far better able to estimate their losses than they proved to be. Thus, the second foundation of the traditional interpretations is shown to be questionable.

The third standard contention, that colonial sex roles were relatively fluid, is rendered at least partially doubtful by other aspects of the same study of Loyalist exiles. The wide variations in the contents of men's and women's Loyalist claims, and the inability or the unwillingness of men to describe household furnishings in the same detail adopted by women, appear to indicate that a fairly rigid line separated masculine and feminine spheres in the colonies. Indeed, the fact that men did not talk about finances with their wives suggests that both sexes had a strong sense of the proper roles of women and men; women did not meddle with politics or economics, which were their husbands' provinces, and men did not interfere with their wives' overseeing of domestic affairs, excluding child rearing, where they did take an active role. Moreover, even though the claims show that some women did engage in business activities, their number was relatively small (fewer than 10 percent of the claimants), and most of them worked in their husbands' enterprises rather than running their own.

That the number of Loyalist women working in masculine areas was not uniquely limited has been suggested by a recent study of Baltimore women in the 1790s, which concludes that only about 5 percent of the female urban population worked outside the home. Thus, it seems likely that eighteenth-century Americans made quite distinct divisions between male and female roles, as reflected in the small numbers of women engaging in masculine occupations and in the fact that men did not normally interfere in the female sphere.

New Issues

Recent scholarship has considered a number of issues not even raised by earlier authors. Interest in these different areas of inquiry owes a great deal to current trends in the study of the history of the American family, of minority groups, and of ordinary people. Although this work has just begun, it is nevertheless already casting innovative light on the subject of colonial women's role in society.

In the first place, it is important to point out that published studies of the lives of colonial women have, with but one or two exceptions, centered wholly on whites. Even though at the time of the Revolution blacks constituted almost 20 percent of the American population, a higher percentage than at any time thereafter, historians have completely neglected the study of female slaves in the colonial era. Therefore, all the statements that women had a relatively good position in the colonies must be immediately qualified to exclude blacks. No one could seriously argue that enslavement was preferable to freedom, especially since female slaves were highly vulnerable to sexual as well as economic exploitation by their masters. Intriguingly, recent work has shown that the sexual imbalance among the earliest African slaves in the South was just as pronounced as that among whites, so that female blacks probably found themselves in a demographic situation comparable to that of their white mistresses. The sex-role definitions applied to whites, though, were never used with respect to blacks. The labor of slave women was too valuable for their masters to pay attention to the niceties of sex; thus, many of them spent their lives laboring in tobacco fields or on sugar plantations alongside their husbands, although others were indeed used as house servants performing typically feminine tasks.

The one concession wise colonial masters made to the sex of female slaves was a recognition of their importance as child-bearers. Since under the law any child of a slave woman was also a slave, masters could greatly increase their human property simply by encouraging their female slaves' fertility. For example, Thomas Jefferson, whose solvency for some years depended on the discreet sale of young blacks, ordered his overseers to allow pregnant and nursing women special privileges, including lighter work loads and separate houses. Since colonial slave women normally bore their first children at the age of 17 or 18, they would experience perhaps 10 or 11 pregnancies (not all of which would result in live births) during their fertile years, which may be contrasted to the standard pattern among white eighteenth-century women, who married perhaps 4 to 6 years later and thus bore fewer children (the average being 6 offspring who lived).

This attention to childbearing patterns has led to a major challenge to the "golden age" theory.... [C]olonial women were either pregnant or nursing during most of their mature years. Such a pattern of constant childbearing was debilitating, even if it was not fatal to as many women as we once thought;

the diaries of white female colonists are filled with references to their continued poor health, and the records of planters show similar consequences among female slaves. Furthermore, the care of so many children must have been exhausting, especially when combined with the extraordinary household demands made on women: production of clothing and time-consuming attention to food preservation and preparation, not to mention candle- and soap-making and doing laundry in heavy iron pots over open fires, with all the water carried by hand from the nearest well or stream. It is questionable how much household power could have been wielded by a woman constantly occupied with such work, even if she was in good health.

It is instructive to stress once again the lack of options in colonial women's lives. Until late in the eighteenth century, marriage was a near-universal experience for women; in an overwhelmingly agricultural society, most female whites ended up as farm wives and most female blacks were farm laborers. For black women burdened with small children, running away was not even the remote chance it was for young unattached male slaves. (In any case, until the Revolution there was no safe place to go, except Spanish Florida, because all the colonies, north and south, allowed slaveholding.)

It might be contended that since most white men were farmers, white women's lack of opportunities was not unique to them. But boys like John Adams, Richard Cranch, and John Shaw had opportunities to gain an education that were closed to their wives, the sisters Abigail, Mary, and Elizabeth Smith. All were exceptionally intelligent and well-informed women, but none received other than a rudimentary formal education, despite the fact that their father was a minister. Since the ability to write a good letter—defined as one that was neat, intelligently constructed, properly grammatical, and carefully spelled—was the mark of a person of substance and standing in colonial America, it is easy to discern the source of the distress Abigail Adams constantly expressed about her inability to write and spell well.

If a white woman did not want to be a farm wife, assuming she had a choice in the matter, then she had only a narrow range of alternatives. In order to take advantage of those alternatives she had to be located in an urban area, where she could support herself in one of three ways: by running a small school in her home; by opening a shop, usually but not always one that sold dry goods; or by in some manner using the household skills she had learned from her mother as a means of making money. This might involve hiring out as a servant, doing sewing, spinning, or weaving for wealthy families, or, if she had some capital, setting up a boardinghouse or inn. There were no other choices, and women who selected one of these occupations—or were compelled by adverse economic circumstances to do so—were frequently regarded as anomalous by their contemporaries.

A major component of the traditional view of American women's history is the assertion that the 40-year period centering on 1800 was a time of retrogression. Joan Hoff Wilson, the most recent proponent of this interpretation, links the setbacks she discerns in women's position explicitly to consequences of the American Revolution. But other work published in the last few years points to an exactly opposite conclusion: It has been suggested (if not yet fully proved) by a number of scholars that the late eighteenth century witnessed a series of advances for women, in some respects at least.

An examination of all extant Massachusetts divorce records seems to indicate, for example, that at the end of the century women seeking divorces were more likely to have their complaints judged fairly and were less likely to be oppressed by application of a sexual double standard than their predecessors had been. In a different area, it has been noted that women's educational opportunities improved dramatically after the mid-1780s.... Finally, extensive research into the patterns of first marriage in one New England town has uncovered changes in marital alliances that can be interpreted as evidence of a greater exercise of independent judgment by girls. Analysis of the records of Hingham, Massachusetts, has shown that in the latter years of the century more daughters married out of birth order and chose spouses whose economic status differed from that of their own parents than had previously been the case. If we assume that both sorts of actions would be contrary to parents' wishes, and couple that assumption with the knowledge that in the same town the premarital conception rate (judged by a comparison of wedding dates with the timing of births of first children) simultaneously jumped to more than 30 percent, we receive the clear impression that parental control of sons and daughters was at a low ebb.

Paradoxically, that last piece of evidence can also be read as suggesting a greater exploitation of women by men. The rise in premarital conception rates, which stretched over the entire eighteenth century and peaked in its last two decades, does not necessarily mean that all the women involved were willing participants seeking what would today be termed sexual fulfillment. On this issue, as on others discussed in this [selection], a great deal more research is needed in order to allow historians to gain a fuller picture of the female experience in colonial America.

POSTSCRIPT

Was the Colonial Period a "Golden Age" for Women in America?

Surveys of American women's history that address the colonial period include June Sochen, *Herstory: A Woman's View of American History* (Alfred A. Knopf, 1974); Mary P. Ryan, *Womenhood in America: From Colonial Times to the Present* (New Viewpoints, 1975); and Nancy Woloch, *Women and the American Experience* (Alfred A. Knopf, 1984). Support for the "golden age" theory can be found in Richard B. Morris, *Studies in the History of American Law*, 2d ed. (Octagon Books, 1964); Elizabeth Anthony Dexter, *Colonial Women of Affairs*, 2d ed. (Houghton Mifflin, 1931); Mary Ritter Beard, *Woman as Force in History* (Macmillan, 1946); Eleanor Flexner, *Century of Struggle* (Belknap Press, 1959); Roger Thompson, *Women in Stuart England and America: A Comparative Study* (Routledge & Kegan Paul, 1974); and Page Smith, *Daughters of the Promised Land: Women in American History* (Little, Brown, 1977).

Many of the scholarly monographs that include discussions of colonial women focus disproportionately on New England. For example, Edmund S. Morgan, *The Puritan Family: Religion and Domestic Relations in Seventeenth-Century New England* (Boston Public Library, 1944) and John Demos, *A Little Commonwealth: Family Life in Plymouth Colony* (Oxford University Press, 1970) both discuss the status of women within the context of the New England family. N. E. H. Hull, *Female Felons: Women and Serious Crime in Colonial Massachusetts* (University of Illinois Press, 1987) and Cornelia Hughes Dayton, *Women Before the Bar: Gender, Law, and Society in Connecticut, 1639–1789* (University of North Carolina Press, 1995) treat the legal status of female New Englanders. Also of interest are Lyle Koehler, *A Search for Power: The Weaker Sex in Seventeenth Century New England* (University of Illinois Press, 1980) and Laurel Thatcher Ulrich, *Good Wives: Image and Reality in the Lives of Women in Northern New England, 1650–1750* (Alfred A. Knopf, 1980).

Women in colonial Virginia are discussed in Darrett B. Rutman and Anita H. Rutman, *A Place in Time: Middlesex County, Virginia, 1650–1750* (W. W. Norton, 1984) and Kathleen M. Brown, *Good Wives, Nasty Wenches, and Anxious Patriarchs: Gender, Race, and Power in Colonial Virginia* (University of North Carolina Press, 1996).

Women in the age of the American Revolution are the focus of Carol Ruth Berkin, *Within the Conjurer's Circle: Women in Colonial America* (General Learning Press, 1974); Linda Grant DePauw and Conover Hunt, *"Remember the Ladies": Women in America, 1750–1815* (Viking Press, 1976); Mary Beth Norton, *Liberty's Daughters: The Revolutionary Experience of American Women, 1750–1800* (Little,

Brown 1980); Linda Kerber, *Women of the Republic: Intellect and Ideology in Revolutionary America* (University of North Carolina Press, 1980); Charles W. Akers, *Abigail Adams: An American Woman* (Little, Brown, 1980); and Joy Day Buel and Richard Buel, Jr., *The Way of Duty: A Woman and Her Family in Revolutionary America* (W. W. Norton, 1984). For the conclusion that the American Revolution failed to advance women's status, see Joan Hoff Wilson, "The Illusion of Change: Women and the American Revolution," in Alfred F. Young, ed., *The American Revolution: Explorations in the History of American Radicalism* (Northern Illinois University Press, 1976).

ISSUE 3

Were Socioeconomic Tensions Responsible for the Witchcraft Hysteria in Salem?

YES: Paul Boyer and Stephen Nissenbaum, from *Salem Possessed: The Social Origins of Witchcraft* (Harvard University Press, 1974)

NO: Laurie Winn Carlson, from *A Fever in Salem* (Ivan R. Dee, 1999)

ISSUE SUMMARY

YES: Historians Paul Boyer and Stephen Nissenbaum argue that the Salem witchcraft hysteria of 1692 was prompted by economic and social tensions that occurred against the backdrop of an emergent commercial capitalism, conflicts between ministers and their congregations, and the loss of family lands, which divided the residents of Salem Town and Salem Village.

NO: Author Laurie Winn Carlson contends that the witchcraft hysteria in Salem was the product of people's responses to physical and neurological behaviors resulting from an unrecognized epidemic of encephalitis.

P rehistoric paintings on the walls of caves throughout Europe reveal that witchcraft was of immediate and serious concern to many of our ancestors. The most intense eruptions in the long history of witchcraft, however, occurred during the sixteenth and seventeenth centuries. There were over 100 witchcraft trials in seventeenth-century New England alone, and 40 percent of the accused were executed. For most Americans the events that began in the kitchen of the Reverend Samuel Parris in Salem, Massachusetts, in 1692 are the most notorious.

A group of young girls, with the assistance of Parris's West Indian slave, Tituba, were attempting to see into the future by "reading" messages in the white of a raw egg they had suspended in a glass. The tragic results of this seemingly innocent diversion scandalized the Salem community and reverberated all the way to Boston. One of the participants insisted she saw the specter of a coffin in the egg white, and soon after, the girls began to display the hysterical symptoms of the possessed. Following intense interrogation by adults, Tituba, Sarah Good, and Sarah Osborne were accused of practicing magic and were arrested. Subsequently, Tituba confessed her guilt and acknowledged the existence of other witches but refused to name them. Accusations spread as paranoia enveloped the community. Between May and September 1692 hundreds of people were arrested for witchcraft. Although two explicit references in the Old Testament (Leviticus 20–27 and Exodus 22:18) condemn witches to death, Salem Christians were willing to spare confessed witches. Ironically, confession, as dangerous as that might have been, ensured acquittal. Those who risked going to trial gambled with their lives. Consequently, 19 people accused of witchcraft were convicted and hanged (not burned at the stake, as is often assumed), and another, a man who refused to admit guilt or innocence, was pressed to death under heavy weights. Finally, Sir William Phips, the new royal governor of the colony, halted court proceedings against the accused (which included his wife), and in May 1693 he ordered the release of those who were still in jail.

Witchcraft accusations tended to follow certain patterns, most of which were duplicated in Salem. Usually, they occurred during periods of political turmoil, economic dislocation, or social stress. In Salem, a political impasse between English authorities and the Massachusetts Bay Colony, economic tensions between commercial and agricultural interests, and disagreements between Salem Town and Salem Village formed the backdrop to the legal drama of 1692. Historians have offered a variety of explanations for the Salem witchcraft hysteria of the late seventeenth century, two of which are presented in the selections that follow.

In the first selection, Paul Boyer and Stephen Nissenbaum detail the socioeconomic conflicts (over such issues as the rise of commercial capitalism, the loss of family lands by third-generation sons, and disputes between local ministers and their congregations) that existed between the residents of Salem Town and Salem Village in the late seventeenth century. By mapping out the residences of those who were accused of witchcraft and those who leveled the charges, Boyer and Nissenbaum conclude that the accusers and the accused generally were not acquainted with one another and that the witchcraft hysteria was based on politics and economics.

Laurie Winn Carlson, on the other hand, insists that previous explanations for the events in Salem fail to take into account the physical and neurological symptoms exhibited by many of the residents of the town. Those symptoms, she argues, correspond very closely to behaviors described during a pandemic of encephalitis lethargica that struck the United States in the early twentieth century and provide a reasonable explanation for many of the unanswered questions about the events in Salem.

Paul Boyer and Stephen Nissenbaum  **YES**

Salem Possessed

1692: Some New Perspectives

Salem witchcraft. For most Americans the episode ranks in familiarity somewhere between Plymouth Rock and Custer's Last Stand. This very familiarity,
though, has made it something of a problem for historians. As a dramatic
package, the events of 1692 are just too neat, highlighted but also insulated
from serious research by the very floodlights which illuminate them. "Rebecca
Nurse," "Ann Putnam," "Samuel Parris"—they all endlessly glide onto the stage,
play their appointed scenes, and disappear again into the void. It is no coin-
cidence that the Salem witch trials are best known today through the work
of a playwright, not a historian. It was, after all, a series of historians from
George Bancroft to Marion Starkey who first treated the event as a dramatic set
piece, unconnected with the major issues of American colonial history. When
Arthur Miller published *The Crucible* in the early 1950's, he simply outdid the
historians at their own game.

After nearly three centuries of retelling in history books, poems, stories,
and plays, the whole affair has taken on a foreordained quality. It is hard to
conceive that the events of 1692 could have gone in any other direction or led
to any other outcome. It is like imagining the *Mayflower* sinking in midpassage,
or General Custer at the Little Big Horn surrendering to Sitting Bull without a
fight.

And yet speculation as to where events might have led in 1692 is one way
of recapturing the import of where they did lead. And if one reconstructs those
events bit by bit, as they happened, without too quickly categorizing them,
it is striking how long they resist settling into the neat and familiar pattern
one expects. A full month, maybe more, elapsed between the time the girls
began to exhibit strange behavior and the point at which the first accusations
of witchcraft were made; and in the haze of those first uncertain weeks, it is
possible to discern the shadows of what might have been.

Bewitchment and Conversion

Imagine, for instance, how easily the finger of witchcraft could have been
pointed back at the afflicted girls themselves. It was they, after all, who first

began to toy with the supernatural. At least one neighboring minister, the Reverend John Hale of Beverly, eventually became convinced that a large measure of blame rested with these girls who, in their "vain curiosity to know their future condition," had "tampered with the devil's tools." And Hale's judgment in the matter was shared by his far more influential colleague Cotton Mather, who pinpointed as the cause of the outbreak the "conjurations" of thoughtless youths, including, of course, the suffering girls themselves.

Why then, during 1692, were the girls so consistently treated as innocent victims? Why were they not, at the very least, chastised for behavior which itself verged on witchcraft? Clearly, the decisive factor was the interpretation which adults—adults who had the power to make their interpretation stick—chose to place on events whose intrinsic meaning was, to begin with, dangerously ambiguous.

The adults, indeed, determined not only the direction the witchcraft accusations would take; it was they, it seems, who first concluded that witchcraft was even in the picture at all. "[W]hen these calamities first began," reported Samuel Parris in March 1692, "... the affliction was several weeks before such hellish operations as witchcraft was suspected." Only in response to urgent questioning—"Who is it that afflicts you?"—did the girls at last begin to point their fingers at others in the Village.

It is not at all clear that the girls' affliction was initially unpleasant or, indeed, that they experienced it as an "affliction" at all. Unquestionably it could be harrowing enough once witchcraft became the accepted diagnosis, but the little evidence available from late February, before the agreed-upon explanation had been arrived at, makes the girls' behavior seem more exhilarated than tormented, more liberating than oppressive. One of the early published accounts of the outbreak, that of Robert Calef in 1700, described the girls' initial manifestations as "getting into holes, and creeping under chairs and stools..., [with] sundry odd postures and antic gestures, [and] uttering foolish, ridiculous speeches which neither they themselves nor any others could make sense of." ...

Some Patterns of Accusation

Pace

By the time the storm subsided in October, several hundred persons had been accused of witchcraft, about 150 of them formally charged and imprisoned, and nineteen executed. But when it first broke out in February, there had been no indication that it would reach such proportions, or that it would be any more serious than the numerous isolated witchcraft outbreaks that had periodically plagued New England since at least 1647—outbreaks that had resulted in a total of only fifteen or so executions. The initial accusation at the end of February had named three witches, and most people outside Salem Village, if they heard of the matter at all, probably assumed that it would end there. But the symptoms of the afflicted girls did not subside, and toward the end of March the girls accused three more persons of tormenting them. Still, by early April (a month and a half after the accusations began) only six people had come under public suspicion of witchcraft.

It was at this time, however, that the pace of accusations picked up sharply, and the whole situation began to assume unusual and menacing proportions. Twenty-two witches were accused in April, thirty-nine more in May. After a dip in June, probably reflecting the impact of the first actual execution on June 10, the arrests picked up again and increased steadily from July through September. Indeed, toward the end of the summer, accusations were being made so freely and widely that accurate records of the official proceedings were no longer kept.

Status
But it was not only in the matter of numbers that the episode changed dramatically as it ran its course; there was a qualitative change as well. The first three women to be accused could be seen as "deviants" or "outcasts" in their community—the kinds of people who anthropologists have suggested are particularly susceptible to such accusations. Tituba... was a West Indian slave; Sarah Good was a pauper who went around the Village begging aggressively for food and lodging; "Gammer" Osborne, while somewhat better off, was a bedridden old woman.

In March, however, a new pattern began to emerge. Two of the three witches accused in that month—the third was little Dorcas Good—were church members (a sign of real respectability in the seventeenth century) and the wives of prosperous freeholders. This pattern continued and even intensified for the duration of the outbreak: the twenty-two persons accused in April included the wealthiest shipowner in Salem (Phillip English) and a minister of the gospel who was a Harvard graduate with a considerable estate in England (George Burroughs). By mid-May warrants had been issued against two of the seven selectmen of Salem Town; and by the end of the summer some of the most prominent people in Massachusetts and their close kin had been accused if not officially charged. These included:

- Several men with "great estates in Boston";
- a wealthy Boston merchant, Hezekiah Usher, and the widow of an even wealthier one, Jacob Sheafe;
- a future representative to the General Court;
- the wife of the Reverend John Hale of Beverly (a man who had himself supported the trials);
- Captain John Alden, one of the best-known men in New England (and son of the now legendary John and Priscilla of Plymouth Colony);
- the two sons of a distinguished old former governor, Simon Bradstreet, who were themselves active in provincial government;
- Nathaniel Saltonstall, a member of the Governor's Council and for a time one of the judges of the witchcraft court;
- and Lady Phips herself, wife of the governor.

Indeed, according to one account, a specter of Cotton Mather and another of his mother-in-law were spied late in the summer. As the attorney who prepared the cases against the accused wrote at the end of May, "The afflicted spare no person of what quality so ever."

True, none of these persons of quality was ever brought to trial, much less executed. Some escaped from jail or house arrest, others were simply never arraigned. Nevertheless, the overall direction of the accusations remains clear: up the social ladder, fitfully but perceptibly, to its very top. Whatever else they may have been, the Salem witch trials cannot be written off as a communal effort to purge the poor, the deviant, or the outcast.

Geography

Just as the accusations thrust steadily upward through the social strata of provincial society, so, too, they pressed outward across geographic boundaries. Beginning within Salem Village itself, the accusations moved steadily into an increasingly wide orbit. The first twelve witches were either residents of the Village or persons who lived just beyond its borders. But of all the indictments which followed this initial dozen, only fifteen were directed against people in the immediate vicinity of Salem Village. The other victims came from virtually every town in Essex County, including the five which surrounded the Village. (In the town of Andover alone, there were more arrests than in Salem Village itself.)

While almost all these arrests were made on the basis of testimony given by the ten or so afflicted girls of Salem Village (although in some cases they merely confirmed the validity of others' accusations), it is clear that the girls themselves did not actually know most of the people they named. The experience of Rebecca Jacobs—arrested only to go unrecognized by her accusers—was far from unique. Captain Alden, for example, later reported that at his arraignment in Salem Village, the afflicted girls who had named him were unable to pick him out until a man standing behind one of them whispered into her ear. After finally identifying Alden, the girl was asked by one of the examiners if she had ever seen the man before; when she answered no, her interrogator asked her "how she knew it was Alden? She said, the man told her so."

Accusers and accused, then, were in many if not most cases personally unacquainted. Whatever was troubling the girls and those who encouraged them, it was something deeper than the kind of chronic, petty squabbles between near neighbors which seem to have been at the root of earlier and far less severe witchcraft episodes in New England.

But if the outbreak's geographic pattern tends to belie certain traditional explanations, it raises other, more intriguing, interpretative possibilities. More than a hundred years ago, Charles W. Upham, a public figure in Salem whose lifelong avocation was the study of the witch trials, published a map which located with some precision the home of nearly every Salem Village resident at the beginning of 1692. Using Upham's careful map as a basis, it is possible to pinpoint the place of residence of every Villager who testified for or against any of the accused witches and also of those accused who themselves lived within the Village bounds. A pattern emerges from this exercise—a pattern which further reinforces the conclusion that neighborhood quarrels, in the narrow sense of the phrase, played a minor role indeed in generating witchcraft accusations:

There were fourteen accused witches who lived within the bounds of Salem Village. Twelve of these fourteen lived in the eastern section of the Village.

There were thirty-two adult Villagers who testified against these accused witches. Only two of these lived in that eastern section. The other thirty lived on the western side. In other words, the alleged witches and those who accused them resided on opposite sides of the Village.

There were twenty-nine Villagers who publicly showed their skepticism about the trials or came to the defense of one or more of the accused witches. Twenty-four of these lived in the eastern part of the Village—the same side on which the witches lived—and only five of them in the west. Those who defended the witches were generally their neighbors, often their immediate neighbors. Those who accused them were not. . . .

Witchcraft and Social Identity

What we have been attempting . . . is to convey something of the deeper historical resonances of our story while still respecting its uniqueness. We see no real conflict between these two purposes. To be sure, no other community was precisely like Salem Village and no other men were exactly like embittered Samuel Parris, cool and ambitious Israel Porter, or Thomas Putnam, Jr., grimly watching the steady diminution of his worldly estate.

This irreducible particularity, these intensely personal aspirations and private fears, fairly leap from the documents these Salem Villagers, and others, left behind them. And had we been able to learn to know them better—heard the timbre of their voices, watched the play of emotion across their faces, observed even a few of those countless moments in their lives which went unrecorded —we might have been able to apprehend with even greater force the pungent flavor of their individuality.

But the more we have come to know these men for something like what they really were, the more we have also come to realize how profoundly they were shaped by the times in which they lived. For if they were unlike any other men, so was their world unlike any other world before or since; and they shared that world with other people living in other places. Parris and Putnam and the rest were, after all, not only Salem Villagers: they were also men of the seventeenth century; they were New Englanders; and, finally, they were Puritans.

If the large concepts with which historians conventionally deal are to have any meaning, it is only as they can be made manifest in individual cases like these. The problems which confronted Salem Village in fact encompassed some of the central issues of New England society in the late seventeenth century: the resistance of back-country farmers to the pressures of commercial capitalism and the social style that accompanied it; the breaking away of outlying areas from parent towns; difficulties between ministers and their congregations; the crowding of third-generation sons from family lands; the shifting locus of authority within individual communities and society as a whole; the very quality of life in an unsettled age. But for men like Samuel Parris and Thomas Putnam, Jr., these issues were not abstractions. They emerged as upsetting personal encounters with people like Israel Porter and Daniel Andrew, and as unfavorable decisions handed down in places like Boston and Salem Town.

It was in 1692 that these men for the first time attempted... to piece together the shards of their experience, to shape their malaise into some broader theoretical pattern, and to comprehend the full dimensions of those forces which they vaguely sensed were shaping their private destinies. Oddly enough, it has been through our sense of "collaborating" with Parris and the Putnams in their effort to delineate the larger contours of their world, and our sympathy, at least on the level of metaphor, with certain of their perceptions, that we have come to feel a curious bond with the "witch hunters" of 1692.

But one advantage we as outsiders have had over the people of Salem Village is that we can afford to recognize the degree to which the menace they were fighting off had taken root within each of them almost as deeply as it had in Salem Town or along the Ipswich Road. It is at this level, indeed, that we have most clearly come to recognize the implications of their travail for our understanding of what might be called the Puritan temper during that final, often intense, and occasionally lurid efflorescence which signaled the end of its century-long history. For Samuel Parris and Thomas Putnam, Jr., were part of a vast company, on both sides of the Atlantic, who were trying to expunge the lure of a new order from their own souls by doing battle with it in the real world. While this company of Puritans were not the purveyors of the spirit of capitalism that historians once made them out to be, neither were they simple peasants clinging blindly to the imagined security of a receding medieval culture. What seems above all to characterize them, and even to help define their identity as "Puritans," is the precarious way in which they managed to inhabit both these worlds at once.

The inner tensions that shaped the Puritan temper were inherent in it from the very start, but rarely did they emerge with such raw force as in 1692, in little Salem Village. For here was a community in which these tensions were exacerbated by a tangle of external circumstances: a community so situated geographically that its inhabitants experienced two different economic systems, two different ways of life, at unavoidably close range; and so structured politically that it was next to impossible to locate, either within the Village or outside it, a dependable and unambiguous center of authority which might hold in check the effects of these accidents of geography.

The spark which finally set off this volatile mix came with the unlikely convergence of a set of chance factors in the early 1690's: the arrival of a new minister who brought with him a slave acquainted with West Indian voodoo lore; the heightened interest throughout New England in fortune telling and the occult, taken up in Salem Village by an intense group of adolescent girls related by blood and faction to the master of that slave; the coming-of-age of Joseph Putnam, who bore the name of one of Salem Village's two controlling families while owing his allegiance to the other; the political and legal developments in

Boston and London which hamstrung provincial authorities for several crucial months early in 1692.

But beyond these proximate causes lie... deeper and more inexorable ones.... For in the witchcraft outburst in Salem Village, perhaps, the most exceptional event in American colonial history, certainly the most bizarre, one finds laid bare the central concerns of the era. And so once again, for a final time, we must return to the Village in the sorest year of its affliction.

Witchcraft and Factionalism

Predictably enough, the witchcraft accusations of 1692 moved in channels which were determined by years of factional strife in Salem Village. The charges against Daniel Andrew and Phillip English, for example, followed closely upon their election as Salem Town selectmen—in a vote which underscored the collapse of the Putnam effort to stage a comeback in Town politics. And Francis Nurse, the husband of accused witch Rebecca Nurse, was a member of the anti-Parris Village Committee which took office in October 1691.

Other accusations, less openly political, suggest a tentative probing around the fringes of the anti-Parris leadership. For example, George Jacobs, Jr. —accused with several members of his family—was a brother-in-law of Daniel Andrew, whose lands he helped farm. Jacobs was close to the Porter group in other ways as well. In 1695, for example, he was on hand as the will of the dying Mary Veren Putnam was drawn up, and his name appears with Israel Porter's as a witness to that controversial document. In May 1692 Daniel Andrew and George Jacobs, Jr., were named in the same arrest warrant, and they evidently went into hiding together.

Another of Daniel Andrew's tenants was Peter Cloyce whose wife, Sarah (a sister of Rebecca Nurse) was among the accused in 1692. And Michael DeRich, whose wife Mary was also charged that year, seems at one time to have been a retainer or servant in the household of the elder John Porter, and his ties to the family may well have continued into the next generation. (Mary DeRich, in turn, was a close relative—perhaps even a sister—of Elizabeth Proctor, convicted of witchcraft along with her husband John.)

Indeed, as the accused are examined from the perspective of Village factionalism, they begin to arrange themselves into a series of interconnected networks. These networks were not formally organized or rigidly structured, but they were nonetheless real enough. The kinds of associations which underlay them were varied: kinship and marriage ties were crucial, but marriage, in all likelihood, was simply the final step, the institutionalization of less tangible bonds built up gradually over a period of time. The traces of such bonds lie buried in a wide variety of sources, including real-estate transactions, court testimony, genealogies, and lists of witnesses and executors in wills and estate settlements. Ultimately, the evidence for these relationships fades off into shadowy associations which are frustratingly difficult to document with precision—although they were certainly well known at the time.

One such network... links Israel Porter with a startling number of "witch" families, most notably the Proctors and the Nurses. Other anti-Parris networks (and, for that matter, pro-Parris networks) could be reconstructed.... Perhaps the nature of these ties provides a key to one of the ways in which political "factions" were established, cemented, and enlarged in Salem Village (and in other communities as well) during the last part of the seventeenth century. If so, the pattern of witchcraft accusations may itself be a more revealing guide than even the maps or tax lists to the origin of political divisions in the Village.

Given all this, it is not surprising to discover a high correlation between Salem Village factionalism and the way the Village divided in 1692 over the witchcraft outbreak. There are forty-seven Villagers whose position can be determined both in 1692 (by their testimonies or other involvement in the witchcraft trials) and in 1695 (by their signatures on one or the other of the two key petitions). Of the twenty-seven of those who supported the trials by testifying against one or more of the accused witches, twenty-one later signed the pro-Parris petition, and only six the anti-Parris document. Of the twenty who registered their opposition to the trials, either by defending an accused person or by casting doubt on the testimony of the afflicted girls, only one supported Parris in 1695, while nineteen opposed him. In short, supporters of the trials generally belonged to the pro-Parris faction, and opponents of the trials were overwhelmingly anti-Parris.

Almost every indicator by which the two Village factions may be distinguished, in fact, also neatly separates the supporters and opponents of the witchcraft trials.... [T]hat part of Salem Village which was an anti-Parris stronghold in 1695 (the part nearest Salem Town) had also been a center of resistance to the witchcraft trials, while the more distant western part of the Village, where pro-Parris sentiment was dominant, contained an extremely high concentration of accusers in 1692.

Similarly with wealth: just as the average member of the anti-Parris faction paid about 40 percent more in Village taxes than his counterpart in the pro-Parris faction, so the average 1695–96 tax of the Villagers who publicly opposed the trials was 67 percent higher than that of those who pushed the trials forward —18.3 shillings as opposed to 11 shillings....

As early as 1689, in his *Memorable Providences Relating to Witchcrafts and Possessions,* Cotton Mather had urged his readers to "shun a frame of discontent" if they wished to avoid becoming witches: "When persons through discontent at their *poverty,* or at their *misery,* shall be always murmuring and repining at the providence of God, the Devils do then invite them to an agreement..., [and d]ownright *witchcraft* is the upshot of it."

From the perspective of those who led the attack in 1692, such an analysis might have seemed to explain not only disruptive malcontents at the lower end of the scale—people like Job Tookey and Sarah Good—but also prospering and upwardly mobile people like John Proctor, John Willard, and Rebecca Nurse. There were, after all, various ways to betray "discontent" with one's natural station: one could turn embittered and spiteful, to be sure; but on the other hand, like the young Proctor and Nurse, one might combine aggressive behavior with good fortune and improve one's status. From a seventeenth century viewpoint, swift economic rise was just as tangible an expression of "discontent" as was muttering or complaining.

Everybody knew that by 1692 John Proctor was wealthier than any of his accusers, yet they also knew that he remained "Goodman" Proctor while Thomas Putnam, by virtue of his father's station, bore the more honorific designation "Mr. Putnam." As Abigail Williams cried out during a spectral visitation in mid-April, running down a list of newly accused witches: "Oh yonder is Goodman Proctor and his wife and Goody Nurse and Goody Cory and Goody Cloyse!" (Abigail's own uncle may not have been receiving his salary at the time, but he was nevertheless "Mr. Parris.") And at the witchcraft examination of Mary Clarke of Haverhill, young Ann Putnam commented sarcastically that even though the accused woman was now addressed at "Mistress Mary Clarke," Ann well knew "that people used to call her Goody Clarke."

All of these people were on the move, socially and economically. Yet to many New Englanders of the seventeenth century, the stability of the social order rested on the willingness of everyone to accept his given station in life. Refusal to do so was more than a personal weakness; it represented a tangible threat to the social fabric itself. When Cotton Mather preached a sermon in 1689 in response to a Boston witchcraft case of that year, he chose a Biblical text which made this very point: *"Rebellion is as the sin of witchcraft."* The rebellion Mather had in mind here was surely not the political sort—not in the very year that he had supported the successful overthrow of Governor Andros!—but the even more menacing variety implicit in both the spiteful turbulence of those who were sliding down the social ladder and the pushy restlessness of those who were climbing up. The feeling that Mather articulated in this 1689 sermon was one shared by many people in Salem Village three years later: the social order was being profoundly shaken by a superhuman force which had lured all too many into active complicity with it. We have chosen to construe this force as emergent mercantile capitalism. Mather, and Salem Village, called it witchcraft.

NO

Laurie Winn Carlson

A Fever in Salem

During the latter part of the seventeenth century, residents of a northeastern Massachusetts colony experienced a succession of witchcraft accusations resulting in hearings, trials, imprisonments, and executions. Between 1689 and 1700 the citizens complained of symptoms that included fits (convulsions), spectral visions (hallucinations), mental "distraction" (psychosis), "pinching, pin pricking and bites" on their skin (clonus), lethargy, and even death. They "barked like dogs," were unable to walk, and had their arms and legs "nearly twisted out of joint."

In late winter and early spring of 1692, residents of Salem Village, Massachusetts, a thinly settled town of six hundred, began to suffer from a strange physical and mental malady. Fits, hallucinations, temporary paralysis, and "distracted" rampages were suddenly occurring sporadically in the community. The livestock, too, seemed to suffer from the unexplainable illness. The randomness of the victims and the unusual symptoms that were seldom exactly the same, led the residents to suspect an otherwordly menace. With the limited scientific and medical knowledge of the time, physicians who were consulted could only offer witchcraft as an explanation.

These New Englanders were Puritans, people who had come to North America to establish a utopian vision of community based upon religious ideals. But, as the historian Daniel Boorstin points out, their religious beliefs were countered by their reliance on English common law. The Puritans did not create a society out of their religious dogma but maintained the rule of law brought from their homeland. They were pragmatic, attempting to adapt practices brought from England rather than reinventing their own as it suited them. When problems arose that were within the realm of the legal system, the community acted appropriately, seeking redress for wrongs within the courts.

Thus when purported witchcraft appeared, church leaders, physicians, and a panicked citizenry turned the problem over to the civil authorities. Witchcraft was a capital crime in all the colonies, and whoever was to blame for it had to be ferreted out and made to stop. Because no one could halt the outbreak of illness, for ten months the community wrestled with sickness, sin, and the criminal act of witchcraft. By September 1692, nineteen convicted

witches had been hanged and more than a hundred people sat in prison await-
ing sentencing when the trials at last faded. The next year all were released and
the court closed. The craze ended as abruptly as it began.

Or did it? There had been similar sporadic physical complaints blamed on
witchcraft going back several decades in New England, to the 1640s when the
first executions for the crime of witchcraft were ordered in the colonies. Evidence indicates that people (and domestic animals) had suffered similar physical symptoms and ailments in Europe in still earlier years. After the witch trials
ended in Salem, there continued to be complaints of the "Salem symptoms"
in Connecticut and New Hampshire, as well as in Boston, into the early eighteenth century. But there were no more hangings. The epidemic and witchcraft
had parted ways.

By examining the primary records left by those who suffered from the
unexplainable and supposedly diabolical ailments in 1692, we get a clear picture
of exactly what they were experiencing. *The Salem Witchcraft Papers*, a three-
volume set compiled from the original documents and preserved as typescripts
by the Works Progress Administration in the 1930s, has been edited for today's
reader by Paul Boyer and Stephen Nissenbaum. It is invaluable for reading the
complete and detailed problems people were dealing with. Like sitting in the
physician's office with them, we read where the pain started, how it disappeared
or progressed, how long they endured it.

A similar epidemic with nearly exact symptoms swept the world from 1916
to 1930. This world-wide pandemic, sleeping sickness, or encephalitis lethargica, eventually claimed more than five million victims. Its cause has never
been fully identified. There is no cure. Victims of the twentieth-century epidemic continue under hospitalization to the present day. An excellent source
for better understanding encephalitis lethargica is Oliver Sacks's book *Awak-
enings*, which is now in its sixth edition and has become a cult classic. A
movie of the same title, based on the book, presents a very credible look at the
physical behaviors patients exhibited during the epidemic. While encephalitis
lethargica, in the epidemic form in which it appeared in the early twentieth
century, is not active today, outbreaks of insect-borne encephalitis do appear
infrequently throughout the country; recent outbreaks of mosquito-borne encephalitis have nearly brought Walt Disney World in Florida to a halt, have
caused entire towns to abandon evening football games, and have made horse
owners anxious throughout the San Joaquin Valley in California.

Using the legal documents from the Salem witch trials of 1692, as well
as contemporary accounts of earlier incidents in the surrounding area, we can
identify the "afflictions" that the colonists experienced and that led to the accusations of witchcraft. By comparing the symptoms reported by seventeenth-
century colonists with those of patients affected by the encephalitis lethargica
epidemic of the early twentieth century, a pattern of symptoms emerges. This
pattern supports the hypothesis that the witch-hunts of New England were a
response to unexplained physical and neurological behaviors resulting from an
epidemic of encephalitis. This was some form of the same encephalitis epidemic
that became pandemic in the 1920s. In fact it is difficult to find anything in the

record at Salem that *doesn't* support the idea that the symptoms were caused by that very disease. . . .

What Happened at Salem?

. . . Historical explanations of witchcraft dwell on what Thomas Szasz calls the "scapegoat theory of witchcraft," which explores who was accused and why in the context of larger societal issues. Inevitably they fail to examine the accusers or the "afflicted," who themselves were often tried for witchcraft.

Sociologists have pointed to community-based socioeconomic problems as the causative agent in the events at Salem. They propose that there were really two Salems: Salem Town (a prosperous sector on the well-developed east side of town) and Salem Village (a less-developed, very swampy and rocky area on the west side). Likening Salem Village to a troubled backwater, the accusations and afflictions emanated from the west side, where the residents directed their animosity toward their wealthier, more powerful eastern counterparts by accusing individuals on the east side of witchcraft. Examining the struggles, failures, broken dreams, and lost hopes of the Salem Village residents, sociologists began to view the village as "an inner city on a hill." Social conflict, in this case between prosperous merchants and struggling subsistence farmers, was examined. In the case of the Salem witch hunts, the theory may better explain who was accused and convicted of witchcraft than why individuals were afflicted. Division along class and religious lines has been well documented in determining criminal accusations.

Other investigators have blamed the situation on village factionalism, claiming that Salem Village was rife with suspicious, disgruntled, jealous settlers whose frustrations had festered for years before exploding in the court record with witchcraft accusations and trials. But that does not explain why twenty-two *other* towns in New England were eventually connected to the proceedings in some way; villagers throughout Maine, New Hampshire, Connecticut, Massachusetts, and Rhode Island were brought into the trial records. Victims, accused witches, and witnesses came from other locales as far away as the Maine frontier. Other locations, such as Connecticut, conducted witch trials that preceded or coincided with those at Salem. Choosing to view the problems as power struggles or personality differences within a small village strikes one as too parochial. Many of the possessed claimants barely knew the people they named as their tormenters, in fact several had never even met the persons they accused of fostering their problems—hardly enough tension to support the idea that the entire uproar was based on long-standing animosities. Socioeconomic divisions did engender problems in the region, and while they ultimately may be used to explain who was accused and why, they do not explain the many physical symptoms or who experienced them.

Carol Karlsen has viewed what happened at Salem in her book *The Devil in the Shape of a Woman*, which relates the events to women's oppressed status within Puritan society. She considers New Englanders' "possession" to have been a cultural performance—a ritual—performed by girls, interpreted by ministers, and observed by an audience as a dramatic event. Karlsen claims the possessed individuals exhibited learned behavior patterns and that words and actions varied only slightly among them. The affected women experienced an inner conflict which was explained by ministers as a struggle between good and evil: God versus Satan. The outcome revolved around whether or not the young women would later lead virtuous lives or fall into sin. Karlsen suggests that a woman's possession was the result of her indecision or ambivalence about choosing the sort of woman she wanted to be. She views the possession as a "collective phenomenon" among women in Connecticut between 1662 and 1663, and in Massachusetts from 1692 to 1693. It was a "ritual expression of Puritan belief and New England's gender arrangements," and a challenge to society. It was ultimately a simple power struggle between women and their oppressors.

As to the physical symptoms: the fits, trances, and paralyzed limbs, among others, Karlsen attributes them to the afflicted girls' actual fear of witches as well as the idea that once they fell into an afflicted state they were free to express unacceptable feelings without reprisal. The swollen throats, extended tongues, and eyes frozen in peripheral stares were manifestations of the inner rage they felt toward society; they were so upset they literally *couldn't* speak. Their paralysis was based on anger over having to work; their inability to walk meant they could not perform their expected labor—in other words, a passive-aggressive response to a situation that incensed them. Karlsen views witchcraft possession in New England as a rebellion against gender and class powers: a psychopathology rooted in female anger.

Misogyny may well explain who was accused of witchcraft, but it lacks an explanation for the wide-ranging symptoms, the ages of the afflicted, and the patterns of symptoms that occurred across time and distance in seventeenth-century New England. Scholars who take this route, however, conveniently ignore the fact that men too were accused, tried, and hanged for witchcraft, both in the colonies and in Europe. In fact, Robin Briggs states that though "every serious historical account recognizes that large numbers of men were accused and executed on similar charges, this fact has never really penetrated to become part of the general knowledge on the subject." His research shows that a misogynistic view of witch-hunts lacks complete credibility.

Many researchers have proposed that mass hysteria affected the young women of Salem. The term *hysteria*, essentially a female complaint, has recently been dropped from use by the psychiatric profession in favor of "conversion symptom," which describes the manner in which neurotic patients suffer emotional stress brought on by an unconscious source. This stress or tension can undergo "conversion" and reveal itself in a variety of physical ailments. Conversion, a very pliable disorder, can be explained by almost any societal pressure in any particular culture. It is a psychological catchall for unexplained neurological or emotional problems. But its victims are always the same, according to analysts: unstable females.

Jean-Martin Charcot, a French physician, worked extensively with epileptic and hysteric female patients at the Salpêtrière Hospital in Paris between 1862 and 1870. He laid the groundwork for hysteria theory, calling it hystero-epilepsy. He accused his patients of being deceitful, clever actresses who delighted in fooling the male physician. Charcot's medical students claimed to be able to transfer diseases from hysterics with the use of magnets, something they called the "metal cure." Eventually his professional standing as a neurologist diminished and faded, and he turned to faith healing. Sigmund Freud, one of his students, began his work under Charcot's direction.

A more modern version of the hysteria complex is called Mass Psychogenic Illness, or MPI, which is defined as the contagious spread of behavior within a group of individuals where one person serves as the catalyst or "starter" and the others imitate the behavior. Used to describe situations where mass illness breaks out in the school or workplace, it is usually connected to a toxic agent —real or imagined—in a less than satisfactory institutional or factory setting. MPI is the sufferer's response to overwhelming life and work stress. It relies on the individual's identification with the index case (the first one to get sick, in effect the "leader") and willingness to succumb to the same illness. A classical outbreak of MPI involves a group of segregated young females in a noisy, crowded, high-intensity setting. It is most common in Southeast Asian factories crowded with young female workers; adults are not usually affected. Symptoms appear, spread, and subside rapidly (usually over one day). Physical manifestations usually include fainting, malaise, convulsions with hyperventilation, and excitement. Transmission is by sight or sound brought about by a triggering factor which affects members of the group, who share some degree of unconscious fantasies. A phenomenon more related to the industrial world of the nineteenth and twentieth centuries than to pastoral village life in colonial New England, MPI does not address the question of why men and young children, who would not have identified emotionally and psychologically with a group of young girls, suffered. The New England colonists scarcely fit the pattern for this illness theory that demands large groups of people of similar age, sex, and personality assembled in one confined location.

Salem's witches cannot, of course, escape Freudian critique. Beyond the hysteria hypothesis, John Demos, in *Entertaining Satan,* looked at the evidence from the perspective of modern psychoanalysis. He pointed out that witchcraft explained and excused people's mistakes or incompetence—a failure or mistake blamed on witches allowed a cathartic cleansing of personal responsibility. Witches served a purpose; deviant people served as models to the rest of society to exemplify socially unacceptable behavior. But Demos's explanation that witch-hunts were an integral part of social experience, something that bound the community together—sort of a public works project—does not address the physical symptoms of the sufferers.

For the most part, examinations of the afflicted individuals at Salem have focused on the young women, essentially placing the blame on them instead of exploring an organic cause for their behaviors. Freudian explanations for the goings-on have attributed the activities of the possessed girls to a quest for attention. Their physical manifestations of illness have been explained as being conversion symptoms due to intrapsychic conflict. Their physical expression of psychological conflict is a compromise between unacceptable impulses and the mind's attempt to ignore them. Demos uses the example of Elizabeth Knapp, whose fits became increasingly severe while strangers gathered to view her behavior. Instead of considering that she was beset by an uncontrollable series of convulsions which were likely worsened by the excited witnesses who refused to leave her alone, he attributes her worsening condition to her exhibitionist tendencies, motivated by strong dependency needs. Elizabeth's writhing on the floor in a fetal position is seen as an oral dependency left over from childhood, causing her regression to infancy.

But "inner conflict" simply does not explain the events at Salem. Neither does the idea that the young afflicted girls were motivated by an erotic attraction to church ministers who were called in to determine whether Satan was involved. The girls' repressed adolescent sexual wishes (one girl was only eleven years old) and their seeking a replacement for absent father figures scarcely explains the toll the disease was taking on victims of both sexes and all ages. No Freudian stone has been left unturned by scholars; even the "genetic reconstruction" of Elizabeth Knapps's past points out that her childhood was filled with unmet needs, her mother's frustration because of an inability to bear additional children, and her father's reputation as a suspected adulterer. "Narcissistic depletion," "psychological transference," "a tendency to fragment which was temporarily neutralized"—the psycho-lingo just about stumbles over itself in attempts to explain the afflicted girls at Salem. But unanswered questions remain: Why the sharp pains in extremities? The hallucinations? The hyperactivity? The periods of calm between sessions of convulsions? Why did other residents swear in court that they had seen marks appear on the arms of the afflicted?

The opinion that the victims were creating their own fits as challenges to authority and quests for fame has shaped most interpretations of what happened in 1692. But would the colonists have strived for public notice and attention? If the afflicted individuals were behaving unusually to garner public notice, why? Did women and men of that era really crave public attention, or would it have put them in awkward, critical, and socially unacceptable situations? How socially redeeming would writhing on the ground "like a hog" and emitting strange noises, "barking like a dog," or "bleating like a calf" be for a destitute young servant girl who hoped to marry above her station? It is difficult to accept that these spectacles, which horrified viewers as well as the participants themselves, were actually a positive experience for the young women. That sort of suspicious activity usually met with social stigma, shunning, or, at the least, brutal whipping from father or master.

Puberty, a time of inner turmoil, is thought to have contributed to the victims acting out through fits, convulsions, and erratic behavior. The victims' inability to eat is explained away as a disorder related to the youthful struggle for individuality: anorexia nervosa. What about the young men who reported symptoms? Freudian interpretation attributes their behavior to rebellion against controlling fathers. How have psycho-social interpretations explained the reason witch trials ended after 1692 in Salem? As communities grew into larger urban units, people no longer knew their neighbors, grudges receded in importance as a factor in social control, and witches were no longer valuable to society. John Demos observes that witchcraft never appeared in cities, and that it lasted longest in villages far removed from urban influence. That linkage between witchcraft outbreaks and agricultural villages is important when establishing a connection with outbreaks of encephalitis lethargica, which appeared largely in small towns and rural areas in the early twentieth century. Rather than accepting the idea that witchcraft receded because it was no longer useful in a community context, one must examine why epidemics occurred in waves and how particular disease affected isolated population groups.

The situation in seventeenth-century New England fails psycho-social explanation because too many questions remain unanswered. Not only can we not make a strong case that infantilism, sexual repression, and a struggle for individuality caused the turmoil in Salem, but a psycho-social explanation does not answer why the symptoms, which were so *obviously physical,* appeared with such force and then, in the autumn of 1692, largely disappeared from Salem.

⋆✦⋆

Because the complexity of psychological and social factors connected with interpreting witchcraft is so absorbing, the existence of a physical pathology behind the events at Salem has long been overlooked. Linnda Caporeal, a graduate student in psychology, proposed that ergot, a fungus that appears on rye crops, caused the hallucinogenic poisoning in Salem. Her article appeared in 1976 in *Science* while Americans were trying to understand the LSD drug phenomenon. Hers is one of the few attempts made to link the puzzling occurrences at Salem with biological evidence.

Ergot was identified by a French scientist in 1676, in an explanation of the relation between ergotized rye and bread poisoning. It is a fungus that contains several potent pharmacologic agents, the ergot alkaloids. One of these alkaloids is lysergic acid amide, which has ten percent of the activity of LSD (lysergic acid diethylamide). This sort of substance causes convulsions or gangrenous deterioration of the extremities. Caporeal proposed that an ergot infestation in the Salem area might explain the convulsions attributed to witchcraft. If grain crops had been infected with ergot fungus during the 1692 rainy season and later stored away, the fungus might have grown in the storage area and spread to the entire crop. When it was distributed randomly among friends and villagers, they would have become affected by the poisoned grain.

Caporeal's innovative thinking was challenged by psychologists Nicholas Spanos and Jack Gottlieb, who were quick to point out that her theory did not explain why, if food poisoning were to blame, families who ate from the same source of grain were not affected. And infants were afflicted who may not have been eating bread grains. Historically, epidemics of ergotism have appeared in areas where there was a severe vitamin A deficiency in the diet. Salem residents had plenty of milk and seafood available; they certainly did not suffer from vitamin A deficiency. Ergotism also involves extensive vomiting and diarrhea, symptoms not found in the Salem cases. A hearty appetite, almost ravenous, follows ergotism; in New England the afflicted wasted away from either an inability to eat or a lack of interest in it. The sudden onset of the Salem symptoms in late winter and early spring would be hard to trace to months of eating contaminated grain. Ergot was never seriously considered as the cause of problems at Salem, even by the colonists themselves who knew what ergotism was (it had been identified sixteen years earlier) and were trying desperately to discover the source of their problems.

An explanation that satisfies many of the unanswered questions about the events at Salem is that the symptoms reported by the afflicted New Englanders and their families in the seventeenth century were the result of an unrecognized epidemic of encephalitis. Comparisons may be made between the afflictions reported at Salem (as well as the rest of seventeenth-century New England) and the encephalitis lethargica pandemic of the early twentieth century. This partial list, created from the literature, reveals how similar the two epidemics were, in spite of the variation in medical terms of the day [see Table 1].

Table 1

1692 *Salem*	1916–1930s *Encephalitis Epidemic*
fits	convulsions
spectral visions	hallucinations
mental "distraction"	psychoses
pinching, pricking	myoclonus of small muscle bundles on skin surface
"bites"	erythmata on skin surface, capillary hemorrhaging
eyes twisted	oculogyric crises: gaze fixed upward, downward, or to the side
inability to walk	paresis: partial paralysis
neck twisted	torticollis: spasm of neck muscles forces head to one side, spasms affect trunk and neck
repeating nonsense words	palilalia: repetition of one's own words

In both times, most of the afflicted were young women or children; the children were hit hardest, several dying in their cradles from violent fits. The afflictions appeared in late winter and early spring and receded with the heat of summer.... Von Economo noted that most encephalitis lethargica epidemics had historically shown the greatest number of acute cases occurring in the first quarter of the year, from midwinter to the beginning of spring. The "pricking and pinching" repeated so often in the court records at Salem can be explained by the way patients' skin surfaces exhibited twitches—quick, short, fluttering sequences of contractions of muscle bundles. Cold temperatures cause them to increase in number and spread over the body. Twitches were seldom absent in cases of hyperkinetic encephalitis lethargica during the 1920s epidemic. The skin surface also exhibited a peculiar disturbance in which red areas appeared due to dilation and congestion of the capillaries. Red marks that bleed through the skin's surface would explain the many references in court documents to suspected bites made by witches.

Examining the colonists' complaints in the trial papers uncovers many other symptom similarities: inability to walk, terrifying hallucinations, sore throat, or choking—the list goes on and on....

Could Encephalitis Lethargica Return?

... The physical symptoms and in particular the psychotic symptoms that accompany encephalitis lethargica fit the complaints and symptoms reported in late-seventeenth-century New England. There would have been no way for the colonists to know what they were dealing with; it was not until the invention of the electron microscope in the 1940s that scientists were able to truly understand viral agents. There would have been no way to heal those who were affected; encephalitis still has no known prevention or cure.

Von Economo clearly believed that his work would be extremely important in later years; he was optimistic that medical professionals who followed him would add to the body of knowledge about encephalitis lethargica and its effects. In fact, no one bothered to do much about it after 1935. Has encephalitis lethargica been relegated to history, much like the black death but slightly more mysterious and less threatening? Perhaps not. Encephalitis lethargica afflicted five million persons worldwide, many who were left crippled for decades. Any disease that widespread and virulent certainly cannot simply be forgotten.

In 1983 English pediatricians were surprised to discover that many of the children brought to the Cambridge University Hospital suffering psychiatric and neurological symptoms appeared to have encephalitis lethargica. They were lethargic, heard "voices," had expressionless faces, experienced double vision and weight loss, attempted suicide, and exhibited oculogyric crises of the eye muscles. Writing in *The Lancet,* English physicians supported the idea that encephalitis lethargica still exists, and they suggested it be considered in children with chronic emotional and behavioral disturbances coinciding with atypical depression.

Professor John Oxford, currently researching the encephalitis lethargica epidemic of the 1920s, has been examining brain samples taken from victims who perished. The tissue samples had been preserved in wax and stored in the basement of a London hospital, in hopes that technology could at some point determine what caused the epidemic. Oxford's research has been unable to detect influenza RNA in the samples, but he has continued the search, exhuming seven coal miners from their permafrost graves in the arctic. One survivor of the epidemic, Philip Leather, remains in a London hospital, and upon his death his body may provide additional answers. Doctors are diagnosing new cases of encephalitis lethargica which will enable researchers to perform detailed studies using these patients. As elusive as encephalitis lethargica is, determining a cause for the disease may take more time and better technology than is currently available. Oxford explains, "We are searching for a ubiquitous virus, present in a wave, which then vanished."

Cheyette and Cummings, in the *Journal of Neuropsychiatry,* point out that study of the 1920s epidemic and the symptoms of encephalitis lethargica may provide insights into many contemporary neuropsychiatric disturbances that look eerily like the symptoms of encephalitis lethargica. They draw comparisons between encephalitis lethargica and contemporary problems such as sleep disorders, tardive dyskinesia, Tourette's syndrome, obsessive-compulsive disorder, depressive disorders, severe conduct disorders in children, and paraphilias (deviant sexual behaviors including pedophilia, transvestism, and rape).

In 1930 von Economo predicted that future epidemics might be unrecognizable, perhaps with mild symptoms that would be ignored. He enjoined psychologists to examine the case descriptions of encephalitis lethargica in order to avoid speculation about psychological manifestations "built on sand." He urged "purely speculative psychologists" to consider the findings regarding encephalitis lethargica from a factual, organic basis. "Every psychiatrist who wishes to probe into the phenomenon of disturbed motility and changes of character, the psychological mechanism of mental inaccessibility, of the neuroses, and etc. must be thoroughly acquainted with the experience gathered from encephalitis lethargica," he wrote. "Encephalitis lethargica can scarcely again be forgotten."

POSTSCRIPT

Were Socioeconomic Tensions Responsible for the Witchcraft Hysteria in Salem?

Although witchcraft and devil worship apparently enjoy a minor vogue today, the last 250 years have witnessed a decline in mystical beliefs. A few witches were tried in the British North American colonies after Salem: in Virginia (1706), North Carolina (1712), and Rhode Island (1728). The last execution for witchcraft in England occurred in 1712 and in Scotland in 1727; on the Continent, royal edicts put an end to such persecutions before the close of the seventeenth century. Documentary evidence of seventeenth-century witchcraft can be examined in Boyer and Nissenbaum's *Witchcraft in Salem Village* (Wadsworth, 1972) and George L. Burr, ed., *Narratives of the Witchcraft Cases, 1648–1706* (Charles Scribner's Sons, 1914). For comparative studies, see George L. Kittridge, *Witchcraft in Old and New England* (Harvard University Press, 1929) and A. D. J. Macfarlane, *Witchcraft in Tudor and Stuart England: A Regional and Comparative Study* (Harper & Row, 1970).

The Salem witch trials represent one of the most thoroughly studied episodes in American history. Several scholars have concluded that the enthusiasm for learning more about the Salem witches and their accusers far outweighs the importance of the event; yet essays and books continue to roll off the presses. The selections by Boyer and Nissenbaum and by Carlson summarize but two of the many interpretations of the incidents at Salem. In her book *The Devil in the Shape of a Woman: Witchcraft in Colonial New England* (Random House, 1987), Carol F. Karlsen offers a gendered explanation of colonial America's witchcraft accusations, insisting that negative views of women as the embodiment of evil were deeply imbedded in the Puritan (and European) worldview. However, through most of the seventeenth century, New Englanders avoided explicit connections between women and witchcraft. Nevertheless, the attitudes that depicted witches as women remained self-evident truths and sprang to the surface in 1692. For more on the relationship between women and witchcraft, see John Putnam Demos, *Entertaining Satan: Witchcraft and the Culture of Early New England* (Oxford University Press, 1982).

Also of value is Demos's earlier essay "Underlying Themes in the Witchcraft of Seventeenth-Century New England," *American Historical Review* (June 1970). More recent studies include Enders A. Robinson, *The Devil Discovered: Salem Witchcraft, 1692* (Hippocrene Books, 1991); Larry Gragg, *The Salem Witch Crisis* (Praeger, 1992); and Bernard Rosenthal, *Salem Story: Reading the Witch Trials of 1692* (Cambridge University Press, 1993).

ISSUE 4

Did Capitalist Values Motivate the American Colonists?

YES: James T. Lemon, from *The Best Poor Man's Country: A Geographical Study of Early Southeastern Pennsylvania* (Johns Hopkins University Press, 1972)

NO: James A. Henretta, from "Families and Farms: *Mentalité* in Pre-Industrial America," *William and Mary Quarterly* (January 1978)

ISSUE SUMMARY

YES: Professor of geography James T. Lemon argues that the liberal, middle-class, white settlers of southeastern Pennsylvania placed individual freedom and material gain at a higher priority than that of the public interest.

NO: Professor of American history James A. Henretta contends that the colonial family determined the character of agrarian life because it was the primary economic and social unit.

Studies completed during the past 80 years that examine the colonies and the earliest local communities can be classified according to three major schools of thought: (1) progressive historians who emphasize the *conflicts* between aristocrats and lower-middle elements; (2) neoconservatives who view the colonists as primarily *middle-class* democrats; and (3) new social historians who stress *family history* through the use of semidemographic models based on the behavioristic theories of other social scientists.

Whether they acknowledge it or not, most historians are influenced by the political and intellectual currents of the times in which they live. During the first half of the twentieth century, American society underwent profound changes as the nation was transformed from a rural and agricultural society into an urban and industrial one. It was also a time when many progressive American reformers focused on rooting out the corruption they perceived in the country's economic and political institutions and worked to bring about change. Professional historians who were active during the Progressive Era read the social and economic conflicts of their own time back into the nation's past.

Rejecting the patriotic views of earlier writers, these progressive historians saw the past in terms of continual conflicts between the forces of liberalism and conservatism, aristocracy and democracy, and the rich and the poor.

There was little doubt as to which side the progressive historians favored. In his study *The Founding of New England* (1921), James Truslow Adams blasted the Puritan establishment for being undemocratic because its religious leaders denied its followers the basic rights of free speech and religious tolerance. Puritans like Roger Williams and Anne Hutchinson, who dissented from the repressive views of the Puritan oligarchy, were, by necessity, banished from Massachusetts Bay Colony.

After World War II, a new generation of historians began to tear down the progressive view of history. There were two reasons for this change. First, the times were better. America had emerged from the depression and the war eras as the strongest nation in the world. Conflicts between the rich and the poor appeared settled; the majority of Americans were middle-class homeowners who shared a common heritage; and a capitalist economy and a democratic government were values that all Americans seemingly shared. A cold war had also been declared. The American system needed to be defended against Russia, an old-fashioned, imperialistic nation that now wanted to spread socialism instead of capitalism and to replace democracy with communism.

A second and more important reason for the breakdown of the progressive synthesis was that it often oversimplified the conflict of America's past and could not withstand the rigors of contemporary scholarship. Robert and Katherine Brown became two of the leading consensus, neoconservative, scholars of the 1950s. In a series of separate studies on Massachusetts and in a joint effort, *Virginia 1705–1786: Democracy or Aristocracy?* (Michigan State University Press, 1964), the Browns concluded that "what now passes in this country as middle-class, representative democracy was well-entrenched in the Old Dominion long before the American Revolution."

A third group of scholars has attempted to rid itself of the ideological biases of its predecessors. Relying upon the attempts of the behavioral sciences to fashion new methodological approaches to the study of the human race, a number of recent scholars have undertaken the study of family history. These new social historians approach history from the bottom up instead of the top down. They attempt to reconstruct the histories of the average colonial family by exploring such quantitative materials as land titles, house deeds, marriage and divorce records, wills, inventories, church listings, voter registrations, and, of course, local and national census data. A number of such studies in 1970 centered upon New England.

In the following selections, James T. Lemon supports the middle-class consensus view of history. According to Lemon, the citizens of southeastern Pennsylvania were of "liberal middle-class orientation" who sought the freedom to pursue "better opportunities for themselves and their families." James A. Henretta denies the importance of the entrepreneurial spirit and argues that the need to maintain a viable family structure determined the character of agrarian life in colonial America.

James T. Lemon

The Best Poor Man's Country

Early Pennsylvania was, in many respects, the prototype of North American development. Its style of life presaged the mainstream of nineteenth-century America; its conservative defense of liberal individualism, its population of mixed national and religious origins, its dispersed farms, county seats, and farm-service villages, and its mixed crop and livestock agriculture served as models for much of the rural Middle West.

To many western Europeans of the late seventeenth and eighteenth centuries Pennsylvania was a veritable paradise and refuge from oppression. Indeed, many commentators referred to it as "the best poor man's country in the world." Without doubt the area was one of the most affluent agricultural societies anywhere. For these reasons as well as for its contribution to the American style of life that followed, early Pennsylvania deserves a great deal more scrutiny than it has hitherto received.

This study in historical geography considers a number of issues bearing on the interplay of society and land in early Pennsylvania and centering on the Pennsylvanians' attachment to the land....

One central conceptual matter needs to be mentioned: the interpretation. In this study a wide range of variables is used to explain the material. Traditionally, students of rural America have tended to present either the cultural background of settlers, or the natural environment, or the frontier as the key to understanding what people did. In Pennsylvania's case the emphasis has been on national or ethnic traditions.

In particular, the "Pennsylvania Dutch" (Germans) have been lauded since Benjamin Franklin's time as better farmers than those from the British Isles. Poor Richard admired the "habitual industry and frugality" of the Germans. Dr. Benjamin Rush, another influential Philadelphian, asserted that German farms could be distinguished "by the fertility of their Fields; the luxuriance of their meadows, and a general appearance of plenty and neatness in everything that belongs to them." Later commentators elaborated the theme until it became a commonplace in the literature. A parallel assertion has been that Ulstermen (usually called Scotch-Irish), though poor farmers, were the "toughest, most adventurous pioneers" on the frontier.

Such a stance accentuates the habitual behavior and the persistence of presumed customs and virtues of these groups. Proponents of national cultural traditions have, therefore, underplayed other cultural, environmental, and social factors. They have not recognized that western Europeans generally shared, for example, a diet emphasizing pork, beef, and small grains. They have not recognized the importance of the new environment.

As is well known, others have used the frontier, or climate, or topography to explain the course of American development. I suspect that some historians think that geographers should talk about the role of, say, mountains in determining the course of settlement, as did Ellen Churchill Semple in her *American History and Its Geographic Conditions,* published in 1903. That is not the perspective taken in this study because it does not give enough due to the people. If cultural determinists made people into pre-programmed automatons who followed custom, then environmentalists imagine people like Pavlovian dogs able only to react to external stimuli.

This study does not deny the power of tradition and environment; but it considers more centrally the decisions of the people and their more immediate social situation. The many decisions that shaped life on the land in early Pennsylvania were the result of how people perceived their situation. Inputs did come from the environment and cultural traditions, but they were interpreted in the light of what people expected to do and what they were able to do. In other words, their ideology (or less strongly, their goals) and their practices determined their actions. So we have to consider the political and economic structures they operated in, the constraints of population growth, developments in western Europe and the Atlantic world, and the status and beliefs of the people who came to the region.

A basic stress in these essays is on the "liberal" middle-class orientation of many of the settlers who elected to leave their European communities. "Liberal" I use in the classic sense, meaning placing individual freedom and material gain over that of public interest. Put another way, the people planned for themselves much more than they did for their communities. Communities, like governments, were necessary evils to support individual fulfillment. This is not to say that the settlers were "economic men," single-minded maximizing materialists. Few could be, or even wanted to be. Nevertheless, they defended their liberal propensities in a tenacious manner. The conservative supporters of individualism were not only the more affluent citizens but also those who moved elsewhere to seek better opportunities for themselves and their families. Undoubtedly their view was fostered by a sense that the environment was "open." As individualists, they were ready in spirit to conquer the limitless continent, to subdue the land. As we now struggle in a "closed" system to find community and to learn to live with a finite nature, we must look at our ancestors to learn how they operated in their environment. We can see the early signs of liberal North America in Pennsylvania as much as anywhere. The interpretation presented here leads us closer, I believe, to understanding of what the people were doing than either the cultural or the environmental or the economic deterministic perspectives can alone....

Society and Environment of Early Pennsylvania

Frederick Brown was a typical (if hypothetical) early Pennsylvanian. Brown came from the Rhineland in 1725 as a boy of ten. With his parents and siblings he settled in Lancaster County near people from Germany and the British Isles. Brown's family was Lutheran; they shared the township with a wide variety of Protestant groups—Quakers, Mennonites, Scotch-Irish Presbyterians, and others. Brown's father established a reasonably successful farm that produced most of the materials needed for a comfortable if not affluent life. When his father retired in 1750 Frederick was married. He took over part of the family farm, carrying on much as his father had, but with increasing economic dependence on the Atlantic world through Lancaster and Philadelphia. As his own sons matured all but one left home, one to a nearby township, the other to the west. Eventually Brown, too, retired from farming in 1780 and became dependent on the support of his eldest son. In 1790 he was buried in the cemetery by the church.

Frederick Brown's life was quite ordinary—ordinary in the sense that he did the sorts of things that many rural Americans did in the eighteenth and nineteenth centuries. But the commonplace qualities of his life and the lives of his fellow Pennsylvanians should not keep us from trying to understand their structure and rhythm, for they stood as a model for later Americans.

The activities of Brown and others grew out of a range of factors including western European cultural traditions, the social characteristics of Pennsylvania life, and the natural qualities of the area. Pennsylvania was a part of western European society, and many of its traditions—the patriarchal family and Christian doctrines, for example—were carried across the Atlantic. Yet the migrants did not represent a cross section of western European life. They were neither the richest nor the poorest Europeans, most were skilled, and perhaps most importantly, most were the kind of people who sought individual satisfaction. To some extent they were entrepreneurs, though not maximizing materialists. Their descendants shared this concern and some imprinted Pennsylvania with a "liberal" image. Pennsylvanians nevertheless were marked by different origins and belonged to different religious groups that helped shape their style of life. The rate of population growth exerted an influence. In their government, they erected structures based on English precedents. They participated in an economic system marked by a strong subsistence component but also by Atlantic trading patterns. Their preindustrial technology used animal and human rather than inanimate sources of energy. These structures affected them all. Moreover, the people had to deal with the Indians and a distinctive set of resources—the climate, the terrain, soil, and forests—that encouraged new methods of land utilization.

These characteristics of tradition, society, and environment combined to create the distinctive Pennsylvanian modes of life. They will be utilized in varying degrees to explain the processes on the land's surface....

In stressing the middle class origins of immigrants and character of Pennsylvania society, the degree of social stratification that developed in the region should not be understated. The inhabitants were conscious of the categories "better," "middling," and "poorer sorts." The distribution of wealth, the number of landless people toward the end of the century, and direct references to poverty tend to support this ranking. By 1800 a fairly wide spread in wealth had arisen between the most affluent and those at the bottom in Chester County. At that time the wealthiest 10 per cent paid 38 per cent of the taxes and the poorest 30 per cent paid only 4 per cent. This was a sharper difference than existed in the 1690s, when the upper 10 per cent held less than 24 per cent of the wealth. Considering that the richer were probably undertaxed, the stratification was probably more marked than the tax lists suggest. In one of the few extant quantitative references to stratification, the assessor of relatively backward and predominantly German Brecknock Township in Lancaster County in 1750 recorded 27 per cent of the people "poor," compared with 40 per cent "middling" and 33 per cent "able," in their capacity to pay taxes. But this is not altogether helpful. The various categories of wealth suggest that probably only three or four persons would be classed as "better sort"; most of 73 per cent called "middling" and "able" were probably "middling." It seems unlikely that most of the "poor" were destitute, but their circumstances are harder to determine. In 1782 nonlandowners in Chester and Lancaster counties totaled about 30 per cent of the population. This category included tenant farmers and "inmates," a designation that might refer to indentured and apprenticed persons, many of whom were born in Pennsylvania and some of whom were married. The most that can be said with certainty, however, is that inmates lived in someone else's house and were craftsmen and laborers rather than farmers. Whatever the facts, the number of landless persons in Lancaster and Chester counties seems to have been high if we presume, as did some in the eighteenth century and later, that land was freely available and that America was a nation of freeholders.

In Pennsylvania, according to reports, poverty was not uncommon, at least in times of recession. In 1747 an observer in Philadelphia noted: "It is remarkable what an increase of the number of Beggars there is about this town this winter, many more than I have before observed." Soon after this, when conditions were quite good, an item in the Lancaster County Commissioners' Book stated that the poor were suffering because the appropriation for squirrel bounties had been curtailed. In the early 1760s redemptioners were little in demand, and money was given to paupers. Agents of the Hamilton family, which owned the town of Lancaster, reported that quit-rents could never be collected from the poor of the town, who were idle "for want of employment," except during harvest time. Mortgages were foreclosed on poorer farmers during difficult times. Toward the end of the century, an Englishman who had expected to see few beggars reported a "great" many in Pennsylvania, and about that time poor houses were established, suggesting either that an endemic situation had finally been recognized or that conditions had recently become worse.

Despite these references to poverty and the acceptance of a tripartite division of society by early Pennsylvanians, we can still affirm that Pennsylvanians were predominantly middle class. Except during times of depression, wages were probably higher throughout the century than in Europe. Even at the end of the century, few tax lists record destitute persons. "Poor tax" records have few entries. If the "holy experiment" did not bring bounty for all, it allowed many to improve their material lot—and if not even if there were many needy, as there were in Pennsylvania in recent years when about 25 per cent of the population could be classed as poor, Pennsylvanians believed that hard work would bring success. In the last analysis, the middle class faith in the right to seek success was the hallmark of the Pennsylvania society and distinguished it somewhat from western Europe, where the landed aristocracy still remained powerful and the many peasants had extremely limited aspirations. Yet it was from western Europe that this liberal philosophy had been carried to fulfillment in America, perhaps most clearly in Pennsylvania.

If the settlers and their descendants were similar in social and economic status, they were varied in language, national origin, and religion. These have contributed to the impression of the society as a pluralistic "mosaic." Many commentators on life in early Pennsylvania have stressed language and national origin, but, these were less relevant to people's action on the land than was previously thought. Religious distinctions, however, were of considerable importance.

On the basis of surname analysis (admittedly an uncertain technique) and other data, the proportions of persons in national groups in 1790 can be estimated. The major groups were Germans and German-speaking Swiss, Englishmen, and Ulstermen, the last called "Irish" by contemporaries and "Scotch-Irish" since the nineteenth century. Even though the distinctiveness of the Scotch-Irish as a cultural group can be questioned, as can that of any English-speaking Celts, in this study I have tried to separate them from the English largely for the sake of argument. . . .

In 1790 persons of German and Swiss background constituted a larger proportion of the population in southeastern Pennsylvania (40 per cent) than in the state as a whole (33 per cent). The English were more numerous in the state than in the region (35 per cent as compared with less than 30), as were the Scotch-Irish and Scots (23 per cent compared with 18 per cent). These proportions can be attributed to continued immigration from the British Isles after 1755, particularly in the early 1770s, and to a dearth of German-speaking migrants after 1755. Estimates of numbers in national groups earlier than 1790 are speculative. Before 1725 the "English" predominated and the Welsh and Swedes were considerably more numerous than they were later. In 1750 the proportion of Germans was probably higher than in 1790.

Language is valid only to distinguish German-speaking from English-speaking persons. Yet many Germans Anglicized themselves. . . . Some Germans, including Mennonites, anxious to have their children learn English, set up schools with English teachers. Although a differentiating characteristic, language was less significant as an influence on social and especially economic processes than has often been stated.

Differences in customs and practices associated with national groups have also been misstated or exaggerated far out of proportion to their significance. . . . The economic status of various national groups did not diverge greatly. A sample of estate inventories, excluding land values, in Lancaster and Chester counties between 1713 and 1790, though an imprecise measure, suggests that differences were not great. The average assessment within a number of townships with substantial numbers in each national group, probably a better yard-stick than inventories shows that in half of eighteen townships the "English" had the edge, but distinctions were not sharp. In 1782 the most affluent were divided among national groups in Lancaster County; only the few Welsh were proportionately more wealthy. In lower income levels differences were not great. Economic status, then, appears to have been much the same among national groups. . . .

Most Pennsylvanians were Protestants, or at least non-Catholic. But denominational affiliations divided the people into groups, and this pluralism was a distinctive mark of the society. Although use of the word "denomination" implies tolerance and an easing of sharp theological conflicts, and although it is clear that groups experienced varying degrees of doctrinal and social metamorphosis throughout the period, some differences remained clear enough to have a significant effect. The critical distinction was between "sects" and "churches." Sectarian "plain folk," notably Friends and Mennonites, were much more prominent than in Europe. Because their values and organizations favored cooperation and discipline, these groups acted on the land in a somewhat different fashion than did Lutheran, Reformed, Anglican, and Presbyterian members. A substantial number of persons were not related to any denomination.

The Friends (mostly from the west of England, the London area, and Wales) and Mennonites (mostly from the lower and middle Rhine Valley and Switzerland) were the most important "sects." During the first forty years of the province these groups, especially the Quakers, were in the majority. In 1790, when Quakers and Mennonites were easily outnumbered by others, they remained substantial minorities in some counties, including Chester, Lancaster, Bucks, and Montgomery. Although the term "sect" is not fully adequate for describing these "plain folk" or others such as the Dunkers, Schwenkfelders, and Moravians, who lived communally for a generation, certain social values set them apart from "church" groups. The Quakers at first stressed the goal of perfecting rather than ignoring the world and encouraged other groups to share in the wealth of the land. But rural Friends and the Mennonites were markedly selective in membership, and as the century passed they relied more on "birthright" than voluntary confession to define membership. This exclusiveness was fostered by a strong sense of self-righteousness, and among the Quakers the notion of perfectibility shifted from the "holy experiment" and society at large to the group. This desire for perfection encouraged a drive for material well-being, possibly to prove their salvation to the world. Paradoxically, then, worldly success for individual members of the group became a goal for those who officially eschewed worldliness. To this end strong local leaders, especially in rural areas, exhorted members to purity of doctrine, society, domestic responsibility, hard work, and mutual help. Thus for the sake of gain, both material and social, Mennonites and Quakers formed societies of discipline, emulation, and mutual aid.

Because of these characteristics, reinforced by their early arrival and their somewhat greater initial affluence, Quakers and Mennonites possessed throughout the period a higher average economic status than members of other denominational groups. In 1782 in Lancaster County, among the sixty Germans paying taxes of £40 or more, thirty-five were Mennonites, a proportion of 58 per cent compared with a Mennonite share of 37 per cent of the German population. In Chester County Quakers headed many tax lists. The tax data are corroborated by contemporary comments. For example, the Anglican clergyman William Smith considered the Mennonites "the most considerable and wealthy sect among the Germans," and another observer asserted, "almost all the Quakers are wealthy people, who never let anyone belonging to their sect be reduced to poverty." Although some poor Quakers and Mennonites lived in the area and members of other groups acquired wealth, the sectarians were generally the most affluent people in rural Pennsylvania.

In spite of the sectarian views held by Quakers and Mennonites, William Penn welcomed other Protestants to Pennsylvania, and Roman Catholics were admitted. This permissive attitude eventually undercut the goal of a clearly structured society based on Quaker principles; but far from making Pennsylvania a failure, as Penn finally felt it might have, this policy resulted in the immigration of many persons who contributed to the growth of the region.

The prominent "church" groups were Presbyterian, Lutheran, Reformed, and Anglican, and to a lesser degree Baptist, Roman Catholic, and eventually Methodist. Their members submitted to looser disciplines and were less inclined to mutual help than the sectarians, partly because they relied on an uncertain supply of ministers from Europe or at least from other communities. In rural areas their average economic status was lower despite the affluence of some....

Because these "church" people, especially the larger Presbyterian, Lutheran, and Reformed memberships, mainly arrived between 1725 and 1755, their influence on the initial patterns of action on the land was less marked than that of Quakers and Mennonites. Without doubt the "church" groups markedly influenced life during the third and subsequent generations. As first arrivals, Quakers and Mennonites were free to choose sites near Philadelphia or on the best soils. Even though substantial numbers of Quakers lived in towns the many rural Quakers and the Mennonites were more tightly clustered geographically and were less mobile than "church" people. The greater wealth of Quakers and Mennonites and other data suggest that on the whole they were better farmers than others. Unlike the communitarian Moravians, however, Quakers and Mennonites lived on family farms rather than in agricultural villages, and most "church" people followed this practice.

Pennsylvanians thus were divided in varying degrees by nationality and language and denomination as well as somewhat by economic status. The divisions varied in importance. Antagonisms among groups and also within groups led to such times of trouble as the debates over the Great Awakening, the controversy over defense against the French and Indians, and the Revolution....

Not only the people's characteristics but their numbers were important in directing their actions on the land. Given limitations in the economic system and backward technologies in agriculture and transportation, the density of population and the rate of growth exerted considerable influence on availability of land and thus on farming opportunities in the areas of initial and later settlement. The population of the region expanded from about 9,000 in

1690 to more than 300,000 a century later. The rate of growth was most rapid before 1700 and was quite marked between 1730 and 1760, a time of substantial immigration. Considerably slower increases occurred in the last third of the century, when fewer immigrants arrived, the birth rate probably was lower, and the region had virtually been occupied, so that many people moved beyond rather than within southeastern Pennsylvania. . . .

Pennsylvanians were involved in two economic systems, the subsistence economic and the Atlantic trading empire centered in London. Few persons were completely self-reliant; few depended entirely on others. Many townsmen kept gardens, orchards, and a cow or two, and remote frontiersmen and laborers bought and sold goods and services in the market. The eighteenth century witnessed an elaboration of the commercial network within the area and with other provinces, Great Britain, and foreign areas, so that Pennsylvania economically was well developed for the time and compared with most areas in Europe. By the third generation, after 1740, farmers of "middling" status sold between a third and a half or more of their production, at least during peacetime. The pattern was preindustrial, however, and farmers did not specialize to the degree they would after 1820 or 1830 when manufacturing and urbanization increased demands for farm products.

The credit and marketing system in the Atlantic world involved many links that gave rise to urban places and a degree of commercial agricultural production. Rural Pennsylvanians were connected by a chain of credit through Philadelphia and Baltimore and through merchants, millers, and shopkeepers in smaller places with London merchants. Although the Atlantic world's economic center was in London, and Pennsylvania exported mostly unprocessed or little-processed agricultural and forest products, Pennsylvania was not locked into a bilateral and dependent pattern to the degree the "staple"-producing southern colonies were. Autonomous connections with other mainland colonies, the West Indies, and southern Europe provided income that helped to compensate for the persistent adverse balance of trade with England. Success in trading encouraged even longer extensions of credit by London merchants confident of Pennsylvania's future growth. Rural Pennsylvanians, especially those west of the Susquehanna River, had the option of dealing with Maryland as well as Philadelphia. In both cases farmers received goods from back-country shopkeepers and merchants, delivered or had delivered their products to Philadelphia or other points, and requested the buyers to credit their dealers' accounts with importers. Even though cash was scarce and banks did not appear until 1783, business was not a barter level. All commodities carried monetary value, and merchants and other wealthy persons acted as bankers. These structures contributed to the development of urban places as the centers of regional activity. Philadelphia, Baltimore, and county seats especially became important.

Pennsylvania's customers were responsible for the kinds of commodities that entered its export trade. The West Indies, New England, southern Europe, Ireland, and ship provisioners demanded flour, bread, and wheat, and to a lesser extent corn, lumber, flaxseed, and many other goods. Because the West Indies opened as a market at about the time Pennsylvania was founded, the Quaker colony was spared the limitations placed on southern colonies by the demands of England for tobacco, rice, and indigo. From the outset it was able to trade outside this bilateral system. Although Pennsylvania supplied England with iron after 1750 and wheat after 1765, encouragement of hemp and silk production as "staples" failed partly because of Pennsylvania's success with other commodities. External markets had a significant bearing on shaping the agricultural system and regional patterns of land use.

Despite the complex commercial connections, internal and external markets were limited by later standards, communication and transport facilities were inadequate, processing operations were unsophisticated, and agricultural tools were primitive. These deficiencies contributed to a continuation of the subsistence aspect of the economy, to a limited specialization of agriculture, and to the existence of the family farm as the chief unit of production.

Information on market conditions outside Pennsylvania was vital for profitable decisions. But four weeks was the minimum travel time from London, so that when prices changed rapidly in Europe and elsewhere Pennsylvanians often could not react as quickly as they might have wished. Within the colonies, even in the late eighteenth century, the overland stage trip between Philadelphia and New York took a minimum of one day. Horse-drawn wagons, the chief means of transporting goods, were slow and costly. Thirty miles was the maximum distance a loaded wagon could cover in a day under favorable weather conditions. Ferriage was also expensive, especially across the Susquehanna. Water transport complemented wagon transportation only to a small extent in Pennsylvania. By 1770 some Pennsylvanians were displeased with their transportation facilities. Yet it appears that more were satisfied with the rate of return from the economy, and therefore not until the early 1790s did the legislature finance the construction of the Lancaster Turnpike. Canals were built even later than this.

The preindustrial character of the economy was nowhere more apparent than in the manufacturing sector. It lacked the diversification, corporate enterprise, and concentration. Many more craftsmen lived in rural areas than scholars have recognized, and Pennsylvania at the time did not trail many parts of Europe in implementing new processing methods. Still, many goods were fabricated by farmers, and most industrial organizations were small and owned by proprietors. Only ironmaking and, toward the end of the century, flour milling and cotton milling foreshadowed nineteenth century corporate structures. Craftsmen and farmers who integrated many operations were the chief manufacturers. The British policy of restriction laws and government subsidies in the wrong areas, such as hemp and silk production, contributed to this state of affairs. But more fundamental factors were the attractions of land investment and of agriculture and other primary production. Investors in England and Pennsylvania were attracted by the certain or higher rates of return in these sectors. The slow development of textile manufacturing in the eighteenth century and well into the nineteenth resulted basically from the diversion of energies and capital to primary production, notably farming, and speculation in land.

Finally, the tools of agriculture limited productivity and encouraged reliance upon the family farm as the basic unit of production. Relatively few innovations—such as the Dutch fan for blowing away chaff—appeared in harvesting and threshing equipment despite recurrent labor shortages and higher labor costs than in Europe. Reformers tried to inform farmers of English methods of improving yields, but aside from perhaps the more affluent sectarians concerned with status, new ideas were not welcomed. Not until the nineteenth century did the agricultural technological revolution occur that has led to the highly capitalized corporate farming of today in many areas. In the eighteenth century, technical limitations both on and off the farm restrained commercialization and caused a large share of production to be consumed at home. Combined with the desire of most settlers to be captains of their own destiny and with the kinds of markets farmers sold to outside the region, these technical constraints encouraged the family farm to thrive as the cornerstone of this agrarian economy....

By the last decade of the eighteenth century the European occupation had dramatically transformed the southeastern Pennsylvania landscape. In 1680 the area was lightly populated by Indians and a few Europeans along the Delaware. In 1800 there were more than 300,000 persons of European descent here, and many others had moved on to other areas. In this 120 years the people organized the space into farms, arrayed their social and political institutions and physical facilities over the area, built towns that became the centers of regional and local activity, and exploited, the land's resources for forestry, mining, and especially agriculture.

Yet in spite of the marked alteration of the surface of the land the Pennsylvanians' mode of living had changed very little. Though their average standard of living had risen, the prosperity, paradoxically, had been achieved through traditional ways. There were few technological advances. Pennsylvanians were perhaps the most liberal people in the world—they believed implicitly, some even explicitly, in individual material success. Yet because many were successful, liberalism (in the traditional sense) became enshrined as a style of life. Many of those who were not so fortunate or were dissatisfied repeated the original movement across the Atlantic by moving to the frontier. They, too, shared the hope of achieving success. Vast resources lay out beyond the settled area, and few persons felt actually limited. (The least stable and successful were sustained by another variation: individual immortality on another frontier.) The openness contributed to making these people conservative, not in the sense of espousing community but in preserving their freedom and privacy. What structures there were, and they were minimal by today's standards, existed for the individual and his family. This can be said even for the more disciplined Quakers and Mennonites. And so the paradox deepens. Their authoritarianism and ideology of hard work existed to prove not only that their groups were viable but that they as individuals were justified in seeking perfection. In this resource-rich environment, what better way could they achieve this than through exploitation of the land?

James A. Henretta

 **NO**

Families and Farms: *Mentalité* in Pre-Industrial America

T he history of the agricultural population of pre-industrial America remains to be written. As a result of quantitative investigations of wealth distribution and social mobility; of rates of birth, marriage, and death; and of patterns of inheritance, officeholding, and church membership, there is an ever-growing mass of data that delineates the *structures* of social existence in the small rural communities that constituted the core of American agricultural society in the North before 1830. But what of the *consciousness* of the inhabitants, the mental or emotional or ideological aspects of their lives? And what of the relationship between the two? Can a careful statistical analysis of people's lives —a precise description of their patterns of social actions—substantiate at least limited statements as to their motivations, values, and goals?

A number of historians have attempted to establish a connection between the subsistence activities of the agricultural population and its institutional, ideological, and cultural existence. Consider, for example, the entrepreneurial interpretation implicit in James T. Lemon's highly regarded quantitative analysis of the eighteenth-century agricultural society of Southeastern Pennsylvania:

> A basic stress in these essays is on the "liberal" middle-class orientation of many of the settlers.... "Liberal" I use in the classic sense, meaning placing individual freedom and material gain over that of public interest. Put another way, the people planned for themselves much more than they did for their communities.... This is not to say that the settlers were "economic men," single-minded maximizing materialists. Few could be, or even wanted to be. Nevertheless, they defended their liberal propensities in a tenacious manner.... Undoubtedly their view was fostered by a sense that the environment was "open." As individualists, they were ready in spirit to conquer the limitless continent, to subdue the land.

However overburdened with reservations and qualifications, the general thrust of this depiction of values and aspirations is clear enough. Lemon's settlers were individualists, enterprising men and women intent upon the pursuit of material advantage at the expense of communal and non-economic goals.

Can the "consciousness" with which Lemon has endowed these early Pennsylvanians be verified by historical evidence? The question is important, for many of the statistical data presented by Lemon do not support this description of the inhabitants' "orientation," "spirit," or "propensities." Take the pattern of residence. It is true that the predominance of isolated farmsteads—rather than nucleated villages—suggests that these men and women were planning "for themselves much more than... for their communities." But what of the presence of clusters of ethnic and religious groups? Such voluntary concentrations of like-minded settlers indicate the importance of *communal* values, of people who preferred to share a religious or ethnic identity. Here the author's evidence contradicts his conclusion. "Most of the people who came during this period," Lemon writes of the years between 1700 and 1730, "settled together in areas and communities defined by nationality or denomination.... Language and creed thus exerted considerable influence on the whereabouts of people. Yet groups were mixed in several areas, for example on the Lancaster Plain."

This exception only confirms the rule. Nearly every historian who has studied ethnic settlement patterns in the colonial period has stressed the existence of communal concentrations. In the Middle Colonies, for example, patterns of spatial segregation appeared among the Dutch in Newark, New Jersey, and to some extent among Quakers and Seventh Day Baptists in the same area. Most of the German immigrants who arrived in Lancaster, Pennsylvania, in 1744 settled on the lots laid out by Dr. Adam Simon Kuhn, the leading German resident, rather than on land offered by the English proprietor, Alexander Hamilton. These linguistic and religious ties extended beyond settlement patterns to encompass economic relationships. Every one of the one hundred names inscribed in the account book of Henry King—shoemaker, butcher, and currier of Second River, in New Jersey in 1775—was of Dutch origin; and the main business connections of the merchants of Lancaster, whether they were Jewish or Quaker or German, were with their coreligionists in Philadelphia.

Is an individualist spirit fully compatible with these communal settlement patterns and this religiously determined economic activity? It is possible, of course, that these ethnic or linguistic preferences facilitated the pursuit of individual economic gain, and that the patronage of the shop of a fellow church member brought preferred treatment and lower prices. But the weight of the evidence indicates that these decisions were not made for narrowly economic or strictly utilitarian reasons: the felt need to maintain a linguistic or religious identity was an important a consideration as the fertility of the soil or the price of the land in determining where a family would settle. The "calculus of advantage" for these men and women was not mere pecuniary gain, but encompassed a much wider range of social and cultural goals.

These ethnic, linguistic, or religious ties did not reflect a coherent ideological system, a planned *communitarian* culture similar to the highly organized Moravian settlement at Bethlehem, Pennsylvania. These bonds among families, neighbors, and fellow church members were informal; nonetheless, they circumscribed the range of individual action among the inhabitants of Pennsylvania and laid the foundations for a rich and diverse cultural existence. These community-oriented patterns of social interaction emerge clearly from

Lemon's quantitative data, yet they do not figure prominently in his conclusion. He has not explained the complexity of the settlers' existence but has forced their lives into the mold of a timeless, placeless concept of "liberal individualism."

A similar discrepancy between data and interpretation appears in Lemon's analysis of the economic goals and achievements of the inhabitants of eighteenth-century Pennsylvania. What becomes of the open environment and the conquering spirit when "tenant farming was much more frequent than we might expect. . . . In 1760 and 1782 about 30 per cent of Lancaster's and Chester's married taxpayers were landless" and an additional 15 percent of the total number of taxpayers in Chester County were single freemen—mostly young men without landed property. With nearly 45 percent of the members of the adult white male population without land of their own, the gap between evidence and conclusion is so obvious that it must be confronted; and what better way than by evoking the spirit of Frederick Jackson Turner? "As long as the frontier was open . . . ," Lemon writes, "many people were able to move, and as a result frustrations were dampened and the liberal values of the original inhabitants of the colony were upheld."

This is an appealing interpretation, especially since it admits the necessary connection between the structure of opportunity offered by a given environment and the consciousness of the inhabitants, but it is not completely satisfactory. It assumes that the migrants came with "liberal" values, with an expectation that most adult males would own a freehold estate and that anything less than this would generate anger and frustration. Neither the basic proposition nor its corollary is acceptable, for both fail to convey the settlers' conception of social reality, their understanding of the structural components of age and wealth.

To be "young" in this agricultural society (as in most) was either to be landless or without sufficient land to support a family. As Philip J. Greven, Daniel Scott Smith, and Robert A. Gross have shown, male parents normally retained legal control of a sizable portion of the family estate until death, in order to ensure their financial well-being in old age, and the economic security of their widows was carefully protected by dower rights. Nor were these cultural restraints on the transmission of improved property the only, or even, the main, obstacle to the economic prospects of the next generation. For the high rate of natural increase constantly threatened to overwhelm the accumulated capital resources of many of these northern farm families. There was never sufficient cleared and improved property, or livestock, or farm equipment, or adequate housing to permit most young men and women to own a farm. In five small agricultural towns in New Jersey in the 1770s, for example, one half of all white males aged eighteen to twenty-five were without land, while another 29 percent of this age group owned fifty acres or less. And in Concord, Massachusetts, the percentage of landless males (many of whom were young) remained at 30 percent from 1750 to 1800. This correlation between age and wealth persisted throughout the life-cycle; all of the males in the lowest quintile of the taxable population in East Guilford, Connecticut, in 1740 were below the age of forty, while every person in the highest quintile was that age or above.

The accumulation of financial resources by aging men brought them higher status and political power. In Concord, between 1745 and 1774, the median age of selectmen at the time of their first election to office was forty-five, a pattern that obtained in Dedham and Watertown as well. Indeed, the correlation among age, wealth, status, and power in these agricultural communities indicates the profound importance of age as a basic principle of social differentiation. And so it appeared to the Reverend William Bentley of Salem on a visit to Andover in 1793; the country people, he noted, assembled to dance "in classes due to their ages, not with any regard to their condition, as in the Seaport Towns." In such an age-stratified society economic "success" was not usual (and not expected) until the age of thirty-five, forty, or even forty-five. Propertied status was the product of one or two decades of work as a laborer or tenant, or of the long-delayed inheritance of the parental farm. The ownership of a freehold estate was the *goal* of young male farmers and their wives; it was not—even in the best of circumstances—a universal condition among adult males at any one point in time. Age stratification thus constituted an important aspect of what Michael Zuckerman has neatly conceptualized as the "social context" of political activity in these small and ethnically homogeneous agricultural settlements. The economic dependence and powerlessness of young adults was a fact of life, the proper definition of social reality.

If cultural norms legitimated an age-stratified society in the minds of most northern farmers, then the character of social and economic life accustomed them to systematic inequalities in the distribution of wealth. Consider the evidence. In southeastern Pennsylvania in 1760 and again in 1782, the top 40 percent of the taxable population owned 70 percent of the assessed wealth, while the top 10 percent controlled 33 percent. On the 1784 tax list of Newtown, Long Island, the proportions were nearly identical, with the top 40 percent owning 73 percent of the wealth, and the richest 10 percent holding 37 percent. In both places, inequality increased steadily from the end of the seventeenth century even as the rate of natural population growth declined—a clear indication of advancing social differentiation (and not simply age stratification). And in Newtown, at least, the bulk of the poor population in 1784 was composed not of "younger sons or older men" but of workers in the prime of their productive lives.

The westward migration of this excess farm population was of crucial importance, although not for the precise reasons suggested by Turner and Lemon. Young men and women without a landed inheritance moved to newly settled communities not as yeomen but as aspirants to that status; they hoped to make the difficult climb up the agricultural "ladder" from laborer to tenant to freeholder. This geographical movement, in turn, helped to maintain social stability in long-settled agricultural towns. One-third of all adult males in Goshen, Connecticut, in 1750 were without land; but two decades later a majority of these men had left the town and 70 percent of those who remained had obtained property through marriage, inheritance, or the savings from their labor. A new landless group of unmarried sons, wage laborers, and tenant farmers had appeared in Goshen by 1771, again encompassing one-third of the adult males. A similar process of out-migration and property accumulation would characterize many of the lives of this landless group, but throughout the northern region there was a steady increase in the number of permanent tenant farmers as the century progressed.

The renewed expropriation of aboriginal lands during the early nineteenth century brought a partial reversal of this trend. Massive westward migration enabled a rapidly growing Euro-American population to *preserve* an agricultural society composed primarily of yeoman freeholding families in many eastern areas, and to *extend* these age and wealth-stratified communities into western regions. This movement did not, however, produce less stratified communities in the Northwest states, nor did it assure the universal ownership of land. Within a few decades of settlement the wealth structure of the frontier states was nearly indistinguishable from that in the agricultural areas of the more densely settled east. In Trempealeau County, Wisconsin, in 1870 the poorest 10 percent of the properties population owned less than 1 percent of all assessed wealth, while the most affluent 10 percent controlled 39 percent. This distribution was almost precisely the same as that in those regions of Vermont from which many of the inhabitants of this farming county had recently migrated. "On no frontier," Neil McNall concludes from an intensive study of the settlement of the rich Genesee Valley in upstate New York between 1790 and 1860, "was there an easy avenue to land ownership for the farmer of limited means."

Evidence from a variety of geographic locations indicates, therefore, that Lemon has presented an overly optimistic description of the agricultural economy of early America and has falsely ascribed a "liberal" consciousness to the inhabitants of eighteenth-century Pennsylvania. His analysis is not unique. A number of historians of colonial New England have offered similar interpretations of an entrepreneurial mentality among the majority of the agricultural population. Sometimes the ascription is implicit and perhaps inadvertent, as in the case of Philip Greven's path-breaking analysis of Andover, which focuses attention on the single economic variable of land transmission. Was the preservation of a landed inheritance the concern of *most* Andover families or only that of the very select group of substantially endowed first settlers and their descendants whom Greven has studied? The pattern of family life, geographic mobility, and economic values may have been very different among later arrivals to Andover—those who had less land to pass on to the next generation—yet this group constituted a majority of the town's population by the eighteenth century. Or what of the pervasive entrepreneurial outlook among Connecticut farmers which is posted by Richard L. Bushman in his stimulating examination of the transition *From Puritan To Yankee?* Bushman's interpretation of the Great Awakening is predicated upon the emergence of an accumulation-oriented pattern of behavior, and yet little—if any—evidence is presented to demonstrate its existence among the mass of the population. . . .

Even in the most market-oriented areas of the Middle Colonies, many farmers participated in the commercial capitalist economy in a much more limited way and with rather different goals. Lacking slaves or indentured servants and unwilling to bid for wage labor, they planted only 8 to 10 acres of wheat each year, a crop that could conveniently be harvested by the farmer, one or two growing sons, and (in some cases) his wife. Of the normal yield of 80 to 100 bushels, 60 would be consumed by the family or saved for seed; the surplus of 20 to 40 bushels would be sold on the Philadelphia market, bringing a cash income in the early 1770s of £5 to £10 sterling. The ordinary male farmer, Lemon concludes, was content to produce "enough for his family and... to sell a surplus in the market to buy what he deemed necessities." There was little innovative, risk-taking behavior; there was no determined pursuit of profit. Indeed, the account books of these farm families indicate that they invariably chose the security of diversified production rather than hire labor to produce more wheat or to specialize in milk production. Economic gain was important to these men and women, yet it was not their dominant value. It was subordinate to (or encompassed by) two other goals: the yearly subsistence and the long-run financial security of the family unit.

Thus, the predominance of subsistence or semi-subsistence productive units among the yeoman farming families of the northern colonies was not only the result of geographic or economic factors—the ready access to a reliable, expanding market. These men and women were enmeshed also in a web of social relationships and cultural expectations that inhibited the free play of market forces. Much of the output of their farms was consumed by the residents, most of whom were biologically or legally related and who were not paid wages for their labor. A secondary group of consumers consisted of the inhabitants of the local area, members of a community often based on ties of kinship, language, religion, or ethnicity. An impersonal price system figured prominently in these transactions, but goods were often bartered for their exchange value or for what was considered a "just price." Finally, a small (but growing) proportion of the total production of these farms was "sold" on an external market through a series of formal commercial transactions.

If freehold ownership and participation in these urban and international markets meant that northern agriculture did not have many of the characteristics of a closed peasant or a pre-capitalist economy, they do not imply that this system of production and exchange was modern or that its members were motivated primarily by liberal, entrepreneurial, individualist, or capitalist values. Nor is it sufficient to describe these farming communities as "transitional" between the ideal-types of traditional and modern or pre-capitalist and capitalist. To adopt such an idealist approach is to substitute typology for analysis, to suggest a teleological model of historical development, and to ignore the specific features of this social and economic system. Rather, one must point to its central features: the community was distinguished by age- and wealth-stratification and (usually) by ethnic or religious homogeneity, while on the family level there was freehold property ownership, a household mode of production, limited economic possibilities and aspirations, and a safety-first subsistence agriculture within a commercial capitalist market structure. And then one must seek an understanding of the "coping strategies" used by individuals, groups, and governments to reconcile the competing demands, the inherent tensions, and the immanent contradictions posed by this particular configuration of historical institutions and cultural values.

It would be premature, at this point, to attempt a complete analysis of the *mentalité* of the pre-industrial yeoman population. Yet a preliminary examination may suggest both a conceptual framework for future research and the character of certain widely accepted values, goals, and behavioral norms. An important, and perhaps controversial, premise should be made explicit at the beginning. It is assumed that the behavior of the farm population constitutes a crucial (although not a foolproof) indicator of its values and aspirations. This epistemological assumption has an interpretive implication, for it focuses attention on those activities that dominated the daily lives of the population—in the case of this particular society, on the productive tasks that provided food, clothing, and shelter.

This process of production and capital formation derived much of its emotive and intellectual meaning from the cultural matrix—from the institutional character of the society. Work was arranged along familial lines rather than controlled communally or through a wage system. This apparently simple organizational fact was a crucial determinant of the historical consciousness of this farming population. For even as the family gave symbolic meaning and emotional significant to subsistence activities, its own essence was shaped by the character of the productive system. There was a complex relationship between the agricultural labor and property system of early America and its rural culture; and it is that matrix of productive activities, organizational structures, and social values which the following analysis attempts (in a very preliminary fashion) to reconstruct.

Because the primary economic unit—the family—was also the main social institution, production activities had an immense impact on the entire character of agrarian life. Family relationships could not be divorced from economic considerations; indeed, the basic question of power and authority within the family hinged primarily on legal control over the land and—indirectly—over the labor needed to work it. The parents (principally the husband) enjoyed legal possession of the property—either as freeholders, tenants or sharecroppers—but they were dependent on their children for economic support in their old age. Their aim, as Greven has pointed out, was to control the terms and the timing of the transfer of economic resources to the succeeding generation.

The intimate relationship between agricultural production and parental values, between economic history and family history, is best approached through a series of case studies. The first of these small family farms began in 1739 with the arrival in Kent, Connecticut, of Joseph Fuller. At one time or another Fuller was an investor in an iron works, a "typical speculative proprietor," and a "rich squatter" who tried to deceive the Connecticut authorities into granting him (and his partner Joshua Lassell) 4,820 acres of provincial land. Fuller's energy ambition, and activities mark him as an entrepreneur, even a "capitalist." Yet his behavior must be seen in the widest possible context, and the motivation assessed accordingly. When this restless man arrived in Kent at the age of forty (with his second wife), he was the father of seven sons, aged two to sixteen; thirteen years later, when his final petition for a land grant was rejected, he had nine sons, aged eleven to twenty-nine years, and five daughters. With fourteen children to provide with land, dowries, or currency,

Fuller *had* to embark on an active career if he wished to keep his children (and himself and his wife in their old age) from a life of landless poverty.

In the event, fecundity overwhelmed the Fullers' financial ingenuity. None of the children of Joseph Fuller ever attained a rating on the tax list equal to the highest recorded for their father, and a similar pattern prevailed among the sons of the third generation. The total resources of the Fuller "clan" (for such it had become) grew constantly over time—with nine second- and twelve third-generation males appearing on the tax lists of Kent—but their per capita wealth declined steadily. The gains of one generation, the slow accumulation of capital resources through savings and invested labor, had been dispersed among many heirs.

Such divisions of limited resources inevitably roused resentment and engendered bitter battles within farm families. Ultimately, the delicate reciprocal economic relationships between parents and children might break down completely. Insufficiency of land meant that most children would have to be exiled —apprenticed to wealthier members of the community or sent out on their own as landless laborers—and that parents would have to endure a harsh old age, sharing their small plot with the remaining heir. High fertility and low mortality threatened each generation of children with the loss of class status; the unencumbered inheritance of a freehold estate was the exception, not the rule.

Even in these circumstances—as a second example will suggest—the ideal for many dispossessed children remained property ownership and eventual control of the transfer process with regard to their own offspring. "My parents were poor," an "Honest Farmer" wrote to the *Pennsylvania Packet* in 1786,

> and they put me at twelve years of age to a farmer, with whom I lived till I was twenty one . . . I married me a wife—and a very working young woman she was—and we took a farm of forty acres on rent. . . . In ten years I was able to buy me a farm of sixty acres on which I became my own tenant. I then, in a manner, grew rich and soon added another sixty acres, with which I am content. My estate increased beyond all account. I bought several lots of out-land for my children, which amounted to seven when I was forty-five years old.
>
> About this time I married my oldest daughter to a clever lad, to whom I gave one hundred acres of my out-land.

Was this "success story" typical? Did the "Honest Farmer" minimize the difficulties of his own ascent and exaggerate the prospects of his seven children, each of whom would have to be provided with land, livestock, or equipment? It is clear, at any rate, that this Pennsylvanian enjoyed a crucial advantage over Joseph Fuller; he could accumulate capital through the regular sale of his surplus production on the market, and offer economic assistance to his children. His grandchildren, moreover, would grow up in the more fully developed commercial economy of the early nineteenth century. Ten years of work as a farm laborer—and an intense commitment to save—would now yield a capital stock of five hundred dollars. With this sum invested in equipment, livestock, and supplies, it would then be feasible to rent a farm, "with the prospect of accumulating money at a rate perhaps double that possible by wage work." To begin with less than five hundred dollars was to increase dependence on the land-lord—to accept a half-and-half division of the produce rather than a two-third share. In either case, there was a high financial and psychological price to be paid. For many years these young adults would be "dependent," would work as wage laborers without security, as sharecroppers without land, or as mortgagors without full independence; their labor would enrich freeholders, landlords, and bankers even as it moved them closer to real economic freedom.

The process is readily apparent in a third case study, an archetypical example of the slow but successful accumulation of productive agricultural property in the mid-nineteenth century. In 1843 a young farmer in Massachusetts bought an old farm of 85 acres for $4,337; "in order to pay for it, I mortgaged it for $4,100, paying only $237, all that I had, after buying my stock." Nine years later it was clear that some progress had been made, for he had "paid up about $600 on the mortgage, and laid out nearly $2,000 in permanent improvements on my buildings and farm." This hard-working farmer was "a little nearer the harbor than I was when I commenced the voyage," but he was still $3,500 in debt and had interest payments of $250 to make each year. These obligations might be met in ten or fifteen years, but by then new debts would have to be incurred in order to provide working capital for his children. This farmer would die a property owner, but ... some of his offspring would face a similarly time-consuming and difficult climb up the agricultural ladder.

Two features of the long-term process of capital formation through agricultural production revealed by these case studies stand out as particularly important, one static and the other dynamic. The recurrent factor was the continual pressure of population on the existing capital stock; the rate of natural increase constantly threatened to outstrip the creation of new productive resources: cleared land, machinery, housing, and livestock. This danger is demonstrable in the case of the Fuller clan, and its specter lurks in the prose of the "Honest Farmer" and his younger accumulation-oriented counterpart in Massachusetts. Economic prosperity was the result of unremitting labor by each generation. Only as farm parents began consciously to limit their fertility were they able to pass on sizable estates to their children—and this occurred primarily after 1830.

What changed—from the seventeenth to the early nineteenth century—was the increased rate of capital formation stemming from the expansion of the market economy; the growing importance of "unearned" profits because of the rise in the value of land and of other scarce commodities; and the extent to which middlemen dominated the processes of agricultural production and of westward migration. These three developments were interrelated. All were aspects of an increasingly important system of commercial agriculture that generated antagonistic social relationships and incipient class divisions. These alterations brought greater prosperity to those farmers whose geographic locations and cultural values were conducive to market activity. . . .

The lineal family—not the conjugal unit and certainly not the unattached individual—thus stood at the center of economic and social existence in northern agricultural society in pre-industrial America. The interlocking relationship between the biological life cycle and the system of agricultural (and domestic) production continued to tie the generations together even as the wider economic structure was undergoing a massive transformation and as the proportion of farming families in the population was steadily declining. Most men, women and children in this yeoman society continued to view the world through the prism of family values. This cultural outlook—this inbred pattern of behavior—set certain limits on personal autonomy, entrepreneurial activity, religious membership, and even political imagery. Lineal family values did not constitute, by any means, the entire world view—the *mentalité*—of the agricultural population, but they did define a central tendency of that consciousness, an abiding core of symbolic and emotive meaning; and, most important of all, they constituted a significant and reliable guide to behavior amid the uncertainties of the world.

POSTSCRIPT

Did Capitalist Values Motivate the American Colonists?

Both Lemon and Henretta defend their positions on the basis of their own research into primary sources. Their opposing interpretations stem from the differing assumptions that both historians make. In the first place, Lemon contends that the settlers of southeastern Pennsylvania placed "individual freedom and material gain over that of public interest. Put another way, the people planned for themselves much more than they did for their communities." Henretta, on the other hand, argues that Lemon has been unduly influenced by the principles of neo-Whig historians writing in the 1950s and has imposed these twentieth-century values onto eighteenth-century settlers. Synthesizing a number of recent studies about the colonial family, Henretta concludes that an "intimate relationship [existed] between agricultural production and parental values, between economic history and family history." Henretta turns Lemon's entrepreneurial argument against him when Lemon admits that language and religious beliefs often exerted a considerable influence on the location and actions of a number of the ethnic groups that settled in southeastern Pennsylvania. Lemon, however, strongly disagrees with this criticism. In his "Comment on James A. Henretta's 'Family and Farms,'" *William and Mary Quarterly* (October 1980), Lemon accuses Henretta of "detaching families from society" and retreating "toward a nostalgic populism of self-sufficient families."

Another area of disagreement in the two readings centers on the timing of historical change. Lemon argues that a middle-class society of expectant capitalists based on the accumulation of property is central from the first settling of America onward. But Henretta views colonial America as a precapitalist society possessing a *mentalité* of traditional Old World religious, family, and agrarian values. He maintains that the transition to a bourgeois industrial society started after 1750 and gradually expanded until it encompassed America in the 1820s and 1830s.

In the survey "The Social Development of Colonial America," *Race, Class and Politics* (University of Illinois Press, 1986), colonial scholar Gary Nash suggests that the argument between Henretta and Lemon may be false because Henretta's evidence comes from his portrait of New England families while Lemon's theory is based upon an intensive study of one portion of a major Pennsylvanian colony. But Nash comes up with an astute geographical explanation of his own that is neglected by both authors. He argues that the geographical differences between thin-soiled New England and Pennsylvania, with its rich, alluvial soil, may explain why the Middle colonists may have been more entrepreneurial as commercial farmers than their New England counterparts. This, Nash says, may be due to the fact that in pre-Columbian times the

Native Americans of the mid-Atlantic left far greater amounts of tillable soil to the future European emigrants than the Algonquians did in the New England area.

A major study synthesizing the past two decades of research on the social structure of colonial America is needed. Jackson Turner Main's *The Social Structure of Revolutionary America* (Princeton University Press, 1965) emphasizes mobility in frontier regions and the subsistence of farming communities, as well as the economic inequalities within the towns and most commercial regions. Main's work is a good starting point, but it is dated, narrow in its time frame, and probably optimistic in its conclusions. More critical and with an excellent introduction to a collection of primary sources and interpretative essays is Nash's *Class and Society in Early America* (Prentice Hall, 1970).

Most research on the class structure of colonial America focuses on case studies of local communities. Nearly everyone agrees that the middle-class democracy thesis perpetuated by neo-Whig historians underestimates income inequalities among the settlers. But the issue is a complex one. Recent research points out how tenancy can be interpreted in a variety of ways. Studies of dissatisfied tenants scorned as the "idle and dissolute" who fall in status and live in permanent poverty can be found in Stephen Innes, "Land Tenancy and Social Order in Springfield, Massachusetts, 1652 to 1702," *William and Mary Quarterly* (October 1978); Gregory Stiverson, *Poverty in a Land of Plenty: Tenancy in Eighteenth-Century Maryland* (Johns Hopkins University Press, 1977); and Edward Countryman, *A People in Revolution: The American Revolution and Political Society in New York, 1760–1790* (Johns Hopkins University Press, 1981). A more favorable view can be found in Sung Bok Kim, *Landlord and Tenant in Colonial New York: Manorial Society, 1664–1775* (University of North Carolina Press, 1978). Lucy Slier reworked some of the same data as Lemon in a very sophisticated analysis of the subject, "Tenancy in Colonial Pennsylvania: The Case of Chester County," *William and Mary Quarterly* (October 1986). She distinguishes among three groups of tenants: *householders,* who were real tenants who rented and occupied the lands or buildings of another, and *inmates* and *freemen,* who were neither land*owners* nor land*holders.*

Finally, both Lemon and Henretta have written broader essays that substantiate their original premises. See, for example, Lemon's "Early Americans and Their Social Environment," *Journal of Historical Geography* (vol. 2, 1980). Sharon V. Salinger has also addressed in great detail the labor question and the shift from lineal to entrepreneurial values near the end of the eighteenth century. As she argues in *To Serve Well and Faithfully: Labor and Indentured Servants in Pennsylvania, 1682–1800* (Cambridge University Press, 1987), "The traditional outlook, in which this mutuality and communal spirit dominated, [began to collapse during the late colonial period] and was replaced by the 'entrepreneurial spirit.'"

ISSUE 5

Was There a Great Awakening in Mid-Eighteenth-Century America?

YES: Patricia U. Bonomi, from *Under the Cope of Heaven: Religion, Society, and Politics in Colonial America* (Oxford University Press, 1986)

NO: Jon Butler, from "Enthusiasm Described and Decried: The Great Awakening as Interpretative Fiction," *The Journal of American History* (September 1982)

ISSUE SUMMARY

YES: Professor of history Patricia U. Bonomi defines the Great Awakening as a period of intense revivalistic fervor that laid the foundation for socioreligious and political reform by spawning an age of contentiousness in the British mainland colonies.

NO: Professor of American history Jon Butler argues that to describe the colonial revivalistic activities of the eighteenth century as the "Great Awakening" is to seriously exaggerate their extent, nature, and impact on pre-Revolutionary American society and politics.

Although generations of American schoolchildren have been taught that the British colonies in North America were founded by persons fleeing religious persecution in England, the truth is that many of those early settlers were motivated by other factors, some of which had little to do with theological preferences. To be sure, the Pilgrims and Puritans of New England sought to escape the proscriptions established by the Church of England. Many New Englanders, however, did not adhere to the precepts of Calvinism and were therefore viewed as outsiders. The Quakers who populated Pennsylvania were mostly fugitives from New England, where they had been victims of religious persecution. But to apply religious motivations to the earliest settlers of Virginia, South Carolina, or Georgia is to engage in a serious misreading of the historical record. Even in New England the religious mission of (the first governor of Massachusetts Bay Colony) John Winthrop's "city upon a hill" began to erode as the colonial settlements matured and stabilized.

90

Although religion was a central element in the lives of the seventeenth- and eighteenth-century Europeans who migrated to the New World, proliferation of religious sects and denominations, emphasis upon material gain in all parts of the colonies, and the predominance of reason over emotion that is associated with the Deists of the Enlightenment period all contributed to a gradual but obvious movement of the colonists away from the church and clerical authority. William Bradford (the second governor of Plymouth Colony), for example, expressed grave concern that many Plymouth residents were following a path of perfidy, and William Penn (the founder of Pennsylvania) was certain that the "holy experiment" of the Quakers had failed. Colonial clergy, fearful that a fall from grace was in progress, issued calls for a revival of religious fervor. Therefore, the spirit of revivalism that spread through the colonies in the 1730s and 1740s was an answer to these clerical prayers.

The episode known as the First Great Awakening coincided with the Pietistic movement in Europe and England and was carried forward by dynamic preachers such as Gilbert Tennant, Theodore Frelinghuysen, and George Whitefield. They promoted a religion of the heart, not of the head, in order to produce a spiritual rebirth. These revivals, most historians agree, reinvigorated American Protestantism. Many new congregations were organized as a result of irremediable schisms between "Old Lights" and "New Lights." Skepticism about the desirability of an educated clergy sparked a strong strain of anti-intellectualism. Also, the emphasis on conversion was a message to which virtually everyone could respond, regardless of age, sex, or social status. For some historians, the implications of the Great Awakening extended beyond the religious sphere into the realm of politics and were incorporated into the American Revolution.

In the following selections, Patricia U. Bonomi writes from the traditional assumption that a powerful revivalistic force known as the Great Awakening occurred in the American colonies in the mid-eighteenth century. Following a survey of the converging forces that served as precursors to this revivalistic movement, she argues that the Great Awakening grew out of clerical disputes among Presbyterians and quickly spread to other denominations throughout the colonies, abetted by dynamic itinerant preachers such as George Whitefield. Before the enthusiasm subsided, she concludes, the Awakening had instilled a tradition of divisiveness that would affect a number of American social, political, and religious structures.

Jon Butler counters that closer scrutiny of the Great Awakening reveals that the revivals were regional episodes that did not affect all of the colonies equally and, hence, had only a modest impact on American colonial religion. Butler suggests that because the mid-eighteenth-century revivals did not produce the kinds of dramatic changes, religious or political, frequently ascribed to them, historians should abandon the concept of the Great Awakening altogether.

Patricia U. Bonomi

 YES

"The Hosannas of the Multitude": The Great Awakening in America

The Great Awakening—that intense period of revivalist tumult from about 1739 to 1745—is one of the most arresting subjects of American history. The eighteenth century, and the latter part of the seventeenth, were of course punctuated with religious episodes that seemed to erupt without warning and draw entire communities into a vortex of religious conversions and agitations of soul. Yet those episodes tended not to spread beyond the individual churches or towns in which they originated. By the third decade of the eighteenth century, however, a number of currents were converging to prepare the way for an unprecedented burst of religious fervor and controversy.

The two major streams of thought shaping western religious belief in the eighteenth century—Enlightenment rationalism and Continental pietism—were by the 1720s reaching increasing numbers of Americans through the world of print, transatlantic learned societies, and such recently arrived spokesmen as the Anglican moderate George Berkeley, on the one side, and the Dutch Reformed pietist Theodore Frelinghuysen, on the other. By the 1730s, American clergymen influenced by the spiritual intensity and emotional warmth of Reformed pietism were vigorously asserting that religion was being corrupted by secular forces; in their view a conversion experience that touched the heart was the only road to salvation. The rationalists demurred, preferring a faith tempered by "an enlightened Mind... not raised Affections." This contest between reason and innate grace was in one sense as old as Christianity itself. In New England, where it was often cast as a competition between Arminians and Antinomians, only the Calvinists' ability to hold the two elements in exquisite balance had averted a schism. Rationalist attitudes... were sufficiently prevalent in the eighteenth-century South to obstruct the development of heart religion there until the later colonial years. In the Middle Colonies, every point of view was heard, though by the 1730s tension was rising between the entrenched ministers of more orthodox opinion and incoming clergymen who insisted on conversion as the *sine qua non* of vital religion.

Adding to currents of religious unease in the early eighteenth century were a number of other developments: an accelerating pace of commercial growth; land shortages as well as land opportunities; the unprecedented diversity of eighteenth-century immigration; and a rapid climb in total population. Population growth now created dense settlements in some rural as well as urban areas, facilitating mass public gatherings. Moreover, the proliferation of churches and sects, intensifying denominational rivalries, and smallpox and earthquake alarms that filled meetinghouses to overflowing all contributed to a sense of quickening in church life.

Into this volatile and expectant environment came some of the most charismatic and combative personalities of the age. And as the electricity of a Tennent crackled, and the thunder of a Whitefield rolled, a storm broke that, in the opinion of many, would forever alter American society. The Great Awakening created conditions uniquely favorable to social and political, as well as religious, reform by piercing the facade of civility and deference that governed provincial life to usher in a new age of contentiousness. By promoting church separations and urging their followers to make choices that had political as well as religious implications, the Awakeners wrought permanent changes in public practices and attitudes. Before it subsided, the revival had unsettled the lives of more Americans and disrupted more institutions than any other single event in colonial experience to that time. To see how a religious movement could overspill its boundaries to reshape cultural understanding and political expectations, we must take a closer look at some of the churches and people caught up in the revival.

Presbyterian Beginnings

The Great Awakening began not as a popular uprising but as a contest between clerical factions. Thus only those churches with a "professional" clergy and organized governing structure—the Presbyterian, Congregational, Dutch Reformed, and eventually the Anglican—were split apart by the revival. The newer German churches and the sects, having little structure to overturn, remained largely outside the conflict. These events have usually been viewed from the perspective of New England Congregationalism, though the first denomination to be involved in the Awakening was the Presbyterian Church in the Middle Colonies. All of the strains and adjustments experienced by other colonial denominations over a longer time span were compressed, in the Presbyterian case, into the fifty years from the beginning of Ulster immigration around 1725 to the Revolution. Thus the Presbyterian example serves as a kind of paradigm of the experience of all churches from their initial formation through the Great Awakening and its aftermath. It reveals too how a dispute between ministers rapidly widened into a controversy that tested the limits of order and introduced new forms of popular leadership that challenged deferential traditions.

Presbyterians looked to the future with reasonably high hopes by the third decade of the eighteenth century. To all appearances they possessed a more stable and orderly church structure than any of their middle-colony competitors. Unlike the Anglicans, they required no bishop to perform the essential rites of ordination and confirmation; nor did they suffer quite the same shortage of ministers as the German churches. The supply of Presbyterian clergy, if never adequate, had at least been sufficient to support the formation of a rudimentary governing structure. Three presbyteries and the Synod of Philadelphia were in place before the first wave of immigration from Ulster reached the Delaware basin, enabling the twenty-five to thirty ministers active in the Middle Colonies to direct growth and protect professional standards in the period of expansion after 1725. Congregations were under the care of laymen ordained to the office of "elder" and, when available, ministers. Supervising presbyteries in each region maintained oversight of local congregations and ordained and disciplined the clergy. At the top was the synod, which provided a forum where clerical disputes over church doctrine and governing authority could be resolved *in camera* [secretly].

Yet the controls imposed by the Presbyterian hierarchy were hardly all that they appeared to be. Beneath orderly processes were tensions which had been expanding steadily before finally bursting forth in fratricidal strife and schism after 1739. Any reading of eighteenth-century Presbyterian records discloses at least three kinds of strains beneath the surface: between parishioners, between people and minister, and within the professional clergy itself.

The Presbyterian Church was the focal point and mediator of Scotch-Irish community life from the late 1720s on, when thousands of Ulster Scots began entering the colonies annually. As the westward-migrating settlers moved beyond the reach of government and law, the Presbyterian Church was the only institution that kept pace with settlement. By stretching resources to the limit, the synod, and especially the presbyteries, kept in touch with their scattered brethren through itinerant preachers and presbyterial visitations. Ministers, invariably the best educated persons on the early frontier, were looked to for leadership in both religious and community affairs, and they often took up multiple roles as doctors, teachers, and even lawyers. So closely did the Scotch-Irish identify with the Kirk [Church] that it was often said they "could not live without it."

But if the church was a vital center it was also an agency of control. Presbyterian ministers—whom some regarded as a "stiff-necked . . . [and] pedantick crew"—expected to guide their parishioners' spiritual growth and moral safety in America as they had done in the Old Country, and at first, by and large, they succeeded. Congregations gathered spontaneously in Scotch-Irish settlements, much as they did in immigrant German communities. A major difference between the two societies was that from an early stage lay Presbyterians submitted themselves to clerical authority. As soon as a Presbyterian congregation was formed, it requested recognition and the supply of a minister from the local presbytery. Often the presbytery could provide only a probationer or itinerant preacher for the Sabbath, and many settlements were fortunate to hear a sermon one or two Sundays a month. The congregations nonetheless proceeded to elect elders, deacons to care for the poor and sick, and trustees to oversee the collection of tithes for the minister's salary. The governing "session," comprised of elders and minister, functioned as a kind of court, hearing charges and ruling on a variety of matters, including disputes between parishioners over land or debt, domestic difficulties, and church doctrine. The main responsibility of the session was to enforce moral discipline. Its rulings could be appealed to the supervising presbytery. The presbytery minutes consequently have much to tell us about the quality of clerical authority. But they also disclose the growing undercurrent of resistance that such authority aroused among the freer spirits in the Scotch-Irish settlements. . . .

New Sides vs. Old Sides

The Great Awakening split the Presbyterian Church apart, and through the cracks long-suppressed steam hissed forth in clouds of acrimony and vituperation that would change the face of authority in Pennsylvania and elsewhere. As the passions of the Awakening reached their height in the early 1740s, evangelical "New Side" Presbyterians turned on the more orthodox "Old Sides" with the ferocity peculiar to zealots, charging them with extravagant doctrinal and moral enormities. The internecine spectacle that ensued, the loss of proportion and professional decorum, contributed to the demystification of the clergy, forced parishioners to choose between competing factions, and overset traditional attitudes about deference and leadership in colonial America.

The division that surfaced in 1740–1741 had been developing for more than a decade. Presbyterian ministers had no sooner organized their central association, the Synod of Philadelphia, in 1715 than the first lines of stress appeared, though it was not until a cohesive evangelical faction emerged in the 1730s that an open split was threatened. Most members of the synod hoped to model American Presbyterianism along orderly lines, and in 1729 an act requiring all ministers and ministerial candidates to subscribe publicly to the Westminster Confession had been approved. In 1738 the synod had further ruled that no minister would be licensed unless he could display a degree from a British or European university, or from one of the New England colleges (Harvard or Yale). New candidates were to submit to an examination by a commission of the synod on the soundness of their theological training and spiritual condition. The emergent evangelical faction rightly saw these restrictions as an effort to control their own activities. They had reluctantly accepted subscription to the Westminster Confession, but synodical screening of new candidates struck them as an intolerable invasion of the local presbyteries' right of ordination.

The insurgents were led by the Scotsman William Tennent, Sr., and his sons, William, Jr., Charles, John, and Gilbert. William, Sr. had been educated at the University of Edinburgh, receiving a bachelor's degree in 1693 and an M.A. in 1695. He may have been exposed to European pietism at Edinburgh, where new ideas of every sort were brewing in the last quarter of the seventeenth century. Though ordained a minister of the Anglican church in 1706, Tennent did not gain a parish of his own, and in 1718 he departed the Old World for the New. When he applied for a license from the Synod of Philadelphia in 1718, Tennent was asked his reasons for leaving the Church of England. He responded that he had come to view government by bishops as anti-scriptural, that he opposed ecclesiastical courts and plural benefices, that the church was leaning toward Arminianism, and that he disapproved of "their ceremonial way of worship." All this seemed sound enough to the Presbyterians, and Tennent was licensed forthwith. Having a strong interest in scholarship and pedagogy, Tennent built a one-room schoolhouse in about 1730 in Neshaminy, Bucks County—the Log College, as it was later derisively called—where he set about training young men for the ministry. Exactly when Tennent began to pull away from the regular synod leadership is unclear, but by 1736 his church at Neshaminy was split down the middle and the anti-evangelical members were attempting to expel him as minister.

In 1739 the synod was confronted with a question on professional standards that brought the two factions closer to a complete break. When the previous year's synod had erected commissions to examine the education of all ministerial candidates not holding degrees from approved universities, Gilbert Tennent had charged that the qualification was designed "to prevent his father's school from training gracious men for the Ministry." Overriding the synod's rule in 1739, the radical New Brunswick Presbytery licensed one John Rowland without reference to any committee, though Rowland had received "a private education"—the synod's euphemism for the Log College. Sharply criticizing the presbytery for its disorderly and divisive action, the synod refused to approve Rowland until he agreed to submit himself for examination, which he in turn refused to do.

⋅⋰⊙⋱⋅

Since education was central to the dispute, it is unfortunate that no Log College records have survived to describe the training given the remarkable group of men that came under William Tennent, Sr.'s tutelage. We do know that they emerged to become leaders of the revivalist movement, and would in turn prepare other religious and educational leaders of the middle and southern colonies. The little existing evidence casts doubt on the synod's charge that Tennent and his followers were "destroyers of good learning" who persisted in foisting unlettered Log College students upon an undiscriminating public. As Gilbert Tennent insisted, the insurgents "desired and designed a well-qualified Ministry as much as our Brethren." To be sure, their theological emphasis was at variance with that of the Old Side clergy, and there may have been parts of the traditional curriculum they did not value as highly, as had been true with the innovative dissenting academies in Britain. But as competition between the two factions intensified, restrained criticism gave way to enmity. Thus when the synod charged that Gilbert Tennent had called "Physicks, Ethicks, Metophysicks and Pnuematicks [the rubric under which Aristotelian philosophy was taught in medieval universities] meer Criticks, and consequently useless," its members could not resist adding that he did so "because his Father cannot or doth not teach them."

Yet there is much that attests to both William Tennent, Sr.'s learning and his pedagogical talents. That he was a polished scholar of the classics, spoke Latin and English with equal fluency, and was a master of Greek was confirmed by many who knew him. He also "had some acquaintance with the... Sciences." A hint of the training Tennent offered comes from the licensing examination given his youngest son Charles in 1736 by the Philadelphia Presbytery, among whose members were several who would later emerge as chief critics of the Tennents. Young Charles was tested on his "ability in prayer [and] in the Languages," in the delivery of a sermon and exegesis, and on his answers to "various suitable questions on the arts and sciences, especially Theology and out of Scripture." He was also examined on the state of his soul. Charles Tennent was apparently approved without question.

The strongest evidence of the quality of a Log College education comes, however, from the subsequent careers and accomplishments of its eighteen to twenty-one "alumni." Their deep commitment to formal education is demonstrated by the number of academies they themselves founded, including Samuel Blair's "classical school" at Faggs Manor in Pennsylvania, Samuel Finley's academy at Nottingham, and several others. Two early presidents of the College of New Jersey (Princeton) were Samuel Finley and Samuel Davies (the latter having been educated by Blair at Faggs Manor). Moreover, the published sermons and essays of Samuel Finley, Samuel Blair, and Gilbert Tennent not only pulse with evangelical passion but also display wide learning. In the opinion of a leading Presbyterian historian the intellectual accomplishments of the Log College revivalists far outshone those of the Old Side opposers, among whom only the scholarly Francis Alison produced significant writings. As George Whitefield observed when he visited Neshaminy in 1739 and saw the rough structure of logs that housed the school: "All that we can say of most universities is, that they are glorious without."

⋅⊙⋅

But the distinction that the Log College men would achieve was still unknown in 1739, when the New Brunswick Presbytery defied the synod by licensing John Rowland. It was at this juncture, moreover, that the twenty-six-year-old English evangelist, George Whitefield, made his sensational appearance. Whitefield's visits to New Jersey and Pennsylvania in the winter of 1739–1740 provided tremendous support for the Presbyterian insurgents, as thousands of provincials flocked to hear him and realized, perhaps for the first time, something of what the American evangelists had been up to. The public support that now flowed to Tennent and the New Side exhilarated its members, inciting them to ever bolder assaults on the synod.

The revivalists had to this point preached only in their own churches or in temporarily vacant pulpits, but that winter they began to invade the territory of the regular clergy. This action raised the issue of itinerant preaching, perhaps the thorniest of the entire conflict, for it brought the parties face to face on the question of who was better qualified to interpret the word of God. It was in this setting that Gilbert Tennent was moved on March 8, 1740 to deliver his celebrated sermon, *The Danger of an Unconverted Ministry,* to a Nottingham congregation engaged in choosing a new preacher. It was an audacious, not to say reckless, attack on the Old Side clergy, and Tennent would later qualify some of his strongest language. But the sermon starkly reveals the gulf that separated the two factions by 1740. It also demonstrates the revivalists' supreme disregard for the traditional limits on public discussion of what amounted to professional questions. . . .

In this influential and widely disseminated sermon Tennent set forth the three principal issues over which Presbyterians would divide: the conversion experience, education of the clergy, and itinerant preaching. While his tone may have owed something to Whitefield's recent influence—humility was never a strong point with the evangelists—it also reflected the growing self-confidence of the insurgents, as a wave of public support lifted them to popular heights. During the synod of 1740 the anti-revivalist clergy, in a demonstration of their reasonableness, agreed to certain compromises on the issues of itinerancy and licensing, but when the revivalists continued to denounce them publicly as carnal and unconverted, their patience came to an end.

The break between Old Side and New Side Presbyterians came during the synod of 1741 when a protest signed by twelve ministers and eight elders demanded that the revivalists be expelled from the synod. In a preemptive move, the New Side clergy voluntarily withdrew from the Philadelphia Synod to their presbyteries, where their work continued with great zeal and met with success that would outshine that of their rivals. In 1745 the evangelical party, joined by other friends of the revival from the Middle Colonies, formed the Synod of New York, which would sustain a lively existence until 1758 when the Presbyterian schism was finally repaired.

❧❦❧

Disagreements over theological emphasis, professional standards, and centralized authority were the most immediate causes of the Presbyterian schism, but other differences between Old and New Sides had the effect of making the conflict sharper. Disparities in education, age (and therefore career expectations), and cultural bias are of special interest.

The twelve Old Sides who moved to expel the revivalist radicals in 1741 have sometimes been labeled the "Scotch-Irish" party for good reason. Nine were born in Northern Ireland, and two in Scotland (the birthplace of the twelfth is unknown). All were educated abroad, mainly in Scotland, and especially at the University of Glasgow. Most came to the colonies between the ages of twenty-eight and thirty-two, after having completed their education. The typical Old Side clergyman was about forty-two at the time of the schism. The New Side ministers who formed the Synod of New York in 1745 numbered twenty-two. Of the twenty-one whose places of birth can be ascertained, ten were born in New England or on eastern Long Island, one in Newark, New Jersey, eight in Northern Ireland (including Gilbert, William, Jr., and Charles Tennent), one in Scotland, and one in England. Most of those born abroad emigrated to the colonies during their middle teens; Charles Tennent was but seven, and the oldest was William Robinson, the son of an English Quaker doctor, who emigrated at about twenty-eight after an ill-spent youth. The educational profile of the New Side preachers is in striking contrast to that of the Old. Of the twenty-two, nine received degrees from Yale College, two were Harvard men, and ten were educated at the Log College. One had probably gone to a Scottish university. The typical New Side minister was about thirty-two at the time of the schism, or a decade younger than his Old Side counterpart.

Several tendencies suggest themselves. The Old Sides, more mature than their adversaries, were also more settled in their professional careers; further, their Scottish education and early professional experiences in Ulster may have instilled a respect for discipline and ecclesiastical order that could not easily be cast aside. They knew it was difficult to keep up standards in provincial societies, especially the heterodox Middle Colonies where competition in religion, as in everything else, was a constant challenge to good order. Still, it was irritating to be treated as intruders by the resident notables, or by such as the Anglicans, who pretended to look down on the Presbyterians as "men of small talents and mean education." There was security in knowing that the first generation of Presbyterian leaders had been educated and licensed in accordance with the most exacting Old World criteria. But the tradition must be continued, for succeeding generations would gain respect only if the ministry were settled on a firm professional base. Though Harvard and Yale were not Edinburgh and Glasgow, they did pattern their curricula after the British universities and to that extent could serve until the Presbyterian Church was able to establish a college of its own. And only if Presbyterian leaders could control the education and admission of candidates to the ministry might they hold their heads high among rival religious groups. A professional ministry was thus crucial to the "Scotch-Irish" party's pride and sense of place.

The New Side party, on the other hand, cared less about professional niceties than about converting sinners. Its members were at the beginning of their careers, and most, being native-born or coming to the colonies in their youth, were not so likely to be imbued with an Old World sense of prerogative and order. They never doubted that an educated clergy was essential, but education had to be of the right sort. By the 1730s Harvard and Yale were being guided, in their view, by men of rationalist leanings who simply did not provide the type of training wanted by the revivalists. Thus the New Sides chafed against the controls favored by their more conservative elders, controls that restricted their freedom of action, slowed their careers, and were in their opinion out of touch with New World ways.

The anti-institutionalism of the revivalists caused some critics to portray them as social levellers, though there were no significant distinctions in social outlook or family background between Old and New Sides. But as with any insurgent group that relies in part on public support for its momentum, the New Sides tended to clothe their appeals in popular dress. At every opportunity they pictured the opposers as "the Noble & Mighty" elders of the church, and identified themselves with the poor and "common People"—images reinforced by the Old Sides' references to the evangelists' followers as an ignorant and "wild Rabble."

The revivalists may not have been deliberate social levellers, but their words and actions had the effect of emphasizing individual values over hierarchical ones. Everything they did, from disrupting orderly processes and encouraging greater lay participation in church government, to promoting mass assemblies and the physical closeness that went with them, raised popular emotions. Most important, they insisted that there were choices, and that the individual himself was free to make them.

The people, it might be suspected, had been waiting for this. The long years of imposed consensus and oversight by the Kirk had taken their toll, and undercurrents of restlessness had strengthened as communities stabilized and Old World values receded. Still, the habit of deferring to the clergy was deeply rooted in Presbyterian culture, making inertia an accomplice of church authority. By 1740, however, with the clergy themselves, or a part of them, openly promoting rebellion, many Presbyterians "in imitation of their example," as it was said, joined the fray. The result was turbulence, shattered and divided congregations, and a rash of slanderous reports against Old Side clergymen. Most such charges were either proved false or are deeply suspect, owing to their connection with the factional conflict. But aspersions against the ministerial character had now become a subject of public debate, suggesting that the schisms of the Awakening were effectively challenging the old structures of authority. . . .

So volatile had the revival become that it could no longer be contained within a single region. Thus when George Whitefield carried the crusade northward, the tumults and divisions that had seized the Presbyterian Church spread to the Congregational meetinghouses of New England.

The "Divine Fire" Kindled in New England

Whitefield's initial visit to Boston in September 1740 was greeted with tremendous interest, for the "Grand Itinerant" was the first figure of international renown to tour the colonies. During an eleven-day period he preached at least nineteen times at a number of different churches and outdoor sites, including New South Church where the huge crowd was thrown into such a panic that five were killed and many more injured. Fifteen thousand persons supposedly heard Whitefield preach on Boston Common. Even allowing for an inflated count, these were surely the largest crowds ever assembled in Boston or any other colonial city. As Samuel Johnson once said, Whitefield would have been adored if he wore a nightcap and preached from a tree. Whitefield's tours outside of Boston, and then into western Massachusetts and Connecticut, were attended by similar public outpourings. No one, it seems, wanted to miss the show. In December Gilbert Tennent arrived in Boston, having been urged by Whitefield to add more fuel to the divine fires he had kindled there. Tennent's preaching, which lacked Whitefield's sweetness but none of his power, aroused a popular fervor that matched or exceeded that inspired by the Englishman.

Most Congregational ministers, including those at Boston, had welcomed Whitefield's tour as an opportunity to stimulate religious piety. Tennent's torrid preaching may have discomfited some, but it was not until 1742 that three events led to a polarization of the clergy into "New Light" supporters and "Old Light" opposers of the Great Awakening. First came the publication in

Boston of Tennent's sermon, *The Danger of an Unconverted Ministry,* which one Old Light would later blame for having "sown the Seeds of all that Discord, Intrusion, Confusion, Separation, Hatred, Variance, Emulations, Wrath, Strife, Seditions, Heresies, &c. that have been springing up in so many of the Towns and Churches thro' the Province...." Another was the publication of White-field's 1740 *Journal,* in which he criticized "most" New England preachers for insufficient piety and observed of Harvard and Yale that "their Light is become Darkness." The final provocation was the arrival in Boston on June 25, 1742 of the Reverend James Davenport, a newly fledged evangelist who already had Connecticut in an uproar and would soon have all Boston by the ears.

Davenport had been expelled from Connecticut on June 3 after being adjudged "disturbed in the rational Faculties of his Mind." Now the twenty-six-year-old evangelist was determined to share his special insights with the people of Boston. Forewarned about Davenport's odd behavior, the ministers of Boston and Charlestown (the majority of whom favored the Awakening) requested that the intruder restrain his "assuming Behavior ... especially in judging the spiritual State of Pastors and People," and decided not to offer him their pulpits. Davenport was undeterred. He preached on the Common and in the rain on Copp's Hill; he proclaimed first three and then nine more of Boston's ministers "by name" to be unconverted; and he announced that he was "ready to drop down dead for the salvation of but one soul." Davenport was followed, according to one critic, by a "giddy Audience ... chiefly made up of idle or ignorant Persons" of low rank. To some of Boston's soberer citizens the crowd appeared "menacing," and one newspaper essayist found Davenport's followers "so red hot, that I verily believe they would make nothing to kill Opposers." Such was the anarchy threatened by religious enthusiasm....

In the months that followed, New Englanders, like middle-colony Presbyterians before them, would witness and then be drawn into a fierce struggle between the two factions, as their once-decorous ministers impugned the intelligence and integrity of their rivals in public sermons and essays. The Old Light writers were especially bellicose, losing no opportunity to rebuke the "enthusiastic, factious, censorious Spirit" of the revivalists. Schisms were threatened everywhere, and as early as 1742 some congregations had "divided into Parties, and openly and scandalously separated from one another." As the Connecticut Old Light, Isaac Stiles, warned, the subversion of all order was threatened when "Contempt is cast upon Authority both Civil and Ecclesiastical." Most distressing to those who believed that "Good Order is the Strength and Beauty of the World," was the Awakening's tendency to splinter New England society. "Formerly the People could bear with each other in Charity when they differ'd in Opinion," recalled one writer, "but they now break Fellowship and Communion with one another on that Account."

Indeed, awakened parishioners were repeatedly urged to withdraw from a "corrupt ministry." "O that the precious Seed might be preserved and *separated* from all gross Mixtures!" prayed the Connecticut New Light Jonathan Parsons. And spurred on by Parsons and other New Lights, withdraw they did. In Plymouth and Ipswich, from Maine to the Connecticut River Valley, the New England separatist movement gained momentum from 1743 onward....

The Great Awakening, as Richard Hofstadter put it, was "the first major intercolonial crisis of the mind and spirit" in eighteenth-century America. No previous occurrence in colonial history compared with it in scale or consequences. True, the floodtide of evangelical fervor soon subsided, but nothing could quite restore the old cultural landscape. The unitary ideal of the seventeenth century continued to be eroded in the post-Awakening years by further church separations. Moreover, as the Reverend William Shurtleff noted in 1745, the "dividing Spirit is not confin'd to those that are Friends" of the revival. Nor was it confined to the religious sphere. That "dividing Spirit" would be manifested everywhere after mid-century in the proliferation of religious and political factions.

NO

Enthusiasm Described and Decried: The Great Awakening as Interpretative Fiction

In the last half century, the Great Awakening has assumed a major role in explaining the political and social evolution of prerevolutionary American society. Historians have argued, variously, that the Awakening severed intellectual and philosophical connections between America and Europe (Perry Miller), that it was a major vehicle of early lower-class protest (John C. Miller, Rhys Isaac, and Gary B. Nash), that it was a means by which New England Puritans became Yankees (Richard L. Bushman), that it was the first "intercolonial movement" to stir "the people of several colonies on a matter of common emotional concern" (Richard Hofstadter following William Warren Sweet), or that it involved "a rebirth of the localistic impulse" (Kenneth Lockridge).

American historians also have increasingly linked the Awakening directly to the Revolution. Alan Heimert has tagged it as the source of a Calvinist political ideology that irretrievably shaped eighteenth-century American society and the Revolution it produced. Harry S. Stout has argued that the Awakening stimulated a new system of mass communications that increased the colonists' political awareness and reduced their deference to elite groups prior to the Revolution. Isaac and Nash have described the Awakening as the source of a simpler, non-Calvinist protest rhetoric that reinforced revolutionary ideology in disparate places, among them Virginia and the northern port cities. William G. McLoughlin has even claimed that the Great Awakening was nothing less than "the Key to the American Revolution."

These claims for the significance of the Great Awakening come from more than specialists in the colonial period. They are a ubiquitous feature of American history survey texts, where the increased emphasis on social history has made these claims especially useful in interpreting early American society to twentieth-century students. Virtually all texts treat the Great Awakening as a major watershed in the maturation of prerevolutionary American society. *The Great Republic* terms the Awakening "the greatest event in the history of religion in eighteenth-century America." *The National Experience* argues that the Awakening brought "religious experiences to thousands of people in every rank of society" and in every region. *The Essentials of American History* stresses how the

From Jon Butler, "Enthusiasm Described and Decried: The Great Awakening as Interpretative Fiction," *The Journal of American History,* vol. 69 (September 1982), pp. 305–314. Copyright © 1982 by The Organization of American Historians. Reprinted by permission of *The Journal of American History.* Notes omitted.

Awakening "aroused a spirit of humanitarianism," "encouraged the notion of equal rights," and "stimulated feelings of democracy" even if its gains in church membership proved episodic. These texts and others describe the weakened position of the clergy produced by the Awakening as symptomatic of growing disrespect for all forms of authority in the colonies and as an important catalyst, even cause, of the American Revolution. The effect of these claims is astonishing. Buttressed by the standard lecture on the Awakening tucked into most survey courses, American undergraduates have been well trained to remember the Great Awakening because their instructors and texts have invested it with such significance.

Does the Great Awakening warrant such enthusiasm? Its puzzling historiography suggests one caution. The Awakening has received surprisingly little systematic study and lacks even one comprehensive general history. The two studies, by Heimert and Cedric B. Cowing, that might qualify as general histories actually are deeply centered in New England. They venture into the middle and southern colonies only occasionally and concentrate on intellectual themes to the exclusion of social history. The remaining studies are thoroughly regional, as in the case of books by Bushman, Edwin Scott Gaustad, Charles Hartshorn Maxson, Dietmar Rothermund, and Wesley M. Gewehr, or are local, as with the spate of articles on New England towns and Jonathan Edwards or Isaac's articles and book on Virginia. The result is that the general character of the Great Awakening lacks sustained, comprehensive study even while it benefits from thorough local examinations. The relationship between the Revolution and the Awakening is described in an equally peculiar manner. Heimert's seminal 1966 study, despite fair and unfair criticism, has become that kind of influential work whose awesome reputation apparently discourages further pursuit of its subject. Instead, historians frequently allude to the positive relationship between the Awakening and the Revolution without probing the matter in a fresh, systematic way.

The gap between the enthusiasm of historians for the social and political significance of the Great Awakening and its slim, peculiar historiography raises two important issues. First, contemporaries never homogenized the eighteenth-century colonial religious revivals by labeling them "the Great Awakening." Although such words appear in Edwards's *Faithful Narrative of the Surprising Work of God,* Edwards used them alternately with other phrases, such as "general awakening," "great alteration," and "flourishing of religion," only to describe the Northampton revivals of 1734–1735. He never capitalized them or gave them other special emphasis and never used the phrase "the Great Awakening" to evaluate all the prerevolutionary revivals. Rather, the first person to do so was the nineteenth-century historian and antiquarian Joseph Tracy, who used Edwards's otherwise unexceptional words as the title of his famous 1842 book, *The Great Awakening.* Tellingly, however, Tracy's creation did not find immediate favor among American historians. Charles Hodge discussed the Presbyterian revivals in his *Constitutional History of the Presbyterian Church* without describing them as part of a "Great Awakening," while the influential Robert Baird refused even to treat the eighteenth-century revivals as discrete and important events, much less label them "the Great Awakening." Baird all but ignored these revivals in the chronological segments of his *Religion in America* and mentioned them elsewhere only by way of explaining the intellectual origins of the Unitarian movement, whose early leaders opposed revivals. Thus, not until the last half of the nineteenth century did "the Great Awakening" become a familiar feature of the American historical landscape.

Second, this particular label ought to be viewed with suspicion, not because a historian created it—historians legitimately make sense of the minutiae of the past by utilizing such devices—but because the label itself does serious injustice to the minutiae it orders. The label "the Great Awakening" distorts the extent, nature, and cohesion of the revivals that did exist in the eighteenth-century colonies, encourages unwarranted claims for their effects on colonial society, and exaggerates their influence on the coming and character of the American Revolution. If "the Great Awakening" is not quite an American Donation of Constantine, its appeal to historians seeking to explain the shaping and character of prerevolutionary American society gives it a political and intellectual power whose very subtlety requires a close inspection of its claims to truth.

How do historians describe "the Great Awakening"? Three points seem especially common. First, all but a few describe it as a Calvinist religious revival in which converts acknowledged their sinfulness without expecting salvation. These colonial converts thereby distinguished themselves from Englishmen caught up in contemporary Methodist revivals and from Americans involved in the so-called Second Great Awakening of the early national period, both of which imbibed Arminian principles that allowed humans to believe they might effect their own salvation in ways that John Calvin discounted. Second, historians emphasize the breadth and suddenness of the Awakening and frequently employ hurricane metaphors to reinforce the point. Thus, many of them describe how in the 1740s the Awakening "swept" across the mainland colonies, leaving only England's Caribbean colonies untouched. Third, most historians argue that this spiritual hurricane affected all facets of prerevolutionary society. Here they adopt Edwards's description of the 1736 Northampton revival as one that touched "all sorts, sober and vicious, high and low, rich and poor, wise and unwise," but apply it to all the colonies. Indeed, some historians go farther and view the Great Awakening as a veritable social and political revolution itself. Writing in the late 1960s, Bushman could only wonder at its power: "We inevitably will underestimate the effect of the Awakening on eighteenth-century society if we compare it to revivals today. The Awakening was more like the civil rights demonstrations, the campus disturbances, and the urban riots of the 1960s combined. All together these may approach, though certainly not surpass, the Awakening in their impact on national life."

No one would seriously question the existence of "the Great Awakening" if historians only described it as a short-lived Calvinist revival in New England during the early 1740s. Whether stimulated by Edwards, James Davenport, or the British itinerant George Whitefield, the New England revivals between 1740 and 1745 obviously were Calvinist ones. Their sponsors vigorously criticized the soft-core Arminianism that had reputedly overtaken New England Congregationalism, and they stimulated the ritual renewal of a century-old society by reintroducing colonists to the theology of distinguished seventeenth-century Puritan clergymen, especially Thomas Shepard and Solomon Stoddard.

Yet, Calvinism never dominated the eighteenth-century religious revivals homogenized under the label "the Great Awakening." The revivals in the middle colonies flowed from especially disparate and international sources. John B. Frantz's recent traversal of the German revivals there demonstrates that they took root in Lutheranism, German Reformed Calvinism (different from the New England variety), and Pietism (however one wants to define it). Maxson stressed the mysticism, Pietism, Rosicrucianism, and Freemasonry rampant in these colonies among both German and English settlers. In an often overlooked observation, Maxson noted that the Tennents' backing for revivals was deeply linked to a mystical experience surrounding the near death of John Tennent and that both John Tennent and William Tennent, Jr., were mystics as well as Calvinists. The revivals among English colonists in Virginia also reveal eclectic roots. Presbyterians brought Calvinism into the colony for the first time since the 1650s, but Arminianism underwrote the powerful Methodist awakening in the colony and soon crept into the ranks of the colony's Baptists as well.

"The Great Awakening" also is difficult to date. Seldom has an "event" of such magnitude had such amorphous beginnings and endings. In New England, historians agree, the revivals flourished principally between 1740 and 1743 and largely ended by 1745, although a few scattered outbreaks of revivalism occurred there in the next decades. Establishing the beginning of the revivals has proved more difficult, however. Most historians settle for the year 1740 because it marks Whitefield's first appearance in New England. But everyone acknowledges that earlier revivals underwrote Whitefield's enthusiastic reception there and involved remarkable numbers of colonists. Edwards counted thirty-two towns caught up in revivals in 1734–1735 and noted that his own grandfather, Stoddard, had conducted no less than five "harvests" in Northampton before that, the earliest in the 1690s. Yet revivals in Virginia, the site of the most sustained such events in the southern colonies, did not emerge in significant numbers until the 1750s and did not peak until the 1760s. At the same time, they also continued into the revolutionary and early national periods in ways that make them difficult to separate from their predecessors.

Yet even if one were to argue that "the Great Awakening" persisted through most of the eighteenth century, it is obvious that revivals "swept" only some of the mainland colonies. They occurred in Massachusetts, Connecticut, Rhode Island, Pennsylvania, New Jersey, and Virginia with some frequency at least at some points between 1740 and 1770. But New Hampshire, Maryland, and Georgia witnessed few revivals in the same years, and revivals were only occasionally important in New York, Delaware, North Carolina, and South Carolina. The revivals also touched only certain segments of the population in the colonies where they occurred. The best example of the phenomenon is Pennsylvania. The revivals there had a sustained effect among English settlers only in Presbyterian churches where many of the laity and clergy also opposed them. The Baptists, who were so important to the New England revivals, paid little attention to them until the 1760s, and the colony's taciturn Quakers watched them in perplexed silence. Not even Germans imbibed them universally. At the same time that Benjamin Franklin was emptying his pockets in response to the preaching of Whitefield in Philadelphia—or at least claiming to do so—the residents of Germantown were steadily leaving their churches, and Stephanie Grauman Wolf reports that they remained steadfast in their indifference to Christianity at least until the 1780s.

Whitefield's revivals also exchanged notoriety for substance. Colonists responded to him as a charismatic performer, and he actually fell victim to the Billy Graham syndrome of modern times: his visits, however exciting, produced few permanent changes in local religious patterns. For example, his appearances in Charleston led to his well-known confrontation with Anglican Commissary Alexander Garden and to the suicide two years later of a distraught follower named Anne LeBrasseur. Yet they produced no new congregations in Charleston and had no documented effect on the general patterns of religious adherence elsewhere in the colony. The same was true in Philadelphia and New York City despite the fact that Whitefield preached to enormous crowds in both places. Only Bostonians responded differently. Supporters organized in the late 1740s a new "awakened" congregation that reputedly met with considerable initial success, and opponents adopted a defensive posture exemplified in the writings of Charles Chauncy that profoundly affected New England intellectual life for two decades.

Historians also exaggerate the cohesion of leadership in the revivals. They have accomplished this, in part, by overstressing the importance of Whitefield and Edwards. Whitefield's early charismatic influence later faded so that his appearances in the 1750s and 1760s had less impact even among evangelicals than they had in the 1740s. In addition, Whitefield's "leadership" was ethereal, at best, even before 1750. His principal early importance was to serve as a personal model of evangelical enterprise for ministers wishing to promote their own revivals of religion. Because he did little to organize and coordinate integrated colonial revivals, he also failed to exercise significant authority over the ministers he inspired.

The case against Edwards's leadership of the revivals is even clearer. Edwards defended the New England revivals from attack. But, like Whitefield, he never organized and coordinated revivals throughout the colonies or even throughout New England. Since most of his major works were not printed in his lifetime, even his intellectual leadership in American theology occurred in the century after his death. Whitefield's lack of knowledge about Edwards on his first tour of America in 1739–1740 is especially telling on this point. Edwards's name does not appear in Whitefield's journal prior to the latter's visit to Northampton in 1740, and Whitefield did not make the visit until Edwards had invited him to do so. Whitefield certainly knew of Edwards and the 1734–1735 Northampton revival but associated the town mainly with the pastorate of Edwards's grandfather Stoddard. As Whitefield described the visit in his journal: "After a little refreshment, we crossed the ferry to Northampton, where no less than three hundred souls were saved about five years ago. Their pastor's name is Edwards, successor and grandson to the great Stoddard, whose memory will be always precious to my soul, and whose books entitled 'A Guide to Christ,' and 'Safety of Appearing in Christ's Righteousness,' I would recommend to all."

What were the effects of the prerevolutionary revivals of religion? The claims for their religious and secular impact need pruning too. One area of concern involves the relationship between the revivals and the rise of the Dissenting denominations in the colonies. Denomination building was intimately linked to the revivals in New England. There, as C. C. Goen has demonstrated, the revivals of the 1740s stimulated formation of over two hundred new congregations and several new denominations. This was accomplished mainly through a negative process called "Separatism," which split existing Congregationalist and Baptist churches along prorevival and antirevival lines. But Separatism was of no special consequence in increasing the number of Dissenters farther south. Presbyterians, Baptists, and, later, Methodists gained strength from former Anglicans who left their state-supported churches, but they won far more recruits among colonists who claimed no previous congregational membership.

Still, two points are important in assessing the importance of revivals to the expansion of the Dissenting denominations in the colonies. First, revivalism never was the key to the expansion of the colonial churches. Presbyterianism expanded as rapidly in the middle colonies between 1710 and 1740 as between 1740 and 1770. Revivalism scarcely produced the remarkable growth that the Church of England experienced in the eighteenth century unless, of course, it won the favor of colonists who opposed revivals as fiercely as did its leaders. Gaustad estimates that between 1700 and 1780 Anglican congregations expanded from about one hundred to four hundred, and Bruce E. Steiner has outlined extraordinary Anglican growth in the Dissenting colony of Connecticut although most historians describe the colony as being thoroughly absorbed by the revivals and "Separatism."

Second, the expansion of the leading evangelical denominations, Presbyterians and Baptists, can be traced to many causes, not just revivalism or "the Great Awakening." The growth of the colonial population from fewer than three hundred thousand in 1700 to over two million in 1770 made the expansion of even the most modestly active denominations highly likely. This was especially true because so many new colonists did not settle in established communities but in new communities that lacked religious institutions. As Timothy L. Smith has written of seventeenth-century settlements, the new eighteenth-century settlements welcomed congregations as much for the social functions they performed as for their religious functions. Some of the denominations reaped the legacy of Old World religious ties among new colonists, and others benefited from local anti-Anglican sentiment, especially in the Virginia and Carolina backcountry. As a result, evangelical organizers formed many congregations in the middle and southern colonies without resorting to revivals at all. The first Presbyterian congregation in Hanover County, Virginia, organized by Samuel Blair and William Tennent, Jr., in 1746, rested on an indigenous lay critique of Anglican theology that had turned residents to the works of Martin Luther, and after the campaign by Blair and Tennent, the congregation allied itself with the Presbyterian denomination rather than with simple revivalism.

The revivals democratized relations between ministers and the laity only in minimal ways. A significant number of New England ministers changed their preaching styles as a result of the 1740 revivals. Heimert quotes Isaac Backus on the willingness of evangelicals to use sermons to "insinuate themselves into the affections' of the people" and notes how opponents of the revivals like Chauncy nonetheless struggled to incorporate emotion and "sentiment" into their sermons after 1740. Yet revivalists and evangelicals continued to draw sharp distinctions between the rights of ministers and the duties of the laity. Edwards did so in a careful, sophisticated way in *Some Thoughts concerning the Present Revival of Religion in New England*. Although he noted that "disputing, jangling, and contention" surrounded "lay exhorting," he agreed that "some exhorting is a Christian duty." But he quickly moved to a strong defense of ministerial prerogatives, which he introduced with the proposition that "the Common people in exhorting one another ought not to clothe themselves with the like authority, with that which is proper for ministers." Gilbert Tennent was less cautious. In his 1740 sermon *The Danger of an Unconverted Ministry*, he bitterly attacked "Pharisee-shepherds" and "Pharisee-teachers" whose preaching was frequently as "unedifying" as their personal lives. But Gilbert Tennent never attacked the ministry itself. Rather, he argued for the necessity of a *converted* ministry precisely because he believed that only preaching brought men and women to Christ and that only ordained ministers could preach. Thus, in both 1742 and 1757, he thundered against lay preachers. They were "of dreadful consequence to the Church's peace and soundness in principle.... [F]or Ignorant Young Converts to take upon them authoritatively to Instruct and Exhort publickly tends to introduce the greatest Errors and the greatest anarchy and confusion."

The 1740 revival among Presbyterians in New Londonderry, Pennsylvania, demonstrates well how ministers shepherded the laity into a revival and how the laity followed rather than led. It was Blair, the congregation's minister, who first criticized "dead Formality in Religion" and brought the congregation's members under "deep convictions" of their "natural unregenerate state." Blair stimulated "soul exercises" in the laity that included crying and shaking, but he also set limits for these exercises. He exhorted them to "moderate and bound their passions" so that the revival would not be destroyed by its own methods. Above this din, Blair remained a commanding, judgmental figure who stimulated the laity's hopes for salvation but remained "very cautious of expressing to People my Judgment of the Goodness of their States, excepting where I had pretty clear Evidences from them, of their being savingly changed." ...

Nor did the revivals change the structure of authority within the denominations. New England Congregationalists retained the right of individual congregations to fire ministers, as when Northampton dismissed Edwards in 1750. But in both the seventeenth and eighteenth centuries, these congregations seldom acted alone. Instead, they nearly always consulted extensively with committees of ordained ministers when firing as well as when hiring ministers. In the middle colonies, however, neither the prorevival Synod of New York nor the antirevival Synod of Philadelphia tolerated such independence in congregations whether in theory or in practice. In both synods, unhappy congregations had to convince special committees appointed by the synods and composed exclusively of ministers that the performance of a fellow cleric was sufficiently dismal to warrant his dismissal. Congregations that acted independently in such matters quickly found themselves censured, and they usually lost the aid of both synods in finding and installing new ministers.

Did the revivals stir lower-class discontent, increase participation in politics, and promote democracy in society generally if not in the congregations? Even in New England the answer is, at best, equivocal. Historians have laid to rest John C. Miller's powerfully stated argument of the 1930s that the revivals were, in good part, lower-class protests against dominant town elites. The revivals indeed complicated local politics because they introduced new sources of potential and real conflict into the towns. New England towns accustomed to containing tensions inside a single congregation before 1730 sometimes had to deal with tensions within and between as many as three or four congregations after 1730. Of course, not all of these religious groups were produced by the revivals, and, as Michael Zuckerman has pointed out, some towns never tolerated the new dissidents and used the "warning out" system to eject them. Still, even where it existed, tumult should not be confused with democracy. Social class, education, and wealth remained as important after 1730 in choosing town and church officers as they had been before 1730, and Edward M. Cook, Jr., notes that after 1730 most new revival congregations blended into the old order: "dissenters [took] their place in town affairs once they stopped threatening the community and symbolically became loyal members of it." . . .

What, then, ought we to say about the revivals of religion in prerevolutionary America? The most important suggestion is the most drastic. Historians should abandon the term "the Great Awakening" because it distorts the character of eighteenth-century American religious life and misinterprets its relationship to prerevolutionary American society and politics. In religion it is a deus ex machina that falsely homogenizes the heterogeneous; in politics it falsely unites the colonies in slick preparation for the Revolution. Instead, a four-part model of the eighteenth-century colonial revivals will highlight their common features, underscore important differences, and help us assess their real significance.

First, with one exception, the prerevolutionary revivals should be understood primarily as regional events that occurred in only half the colonies. Revivals occurred intermittently in New England between 1690 and 1745 but became especially common between 1735 and 1745. They were uniformly Calvinist and produced more significant local political ramifications—even if they did not democratize New England—than other colonial revivals except those in Virginia. Revivals in the middle colonies occurred primarily between 1740 and 1760. They had remarkably eclectic theological origins, bypassed large numbers of settlers, were especially weak in New York, and produced few demonstrable political and social changes. Revivals in the southern colonies did not occur in significant numbers until the 1750s, when they were limited largely to Virginia, missed Maryland almost entirely, and did not occur with any regularity in the Carolinas until well after 1760. Virginia's Baptist revivalists stimulated major political and social changes in the colony, but the secular importance of the other revivals has been exaggerated. A fourth set of revivals, and the exception to the regional pattern outlined here, accompanied the preaching tours of the Anglican itinerant Whitefield. These tours frequently intersected with the regional revivals in progress at different times in New England, the middle colonies, and some parts of the southern colonies, but even then the fit was imperfect. Whitefield's tours produced some changes in ministerial speaking styles but few permanent alterations in institutional patterns of religion, although his personal charisma supported no less than seven tours of the colonies between 1740 and his death in Newburyport, Massachusetts, in 1770.

Second, the prerevolutionary revivals occurred in the colonial backwaters of Western society where they were part of a long-term pattern of erratic movements for spiritual renewal and revival that had long characterized Western Christianity and Protestantism since its birth two centuries earlier. Thus, their theological origins were international and diverse rather than narrowly Calvinist and uniquely American. Calvinism was important in some revivals, but Arminianism and Pietism supported others. This theological heterogeneity also makes it impossible to isolate a single overwhelmingly important cause of the revivals. Instead, they appear to have arisen when three circumstances were present—internal demands for renewal in different international Christian communities, charismatic preachers, and special, often unique, local circumstances that made communities receptive to elevated religious rhetoric.

Third, the revivals had modest effects on colonial religion. This is not to say that they were "conservative" because they did not always uphold the traditional religious order. But they were never radical, whatever their critics claimed. For example, the revivals reinforced ministerial rather than lay authority even as they altered some clergymen's perceptions of their tasks and methods. They also stimulated the demand for organization, order, and authority in the evangelical denominations. Presbyterian "New Lights" repudiated the conservative Synod of Philadelphia because its discipline was too weak, not too strong, and demanded tougher standards for ordination and subsequent service. After 1760, when Presbyterians and Baptists utilized revivalism as part of their campaigns for denominational expansion, they only increased their stress on central denominational organization and authority.

Indeed, the best test of the benign character of the revivals is to take up the challenge of contemporaries who linked them to "outbreaks of enthusiasm" in Europe. In making these charges, the two leading antirevivalists in the colonies, Garden of Charleston and Chauncy of Boston, specifically compared the colonial revivals with those of the infamous "French Prophets" of London, exiled Huguenots who were active in the city between 1706 and about 1730. The French Prophets predicted the downfall of English politicians, raised followers from the dead, and used women extensively as leaders to prophesy and preach. By comparison, the American revivalists were indeed "conservative." They prophesied only about the millennium, not about local politicians, and described only the necessity, not the certainty, of salvation. What is most important is that they eschewed radical change in the position of women in the churches. True, women experienced dramatic conversions, some of the earliest being described vividly by Edwards. But, they preached only irregularly, rarely prophesied, and certainly never led congregations, denominations, or sects in a way that could remotely approach their status among the French Prophets.

Fourth, the link between the revivals and the American Revolution is virtually nonexistent. The relationship between prerevolutionary political change and the revivals is weak everywhere except in Virginia, where the Baptist revivals indeed shattered the exclusive, century-old Anglican hold on organized religious activity and politics in the colony. But, their importance to the Revolution is weakened by the fact that so many members of Virginia's Anglican aristocracy also led the Revolution. In other colonies the revivals furnished little revolutionary rhetoric, including even millennialist thought, that was not available from other sources and provided no unique organizational mechanisms for anti-British protest activity. They may have been of some importance in helping colonists make moral judgments about eighteenth-century English politics, though colonists unconnected to the revivals made these judgments as well.

In the main, then, the revivals of religion in eighteenth-century America emerge as nearly perfect mirrors of a regionalized, provincial society. They arose erratically in different times and places across a century from the 1690s down to the time of the Revolution. Calvinism underlay some of them, Pietism and Arminianism others. Their leadership was local and, at best, regional, and they helped reinforce—but were not the key to—the proliferation and expansion of still-regional Protestant denominations in the colonies. As such, they created no intercolonial religious institutions and fostered no significant experiential unity in the colonies. Their social and political effects were minimal and usually local, although they could traumatize communities in which they upset, if only temporarily, familiar patterns of worship and social behavior. But the congregations they occasionally produced usually blended into the traditional social system, and the revivals abated without shattering its structure. Thus, the revivals of religion in prerevolutionary America seldom became proto-revolutionary, and they failed to change the timing, causes, or effects of the Revolution in any significant way.

Of course, it is awkward to write about the eighteenth-century revivals of religion in America as erratic, heterogeneous, and politically benign. All of us have walked too long in the company of Tracy's "Great Awakening" to make our journey into the colonial past without it anything but frightening. But as Chauncy wrote of the Whitefield revivals, perhaps now it is time for historians "to see that Things have been carried too far, and that the Hazard is great ... lest we should be over-run with *Enthusiasm*."

POSTSCRIPT

Was There a Great Awakening in Mid-Eighteenth-Century America?

Butler's critique of efforts to link the Great Awakening with the American Revolution is part of a longstanding debate. He suggests that there is not enough evidence to support, for example, William McLoughlin's thesis that the revivals were a "key" that opened the door to the War for Independence. He emphasizes the regional element in revivalist activities, suggesting that they did not have a broad impact. If Butler is correct, however, there is still room to argue that the Revolution was not without its religious elements.

In his book *Religion in America: Past and Present* (Prentice Hall, 1961), Clifton E. Olmstead argues for a broader application of religious causes to the origins of the American Revolution. First, Olmstead contends that the Great Awakening did foster a sense of community among American colonists, thus providing the unity required for an organized assault on English control. Moreover, the Great Awakening further weakened existing ties between the colonies and England by drawing adherents of the Church of England into the evangelical denominations that expanded as a result of revivalistic Protestantism. Second, tensions were generated by the demand that an Anglican bishop be established in the colonies. Many evangelicals found in this plan evidence that the British government wanted further control over the colonies. Third, the Quebec Act, enacted by Parliament in 1774, not only angered American colonists by nullifying their claims to western lands, but it also heightened religious prejudice in the colonies by granting tolerance to Roman Catholics. Fourth, ministers played a significant role in encouraging their parishioners to support the independence movement. Finally, many of the revolutionaries, imbued with the American sense of mission, believed that God was ordaining their activities.

Further support for each of these views can be found in Rhys Isaac, *The Transformation of Virginia, 1740–1790* (University of North Carolina Press, 1982); Ruth H. Bloch, *Visionary Republic* (Cambridge University Press, 1985); and Harry S. Stout, *The New England Soul: Preaching and Religious Culture in Colonial New England* (Oxford University Press, 1986). Students interested in further analyses of the Great Awakening should consult Edwin Scott Gaustad, *The Great Awakening in New England* (Peter Smith, 1957) and Marilyn J. Westerkamp, *Triumph of the Laity: Scots-Irish Piety and the Great Awakening, 1625–1760* (Oxford University Press, 1987).

An Internet site devoted to some spiritual leaders of the Great Awakening can be found at http://dylee.keel.econ.ship.edu/ubf/leaders/leaders.htm.

On the Internet . . .

The Constitution of the United States

Sponsored by the National Archives and Records Administration, this site presents a wealth of information on the U.S. Constitution. From here you can link to the biographies of the 55 delegates to the Constitutional Convention, take an in-depth look at the convention and the ratification process, read a transcription of the complete text of the Constitution, and view high-resolution images of each page of the Constitution.

http://www.nara.gov/exhall/charters/constitution/
conmain.html

A Revolutionary People, 1775–1828

Susan Butler, who teaches American and women's history at Cerritos College, has gathered together an impressive list of sites on the revolutionary period. Included are more than two dozen links to sites on Thomas Jefferson.

http://www3.cerritos.edu/sbutler/part2rev.htm

History of Compromise Legislation: An Annotated Chronology

This page links to sources on compromise legislation in the United States, from the Northwest Ordinance in 1787 to the *Dredd Scott* decision in 1856. Much of the focus is on slavery, but it also examines the first two-party system, Indian removal policies of the 1830s, and the First and Second Banks of the United States.

http://www.wfu.edu/~zulick/340/compromise.html

PART 2

Revolution and the New Nation

*T*he American Revolution led to independence from England and to
the establishment of a new nation. As the United States matured, its people and leaders struggled to implement fully the ideals that had sparked
the Revolution. What had been abstractions before the formation of
the new government had to be applied and refined in day-to-day practice. The nature of post–Revolutionary America, government stability,
the transition of power against the backdrop of political factionalism,
and the extension of democracy had to be worked out.

- Was the American Revolution a Conservative Movement?

- Were the Founding Fathers Democratic Reformers?

- Was Thomas Jefferson Committed to Bringing an End to Chattel
  Slavery?

- Was Andrew Jackson's Indian Removal Policy Motivated by
  Humanitarian Impulses?

ISSUE 6

Was the American Revolution a Conservative Movement?

YES: Carl N. Degler, from *Out of Our Past: The Forces That Shaped Modern America*, rev. ed. (Harper & Row, 1970)

NO: Gordon S. Wood, from *The Radicalism of the American Revolution* (Alfred A. Knopf, 1991)

ISSUE SUMMARY

YES: Pulitzer Prize–winning author Carl N. Degler argues that upper-middle-class colonists led a conservative American Revolution that left untouched the prewar economic and social class structure of an upwardly mobile people.

NO: Prize-winning historian Gordon S. Wood argues that the American Revolution was a far-reaching, radical event that produced a unique democratic society in which ordinary people could make money, pursue happiness, and be self-governing.

W as the American Revolution a true revolution? The answer may depend on how the term *revolution* is defined. *Strict constructionists,* for example, perceive revolution as producing significant and deep societal change, while *loose constructionists* define the term as "any resort to violence within a political order to change its constitution, rulers, or policies." Historians agree that American Revolutionaries fulfilled the second definition because they successfully fought a war that resulted in the overthrow of their British rulers and established a government run by themselves. However, historians disagree over the amount of social and economic changes that took place in America.

Early historians did not concern themselves with the social and economic aspects of the American Revolution. They instead argued over the causes of the Revolution and refought the political arguments advanced by the rebelling colonists and the British government. George Bancroft was the first historian to advance the *Whig,* or *pro-American,* interpretation of the war. America won, he said, because God was on our side.

Bancroft's view remained unchallenged until the beginning of the twentieth century, when a group of *imperialist* historians analyzed the Revolution from the perspective of the British empire. These historians tended to be sympathetic to the economic and political difficulties that Great Britain faced in running an empire in the late eighteenth century.

Both the Whig and the imperialist historians assumed that the Revolution was an *external* event whose primary cause was the political differences between the colonists and their British rulers. In 1909, however, historian Carl Becker paved the way for a different interpretation of the Revolution when he concluded in his study of colonial New York that an *internal* revolution had taken place. The American Revolution, said Becker, created a struggle not only for home rule but also one for who should rule at home. This *progressive*, or *conflict*, interpretation dominated most of the writings on the American Revolution from 1910 through 1945. During this time progressive historians searched for the social and economic conflicts among groups struggling for political power.

Since World War II, most professional historians have rejected what they considered to be an oversimplified conflict interpretation of the Revolution by the previous generation of progressive historians. Robert E. Brown, in his studies on colonial Massachusetts and Virginia, argued that America had become a middle-class democracy before the American Revolution. Consequently, Brown maintained, there was no need for a social revolution. Most influential have been the works of Harvard University professor Bernard Bailyn, who used a neoconservative approach in analyzing the Revolution. In his *Ideological Origins of the American Revolution* (Harvard University Press, 1968), Bailyn took ideas seriously once again and saw the colonists implementing the views of radical British thinkers in their struggle for independence. The most recent statement on the American Revolution from the neoconservative perspective is *Becoming America: The Revolution Before 1776* by Jon Butler (Howard University Press, 2000). In it, Butler argues that American colonial society—politically, socially, and economically—was dramatically transformed between 1680 and 1770.

In the first of the following selections, Carl N. Degler argues the neoconservative view of the American Revolution, maintaining that the upper-middle-class colonists led a conservative Revolution that left untouched the prewar economic and social class structure of an upwardly mobile people. This essay is an excellent example of the loose constructionist definition of revolution.

Since the late 1960s, historians have written a great deal about blacks, women, Native Americans, and "ordinary" people. This neoprogressive interpretation of America's past has also made views on the events surrounding the Revolution more complicated. See the collection of articles in *The American Revolution: Explorations in the History of American Radicalism* edited by Alfred F. Young (Northern Illinois University Press, 1976).

Gordon S. Wood has given a new dimension to the neoprogressive studies of the Revolutionary era. In his book *The Radicalism of the American Revolution*, he argues the strict constructionist view that the Revolution produced major social changes. In the second selection, taken from this book, Wood maintains that the American Revolution was a radical event because America was the first nation to hold democratic values, allowing ordinary people to make money, pursue happiness, and rule themselves.

Carl N. Degler  **YES**

A New Kind of Revolution

Conservatives Can Be Innovators

Like fabled genii grown too big to be imprisoned in their bottles, wars and revolutions frequently take on a life of their own irrespective of their first purposes. The overarching considerations of survival or victory distort or enlarge the narrow and limited aims for which the conflict was begun. The American War for Independence was such an event. Begun for only limited political and constitutional purposes, the war released social forces which few of the leaders ever anticipated, but which have helped to mold the American tradition.

One such unforeseen result was the rapid and final disestablishment of the Anglican Church, heretofore the state-supported religion in all of the colonies south of Mason and Dixon's Line and in parts of New York and New Jersey as well.[1] In knocking out the props of the State from beneath the Anglican Church, the states provided the occasion for wider and more fundamental innovations. Virginia in 1786, in disestablishing the Anglican Church, put no other church in its place and instead passed a law guaranteeing religious freedom. This law, with which Madison and Jefferson had so much to do, prepared the ground for the ultimate triumph of the American doctrine of separation of Church and State.

The ratification of the federal Constitution in 1788 constituted the first step in the acceptance of the principle that a man's religion was irrelevant to government, for the Constitution forbade all religious tests for officeholding.[2] Then in 1791, when the first ten amendments were added, Congress was enjoined from legislating in any manner "respecting an establishment of religion or prohibiting the free exercise thereof." These legalistic and now commonplace phrases had centuries of man's religious history packed within them; upon their implementation western Christendom reached a milestone in its long quest for a viable accommodation between man's religious conscience and *raison d'état*.

For millennia a man's religion had been either a passport or a barrier to his freedom and the opportunity to serve his State; it had always mattered how a man worshiped God. Since Emperor Theodosius in the fourth century of the Christian era, religious orthodoxy had been considered necessary for good citizenship and for service to the state. All this weighty precedence was boldly overthrown by Americans in 1789–91 when they erected a government wherein "a man's religious tenets will not forfeit the protection of the Laws nor deprive him of the right of attaining and holding the highest offices that are known in the United States," as George Washington said.

In the course of the early nineteenth century, the federal example of a strict divorce of State and Church was emulated by the individual states. At the time of the Revolution many states had demanded Christian and often Protestant affiliations for officeholding, and some had even retained a state-supported Church. Gradually, however, and voluntarily—Massachusetts was last in 1833—all the states abandoned whatever connections they might have had with the churches. The doctrine of separation has been more deeply implanted in our tradition in the twentieth century by the Supreme Court, which has declared that separation is a freedom guaranteed by the Fourteenth Amendment to the Constitution and therefore obligatory upon the states as well as the federal government. Thus the two extremes of the American political spectrum— the popular state governments and the august Supreme Court—have joined in sanctioning this doctrine born out of the Revolution by the liberalism of the Enlightenment.

It was a remarkably novel and even unique approach to the question of the relation between the State and religion. Although the doctrine repudiates any connection between the State and the Church, the American version has little in common with the practice in countries like revolutionary France and Mexico and atheistic Soviet Russia, where separation has been so hostile to religion as to interfere, at times, with freedom of worship. The American conception is not antireligious at all. Our Presidents invoke the Deity and offer Thanksgiving prayers, our armies and legislatures maintain chaplains, and the state and federal governments encourage religion through the remission of taxes. In America the State was declared to be secular, but it continued to reflect the people's concern with religion. The popular interest in religion was still evident in 1962 and 1963 when the Supreme Court invoked the principle of separation of church and state to ban prayers and Bible-reading from the public schools. In both Congress and the public press there was a loud protest against such a close and allegedly antireligious interpretation of the principle. But efforts to amend the Constitution in order to circumvent the Supreme Court's interpretation failed.

In the eighteenth century the American principle of separation of Church and State was indeed an audacious experiment. Never before had a national state been prepared to dispense with an official religion as a prop to its authority and never before had a church been set adrift without the support of the state. Throughout most of American history the doctrine has provided freedom for religious development while keeping politics free of religion. And that, apparently, had been the intention of the Founding Fathers.

As the principle of the separation of Church and State was a kind of social side effect of the Revolution, so also was the assertion in the Declaration of Independence that "all men are created equal." These five words have been sneered at as idealistic, refuted as manifestly inaccurate, and denied as preposterous, but they have, nonetheless, always been capable of calling forth deep emotional response from Americans. Even in the Revolutionary era, their power was evident. In 1781 the Supreme Judicial Court of Massachusetts declared slavery at an end in that state because it "is inconsistent with our own conduct and Constitution" which "set out with declaring that all men are born free and equal...." The Reverend Samuel Hopkins told the Continental Congress that it was illogical to "be holding so many hundreds of blacks in slavery... while we are maintaining this struggle for our own and our Children's liberty." In 1782 William Binford of Henrico County, Virginia, set free twelve slaves because he was "fully persuaded that freedom is the natural right of all mankind." Another Virginian, a few years later, freed all his slaves which had been "born after the Declaration of Independence." Such efforts to reconcile the theory of the Declaration with the practices of life represent only the beginnings of the disquieting echoes of the celebrated phrase.

It is wrong to assume, however, that the mere inclusion of that phrase in the Declaration worked the mighty influence implied in the foregoing examples; social values are not created so deliberately or so easily. Like so much else in the Declaration, this sentence was actually the distillation of a cherished popular sentiment into a ringing phrase, allegiance to which stemmed from its prior acceptance rather than from its eloquence. The passionate belief in social equality which commentators and travelers in Jacksonian America would later find so powerful was already emergent in this earlier period. Indeed, we have already seen its lineaments during the colonial period. After 1776 the conviction was reinforced by the success of the Revolution and by the words of the great Declaration itself.

It was also supported by the facts of American social life. Despite the lowly position accorded the Negro, wrote the French traveler [Jacques-Pierre] Brissot in 1788, it still must be admitted "that the Americans more than any other people are convinced that all men are born free and equal." Moreover, he added, "we must acknowledge, that they direct themselves generally by this principle of equality." German traveler Johann Schoepf noticed that in Philadelphia "rank of birth is not recognized, is resisted with a total force.... People think, act, and speak here precisely as it prompts them...."[3] And in the privacy of the Federal Convention of 1787, Charles Pinckney of South Carolina urged his fellow delegates to recognize the uniqueness of their country. "There is more equality of rank and fortune in America than in any other country under the sun," he told them.

There were other signs of what an earlier generation would have stigmatized as "leveling tendencies" in the new post-Revolutionary society. The attacks made by the Democratic-Republican societies upon the privileged Order of the Cincinnati, because it was secret and confined to Revolutionary officers and their descendants, were obviously inspired by a growing egalitarian sentiment. French traveler Moreau de Saint-Méry recalled with disgust how Americans proudly told him that the hotel custom of putting strange travelers together in the same bed was "a proof of liberty." By the end of the century old social distinctions like rank-seating in churches and the differentiating title of esquire were fast passing out of vogue. On an economic level, this abiding American faith was translated as equality of opportunity, and here dour Federalist Fisher Ames could lock arms with his Republican opponents when he averred that "all cannot be rich, but all have a right to make the attempt."

Though economic grievances seem to have played a negligible role in bringing on the Revolution, this is not to say that there were no economic consequences. The economic stimulus afforded by the war demands and the freedom from English mercantilistic restrictions which victory made permanent provided adventuresome American merchants and entrepreneurs with wide opportunities for gaining new markets and new sources of profit. The expansion of the American economy, which was to be characteristic all through the nineteenth century, was thus begun.

But even when one has added together the new constitutions, the enlightened religious innovations, and the stimulus to equality, it is quickly apparent that the social consequences of the Revolution were meager indeed. In both purpose and implementation they were not to be equated with the massive social changes which shook France and Russia in later years. For the most part, the society of post-Revolutionary America was but the working out of social forces which were already evident in the colonial period.

It is significant, for example, that no new social class came to power through the door of the American Revolution. The men who engineered the revolt were largely members of the colonial ruling class. Peyton Randolph and Patrick Henry were well-to-do members of the Virginia Assembly; Washington, reputed to be the richest man in America, was an officer in the Virginia militia. The New York leaders John Morin Scott and Robert Livingston were judges on the Supreme Court of the colony, while William Drayton, a fire-eating radical of South Carolina, was a nephew of the lieutenant governor of the province, and himself a member of the Governor's Council until his anti-British activities forced his removal. Certainly Benjamin Franklin, citizen of the Empire, celebrated scientist, and long retired, well-to-do printer, was no submerged member of Philadelphia's society—or London's for that matter. Moreover, Franklin's natural son, William, was a Royal Governor at the outbreak of the Revolution. Hancock of Boston and Christopher Gadsden of Charleston were only two of the many respected and wealthy merchants who lent their support to the patriot cause. In fact, speaking of wealth, the Revolution in Virginia was made and led by the great landed class, and its members remained to reap the benefits. Farther down the social scale, in the backwoods of Massachusetts, it has been shown that the chief revolutionists in the western counties were the old leaders, so that no major shift in leadership took place there either, as a result of the Revolution.

This emphasis on position and wealth among the Revolutionary leaders should not be taken as a denial that many men of wealth and brains left the colonies in the exodus of the Loyalists. Certainly few patriots were the peers of Jared Ingersoll in the law, Jonathan Boucher in the Church, and Thomas Hutchinson and James Galloway in government. But the Loyalist departure did not decapitate the colonial social structure, as some have suggested—it only removed those most attached to the mother country.[4] A large part of the governing class remained to guide the Revolution and reap its favors. It is true, that in the states of Georgia and Pennsylvania, where the radical democrats held sway in the early years of the Revolution, new men seemed to occupy positions of power. But these men were still unknowns on the periphery of government and business, and generally remained there; they cannot be compared with the Robespierres and the Dantons, the Lenins and the Trotskys, of the great continental eruptions.

A convenient gauge of the essential continuity of the governing class in America before and after the Revolution is to be found in an examination of the careers of the signers of the Declaration of Independence. Surely these fifty-five men are important patriot leaders and presumably among the chief beneficiaries of the Revolution they advocated. Yet they were by no means a disadvantaged lot. Fully 40 per cent of them attended college or one of the Inns of Court in England at a time when such a privilege was a rarity. An additional 21 per cent of them came from important families of their respective colonies, or, like Robert Morris and Joseph Hewes, were men of acquired wealth. Over 69 per cent of them held office under the colonial regimes, 29 per cent alone holding some office within the executive branch; truly these were not men held at arm's length from the plums of office.

Most striking about the careers of these men is the fact that so many of them held office before and after the dividing line of the Revolution. Of those who held an office under the state governments after the Revolution, 75 per cent had occupied offices before 1774, proving, if need be, that service in the colonial governments before the Revolution was no obstacle to political preferment for a patriot afterward. If those who held no office before 1774 are not counted—and several might be considered too young to be expected to have held office—then the continuity shows up even more clearly. Eighty-nine per cent of those who filled an office before the Revolution also occupied an office under one of the new state governments. And if federal office after 1789 is included, then the proportion rises to 95 per cent. Add to this the fact that other leaders, not included in the group of signers, had similarly good social backgrounds—men like Washington, Robert Livingston, Gouverneur Morris, Philip Schuyler, and a dozen more—and the conclusion that the Revolution was a thoroughly upper-middle-class affair in leadership and aim is inescapable.

A further and perhaps more important conclusion should be drawn from this analysis of the political careers of the signers after the Revolution. These conservative, upper-class leaders who proclaimed the Revolution suffered no repudiation in the course of the struggle; no mass from the bottom rose and seized control of the Revolutionary situation to direct the struggle into new channels. Rather these men merely shifted, as it were, from their favored status under the colonial regimes to comparable, if not improved, positions after the Revolution.

As a colonial revolt against an alien power, such a development is not surprising. But certainly—for better or for worse—the continuity brought a degree of social and political stability to the new nation rarely associated with the word "revolution" and serves, once again, to illustrate the truly conservative nature of the American revolt.

Similarly, in the redistribution of land, which played such a crucial role in France and Russia, the American Revolution set no example of social motivation or consequence. The Crown's lands, it is true were confiscated, and—of greater import—so were the lands of the proprietors and those of the literally thousands of Tories. But the disposition of these lands hardly constitutes a social revolution of major proportions. One can collect, of course, examples of the breakup of great estates, like the De Lancey manor in New York, which was sold to 275 individuals, or the 40,000-acre estate in North Carolina which was carved into scores of plots averaging 200 acres apiece, or the vast 21,000,000-acre proprietary lands of the Penns. But the more significant question to be answered is who got the land. And, from the studies which have been made, it would appear that most often the land went to speculators or men already possessing substantial acreage, not to the landless or even to the small holder. To be sure, much Tory land which first fell under the auctioneer's hammer to a speculator ultimately found its way into the hands of a yeoman, but such a procedure is a rather slow and orderly process of social revolution.

Furthermore, it is obvious from the Confiscation Acts in the several states and the commissioners who operated pursuant to them that the motive behind the acquisition of Tory lands was enhancement of the state revenues—as, indeed, the original resolution from Congress had suggested. Under such circumstances, pecuniary motives, not democratic theories of society, determined the configuration distribution would take. And it is here that we begin to touch upon the fundamental reason why the confiscation of the royal, proprietary, and Loyalist lands never assumed crucial social importance. Land was just too plentiful in America for these acres to matter. Speculators were loaded down with it; most men who wanted it already possessed it, or were on the way toward possession. One recent investigator of the confiscations in New York, for example, has pointed out that land there could be bought cheaper from speculators than from a former Tory estate.

Even the abolition of primogeniture in all the southern states by 1791 cannot be taken as a significant example of the Revolution's economic influence. The fact of the matter is that primogeniture had never appreciably affected land distribution, since it came into play only when the owner died intestate. Considering the notorious litigiousness of eighteenth-century Americans, it is hardly to be doubted that partible inheritance was the practice, if not the theory, long before primogeniture was wiped from the statute books. Furthermore, in almost half of the country—New Jersey, Pennsylvania, and all of the New England states—primogeniture never prevailed anyway.

As for the abolition of entail, it was frequently welcomed by owners of entailed estates, as was the case in Jefferson's Virginia, since it would permit the sale of otherwise frozen assets. These laws had not created a landed aristocracy in America and their repeal made no significant alteration in the social landscape.

Instead of being an abrupt break, the Revolution was a natural and even expected event in the history of a colonial people who had come of age. It is true that social and political changes accompanied the Revolution, some of which were destined to work great influence upon American institutions in the future, but these had been implicit in the pre-Revolutionary society. Moreover, important social institutions were left untouched by the Revolution: the class structure, the distribution of property, the capitalistic economy, the ideas of the people concerning government.

This lack of profound and widespread social and economic change is not surprising. These Americans, for all their talk, had been a contented and prosperous people under the British Crown and they were, therefore, contented revolutionaries who wanted nothing more than to be undisturbed in their accustomed ways. They are in no wise to be compared with the disgruntled lawyers, the frustrated bourgeois, the tyrannized workers, and the land-hungry peasants of the *anciens régimes* of France and Russia.

Yet, in conclusion, it is perhaps fitting to recall that America was born in revolution, for this fact has become embedded in our folk and sophisticated traditions alike. It was apparent in the self-conscious, often naïve enthusiasm displayed by American statesmen and people in support of the colonial rebellions in South America and in Greece in the first two decades of the nineteenth century. Revolutionaries of the middle of the century, like Louis Kossuth [Hungary] and [Giuseppe] Garibaldi [Italy], garnered moral and material benefits from this continuing American friendship for rebellion. European exiles and revolutionaries of 1848 were entertained at the London residence of United States Minister James Buchanan. And it is still apparent today. The declarations of independence of Ho Chi Minh's Democratic Republic of (North) Vietnam in 1945 and Ian Smith's Rhodesia in 1965 both begin with quotations from the United States Declaration of Independence! And [President Gamal Abdel] Nasser of Egypt, at the time of the United States intervention in Lebanon in July, 1958, taunted Americans with their revolutionary tradition. "How can the United States, which pushed off British colonialism many years ago, forget its history?" he shouted to a crowd in Damascus.

An anticolonial tradition of such weight could not fail to leave its stamp upon American attitudes.... It was invoked again and again in debates over American foreign policy, and its continuing influence is evident in the movement of former colonies like Hawaii and Alaska into statehood and the Philippines into independence. Long before, in the era of the Revolution, American leaders, profiting from the lessons of Britain's imperial problems, agreed in the Ordinance of 1787 and the Constitution that newly acquired territories could attain, in the natural course of events, equal constitutional status with the original thirteen states. Thus, in a single stroke, Americans sidestepped the tensions and divisions attendant upon a colonial empire and laid the enduring foundations for an expanding and united country.

Constitutional devices, however, no matter how clever or farsighted, cannot of themselves create a new people. The forces of economics and geography can wreak havoc with the best laid plans of Founding Fathers. Whether Americans would retain their independence and become a truly united people was to be determined only by time and the people themselves.

Notes

1. This is not to say, however, that disestablishment of all churches was brought about by the Revolution. All of the New England states, with the exception of

Rhode Island—still loyal to Roger Williams in this respect—continued to support the Congregational Church.

2. Just because the so-called conservatives dominated the Constitutional Convention, such religious indifference was possible. Generally the radials during the Revolutionary era were in favor of state support or recognition of some religion. Thus in the states where the radicals dominated, religious tests were part of the Constitution: Georgia (all members of the legislature had to be Protestants); North Carolina (no one could hold office who denied "God or the truth of the Protestant religion"); and Pennsylvania (the test oath demanded a belief in one God and his rewarding and punishing, and the acknowledgment that the Old and New Testaments were "given by Divine Inspiration"). The contrast with the Constitutional Convention of 1787 is striking. The Continental Congress, which had been dominated by the radicals, always opened its deliberations with chaplain-led prayers; the Convention of 1787, however, failed to have either a chaplain or prayers, though Franklin made an eloquent plea for both. He wrote later that "the Convention except three or four persons thought Prayers unnecessary." Whereas the Declaration of Independence refers to "God" and "Divine Providence," such words are completely absent from the "conservative" Constitution—much to the mystification of modern conservatives.

3. Schoepf, interestingly enough, discovered in the economic opportunities available in America the source of the social equality. "Riches make no positive material difference," he wrote concerning Philadelphia society, "because in this regard every man expects at one time or another to be on a footing with his rich neighbor, and in this expectation shows him no knavish reverence, but treats him with an open, but seemly familiarity."

4. William Nelson, *American Tory* (Oxford, 1961), suggests in his last chapter that America lost an organic or conservative view of society with the departure of the Loyalists. Insofar as that is true, it would reinforce the liberal bias that has been so characteristic of American political and social thought.

Gordon S. Wood

 **NO**

The Radicalism of the
American Revolution

We Americans like to think of our revolution as not being radical; indeed, most of the time we consider it downright conservative. It certainly does not appear to resemble the revolutions of other nations in which people were killed, property was destroyed, and everything was turned upside down. The American revolutionary leaders do not fit our conventional image of revolutionaries —angry, passionate, reckless, maybe even bloodthirsty for the sake of a cause. We can think of Robespierre, Lenin, and Mao Zedong as revolutionaries, but not George Washington, Thomas Jefferson, and John Adams. They seem too stuffy, too solemn, too cautious, too much the gentlemen. We cannot quite conceive of revolutionaries in powdered hair and knee breeches. The American revolutionaries seem to belong in drawing rooms or legislative halls, not in cellars or in the streets. They made speeches, not bombs; they wrote learned pamphlets, not manifestos. They were not abstract theorists and they were not social levelers. They did not kill one another; they did not devour themselves. There was no reign of terror in the American Revolution and no resultant dictator—no Cromwell, no Bonaparte. The American Revolution does not seem to have the same kinds of causes—the social wrongs, the class conflict, the impoverishment, the grossly inequitable distributions of wealth—that presumably lie behind other revolutions. There were no peasant uprisings, no jacqueries, no burning of châteaux, no storming of prisons.

Of course, there have been many historians—Progressive or neo-Progressive historians, as they have been called—who have sought, as Hannah Arendt put it, "to interpret the American Revolution in the light of the French Revolution," and to look for the same kinds of internal violence, class conflict, and social deprivation that presumably lay behind the French Revolution and other modern revolutions. Since the beginning of the twentieth century these Progressive historians have formulated various social interpretations of the American Revolution essentially designed to show that the Revolution, in Carl Becker's famous words, was not only about "home rule" but also about "who was to rule at home." They have tried to describe the Revolution essentially as a social struggle by deprived and underprivileged groups against entrenched elites. But, it has been correctly pointed out, despite an extraordinary amount

From Gordon S. Wood, *The Radicalism of the American Revolution* (Alfred A. Knopf, 1991). Copyright © 1991 by Gordon S. Wood. Reprinted by permission of Alfred A. Knopf, a division of Random House, Inc. Notes omitted.

of research and writing during a good part of this century, the purposes of these Progressive and neo-Progressive historians—"to portray the origins and goals of the Revolution as in some significant measure expressions of a peculiar economic malaise or of the social protests and aspirations of an impoverished or threatened mass population—have not been fulfilled." They have not been fulfilled because the social conditions that generically are supposed to lie behind all revolutions—poverty and economic deprivation—were not present in colonial America. There should no longer be any doubt about it: the white American colonists were not an oppressed people; they had no crushing imperial chains to throw off. In fact, the colonists knew they were freer, more equal, more prosperous, and less burdened with cumbersome feudal and monarchical restraints than any other part of mankind in the eighteenth century. Such a situation, however, does not mean that colonial society was not susceptible to revolution.

Precisely because the impulses to revolution in eighteenth-century America bear little or no resemblance to the impulses that presumably account for modern social protests and revolutions, we have tended to think of the American Revolution as having no social character, as having virtually nothing to do with the society, as having no social causes and no social consequences. It has therefore often been considered to be essentially an intellectual event, a constitutional defense of American rights against British encroachments ("no taxation without representation"), undertaken not to change the existing structure of society but to preserve it. For some historians the Revolution seems to be little more than a colonial rebellion or a war for independence. Even when we have recognized the radicalism of the Revolution, we admit only a political, not a social radicalism. The revolutionary leaders, it is said, were peculiar "eighteenth-century radicals concerned, like the eighteenth-century British radicals, not with the need to recast the social order nor with the problems of the economic inequality and the injustices of stratified societies but with the need to purify a corrupt constitution and fight off the apparent growth of prerogative power." Consequently, we have generally described the Revolution as an unusually conservative affair, concerned almost exclusively with politics and constitutional rights, and, in comparison with the social radicalism of the other great revolutions of history, hardly a revolution at all.

If we measure the radicalism of revolutions by the degree of social misery or economic deprivation suffered, or by the number of people killed or manor houses burned, then this conventional emphasis on the conservatism of the American Revolution becomes true enough. But if we measure the radicalism by the amount of social change that actually took place—by transformations in the relationships that bound people to each other—then the American Revolution was not conservative at all; on the contrary: it was as radical and as revolutionary as any in history. Of course, the American Revolution was very different from other revolutions. But it was no less radical and no less social for being different. In fact, it was one of the greatest revolutions the world has known, a momentous upheaval that not only fundamentally altered the character of American society but decisively affected the course of subsequent history.

It was as radical and social as any revolution in history, but it was radical and social in a very special eighteenth-century sense. No doubt many of the concerns and much of the language of that premodern, pre-Marxian eighteenth century were almost entirely political. That was because most people in that very different distant world could not as yet conceive of society apart from government. The social distinctions and economic deprivations that we today think of as the consequence of class divisions, business exploitation, or various isms—capitalism, racism, etc.—were in the eighteenth century usually thought to be caused by the abuses of government. Social honors, social distinctions, perquisites of office, business contracts, privileges and monopolies, even excessive property and wealth of various sorts—all social evils and social deprivations—in fact seemed to flow from connections to government, in the end from connections to monarchical authority. So that when Anglo-American radicals talked in what seems to be only political terms—purifying a corrupt constitution, eliminating courtiers, fighting off crown power, and, most important, becoming republicans—they nevertheless had a decidedly social message. In our eyes the American revolutionaries appear to be absorbed in changing only their governments, not their society. But in destroying monarchy and establishing republics they were changing their society as well as their governments, and they knew it. Only they did not know—they could scarcely have imagined—how much of their society they would change. J. Franklin Jameson, who more than two generations ago described the Revolution as a social movement only to be roundly criticized by a succeeding generation of historians, was at least right about one thing: "the stream of revolution, once started, could not be confined within narrow banks, but spread abroad upon the land."

By the time the Revolution had run its course in the early nineteenth century, American society had been radically and thoroughly transformed. One class did not overthrow another; the poor did not supplant the rich. But social relationships—the way people were connected one to another—were changed, and decisively so. By the early years of the nineteenth century the Revolution had created a society fundamentally different from the colonial society of the eighteenth century. It was in fact a new society unlike any that had ever existed anywhere in the world.

That revolution did more than legally create the United States; it transformed American society. Because the story of America has turned out the way it has, because the United States in the twentieth century has become the great power that it is, it is difficult, if not impossible, to appreciate and recover fully the insignificant and puny origins of the country. In 1760 America was only a collection of disparate colonies huddled along a narrow strip of the Atlantic coast—economically underdeveloped outposts existing on the very edges of the civilized world. The less than two million monarchical subjects who lived in these colonies still took for granted that society was and ought to be a hierarchy of ranks and degrees of dependency and that most people were bound together by personal ties of one sort or another. Yet scarcely fifty years later these insignificant borderland provinces had become a giant, almost continent-wide republic of nearly ten million egalitarian-minded bustling citizens who not only had thrust themselves into the vanguard of history but had fundamentally altered their society and their social relationships. Far from remaining monarchical, hierarchy-ridden subjects on the margin of civilization, Americans had become almost overnight, the most liberal, the most democratic, the most commercially minded, and the most modern people in the world.

And this astonishing transformation took place without industrialization, without urbanization, without railroads, without the aid of any of the great forces we usually invoke to explain "modernization." It was the Revolution that was crucial to this transformation. It was the Revolution, more than any other single event, that made America into the most liberal, democratic, and modern nation in the world.

Of course, some nations of Western Europe likewise experienced great social transformations and "democratic revolutions" in these same years. The American Revolution was not unique; it was only different. Because of this shared Western-wide experience in democratization, it has been argued by more than one historian that the broader social transformation that carried Americans from one century and one kind of society to another was "inevitable" and "would have been completed with or without the American Revolution." Therefore this broader social revolution should not be confused with the American Revolution. America, it is said, would have emerged into the modern world as a liberal, democratic, and capitalistic society even without the Revolution. One could, of course, say the same thing about the relationship between the French Revolution and the emergence of France in the nineteenth century as a liberal, democratic, and capitalistic society; and indeed, much of the current revisionist historical writing on the French Revolution is based on just such a distinction. But in America, no more than in France, that was not the way it happened: the American Revolution and the social transformation of America between 1760 and the early years of the nineteenth century were inextricably bound together. Perhaps the social transformation would have happened "in any case," but we will never know. It was in fact linked to the Revolution; they occurred together. The American Revolution was integral to the changes occurring in American society, politics, and culture at the end of the eighteenth century.

These changes were radical, and they were extensive. To focus, as we are today apt to do, on what the Revolution did not accomplish—highlighting and lamenting its failure to abolish slavery and change fundamentally the lot of women—is to miss the great significance of what it did accomplish; indeed, the Revolution made possible the anti-slavery and women's rights movements of the nineteenth century and in fact all our current egalitarian thinking. The Revolution not only radically changed the personal and social relationships of people, including the position of women, but also destroyed aristocracy as it had been understood in the Western world for at least two millennia. The Revolution brought respectability and even dominance to ordinary people long held in contempt and gave dignity to their menial labor in a manner unprecedented in history and to a degree not equaled elsewhere in the world. The Revolution did not just eliminate monarchy and create republics; it actually reconstituted what Americans meant by public or state power and brought about an entirely new kind of popular politics and a new kind of democratic officeholder. The Revolution not only changed the culture of Americans—making over their art, architecture, and iconography—but even altered their understanding of history, knowledge, and truth. Most important, it made the interests and prosperity of ordinary people—their pursuits of happiness—the goal of society and government. The Revolution did not merely create a political and legal environment conducive to economic expansion; it also released powerful popular entrepreneurial and commercial energies that few realized existed and transformed the economic landscape of the country. In short, the Revolution was the most radical and most far-reaching event in American history. . . .

。◆◆。

By the late 1760s and early 1770s a potentially revolutionary situation existed in many of the colonies. There was little evidence of those social conditions we often associate with revolution (and some historians have desperately sought to find): no mass poverty, no seething social discontent, no grinding oppression. For most white Americans there was greater prosperity than anywhere else in the world; in fact, the experience of that growing prosperity contributed to the unprecedented eighteenth-century sense that people here and now were capable of ordering their own reality. Consequently, there was a great deal of jealousy and touchiness everywhere, for what could be made could be unmade; the people were acutely nervous about their prosperity and the liberty that seemed to make it possible. With the erosion of much of what remained of traditional social relationships, more and more individuals had broken away from their families, communities, and patrons and were experiencing the anxiety of freedom and independence. Social changes, particularly since the 1740s, multiplied rapidly, and many Americans struggled to make sense of what was happening. These social changes were complicated, and they are easily misinterpreted. Luxury and conspicuous consumption by very ordinary people were increasing. So, too, was religious dissent of all sorts. The rich became richer, and aristocratic gentry everywhere became more conspicuous and self-conscious; and the numbers of poor in some cities and the numbers of landless in some areas increased. But social classes based on occupation or wealth did not set themselves against one another, for no classes in this modern sense yet existed. The society was becoming more unequal, but its inequalities were not the source of the instability and anxiety. Indeed, it was the pervasive equality of American society that was causing the problems. . . .

This extraordinary touchiness, this tendency of the colonists in their political disputes to argue "with such vehemence as if all had been at Stake," flowed from the precariousness of American society, from its incomplete and relatively flattened character, and from the often "rapid ascendency" of its aristocracy, particularly in the Deep South, where families "in less than ten years have risen from the lowest rank, have acquired upward of £100,000 and have, moreover, gained this wealth in a simple and easy manner." Men who had quickly risen to the top were confident and aggressive but also vulnerable to challenge, especially sensitive over their liberty and independence, and unwilling to brook any interference with their status or their prospects.

For other, more ordinary colonists the promises and uncertainties of American life were equally strong. Take, for example, the lifelong struggle of farmer and sawmill owner Moses Cooper of Glocester, Rhode Island, to rise from virtual insignificance to become the richest man in the town. In 1767–68, at the age of sixty, Cooper was finally able to hire sufficient slaves and workers to do all his manual labor; he became a gentleman and justice of the peace and appended "Esq." to his name. Certainly by this date he could respond to the rhetoric of his fellow Rhode Islanders talking about their colony as "the promised land... a land of milk and honey and wherein we eat bread to the full... a land whose stones are iron... and... other choice mines and minerals; and a land whose rivers and adjacent seas are stored with the best of fish." And Cooper might well have added, "whose forests were rich with timber," for he had made his money from lumber. Yet at the same time Cooper knew only too well the precariousness of his wealth and position and naturally feared what Britain's mercantile restrictions might mean for his lumber sales to the West Indies. What had risen so high could as readily fall: not surprisingly, he became an enthusiastic patriot leader of his tiny town of Glocester. Multiply Cooper's experience of uneasy prosperity many thousandfold and we have the stuff of a popular revolutionary movement.

... The great social antagonists of the American Revolution were not poor vs. rich, workers vs. employers, or even democrats vs. aristocrats. They were patriots vs. courtiers—categories appropriate to the monarchical world in which the colonists had been reared. Courtiers were persons whose position or rank came artificially from above—from hereditary or personal connections that ultimately flowed from the crown or court. Courtiers, said John Adams, were those who applied themselves "to the Passions and Prejudices, the Follies and Vices of Great Men in order to obtain their Smiles, Esteem, and Patronage and consequently their favors and Preferments. Patriots, on the other hand, were those who not only loved their country but were free of dependent connections and influence; their position or rank came naturally from their talent and from below, from recognition by the people. "A real patriot," declared one American in 1776, was "the most illustrious character in human life. Is not the interest and happiness of his fellow creatures his care?" ...

It is in this context that we can best understand the revolutionaries' appeal to independence, not just the independence of the country from Great Britain, but, more important, the independence of individuals from personal influence and "warm and private friendship." The purpose of the Virginia constitution of 1776, one Virginian recalled, was "to prevent the undue and overwhelming influence of great landholders in elections." This was to be done by disfranchising the landless "tenants and retainers" who depended "on the breath and varying will" of these great men and by ensuring that only men who owned their own land could vote.

A republic presumed, as the Virginia declaration of rights put it, that men in the new republic would be "equally free and independent," and property would make them so. Property in a republic was still conceived of traditionally —in proprietary terms—not as a means of personal profit or aggrandizement but rather as a source of personal authority or independence. It was regarded not merely as a material possession but also as an attribute of a man's personality that defined him and protected him from outside pressure. A carpenter's skill, for example, was his property. Jefferson feared the rabble of the cities precisely because they were without property and were thus dependent.

All dependents without property, such as women and young men, could be denied the vote because, as a convention of Essex County, Massachusetts, declared in 1778, they were so situated as to have no wills of their own." Jefferson was so keen on this equation of property with citizenship that he proposed in 1776 that the new state of Virginia grant fifty acres of land to every man that did not have that many. Without having property and a will of his own —without having independence—a man could have no public spirit; and there could be no republic. For, as Jefferson put it, "dependence begets subservience and venality, suffocates the germ of virtue, and prepares fit tools for the designs of ambition."

In a monarchical world of numerous patron-client relations and multiple degrees of dependency, nothing could be more radical than this attempt to make every man independent. What was an ideal in the English-speaking world now became for Americans an ideological imperative. Suddenly, in the eyes of the revolutionaries, all the fine calibrations of rank and degrees of unfreedom of the traditional monarchical society became absurd and degrading. The Revolution became a full-scale assault on dependency.

At the beginning of the eighteenth century the English radical whig and deist John Toland had divided all society into those who were free and those who were dependent. "By *Freeman*," wrote Toland, "I understand men of property, or persons that are able to live of themselves; and those who cannot subsist in this independence, I call *Servants*." In such a simple division everyone who was not free was presumed to be a servant. Anyone tied to someone else, who was someone's client or dependent, was servile. The American revolutionary movement now brought to the surface this latent logic in eighteenth-century radical whig thinking.

Dependency was now equated with slavery, and slavery in the American world had a conspicuous significance. "What is a slave," asked a New Jersey writer in 1765, "but one who depends upon the will of another for the enjoyment of his life and property?" "Liberty," said Stephen Hopkins of Rhode Island, quoting Algernon Sidney, "solely consists in an independency upon the will of another; and by the name of slave we understand a man who can neither dispose of his person or goods, but enjoys all at the will of his master." It was left to John Adams in 1775 to draw the ultimate conclusion and to destroy in a single sentence the entire conception of society as a hierarchy of graded ranks and degrees. "There are," said Adams simply, "but two *sorts* of men in the world, freemen and slaves." Such a stark dichotomy collapsed all the delicate distinctions and dependencies of a monarchical society and created radical and momentous implications for Americans.

Independence, declared David Ramsay in a memorable Fourth of July oration in 1778, would free Americans from that monarchical world where "favor is the source of preferment," and where "he that can best please his superiors, by the low arts of fawning and adulation, is most likely to obtain favor." The revolutionaries wanted to create a new republican world in which "all offices lie open to men of merit, of whatever rank or condition." They believed that "even the reins of state may be held by the son of the poorest men, if possessed of abilities equal to the important station." They were "no more to look up for the blessings of government to hungry courtiers, or the needy dependents of British nobility"; but they had now to educate their "own children for these exalted purposes." Like Stephen Burroughs, the author of an extraordinary memoir of these years, the revolutionaries believed they were "so far republican" that they considered "a man's merit to rest entirely with himself, without any regard to family, blood, or connection." We can never fully appreciate the emotional meaning these commonplace statements had for the revolutionaries until we take seriously their passionate antagonism to the prevalence of patronage and family influence in the *ancien régime*.

Of course, the revolutionary leaders did not expect poor, humble men—farmers, artisans, or tradesmen—themselves to gain high political office. Rather, they expected that the sons of such humble or ungenteel men, if they had abilities, would, as they had, acquire liberal and genteel republican attributes, perhaps by attending Harvard or the College of New Jersey at Princeton, and would thereby rise into the ranks of gentlemen and become eligible for high political office. The sparks of genius that they hoped republicanism would fan and kindle into flame belonged to men like themselves—men "drawn from obscurity" by the new opportunities of republican competition and emulation into becoming "illustrious characters, which will dazzle the world with the splendor of their names." Honor, interest, and patriotism together called them to qualify themselves and posterity "for the 'bench, the army, the navy, the learned professions, and all the departments of civil government." They would become what Jefferson called the "natural aristocracy"—liberally educated, enlightened gentlemen of character. For many of the revolutionary leaders this was the emotional significance of republicanism—a vindication of frustrated talent at the expense of birth and blood. For too long, they felt, merit had been denied. In a monarchical world only the arts and sciences had recognized talent as the sole criterion of leadership. Which is why even the eighteenth-century *ancien régime* called the world of the arts and sciences "the republic of letters." Who, it was asked, remembered the fathers or sons of Homer and Euclid? Such a question was a republican dagger driven into the heart of the old hereditary order. "Virtue," said Thomas Paine simply, "is not hereditary." . . .

In their revolutionary state constitutions and laws the revolutionaries struck out at the power of family and hereditary privilege. In the decades following the Revolution all the new states abolished the legal devices of primogeniture and entail where they existed, either by statute or by writing the abolition into their constitutions. These legal devices, as the North Carolina statute of 1784 stated, had tended "only to raise the wealth and importance of particular families and individuals, giving them an unequal and undue influence in a republic, and prove in manifold instances the source of great contention and injustice." Their abolition would therefore "tend to promote that equality of property which is of the spirit and principle of a genuine republic." . . .

Women and children no doubt remained largely dependent on their husbands and fathers, but the revolutionary attack on patriarchal monarchy made all other dependencies in the society suspect. Indeed, once the revolutionaries collapsed all the different distinctions and dependencies of a monarchical society into either freemen or slaves, white males found it increasingly impossible to accept any dependent status whatsoever. Servitude of any sort suddenly became anomalous and anachronistic. In 1784 in New York, a group believing that indentured servitude was "contrary to... the idea of liberty this country has so happily established" released a shipload of immigrant servants and arranged for public subscriptions to pay for their passage. As early as 1775 in Philadelphia the proportion of the work force that was unfree—composed of servants and slaves—had already declined to 13 percent from the 40 to 50 percent that it had been at mid-century. By 1800 less than 2 percent of the city's labor force remained unfree. Before long indentured servitude virtually disappeared....

One obvious dependency the revolutionaries did not completely abolish was that of nearly a half million Afro-American slaves, and their failure to do so, amidst all their high-blown talk of liberty, makes them seem inconsistent and hypocritical in our eyes. Yet it is important to realize that the Revolution suddenly and effectively ended the cultural climate that had allowed black slavery, as well as other forms of bondage and unfreedom, to exist throughout the colonial period without serious challenge. With the revolutionary movement, black slavery became excruciatingly conspicuous in a way that it had not been in the older monarchical society with its many calibrations and degrees of unfreedom; and Americans in 1775–76 began attacking it with a vehemence that was inconceivable earlier.

For a century or more the colonists had taken slavery more or less for granted as the most base and dependent status in a hierarchy of dependencies and a world of laborers. Rarely had they felt the need either to criticize black slavery or to defend it. Now, however, the republican attack on dependency compelled Americans to see the deviant character of slavery and to confront the institution as they never had to before. It was no accident that Americans in Philadelphia in 1775 formed the first anti-slavery society in the world. As long as most people had to work merely out of poverty and the need to provide for a living, slavery and other forms of enforced labor did not seem all that different from free labor. But the growing recognition that labor was not simply a common necessity of the poor but was in fact a source of increased wealth and prosperity for ordinary workers made slavery seem more and more anomalous. Americans now recognized that slavery in a republic of workers was an aberration, "a peculiar institution," and that if any Americans were to retain it, as southern Americans eventually did, they would have to explain and justify it in new racial and anthropological ways that their former monarchical society had never needed. The Revolution in effect set in motion ideological and social forces that doomed the institution of slavery in the North and led inexorably to the Civil War.

With all men now considered to be equally free citizens, the way was prepared as well for a radical change in the conception of state power. Almost at a stroke the Revolution destroyed all the earlier talk of paternal or maternal government, filial allegiance, and mutual contractual obligations between rulers and ruled. The familial image of government now lost all its previous relevance, and the state in America emerged as something very different from what it had been.

POSTSCRIPT

Was the American Revolution a Conservative Movement?

In arguing that the American Revolution was a conservative affair, Degler compares the American colonial leadership classes of lawyers, merchants, and planters with those who led similar revolutions later in France, Russia, and China. The American leadership was different, maintains Degler, because most held positions in government both before and after the Revolution. The goals of the American leaders also appear tame compared to revolutionaries in other countries. The Americans got rid of mercantilism but preserved capitalism. Also, loyalists were dispatched to Canada and England, but an upper middle class of pre-Revolutionary leaders remained in power.

Degler challenges the views of the earlier progressive historian J. Franklin Jameson, who argues in *The American Revolution Considered as a Social Movement* (Princeton University Press, 1926, 1967) that a radical transformation had taken place in the postwar distribution of land. Jameson also argues that the abolition of the slave trade and the separation of church and state were radical results of the American Revolution. And if the abolition of slavery and the attainment of equal rights for women were to come later, its roots were in the Revolutionary period.

Wood concedes that the American Revolution was not radical in the strict constructionist definition of the term. There were no major land reforms or political upheavals. Tories such as Massachusetts governor Thomas Hutchinson were given a one-way ticket to England—not a trip to the guillotine. Nevertheless, Wood argues that the Revolution was radical and social in a special eighteenth-century, premodern, pre-Marxian sense. Prior to the Industrial Revolution, class divisions and economic exploration of the people resulted from abuses by corrupt, tyrannical governments run by various kings and queens. Once the monarchy was overthrown, says Wood, the American Revolution created "a society fundamentally different from the colonial society of the eighteenth century."

Although Degler and Wood disagree on whether the American Revolution was radical or conservative, their arguments converge in several areas. Degler sees the disestablishment of the Anglican Church and the acceptance of the separation of the church from the state as an unintended result of the Revolution. Both Degler and Wood concede that deference to authority was weakened and that small farmers entered state legislatures, a number of state capitals were moved west, and legislative sessions were opened to the public. Obviously, the new social history caused both historians to think about the long-range effects of the Revolution on the rights of women and the eventual abolition of slavery.

For a contrary view, see Linda De Pauw, "Land of the Unfree: Legal Limitations on Liberty in Pre-Revolutionary America," *Maryland Historical Magazine* (Winter 1973).

Neo-Left historians such as Alfred F. Young, Gary B. Nash, and Edward Countryman have written books and articles that stress racial, ethnic, and especially class conflicts that took place in the colonies in the 1760s and 1770s. In *The Urban Crucible: Social Change, Political Consciousness, and the Origins of the American Revolution* (Harvard University Press, 1979), for example, Nash interprets colonial life and the origins of the American Revolution in a comparative history of the three largest seaport cities in the colonies—Boston, New York, and Philadelphia.

Students who wish to explore Degler's suggestion that the American Revolution established "a new model for mankind" and influenced other revolutions by fighting the first successful anticolonial war of national liberation should read Richard B. Morris, *The Emerging Nations and the American Revolution* (Harper & Row, 1970) and the appropriate sections of Robert R. Palmer, *The Age of the Democratic Revolution* (Princeton University Press, 1959, 1964). A contrary view is advanced by Sung Bok Kim in "The American Revolution and the Modern World," in Larry R. Gerlach, James A. Dolph, and Michael L. Nicholls, eds., *Legacies of the American Revolution* (Utah State University Press, 1978). Kim concludes that the French Revolution had a greater impact on world history because the American Revolution established a society that values civil liberties and private ownership of property.

There are numerous anthologies that offer a diverse range of interpretations about the American Revolution. Two of the best-edited collections are George Athan Billias, *The American Revolution: How Revolutionary Was It?* (Holt, Rinehart & Winston, 1980) and Richard M. Fulton, *The Revolution That Wasn't: A Contemporary Assessment of 1776* (Kennikat Press, 1981), which discusses numerous theories of revolution. Among the most recent edited collections is Kirk D. Werner, ed., *The American Revolution* (Greenhaven Press, 2000). William Dudley has edited some of the most useful primary sources to a reasonable length in *The American Revolution: Opposing Viewpoints* (Greenhaven Press, 1992). Finally, Alfred F. Young provides a massive annotated and interpretative bibliography of works on the American Revolution in Ronald Hoffman and Peter J. Albert, eds., *The Transforming Hand of Revolution: Reconsidering the American Revolution as a Social Movement* (University Press of Virginia, 1995).

ISSUE 7

Were the Founding Fathers Democratic Reformers?

YES: John P. Roche, from "The Founding Fathers: A Reform Caucus in Action," *American Political Science Review* (December 1961)

NO: Alfred F. Young, from "The Framers of the Constitution and the 'Genius' of the People," *Radical History Review* (vol. 42, 1988)

ISSUE SUMMARY

YES: Political scientist John P. Roche asserts that the Founding Fathers were not only revolutionaries but also superb democratic politicians who created a Constitution that supported the needs of the nation and at the same time was acceptable to the people.

NO: Historian Alfred F. Young argues that the Founding Fathers were an elite group of college-educated lawyers, merchants, slaveholding planters, and "monied men" who strengthened the power of the central government yet, at the same time, were forced to make some democratic accommodations in writing the Constitution in order to ensure its acceptance in the democratically controlled ratifying conventions.

The United States possesses the oldest written constitution of any major power. The 55 men who attended the Philadelphia Convention of 1787 could scarcely have dreamed that 200 years later the nation would venerate them as the most "enlightened statesmen" of their time. James Madison, the principal architect of the document, may have argued that the Founding Fathers had created a system that might "decide forever the fate of Republican Government which we wish to last for ages," but Madison also told Thomas Jefferson in October 1787 that he did not think the document would be adopted, and if it was, it would not work.

The enlightened statesmen view of the Founding Fathers, presented by nineteenth-century historians like John Fiske, became the accepted interpretation among the general public until the Progressive Era. In 1913 Columbia University professor Charles A. Beard's *An Economic Interpretation of the Constitution of the United States* (Free Press, 1913, 1986) caused a storm of controversy because it questioned the motivations of the Founding Fathers. The Founding Fathers supported the creation of a stronger central government, argued Beard, not for patriotic reasons but because they wanted to protect their own economic interests.

Beard's research method was fairly simple. Drawing upon a collection of old, previously unexamined treasury records in the National Archives, he discovered that a number of delegates to the Philadelphia Convention and, later, the state ratifying conventions, held substantial amounts of continental securities that would sharply increase in value if a strong national government were established. In addition to attributing economic motives to the Founding Fathers, Beard included a Marxist class conflict interpretation in his book. Those who supported the Constitution, he said, represented "personalty interests which had been adversely affected under the Articles of Confederation: money, public securities, manufactures, and trade and shipping." Those who opposed ratification of the Constitution were the small farmers and debtors.

Beard's socioeconomic conflict interpretation of the supporters and opponents of the Constitution raised another issue: How was the Constitution ratified if the majority of Americans opposed it? Beard's answer was that most Americans could not vote because they did not own property. Therefore, the entire process, from the calling of the Philadelphia Convention to the state ratifying conventions, was nonrepresentative and nondemocratic.

An Economic Interpretation was a product of its times. Economists, sociologists, and political scientists had been analyzing the conflicts that resulted from the Industrial Revolution, which America had been experiencing at the turn of the twentieth century. Beard joined a group of progressive historians who were interested in reforming the society in which they lived and who also shared his discontent with the old-fashioned institutional approach. The role of the new historians was to rewrite history and discover the real reason why things happened. For the progressive historians, reality consisted of uncovering the hidden social and economic conflicts within society.

In the years between the world wars, the general public held steadfastly to the enlightened statesmen view of the Founding Fathers, but Beard's thesis on the Constitution became the new orthodoxy in most college texts on American history and government. The post–World War II period witnessed the emergence of the neoconservative historians, who viewed the Beardian approach to the Constitution as overly simplistic.

In the first of the following selections, which is a good example of consensus history, John P. Roche contends that although the Founding Fathers may have been revolutionaries, they were also superb democratic politicians who framed a Constitution that supported the needs of the nation and at the same time was acceptable to the people. A good example of Beard's influence lasting into the 1990s can be found in the second selection, in which Alfred F. Young argues that although the Constitution may have strengthened the powers of the central government, the Founding Fathers were forced to make concessions to the people in the final document. Otherwise, the delegates to the state ratifying conventions would have rejected the new Constitution.

John P. Roche

 **YES**

The Founding Fathers:
A Reform Caucus in Action

The work of the Constitutional Convention and the motives of the Founding Fathers have been analyzed under a number of different ideological auspices. To one generation of historians, the hand of God was moving in the assembly; under a later dispensation, the dialectic (at various levels of philosophical sophistication) replaced the Deity: "relationships of production" moved into the niche previously reserved for Love of Country.... The Framers have undergone miraculous metamorphoses: at one time acclaimed as liberals and bold social engineers, today they appear in the guise of sound Burkean conservatives, men who in our time would subscribe to *Fortune*....

The "Fathers" have thus been admitted to our best circles; the revolutionary ferocity which confiscated all Tory property in reach... has been converted... into a benign dedication to "consensus" and "prescriptive rights."...
It is not my purpose here to argue that the "Fathers" were, in fact, radical revolutionaries; that proposition has been brilliantly demonstrated.... My concern is with the further position that not only were they revolutionaries, but also they were democrats. Indeed, in my view, there is one fundamental truth about the Founding Fathers...: They were first and foremost superb democratic politicians.... As recent research into the nature of American politics in the 1780s confirms, they were committed (perhaps willy-nilly) to working within the democratic framework, within a universe of public approval.... The Philadelphia Convention was not a College of Cardinals or a council of Platonic guardians working within a manipulative, pre-democratic framework; it was a nationalist reform caucus which had to operate with great delicacy and skill in a political cosmos full of enemies to achieve the one definitive goal—popular approbation....

What they did was to hammer out a pragmatic compromise which would both bolster the "national interest" and be acceptable to the people. What inspiration they got came from their collective experience as professional politicians in a democratic society. As John Dickinson put it to his fellow delegates on August 13, "Experience must be our guide. Reason may mislead us."

In this context, let us examine the problems they confronted and the solutions they evolved. The Convention has been described picturesquely as a

From John P. Roche, "The Founding Fathers: A Reform Caucus in Action," *American Political Science Review*, vol. 55 (December 1961). Copyright © 1961 by The American Political Science Association. Reprinted by permission.

counter-revolutionary junta and the Constitution as a coup d'état, but this has been accomplished by withdrawing the whole history of the movement for constitutional reform from its true context. No doubt the goals of the constitutional elite were "subversive" to the existing political order, but it is overlooked that their subversion could only have succeeded if the people of the United States endorsed it by regularized procedures.…

I

When the Constitutionalists went forth to subvert the Confederation, they utilized the mechanisms of political legitimacy. And the roadblocks which confronted them were formidable. At the same time, they were endowed with certain potent political assets. The history of the United States from 1786 to 1790 was largely one of a masterful employment of political expertise by the Constitutionalists as against bumbling, erratic behavior by the opponents of reform. Effectively, the Constitutionalists had to induce the states, by democratic techniques of coercion, to emasculate themselves.… And at the risk of becoming boring, it must be reiterated that the only weapon in the Constitutionalist arsenal was an effective mobilization of public opinion.

The group which undertook this struggle was an interesting amalgam of a few dedicated nationalists with the self-interested spokesmen of various parochial bailiwicks. The Georgians, for example, wanted a strong central authority to provide military protection for their huge, underpopulated state against the Creek Confederacy; Jerseymen and Connecticuters wanted to escape from economic bondage to New York; the Virginians hoped to establish a system which would give that great state its rightful place in the councils of the republic. The dominant figures in the politics of these states therefore cooperated in the call for the Convention. In other states, the thrust towards national reform was taken up by opposition groups who added the "national interest" to their weapons system; in Pennsylvania, for instance, the group fighting to revise the Constitution of 1776 came out four-square behind the Constitutionalists, and in New York, [Alexander] Hamilton and the Schuyler [family] ambiance took the same tack against George Clinton. There was, of course, a large element of personality in the affair: there is reason to suspect that Patrick Henry's opposition to the Convention and the Constitution was founded on his conviction that Jefferson was behind both, and a close study of local politics elsewhere would surely reveal that others supported the Constitution for the simple (and politically quite sufficient) reason that the "wrong" people were against it.…

What distinguished the leaders of the Constitutionalist caucus from their enemies was a "Continental" approach to political, economic and military issues. To the extent that they shared an institutional base of operations, it was the Continental Congress (thirty-nine of the delegates to the Federal Convention had served in Congress), and this was hardly a locale which inspired respect for the state governments.… Membership in the Congress under the Articles of Confederation worked to establish a continental frame of reference, that a Congressman from Pennsylvania and one from North Carolina would share.… This was particularly true with respect to external affairs: the average state legislator was probably about as concerned with foreign policy than as he is today, but Congressmen were constantly forced to take the broad view of American prestige, were compelled to listen to the reports of Secretary John Jay and to the dispatches and pleas from their frustrated envoys in Britain, France and Spain. From considerations such as these, a "Continental" ideology developed which seems to have demanded a revision of our domestic institutions primarily on the ground that only by invigorating our general government could we assume our rightful place in the international arena. . . .

Note that I am not endorsing the "Critical Period" thesis; on the contrary, Merrill Jensen seems to me quite sound in his view that for most Americans, engaged as they were in self-sustaining agriculture, the "Critical Period" was not particularly critical. In fact, the great achievement of the Constitutionalists was their ultimate success in convincing the elected representatives of a majority of the white male population that change was imperative. A small group of political leaders with a Continental vision and essentially a consciousness of the United States' international impotence, provided the matrix of the movement. To their standard other leaders rallied with their own parallel ambitions. Their great assets were (1) the presence in their caucus of the one authentic American "father figure," George Washington, whose prestige was enormous; (2) the energy and talent of their leadership (in which one must include the towering intellectuals of the time, John Adams and Thomas Jefferson, despite their absence abroad), and their communications "network," which was far superior to anything on the opposition side; (3) the preemptive skill which made "their" issue The Issue and kept the locally oriented opposition permanently on the defensive; and (4) the subjective consideration that these men were spokesmen of a new and compelling credo: American nationalism, that ill-defined but nonetheless potent sense of collective purpose that emerged from the American Revolution. . . .

The Constitutionalists got the jump on the "opposition" (a collective noun: oppositions would be more correct) at the outset with the demand for a Convention. Their opponents were caught in an old political trap: they were not being asked to approve any specific program of reform, but only to endorse a meeting to discuss and recommend needed reforms. If they took a hard line at the first stage, they were put in the position of glorifying the status quo and of denying the need for any changes. Moreover, the Constitutionalists could go to the people with a persuasive argument for "fair play"—"How can you condemn reform before you know precisely what is involved?" Since the state legislatures obviously would have the final say on any proposals that might emerge from the Convention, the Constitutionalists were merely reasonable men asking for a chance. Besides, since they did not make any concrete proposals at that stage, they were in a position to capitalize on every sort of generalized discontent with the Confederation.

Perhaps because of their poor intelligence system, perhaps because of over-confidence generated by the failure of all previous efforts to alter the Articles, the opposition awoke too late to the dangers that confronted them in 1787. Not only did the Constitutionalists manage to get every state but Rhode Island . . . to appoint delegates to Philadelphia, but when the results were in, it appeared that they dominated the delegations. Given the apathy of the opposition, this was a natural phenomenon: in an ideologically nonpolarized political atmosphere those who get appointed to a special committee are likely to be the men who supported the movement for its creation.... Much has been made of the fact that the delegates to Philadelphia were not elected by the people; some have adduced this fact as evidence of the "undemocratic" character of the gathering. But put in the context of the time, this argument is wholly specious: the central government under the Articles was considered a creature of the component states and in all the states but Rhode Island, Connecticut and New Hampshire, members of the national Congress were chosen by the state legislatures. This was not a consequence of elitism or fear of the mob; it was a logical extension of states'-rights doctrine to guarantee that the national institution did not end-run the state legislatures and make direct contact with the people.

II

With delegations safely named, the focus shifted to Philadelphia. While waiting for a quorum to assemble, James Madison got busy and drafted the so-called Randolph or Virginia Plan with the aid of the Virginia delegation. This was a political master-stroke. Its consequence was that once business got under way, the framework of discussion was established on Madison's terms. There was no interminable argument over agenda; instead the delegates took the Virginia Resolutions—"just for purposes of discussion"—as their point of departure. And along with Madison's proposals, many of which were buried in the course of the summer, went his major premise: a new start on a Constitution rather than piecemeal amendment....

Standard treatments of the Convention divide the delegates into "nationalists" and "states'-righters" with various improvised shadings ("moderate nationalists," etc.), but these are a posteriori categories which obfuscate more than they clarify. What is striking to one who analyzes the Convention as a case-study in democratic politics is the lack of clear-cut ideological divisions in the Convention. Indeed, I submit that the evidence—Madison's Notes, the correspondence of the delegates, and debates on ratification—indicates that this was a remarkably homogeneous body on the ideological level. [Robert] Yates and [John] Lansing [of New York], who favored the New Jersey Plan]... left in disgust on July 10.... Luther Martin, Maryland's bibulous narcissist, left on September 4 in a huff when he discovered that others did not share his self-esteem; others went home for personal reasons. But the hard core of delegates accepted a grinding regimen throughout the attrition of a Philadelphia summer precisely because they shared the Constitutionalist goal.

Basic differences of opinion emerged, of course, but these were not ideological; they were structural. If the so-called "states'-rights" group had not accepted the fundamental purposes of the Convention, they could simply have pulled out and by doing so have aborted the whole enterprise. Instead of bolting, they returned day after day to argue and to compromise. An interesting symbol of this basic homogeneity was the initial agreement on secrecy: these professional politicians did not want to become prisoners of publicity; they wanted to retain that freedom of maneuver which is only possible when men are not forced to take public stands in the preliminary stages of negotiation. There was no legal means of binding the tongues of the delegates: at any stage in the game a delegate with basic principled objections to the emerging project could have taken the stump (as Luther Martin did after his exit) and denounced the convention to the skies. Yet... the delegates generally observed the injunction. Secrecy is certainly uncharacteristic of any assembly marked by strong ideological polarization....

Commentators on the Constitution who have read *The Federalist* in lieu of reading the actual debates have credited the Fathers with the invention of a sublime concept called "Federalism."... Federalism, as the theory is generally defined, was an improvisation which was later promoted into a political theory. Experts on "federalism" should take to heart the advice of David Hume, who warned... "there is no subject in which we must proceed with more caution than in [history], lest we assign causes which never existed and reduce what is merely contingent to stable and universal principles." In any event, the final balance in the Constitution between the states and the nation must have come as a great disappointment to Madison....

It is indeed astonishing how those who have glibly designated James Madison the "father" of Federalism have overlooked the solid body of fact which indicates that he shared Hamilton's quest for a unitary central government. To be specific, they have avoided examining the clear import of the Madison-Virginia Plan, and have disregarded Madison's dogged inch-by-inch retreat from the bastions of centralization. The Virginia Plan envisioned a unitary national government effectively freed from and dominant over the states. The lower house of the national legislature was to be elected directly by the people of the states with membership proportional to population. The upper house was to be selected by the lower and the two chambers would elect the executive and choose the judges. The national legislature was to be empowered to disallow the acts of state legislatures, and the central government was vested, in addition to the powers of the nation under which the Articles of Confederation, with plenary authority wherever "... the separate States are incompetent or in which the harmony of the United States may be interrupted by the exercise of individual legislation." Finally, just to lock the door against state intrusion, the national Congress was to be given the power to use military force on recalcitrant states. This was Madison's "model" of an ideal national government, though it later received little publicity in *The Federalist*.

The interesting thing was the reaction of the Convention to this militant program for a strong autonomous central government. Some delegates were startled, some obviously leery of so comprehensive a project of reform, but nobody set off any fireworks and nobody walked out. Moreover, in the two weeks that followed, the Virginia Plan received substantial endorsement *en principe;* the initial temper of the gathering can be deduced from the approval "without debate or dissent," on May 31, of the Sixth Resolution which granted Congress the authority to disallow state legislation "... contravening in its opinion the

Articles of Union." Indeed, an amendment was included to bar states from contravening national treaties.

The Virginia Plan may therefore be considered, in ideological terms, as the delegates' Utopia, but as the discussions continued and became more specific, many of those present began to have second thoughts.... They were practical politicians in a democratic society, and no matter what their private dreams might be, they had to take home an acceptable package and defend it—and their own political futures—against predictable attack. On June 14 the breaking point between dream and reality took place. Apparently realizing that under the Virginia Plan, Massachusetts, Virginia and Pennsylvania could virtually dominate the national government—and probably appreciating that to sell this program to "the folks back home" would be impossible—the delegates from the small states dug in their heels and demanded time for a consideration of alternatives....

Now the process of accommodation was put into action smoothly—and wisely, given the character and strength of the doubters. Madison had the votes, but this was one of those situations where the enforcement of mechanical majoritarianism could easily have destroyed the objectives of the majority: the Constitutionalists were in quest of a qualitative as well as a quantitative consensus; ... it was a political imperative if they were to attain ratification.

III

According to the standard script, at this point the "states'-rights" group intervened in force behind the New Jersey Plan, which has been characteristically portrayed as a revision to the status quo under the Articles of Confederation with but minor modifications. A careful examination of the evidence indicates that only in a marginal sense is this an accurate description. It is true that the New Jersey Plan put the states back into the institutional picture, but one could argue that to do so was a recognition of political reality rather than an affirmation of states'-rights. A serious case can be made that the advocates of the New Jersey Plan, far from being ideological addicts of states'-rights, intended to substitute for the Virginia Plan a system which would both retain strong national power and have a chance of adoption in the states. The leading spokesman for the project asserted quite clearly that his views were based more on counsels of expediency than on principle.... In his preliminary speech on June 9, Paterson had stated " ... to the public mind we must accommodate ourselves," and in his notes for this and his later effort as well, the emphasis is the same. The structure of government under the Articles should be retained:

> 2. Because it accords with the Sentiments of the People

>> [Proof:] 1. Coms. [Commissions from state legislatures defining the jurisdiction of the delegates]
>> 2. News-papers—Political Barometer. Jersey never would have sent Delegates under the first [Virginia] Plan—

> Not here to sport Opinions of my own. Wt. [What] can be done. A little practicable Virtue preferrable to Theory.

This was a defense of political acumen, not of states'-rights....

In other words, the advocates of the New Jersey Plan concentrated their fire on what they held to be the political liabilities of the Virginia Plan—which were matters of institutional structure—rather than on the proposed scope of national authority. Indeed, the Supremacy Clause of the Constitution first saw the light of day in Paterson's Sixth Resolution; the New Jersey Plan contemplated the use of military force to secure compliance with national law; and finally Paterson made clear his view that under either the Virginia or the New Jersey systems, the general government would "... act on individuals and not on states." From the states'-rights viewpoint, this was heresy: the fundament of that doctrine was the proposition that any central government had as its constituents the states, not the people, and could only reach the people through the agency of the state government.

Paterson then reopened the agenda of the Convention, but he did so within a distinctly naturalist framework. Paterson's position was one of favoring a strong central government in principle, but opposing one which in fact put the big states in the saddle.

How attached would the Virginians have been to their reform principles if Virginia were to disappear as a component geographical unit (the largest) for representational purposes? Up to this point, the Virginians had been in the happy position of supporting high ideals with that inner confidence born of knowledge that the "public interest" they endorsed would nourish their private interest. Worse, they had shown little willingness to compromise. Now the delegates from the small states announced that they were unprepared to be offered up as sacrificial victims to a "national interest" which reflected Virginia's parochial ambition. Caustic Charles Pinckney was not far off when he remarked sardonically that "... the whole [conflict] comes to this: Give N. Jersey an equal vote, and she will dismiss her scruples, and concur in the Natil. system." What he rather unfairly did not add was that the Jersey delegates were not free agents who could adhere to their private convictions; they had to take back, sponsor and risk their reputations on the reforms approved by the Convention—and in New Jersey, not in Virginia....

IV

On Tuesday morning, June 19, ... James Madison led off with a long, carefully reasoned speech analyzing the New Jersey Plan which, while intellectually vigorous in its criticisms, was quite conciliatory in mood. "The great difficulty," he observed, "lies in the affair of Representation; and if this could be adjusted, all others would be surmountable." (As events were to demonstrate, this diagnosis was correct.) When he finished, a vote was taken on whether to continue with the Virginia Plan as the nucleus for a new constitution: seven states voted "Yes"; New York, New Jersey, and Delaware voted "No"; and Maryland, whose position often depended on which delegates happened to be on the floor, divided. Paterson, it seems, lost decisively; yet in a fundamental sense he and his allies had achieved their purpose: from that day onward, it could never be forgotten that the state governments loomed ominously in the background.... Moreover, nobody bolted the convention: Paterson and his colleagues took their defeat in stride and set to work to modify the Virginia Plan, particularly with respect to its provisions on representation in the national legislature. Indeed, they won an immediate rhetorical bonus; when Oliver Ellsworth of Connecticut rose to move that the word "national" be expunged from the Third Virginia Resolution ("Resolved that a national Government ought to be established consisting of a supreme Legislative, Executive and Judiciary"), Randolph agreed and the motion passed unanimously. The process of compromise had begun.

For the next two weeks, the delegates circled around the problem of legislative representation. The Connecticut delegation appears to have evolved a possible compromise quite early in the debates, but the Virginians and particularly Madison (unaware that he would later be acclaimed as the prophet of "federalism") fought obdurately against providing for equal representation of states in the second chamber.... On July 2, the ice began to break when through a number of fortuitous events—and one that seems deliberate—the majority against equality of representation was converted into a dead tie. The Convention had reached the stage where it was "ripe" for a solution (presumably all the therapeutic speeches had been made), and the South Carolinians proposed a committee. Madison and James Wilson wanted none of it, but with only Pennsylvania dissenting, the body voted to establish a working party on the problem of representation.

The members of this committee, one from each state, were elected by the delegates—and a very interesting committee it was. Despite the fact that the Virginia Plan had held majority support up to that date, neither Madison nor Randolph was selected (Mason was the Virginian) and Baldwin of Georgia, whose shift in position had resulted in the tie, was chosen. From the composition, it was clear that this was not to be a "fighting" committee: the emphasis in membership was on what might be described as "second-level political entrepreneurs." On the basis of the discussions up to that time, only Luther Martin of Maryland could be described as a "bitter-ender." Admittedly, some divination enters into this sort of analysis, but one does get a sense of the mood of the delegates from these choices—including the interesting selection of Benjamin Franklin, despite his age and intellectual wobbliness, over the brilliant and incisive Wilson or the sharp, polemical Gouverneur Morris, to represent Pennsylvania. His passion for conciliation was more valuable at this juncture than Wilson's logical genius, or Morris' acerbic wit....

It would be tedious to continue a blow-by-blow analysis of the work of the delegates; the critical fight was over representation of the states and once the Connecticut Compromise was adopted on July 17, the Convention was over the hump. Madison, James Wilson, and Gouverneur Morris of New York (who was there representing Pennsylvania!) fought the compromise all the way in a last-ditch effort to get a unitary state with parliamentary supremacy. But their allies deserted them.... Moreover, once the compromise had carried (by five states to four, with one state divided), its advocates threw themselves vigorously into the job of strengthening the general government's substantive powers—as might have been predicted, indeed, from Paterson's early statements. It nourishes an increased respect for Madison's devotion to the art of politics, to realize that this dogged fighter could sit down six months later and prepare essays for *The Federalist* in contradiction to his basic convictions about the true course the Convention should have taken.

V

Two tricky issues will serve to illustrate the later process of accommodation. The first was the institutional position of the Executive. Madison argued for an executive chosen by the National Legislature and on May 29 this had been adopted with a provision that after his seven-year term was concluded, the chief magistrate should not be eligible for reelection. In late July this was reopened and for a week the matter was argued from several different points of view.... One group felt that the states should have a hand in the process; another small but influential circle urged direct election by the people. There were a number of proposals: election by the people, election by state governors, by electors chosen by state legislatures, by the National legislature, ... and there was some resemblance to three-dimensional chess in the dispute because of the presence of two other variables, length of tenure and reeligibility. Finally, after opening, reopening, and re-reopening the debate, the thorny problem was consigned to a committee for resolution.

The Brearley Committee on Postponed Matters was a superb aggregation of talent and its compromise on the Executive was a masterpiece of political improvisation. (The Electoral College, its creation, however, had little in its favor as an institution—as the delegates well appreciated.) The point of departure for all discussion about the presidency in the Convention was that in immediate terms, the problem was non-existent; in other words, everybody present knew that under any system devised, George Washington would be President. Thus they were dealing in the future tense and to a body of working politicians the merits of the Brearley proposal were obvious: everybody got a piece of cake. (Or to put it more academically, each viewpoint could leave the Convention and argue to its constituents that it had really won the day.) First, the state legislatures had the right to determine the mode of selection of the electors; second, the small states received a bonus in the Electoral College in the form of a guaranteed minimum of three votes while the big states got acceptance of the principle of proportional power; third, if the state legislatures agreed (as six did in the first presidential election), the people could be involved directly in the choice of electors; and finally, if no candidate received a majority in the College, the right of decision passed to the National Legislature with each state exercising equal strength. (In the Brearley recommendation, the election went to the Senate, but a motion from the floor substituted the House; this was accepted on the ground that the Senate already had enough authority over the executive in its treaty and appointment powers.)

This compromise was almost too good to be true, and the Framers snapped it up with little debate or controversy. No one seemed to think well of the College as an institution; indeed, what evidence there is suggests that there was an assumption that once Washington had finished his tenure as President, the electors would cease to produce majorities and the chief executive would usually be chosen in the House. George Mason observed casually that the selection would be made in the House nineteen times in twenty and no one seriously disputed this point. The vital aspect of the Electoral College was that it got the Convention over the hurdle and protected everybody's interests. . . .

In short, the Framers did not in their wisdom endow the United States with a College of Cardinals—the Electoral College was neither an exercise in applied Platonism nor an experiment in indirect government based on elitist distrust of the masses. It was merely a jerry-rigged improvisation which has subsequently been endowed with a high theoretical content. . . .

The second issue on which some substantial practical bargaining took place was slavery. The morality of slavery was, by design, not at issue; but in its other concrete aspects, slavery colored the arguments over taxation, commerce, and representation. The "Three-Fifths Compromise," that three-fifths of the slaves would be counted both for representation and for purposes of direct taxation (which was drawn from the past—it was a formula of Madison's utilized by Congress in 1783 to establish the basis of state contributions to the Confederation treasury) had allayed some Northern fears about Southern over-representation. . . . The Southerners, on the other hand, were afraid that Congressional control over commerce would lead to the exclusion of slaves or to their excessive taxation as imports. Moreover, the Southerners were disturbed over "navigation acts," i.e., tariffs or special legislation providing, for example, that exports be carried only in American ships; as a section depending upon exports, they wanted protection from the potential voracity of their commercial brethren of the Eastern states. To achieve this end, Mason and others urged that the Constitution include a proviso that navigation and commercial laws should require a two-thirds vote in Congress.

These problems came to a head in late August and, as usual were handed to a committee in the hope that, in Gouverneur Morris' words, " . . . these things may form a bargain among the Northern and Southern states." The Committee reported its measures of reconciliation on August 25, and on August 29 the package was wrapped up and delivered. What occurred can best be described in George Mason's dour version (he anticipated Calhoun in his conviction that permitting navigation acts to pass by majority vote would put the South in economic bondage to the North—it was mainly on this ground that he refused to sign the Constitution):

> The Constitution as agreed to till a fortnight before the Convention rose was such a one as he would have set his hand and heart to. . . . [Until that time] The 3 New England States were constantly with us in all questions . . . so that it was these three States with the 5 Southern ones against Pennsylvania, Jersey and Delaware. With respect to the importation of slaves, [decision-making] was left to Congress. This disturbed the two Southernmost States who knew that Congress would immediately suppress the importation of slaves. Those two States therefore struck up a bargain with the three New England States. If they would join to admit slaves for some years, the two Southern-most States would join in changing the clause which required the 2/3 of the Legislature in any vote [on navigation acts]. It was done.

On the floor of the Convention there was a virtual love-feast on this happy occasion. Charles Pinckney of South Carolina attempted to overturn the committee's decision, when the compromise was reported to the Convention, by insisting that the South needed protection from the imperialism of the Northern states. But his Southern colleagues were not prepared to rock the boat and General C. C. Pinckney arose to spread oil on the suddenly ruffled waters; he admitted that:

> It was in the true interest of the S[outhern] States to have no regulation of commerce; but considering the loss brought on the commerce of the Eastern States by the Revolution, their liberal conduct towards the views of South Carolina [on the regulation of the slave trade] and the interests the weak Southn. States had in being united with the strong Eastern states, he thought it proper that no fetters should be imposed on the power of making commercial regulations; and that his constituents, though prejudiced against the Eastern States, would be reconciled to this liberality. He had himself prejudices against the Eastern States before he came here, but would acknowledge that he had found them as liberal and candid as any men whatever.

Pierce Butler took the same tack, essentially arguing that he was not too happy about the possible consequences, but that a deal was a deal. . . .

VI

Drawing on their vast collective political experience, utilizing every weapon in the politician's arsenal, looking constantly over their shoulders at their constituents, the delegates put together a Constitution. It was a makeshift affair; some sticky issues (for example, the qualification of voters) they ducked entirely; others they mastered with that ancient instrument of political sagacity, studied ambiguity (for example, citizenship), and some they just overlooked. In this last category, I suspect, fell the matter of the power of the federal courts to determine the constitutionality of acts of Congress. When the judicial article was formulated (Article III of the Constitution), deliberations were still in the stage where the legislature was endowed with broad power under the Randolph formulation, authority which by its own terms was scarcely amenable to judicial review. In essence, courts could hardly determine when " . . . the separate States are incompetent or . . . the harmony of the United States may be interrupted"; the National Legislature, as critics pointed out, was free to define its own jurisdiction. Later the definition of legislative authority was changed into the form we know, a series of stipulated powers, but the delegates never seriously reexamined the jurisdiction of the judiciary under this new limited formulation. All arguments on the intention of the Framers in this matter are thus deductive and a posteriori, though some obviously make more sense than others.

The Framers were busy and distinguished men, anxious to get back to their families, their positions, and their constituents. . . . They were trying to do an important job, and do it in such a fashion that their handiwork would be acceptable to very diverse constituencies. No one was rhapsodic about the final document, but it was a beginning, a move in the right direction, and one they had reason to believe the people would endorse. In addition, since they had modified the impossible amendment provisions of the Articles... to one demanding approval by only three-quarters of the states, they seemed confident that gaps in the fabric which experience would reveal could be rewoven without undue difficulty.

So with a neat phrase introduced by Benjamin Franklin (but devised by Gouverneur Morris) which made their decision sound unanimous, and an in-spired benediction by the Old Doctor urging doubters to doubt their own infallibility, the Constitution was accepted and signed. Curiously, Edmund Randolph, who had played so vital a role throughout, refused to sign, as did his fel-low Virginian George Mason and Elbridge Gerry of Massachusetts. Randolph's behavior was eccentric;... the best explanation seems to be that he was afraid that the Constitution would prove to be a liability in Virginia politics, where Patrick Henry was burning up the countryside with impassioned denunciations. Presumably, Randolph wanted to check the temper of the populace before he risked his reputation, and perhaps his job, in a fight with both Henry and Richard Henry Lee. Events lend some justification to this speculation: after much temporizing... Randolph endorsed ratification in Virginia and ended up getting the best of both worlds....

The Constitution, then, was an apotheosis of "constitutionalism," a tri-umph of architectonic genius; it was a patchwork sewn together under the pressure of both time and events by a group of extremely talented democratic politicians. They refused to attempt the establishment of a strong, centralized sovereignty on the principle of legislative supremacy for the excellent reason that the people would not accept it. They risked their political fortunes by opposing the established doctrines of state sovereignty because they were con-vinced that the existing system was leading to national impotence and probably foreign domination. For two years, they worked to get a convention established. For over three months, in what must have seemed to the faithful participants an endless process of give-and-take, they reasoned, cajoled, threatened, and bar-gained amongst themselves. The result was a Constitution which the people, in fact, by democratic processes, did accept, and a new and far better national government was established....

To conclude, the Constitution was neither a victory for abstract theory nor a great practical success. Well over half a million men had to die on the battle-fields of the Civil War before certain constitutional principles could be defined —a baleful consideration which is somehow overlooked in our customary trib-utes to the farsighted genius of the Framers and to the supposed American talent for "constitutionalism." The Constitution was, however, a vivid demonstration of effective democratic political action, and of the forging of a national elite which literally persuaded its countrymen to hoist themselves by their own boot straps.

The Framers of the Constitution
and the "Genius" of the People

On June 18, 1787, about three weeks into the Constitutional Convention at Philadelphia, Alexander Hamilton delivered a six-hour address that was easily the longest and most conservative the Convention would hear. Gouverneur Morris, a delegate from Pennsylvania, thought it was "the most able and impressive he had ever heard."

Beginning with the premise that "all communities divide themselves into the few and the many," "the wealthy well born" and "the people," Hamilton added the corollary that the "people are turbulent and changing; they seldom judge or determine right." Moving through history, the delegate from New York developed his ideal for a national government that would protect the few from "the imprudence of democracy" and guarantee "stability and permanence": a president and senate indirectly elected for life ("to serve during good behavior") to balance a house directly elected by a popular vote every three years. This "elective monarch" would have an absolute veto over laws passed by Congress. And the national government would appoint the governors of the states, who in turn would have the power to veto any laws by the state legislatures.

If others quickly saw a resemblance in all of this to the King, House of Lords and House of Commons of Great Britain, with the states reduced to colonies ruled by royal governors, they were not mistaken. The British constitution, in Hamilton's view, remained "the best model the world has ever produced."

Three days later a delegate reported that Hamilton's proposals "had been praised by everybody," but "he has been supported by none." Acknowledging that his plan "went beyond the ideas of most members," Hamilton said he had brought it forward not "as a thing attainable by us, but as a model which we ought to approach as near as possible." When he signed the Constitution the framers finally agreed to on September 17, 1787, Hamilton could accurately say, "no plan was more remote from his own."

Why did the framers reject a plan so many admired? To ask this question is to go down a dark path into the heart of the Constitution few of its celebrants care to take. We have heard so much in our elementary and high

From Alfred F. Young, "The Framers of the Constitution and the 'Genius' of the People," *Radical History Review*, vol. 42 (1988). Copyright © 1988 by Cambridge University Press. Reprinted by permission.

school civics books about the "great compromises" within the Convention—between the large states and the small states, between the slaveholders and non-slaveholders, between North and South—that we have missed the much larger accommodation that was taking place between the delegates as a whole at the Convention and what they called "the people out of doors."

The Convention was unmistakably an elite body. [In 1987] the official exhibit for the bicentennial, "Miracle at Philadelphia," [opened] appropriately enough with a large oil portrait of Robert Morris, a delegate from Philadelphia, one of the richest merchants in America, and points out elsewhere that 11 out of 55 delegates were business associates of Morris'. The 55 were weighted with merchants, slaveholding planters and "monied men" who loaned money at interest. Among them were numerous lawyers and college graduates in a country where most men and only a few women had the rudiments of a formal education. They were far from a cross section of the four million or so Americans of that day, most of whom were farmers or artisans, fishermen or seamen, indentured servants or laborers, half of whom were women and about 600,000 of whom were African-American slaves.

The First Accommodation

Why did this elite reject Hamilton's plan that many of them praised? James Madison, the Constitution's chief architect, had the nub of the matter. The Constitution was "intended for the ages." To last it had to conform to the "genius" of the American people. "Genius" was a word eighteenth-century political thinkers used to mean spirit: we might say character or underlying values.

James Wilson, second only to Madison in his influence at Philadelphia, elaborated on the idea. "The British government cannot be our model. We have no materials for a similar one. Our manners, our law, the abolition of entail and primogeniture," which made for a more equal distribution of property among sons, "the whole genius of the people, are opposed to it."

This was long-range political philosophy. There was a short-range political problem that moved other realistic delegates in the same direction. Called together to revise the old Articles of Confederation, the delegates instead decided to scrap it and frame an entirely new constitution. It would have to be submitted to the people for ratification, most likely to conventions elected especially for the purpose. Repeatedly, conservatives recoiled from extreme proposals for which they knew they could not win popular support.

In response to a proposal to extend the federal judiciary into the states, Pierce Butler, a South Carolina planter, argued, "the people will not bear such innovations. The states will revolt at such encroachments." His assumption was "we must follow the example of Solomon, who gave the Athenians not the best government he could devise but the best they would receive."

The suffrage debate epitomized this line of thinking. Gouverneur Morris, Hamilton's admirer, proposed that the national government limit voting for the House to men who owned a freehold, i.e. a substantial farm, or its equivalent. "Give the vote to people who have no property and they will sell them to the rich who will be able to buy them," he said with some prescience. George Mason, author of Virginia's Bill of Rights, was aghast. "Eight or nine states have extended the right of suffrage beyond the freeholders. What will people there say if they should be disfranchised?"

Benjamin Franklin, the patriarch, speaking for one of the few times in the convention, paid tribute to "the lower class of freemen" who should not be disfranchised. James Wilson explained, "it would be very hard and disagreeable for the same person" who could vote for representatives for the state legislatures "to be excluded from a vote for this in the national legislature." Nathaniel Gorham, a Boston merchant, returned to the guiding principle: "the people will never allow" existing rights to suffrage to be abridged. "We must consult their rooted prejudices if we expect their concurrence in our propositions."

The result? Morris' proposal was defeated and the convention decided that whoever each state allowed to vote for its own assembly could vote for the House. It was a compromise that left the door open and in a matter of decades allowed states to introduce universal white male suffrage.

Ghosts of Years Past

Clearly there was a process of accommodation at work here. The popular movements of the Revolutionary Era were a presence at the Philadelphia Convention even if they were not present. The delegates, one might say, were haunted by ghosts, symbols of the broadly based movements elites had confronted in the making of the Revolution from 1765 to 1775, in waging the war from 1775 to 1781 and in the years since 1781 within their own states.

The first was the ghost of Thomas Paine, the most influential radical democrat of the Revolutionary Era. In 1776 Paine's pamphlet *Common Sense* (which sold at least 150,000 copies), in arguing for independence, rejected not only King George III but the principle of monarchy and the so-called checks and balances of the unwritten English constitution. In its place he offered a vision of a democratic government in which a single legislature would be supreme, the executive minimal, and representatives would be elected from small districts by a broad electorate for short terms so they could "return and mix again with the voters." John Adams considered *Common Sense* too "democratical," without even an attempt at "mixed government" that would balance "democracy" with "aristocracy."

The second ghost was that of Abraham Yates, a member of the state senate of New York typical of the new men who had risen to power in the 1780s in the state legislatures. We have forgotten him; Hamilton, who was very conscious of him, called him "an old Booby." He had begun as a shoemaker and was a self-taught lawyer and warm foe of the landlord aristocracy of the Hudson Valley which Hamilton had married into. As James Madison identified the "vices of the political system of the United States" in a memorandum in 1787, the Abraham Yateses were the number-one problem. The state legislatures had "an itch for paper money" laws, laws that prevented foreclosure on farm mortgages, and tax laws that soaked the rich. As Madison saw it, this meant that "debtors defrauded their creditors" and "the landed interest has borne hard on the mercantile interest." This, too, is what Hamilton had in mind when he spoke of the "depredations which the democratic spirit is apt to make on property" and what others meant by the "excess of democracy" in the states.

The third ghost was a very fresh one—Daniel Shays. In 1786 Shays, a captain in the Revolution, led a rebellion of debtor farmers in western Massachusetts which the state quelled with its own somewhat unreliable militia. There were "combustibles in every state," as George Washington put it, raising the specter of "Shaysism." This Madison enumerated among the "vices" of the system as "a want of guaranty to the states against internal violence." Worse still, Shaysites in many states were turning to the political system to elect their own kind. If they succeeded they would produce legal Shaysism, a danger for which the elites had no remedy.

The fourth ghost we can name was the ghost of Thomas Peters, although he had a thousand other names. In 1775, Peters, a Virginia slave, responded to a plea by the British to fight in their army and win their freedom. He served in an "Ethiopian Regiment," some of whose members bore the emblem "Liberty to Slaves" on their uniforms. After the war the British transported Peters and several thousand escaped slaves to Nova Scotia from whence Peters eventually led a group to return to Africa and the colony of Sierra Leone, a long odyssey to freedom. Eighteenth-century slaveholders, with no illusions about happy or contented slaves, were haunted by the specter of slaves in arms.

Elite Divisions

During the Revolutionary Era elites divided in response to these varied threats from below. One group, out of fear of "the mob" and then "the rabble in arms," embraced the British and became active Loyalists. After the war most of them went into exile. Another group who became patriots never lost their obsession with coercing popular movements....

Far more important, however, were those patriot leaders who adopted a strategy of "swimming with a stream which it is impossible to stem." This was the metaphor of Robert R. Livingston, Jr., ... a gentleman with a large tenanted estate in New York. Men of his class had to learn to "yield to the torrent if they hoped to direct its course."

Livingston and his group were able to shape New York's constitution, which some called a perfect blend of "aristocracy" and "democracy." John Hancock, the richest merchant in New England, had mastered this kind of politics and emerged as the most popular politician in Massachusetts. In Maryland Charles Carroll, a wealthy planter, instructed his anxious father about the need to "submit to partial losses" because "no great revolution can happen in a state without revolutions or mutations of private property. If we can save a third of our personal estate and all of our lands and Negroes, I shall think ourselves well off."

The major leaders at the Constitutional Convention in 1787 were heirs to both traditions: coercion and accommodation—Hamilton and Gouverneur Morris to the former, James Madison and James Wilson much more to the latter.

They all agreed on coercion to slay the ghosts of Daniel Shays and Thomas Peters. The Constitution gave the national government the power to "suppress insurrections" and protect the states from "domestic violence." There would be a national army under the command of the president, and authority to nationalize the state militias and suspend the right of habeas corpus in "cases of rebellion or invasion." In 1794 Hamilton, as secretary of the treasury, would exercise such powers fully (and needlessly) to suppress the Whiskey Rebellion in western Pennsylvania.

Southern slaveholders correctly interpreted the same powers as available to shackle the ghost of Thomas Peters. As it turned out, Virginia would not need a federal army to deal with Gabriel Prosser's insurrection in 1800 or Nat Turner's rebellion in 1830, but a federal army would capture John Brown after his raid at Harpers Ferry in 1859.

But how to deal with the ghosts of Thomas Paine and Abraham Yates? Here Madison and Wilson blended coercion with accommodation. They had three solutions to the threat of democratic majorities in the states.

Their first was clearly coercive. Like Hamilton, Madison wanted some kind of national veto over the state legislatures. He got several very specific curbs on the states written into fundamental law: no state could "emit" paper money or pass "laws impairing the obligation of contracts." Wilson was so overjoyed with these two clauses that he argued that if they alone "were inserted in the Constitution I think they would be worth our adoption."

But Madison considered the overall mechanism adopted to curb the states "short of the mark." The Constitution, laws and treaties were the "supreme law of the land" and ultimately a federal court could declare state laws unconstitutional. But this, Madison lamented, would only catch "mischiefs" after the fact. Thus they had clipped the wings of Abraham Yates but he could still fly.

The second solution to the problem of the states was decidedly democratic. They wanted to do an end-run around the state legislatures. The Articles of Confederation, said Madison, rested on "the pillars" of the state legislatures who elected delegates to Congress. The "great fabric to be raised would be more stable and durable if it should rest on the solid grounds of the people themselves"; hence, there would be popular elections to the House.

Wilson altered only the metaphor. He was for "raising the federal pyramid to a considerable altitude and for that reason wanted to give it as broad a base as possible." They would slay the ghost of Abraham Yates with the ghost of Thomas Paine.

This was risky business. They would reduce the risk by keeping the House of Representatives small. Under a ratio of one representative for every 30,000 people, the first house would have only 65 members; in 1776 Thomas Paine had suggested 390. But still, the House would be elected every two years, and with each state allowed to determine its own qualifications for voting, there was no telling who might end up in Congress.

There was also a risk in Madison's third solution to the problem of protecting propertied interests from democratic majorities: "extending the sphere" of government. Prevailing wisdom held that a republic could only succeed in a small geographic area; to rule an "extensive" country, some kind of despotism was considered inevitable.

Madison turned this idea on its head in his since famous *Federalist* essay No. 10. In a small republic, he argued, it was relatively easy for a majority to gang up on a particular "interest." "Extend the sphere," he wrote, and "you take in a greater variety of parties and interests." Then it would be more difficult for a majority "to discover their own strength and to act in unison with each other."

This was a prescription for a non-colonial empire that would expand across the continent, taking in new states as it dispossessed the Indians. The risk was there was no telling how far the "democratic" or "leveling" spirit might go in such likely would-be states as frontier Vermont, Kentucky and Tennessee.

Democratic Divisions

In the spectrum of state constitutions adopted in the Revolutionary era, the federal Constitution of 1787 was, like New York's, somewhere between "aristocracy" and "democracy." It therefore should not surprise us—although it has eluded many modern critics of the Constitution—that in the contest over ratification in 1787–1788, the democratic minded were divided.

Among agrarian democrats there was a gut feeling that the Constitution was the work of an old class enemy. "These lawyers and men of learning and monied men," argued Amos Singletary, a working farmer at the Massachusetts ratifying convention, "expect to be managers of this Constitution and get all the power and all the money into their own hands and then will swallow up all of us little folks ... just as the whale swallowed up Jonah."

Democratic leaders like Melancton Smith of New York focused on the small size of the proposed House. Arguing from Paine's premise that the members of the legislature should "resemble those they represent," Smith feared that "a substantial yeoman of sense and discernment will hardly ever be chosen" and the government "will fall into the hands of the few and the great." Urban democrats, on the other hand, including a majority of the mechanics and tradesmen of the major cities who in the Revolution had been a bulwark of Paineite radicalism, were generally enthusiastic about the Constitution. They were impelled by their urgent stake in a stronger national government that would advance ocean-going commerce and protect American manufacturers from competition. But they would not have been as ardent about the new frame of government without its saving graces. It clearly preserved their rights to suffrage. And the process of ratification, like the Constitution itself, guaranteed them a voice. As early as 1776 the New York Committee of Mechanics held it as "a right which God has given them in common with all men to judge whether it be consistent with their interest to accept or reject a constitution."

Mechanics turned out en masse in the parades celebrating ratification, marching trade by trade. The slogans and symbols they carried expressed their political ideals. In New York the upholsterers had a float with an elegant "Federal Chair of State" flanked by the symbols of Liberty and Justice that they identified with the Constitution. In Philadelphia the bricklayers put on their banner "Both buildings and rulers are the work of our hands."

Democrats who were skeptical found it easier to come over because of the Constitution's redeeming features. Thomas Paine, off in Paris, considered the Constitution "a copy, though not quite as base as the original, of the form of the British government." He had always opposed a single executive and he objected to the "long duration of the Senate." But he was so convinced of "the absolute necessity" of a stronger federal government that "I would have voted for it myself had I been in America or even for a worse, rather than have none." It was crucial to Paine that there was an amending process, the means of "remedying its defects by the same appeal to the people by which it was to be established."

The Second Accommodation

In drafting the Constitution in 1787 the framers, self-styled Federalists, made their first accommodation with the "genius" of the people. In campaigning for its ratification in 1788 they made their second. At the outset, the conventions in the key states—Massachusetts, New York and Virginia—either had an anti-Federalist majority or were closely divided. To swing over a small group of "antis" in each state, Federalists had to promise that they would consider amendments. This was enough to secure ratification by narrow margins in Massachusetts, 187 to 168; in New York, 30 to 27; and in Virginia, 89 to 79.

What the anti-Federalists wanted were dozens of changes in the structure of the government that would cut back national power over the states, curb the powers of the presidency as well as protect individual liberties. What they got was far less. But in the first Congress in 1789, James Madison, true to his pledge, considered all the amendments and shepherded 12 amendments through both houses. The first two of these failed in the states; one would have enlarged the House. The 10 that were ratified by December 1791 were what we have since called the Bill of Rights, protecting freedom of expression and the rights of the accused before the law. Abraham Yates considered them "trivial and unimportant." But other democrats looked on them much more favorably. In time the limited meaning of freedom of speech in the First Amendment was broadened far beyond the framers' original intent. Later popular movements thought of the Bill of Rights as an essential part of the "constitutional" and "republican" rights that belonged to the people.

The "Loser's" Role

There is a cautionary tale here that surely goes beyond the process of framing and adopting the Constitution and Bill of Rights from 1787 to 1791. The Constitution was as democratic as it was because of the influence of popular movements that were a presence, even if not present. The losers helped shape the results. We owe the Bill of Rights to the opponents of the Constitution, as we do many other features in the Constitution put in to anticipate opposition.

In American history popular movements often shaped elites, especially in times of crisis when elites were concerned with the "system." Elites have often divided in response to such threats and according to their perception of the "genius" of the people. Some have turned to coercion, others to accommodation. We run serious risk if we ignore this distinction. Would that we had fewer Gouverneur Morrises and Alexander Hamiltons and more James Madisons and James Wilsons to respond to the "genius" of the people.

POSTSCRIPT

Were the Founding Fathers Democratic Reformers?

Roche stresses the political reasons for writing a new Constitution. In a spirited essay that reflects great admiration for the Founding Fathers as enlightened politicians, Roche describes the Constitution as "a triumph of architectonic genius; it was a patch-work sewn together under the pressure of both time and events by a group of extremely talented democratic politicians."

Roche narrates the events of the convention of 1787 with a clarity rarely seen in the writings on this period. He makes the telling point that once the dissenters left Philadelphia, the delegates were able to hammer out a new Constitution. All the Founding Fathers agreed to create a stronger national government, but differences centered around the shape the new government would take. The delegates' major concern was to create as strong a national government as possible that would be acceptable to all states. Had the ratifying conventions rejected the new Constitution, the United States might have disintegrated into 13 separate countries.

Young asserts that the Constitution was written by an elite group of people to strengthen the powers of the national government against those of the people. He believes that four ghosts that made their presence felt at the Philadelphia Convention caused the Founding Fathers to react in a paradoxical manner. On the one hand, the shadows of the radical Democrat Thomas Paine and arch Anti-Federalist Abraham Yates of the New York State senate forced the Founding Fathers to support universal white male suffrage, a House of Representatives directly elected by the people every two years, and a bill of rights to protect the individual liberties of people from a tyrannical government. On the other hand, the national government was able to quell the ghosts of Daniel Shays and ex-slave Thomas Peters with its power to "suppress insurrections" and protect the states from "domestic violence."

Historian Gordon S. Wood tries to recapture the eighteenth-century world in *The Creation of the American Republic, 1776–1787* (University of North Carolina Press, 1969), a seminal work that has replaced Beard as the starting point for scholarship on this topic. A devastating critique of the methodological fallacies of Wood and other intellectual writers on this period can be found in Ralph Lerner's "The Constitution of the Thinking Revolutionary," in Richard Beeman et al., eds., *Beyond Confederation: Origins of the Constitution and American National Identity* (University of North Carolina Press, 1987). Also see Richard B. Morris, *The Forging of the Union, 1781–1789* (Harper & Row, 1987) and Michael Kammen, *A Machine That Would Go of Itself: The Constitution in American Culture* (Alfred A. Knopf, 1986).

ISSUE 8

Was Thomas Jefferson Committed to Bringing an End to Chattel Slavery?

YES: Dumas Malone, from *Jefferson and His Time, vol. 6: The Sage of Monticello* (Little, Brown, 1981)

NO: William Cohen, from "Thomas Jefferson and the Problem of Slavery," *The Journal of American History* (December 1969)

ISSUE SUMMARY

YES: American historian Dumas Malone (1892–1986) asserts that, although he did not live to see slavery abolished, Thomas Jefferson sincerely deplored the slave system as unjust to its victims and injurious to the masters. Malone maintains that Jefferson was one of the first Americans to propose a specific plan for emancipation.

NO: American historian William Cohen contends that libertarian views had virtually no impact on Jefferson's actions after 1784 and that his behavior as a slave owner differed little from that of Virginia planters who opposed his antislavery speculations and who were committed to protecting their chattel property.

T homas Jefferson still survives," former president John Adams uttered as he died on July 4, 1826. Unknown to Adams, however, Jefferson had passed away a few hours earlier that same day—the 50th anniversary of the adoption of the Declaration of Independence. But Jefferson never really died; rather, he became a living American legend. In 1968 *Esquire* magazine polled 174 members of Congress, asking each, "What idea, work, or thinker most influenced your present political philosophy?" While a number of the respondents named either Abraham Lincoln or Woodrow Wilson as their most admired thinker, the individual most commonly selected was Thomas Jefferson. Indeed, the variety of congressional representatives—Democrats and Republicans, liberals and conservatives, northerners and southerners—who chose Jefferson reveals his amazing ability to be many things to many different people.

There were at least two Jeffersons. One was a man of ideas. As a philosopher who spoke to posterity, he waxed eloquent in his writings about civil liberties, the rights of man, strict construction of the Constitution, states' rights, and the virtues of the agrarian way of life. Many observers have noted that Jefferson possessed a tremendous penchant for theoretical analysis. His was a giant intellect recognized most famously by President John F. Kennedy, who, during a White House dinner honoring recipients of the Nobel Prize, toasted his guests by describing them as "the most extraordinary collection of talent, of human knowledge, that has ever been gathered together at the White House, with the possible exception of when Thomas Jefferson dined alone."

In addition, Jefferson was a true Renaissance man who knew a little about everything. A practical man in both his daily life and in politics, he was an architect of the nation's capital, the University of Virginia, and his own home. Visitors to Monticello are amazed by the elaborate pulley and drainage systems that he devised. When he traveled, he recorded everything he observed in detailed journals. The newest inventions—steam engines, thermometers, elevators —fascinated him. "Not a sprig of grass shoots uninteresting to me," he once wrote to one of his daughters.

Jefferson's practicality extended to his career in politics and prevented him from being held captive to his ideology. For example, despite his ideological commitment to strict construction of the Constitution, Jefferson was able to set aside his preference for limited government in order to complete the negotiations for the Louisiana Purchase. While questioning the constitutionality of the Bank of the United States, as president he did nothing to tamper with the Bank's operations. And though firmly tied to the nation's agrarian interests, Jefferson nevertheless realized during his presidential terms that he needed the support of commercial and manufacturing interests to strengthen the country's economic position.

Perhaps nowhere is the contrast between ideas and practice more evident in Jefferson's life than on the question of slavery. A respected member of the Virginia aristocracy who owned about 10,000 acres and between 100 and 200 slaves, Jefferson attempted to operate his plantation in a self-sufficient manner and carefully studied the efficiency of employing slave labor. It is one of the great ironies of American history, then, that a man who abhorred the institution of slavery and who, as the chief architect of the Declaration of Independence, expressed the view that "all men are created equal," was himself a slave owner.

In the selections that follow, two historians analyze Thomas Jefferson's commitment to the institution of slavery. Jefferson's chief biographer, Dumas Malone, emphasizes that "the sage of Monticello" clearly recognized the contradiction posed by the presence of chattel slavery in a nation committed to freedom and liberty. Focusing on Jefferson's public record and private correspondence, Malone concludes that Jefferson sought an end to slavery but realized that the duty of relieving the South of this moral stigma would lay with a future generation. According to William Cohen, however, Jefferson's world depended upon slave labor for its existence. By examining Jefferson's treatment of fugitive slaves, his sale of slaves, and his attitude toward manumission (emancipation from slavery), Cohen concludes that Jefferson's actions, motivated by prevailing racial attitudes and economic considerations, differed little from those of his Virginia planter counterparts.

The Hopes and Fears of a Slaveholder

In one of the last letters he ever wrote, Jefferson said that the subject of slavery was one on which he did not permit himself to express an opinion except when "time, place, and occasion" could give it "some favorable effect." He added that his sentiments had been before the public for forty years. He must have been referring primarily to what he said in his *Notes on Virginia*, which appeared during his ministry in France. After his return to America in 1789, he seems never again to have expressed himself publicly on the subject of domestic slavery. Throughout the rest of his life he responded candidly to private inquiries about his views, and he elaborated on them somewhat in private letters. They remained essentially unchanged, but nowhere were they so vividly presented as in the book he published and the letters he wrote to men of learning while in the Old World.

He deplored the institution of slavery as unjust to its victims and injurious to the characters of its ostensible beneficiaries. The lurid picture he drew in the *Notes* of a raging master and hapless slave could hardly have been matched in later abolitionist literature. A few years after his retirement it was criticized by John Taylor of Caroline as extravagant and atypical. However, he did not disown it, nor did he try to tone it down.

His moral indignation was never more strikingly displayed than in certain comments he made when in Paris to the editor of the *Encyclopédie Méthodique*:

> What a stupendous, what an incomprehensible machine is man! Who can endure toil, famine, stripes, imprisonment or death itself in vindication of his own liberty, and the next moment... inflict on his fellow men a bondage, one hour of which is fraught with more misery than ages of that which he rose in rebellion to oppose.

Judging from other words of his, he did not believe that his own slaves were in constant misery, but the contradiction that he observed in human nature and in his native society deeply troubled him as a rational and humane being. He clearly perceived that this contradiction could be resolved only by the abolition of legalized slavery.

He was one of the first Americans to propose a specific plan of emancipation. He said he devised it when engaged in the revision of the laws of

Virginia during the American Revolution. The plan called for the freeing of all slaves born in his state after a specified date, for their training in useful pursuits under public authority, and for their removal to another locality on reaching maturity. The time did not seem ripe to present the plan to the legislature, nor did anything come of his draft of a constitution for Virginia (1783), containing a provision for the emancipation of slaves born after 1800. Both of these proposals appeared in print in his *Notes on Virginia.*

As designed by Jefferson, emancipation was to be a gradual process and, under his plan, the freed slaves were to go through a long period of preparation for economic independence and self-support. The wisdom of this provision could hardly have been questioned, whatever might have been said about its feasibility. He himself thought that someone would probably ask why he proposed that the emancipated blacks be ultimately deported instead of being incorporated into the state. This generally optimistic man did not believe that the whites and blacks could live together peaceably on the basis of equality. In a memorable passage in his *Notes on Virginia,* he said:

> Deep rooted prejudices entertained by the whites; ten thousand recollections, by the blacks, of the injuries they have sustained; new provocations; the real distinctions which nature has made; and many other circumstances, will divide us into parties, and produce convulsions which will probably never end but in the extermination of the one or the other race.

He may never again have spoken so strongly about racial conflict, but he never lost his fear of it. And he spoke for himself as well as for his society when he said: "This unfortunate difference of color and perhaps of faculty is a powerful obstacle to the emancipation of these people." He was well aware of the obstacle which most people probably regarded as the main one—the financial interest of slave-owners. The statement he made to Dr. Richard Price while in France, that the contest in Virginia would be between justice and avarice, was an over-simplification, as other comments of his clearly show. In his early years of service in the House of Burgesses, however, he had gained impressions of complacent self-interest that remained vivid in his memory. Speaking years later of the attitude of planters of the pre-Revolutionary generation toward their slaves, he said:

> Nursed and educated in the daily habit of seeing the degraded condition, both bodily and mental, of those unfortunate beings, ... few minds had yet doubted but that they were as legitimate subjects of property as their horses and cattle.

He resented the designation of these unfortunate human beings as property. He did not even like to call them slaves. When referring to those in his own possession, he generally spoke of them as servants or as his "people."

Until the end of his life he claimed that he would gladly bear the financial loss from emancipation if a practicable plan could be adopted. Since he was never put to the test, his dismissal of financial considerations as unworthy may be regarded by latter-day critics as an empty gesture, but it was an indication of his scale of values. No doubt he was viewed by many of his fellows as a dreamer. At any rate, he realized that planters who grew up in colonial Virginia took slavery as a matter of course. Such hopes as he had of relieving his state of the moral stigma of slavery lay with the rising generation, whose members had imbibed or should have imbibed the spirit of freedom with their mothers' milk. As things turned out, they were as apathetic as their fathers and more fearful.

In later years Jefferson said that if he had remained in the service of his state the problem of slavery would have been a major object of his attention. What the results might have been we can only guess, but judging from his own report of what happened before and after he went to France, he might have expected severe rebuffs. Actually, his public service was on the federal level until his retirement from the presidency in 1809, while domestic slavery was regarded by virtually everybody as solely subject to state authority. It was not a national issue when he became secretary of state, and his public silence on the question afterwards should not be surprising.

Jefferson never ceased to believe that the condition of mankind would progressively improve with the growth and spread of knowledge. He was keenly sensitive to public opinion and was notably patient as well as persistent in the pursuit of goals. The purpose of all government, as he saw it, was to secure human rights, and throughout life he sought to broaden the concept of humanity. As a public servant, however, he had to devote himself to the business at hand—most importantly, the completion and preservation of American independence, along with the maintenance of true republicanism. As a party chieftain he was faced with the task of unifying his followers, and as President with that of holding the nation together.

When in France he went to considerable pains to point out the obstacles to emancipation in his own country. These by no means disappeared in the score of years after his return to America. Although early in 1805 he observed that slavery was becoming undesirable on economic grounds, slaves actually constituted a larger percentage of the total population of Virginia in this decade than at any other in Jefferson's lifetime. The Gabriel revolt early in his administration proved abortive, but the revolution in St. Domingo was unquestionably successful. The massacre of the whites and mulattoes by the triumphant blacks bore out Jefferson's direful forebodings of racial conflict.

Added to the fear occasioned in his state by this revolution was a growing distrust of free blacks. Their numbers had increased since the passage of the liberal manumission law of 1782. Stories of their idleness and corruption could easily have been exaggerated, but these were not confined to the slave states. Near the end of Jefferson's days, the editor of the *North American Review* in Boston referred to "the living pestilence of a free black population." In 1806 the General Assembly of Virginia had tried to avoid this by amending the manumission law of 1782. Henceforth an emancipated slave was required to leave the state within a year.

As President, Jefferson followed a policy of non-involvement in state and local affairs, believing that his intervention would be resented and that his advocacy of a particular cause or measure might do it more harm than good. His private letters show that he regarded the abolition of slavery as inevitable, but he had no hope that peaceful emancipation would be effected or even begun in any southern state in the near future. Midway in his presidency he frankly described the policy he had imposed on himself in these circumstances. He told a Quaker abolitionist that he had "most carefully avoided every public action or manifestation" on the subject of slavery. He added that if an occasion should arise when he "could speak with decisive effect," he would do his duty.

As the responsible head of the Republic, he was probably wise in avoiding futile gesticulation, and he availed himself of one opportunity to act decisively. As the time neared when the legal importation of slaves could be terminated, he recommended that Congress put an end to this long-continued violation of the rights of the "unoffending inhabitants" of Africa. A law was passed, but neither he nor anybody else made much of it in that time of world war.

Abolition did not become a live issue during the years immediately following Jefferson's retirement from public office, when he was personally directing agricultural operations at Monticello and trying to straighten out his tangled financial affairs. As in the past, he received occasional letters relating to slavery. In the last summer of the war (1814), he had one from a fellow Virginian on the question that he himself had refrained from discussing in public. The writer was Edward Coles of Albemarle County, then in his late twenties, who was now secretary to President Madison, as his elder brother Isaac had been to Jefferson.

In a deferential letter his young friend urged the former President to devise and promote a plan for the general emancipation of the slaves in their state. To perform this difficult task Jefferson was pre-eminently qualified, he said, because of that patriot's avowed principles and conspicuous services to the cause of human rights. He believed that the author of the Declaration of Independence could do more than anybody else to bring the "hallowed principles" of this document into full effect. Coles urged Jefferson not to be deterred by fear of failure, saying that the influence of his example would be even greater after death than in life, and that he would be on the side of emancipation in future conflict. Speaking for himself, Coles, who had recently inherited a score of slaves, said he found the system so repugnant that he was determined to leave the state. He said nothing about taking slaves with him, giving the impression, unwittingly no doubt, that he was abandoning them along with his land, his relatives, and his neighbors.

When Jefferson replied to this letter, about three weeks after he got it, he did not know that the British were sacking Washington. He did knew that all the young men in his family had gone to the defense of Richmond, and at seventy-one he was feeling old. Under the confused circumstances of the time his answer was slow in reaching Coles, but before the end of another month the young man learned that his own letter had been read with "peculiar pleasure." Its sentiments did honor to both the head and the heart of its writer, said Jefferson. He himself regarded it as shameful that Virginians had made no effort whatsoever to rid themselves of their condition of "moral and political reprobation." (Apparently he did not think that his own proposals should be described as "efforts." They had resulted in no action and could be considered as no more than an expression of personal opinion.) Early in his public career he had concluded that nothing could be expected of masters of slaves who had attained the fullness of age in the period of colonial subservience. Furthermore, on the basis of his own experience he could testify that anyone seeking to alleviate the conditions of the slaves would probably be considered an enemy of his society. Despairing of the old, he had placed his hopes on the young, but they in turn had disappointed him. His statement that only the voice of Coles had broken the silence may not have been literally true, but there could be no doubt of the general apathy.

An element of fatalism marks Jefferson's attitude toward emancipation. In his letter he said that only time would show whether it would be brought about by the "generous energy" of their own minds or by the "bloody process" of St. Domingo. When asking him to devise a plan, Coles made no mention of the one described in the *Notes on Virginia*. Still believing that this offered the most expedient method of relieving their commonwealth of the burden of slavery, Jefferson summarized it for the benefit of his idealistic young friend. It was a rational plan, designed to transform the economy of the state by the gradual replacement of black slaves with free white workmen. But its practically was open to serious question, and public support for it would certainly have been hard to gain.

Coles had made his request at a particularly unpropitious moment in Jefferson's personal history and in that of the Republic, but the orderly transformation of their society according to Jefferson's ideas would have been a slow operation under the most favorable circumstances. He asserted that it was no task for an old man to assume. Priam should not be asked to buckle on the armor of Hector, he said. Coles had referred to the possibility that Jefferson might fail in his own lifetime, but the old warrior did not go so far as to remind Coles of young Hector's fate before the walls of Troy. Instead he invited him to remain in Virginia and become a "missionary" of the principles he professed. Speaking of his own slaves, he said:

> My opinion has ever been that, until more can be done for them, we should endeavor with those whom fortune has thrown on our hands, to feed and clothe them well, protect them from all ill usage, require such reasonable labor only as is performed voluntarily by freemen, & be led by no repugnancies to abdicate them, and our duties to them. The laws do not permit us to turn them loose, if that were for their good: and to commute them for other property is to commit them to those whose usage of them we cannot control.

Coles appreciated Jefferson's desire to retain him as a neighbor and was not offended by the intimation that he was trying to escape his responsibilities to the state and to his own slaves. In his reply to Jefferson's letter he said he would gladly remain in Virginia if he thought he could do anything at all to promote the cause of general emancipation. He assured his solicitous correspondent that he was not planning to abandon his slaves. He expected to take them with him to the territory northwest of the Ohio River where they could live in freedom. (This he did five years later.) He had chosen the only sure way of escape for himself and for them from the system into which they had all been born. If he had decided to remain in Albemarle County, he could not have manumitted his slaves and employed them for wages because they would have been required by law to leave the state within a year.

His claim that he could do nothing for general emancipation in Virginia suggests that Coles regarded the prospects of the cause as bleak, and no doubt he was correct in believing that only a recognized leader could hope to arouse Virginia society from its apathy. Jefferson said that at his age he had only prayers to contribute. Like many other elderly people he may have talked too much about his age and infirmity. But he had other reasons for declining to follow the suggestion of Coles. His personal finances were in a precarious state, and after forty years of public service he was determined to be a private man.

Despite his belief that, as a rightful cause, emancipation was sure to triumph eventually, it was forlorn cause in their state at that time. We may properly ask just what he could have done to advance it. Judging from his suggestions to Coles as a prospective "missionary," the situation called for a long educational campaign, and there is no reason to believe that he thought himself capable of doing anything decisive. The predictable outcome of any crusade for abolition in Virginia was failure and opprobrium for those engaged in it. Virginians were less fearful of abolitionists than they afterwards became, but opponents of the slavery system were actually faced with a choice between exile, martyrdom, and quiescence.

Edward Coles, who was a bachelor, chose exile. The ex-President, who was more deeply rooted in their native soil and had far greater personal responsibilities, chose quiescence. His aversion to slavery may have been less known to his fellow Virginians than he claimed, but, judging from the private letters he received during the rest of his life, it was widely recognized in the nation. At this time, when the cause of abolition was so feeble, his interest in it may have been described not improperly as theoretical. In view of the immediate circumstances and his total record, however, he does not deserve the censure he has received from some modern historians of the antislavery movement. One of the best of them has said: "The exchange with Edward Coles dramatized Jefferson's fundamental commitment to his 'country' as well as his extraordinary capacity to sound like an enlightened reformer while upholding the interests of the planter class."

Though Jefferson was unquestionably committed to his state and concerned for its welfare, he never sought to promote the interests of the planters as a class. He prided himself on the blows against the landed aristocracy that he struck during the American Revolution, and he consistently tried to increase the opportunities and advance the interests of small, independent farmers. Though he had a healthy respect for real property, he believed that the best and happiest society was one where inequalities of conditions were not great.

At just this time he said that in the United States the wealthy knew nothing of luxury in the European sense. They had only somewhat more of the comforts of life than the workers who provided them. He was not comparing his state with any other in the Union, but he claimed that even the enslaved blacks were "better fed ..., warmer clothed, and labored less than the journeymen or day-laborers of England." Also, unlike the wretched poor of England, they were secure from want as long as they lived. It was true that they were subject to physical coercion, but so were British soldiers and seamen. The latter had also been brought into subjection by force—that is, by the press gang. He said he did not condone wrong committed by Americans against Africans because of those committed by Englishmen against their own kind, but we may be sure that many of his countrymen did. Also, these private reflections may have constituted a form of self-justification, even though he did not admit it. While he prized industry, he disliked severity. That there was less of this on his farms than on others we cannot say, but he is reputed to have been a kindly master, and there can be no doubt of his solicitude for his "people." He was sure that, with rare exceptions, they were wholly unprepared for self-government and he liked to think that for the present they were safe and relatively comfortable.

Jefferson never ceased to urge the necessity of a "practicable" plan of emancipation and to say that he knew of none better than his own. As an advocate of self-government he not only insisted that the slaves be prepared for it. He assumed that the consent of the owners must be gained. He was proposing no compensation and seems to have been relying entirely on moral suasion to overcome the "obstacles of self-interest" in the minds of the masters. He recognized that this would require much time and patience, but he sounded a note of hope in many a private letter on the subject. Considering the circumstances, that persistent hope is as noteworthy as his desire to maintain silence in public.

He told William Short that his repugnance to the "political pen" was insuperable. His former secretary wanted him to protest against the "foul traffic" in slaves which was being openly carried on, especially by certain "scoundrels" from Rhode Island. Jefferson's record of opposition to the foreign slave trade was clear and consistent, but Short said that some people were unaware of it and thought that a public communication from him might be helpful. He had entered his seventy-fourth year several months before he received this suggestion. When rejecting it he asserted that the problem could be safely left to his juniors and that it was their responsibility anyway. "The concerns of each generation are their own care," he said. Until the end of his days, however, his juniors continued to seek his opinion and they often published his private letters.

A few weeks after Jefferson replied to Short, his name was evoked and his words were employed to promote the colonization movement. In the House of Delegates of Virginia in December, 1816, Charles F. Mercer obtained a resolution calling on the federal government to secure territory outside the United States as a refuge for free blacks. In support of this resolution Mercer produced hitherto unpublished correspondence of 1801–1802 between President Jefferson and Governor Monroe regarding the possible establishment of a settlement for deported blacks. In this correspondence the inquiries that Jefferson made at the request of the legislature were reported.

At almost the same time that these events occurred in Richmond, the American Colonization Society was being independently organized in Washington by Dr. Robert Finley of New Jersey, a Presbyterian minister. On January 1, 1817, officers of the society were elected. Jefferson seems never to have specifically endorsed this organization, but an earlier letter of his (January 21, 1811), supporting colonization, was published in the *Richmond Enquirer* on April 11,

1817. When the national society met on its first anniversary, Henry Clay introduced the letter into the records as evidence of Jefferson's support of the cause. At the same meeting, Mercer introduced the Monroe-Jefferson correspondence. All of this was published in the society's *First Annual Report.*

Early in 1817 Jefferson privately expressed approval of the proposal to establish a refuge for free blacks on the coast of Africa, which was made at this time and carried into effect five years later. But his own hopes went far beyond this. In his mid-seventies, while somewhat encouraged, he saw no sign that a practicable plan of general emancipation would be adopted in his day.

As Jefferson foresaw, he was doomed to spend the rest of his life in a society that was based on slave labor, but his friend Edward Coles finally managed to escape from it. This was about four and a half years after he informed the older man of his intention to emigrate from Virginia. Coles had carefully arranged his affairs, making two exploratory trips to the western country, selling his Virginia property, and obtaining an appointment as registrar of the United States land office at Edwardsville, Illinois. In the spring of 1819 he made his move. Two of his slaves were old women whom he left behind after he had provided for their needs. Ten of the others he emancipated en route to Illinois, granting each of the three families involved 160 acres of land in the southern part of the state. To provide for his remaining slaves, a woman and her five small children, he purchased the woman's husband from a Virginia neighbor. They were allowed to settle in St. Louis, Missouri, where they were legally freed in 1825.

In effecting an escape from a system he deplored, Coles had fully assumed his responsibilities to the human beings he had inherited as property. Jefferson could not have failed to approve of what he did for the freed blacks. Madison commended his former secretary for having provided the families in southern Illinois with land but made the realistic observation that he could not assure their enjoyment of all the rights of white Americans without changing the color of their skins. Despite its illegality, slavery actually existed in that region, and the introduction of free blacks was resented by many settlers. The former slaves of Coles were ushered into an unfriendly world, and he himself suffered much unpleasantness because of his sentiments.

Into the details of his career in Illinois we cannot enter here, but we should note that he published part of Jefferson's letter in 1814 in justification of his antislavery position. This was in the course of his successful campaign for the governorship a few years after his arrival. There appear to be no recorded comments of Jefferson's on the activities of Coles in Illinois, but the high regard the two men had for each other seems never to have diminished. Much as he regretted the loss that the state suffered when this promising young man left it, there is no reason to believe that he tried to discourage Cole's generous act of manumission. It released one owner and his particular slaves from a detested system, but no such way of escape was open to Jefferson and his slaves at Monticello and Poplar Forest. For him exile from Virginia was unthinkable, even if it had been feasible, and his unavoidable problem at this stage of drought and depression was not how to free his slaves, but how to feed them.

Thomas Jefferson and the Problem of Slavery

[Thomas] Jefferson's views on slavery and race suggest that his libertarian sentiments were more than counterbalanced by his conviction that Negroes were members of a race so alien and inferior that there was no hope that whites and blacks could coexist side by side on terms of equality. Jefferson's libertarian views, however, had virtually no impact upon his actions after 1784, and his belief in the inferiority of the slaves was completely congruent with his behavior as both a planter and a politician.

In his daily life there were few differences between Jefferson's behavior as an owner of men and that of Virginia plantation masters who opposed his antislavery speculations. His bondsmen were well fed and clothed, and their work load was comparable to that of white freemen. In this regard their lot may have been easier than that of many other slaves in the state. Nevertheless, when he dealt with runaways, sales of slaves, breeding, flogging, and manumissions, his behavior did not differ appreciably from that of other enlightened slaveholders who deplored needless cruelty, but would use whatever means they felt necessary to protect their peculiar form of property.

During Jefferson's adult lifetime, more than forty of his Negroes attempted to escape. Thirty of these were mentioned by him in a letter to an Englishman, Dr. William Gordon, who had fought on the American side in the Revolution and returned to Great Britain in 1786. Jefferson described the depredations of Lord Cornwallis and his troops when they overran his estate in 1781 and added: "he carried off also about thirty slaves; had this been to give them their freedom, he would have done right, but it was to consign them to inevitable death from the smallpox and putrid fever then raging in his camp."

This account differs markedly from the cold facts recorded in his "Farm Book" when these events took place. In that document, which was not intended for the public eye, he listed the names of the slaves that he had lost and described what had befallen them. Next to eight entries in a group he wrote: "fled to the enemy and died." Another two slaves were said to have "joined the enemy and died"; while four more, "joined the enemy, returned and died." Beside three names he wrote laconically: "joined enemy"; and it is presumed that they managed to survive the war. One slave, Barnaby, was described as having "run

From William Cohen, "Thomas Jefferson and the Problem of Slavery," *The Journal of American History*, vol. 56, no. 3 (December 1969). Copyright © 1969 by The Organization of American Historians. Reprinted by permission of *The Journal of American History*. Notes omitted.

away, returned and died." Four slaves were said to have "joined the enemy, but came back again and lived." Nowhere in this account is the term "carried off" seen, and Jefferson's later use of the phrase glosses over the fact that more than one seventh of his blacks chose to desert him.

Jefferson's statement that Cornwallis would have done right if he had taken the Negroes to free them is at variance with the Virginian's behavior both before and after 1781. In 1769 he placed an advertisement in the *Virginia Gazette* asking for the return of a runaway slave named Sandy. Throughout his life Jefferson hired slave catchers and asked his friends to keep an eye peeled for his thralls when they struck out for freedom. In early September 1805, Jame Hubbard, a stout Negro who worked in the plantation nail factory, ran away, but was soon apprehended and returned. About five years later, he escaped again. A year passed before Jefferson learned that Hubbard was living in the area of Lexington and dispatched Isham Chisolm to retrieve the bondsman. It was too late, however; Hubbard had departed only a few days earlier for parts unknown. When Chisolm returned empty-handed, Jefferson offered him a bonus of twenty-five dollars to go after the man a second time. This time Hubbard was caught and brought back in irons, and Jefferson reported: "I had him severely flogged in the presence of his old companions. . . ." He then added that he was convinced that Hubbard "will never again serve any man as a slave. the [sic] moment he is out of jail and his irons he will be off himself." Before Jefferson could implement plans to have him sold out of the state, Hubbard disappeared again.

In the abstract Jefferson did not believe one man had a right to own another, and, hence, no man had a right to sell another. He repeatedly expressed his dislike for this commerce, and he tried to avoid selling his human property except for misbehavior or at their own request. Nevertheless, slaves were sold when he was pressed for cash, regardless of their wishes in the matter. In 1787, deeply in debt as the result of obligations which he had inherited from his father-in-law, Jefferson wrote to his plantation manager:

> The torment of mind I endure till the moment shall arrive when I shall not owe a shilling on earth is such really as to render life of little value. I cannot decide to sell my lands. I have sold too much of them already, and they are the only sure provision for my children, nor would I willingly sell the slaves as long as there remains any prospect of paying my debts with their labor. In this I am governed solely by views to their happiness which will render it worth their while to use extraordinary exertions for some time to enable me to put them ultimately on an easier footing, which I will do the moment they have paid the debts due from the estate, two thirds of which have been contracted by purchasing them.

These remarks may appear to confirm the view that Jefferson's primary concern was the welfare of his bondsmen, but just the opposite is true. The underlying assumption in this letter is that the slaves owe him a living and that, if they do not provide it, they will be the ones to suffer. A second implication is that he has the right to dispose of them as he thinks best. Acting upon this view in the years 1783–1794, he reluctantly sold about fifty slaves.

When selling slaves, Jefferson did his best to keep families together if it did not entail a financial hardship for him. In 1792, he sold two males named

York and Jame and offered to throw their superannuated parents, Judy and Will, into the bargain if they wished to go along with their sons. His gesture might have saved him money by taking from his shoulders the burden of caring for the old couple who were no longer good for much work. That Jefferson did not let scruples about breaking up families interfere with his business is shown by the fact that in the same lot of slaves with Jame and York was Dilcey, a twenty-three-year-old woman, whose valuable parents remained his property.

The eleven males to be sold in this lot were insufficient in number to make a sale by themselves, and Jefferson instructed his agents to carry them "to some other sale in that part of the country to be sold." Jefferson had yet another reason for selling them elsewhere: "I do not (while in public life) like to have my name annexed in the public papers to the sale of property." Whether he was referring specifically to slave property or to property in general is not clear.

Whenever it could be done without seriously inconveniencing himself, Jefferson tried to unite husbands and wives; and he would buy or sell one partner of a marriage to enable the two of them to live together. He expressed himself as "always willing to indulge connections seriously formed by those people, where it can be done reasonably." In 1792, when he needed to sell a few more slaves to pay his debts, Jefferson offered to sell a slave and her children to his brother who owned her husband. The bondswoman had been asking to be united with her husband for some time but her wishes in the matter had had to await Jefferson's convenience.

In November 1806, Jefferson noted that he had always intended to buy the wife of his slave, Moses, when he could "spare the money," but he could not do so at that time. He said he was willing to hire her, but feared that she had not been brought up to field labor. However, he told his manager that it would be permissible to employ her if she could earn her keep. She was not hired, and Moses and his wife remained apart for the next six months. At the end of that time, however, Jefferson did purchase the woman and her children.

It may be argued that, although Jefferson deplored the institution of slavery and particularly the buying and selling of men, the purchases and sales he made were impossible to avoid, since they were for the purpose of paying off debts or uniting families. But in 1805, he said that he was "endeavoring to purchase young and able negro men" for his plantation. Clearly then, he was not merely engaged in a holding operation designed to protect his slaves from a cruel and inhospitable world.

Like any other entrepreneur, Jefferson was concerned with the problem of increasing his capital assets—land and Negroes. Because he was always short of cash, it was difficult for him to increase his land holdings; and he never did. Slaves, however, increased of their own accord, and Jefferson took pains to make sure that this source of profit was not lost through shortsightedness. In 1819 he instructed his manager:

> I have no reason to believe that any overseer, since Griffin's time has over worked them. accordingly, the deaths among the grown ones seems ascribable to natural causes, but the loss of 5 little ones in 4 years induces me to fear that the overseers do not permit the women to devote as much time as is necessary to the care of their children: that they view their labor as the 1st

object and the raising their child but as secondary. I consider the labor of a breeding woman as no object, and that a child raised every 2 years is of more profit than the crop of the best laboring man. in this, as in all other cases, providence has made our interests and our duties coincide perfectly.... I must pray you to inculcate upon the overseers that it is not their labor, but their increase which is the first consideration with us.

Between 1810 and 1822, about 100 slaves were born to Jefferson's "breeding women"; while only a total of thirty Negroes died, were sold, or ran away.

Throughout his life, Jefferson appears to have emancipated only two slaves; and one of them bought his freedom in 1792 at the price of £60. Upon his death in 1826, Jefferson manumitted five more Negroes and willed over 260 bondsmen to his heirs. Of the total of seven slaves that he freed, at least five were members of a mulatto family named Hemings; and it seems well established that these favored individuals were directly descended from Jefferson's father-in-law. Nevertheless, several of them remained in servitude after Jefferson died. In 1822, two Hemings girls, tired of waiting for their freedom, ran away to Washington.

Apparently, Jefferson's unwillingness to manumit his bondsmen arose, at least in part, from his reluctance to alter his standard of living and to bring his practices into line with his principles. He took much pride in the fine wines, good books, and generous hospitality to be found at Monticello; and he went to great lengths to preserve intact this inheritance for his posterity. It may be argued that Jefferson did not believe in emancipation unless it was accompanied by colonization, and this is true enough. But if this had been the only obstacle to the emancipation of his slaves, he could have made arrangements for the expatriation of those who might choose freedom.

Although manumissions were infrequent in Virginia at this time, they were by no means unknown. When George Washington died in 1799, he gave his slaves their freedom, and so did Jefferson's mentor, George Wythe, who passed away in 1806. Coles, a young planter who had served as private secretary to President James Madison, went still further and in 1819 migrated to Illinois with his slaves and gave 160 acres of land to each family along with its freedom. When the eccentric John Randolph of Roanoke died in 1833 (seven years after Jefferson), his will contained a provision for the emancipation of his 400 bondsmen.

If self-interest played a major role in determining Jefferson's behavior as a plantation owner, it was equally important in shaping his stance as a national leader on questions involving slavery. After 1784, he refrained from discussing the issue publicly for political reasons, but the matter came up occasionally in the course of his official duties. As ambassador to France, he zealously sought to justify the American claim to compensation for slaves taken by the British in 1783; and he continued to press for satisfaction on this issue when he served as secretary of state. He then pressured the Spanish government into denying sanctuary in Florida to fugitive slaves from Georgia.

Although Jefferson embraced the French Revolution, he shuddered with fear in August 1791 when slaves on the island of Santo Domingo revolted for their liberty, and he approved a grant of arms and ammunition to their embattled Gallic masters. The situation grew more complicated when it became apparent that a second and larger grant might provoke the resentment of the French mother country; and Jefferson insisted that future applications for aid be routed through Paris. Nevertheless, he continued to sympathize with the island aristocracy; and, when in 1793 many of them fled to the United States, he argued that they be generously aided. True to his states' rights convictions, he denied the power of the federal government to apply money to such a purpose, but he denied it "with a bleeding heart." He implored James Monroe to urge the government of Virginia to make a large donation to the refugees and said: "never was so deep a tragedy presented to the feelings of men."

The upheaval in Santo Domingo struck a responsive chord in Jefferson, for he feared that Virginia would eventually see the same kind of murderous violence. He warned Monroe that "it is high time we should foresee the bloody scenes which our children certainly, and possibly ourselves . . . [will] have to wade through, and try to avert them." Four years afterward, in 1797, he again urged that "if something is not done and soon done we shall be the murderers of our own children."

Three years later, his worst fears seemed about to be realized when a Virginia slave revolt, which may have involved as many as 1,000 Negroes, was aborted. Monroe informed Jefferson that ten of the rebels had already been hanged and wondered what to do about the remaining conspirators. Jefferson, advising against any further executions, cautioned that "the other states and the world at large will forever condemn us if we indulge a principle of revenge, or go one step beyond absolute necessity. They cannot lose sight of the rights of the two parties, and the object of the unsuccessful one." This was good advice, but it did not prevent the execution of about twenty-five more Negroes involved in the plot.

Within a few months Jefferson became President, and he failed to use his office to avert the bloody scenes which he had predicted. Deeply worried by the slave revolt of 1800, the Virginia legislature requested Governor Monroe to consult with the President about means of deporting Negroes involved in future outbreaks. Jefferson, a longtime colonizationist, then asked the American minister to England to negotiate with the Sierra Leone Company for the "reception of such of these people as might be colonized thither." After learning that the Company was unwilling to consider the proposal, the President abandoned his colonization efforts for the duration of his term.

Jefferson's proslavery actions were particularly evident in the area of foreign policy, and the treaty which granted the Louisiana Territory to the United States contained a provision protecting the right of the Spanish and French inhabitants in the area to keep their slaves. The French insistence upon such a condition was understandable, and so was its acceptance by the United States, but the author of the Ordinance of 1784 made no move to limit the further introduction of bondage into the area.

Napoleon had given up Louisiana largely because of his inability to crush the rebel forces on Santo Domingo. By 1806, he again entertained the hope of reconquering the island, and he asked the American government to cooperate by cutting off all trade with the black nation. Jefferson complied with this request and commended the measure to Congress, where it passed in the House by a vote of 93–26. The President supported France in this venture because he hoped that Napoleon would reciprocate by aiding the United States to acquire Florida, but Jefferson was surely aware of the fact that if the plan succeeded it would destroy the island's Negro regime, which stood as a beacon of hope to American slaves.

Despite these actions, the dominant theme of Jefferson's administration on the subject of slavery was discreet silence. When citizens in the Indiana Territory were demanding that slavery be permitted throughout the Northwest Territory, the President made no comment. Although Jefferson privately continued to represent himself as a foe of human bondage and on rare occasions during his presidency voiced such sentiments in letters to men who shared his views, he was exceedingly careful to keep these thoughts from reaching the public. When he received an emancipation tract from Thomas Brannagan, a slave trader-turned-abolitionist, Jefferson did not directly reply to the author's request for an endorsement. Instead, he wrote to Dr. George Logan:

> The cause in which he embarks is so holy, the sentiments he expresses in his letter so friendly that it is highly painful to me to hesitate on a compliance which appears so small. But that is not its true character, and it would be injurious even in his views, for me to commit myself on paper by answering his letter. I have most carefully avoided every public act or manifestation on that subject. Should an occasion occur in which I can interpose with decisive effect, I shall certainly know and do my duty with promptitude and zeal.

In fact, by the time he wrote these words, Jefferson had already given up "the expectation of any early provision for the extinguishment of slavery among us," and his actions appear to have been designed more to mute the issue than to resolve it.

Ten years after he left office, as the Missouri issue was dividing the nation, Jefferson again demonstrated his ability to mix vague abolition sentiments with a position that worked to the advantage of the slave states. Recognizing that the dispute over the admission of Missouri heralded an era of increasing national division over the slavery issue, he likened the controversy to a "fire bell in the night" and warned of impending disaster for the Union. Speaking of slavery, he implicitly endorsed the moral position of the North when he described the dilemma of the South: "We have the wolf by the ears and can neither hold him, nor safely let him go. Justice is in the one scale, and self-preservation in the other." He indicated his willingness to give up his bondsmen if any *"practicable"* way of achieving their "emancipation and *expatriation"* could be found.

Nevertheless, he endorsed the southern position and charged the Federalists with creating a geographical division based on an ostensibly moral question as a means of regaining their influence. He then denied that morality was involved because the limitation of the area of bondage would free no one. He also denied that the federal government could regulate the "condition of different descriptions of men composing a State," and he ruled out the only practical means by which emancipation might eventually have been brought about.

It may be argued that Jefferson's position on the Missouri issue and also his inactivity as President may have been dictated by his strict construction of the Constitution. When the object was large enough, however, Jefferson could be quite flexible; and he did not allow such scruples to prevent the acquisition of the Louisiana Territory. Moreover, he believed that the expatriation of America's blacks was a subject which merited a similar elasticity.

Despite his support for the southern position on the issue of Missouri, in 1821 Jefferson could still write: "Nothing is more certainly written in the book of fate than that these people are to be free, Nor is it less certain that the two races, equally free, cannot live in the same government." Thus, in the last years of his life he continued to insist that emancipation must be accompanied by expatriation. Nevertheless, he lacked enthusiasm about the plan to resettle the Negroes in Africa and believed that the distance of that continent would make it impossible for such an operation to succeed.

In 1824 Jefferson argued that there were a million and a half slaves in the nation and that no one conceived it to be "practicable for us, or expedient for them" to send all the blacks away at once. He then went on to calculate:

> Their estimated value as property, in the first place, (for actual property has been lawfully vested in that form, and who can lawfully take it from the possessors?) at an average of two hundred dollars each ... would amount to six hundred millions of dollars which must be paid or lost by somebody. To this add the cost of their transportation by land and sea to Mesurado, a year's provision of food and clothes, implements of husbandry and of their trades, which will amount to three hundred millions more ... and it is impossible to look at the question a second time.

Since African colonization seemed an impossibility, Jefferson suggested a plan which entailed "emancipating the afterborn, leaving them, on due compensation, with their mothers, until their services are worth their maintenance, and putting them to industrious occupations until a proper age for deportation." The individuals who would be "freed" immediately after their birth would eventually be sent to Santo Domingo which, according to the newspapers, had recently offered to open its doors to such persons. In effect, Jefferson was proposing that the federal government buy all newborn slaves from their owners (at twelve dollars and fifty cents each) and that it pay for their "nurture with the mother [for] a few years." Beyond this, the plan would not cost the government anything, for the young blacks would then work for their maintenance until deported. Santo Domingo had offered to bear the cost of passage.

Jefferson noted that a majority of Americans then living would live to see the black population reach six million and warned that "a million and a half are within their control; but six millions, ... and one million of these fighting men, will say, 'we will not go.' " The Virginia statesman concluded his proposal by urging that neither constitutional problems nor human sentiment ought to be allowed to stand in its way:

> I am aware that this subject involves some constitutional scruples. But a liberal construction, justified by the object, may go far, and an amendment of the constitution, the whole length necessary. The separation of infants from their mothers, too, would produce some scruples of humanity. But this would be straining at a gnat, and swallowing a camel.

Thus, only two and a half years before his death, Jefferson reiterated his long held belief that emancipation was imperative for the sake of the nation, but that it must be accompanied by colonization. Even here, however, his theory differed from his practice; and in this case his inconsistency would follow him beyond the grave for he did not offer to free his slaves on the condition that they leave the country. On the contrary, in his will he reported the Virginia legislature to grant special permission to the five slaves he manumitted to continue to live in the state.

Jefferson was a man of many dimensions, and any explanation of his behavior must contain a myriad of seeming contradictions. He was a sincere and dedicated foe of the slave trade who bought and sold men whenever he found it personally necessary. He believed that all men were entitled to life and liberty regardless of their abilities, yet he tracked down those slaves who had the courage to take their rights by running away. He believed that slavery was morally and politically wrong, but still he wrote a slave code for his state and opposed a national attempt in 1819 to limit the further expansion of the institution. He believed that one hour of slavery was worse than ages of British oppression, yet he was able to discuss the matter of slave breeding in much the same terms that one would use when speaking of the propagation of dogs and horses.

From an intellectual point of view, his strong "suspicion" that the Negroes were innately inferior is probably of great significance in explaining his ability to ignore his own strictures about their rights. Thinking of them as lesser men, he was able to convince himself that his behavior toward them was benevolent and humane; and indeed it was, when judged by the traditional assumptions of the slaveholders. It is a mistake, however, to treat Jefferson's relationship to slavery in intellectual or psychological terms alone, for the institution shaped the warp and woof of life at Monticello and his abstract speculations about human freedom carried little weight when balanced against the whole pattern of his existence there.

Interacting with one another as both cause and effect to produce Jefferson's proslavery behavior was a complex set of factors which included his belief in Negro inferiority, a societal environment which took for granted the enslavement of one race by another, and the fact that he owned 10,000 acres of land and over 200 slaves. His wealth, his status, and his political position were tied to the system of slavery, and never once did he *actively* propose a plan that would have jeopardized all this. More often than not, the actions he took with regard to slavery actually strengthened the institution. This can be seen in his authorship in 1778 of Virginia's slave code, in his support of the plantation owners of Santo Domingo, and in his position on the Missouri question.

Monticello was the workshop of the maker of the "agrarian dream." It was here that Jefferson conducted his agricultural and scientific experiments and offered a generous hospitality to visitors. It was here that he lived a bustling, but gracious life far from the money changers in the cities of the North. This was the life that he sought to preserve against the incursions of the forces of commerce and industry. But it should not be forgotten that Jefferson's world depended upon forced labor for its very existence.

POSTSCRIPT

Was Thomas Jefferson Committed to Bringing an End to Chattel Slavery?

There is no doubt that Thomas Jefferson advocated human liberty and anticipated the end of the slave system in the United States. In fact, he played a key role in preventing the expansion of slavery into the Northwest Territory in the 1780s. He clearly recognized the potential danger for the nation posed by the growing ideological battle over the institution. Reacting to the introduction of the slavery issue into the debate over the admission of Missouri as a new state, Jefferson lamented that the battle over the slavery question "like a firebell in the night awakened and filled me with terror."

It is one of the great ironies of history, however, that a person who abhorred the institution of slavery and who, in the Declaration of Independence, expressed the idea that "all men are created equal," both held slaves and stated his personal belief in the innate inferiority of blacks to whites. Jefferson did not think that any person should be enslaved, and he expressed deep personal guilt about his own slaveholding. Still, unlike some of his planter contemporaries, such as George Washington, Jefferson did not arrange for the wholesale manumission of his human chattel even through his will.

This curious contrast of images of Jefferson either as architect of equality or as racist owner of other human beings is made even more compelling by the recent resurfacing of highly publicized accusations that the "sage of Monticello" fathered several children by his slave Sally Hemings. These accusations, which date back two centuries, have been proven true in the minds of some scholars by the results of DNA tests, though many others continue to express doubts.

Two older works are good starting points for a study of Jefferson: Henry Adams's *History of the United States During the Administrations of Thomas Jefferson and James Madison* (1889–1891) and Richard Hofstadter's cogent essay "Thomas Jefferson: The Aristocrat as Democrat," from his *American Political Tradition and the Men Who Made It* (Alfred A. Knopf, 1948). The definitive biographical study is Malone's *Jefferson and His Time*, 6 vols. (Little, Brown, 1948–1981). Other interesting biographical treatments include Saul K. Padover, *Jefferson* (Harcourt Brace Jovanovich, 1942); Forrest McDonald, *The Presidency of Thomas Jefferson* (University Press of Kansas, 1976); and Joseph J. Ellis, *American Sphinx: The Character of Thomas Jefferson* (Alfred A. Knopf, 1997). Merrill D. Peterson's *The Jeffersonian Image in the American Mind* (Oxford University Press, 1960) brilliantly describes Jefferson's influence on generations of American citizens in the century following his death.

ISSUE 9

Was Andrew Jackson's Indian Removal Policy Motivated by Humanitarian Impulses?

YES: Robert V. Remini, from *Andrew Jackson and the Course of American Freedom, 1822–1832, vol. 2* (Harper & Row, 1981)

NO: Anthony F. C. Wallace, from *The Long, Bitter Trail: Andrew Jackson and the Indians* (Hill & Wang, 1993)

ISSUE SUMMARY

YES: Historical biographer Robert V. Remini argues that Andrew Jackson did not seek to destroy Native American life and culture. He portrays Jackson as a national leader who sincerely believed that the Indian Removal Act of 1830 was the only way to protect Native Americans from annihilation at the hands of white settlers.

NO: Historian and anthropologist Anthony F. C. Wallace contends that Andrew Jackson oversaw a harsh policy with regard to Native Americans. This policy resulted in the usurpation of land, attempts to destroy tribal culture, and the forcible removal of Native Americans from the southeastern United States to a designated territory west of the Mississippi River.

Andrew Jackson's election to the presidency in 1828 ushered in an era marked by a growing demand for political and economic opportunities for the "common man." As the "people's president," Jackson embodied the democratic ideal in the United States. In his role as chief executive, Jackson symbolized a strong philosophical attachment to the elimination of impediments to voting (at least for adult white males), the creation of opportunities for the common man to participate directly in government through officeholding, and the destruction of vestiges of economic elitism that served only the rich, well-born, and able. In addition, Jackson was a nationalist who defended states' rights as long as those rights did not threaten the sanctity of the Union.

The rise of Jacksonian democracy occurred during a dramatic territorial growth increase in the years immediately following the War of 1812. A new state joined the Union each year between 1816 and 1821. As the populations of these states increased, white citizens demanded that their governments, at both the state and national levels, do something about the Native American tribes in their midst who held claims to land in these regions by virtue of previous treaties. (Jackson had negotiated several of these treaties. Some included provisions for the members of the southern tribes to remain on their lands in preparation for obtaining citizenship.) Most white settlers preferred the removal of Native Americans to western territories where, presumably, they could live unencumbered forever. The result was the "Trail of Tears," the brutal forced migration of Native Americans in the 1830s that resulted in the loss of thousands of lives.

According to historian Wilcomb Washburn, "No individual is more closely identified with... the policy of removal of the Indians east of the Mississippi to lands west of the river—than President Andrew Jackson." While most historians are in agreement with the details of Jackson's Indian removal policy, there is significant debate with respect to his motivation. Did Jackson's racist antipathy to the Indians pave the way for the "Trail of Tears"? Or did he support this policy out of a humanitarian desire to protect Native Americans from the impending wrath of white settlers and their state governments who refused to negotiate with the southern tribes as sovereign nations?

In the following selection, Robert V. Remini, Jackson's foremost biographer, states that the criticism of Jackson's Indian Removal Act is unfair. He argues that Jackson firmly believed that removal was the only policy that would prevent the decimation of Native Americans. Remini concludes that Jackson attempted to deal as fairly as possible with the representatives of the Choctaws, Cherokees, Chickasaws, Creeks, and Seminoles, known then as the "Five Civilized Tribes."

In the second selection, Anthony F. C. Wallace maintains that Jackson viewed Native Americans as savages and, while not proposing their extermination, he supported a policy of coercion to force their removal from the southeastern states. This approach, according to Wallace, was consistent with several powerful forces in Democratic politics, including the exaltation of the common white man, expansionism, and open acceptance of racism.

Robert V. Remini

 **YES**

"Brothers, Listen . . . You Must Submit"

It is an awesome contradiction that at the moment the United States was entering a new age of economic and social betterment for its citizens—the industrial revolution underway, democracy expanding, social and political reforms in progress—the Indians were driven from their homes and forced to seek refuge in remote areas west of the Mississippi River. [Andrew] Jackson, the supreme exponent of liberty in terms of preventing government intervention and intrusion, took it upon himself to expel the Indians from their ancient haunts and decree that they must reside outside the company of civilized white men. It was a depressing and terrible commentary on American life and institutions in the 1830s.

The policy of white Americans toward Indians was a shambles, right from the beginning. Sometimes the policy was benign—such as sharing educational advantages—but more often than not it was malevolent. Colonists drove the Indians from their midst, stole their lands and, when necessary, murdered them. To the colonists, Indians were inferior and their culture a throwback to a darker age.

When independence was declared and a new government established committed to liberty and justice for all, the situation of the Indians within the continental limits of the United States contradicted the ennobling ideas of both the Declaration and the Constitution. Nevertheless, the Founding Fathers convinced themselves that men of reason, intelligence and good will could resolve the Indian problem. In their view the Indians were "noble savages," arrested in cultural development, but they would one day take their rightful place beside white society. Once they were "civilized" they would be absorbed.

President George Washington formulated a policy to encourage the "civilizing" process, and Jefferson continued it. They presumed that once the Indians adopted the practice of private property, built homes, farmed, educated their children, and embraced Christianity these Native Americans would win acceptance from white Americans. Both Presidents wished the Indians to become cultural white men. If they did not, said Jefferson, then they must be driven to the Rocky Mountains.

The policy of removal was first suggested by Jefferson as the alternative to the "civilizing" process, and as far as many Americans were concerned removal

From Robert V. Remini, *Andrew Jackson and the Course of American Freedom, 1822–1832, vol. 2* (Harper & Row, 1981). Copyright © 1981 by Robert V. Remini. Reprinted by permission of Harper-Collins Publishers, Inc. Notes omitted.

made more sense than any other proposal. Henry Clay, for example, insisted that it was impossible to civilize these "savages." They were, he argued, inferior to white men and "their disappearance from the human family. would be no great loss to the world."

Despite Clay's racist notions—shared by many Americans—the government's efforts to convert the Indians into cultural white men made considerable progress in the 1820s. The Cherokees, in particular, showed notable technological and material advances as a result of increased contact with traders, government agents, and missionaries, along with the growth of a considerable population of mixed-bloods.

As the Indians continued to resist the efforts to get rid of them—the thought of abandoning the land on which their ancestors lived and died was especially painful for them—the states insisted on exercising jurisdiction over Indian lands within their boundaries. It soon became apparent that unless the federal government instituted a policy of removal it would have to do something about protecting the Indians against the incursions of the states. But the federal government was feckless. It did neither. Men like President John Quincy Adams felt that removal was probably the only policy to follow but he could not bring himself to implement it. Nor could he face down a state like Georgia. So he did nothing. Many men of good will simply turned their faces away. They, too, did nothing.

Not Jackson. He had no hesitation about taking action. And he believed that removal was indeed the only policy available if the Indians were to be protected from certain annihilation. His ideas about the Indians developed from his life on the frontier, his expansionist dreams, his commitment to states' rights, and his intense nationalism. He saw the nation as an indivisible unit whose strength and future were dependent on its ability to repel outside foes. He wanted all Americans from every state and territory to participate in his dream of empire, but they must acknowledge allegiance to a permanent and indissoluble bond under a federal system. Although devoted to states' rights and limited government in Washington, Jackson rejected any notion that jeopardized the safety of the United States. That included nullification and secession. That also included the Indians. . . .

The Indian Removal Act of 1830 authorized Jackson to carry out the policy outlined in his first message to Congress. He could exchange unorganized public land in the trans-Mississippi west for Indian land in the east. Those Indians who moved would be given perpetual title to their new land as well as compensation for improvements on their old. The cost of their removal would be absorbed by the federal government. They would also be given assistance for their "support and subsistence" for the first year after removal. An appropriation of $500,000 was authorized to carry out these provisions.

This monumental piece of legislation spelled the doom of the American Indian. It was harsh, arrogant, racist—and inevitable. It was too late to acknowledge any rights for the Indians. As [Senator Theodore] Frelinghuysen [of New Jersey] remarked, all the white man had ever said to the Indian from the moment they first came into contact was "give!" Once stripped of his possessions the Indian was virtually abandoned.

Of the many significant predictions and warnings voiced during the debates in Congress that eventually came true, two deserve particular attention. One of them made a mockery of Jackson's concern for freedom. The President insisted that the Indians would not be forced to remove. If they wished to reside within the state they might do so but only on condition that they understood they would be subject to state law. He would never force them to remove, never compel them to surrender their lands. That high and noble sentiment as interpreted by land-greedy state officials meant absolutely nothing. Fraud and deception also accompanied the exchange of land. Jackson himself tried desperately to discourage corruption among the government agents chosen to arrange the removal, but the events as they actually transpired ran totally opposite to what he expected and promised.

The other prediction that mocked Jackson's commitment to economy was the cost of the operation. In the completed legislation the Congress had appropriated $500,000 but the actual cost of removal is incalculable. For one thing the process extended over many years and involved many tribes. Naturally some Indians resisted Jackson's will and the government was required to apply force. The resulting bloodshed and killing and the cost of these Indian wars cannot be quantified. For a political party that prized economy above almost everything else the policy of Indian removal was a radial departure from principle. Still many Democrats argued that the actual cost was a small price to pay for the enormous expanse of land that was added to the American empire. In Jackson's eight years in office seventy-odd treaties were signed and ratified, which added 100 million acres of Indian land to the public domain at a cost of roughly $68 million and 32 million acres of land west of the Mississippi River. The expense was enormous, but so was the land-grab.

Andrew Jackson has been saddled with a considerable portion of the blame for this monstrous deed. He makes an easy mark. But the criticism is unfair if it distorts the role he actually played. His objective was not the destruction of Indian life and culture. Quite the contrary. He believed that removal was the Indian's only salvation against certain extinction. Nor did he despoil Indians. He struggled to prevent fraud and corruption, and he promised there would be no coercion in winning Indian approval of his plan for removal. Yet he himself practiced a subtle kind of coercion. He told the tribes he would abandon them to the mercy of the states if they did not agree to migrate west.

The Indian problem posed a terrible dilemma and Jackson had little to gain by attempting to resolve it. He could have imitated his predecessors and done nothing. But that was not Andrew Jackson. He felt he had a duty. And when removal was accomplished he felt he had done the American people a great service. He felt he had followed the "dictates of humanity" and saved the Indians from certain death.

Not that the President was motivated by concern for the Indians—their language or customs, their culture, or anything else. Andrew Jackson was motivated principally by two considerations: first, his concern for the military safety of the United States, which dictated that Indians must not occupy areas that might jeopardize the defense of this nation; and second, his commitment to the principle that all persons residing within states are subject to the jurisdiction and laws of those states. Under no circumstances did Indian tribes constitute sovereign entities when they occupied territory within existing state boundaries. The quickest way to undermine the security of the Union, he argued, was to jeopardize the sovereignty of the states by recognizing Indian tribes as a third sovereignty.

But there was a clear inconsistency—if not a contradiction—in this argument. If the tribes were not sovereign why bother to sign treaties (requiring Senate approval) for their land? Actually Jackson appreciated the inconsistency, and it bothered him. He never really approved of bargaining or negotiating with tribes. He felt that Congress should simply determine what needed to be done and then instruct the Indians to conform to it. Congress can "occupy and possess" any part of Indian territory, he once said, "whenever the safety, interest or defence of the country" dictated. But as President, Jackson could not simply set aside the practice and tradition of generations because of a presumed contradiction. So he negotiated and signed treaties with dozens of tribes, at the same time denying that they enjoyed sovereign rights.

The reaction of the American people to Jackson's removal policy was predictable. Some were outraged, particularly the Quakers and other religious groups. Many seemed uncomfortable about it but agreed that it had to be done. Probably a larger number of Americans favored removal and applauded the President's action in settling the Indian problem once and for all. In short, there was no public outcry against it. In fact it was hardly noticed. The horror of removal with its "Trail of Tears" came much later and after Jackson had left office.

Apart from everything else, the Indian Removal Act served an important political purpose. For one thing it forced Jackson to exercise leadership as the head of the Democratic party within Congress. It prepared him for even bigger battles later on. For another it gave "greater ideological and structural coherence" to the party. It separated loyal and obedient friends of the administration from all others. It became a "distinguishing feature" of Jacksonian Democrats....

According to the Treaty of Dancing Rabbit Creek, the Choctaws agreed to evacuate all their land in Mississippi and emigrate to an area west of the Arkansas Territory to what is now Oklahoma. In addition the Indians would receive money, household and farm equipment, subsistence for one year, and reimbursement for improvements on their vacated property. In effect the Choctaws ceded to the United States 10.5 million acres of land east of the Mississippi River. They promised to emigrate in stages: the first group in the fall of 1831, the second in 1832, and the last in 1833.

Jackson immediately submitted the treaty to Congress when it reconvened in December, 1830, and [Secretary of War John] Eaton, in his annual report, assured the members that agreement was reached through persuasion only. No secret agreements, no bribes, no promises. Everything had been open and aboveboard! The Senate swallowed the lie whole and ratified the treaty on February 25, 1831, by a vote of 35 to 12. Said one Choctaw chief: "Our doom is sealed."

Since the Treaty of Dancing Rabbit Creek was the first to win Senate approval the President was very anxious to make it a model of removal. He wanted everything to go smoothly so that the American people would understand that removal was humane and beneficial to both the Indians and the American nation at large. Furthermore, he hoped its success would encourage other tribes to capitulate to his policy and thereby send a veritable human tide streaming across the Mississippi into the plains beyond.

The actual removal of the Choctaw Nation violated every principle for which Jackson stood. From start to finish the operation was a fraud. Corruption, theft, mismanagement, inefficiency—all contributed to the destruction of a once-great people. The Choctaws asked to be guided to their new country by General George Gibson, a man they trusted and with whom they had scouted their new home. Even this was denied them. The bureaucracy dictated another choice. So they left the "land of their fathers" filled with fear and anxiety. To make matters worse the winter of 1831–1832 was "living hell." The elements conspired to add to their misery. The suffering was stupefying. Those who watched the horror never forgot it. Many wept. The Indians themselves showed not a single sign of their agony.

Jackson tried to prevent this calamity but he was too far away to exercise any real control, and the temptations and opportunities for graft and corruption were too great for some agents to resist. When he learned of the Choctaw experience and the suffering involved, Jackson was deeply offended. He did what he could to prevent its recurrence. He proposed a new set of guidelines for future removals. He hoped they would reform the system and erase mismanagement and the opportunity for theft.

To begin with, the entire operation of Indian removal was transferred from civilian hands to the military. Then the office of commissioner of Indian affairs was established under the war department to coordinate and direct all matters pertaining to the Indians. In large part these changes reflected Jackson's anguish over what had happened to the Choctaws, but they also resulted from his concern over public opinion. Popular outrage could kill the whole program of removal. . . .

The experience of removal is one of the horror stories of the modern era. Beginning with the Choctaws it decimated whole tribes. An entire race of people suffered. What it did to their lives, their culture, their language, their customs is a tragedy of truly staggering proportions. The irony is that removal was intended to prevent this calamity.

Would it have been worse had the Indians remained in the East? Jackson thought so. He said they would "disappear and be forgotten." One thing does seem certain: the Indians would have been forced to yield to state laws and white society. Indian Nations *per se* would have been obliterated and possibly Indian civilization with them.

In October, 1832, a year and a half after the Choctaw treaty was ratified, General [John] Coffee signed a treaty with the Chickasaws that met Jackson's complete approval. "Surely the religious enthusiasts," wrote the President in conveying his delight to Coffee, "or those who have been weeping over the oppression of the Indians will not find fault with it for want of liberality or justice to the Indians." By this time Jackson had grown callous. His promise to economize got the better of him. "The stipulation that they remove at their own expence and on their own means, is an excellent feature in it. The whole treaty is just. We want them in a state of safety removed from the states and free from colision with the whites; and if the land does this it is well disposed of and freed from being a corrupting source to our Legislature."

Coffee's success with the Chickasaws followed those with the Creeks and Seminoles. On March 24, 1832, the destruction of the Creek Nation begun with the Treaty of Fort Jackson in 1814 was completed when the chiefs signed an agreement to remove rather than fight it out in the courts. The Seminoles accepted a provisional treaty on May 9, 1832, pending approval of the site for relocation. Thus, by the close of Jackson's first administration the Choctaws, Creeks, Chickasaws, and Seminoles had capitulated. Of the so-called Five Civilized Tribes only the Cherokees held out.

Not for long. They found small consolation from the courts. The Cherokees' lawyer, William Wirt, sued in the Supreme Court for an injunction that would permit the Indians to remain in Georgia unmolested by state law. He argued that the Cherokees had a right to self-government as a foreign nation and that this right had long been recognized by the United States in its treaties with the Indians. He hoped to make it appear that Jackson himself was the nullifier of federal law. In effect he challenged the entire removal policy by asking for a restraining order against Georgia.

Chief Justice John Marshall in the case *Cherokee Nation* v. *Georgia* handed down his opinion on March 18, 1831. He rejected Wirt's contention that the Cherokees were a sovereign nation. He also rejected Jackson's insistence that they were subject to state law. The Indians, he said, were "domestic dependent nations," subject to the United States as a ward to a guardian. They were not subject to individual states, he declared. Indian territory was in fact part of the United States.

The Indians chose to regard the opinion as essentially favorable in that it commanded the United States to protect their rights and property. So they refused to submit—either to Georgia or to Jackson. Meanwhile, Georgia passed legislation in late December, 1830, prohibiting white men from entering Indian country after March 1, 1831, without a license from the state. This was clearly aimed at troublesome missionaries who encouraged Indians in their "disobedience." Samuel A. Worcester and Dr. Elizur Butler, two missionaries, defied the law; they were arrested and sentenced to four years imprisonment in a state penitentiary. They sued, and in the case *Worcester* v. *Georgia* the Supreme Court decided on March 3, 1832, that the Georgia law was unconstitutional. Speaking for the majority in a feeble voice, John Marshall croaked out the court's decision. All the laws of Georgia dealing with the Cherokees were unconstitutional, he declared. He issued a formal mandate two days later ordering the Georgia Superior Court to reverse its decision.

Georgia, of course, had refused to acknowledge the court's right to direct its actions and had boycotted the judicial proceedings. The state had no intention of obeying the court's order. Since the court adjourned almost immediately after rendering its decision nothing further could be done. According to the Judiciary Act of 1789 the Supreme Court could issue its order of compliance only when a case had already been remanded without response. Since the court would not reconvene until January, 1833, no further action by the government could take place. Thus, until the court either summoned state officials before it for contempt or issued a writ of habeas corpus for the release of the two missionaries there was nothing further to be done. The President was under no obligation to act. In fact there is some question as to whether the court itself could act since the existing habeas corpus law did not apply in this case because the missionaries were not being detained by federal authorities. And since the Superior Court of Georgia did not acknowledge in writing its refusal to obey, Marshall's decision could not be enforced. Jackson understood this. He knew there was nothing for him to do. "The decision of the supreme court has fell still born," he wrote John Coffee, "and they find that it cannot coerce Georgia to yield to its mandate."

It was later reported by Horace Greeley that Jackson's response to the Marshall decision was total defiance. "Well: John Marshall has made his decision: *now let him enforce it!*" Greeley cited George N. Briggs, a Representative from Massachusetts, as his source for the statement. The quotation certainly sounds like Jackson and many historians have chosen to believe that he said it. The fact is that Jackson did not say it because there was no reason to do so. There was nothing for him to enforce. Why, then, would he refuse an action that no one asked him to take? As he said, the decision was stillborn. The court rendered an opinion which abandoned the Indians to their inevitable fate. "It cannot coerce Georgia to yield to its mandate," said Jackson, "and I believe [Major John] Ridge has expressed despair, and that it is better for them [the Cherokees] to treat and move."

Even if Jackson did not use the exact words Greeley put into his mouth, even if no direct action was required at the moment, some historians have argued that the quotation represents in fact Jackson's true attitude. There is evidence that Jackson "sportively said in private conversation" that if summoned "to support the decree of the Court he will call on those who have brought about the decision to enforce it." Actually nobody expected Jackson to enforce the decision, including the two missionaries, and therefore a lot of people simply assumed that the President would defy the court if pressured. In the rush to show Jackson as bombastic and blustery, however, an important point is missed. What should be remembered is that Jackson reacted with extreme caution to this crisis because a precipitous act could have triggered a confrontation with Georgia. Prudence, not defiance, characterized his reaction to both the challenge of Georgia and later the threat of nullification by South Carolina. As one historian has said, Jackson deserves praise for his caution in dealing with potentially explosive issues and should not be condemned for his so-called inaction.

Still the President had encouraged Georgia in its intransigence. He shares responsibility in producing this near-confrontation. He was so desperate to achieve Indian removal that he almost produced a crisis between federal and state authorities. Nor can it be denied, as one North Carolina Congressman observed, that "Gen Jackson could by a nod of the head or a crook of the finger induce Georgia to submit to the law. It is by the promise or belief of his countenance and support that Georgia is stimulated to her disorderly and rebellious conduct."

Jackson chose not to nod his head or crook his finger for several reasons, the most important of which was his determination to remove the Cherokees. But he had other concerns. As the time neared for the Supreme Court to reconvene and deliberate on Georgia's defiance, a controversy with South Carolina over nullification developed. Jackson had to be extremely careful that no action of his induced Georgia to join South Carolina in the dispute. Nullification might lead to secession and civil war. He therefore maneuvered to isolate South Carolina and force Georgia to back away from its position of confrontation. He needed to nudge Georgia into obeying the court order and free the two missionaries. Consequently he moved swiftly to win removal of the Indians. His secretary of war worked quietly to convince the legal counsel for the missionaries and the friends of the Cherokees in Congress, such as Theodore Frelinghuysen, that the President would not budge from his position nor interfere in the operation of Georgia laws and that the best solution for everyone was for the Indians to remove. Meanwhile the Creeks capitulated, and a treaty of removal was ratified by the Senate in April, 1832.

Although Senator Frelinghuysen "prayed to God" that Georgia would peacefully acquiesce in the decision of the Supreme Court he soon concluded that the Cherokees must yield. Even Justice John McLean, who wrote a concurring opinion in the *Worcester* case, counseled the Cherokee delegation in Washington to sign a removal treaty. Van Buren's Albany Regency actively intervened because of their concern over a possible southern backlash against their leader. Van Buren himself encouraged his friend Senator John Forsyth to intercede with the newly elected governor of Georgia, Wilson Lumpkin, keeping Jackson carefully informed of his actions. More significant, however, were the letters written by the secretary of war to Lumpkin. These letters pleaded for a pardon for the two missionaries and stated that the President himself gave his unconditional endorsement of the request. Finally Forsyth conferred with William Wirt who in turn conferred with a representative of the two missionaries, and they all agreed to make no further motion before the Supreme Court. That done, Governor Lumpkin ordered the "keeper" of the penitentiary on January 14, 1833 to release Worcester and Butler under an arrangement devised by Forsyth. Thus, while the President held steady to his course and directed the activities of the men in contact with Lumpkin, both the problem of Georgia's defiance and the fate of the two missionaries were quietly resolved without injurious consequences to the rest of the nation. It was one of Jackson's finest actions as a statesman.

Ultimately, the Cherokees also yielded to the President. On December 29, 1835, at New Echota a treaty was signed arranging an exchange of land. A protracted legal argument had gained the Indians a little time but nothing else. Removal now applied to all eastern Indians, not simply the southern tribes. After the Black Hawk War of 1832 Jackson responded to the demands of Americans in the northwest to send all Indians beyond the Mississippi. A hungry band of Sac and Fox Indians under the leadership of Black Hawk had recrossed the Mississippi in the spring of 1832 to find food. People on the frontier panicked and Governor John Reynolds of Illinois called out the militia and appealed to Jackson for assistance. Federal troops were immediately dispatched under Generals Winfield Scott and Henry Atkinson. A short and bloody war resulted, largely instigated by drunken militia troops, and when it ended the northwestern tribes were so demoralized that they offered little resistance to Jackson's steady pressure for their removal west of the Mississippi. The result of the Black Hawk War, said the President in his fourth message to Congress, had been very "creditable to the troops" engaged in the action. "Severe as is the lesson to the Indians," he lectured, "it was rendered necessary by their unprovoked aggressions, and it is to be hoped that its impression will be permanent and salutary."

It was useless for the Indians to resist Jackson's demands. Nearly 46,000 of them went west. Thousands died in transit. Even those under no treaty obligation to emigrate were eventually forced to remove. And the removal experiences were all pretty much like that of the Choctaws—all horrible, all rife with corruption and fraud, all disgraceful to the American nation.

The policy of removal formed an important part of Jackson's overall program of limiting federal authority and supporting states' rights. Despite the accusation of increased executive authority, Jackson successfully buttressed state sovereignty and jurisdiction over all inhabitants within state boundaries. This is a government of the people, Jackson argued, and the President is the agent of the people. The President and the Congress exercise their jurisdiction over "*the people of the union.* [W]ho are the people of the union?" he asked. Then, answering his own question, he said: "all those subject to the jurisdiction of the sovereign states, none else." Indians are also subject to the states, he went on. They are subject "to the sovereign power of the state within whose sovereign limits they reside." An "absolute independence of the Indian tribes from state authority can never bear an intelligent investigation, and a quasi independence of state authority when located within its Territorial limits is *absurd.*"

In addition to establishing the removal policy Jackson also restructured the bureaucracy handling Indian problems. Since 1824 a Bureau of Indian Affairs headed by Thomas L. McKenney had supervised the government's relations with the Indians. By the time Jackson assumed the presidency the Bureau had become an "enormous quagmire" from an administrative point of view. McKenney was retained in office to take advantage of his reputation to win passage of the Removal bill. Once Removal passed, McKenney was dismissed. (For one thing he had supported Adams in 1828). Then the Bureau was reorganized. On June 30, 1834, Congress passed the necessary legislation establishing the Office of Indian Affairs under an Indian commissioner, and this administrative machinery remained in place well into the twentieth century. The Indian service was restructured into a more cohesive operation than had previously been the case. It regularized procedures that had been practiced as a matter of custom rather than law.

Ultimately Jackson's policy of removal and reorganization of the Indian service won acceptance by most Americans. The President was seen as a forceful executive who addressed one of the nation's most bedeviling problems and solved it. Even Americans who fretted over the fate of the Indians eventually went along with removal. The policy seemed enlightened and humane. It seemed rational and logical. It constituted, Americans thought, the only possible solution to the Indian problem.

The Long, Bitter Trail: Andrew Jackson and the Indians

Georgia in the late 1820s was a prosperous and rapidly developing common-wealth. The state government encouraged the growth of an extensive system of private banks that lent money to aspiring farmers and entrepreneurs. Family farms were the norm; there were few cotton plantations larger than 500 acres. Railroads and shallow-draft steamboats were opening up the agricul-tural interior and connecting the cotton country with seaports at Savannah and Brunswick, through which passed the trade not only with Great Britain but also with the industrial Northern states. Georgia was less inclined than her neighbor South Carolina to espouse the doctrine of nullification, so hateful to President Jackson, propounded by that state's legislature and advocated by her native son Vice President John C. Calhoun. Increasingly, too, the Georgia electorate was turning away from the faction headed by Jackson's old political rival, William H. Crawford, and was favoring the party more friendly to the President. Jackson had motives for rewarding Georgia that went beyond his commitment to Indian removal.

Thus Georgians felt that they had the right to claim the President's sym-pathetic attention in time of need. And now was that time. The Cherokee constitution in effect nullified Georgia law and made the Indian nation a "state within a state." Left to themselves, the Cherokees would become a prosperous, independent commonwealth, and they would never sell their land (indeed, by Cherokee law, the further sale of land to the United States was a crime). On De-cember 20, 1828, immediately after the election of Andrew Jackson as President of the United States, the Georgia legislature passed a law extending the state's jurisdiction—i.e., its laws, its police powers, and its courts—over the Cherokees living within the state. Enforcement was to be deferred until June 1, 1830, to give the President and Congress time to act in support of Georgia.

Georgia's action forced the President's hand. He must see to it that a removal policy long covertly pursued by the White House would now be enacted into law by the Congress. The new President quickly took steps to implement a removal program that would, among other things, resolve the Georgia crisis. As his Secretary of War he appointed his old friend and political supporter from Tennessee, Senator John Eaton. No doubt with the advice of Superintendent McKenney, who had convinced himself of the need for removal, Eaton included in his first (1829) Report to the President a recommendation for wholesale removal of the Eastern Indians to a self-governing "Indian territory" in the West, where the U.S. Army would protect them from intruding whites and keep the peace among the tribes.

The Twenty-first Congress convened for its first session in December 1829, and as was (and still is) the custom, the President delivered to it a message reporting on the State of the Union and making recommendations for new legislation. Not unexpectedly, he paid considerable attention to the Indian question.... About half the discussion of Indian affairs was devoted to the constitutional issue raised by the Cherokee claim to independence and political sovereignty within the state of Georgia. Jackson stated that in his view the Native Americans residing within the boundaries of old or new states were subject to the laws of those states. He recognized the efforts of some tribes to become "civilized" but saw the only hope for their survival to be removal to a Western territory. The rhetoric was candid but compassionate in tone, no doubt intended to disarm criticism, suggesting that removal was not merely legally justified but morally necessary, and that he was responding not to the greed of land speculators and would-be settlers but to a moral imperative to save the Indians from extinction. Emigration, of course, should be strictly voluntary with individuals. Those who chose to leave would be provided with an "ample district West of the Mississippi," to be guaranteed to them as long as they occupied it. Each tribe would have its own territory and its own government and would be free to receive "benevolent" instructors in the "arts of civilization." In the future, there might arise "an interesting commonwealth, destined to perpetuate the race, and to attest the humanity and justice of this Government." For those who chose to remain, he gave assurance that they would "without doubt" be allowed to keep possession of their houses and gardens. But he warned them that they must obey the laws of the states in which they lived, and must be prepared to give up all claims to "tracts of country on which they have neither dwelt nor made improvements, merely because they have seen them from the mountain, or passed them in the chace." Eventually, those who stayed behind could expect to "become merged in the mass of our population."

On February 24, 1830, a removal bill was reported out from the House Committee on Indian Affairs (John Bell of Tennessee, chairman). The same bill was also introduced into the Senate by its Indian Committee (also chaired by a Jackson man from Tennessee). The text of the bill... was briefer than the President's message recommending it. In eight sections, it authorized the President to set aside an Indian territory on public lands west of the Mississippi; to exchange districts there for land now occupied by Indians in the East; to grant the tribes absolute ownership of their new homes "forever"; to treat with tribes for the rearrangement of boundaries in order to effect the removal; to ensure that property left behind by emigrating Indians be properly appraised and fair compensation be paid; to give the emigrants "aid and assistance" on their journey and for the first year after their arrival in their new country; to protect the emigrants from hostile Indians in the West and from any other intruders; to continue the "superintendence" now exercised over the Indians by the Trade and Intercourse Laws. And to carry out these responsibilities, the Congress appropriated the sum (soon to prove woefully inadequate) of $500,000.

The debate on the bill was long and bitter, for the subject of Indian removal touched upon a number of very emotional issues: the constitutional question of states' rights versus federal prerogatives, Christian charity, national honor, racial and cultural prejudices, manifest destiny, and of course just plain greed. The opening salvo was the Report of the Indian Committee of the House. The report defended the constitutional right of the states to exercise sovereignty over residents, including Indians, within their borders. It discussed the nature of Indian title, naïvely asserting that in pre-Columbian times "the whole country was a common hunting ground"; they claimed as private or tribal property only their "moveable wigwams" and in some parts of the continent "their small corn patches." The committee declared that the Indians were incapable of "civilization," despite their recent "extravagant pretensions," so loudly touted by misguided zealots opposed to emigration. Among the Cherokees, the report asserted, only a small oligarchy of twenty-five or thirty families controlled the government and only these, and about two hundred mixed-blood families who made up what the report referred to as a "middle class," could claim to have made any progress toward what the committee regarded as "civilization." These favored few opposed emigration. But the remainder, allegedly living in indolence, poverty, and vice, were generally in favor of removal as the only way to escape destitution and eventual annihilation. Obviously, in the committee's view, it was not merely justifiable but morally imperative to save the Southern tribes from extinction by helping them to emigrate to the West.

Both Houses of Congress were deluged by hundreds of petitions and memorials, solicited by religious groups and benevolent societies opposed to Indian removal. Town meetings were held, particularly in the Northern states, demanding justice for the Native Americans. Joseph Hemphill, congressman from Pennsylvania, published a review of Cass's article "Indian Reform," excoriating him for recommending an oppressive policy toward the Indians; and he included in his condemnation the Reverend Isaac McCoy, who had written a book, *The Practicability of Indian Reform*, urging removal as the only means of civilizing the natives. The American Board of Commissioners exerted wide influence on Protestant denominations in the cause of Indian rights. Not to be outdone, friends of Jackson organized their own pro-removal missionary society, its masthead adorned with the names of prominent officials and clergymen who favored the bill. Its efforts were eclipsed by the older American Board, however, whose leader, Jeremiah Evarts, under the *nom de plume* William Penn, had already published his *Essays on the Present Crisis in the Condition of the American Indians*.

In the spring of 1830, active debate began in the chambers of Congress. The attack on the bill was launched in the Senate by Theodore Frelinghuysen of New Jersey, a distinguished lawyer whose deep religious convictions had already earned him the respect of colleagues in both parties. Frelinghuysen, a Whig, was an example of the "Christian party in politics," for at one time or another he was president of the American Board of Commissioners for Foreign Missions (sixteen years), president of the American Bible Society (sixteen years), president of the American Tract Society (six years), vice president of the American Sunday School Union (fifty years), and for many years an officer of the American Temperance Union and the American Colonization Society. His stand on the Indian question was to earn him a national reputation as "the Christian statesman" and in 1844 a place on the Whig ticket as (unsuccessful) candidate for Vice President of the United States, along with Henry Clay for President. Senator Frelinghuysen's speech, which took three days to deliver, pointed out that the Indian policy of the United States, from the time of Washington on, had been based on the principle that the United States was obligated to protect peaceful natives living in unceded territory from intrusion by whites under any pretext, by force if necessary. Treaties with the Native Americans, according to the Constitution, were, like other treaties, the law of the land. The Jackson Administration, by refusing to enforce existing treaties, was violating the Constitution.

Why was more Indian land needed now, when annual sales of public lands amounted to no more than 1 million acres? The Indian occupants of the continent had already peacefully sold more than 214 million acres, and much of that remained vacant. To be sure, hunters would eventually sell to agriculturists, but willingly and in response to reasonable argument, not by coercion, as this bill, in the hands of this administration, promised. Furthermore, many of the Native Americans, in response to the official reform policy of the United States government, were adopting white customs and could be expected to amalgamate with the whites, if left alone where they were. Frelinghuysen concluded with an essentially moral appeal:

> Sir, if we abandon these aboriginal proprietors of our soil, these early allies and adopted children of our forefathers, how shall we justify it to our country? . . . How shall we justify this trespass to ourselves? . . . Let us beware how, by oppressive encroachments upon the sacred privileges of our Indian neighbors, we minister to the agonies of future remorse.

The pro-removal reply to Frelinghuysen was delivered by Senator John Forsyth of Georgia. Like his opponent, Forsyth was a lawyer and a former attorney general of his state. He had served as a representative in Congress, as minister to Spain (he secured the King's ratification of the 1819 treaty ceding Florida to the United States), and, most recently, he had served as governor of Georgia (1827–29). He was a loyal Jackson follower, would later support Jackson and oppose Calhoun over nullification, and in 1834 he was rewarded by appointment as Secretary of State. He was a skilled orator and had the reputation of being the best debater of his time.

Forsyth dismissed Frelinghuysen's words as a mere self-interested plea by the "Christian party in politics" to create unwarranted sympathy for the Indians, among whom their missionaries lived so prosperously. He pointed to the deplorable conditions under which the Native Americans now lived and to the long history of the removal policy. Forsyth, as a true friend of the Indians, had long had doubts that removal would promote their civilization, but he would vote for this bill because it would relieve the states "from a population useless and bothersome" and would place these wild hunters in a country better supplied with game. But most of Forsyth's time was spent on legal arguments about states' rights (particularly Georgia's) to exercise sovereignty over Indians, about old treaties and proclamations, and about natural law. He concluded that Georgia had a right to expect the United States to remove the Indians (without coercion, of course) to a happier hunting ground west of the Mississippi.

The debate raged for weeks in both the Senate and the House. Amendments were proposed in the Senate that would have weakened the bill by protecting the Indians' interests; three times these amendments were defeated by a single vote. In general, delegates from the Northern and Eastern states, many of them National Republicans, anti-Masons, and moral reformers, stood against the bill, and Southern and Western delegates—many, like Jackson, with little interest in evangelical Christianity—favored it. Eventually, on April 23, 1830, the Senate voted 28 to 19 to pass the measure. On May 24, the House passed the bill by a narrower margin, 102 to 97.

President Jackson signed the Removal Act on the same day. It was, some maintained, the "leading measure" of his administration; indeed, "the greatest question that ever came before Congress, short of the question of peace and war." Jackson himself said that Indian removal was the "most arduous part of my duty" as President.

A fairly clear federal policy with regard to the transfer to white owners of title to newly purchased Indian lands, based on a generation of experience, was already in place when the Removal Act was passed and signed. In some cessions, individual Indians were allowed to retain small tracts, called "allotments" (in distinction to tribally owned "reservations"), generally small parcels of land around their residences. These allotments could be sold by their Indian owners to settlers or land companies by government-approved contract. The remainder of the ceded territory became part of the public lands of the United States (except for Georgia, where, by special agreement, lands purchased by the United States were turned over to the state). The usual practice of the federal government was to dispose of the public lands as quickly as possible. The lands were first surveyed and then sold, a large proportion initially at public auction at a minimum price of $1.25 an acre, and the remainder at subsequent privately arranged sales.

Meanwhile, "actual settlers" would be entering these public lands, staking out claims, building cabins, making improvements. Along with the squatters, "land lookers" sent by land companies were prowling about, identifying the best locations for speculative investment. The government did not try to stop the squatters, who often were tacitly accorded a "preemption right" to 80 or 160 acres around their improvements at the minimum price of $1.25 an acre.

"Speculator" land companies, while they were condemned in political rhetoric as unfair monopolistic competitors of the "actual settler," at least sometimes supported the settlers' interests. Government did not really want to discourage the speculators any more than the settlers. After all, many politicians and officials (as we have seen, including Jackson and his friends) were speculators in Indian lands themselves, and anyway, there were rarely enough settlers on hand to buy up all the land offered for sale. Besides, some tracts like town sites required expensive development before resale to "actual settlers."

The government did not expect to realize much if any profit from the sale of the public lands. Some of the less desirable tracts, slow to move, eventually went for as little as 12½ cents an acre after languishing for up to five years. Some of the more attractive sites, on the other hand, might bring prices at auction well above the $1.25-an-acre minimum. But even though the Indians would be given only a few cents an acre for their land, the government was likely to agree to pay for the expense of their relocation out of the proceeds from the sale of their former domain. And there were costs associated with preparing the public lands for sale: surveys, the opening of roads, and the operations of the Land Office itself, both in Washington and in the field. Public policy was to get the public lands into private hands, for economic development, as quickly as possible.

Thus the Jackson administration was ready to do its "land-office business" as soon as the Indians could be persuaded to sell and agree to remove. In fact, efforts to that end were already under way.

The Trail of Tears

Responsibility for arranging the actual removal of the Indians was now in the hands of the administration. Jackson had in place a removal team: his protégé John Eaton, the Secretary of War; Thomas McKenney, Superintendent of the Indian Office, a declared supporter of removal; General Coffee, his old comrade-in-arms, always ready to serve as the situation demanded—as Indian fighter, treaty negotiator, or surveyor of purchased lands. He also had available the staff of Indian agents who served under McKenney. But McKenney, despite his support for the principle of voluntary removal, soon balked at the harassment tactics of the administration. He was removed from office in August 1830. In 1831, after another official had served for a year, the position was filled by a loyal Jacksonite, Elbert Herring, who supported the removal policy until he left in 1836. Along with McKenney, about half the experienced Indian agents in the field were replaced by Jackson men. They could be counted on to execute administration policy more readily than those whose long acquaintance with Native Americans had made them too sympathetic. In 1831, Eaton, mired in an embarrassing domestic scandal, was replaced as Secretary of War by Lewis Cass, who ... was not only a loyal Democrat but also a leading advocate of removal. Not incidentally, his political leadership in the Michigan Territory, which was about to become a state, would come in handy at election time in 1832.

It was the team of Jackson, Cass, and Herring that supervised the removal of most of the Southern Indians from 1830 through 1836. By the end of 1836, the Choctaws and Creeks had emigrated, and by the close of 1837 the Chickasaws had followed. Cherokee resistance was not broken, however, until 1839, and the Seminoles were not removed until 1842, after a long and bloody war.

                        ᴥ◉ᴥ

In principle, emigration was to be voluntary; the Removal Act did not require Native Americans to emigrate, and those who wished to remain could do so. But the actual policy of the administration was to encourage removal by all possible means, fair or foul.

Jackson as usual spoke publicly in a tone of friendship and concern for Indian welfare. In a letter of instruction to an agent who was to visit the Choctaws in October 1829 (even before the Removal Act was passed) he outlined the message from "their father," the President, urging them to emigrate. The threats were veiled. "They and my white children are too near each other to live in harmony and peace." The state of Mississippi had the right to extend a burdensome jurisdiction over them, and "the general government will be obliged to sustain the States in the exercise of their right." He, as President, could be their friend only if they removed beyond the Mississippi, where they should have a "land of their own, which they shall possess as long as Grass grows or water runs . . . and I never speak with forked tongue."

A harsh policy was nevertheless quickly put in place. To weaken the power of the chiefs, many of whom opposed removal, the traditional practice of paying annuities in a lump sum, to be used by the chiefs on behalf of the tribe for capital improvements and education, was terminated and annuities were doled out piecemeal to individual Indians. The amounts were pitifully small—each Cherokee was to receive forty-four cents per year, for example, and even that was to be withheld until he reached the West. Some annuities were not paid at all, being diverted by local agents to pay spurious damage claims allowed by state courts against Indians.

The principal acts of harassment, however, were carried out by the governments and citizens of the Southern states. The extension of state sovereignty over the tribes within their borders led quickly to the passage of destructive legislation. The tribal governments, so carefully organized in imitation of white institutions, were simply abolished; it became illegal for tribes to establish their own laws and to convict and punish lawbreakers. The chiefs were to have no power. Tribal assemblies were banned. Indians were subject to state taxes, militia duty, and suits for debt. Indians were denied the right to vote, to bring suit, even to testify in court (as heathens all—despite the evidence of conversion for many—they could not swear a Christian oath). Intruders were encouraged to settle on Indian territory; lands were sold even before they had been ceded. In Georgia, after gold was discovered on Cherokee property, the Indians were prohibited from digging or mining gold on their own land, while hundreds of white prospectors were allowed to trespass and steal the gold with impunity.

And all the while, the federal government stood idly by, refusing to intervene in the application of state laws. The result was chaos. Thousands of intruders swarmed over the Indian country in a frenzied quest for land and gold, destroying Indian farms and crops. The missionaries tried to persuade their Indian friends to stand firm against removal. But Georgia passed a law requiring missionaries to take an oath of loyalty to the state or leave the Indian country, and when a number refused, they were seized, imprisoned, tried, convicted, and sentenced to long prison terms. All but two were pardoned after they signed a pledge to obey the laws of Georgia. The recalcitrant ones, the famous Samuel Worcester, former head of the American Board's school at Brainerd, publisher of *The Cherokee Phoenix,* and an ardent anti-removal advocate, and an assistant missionary, Elizur Butler, chose to appeal their convictions. While they languished in prison, the case wound its way up to the Supreme Court, where the issue was interpreted in the context of Georgia's claim of state sovereignty. The Supreme Court found against Georgia's right to supersede federal authority over Indian tribes and thus set aside Georgia's assertion of state sovereignty over the Cherokees and their missionaries. Jackson was not impressed, however, and is reputed to have said, "Justice Marshall has made his decision, now let him enforce it." Whether he actually used these words has been questioned; but they represent his sentiments, for the administration did nothing to aid the missionaries or effectively to deter intruders. Worcester was not released from prison until the following year (1833).

The other major legal challenge to the state's sovereignty was an earlier suit pressed by the Cherokee nation that directly challenged the constitutionality of Georgia's attempt to execute state law within the Indian country. Former Attorney General William Wirt (who also represented Samuel Worcester) applied to the Supreme Court for an injunction. But this case was dismissed on the technical ground that an Indian nation was not a foreign state but a "domestic dependent nation," a "ward" of its "guardian," the United States, and therefore could not bring suit before the Supreme Court.

It is abundantly clear that Jackson and his administration were determined to permit the extension of state sovereignty because it would result in the harassment of Indians, powerless to resist, by speculators and intruders hungry for Indian land. Jackson, of course, was not always so indulgent of states' rights, as is shown by his famous threat later on to use military force against South Carolina if that state acted on John Calhoun's doctrine of nullification.

POSTSCRIPT

Was Andrew Jackson's Indian Removal Policy Motivated by Humanitarian Impulses?

One of the interesting sidelights of the federal government's efforts to develop a policy with regard to Native American tribes residing in individual states revolved around the questions of tribal sovereignty versus states' rights. The Cherokee, in particular, proved troublesome in this regard. Since 1791 the United States had recognized the Cherokee as a nation in a number of treaties, and in 1827 delegates of this tribe initiated action to draft a constitution that would more formally recognize this status. In doing so, Native Americans confronted a barrier in the U.S. Constitution that prohibited the establishment of a new state in a preexisting state without the latter's approval. In response, Georgia, where most of the Cherokee lived, opposed the plan and called for the removal of all Native Americans. At this juncture, Cherokee leaders sought an injunction to prevent the state of Georgia from enforcing its laws within Native American territory. The case reached the U.S. Supreme Court, which, in *Cherokee Nation v. Georgia* (1831), expressed sympathy for the Native Americans' position but denied that the Cherokee held the status of a foreign nation. The following year, in the midst of efforts to remove all Native Americans from the southeastern United States, Chief Justice John Marshall, in *Worcester v. Georgia* (1832), ruled that the state had no right to extend sovereignty over the Cherokees within its borders.

Major studies of the Indian removal policy in Jacksonian America include Angie Debo's classic *And Still the Waters Run: The Betrayal of the Five Civilized Tribes* (University of Oklahoma Press, 1940); Allen Guttman, *States Rights and Indian Removal: The Cherokee Nation vs. the State of Georgia* (D. C. Heath, 1965); John Ehle, *Trail of Tears: The Rise and Fall of the Cherokee Nation* (Doubleday, 1988); Mary E. Young, *Redskins, Ruffleshirts, and Rednecks: Indian Allotments in Alabama and Mississippi, 1830–1860* (University of Oklahoma Press, 1961); and Arthur H. DeRosier, Jr., *The Removal of the Choctaw Indians* (University of Tennessee Press, 1970). Perhaps the best analysis of Jackson's sometimes ambiguous attitude toward Native Americans is Michael Paul Rogin, *Fathers and Children: Andrew Jackson and the Subjugation of the American Indian* (Alfred A. Knopf, 1975).

For general studies of Native American history that include discussions of Jackson's attitudes and policies with regard to Native Americans, see Wilcomb E. Washburn, *The Indian in America* (Harper & Row, 1975); Robert F. Berkhofer, Jr., *The White Man's Indian: Images of the American Indian From Columbus to the*

Present (Alfred A. Knopf, 1978); and Francis Paul Prucha's edited collection of readings *The Indian in American History* (Holt, Rinehart & Winston, 1971).

The historical literature on Jacksonian philosophy and policies is extensive. Remini is Jackson's definitive, generally sympathetic biographer. His three-volume study, *Andrew Jackson and the Course of American Empire, 1767–1821* (Harper & Row, 1977); *Andrew Jackson and the Course of American Freedom, 1822–1832* (Harper & Row, 1981); and *Andrew Jackson and the Course of American Democracy, 1833–1845* (Harper & Row, 1984), is the culmination of a long career of study and writing. Older though equally excellent studies include Arthur Schlesinger, Jr., *The Age of Jackson* (Little, Brown, 1946); John William Ward, *Andrew Jackson: Symbol for an Age* (Oxford University Press, 1955); and Marvin Meyers, *The Jacksonian Persuasion: Politics and Belief* (Stanford University Press, 1957). Useful primary sources on the "age of Jackson" are collected in Edward Pessen, ed., *Jacksonian Panorama* (Bobbs-Merrill, 1976). The period is also explored in Glyndon G. Van Deusen, *The Jacksonian Era, 1828–1848* (Harper & Row, 1959); Edward Pessen, *Jacksonian America: Society, Personality, and Politics* (Dorsey Press, 1969); and Henry L. Watson, *Liberty and Power: The Politics of Jacksonian America* (Hill & Wang, 1990). Finally, Alexis de Tocqueville's classic *Democracy in America* (HarperCollins, 1988) sheds a great deal of light on the still-young nation of Jackson's time from the perspective of a foreign observer.

On the Internet ...

African-American Mosaic: Abolition

The Library of Congress created this Web site on abolition. This site consists of a list of writings on the subject and shows the great deal of public support for abolition. Also included is a handbill opposing abolition. Photos of publications as well as summaries are provided, and one is able to read abolitionist pamphlets that were designed specifically for women and children.

`http://lcweb.loc.gov/exhibits/african/afam005.html`

Black Resistance: Slavery in the United States

This slavery exhibit is part of Afro-America's Black History Museum. Compiled by Carolyn L. Bennett and designed by Matt Evans, it offers a chronology of events, a brief introduction to the transport of Africans to America, and some commentary on the attitudes of slaves.

`http://www.afroam.org/history/slavery/main.html`

ReenactorsWorldPlus.com

ReenactorsWorldPlus.com is dedicated to the tens of thousands of men, women, and children around the world who bring our historical heritage alive through education in our schools, living history events, and other public areas. This page is dedicated to the Mexican-American War.

`http://reenactorsworldplus.com/mexican.htm`

Historical Text Archive: Women's History

This archive contains an impressive collection of links related to women and their roles in history. Topics include women on the frontier in the 1800s, women and social movements in the United States, and women during the Civil War.

`http://www.geocities.com/Athens/Forum/9061/USA/women.html`

PART 3

Antebellum America

*P*ressures and trends that began building in the early years of the American nation continued to gather momentum until conflict was almost inevitable. Population growth and territorial expansion brought the country into conflict with other nations. The United States had to respond to challenges from Americans who felt alienated from or forgotten by the new nation because the ideals of human rights and democratic participation that guided the founding of the nation had been applied only to selected segments of the population.

- Were the Abolitionists "Unrestrained Fanatics"?

- Was Slavery Profitable?

- Was the Mexican War an Exercise in American Imperialism?

- Did the Westward Movement Transform the Traditional Roles of Women in the Mid-Nineteenth Century?

ISSUE 10

Were the Abolitionists "Unrestrained Fanatics"?

YES: Avery Craven, from *The Coming of the Civil War*, 2d ed. (University of Chicago Press, 1957)

NO: Irving H. Bartlett, from "The Persistence of Wendell Phillips," in Martin Duberman, ed., *The Antislavery Vanguard: New Essays on the Abolitionists* (Princeton University Press, 1965)

ISSUE SUMMARY

YES: Historian Avery Craven asserts that the fanaticism of the abolitionist crusade created an atmosphere of crisis that resulted in the outbreak of the Civil War.

NO: Irving H. Bartlett, a retired professor of American civilization, differentiates between agitation and fanaticism and states that abolitionists like Wendell Phillips were deeply committed to improving the quality of life for all Americans, including African Americans held as slaves.

Opposition to slavery in the area that became the United States dates back to the seventeenth and eighteenth centuries, when Puritan leaders, such as Samuel Sewall, and Quakers, such as John Woolman and Anthony Benezet, published a number of pamphlets condemning the existence of the slave system. This religious link to antislavery sentiment is also evident in the writings of John Wesley as well as in the decision of the Society of Friends in 1688 to prohibit their members from owning bondservants. Slavery was said to be contrary to Christian principles. These attacks, however, did little to diminish the institution. In fact, efforts to force emancipation gained little headway in the colonies until the outbreak of the American Revolution. Complaints that the English government had instituted a series of measures that "enslaved" the colonies in British North America raised thorny questions about the presence of real slavery in those colonies. How could Americans demand their freedom from King George III, who was cast in the role of oppressive master, while denying freedom and liberty to African American bondsmen? Such a contradiction inspired a gradual emancipation movement in the North, which was often accompanied by compensation for the former slave owners.

In addition, antislavery societies sprang up throughout the nation to continue the crusade against bondage. Interestingly, the majority of these organizations were located in the South. Prior to the 1830s the most prominent antislavery organization was the American Colonization Society, which offered a two-fold program: (1) gradual, compensated emancipation of slaves, and (2) exportation of the new freedmen to colonies outside the boundaries of the United States, mostly to Africa.

In the 1830s antislavery activity underwent an important transformation. A new strain of antislavery sentiment expressed itself in the abolitionist movement. Drawing momentum from both the revivalism of the Second Great Awakening and the example set by England (which prohibited slavery in its imperial holdings in 1833), abolitionists called for the immediate end to slavery without compensation to masters for the loss of their property. Abolitionists viewed slavery not so much as a practical problem to be resolved, but rather as a moral offense incapable of resolution through traditional channels of political compromise. In January 1831 William Lloyd Garrison, who for many came to symbolize the abolitionist crusade, published the first issue of *The Liberator*, a newspaper dedicated to the immediate end of slavery. In his first editorial, Garrison expressed the indignation of many in the abolitionist movement when he warned slaveholders and their supporters to "urge me not to use moderation in a cause like the present. I am in earnest—I will not equivocate—I will not excuse —I will not retreat a single inch—AND I WILL BE HEARD."

Unfortunately for Garrison, relatively few Americans were inclined to respond positively to his call. His newspaper generated little interest outside Boston, New York, Philadelphia, and other major urban centers of the North. This situation, however, changed within a matter of months. In August 1831 a slave preacher named Nat Turner led a rebellion of slaves in Southampton County, Virginia, that resulted in the death of 58 whites. Although the revolt was quickly suppressed and Turner and his supporters were executed, the incident spread fear throughout the South. Governor John B. Floyd of Virginia turned an accusatory finger toward the abolitionists when he concluded that the Turner uprising was "undoubtedly designed and matured by unrestrained fanatics in some of the neighboring states." Moreover, it would be charged, these abolitionists contributed to a crisis environment that degenerated over the next generation and ultimately produced civil war.

Some historians have accepted the view that abolitionist fanaticism, expressed through attacks on Southern slavery, led to political deterioration in the United States which culminated in secession and war. In the following selection, for example, Avery Craven blames abolitionists for inciting volatile emotions by characterizing slaveholders as sinful aristocrats who were willing to distort the American dream of freedom to preserve their peculiar institution.

In the second selection, Irving H. Bartlett surveys the abolitionist career of Wendell Phillips and concludes that he was not a fanatic but rather a practical agitator, an intellectual, and a committed philosopher of reform who clearly understood the difference between agitation and demagoguery.

 **YES**

The Northern Attack on Slavery

The abolition movement... was closely related in origins, leadership, and expression to the peace movement, the temperance crusade, the struggles for women's rights, prison and Sabbath reform, and the improvement of education. It was not unrelated to the efforts to establish communities where social-economic justice and high thinking might prevail. It was part of the drive to unseat aristocrats and re-establish American democracy according to the Declaration of Independence. It was a clear-cut effort to apply Christianity to the American social order.

The anti-slavery effort was at first merely one among many. It rose to dominance only gradually. Fortunate from the beginning in leadership, it was always more fortunate in appeal. Human slavery more obviously violated democratic institutions than any other evil of the day; it was close enough to irritate and to inflame sensitive minds, yet far enough removed that reformers need have few personal relations with those whose interests were affected. It rasped most severely upon the moral senses of a people whose ideas of sin were comprehended largely in terms of self-indulgence and whose religious doctrines laid emphasis on social usefulness as the proper manifestation of salvation. And, what was more important, slavery was now confined to a section whose economic interests, and hence political attitudes, conflicted sharply with those of the Northeast and upper Northwest.

Almost from the beginning of the new anti-slavery movement, two distinct centers of action appeared, each with its distinct and individual approach to the problem. One developed in the industrial areas of New England. Its most important spokesman was William Lloyd Garrison, founder and editor of a Boston abolition paper called the *Liberator*. Garrison at first accepted the old idea that slavery was an *evil* to be pointed out and gradually eradicated by those among whom it existed, but he shifted his position in the early 1830's and denounced slavery as a damning crime to be unremittingly assailed and immediately destroyed. The first issue of his paper announced a program from which he never deviated: " ... *I do not wish to think or speak or write with moderation. I will not retreat a single inch, and I will be heard.*" The problem, as Garrison saw it, was one of abstract right and wrong. The Scriptures and the Declaration of Independence had already settled the issue. Slavery could have no legal status in a Christian democracy. If the Constitution recognized it, then the Constitution should be destroyed. Slaveholders were both sinners and criminals. They could lay no claim to immunity from any mode of attack. . . .

The extreme and impractical nature of the Garrison anti-slavery drive served to attract attention and arouse antagonism rather than to solve the problem. It did, however, show how profoundly the conditions of the time had stirred the reform spirit and how wide the door had been opened to the professional reformers—men to whom the question was not so much "how shall we abolish slavery, as how shall we best discharge our duty . . . to ourselves." Garrison may be taken as typical of the group. His temperament and experiences had combined to set him in most relationships against the accepted order of things. His life would probably have been spent in protesting even if slavery had never existed. From childhood he had waged a bitter fight *against* obstacles and *for* a due recognition of his abilities. A drunken father had abandoned the family to extreme poverty before William was three years old, and the boy, denied all but the rudiments of an education, had first been placed under the care of Deacon Bartlett, and then apprenticed for seven years to one Ephraim Allen to learn the printing trade. His first venture after his apprenticeship was over failed. His second gave him the opportunity to strike back at an unfair world. He became an editor of the *National Philanthropist,* a paper devoted to the suppression of "intemperance and its Kindred vices." This publication served also as a medium through which to attack lotteries, Sabbath-breaking, and war. A new Garrison began to emerge. His personality, given opportunity for expression, asserted itself. Attending a nominating caucus in Boston, he made bold to speak, and, being resented as an upstart, he replied to his critic in a letter to the Boston *Courier:*

> It is true my acquaintance in this city is limited. . . . Let me assure him, however, that if my life be spared, my name shall one day be known to the world—at least to such an extent that common inquiry shall be unnecessary.

To another critic he reiterated this statement, adding these significant words: "I speak in the spirit of prophecy, not of vainglory—with a strong pulse, a flashing eye, and a glow of the heart. The task may be yours to write my biography."

Anti-slavery efforts entered the Garrison program when Benjamin Lundy, the pioneer abolitionist, invited him to help edit the *Genius of Universal Emancipation* in Baltimore. Hostile treatment there, climaxed by imprisonment for libel, together with the influence of extreme British opinion, changed a moderate attitude which admitted "that immediate and complete emancipation is not desirable . . . no rational man cherishes so wild a vision," into the extreme and uncompromising fanaticism expressed only two years later in the *Liberator.* From that time on Garrison was bothered only by the fact that the English language was inadequate for the expression of his violent opinions. Southerners in Congress were desperados.

> We would sooner trust the honor of the country . . . in the hands of the inmates of our penitentiaries and prisons than in their hands . . . they are the meanest of thieves and the worst of robbers. . . . We do not acknowledge them to be within the pale of Christianity, or republicanism, or humanity!

Hatred of the South had supplanted love for the Negro!

In such an approach as this, there could be no delay, no moderation. Right was right, and wrong was wrong. The Slaveholder could not be spared or given time to learn the evil of his ways. Action immediate and untempered was demanded. Yet this was the same William Lloyd Garrison who, in 1877, replied to Susan B. Anthony's request for aid to Women's Suffrage:

> You desire me to send you a letter, to be read at the Washington Convention of the National Woman Suffrage Association, in favor of a petition to Congress, asking that body to submit to the several States a 16th Amendment for the Constitution of the United States, securing suffrage for all, irrespective of sex. On fully considering the subject, I must decline doing so, because such a petition I deem to be quite premature. If its request were complied with by the present Congress—a supposition simply preposterous —the proposed Amendment would be rejected by every State in the Union, and in nearly every instance by such an overwhelming majority as to bring the movement into needless contempt. Even as a matter of "agitation," I do not think it would pay. Look over the whole country, and see in the present state of public sentiment on the question of woman suffrage what a mighty primary work remains to be done in enlightening the masses, who know nothing and care nothing about it, and consequently are not at all prepared to cast their votes for any such thing. . . .

Evidently circumstances alter cases in reform as drastically as in other lines of human endeavor!

The second center of anti-slavery effort was in upper New York and the farther Northwest. Influences from this center included in their sweep, however, much of rural New England and the Middle States and the movement found liberal financial help in New York City. Benjamin Lundy and other Quaker leaders started the crusade, but it did not come to full and wide expression until Theodore Weld, already the ablest temperance orator in the Northwest, set about cultivating the great field prepared for social reform by the Finney revivals.

Weld was, like Garrison, unusual both in abilities and in personal characteristics. He was much given to "anti-meat, -butter, -tea, and -coffee, etc. -ism[s]." He indulged in excessive self-effacement and in extravagant confessions of selfishness, pride, impatience of contradiction, personal recklessness, and "a bad, unlovely temper." Of his pride, "the great besetment of my soul," he wrote:

> I am too proud to be ambitious, too proud to seek applause, too proud to tolerate it when lavished upon me, proud as Lucifer that I can and do scorn applause and spurn flattery, and indignantly dash down and shiver to atoms the censer in which others would burn incense to me; too proud to betray emotions, too proud ever for an instant to lose my self possession whatever the peril, too proud to ever move a hair for personal interest, too proud ever to defend my character when assailed or my motives when impeached, too proud ever to wince when the hot iron enters my soul and passes thro it.

He wrote also of his contempt of opponents—"one of the *trade* winds of my nature [which] very often . . . *blows a hurricane*," and he listed by name those "who strangely and stupidly idolize me... and yield themselves to my sway in all confidence and love." He boasted of his daring and told of how as a child a tremendous thunderstorm would send him whooping and hallooing through the fields like a wild Indian. He had the Puritan's love of enduring; the saint's "right" to intolerance. He was, in fact, always a revivalist—a man with a mission to perform in the great West—"the battlefield of the World."

The campaign which he launched was but an expansion of the benevolence crusade already a part of the Western revival effort. As W. C. Preston said: "Weld's agents made the anti-slavery cause 'identical with religion,' and urged men, by all they esteem[ed] holy, by all the high and exciting obligations of duty to man and God... to join the pious work of purging the sin of slavery from the land." The movement, as it developed, was generally temperate in tone, and tended to function through the existing agencies of religion and politics. Lane Theological Seminary, founded in Cincinnati to train leaders in the Finney tradition, became the center from which Weld worked. Here, in a series of debates, he shaped the doctrine of gradual immediatism which by insisting that *gradual emancipation* begin *at once,* saved the movement from Garrison's extremes; from here he went out to win a group of converts which included James G. Birney, Joshua Giddings, Edwin M. Stanton, Elizur Wright, and Beriah Green; and here he adapted the revival technique to the abolition crusade and prepared the way for his loyal band of Seventy to carry that crusade throughout the whole Northwest.

There was, however, another aspect to the movement in this region—a very hard-headed practical aspect. Its leaders believed in action as well as agitation. And action here meant political action. Western men had a way of viewing evil as something there ought to be a law against. They thought it was the business of government to secure morality as well as prosperity. They were even inclined to regard the absence of prosperity as the result of the existence of evil. Naturally, therefore, in spite of the revival-meeting procedure used to spread the gospel of abolition, action against slavery followed political precedent. This action began with petitions to Congress for such a practical end as the abolition of slavery in the District of Columbia. When Southern resentment of such a measure brought the adoption of gag rule methods, the contest was broadened into a fight on the floors of Congress for the constitutional rights of petition and free speech. This proved to be an excellent way to keep the slavery question before the public and to force slaveholders to reveal their undemocratic attitudes. Petitions arrived in such quantities as to clog the work of Congress. A Washington organization for agitation and lobbying became necessary. Weld himself went to Washington to advise with John Quincy Adams and his fellow workers. Slavery thus again entered national politics, this time by way of the Northwest. Anti-slavery politicians, such as Joshua Giddings and Salmon P. Chase of Ohio, quickly proved the value of the cause as a stepping-stone to public office....

With the new growth and new importance of the movement, the technique of its propaganda also reached new efficiency. Never before or since has a cause been urged upon the American people with such consummate skill and such lasting effects. Every agency possible in that day was brought into use;

even now the predominating opinions of most of the American people regarding the ante-bellum South and its ways are the product of that campaign of education.

Indoctrination began with the child's A B C's which were learned from booklets containing verses like the following:

> **A** is an Abolitionist
> A man who wants to free
> The wretched slave, and give to all
> An equal liberty.
>
> **B** is a Brother with a skin
> Of somewhat darker hue,
> But in our Heavenly Father's sight,
> He is as dear as you.
>
> **C** is the Cotton field, to which
> This injured brother's driven,
> When, as the white man's *slave,* he toils
> From early morn till even.
>
> **D** is the Driver, cold and stern,
> Who follows, whip in hand,
> To punish those who dare to rest,
> Or disobey command.
>
> . . . .
>
> **I** is the Infant, from the arms
> Of its fond mother torn,
> And at a public auction sold
> With horses, cows, and corn.
>
> . . . .
>
> **Q** is the Quarter, where the slave
> On coarsest food is fed
> And where, with toil and sorrow worn
> He seeks his wretched bed.
>
> . . . .
>
> **W** is the Whipping post,
> To which the slave is bound,
> While on his naked back, the lash
> Makes many a bleeding wound.

. . . .

Z is a Zealous man, sincere,
Faithful, and just, and true;
An earnest pleader for the slave—
Will you not be so too?

For children able to read, a wider variety of literature was written. One volume in verse urged "little children" to "plead with men, that they buy not slaves again" and called attention to the fact that

They may harken what *you* say,
Though from *us* they turn away.

Another verse suggested that:

Sometimes when from school you walk,
You can with your playmates talk,
Tell them of the slave child's fate,
Motherless and desolate.
And you can refuse to take
Candy, sweetmeat, pie or cake,
Saying "No"—unless 'tis free—
"The slave shall not work for me."

Juvenile story books, with some parts written in verse and printed in large and bold type and the rest written in prose and set in smaller type, were issued with the explanation that the verses were adapted to the capacity of the youngest reader, while the prose was well suited for being read aloud in the family circle. "It is presumed," said the preface, "that [with the prose] our younger friends will claim the assistance of their older brothers and sisters, or appeal to the ready aid of their mamma." Such volumes might contain pictures and stories from *Uncle Tom's Cabin* or they might consist of equally appealing tales of slave children cruelly torn from their parents or tortured by ingenious methods.

For adults the appeal was widened. No approach was neglected. Hymn books offered abolition songs set to familiar tunes. To the strains of "Old Hundred" eager voices invited "ye Yeomen brave" to rescue "the bleeding slave," or, to the "Missionary Hymn," asked them to consider

The frantic mother
Lamenting for her child,
Till falling lashes smother
Her cries of anguish wild!

Almanacs, carrying the usual information about weather and crops, filled their other pages with abolition propaganda. In one of these, readers found the story of Liburn Lewis, who, for a trifling offense, bound his slave, George, to a meat block and then, while all the other slaves looked on, proceeded slowly to chop him to pieces with a broad ax, and to cast the parts into a fire. Local, state, and national societies were organized for more efficient action in petitioning, presenting public speakers, distributing tracts, and publishing anti-slavery periodicals. The American Anti-Slavery Society "in the year 1837–38, published 7,877 bound volumes, 47,256 tracts and pamphlets, 4,100 circulars, and 10,490 prints. Its quarterly *Anti-Slavery Magazine* had an annual circulation of 9,000; the *Slave Friend,* for children, had 131,050; the monthly *Human Rights*, 189,400, and the weekly *Emancipator,* 217,000." From 1854 to 1858 it spent $3281 on a series of tracts discussing every phase of slavery, under such suggestive titles as "Disunion, our Wisdom and our Duty," "Relations of Anti-Slavery to Religion," and "To Mothers in the Free States." Its "several corps of lecturers of the highest ability and worth... occupied the field" every year in different states. Its Annual Reports, with their stories of atrocities and their biased discussion of issues, constituted a veritable arsenal from which weapons of attack could be drawn. Like other anti-slavery societies, it maintained an official organ, issued weekly, and held its regular conventions for the generation of greater force.

Where argument and appeal to reason failed, the abolitionists tried entertainment and appeal to emotion. *Uncle Tom's Cabin* was written because its author, "as a woman, as a mother," was "oppressed and broken hearted, with the sorrows & injustice" seen, and "because as a Christian" she "felt the dishonor to Christianity—because as a lover of [her] country, [she] trembled at the coming day of wrath." It became a best seller in the most complete sense. Only the Bible exceeded it in numbers sold and in the thoroughness with which it was read in England and America. Editions were adapted to every pocketbook, and translations carried it throughout the world. Dramatized and put on the stage, it did more to make the theatre respectable in rural America than any other single influence. The fictitious Uncle Tom became the stereotype of all American Negro slaves; Simon Legree became the typical slaveholder. A generation and more formed its ideas of Southern life and labor from the pages of this novel. A romantic South, of planter-gentlemen and poor whites, of chivalry and dissipation, of "sweet but worthless" women, was given an imaginative reality so wide and so gripping that no amount of patient research and sane history writing could alter it. Other novels, such as *Our World: or the Slaveholder's Daughter,* built their plots about the love affairs of Southern planters with their Negro slaves. Jealousies between wives and mistresses, struggles between brothers for the possession of some particularly desirable wench, or the inner conflict of a master over his obligation to his mulatto bastards, constituted the main appeal in such works. The object was always the same: to reveal the licentious character of Southern men, the unhappy status of Southern homes, and the horrible violation of Negro chastity everywhere existing under slavery.

Reformed slaveholders and escaped slaves were especially valuable in the crusade. Under the warming influence of sympathetic audiences their stories of cruelty and depravity grew apace. Persecution and contempt from old friends increased their zeal. Birney, the Grimké sisters, Frederick Douglass, and many others influenced the movement and were influenced by it in a way comparable only to the relation of reformed drunkards to the temperance cause.

By means of such agencies and methods a well-defined picture of the South and slavery became slowly fixed in Northern minds. The Southern people were divided into two distinct classes—slaveholders and poor whites. The former constituted an aristocracy, living in great white-pillared houses on extended plantations. The latter, ignorant and impotent, made up a rural slum which clung hopelessly to the pine barrens or the worn-out acres on the fringes of the plantations. Planters, who lived by the theft of Negro labor, completely dominated the section. They alone were educated; they alone held office. Non-slaveholders were too poor to "buy an education for themselves and their children," and the planters, not wishing to "endanger their supremacy," refused to establish public schools. Few poor whites could either read or write. They gained their opinions and their principles from "stump speeches and tavern conversations." They were "absolutely in the slaveholder's power." He sent "them to the polls to vote him into office and in so doing to vote down their own rights and interests...." They knew "no more what they [were] about, than so many children or so many Russian serfs...."

Social-economic conditions in the South were described as tumble-down and backward. The slave, lacking the incentive of personal gain, was inefficient. The master, ruined by power, self-indulgence, and laziness, was incapable of sound management. James Birney described the section as one

> whose Agriculture is desolation—whose Commerce is mainly confined to a crazy wagon and half fed team of oxen or mules as a means of carrying it on —whose manufacturing "Machinery" is limited to the bones and sinews of reluctant slaves—whose currency is individual notes always to *be* paid (it may be at some broken bank) and mortgages on men and women and children who may run away or die, and on land, which without them is of little value....

Others went so far as to charge the panic of 1837 to Southern profligacy. "The existence of Slavery," resolved the American Anti-Slavery Society in 1840, "is the grand cause of the pecuniary embarrassments of the country; and... no real or permanent relief is to be expected... until the total abolition of that execrable system." Joshua Leavitt called the slave system "a bottomless gulf of extravagance and thriftlessness." Another explained its "withering and impoverishing effect["] by the fact that it was the "rule of violence and arbitrary will.... It would be quite in character with its theory and practice," he said, "if slave-drivers should refuse to pay their debts and meet the sheriff with dirk and pistol." Leavitt estimated that the South had "taken from the North, within five years, more than $100,000,000, by notes which will never be paid," and quoted an English writer to the effect that "planters are always in debt. The system of society in a slaveholding community is such as to lead to the contraction of debt, which the system itself does not furnish the means of paying...."

Nor did the Southern shortcomings, according to the anti-slavery view, end with things material. Moral weaknesses were even more offensive. Sexual virtue was scarcely known. "The Slave States," wrote an abolitionist, "are Sodoms, and almost every village family is a brothel." Another writer declared that "in the slaveholding settlements of Middle and Southern Mississippi... there [was] not a virtuous young man of twenty years of age." "To send a lad to a male academy in Mississippi," he said, "is moral murder." An anti-slavery pamphlet told of "a million and a half of slave women, some of them without even the tinge of African blood... given up a lawful prey to the unbridled lusts of their masters." Another widely circulated tract described a slave market in which one dealer "devoted himself exclusively to the sale of young mulatto women." The author pictured the sale of "the most beautiful woman I ever saw," without *"a single trace of the African about her features"* and with "a pair of eyes that pierced one through and through" to "one of the most lecherous-looking old brutes" that he had ever seen. The narrative closed with the shrieking appeal: "God shield the helpless victim of that bad man's power—it may be, ere now, that bad man's lust!" The conclusion was inescapable. Slavery and unrestrained sexual indulgence at Negro expense were inseparable.

In such a section and in the hands of such men, abolitionists assumed that slavery realized its most vicious possibilities. Anti-slavery men early set themselves to the task of collecting stories of cruelty. These were passed about from one to another, often gaining in ferocity as they travelled. Weld gathered them together in a volume entitled *American Slavery As It Is* and scattered them broadcast over the North. The annual reports of the anti-slavery societies, their tracts and periodicals, also revelled in atrocities, asking no more proof of their absolute truth than the word of a fellow fanatic.

The attempt to picture slavery "as it was," therefore, came to consist almost entirely of a recital of brutalities. Now and then a kind master and seemingly contented slaves were introduced for the purpose of contrast—as a device to deepen shadows. But, as a rule, Southerners, according to these tracts, spent their time in idleness broken only by brutal cock-fights, gander pullings, and horse races so barbarous that "the blood of the tortured animal drips from the lash and flies at every leap from the stroke of the rowel." Slavery was one continual round of abuse. The killing of a slave was a matter of no consequence. Even respectable ladies might cause "several to be *whipped to death*." Brandings, ear cropping, and body-maiming were the rule. David L. Child honestly declared: "From all that I have read and heard upon the subject of whipping done by masters and overseers to slaves... I have come to the conclusion that some hundreds of *cart whips* and cowskin instruments, which I am told make the skin fly like feathers, and cut frequently to the bone, are in *perpetual daily motion* in the slave states." John Rankin told of Negroes stripped, hung up and stretched and then "whipped until their bodies [were] covered with blood and mangled flesh," some dying "under the lash, others linger[ing] about for a time, and at length die[ing] of their *wounds....*" The recital was indeed one of *"groans, tears, and blood."*

To abuse was added other great wrongs. Everywhere slaves were overworked, underfed, and insufficiently clothed and sheltered. Family ties were cut without the slightest regard for Negro feelings—infants were torn from the mother's breast, husbands separated from their wives and families. Marriage was unknown among slaves, and the right to worship God generally denied. Strangely enough, little was said of slave-breeding for market. That charge was largely left to the politicians of the next decades and to the historians of a later day.

Two principal assumptions stood out in this anti-slavery indictment of the slaveholder. He was, in the first place, the arch-aristocrat. He was the great enemy of democracy. He was un-American, the oppressor of his fellow men, the exploiter of a weaker brother. Against him could be directed all the complaints and fears engendered by industrial captains and land speculators. He, more than any other aristocrat, threatened to destroy the American democratic dream.

In the second place, he was a flagrant sinner. His self-indulgence was unmatched. His licentious conduct with Negro women, his temperance in the use of intoxicating liquors, his mad dueling, and his passion for war against the weak were enough to mark him as the nation's moral enemy number one! The time for dealing moderately had passed. Immediate reform was imperative.

Thus it was that the slaveholder began to do scapegoat service for all aristocrats and all sinners. To him were transferred resentments and fears born out of local conditions. Because it combined in itself both the moral and the democratic appeal, and because it coincided with sectional rivalry, the abolition movement gradually swallowed up all other reforms. The South became the great object of all efforts to remake American society. Against early indifference and later persecution, a handful of deadly-in-earnest men and women slowly built into a section's consciousness the belief in a Slave Power. To the normal strength of sectional ignorance and distrust they added all the force of Calvinistic morality and American democracy and thereby surrounded every Northern interest and contention with holy sanction and reduced all opposition to abject depravity. When the politician, playing his risky game, linked expansion and slavery, Christian common folk by the thousands, with no great personal urge for reforming, accepted the Abolition attitudes toward both the South and slavery. Civil war was then in the making.

The Persistence of Wendell Phillips

"The antislavery agitation is an important, nay, an essential part of the machinery of the state. It is not a disease nor a medicine. No; it is the normal state,—The normal state of the nation."

— *Lecture on Public Opinion*

Wherever Wendell Phillips walked on the Harvard campus he carried the aura of Beacon Hill with him. He was as well born as any Winthrop or Saltonstall and had been brought up in an imposing brick mansion on Beacon Hill only a few steps from the State House. The son of Boston's first mayor, a man universally respected for sound conservative principles, young Phillips seemed intent on following in his father's footsteps. He gained a reputation as being "the pet of the aristocracy," and in orations at the college exhibitions went out of his way to attack reformers and defend the standing order. One of his friends later recalled that Phillips would probably have been chosen by his classmates as the man *"least likely* to give the enthusiasm and labor of [his life] to the defense of popular rights."

Fifteen years after he left Harvard Phillips was asked by the secretary of the class of 1831 to fill out a questionnaire. He noted that he was in good health but growing bald. Under occupation he said he had prepared for the law "but grew honest and quitted what required an oath to the Constitution of the United States." Asked to note any other remarks that might be interesting to his classmates, he wrote: "My main business is to forward the abolition of slavery. I hold that the world is wrong side up and maintain the propriety of turning it upside down. I go for Disunion and have long since abjured that contemptible mockery, the Constitution of the United States."

To understand Phillips' career as an abolitionist and free-lance radical it is first necessary to account for his transformation from gentility to "fanaticism." Certainly it was not a natural development. After graduating from Harvard College Phillips entered the Harvard Law School. His career there and later as a practicing attorney was uneventful. Like most of the other sons of the old Federalists, he was happy to follow Daniel Webster into the Whig party which continued to serve the bulwarked conservatism of Massachusetts. He shared an

From Irving H. Bartlett, "The Persistence of Wendell Phillips," in Martin Duberman, ed., *The Antislavery Vanguard: New Essays on the Abolitionists* (Princeton University Press, 1965). Copyright © 1965, 1993 by Princeton University Press. Reprinted by permission. Notes omitted.

office at this time with a man who later led a mob against abolitionists, and most of his social contacts were with the old aristocratic families who, if they knew anything about William Lloyd Garrison, naturally "supposed him to be a man who ought to be hung," and were unanimously determined to outlaw anyone, even the saintly William Ellery Channing, for expressing the slightest sympathy with his principles.

Phillips' first personal encounter with the antislavery movement came in October 1835, when he stood on a Boston street corner and watched a jeering mob drag Garrison through the street at the end of a rope. A few weeks later he met Ann Terry Greene, one of Garrison's disciples, and in less than a year, to the consternation of his mother and most of Boston society, married her. A few months later he made his first antislavery speech.

As with most of the early abolitionists, religion played a dominant role in making Phillips an abolitionist. We will never know how successful he might have been in law or politics, but his advantages in family background and education, his intelligence, and his remarkable oratorical talent suggest that the achievements of a Webster, Choate, or Sumner were not beyond his reach. The fact is, however, that between the time he graduated from college and met his wife, Phillips appears to have been in a melancholy state of mind largely because he lacked a sense of vocation. He had been brought up as a devout Calvinist, and it was a fundamental article in his belief that a man must make his life count for something. Like all new lawyers he found it slow going to get a practice started, but even more important he found no great satisfaction in the profession. He needed to find a calling. As it turned out he fell in love and found his calling at the same time. His bride introduced him to William Lloyd Garrison and other Boston abolitionists, and in the early days of their marriage, when her health permitted, accompanied him to antislavery meetings. Phillips had undergone religious conversion years before under the powerful preaching of Lyman Beecher. As he joined hands with the abolitionists he felt he was being born a third time. "None know what it is to live," he wrote in 1841, "till they redeem life from its seeming monotony by laying it a sacrifice on the altar of some great cause."

Phillips never forgot the importance of religion to the antislavery movement. "Our enterprise is eminently a religious one," he said, "dependent for success entirely on the religious sentiment of the people." When Phillips refused to take an oath to support the "proslavery constitution" of the United States, he thought of himself as following in the tradition of his forbear, the Reverend George Phillips, who had come to America in 1630 to put the Atlantic Ocean "between himself and a corrupt church." He did not think of himself as an ordinary lecturer or orator, but as a kind of minister to the public, preaching the gospel of reform. When he was called to fill Theodore Parker's pulpit in the Boston Music Hall in 1860, it was natural for him to begin a sermon by announcing that "Christ preached on the last political and social item of the hour; and no man follows in his footsteps who does not do exactly the same thing." Phillips' sermons before Parker's congregation were the same sermons that he preached in Faneuil Hall before antislavery meetings, and he was convinced that he did his duty to God in both places by flaying the public sinners of the day whether their names were Webster, Everett, Jefferson Davis, or Abraham Lincoln.

The idealism of the American revolutionary tradition also played a decisive role in shaping Phillips' career. When he was a boy, he remembered later, the Boston air still "trembled and burned with Otis and Sam Adams." He had been born practically next door to John Hancock's mansion, within [sight] of Bunker Hill and only a few steps from the site of the Boston massacre. When he was thirteen years old and a student at the Boston Latin School he stood for hours in a crowd on the Common to catch a glimpse of Lafayette upon his visit to the city. Two years later, while poring over his lessons at the school, the sound of tolling bells came through the open windows announcing the deaths of Thomas Jefferson and John Adams.

Phillips never doubted that the revolutionary fathers were on his side. His first antislavery speech was given to support John Quincy Adams in his fight to get the Congress to hear petitions attacking slavery. Phillips argued that the right of petition was a traditional right for free men and that in attacking it the South threatened the freedom of all men. "This is the reason we render to those who ask us why we are contending against southern slavery," he said, "*that it may not result in northern slavery* ... it is our own rights which are at issue."

The speech which made Phillips famous in Boston was given at a Faneuil Hall meeting to honor the memory of Elijah Lovejoy who had been killed by a mob in Alton, Illinois. The meeting was called to pay tribute to Lovejoy, but the abolitionists almost lost control of it when James Austin, the Attorney General for Massachusetts, stood up and made a violent speech attacking Lovejoy for having published an incendiary antislavery newspaper. Austin likened the mob which destroyed Lovejoy and his press to the patriots responsible for the Boston Tea Party. Phillips was able to get the floor after Austin, and overcome the hooting and jeering of the proslavery faction in the audience with an eloquent defense of Lovejoy. Again Phillips was defending a traditional American right, freedom of the press, and he insisted that the spirit of the American revolution supported him.

> Sir, when I heard the gentleman lay down principles which place the murderers of Alton side by side with Otis and Hancock, with Quincy Adams, I thought those pictured lips would have broken into voice to rebuke the recreant American,—The slanderer of the dead.... In the sentiments he has uttered, on soil consecrated by the prayers of Puritans and the blood of patriots, the earth should have yawned and swallowed him up.

In his reliance on religion and the spirit of the Declaration of Independence, Phillips was like most other abolitionists. As an orator, however, despite the fact that he was part of a movement full of celebrated speakers, his uniqueness is unchallenged.

For at least a quarter of a century, from 1850 to 1875, Wendell Phillips was the commanding figure on the American lecture platform. Not only was he a spectacular success on the Lyceum circuit, but during the critical years surrounding the Civil War, his reputation as a critic of public policy was so great that each of his major addresses became a national event widely reported by the Boston and New York press and copied in papers throughout the northern and western states. Chauncey Depew, who lived to be ninety and claimed to have heard all the great speakers including Webster and Clay, declared that Phillips was "the greatest of all American orators." Thomas Wentworth Higginson placed Phillips and Webster together as the two most powerful orators in the post-revolutionary period, while Bronson Alcott said that Phillips' speeches "in range of thought, cleverness of statement, keen satire, brilliant wit, personal anecdote, wholesome moral sentiments, patriotism and Puritan spirit" were "unmatched by any of the great orators of the day." A critical piece in the *New Englander* in 1850 may be considered typical of the way in which a performance by Phillips was reviewed. Taking pains to disassociate himself from the speaker's radical doctrines, the writer went on to say that he was a "more instructive and more interesting speaker" than Clay, Webster, Choate, Adams, or Benton. Nor was Phillips' power entirely lost on the generation which grew up after his death in 1884, for as late as 1927 Senator William E. Borah, one of the few great American orators of this century, confessed to the habit of reading one of Phillips' speeches every three weeks or so to keep the famous radical's "style" fresh in his mind.

What sets Phillips off from the other lecturers within the Garrisonian camp, such colorful individuals as Parker Pillsbury and Stephen and Abby Kelly Foster, is that Phillips alone was consistently recognized as great even by those who detested his ideas. After hearing him declare in what was perhaps an unconscious parody of Webster's famous words, that he hoped to witness before he died "the convulsion of a sundering Union and a dissolving church," a New York reporter remarked that Phillips' sentiments "however repugnant to general opinion were expressed with a clear and lofty eloquence and extraordinary felicity and beauty of illustration." In Boston, where Phillips was loved and hated the most, a writer for the *Courier* made the same point in plain language. "It is a dish of tripe and onions served on silver," he wrote, "or black-strap presented in a goblet of Bohemian glass... Mr. Phillips thinks like a Billingsgate fishwoman, or a low pothouse bully, but he speaks like Cicero."

The sources of Phillips' power on the platform were deceptive. Those seeing him for the first time were invariably surprised to discover that he was not an orator in the grand manner. Shortly before the Civil War an Andover student, hearing that Phillips was to lecture in Boston, made a twenty-two-mile pilgrimage on foot to hear him. At first the trip seemed hardly worthwhile, for Phillips stood on the platform, one hand lightly resting on a table, talked for what seemed about twenty minutes and suddenly sat down. When the astonished young man consulted his watch he found that he had been listening for an hour and a half.

There was, as the Andover student discovered, nothing ponderous about Phillips as a speaker, no bombast, no flights of empty rhetoric. He spoke almost conversationally; his appearance was invariably one of calm poise, and he relied little on the kind of theatrics that led Henry Ward Beecher to auction off a slave girl from the pulpit. "The most prolonged applause could not disturb a muscle in his countenance," one listener remembered, "and a storm of hisses seemed to have as little effect on him." His customary serenity enhanced the effect of those few occasions when Phillips did make some spectacular gesture, as for example, when after mentioning the name of the fugitive slave commissioner George Ticknor Curtis, he would rinse his mouth out with water and spit it on the floor.

Webster with his bull-like body and cavernous, smoldering eyes could overpower an audience with sheer physical magnetism. Phillips did not have this power. He was a man of average height, rather slightly built, with finely drawn features which most easily lent themselves to expressions of scorn and resolution. What everyone did notice about him was his aristocratic bearing. An Englishman visiting Boston saw Phillips and Edmund Quincy walking together down Park Street and remarked that they were the only men he had seen in this country "who looked like Gentlemen." As a matter of fact, Phillips came as close to being a native-born aristocrat as any American could. And his assurance on the platform was undoubtedly related to the fact that he did not have to make a name for himself. He had a way of treating his opponents as if they were socially beneath him as well as morally loathsome. Because of this he was nearly immune to criticism, and absolutely invulnerable to a heckling audience. He would never lose his temper, but would reply to his critics in a tone so witheringly contemptuous that it was like a blast of air from an iceberg. Neither rotten eggs nor brickbats could startle him, and hissing so consistently aroused him to his best effort that his admirers sometimes sat in a back row and hissed merely to make him warm to the subject.

By far the most sensational characteristic of Phillips as a speaker was the contrast between his perfectly controlled, poised, almost dispassionate manner, and the inflammatory language he employed. It was the apparent effortlessness of his delivery that impressed many listeners most. "Staples said the other day that he heard Phillips speak at the State House," wrote Thoreau in his *Journal.* "By thunder! he never heard a man that could speak like him. His words come so easy. It was just like picking up chips." In an effort to explain how the speaker remained somehow detached from his own eloquence, another observer compared him to "a cold but mysteriously animated statue of marble." Time and time again when Phillips was on tour, talking before new audiences, the reporter would register the audience's surprise. "They had conceived him to be a ferocious ranter and blustering man of words. They found him to be a quiet, dignified and polished gentleman and scholar, calm and logical in his argument."

One of the reasons why abolitionist meetings in the middle and later 1850's began to draw impressively large crowds, as the critics of the abolitionists pointed out, was that for many people an antislavery meeting had all the elements of a theatrical performance. The star performer was usually Wendell Phillips, and his stock in trade, according to the unconverted, was "personal abuse." To the abolitionists themselves he was, as his publisher remarked, the greatest "master of invective" in the nineteenth century. With sublime confidence, almost as if he were reading from a sheaf of statistics or reciting a series of scientific facts, Phillips would take the platform to announce that Daniel Webster was "a great mass of dough," Edward Everett "a whining spaniel," Massachusetts Senator Robert C. Winthrop "a bastard who had stolen the name of

Winthrop," and the New England churches an ecclesiastical machine to manufacture hypocrisy "just as really as Lowell manufactures cotton." It was the way Phillips uttered his epithets that fascinated most critics. The shrewd Scottish traveler David Macrae who had been led "from the ferocity of his onslaughts on public men and public measures... to form a false conception of his delivery" noted with surprise that vehemence and declamation were replaced by sarcasm, "cold, keen, withering." Macrae was impressed by the relentless manner in which Phillips pursued his opponents. "He follows an enemy like an Indian upon the trail.... When he comes to strike, his strokes are like galvanic shocks; there is neither noise nor flash but their force is terrible."

A writer for an English paper who was contrasting Phillips' speeches with "the rounded periods of Mr. Seward" and "the finished artistic rhetoric of the patriotic Mr. Everett" noted one quality which grated on European ears, and that was "the concentrated bitterness, the intense spirit of hatred with which they are frequently suffused." Because Phillips did not like to talk in general terms about issues, because he always took dead aim on personalities and heaped "the concentrated bitterness" of his rhetoric upon the heads of men prominent in public life, and because the people turned out in droves to hear him, Robert C. Winthrop believed that Phillips had "gradually educated our people to relish nothing but the 'eloquence of abuse.'"

A good many later critics have been much harsher than Winthrop in criticizing Phillips. Theodore Roosevelt called him a wild-eyed fanatic and Professor [James G.] Randall has dismissed his speeches as "a kind of grandiloquent, self-righteous raving." A careful reading of his career shows these estimates to be incorrect. What distinguishes Phillips from the other abolitionists more significantly than anything else is that he was an intellectual, a philosopher of reform as well as a practical agitator. It is impossible to understand him, therefore, without knowing more about his political ideas and his conception of the role of the reformer in America.

Like other abolitionists Phillips believed in the Higher Law and judged every public question from an absolute moral standard. He believed that a man's first duty was to God, and that men should do their duty at whatever cost. He was convinced that anything right in principle had to be right in practice. He accepted Garrison's demand for immediate emancipation without question. Phillips' Calvinism, his belief in Divine Providence, made it possible for him to dismiss whatever doubts he might have had about the practicality of this radical solution. "No matter if the charter of emancipation was written in blood," he said in one of his early speeches, "and anarchy stalk abroad with giant strides— if God commanded, it was right." Phillips' Calvinism reinforced his radicalism. He did not have to worry about the consequences of his agitation. A man could only do his duty and let God do the rest.

As the most eloquent and intellectual of all the radicals, Phillips was called upon to defend the position that abolitionists should not support a constitution or government which supported slavery. Although the refusal of the radical abolitionists to vote or hold office, and their continued agitation to get the North to secede from the union seemed incomprehensible to most people, the position was perfectly consistent with Phillips' principles. Slavery was evil and this evil was supported by a Federal government which protected slave states from insurrection, undertook to return their fugitives and gave them special representation in Congress. Therefore anything voluntarily done in support of this government (i.e. taking an oath to support the Constitution or voting for a candidate who would be required to take such an oath), supported slavery also and was evil.

Despite the fact that his position was condemned in the public mind from the beginning, Phillips, through pamphlets and lectures, did as much as anyone could do to persuade people of its worth. He never once doubted its soundness. When friends like Charles Sumner argued that the course he advocated would impede the struggle for emancipation, he replied that "honesty and truth are more important than even freeing slaves." When Sumner asked how he could consistently pay taxes or even remain in the country, he reminded him that a man's choices were always limited by the social and historical situation in which God placed him. A man had to live in the world, but he did not have to collaborate with the devil, which is what Sumner and all other "loyal citizens" were doing. "To live where God sent you and protest against your neighbor— this is certainly different from *joining him* in sinning, which the office holder of this country does."

Phillips' moralism supplied the ballast for his career. His solutions to difficult problems were both "right" and simple. When he continued to badger the government long after Garrison and other abolitionists had retired from the field after the war, it was because he sought "*justice*—absolute, immediate, unmixed justice to the negro." He did not, however, live by shibboleths alone, and his tactics as a reformer were based on a surprisingly sophisticated conception of American politics and society.

Phillips recognized that slavery was a threat to the freedom of all Americans. This conviction developed gradually out of his early experiences. He had the grisly reminiscences of the Grimké sisters to remind him of the evils of slavery in the south—the whippings and mutilations, the ruthless separation of husband and wife, of parent and child. Closer to his personal experience was what slavery had done to supposedly free American citizens. It had jailed Prudence Crandall for opening a school for Negro girls. It had publicly whipped Amos Dresser for daring to distribute antislavery literature. It had tried to gag John Quincy Adams in Congress, had mobbed Garrison within the shadow of Faneuil Hall, and had finally killed Lovejoy. The pattern seemed always to be the same; principle was overcome by power. For the first time Phillips sensed the demonic possibilities of a slave power supported by public opinion in America.

> A lawyer, bred in all the technical reliance on the safeguards of Saxon liberty, I was puzzled, rather than astounded, by the fact that, outside of the law and wholly unrecognized in the theory of our institutions, was a mob power —an abnormal element which nobody had counted in, in the analysis of the system, and for whose irregular actions no check, no balance, had been provided. The gun which was aimed at the breast of Lovejoy on the banks of the Mississippi brought me to my feet conscious that I stood in the presence of a power whose motto was victory or death.

Having recognized the importance of public opinion in America Phillips began to examine American institutions more closely. He distinguished a fundamental tension between the American ideal, a society based on the rights of man, and an American political system based on numbers. "The majority rules, and law rests on numbers, not on intellect or virtue," thus "while theoretically holding that no vote of the majority can authorize injustice, we practically consider public opinion the real test of what is true and what is false; and hence, as a result, the fact which Tocqueville has noticed, that practically our institutions protect, not the interest of the whole community but the interests of the majority."

Phillips was acute enough to see that while the tyranny of the majority might occasionally express itself violently, as in the lynching of Lovejoy, a more common and insidious threat to liberty came through the intimidation of citizens holding unpopular ideas. "Entire equality and freedom in political forms" naturally tended to "make the individual subside into the mass, and lose his identity in the general whole." In an aristocratic society like England a man could afford to "despise the judgment" of most people so long as he kept the good opinion of those in his own class. In America there was no refuge. Every citizen "in his ambition, his social life, or his business" depended on the approbation and the votes of those around him. Consequently, Phillips said, "instead of being a mass of individuals, each one fearlessly blurting out his own convictions,—as a nation, compared with other nations, we are a mass of cowards. More than any other people, we are afraid of each other."

Although Phillips knew that in some nations public opinion was shaped by political leaders, he could find nothing to show that this was true in the American experience. Theoretically every American male citizen was supposed to be eligible for office, but in practice, "with a race like ours, fired with the love of material wealth," the best brains were drawn into commerce. As a result politics took up with small men, "men without grasp enough for large business... men popular because they have no positive opinions." Even if an occasional man of the first rank (a Charles Sumner for example), did emerge in politics, he would be lost to the reformer because the whole art of politics in America was based on the ability to compromise. "The politician must conceal half his principles to carry forward the other half," Phillips said, "must regard, not rigid principle and strict right, but only such a degree of right as will allow him at the same time to secure *numbers.*"

These considerations led Phillips to conclude that the reformer in America had to confront the people directly. "Our aim," he said in his lecture *The Philosophy of Abolitionism,* "is to alter public opinion." Slavery endured and abolitionists were mobbed because a majority of Americans refused to face the moral issues involved. Phillips was too much of a realist to believe that he could suddenly convert the nation, but he did feel that he could force the issue and change the public attitude toward slavery.

Phillips knew that most people in the North disliked slavery, but he also knew that it was to their self-interest to leave it alone. To stir up controversy was dangerous: no one wanted to be known as a troublemaker; mill owners were concerned for their capital; mill hands were concerned for their jobs; the respectable middle class was concerned for its reputation. The easy thing for everyone was to turn away from the problem. The abolitionist's job was to scatter thorns on the easy road by dramatizing the moral issue and insisting that every man who did not throw his whole influence into the scales against slavery was as guilty as the slaveholder. "We will gibbet the name of every apostate so black and high," Phillips warned, "that his children's children shall blush to hear it. Yet we bear no malice—cherish no resentment. We thank God that the love of fame is shared by the ignoble."

What this could mean in practice is perhaps best seen in Phillips' criticism of Henry Gardner, a Boston politician who was the leader of Know-Nothingism in Massachusetts and Governor of the Commonwealth from 1855 to 1858. Gardner usually made a few antislavery sounds during election campaigns, but his great appeal was to nativism, and it was he who had blocked Phillips' attempt to get Judge Edward Loring recalled after the rendition of Anthony Burns. Phillips believed that Gardner dabbled in antislavery politics for personal gain and frustrated the abolitionists' effort to educate the public. He called the Governor "a consummate hypocrite, a man who if he did not have some dozen and distinct reasons for telling the truth would naturally tell a lie." On another occasion he said, "Our course is a perfect copy of Sisyphus. We always toil up, up, up the hill until we touch the soiled sandals of some Governor Gardner, and then the rock rolls down again. Always some miserable reptile that has struggled into power in the corruption of parties—reptiles who creep where *man* disdains to climb; some slight thing of no consequence till its foul mess blocks our path; and dashes our hopes at the last minute."

The denunciation could hardly have been more savage. Phillips insisted, however, that there was nothing personal in it.

> Do not say I am personal in speaking thus of Governor Gardner. . . . Do not blame me when I speak thus of Henry J. Gardner. What is the duty of the minority . . . what is the duty of a minority in this country? A minority has no right to rebel . . . the majority have said the thing shall be so. It is not to resist, it is to convert. And how shall we convert? If the community is in love with some monster, we must paint him truly. The duty of a minority being to convert, every tool which the human mind knows, it is their right and duty to use; a searching criticism, pitiless sarcasm, bitter invective, rigid analysis of motives, constant recurrence to the admitted facts of a man's career,—these are our rights, if our function is to save the people from delusion.

Phillips was not a fanatic. He used the most violent language dispassionately as a surgeon uses the sharpest steel. He could not actually cut away the diseased tissue with his rhetoric, but he could expose it. Thus when he called Lincoln a "slave hound" he was reminding his listeners and readers that as a Congressman Lincoln had supported a bill which would have enforced the return of fugitive slaves escaping into the District of Columbia. This was the man who expected to get the antislavery vote. Phillips' intention in attacking Lincoln so savagely was simply to dramatize the rottenness of the American conscience by showing that only a "slave hound" could be elected President. His reply to those who accused him of extravagance and distortion was that "there are far more dead hearts to be quickened, than confused intellects to be cleared up—more dumb dogs to be made to speak than doubting consciences to be enlightened. We have use, then, for something beside argument."

The easiest way to treat nettlesome reformers like the abolitionists is to dismiss them as cranks. Nothing irritated Phillips more than the attempts of his opponents to thrust him outside the mainstream of American life. The anti-slavery agitation, he insisted, was "an essential part of the machinery of the state... not a disease nor a medicine... the normal state of the nation."

The preceding statement takes us to the heart of Phillips' philosophy of reform. He recognized that American ideals could ultimately be translated into practice only through politics. At the same time he knew that the American politician's ability to gain and hold power was largely determined by his ability to effect compromises that appealed to numbers rather than to principle. He added to these corruptive tendencies the fact that people in a democracy always tend to have as high an opinion of themselves as possible—always tremble on the edge of national idolatry. The result, Phillips argued, was that "every government is always growing corrupt. Every Secretary of State is by the very necessity of his position an apostate." A democratic society that trusted to constitutions and political machinery to secure its liberties never would have any. "The people must be waked to a new effort," he said, "just as the church has to be regenerated in each age." In the middle of the nineteenth century the abolitionist was the agency of national regeneration, but even after he had vanished his function in the American system would still remain.

> Eternal vigilance is the price of liberty: power is ever stealing from the many to the few. The manna of popular liberty must be gathered each day, or it is rotten.... The hand entrusted with power becomes, either from human depravity or *esprit de corps,* the necessary enemy of the people. Only by continual oversight can the democrat in office be prevented from hardening into a despot: only by unintermitted agitation can a people be kept sufficiently awake to principle not to let liberty be smothered in material prosperity. All clouds, it is said, have sunshine behind them, and all evils have some good result; so slavery, by the necessity of its abolition, has saved the freedom of the white race from being melted in luxury or buried beneath the gold of its own success. Never look, therefore, for an age when the people can be quiet and safe. At such times despotism, like a shrouding mist, steals over the mirror of Freedom.

It should be clear now that Phillips believed the radical abolitionist to be justified as much by his radicalism as by his abolitionism. Phillips preferred the word agitator to radical, and since he himself was frequently accused of demagoguery, he took pains to point out the difference between the demagogue and agitator. A demagogue (he used Robespierre as an example), "rides the storm; he has never really the ability to create one. He uses it narrowly, ignorantly, and for selfish ends. If not crushed by the force which, without his will, has flung him into power, he leads it with ridiculous miscalculation against some insurmountable obstacle that scatters it forever. Dying, he leaves no mark on the elements with which he has been mixed." Quoting Sir Robert Peel, Phillips defined agitation as "the marshalling of the conscience of a nation to mould its laws." Daniel

O'Connell who, after thirty years of "patient and sagacious labor," succeeded in creating a public opinion and unity of purpose to free Ireland from British tyranny was one of Phillips' models as a successful agitator.

It was because Phillips thought of himself primarily as an agitator and Garrison thought of himself primarily as an abolitionist that the two came to a parting of the ways in 1865. With the war over and slavery prohibited by the passage of the thirteenth amendment, Garrison felt that the "covenant with death" had been annulled. The American nation had become "successor to the abolitionists," and the American Anti-Slavery Society had lost its excuse for being. Phillips did not agree. He argued that the nation needed "the constant, incessant discriminating criticism of the abolitionists as much as ever." The debate grew rancorous and resulted in Garrison's quitting the Society. Phillips was elected President in his place, and for the next five years continued to agitate as fiercely for Negro suffrage as he had for emancipation. Only after the fifteenth amendment was passed did he allow the organization to be dissolved.

Even then Phillips did not relax his efforts. He denounced the decision to remove Federal troops from the South as vehemently as he had the Fugitive Slave Law, and predicted that a " 'solid south'—the slave power under a new name" would soon control national politics. Most of the other surviving abolitionists had long since gone over to the Republican party lock, stock, and barrel, but Phillips saw through the moral pretensions of the Republicans as clearly as anyone in the country. They had waved the bloody flag with regularity, but had been unwilling to make the sacrifices and the long-term commitments in reconstruction that were necessary if the moral legacy of the war was not to be squandered away. Accusing the Republicans of "a heartless and merciless calculation" to exploit war memories and Ku Klux Klan atrocities for party purposes, Phillips claimed that no party in history had ever "fallen from such a height to such a depth of disgrace."

The rhetoric was the same but the response was not. The people had grown tired of the war, and newspapers that would have praised him in the sixties now wrote about "Mr. Phillips' Last Frenzy" and called him "the apostle of unforgiving and relentless hate."

Meanwhile, even as he decried the growing popularity of the illusion that the Negro might be safe in the hands of his old master, Phillips turned his attention to the struggle of free labor in the North. "While this delusion of peace without purity persists," he was saying in 1878, "labor claims every ear and every hand." And so, in the declining years of his life, Wendell Phillips, true to his belief that agitation was "an essential part of the machinery of the state," poured his whole influence into the struggle for social justice in an industrial society. His solutions were still simple—passage of an eight-hour law—the unlimited issuance of Greenbacks. His tactics were the same. "The only way to accomplish our object," he said, "is to shame greedy men into humanity. Poison their wealth with the tears and curses of widows and orphans. In speaking of them call things by their right names. Let men shrink from them as from slave dealers and pirates." And the response was the same he had received during the hard, bitter years before the war. If anything Phillips was even more of an outsider now than he had been then. His support of unions, the right to strike, shorter hours of work, a graduated income tax, and his derision of laissez-faire ("the bubble and chaff of 'supply and demand' ") offended even the old abolitionists. If Phillips had acted "with ordinary common sense and good temper when slavery was abolished and had gone into politics," Edmund Quincy thought, "he might have been the next Senator . . . but he is 'played out' as we say, and will be merely a popular lecturer and a small demagogue for the rest of his life."

Quincy was a retired reformer. Like most of his contemporaries and most of the American historians who have followed, he could not appreciate Wendell Phillips, a gentleman who understood the difference between agitation and demagoguery, and knew that the radical in America could never retire.

POSTSCRIPT

Were the Abolitionists "Unrestrained Fanatics"?

One of the weaknesses of most studies of abolitionism, which is reflected in both of the preceding essays, is that they are generally written from a monochromatic perspective. In other words, historians typically discuss whites within the abolitionist crusade and give little, if any, attention to the roles that blacks played in the movement. Whites are portrayed as the active agents of reform, while blacks are depicted as the passive recipients of humanitarian efforts to eliminate the scourge of slavery. Students should be aware that African Americans, slave and free, also rebelled against the institution of slavery both directly and indirectly.

Benjamin Quarles, in *Black Abolitionists* (Oxford University Press, 1969), describes a wide range of roles played by African Americans in the abolitionist movement. For example, as Garrison's *Liberator* struggled to survive in the early months of 1831, African American subscribers in the North kept the paper afloat. In addition, African Americans organized themselves into local antislavery societies, became members of national abolitionist organizations (particularly the American Anti-Slavery Society and the American and Foreign Anti-Slavery Society), contributed funds to the operations of these societies, made black churches available for abolitionist meetings, and promoted abolitionism through pamphlet-writing and speaking engagements. Between 1830 and 1835 the Negro Convention Movement sponsored annual meetings of African Americans in which protests against slavery were a central feature.

Studies that discuss the role of black abolitionists in the antislavery movement include Ronald K. Burke, *Samuel Ringgold Ward: Christian Abolitionist* (Garland, 1995) and Nell Irvin Painter, *Sojourner Truth: A Life, A Symbol* (W. W. Norton, 1997).

For general discussions of the abolitionist movement, see Gerald Sorin, *Abolitionism: A New Perspective* (Praeger, 1972); Lewis Perry, *Radical Abolitionism: Anarchy and the Government of God in Antislavery Thought* (Cornell University Press, 1973); Merton L. Dillon, *The Abolitionists: The Growth of a Dissenting Minority* (Northern Illinois University Press, 1974); James Brewer Stewart, *Holy Warriors: The Abolitionists and American Slavery* (Hill & Wang, 1976); Ronald G. Walters, *The Antislavery Appeal: American Abolitionism After 1830* (Johns Hopkins University Press, 1978); Lawrence J. Friedman, *Gregarious Saints: Self and Community in American Abolitionism, 1830–1870* (Cambridge University Press, 1982); and Stanley Harrold, *The Abolitionists in the South, 1831–1861* (University Press of Kentucky, 1995).

ISSUE 11

Was Slavery Profitable?

YES: Kenneth M. Stampp, from *The Peculiar Institution: Slavery in the Ante-Bellum South* (Alfred A. Knopf, 1956)

NO: Eugene D. Genovese, from *The Political Economy of Slavery: Studies in the Economy and Society of the Slave South* (Vintage Books, 1965)

ISSUE SUMMARY

YES: Kenneth M. Stampp, a professor emeritus of history, contends that although slaveholding did not guarantee affluence, slave labor held a competitive advantage over free white labor. He finds ample evidence that the average slaveholder earned a reasonably satisfactory return from his investment in slaves.

NO: Historian Eugene D. Genovese maintains that poorly fed and inadequately trained slaves lacked the versatility and incentive to be particularly productive agricultural laborers and, consequently, contributed to the backwardness of the antebellum southern economy.

By the time the Thirteenth Amendment abolished slavery in 1865, the history of that peculiar institution in British North America had stretched back for over two centuries. It was as old as the House of Burgesses in Virginia and Harvard University in New England. Those institutions were not at all unique to the New World, however, having their roots in Parliament and the universities at Oxford and Cambridge, respectively. Slavery, on the other hand, did not exist in England at this time, so why did it develop in settlements established by English people searching for political, economic, and religious freedom?

The London companies whose investments underwrote the colonization of Virginia and Massachusetts intended to earn a profit on their capital. Moreover, slavery had always held an attraction for entrepreneurs who believed that the costs of labor determined prices. When European settlers determined that Native Americans were unsuited to enslavement and that white indentured servants failed to provide a permanent labor supply, rather than abandoning their interest in forced servitude, they imported sub-Saharan Africans as chattel slaves. Starting in 1502, when the Spanish slave trade commenced, 10 to 15 million Africans arrived in the Americas via the forced overseas migration known as the Middle Passage. By 1750 the institution of slavery was embedded in all of the original 13 English colonies along the Atlantic seaboard, and by 1800, despite the encouragement for emancipation spawned by the Enlightenment and the revolutionary rhetoric of the American independence movement, the slave system remained firmly entrenched in the southern states.

The South lacked workers in the same way other regions did but particularly because of the kind of agriculture developed there. Labor-intensive staple crops, such as tobacco, rice, indigo, cotton, and sugar, dominated the southern economy. The toil required to transplant tobacco seedlings on wet days or to pick hornworms off the maturing leaves partially explains why a subservient and cowed workforce appeared attractive. Workers with any semblance of choice avoided not only the tobacco fields but also the cultivation of rice and indigo, which were often grown on the same plantations. Both kinds of work were tedious and unhealthy. Rice was planted in reclaimed swampland, and slaves worked from dawn to dusk. The processing of indigo blooms, cotton, and sugar cane demanded around-the-clock labor.

Despite the assumed necessity of slave labor, however, southern plantation owners frequently complained that the high cost of upkeep, measured by the expense parceled out for food, clothing, housing, and medical attention, overrode any sensible explanation for perpetuating the system of chattel slavery. Maintaining a slave workforce, they insisted, simply was not worth the trouble. Or was it? Was slavery profitable for southern plantation owners, or did it saddle them with the burdensome task of providing for an undesirable pool of laborers whose upkeep drove them into debt?

In the following selection, Kenneth M. Stampp examines several of what he describes as "myths" concerning the unprofitability of slavery and rejects the view that the use of slave labor was responsible for increasing the mountain of debt endured by plantation owners, compounding the decline of soil fertility, retarding industrialization and urbanization in the South, and decreasing agricultural productivity. In fact, says Stampp, slave labor had a competitive advantage over free white labor, and there is ample evidence that the average antebellum slaveholder earned a reasonably satisfactory return upon his investment in human property.

Eugene D. Genovese, in the second selection, offers an interpretation that focuses on the low productivity of slave labor. Several factors, Genovese argues, including poor diet, insufficient supervision and training, and inadequate work incentives, led to careless and wasteful labor practices on the part of slaves that adversely affected the plantation economy. In addition, he says, slavery retarded technological progress in the South by inhibiting economic diversification, division of labor, and the improvement of farm implements and machines.

Kenneth M. Stampp

 **YES**

Profit and Loss

If one is to investigate the profitability or unprofitability of slavery, it is essential to define the problem precisely. Profitable for whom? Bondage was obviously not very profitable for the bondsmen whose standard of living was kept at the subsistence level; but bondage was not designed to enrich its victims. Nor was it introduced or preserved to promote the general welfare of the majority of white Southerners, who were nonslaveholders. The question is not whether the great mass of southern people of both races profited materially from slavery.

Moreover, the question is not whether a Southerner would have gained by selling his slaves, leaving his section, settling somewhere in the North, and investing in commerce or industry. He might have, but this involves the question of whether agriculture, in the long run, ever yields profits equal to those gained from manufacturing and trade. With or without slavery, planters and farmers were the victims of uncontrolled and wildly fluctuating prices, of insect pests, and of the weather. The year 1846, mourned one Mississippi planter, "will ever be memorable in the history of cotton planting from the ravages of the army worm which has no doubt curtailed the crop... at least Six Hundred Thousand Bales, worth Twenty Millions of Dollars." A rice planter surveyed the ruin following a "violent gale accompanied by immense rain.... The little that remained of the Crop after the two last gales, may now be abandoned. Not even the fragments of the wreck are left. Such is planting." Time after time the growers of southern staples saw their crops wither in severe droughts during the growing season—or rot in heavy rains at harvest time. Everything, concluded a discouraged planter, "seems to be against Cotton, not only the Abolitionists: but frost, snow, worms, and water." These were the hazards of husbandry in an age without crop insurance, price supports, or acreage restrictions. But they had no bearing upon the question of whether those who chose to risk them found it profitable to employ slave labor.

Here, then, is the problem: allowing for the risks of a laissez-faire economy, did the average ante-bellum slaveholder, over the years, earn a reasonably satisfactory return from his investment? One must necessarily be a little vague about what constitutes a satisfactory return—whether it is five per cent, or eight, or more—because any figure is the arbitrary choice of the person who picks it.

From Kenneth M. Stampp, *The Peculiar Institution: Slavery in the Ante-Bellum South* (Alfred A. Knopf, 1956). Copyright © 1956 by Kenneth M. Stampp. Reprinted by permission of Alfred A. Knopf, a division of Random House, Inc. Notes omitted.

The slaveholders themselves drew no clear and consistent line between satisfactory and unsatisfactory returns. In an absolute sense, of course, anything earned above operating expenses and depreciation is a profit. The question is whether it was substantial enough to be satisfactory.

It may be conceded at the outset that possession of a supply of cheap slave labor carried with it no automatic guarantee of economic solvency, much less affluence. An incompetent manger moved with steady pace toward insolvency and the inevitable execution sale. Even an efficient manager found that his margin of profit depended upon the fertility of his land, proximity to cheap transportation, and the ability to benefit from the economies of large-scale production. Moreover, nearly every slaveholder saw his profits shrink painfully during periods of agricultural depression such as the one following the Panic of 1837; and many who had borrowed capital to speculate in lands and slaves were ruined. In short, there were enormous variations in the returns upon investments in slave labor from master to master and from year to year. For the "average slaveholder" is, of course, an economic abstraction, albeit a useful one.

The adversities that at some time or other overtook most slaveholders, the anxieties to which their business operations subjected them, and the bankruptcy that was the ultimate reward of more than a few, have produced an uncommon lot of myths about the economic consequences of slavery for both the slaveholder and the South as a whole. One of the most durable of these myths is that the system unavoidably reduced masters to the desperate expedients of carrying a heavy burden of mortgage indebtedness and of living upon credit secured by the next crop. Actually, the property of most slaveholders was not mortgaged; and when they were troubled with debt, slavery was not necessarily the cause. Many of the debt-burdened planters gave evidence not of the unprofitability of slavery but of managerial inefficiency or of a tendency to disregard the middle-class virtue of thrift and live beyond their means. "There is a species of pride," complained one Southerner, "which prompts us to... imitate, if not exceed, the style of our neighbors... and it very often occurs that the deeper we are involved, the more anxious do we become to conceal it from the world, and the more strenuous to maintain the same showy appearance.... We cannot bear the thought that the world should know that we are not as wealthy, as it was willing to believe us to be, and thus lose the importance attached to our riches." Even during the depression years of the early nineteenth century, thriftless Virginia planters still hired tutors for their children, surrounded themselves with an army of servants, and entertained on a grand scale. It was not slavery itself but the southern culture that required these extravagances.

Other slaveholders went into debt to begin or to enlarge their agricultural operations. So long as their investments were sound, there was nothing reckless about launching an enterprise or expanding it on borrowed capital. Indeed, many of them deliberately remained in debt because their returns from borrowed capital far exceeded the interest charges. But the planter often was unable to resist the temptation to overextend himself, especially in the thriving regions of the Southwest. "This credit system is so fascinating," confessed a Mississippian, that it entices "a man [to] go farther than prudence would dictate." A critic of the Louisiana planters claimed that one of their "leading characteristics" was "an apparent determination to be always in debt; notwithstanding the sufficiency of their ordinary incomes to support them in ease and affluence." It seemed to this conservative critic that a planter ought not to become obsessed with "rearing up a mammoth estate, to add to his cares and anxieties in this world"; rather, he "should be satisfied with an income of 15 or $20,000"! When a sudden decline of staple prices caused the speculative bubble to burst, the ambitious Louisianian, like the extravagant Virginian, was the victim of forces that were entirely unrelated to slavery. The frontier boomer and the reckless speculator were in no sense evils spawned by the South's labor system.

The slaveholder who expanded his enterprise with his own profits was obviously more fortunate and more secure than those who borrowed for this purpose. A fall in prices merely reduced his income but seldom threatened him with bankruptcy. Yet the condition of even this thoroughly solvent entrepreneur has been misunderstood. Such a planter, it has often been said, was caught in a vicious circle, because he "bought lands and slaves wherewith to grow cotton, and with the proceeds ever bought more slaves to make more cotton." Surely this was not the essence of economic futility, for an entrepreneur could hardly be considered trapped by a system which enabled him to enlarge his capital holdings out of surplus profits. As long as the slaveholder earned returns sufficient to supply his personal needs, meet all operating expenses, and leave a balance for investment, he might count himself fortunate indeed!

The economic critics also blamed slavery for one of the South's chronic problems: the declining fertility of the land. This form of labor, they argued, was only adaptable to a one-crop system which used crude, unscientific methods and led relentlessly to soil exhaustion. Slaves, wrote Cairnes, were incapable of working with modern agricultural implements; lacking versatility, they could be taught little more than the routine operations required in the growth of a single staple. "Slave cultivation, therefore, precluded the conditions of rotation of crops or skillful management, tends inevitably to exhaust the land of a country, and consequently requires for its permanent success not merely a fertile soil but a practically unlimited extent of it."

The proof seemed to be everywhere at hand, not only in the older tobacco and cotton districts on the Atlantic coast but also, by the last two ante-bellum decades, in areas that had not been settled until the nineteenth century. A Georgian described the "barren waste" into which parts of Hancock Country had been transformed by careless husbandry: "Fields that once teemed with luxuriant crops... are disfigured with gaping hill-sides, chequered with gullies, coated with broom straw and pine, the sure indices of barrenness and exhaustion—all exhibiting a dreary desolation." In 1859, a Southerner noted that the process of soil exhaustion was far advanced in Mississippi and Alabama, and that the slaveholders were now ready "to wear out the Mississippi bottom, ... Arkansas, Texas and all other slave soil in creation." Even in Texas Olmsted often observed "that spectacle so familiar and so melancholy... in all the older Slave States": the abandoned plantation with its worn-out fields. By way of explanation a northern agricultural expert affirmed that "in many of the cotton plantations, the most destructive system of farming is pursued that I ever saw."

If slavery had been the cause of soil exhaustion, this would provide convincing evidence that it was a general economic blight upon the South; but even this would not necessarily be relevant to the question of whether slavery was profitable to individual masters. For many of them found it highly rewarding to exhaust their lands within a few years and then move on to fresh lands. However, there was in reality little connection between slavery and the extensive, soil-mining type of agriculture that characterized the ante-bellum South. How else account for the fact that many nonslaveholders, North and South, used the same wasteful methods in the cultivation of their farms? The explanation in both cases was that land was relatively cheap and abundant and labor relatively expensive and scarce; and in an agricultural milieu such as this landowners were reluctant to employ labor in the manuring of exhausted fields to restore their fertility. The one-crop system prevailed throughout much of the South, because one or another of the great staples seemed to promise the largest returns on capital investments. The expectation of profits from staple production, not the limitations of slavery, led to specialization rather than diversification, and caused some planters to fail to produce enough food for their own needs. Nor can slavery be blamed for the managerial inefficiency of unsupervised overseers who introduced slovenly agricultural methods on many estates. "Depend upon it that it is not our negroes, but our white managers, who stand in the way of improvement," asserted a South Carolinian. Finally, soil erosion was not the product of slavery but of the hilly, rolling terrain, of heavy rains, and of the failure to introduce contour plowing and proper drainage. This trouble, too, afflicted slaveholders and nonslaveholders alike.

As conditions changed in the other parts of the South, tillage methods also changed. Out of economic depression, which resulted from declining staple prices and rising production costs on depleted lands, there appeared an increasingly obvious need for agricultural reform. "Formerly, when lands were fresh and cotton high," observed a Southerner, "planters had very little difficulty in getting along, and with the least industry and economy, accumulated property rapidly.... Twenty cents a pound for cotton cured all defects in management, and kept the sheriff at bay; but six cents a pound for cotton is quite another thing." Then, for the first time, some of those who had been mining the southern soil began to show an interest in conserving it.

And wherever in the South improved methods were adopted, the slaveholders usually took the lead. They promoted the organization of local agricultural societies, sponsored essay contests on agricultural topics, and provided most of the support for the numerous periodicals which preached reform. They did most of the experimenting with new crops, with systems of crop rotation, with new implements and techniques, and with fertilizers. In Virginia, slaveholders such as Edmund Ruffin, Hill Carter, and John Seldon abandoned tobacco, or at least rotated tobacco with wheat and clover; they were the first to enrich their lands with marl and with animal and vegetable manures. In short, they were responsible for the agricultural renaissance that Virginia enjoyed during the generation before 1860. "It is true," admitted Ruffin, "that *good farming* is rare here; and so it is elsewhere." But, he added, "our best farming in lower and middle Virginia is always to be found in connection with... [the] use of slave labor."

In the Deep South, slaveholding planters such as James H. Hammond, of South Carolina, and Dr. Martin W. Phillips, of Mississippi, led similar movements to save the soil. Throughout the South, most of the improved farming was being done on lands worked by bondsmen; the "model" farms and plantations were almost invariably operated with their labor. Thus a substantial minority of the landowners demonstrated that slaves could be used efficiently in a system of intensive, scientific, and diversified agriculture. It is a mistake, therefore, to attribute soil exhaustion to slavery, or to assume that the institution was working such general economic havoc as to be rushing headlong toward destruction.

But slavery was alleged to be economically injurious to the South not only because it fostered one-crop agriculture but also because it produced a generally unbalanced economy. Southerners, according to this argument, had never been able to accumulate capital for manufacturing, because so much of their wealth was invested in their labor force. Critics such as Cairnes insisted that slaves were, "from the nature of the case, unskilled" and hence could not "take part with efficiency in the difficult and delicate operations which most manufacturing and mechanical processes involve." Slaves, concluded Cairnes, have "never been, and can never be, employed with success in manufacturing industry."

It is doubtful, however, that slavery in any decisive way retarded the industrialization of the South. After the African slave trade was legally closed, the southern labor system absorbed little new capital that might have gone into commerce or industry. Then only the illegal trade carried on by northern and foreign merchants drained off additional amounts of the South's liquid assets. The domestic slave trade involved no further investment; it merely involved the transfer of a portion of the existing one between individuals and regions. Obviously, when one Southerner purchased slaves another liquidated part of his investment in slaves and presumably could have put his capital in industry if he cared to. To define the cost of raising a young slave to maturity as a new capital investment is quite misleading. It would be more logical to call this a part of the "wage" a slave received for his lifetime of labor; or to call it—as most slaveholders did—a part of the annual operating expense. Southerners *did* have capital for investment in industry, and the existence of slavery was not the reason why so few of them chose to become industrialists.

After innumerable experiments had demonstrated that slaves could be employed profitably in factories, Southerners were still divided over the wisdom of such enterprises. Some of the opponents were devoted to the agrarian tradition and contended that industrialization was an evil under all circumstances. Others insisted that nonagricultural occupations should be reserved for free white labor and that white men should not be degraded by slave competition. In addition, many feared that removing slaves from the farms and plantations and increasing their numbers in the cities would undermine the peculiar institution. "Whenever a slave is made a mechanic, he is more than half freed," argued one master. "Wherever slavery has decayed, the first step... has been the elevation of the slaves to the rank of artisans and soldiers."

Those who favored employing slaves in industry believed that this was the most practical way for the South to diversify its economy and to become more nearly self-sufficient. They protested that the attempt to confine slaves to agriculture was an attack upon slavery itself. It was the work of abolitionists. To prohibit masters from training slaves for any occupation "in which they may be profitably employed... would be fatal to the institution of Slavery, and an infringement on the rights of those on whom has developed the responsibility of taking care of dependents." Finally, promoters of industry pointed to the record of successes where slaves were being used in mines, cotton mills, iron foundries, and tobacco factories.

The appeal of such promoters had little effect, however, for Southerners put only a small amount of capital into industry before the Civil War. Many of those who sold slaves to the traders used the money to support an extravagant standard of living rather than for new investments. But in the nineteenth century most of the South's surplus capital went into land and agricultural improvements; and the reason for this way simply that in the competition for funds agriculture was able to outbid industry. Men invested in land not only because of the agrarian tradition and the prestige derived from the ownership of real estate, but also because the production of one of the staples seemed to be the surest avenue to financial success. Besides, southern industry faced the handicap of competition from northern industry which enjoyed the advantages of greater experience, more efficient management, more concentrated markets, more numerous power sites, and better transportation. All of these factors destined the South, with or without slavery, to be a predominantly agricultural region—and so it continued to be for many years after emancipation.

Another supposed disadvantage of the southern labor system was that slaves were less productive than free workers and therefore more expensive to their employers. Cairnes explained that since slaves could be offered no incentives, "fear is substituted for hope, as the stimulus to exertion. But fear is ill calculated to draw from a labourer all the industry of which he is capable." A second critic declared, "Half the population of the South is employed in seeing that the other half do their work, and they who do work, accomplish half what they might do under a better system." After visiting a number of plantations in Virginia, Olmsted concluded that slaves "can not be driven by fear of punishment to do that which the laborers in free communities do cheerfully from their sense of duty, self-respect, or regard for their reputation and standing with their employer."

To be sure, the slave's customary attitude of indifference toward his work, together with the numerous methods he devised to resist his enslavement, sharply reduced the master's potential profits. It does not follow, however, that a slaveholder who was a reasonably efficient manager would have found free labor cheaper to employ. Slavery's economic critics overlooked the fact that physical coercion, or the threat of it, proved to be a rather effective incentive, and that the system did not prevent masters from offering tempting rewards for the satisfactory performance of assigned tasks.

Besides, slave labor had several competitive advantages over free white labor. In the first place, it was paid less: the average wage of a free laborer exceeded considerably the investment and maintenance costs of a slave. In the second place, masters exploited women and children more fully than did the employers of free labor. Finally, the average bondsman worked longer hours and was subjected to a more rigid discipline. Slaveholders were less troubled with labor "agitators" and less obligated to bargain with their workers. The crucial significance of this fact was dramatically demonstrated by a Louisiana sugar planter who once experimented with free labor, only to have his gang strike for double pay during the grinding season. "Slave labor is the most constant form of labor," argued a Southerner. "The details of cotton and rice culture could not be carried on with one less constant." No conviction was more firmly embedded in the mind of the planter than this. Many employers "hire slaves in preference to other laborers," explained a southern judge, "because they believe the contract confers an absolute right to their services during its continuation." These advantages more than compensated for whatever superiority free labor had in efficiency.

Indeed, some southern landowners who employed Irish immigrants or native whites even doubted that they were more diligent than slaves. One employer complained that no matter how well white workers were treated, "except when your eyes are on them they cheat you out of the labor due you, by lounging under the shade of the trees in your field." A Maryland planter assured Olmsted that "at hoeing and any steady field-work" his slaves accomplished twice as much, and with less personal supervision, than the Irish laborers he had used. North Carolina farmers told him that poor whites were "even more inefficient and unmanageable than ... slaves." Clearly, the productivity and efficiency of free labor was not so overwhelmingly superior as to make the doom of slavery inevitable.

Still another argument of the economic critics was that owners of slaves had to bear certain costs that employers of free labor did not bear. In a free labor system workers were hired and fired as they were needed; in a slave labor system workers had to be supported whether or not they were needed. In a free labor system the employer had no obligation to support the worker's dependents, or the worker himself during illness and in old age; in a slave labor system the employer was legally and morally obligated to meet these costs. Thus, presumably, slavery was at once more humane and more expensive.

This, too, is a myth. Employers of free labor, through wage payments, did in fact bear most of the expense of supporting the children of their workers, as well as the aged and infirm. Government and private charities assumed only a small part of this burden. Moreover, the amount that slaveholders spent to maintain these unproductive groups was not a substantial addition to their annual operating costs. The maintenance of disabled and senile slaves was a trivial charge upon the average master; and the market value of a young slave far exceeded the small expense of raising him.

Nor was the typical slaveholder faced with the problem of feeding and clothing surplus laborers; rather, his persistent problem was that of a labor shortage, which became acute during the harvest. Only a few masters had difficulty finding work for all available hands throughout the year. As for the need to support workers in time of economic depression, it must be remembered that the nineteenth-century agriculturist (unlike the manufacturer) did not ordinarily stop, or even curtail, production when demand and prices declined. Instead, he continued his operations—and sometimes even expanded them in an effort to augment his reduced income. During the depression of the 1840's, for example, both slaveholders and nonslaveholders strove for maximum production, and as a result there were few unemployed agricultural workers. Slave prices declined because nearly all prices declined, not because masters deliberately flooded the market with Negroes for whom there was no work. Rarely, then, did slaveholders pay for the support of idle hands.

But were there not other costs burdening the employer of slave labor which the employer of free labor escaped? The slaveholder, said the critics, bore the initial expense of a substantial investment in his laborers, the annual expense of interest and depreciation upon his investment, and the constant risk of loss through death by accident or disease. The employer of free labor, on the other hand, bore neither of these expenses and lost nothing when a worker died or was disabled. Here, many thought, was the most convincing evidence that slave labor was more costly than free.

It is true that the purchase of slaves (which involves the capitalization of future income from their labor) increased the size of the capital investment in a business enterprise—and that most southern whites lacked the cash or credit to gain title to this form of labor. It is also true that an investment in slaves entailed the risk of serious losses, especially for the small slaveholder. Though most masters continued to assume this risk, late in the ante-bellum period a few began to protect themselves from such disasters by insuring the lives of slaves. More important, however, is the fact that in the general pricing of slaves these risks were discounted. Such dangers as death, long illness, permanent disability, rebelliousness, and escape were all weighed when a purchaser calculated the price he was willing to pay. Only an unfortunate minority, therefore, suffered severe losses from an investment in slaves.

Depreciation on slave capital was not an operational expense for the average master. Not only were slave prices increasing, but with reasonable luck an investment in slaves was self-perpetuating. As one Southerner observed, "slaves . . . are not wasted by use, and if they are, that waste is supplied by their issue." Another added, "Their perpetuation by natural increase bears a strong resemblance to the permanency of Lands." Most slaveholders, in fact, were more fortunate than this, for their slave forces actually grew in size. With proper use, a master found his investment in slaves (sometimes in land too), unlike his investment in tools and buildings, appreciating rather than depreciating. This natural increase was a significant part of his profit.

The southern master's capitalization of his labor force has caused more confusion than anything else about the comparative cost of free and slave labor. This capital investment was not an added expense; it was merely the payment in a lump sum of a portion of what the employer of free labor pays over a period of years. The price of a slave, together with maintenance, was the cost of a lifetime claim to his labor; it was part of the wage an employer could have paid a free laborer. The price was what a master was willing to give for the right to maintain his workers at a subsistence level, and to gain full control over their time and movements. The interest he expected to accrue from his investment was not an operational expense to be deducted from profits, as it has often been called, unless the slaves were purchased on credit and interest therefore had to be paid to someone else. To deduct from the master's profit an amount equal to interest on his own capital invested in slaves is to create a fictitious expense and to underestimate his total earnings. There would be less confusion if this amount were called "profit on investment" rather than "interest on investment"; for as long as he earned it, this was a portion of his reward for risking his capital and managing his enterprise. With scarcely an exception, southern slaveholders, like entrepreneurs generally, not only considered interest earned on investment as part of their total profit but lumped all sources of profit together without artificial and arbitrary divisions.

Calculated on this basis, discounting the myths, there is ample evidence that the average slaveholder earned a reasonably satisfactory return upon his investment in slaves.

NO

Eugene D. Genovese

The Low Productivity of
Southern Slave Labor

The economic backwardness that condemned the slaveholding South to defeat in 1861–1865 had at its root the low productivity of labor, which expressed itself in several ways. Most significant was the carelessness and wastefulness of the slaves. Bondage forced the Negro to give his labor grudgingly and badly, and his poor work habits retarded those social and economic advances that could have raised the general level of productivity. Less direct were limitations imposed on the free work force, on technological development, and on the division of labor.

Although the debate on slave productivity is an old one, few arguments have appeared during the last hundred years to supplement those of contemporaries like John Elliott Cairnes and Edmund Ruffin. Cairnes made the much-assailed assertion that the slave was so defective in versatility that his labor could be exploited profitably only if he were taught one task and kept at it. If we allow for exaggeration, Cairnes's thesis is sound. Most competent observers agreed that slaves worked badly, without interest or effort. Edmund Ruffin, although sometimes arguing the reverse, pointed out that whereas at one time cheap, fertile farmland required little skill, soil exhaustion had finally created conditions demanding the intelligent participation of the labor force. Ruffin neither developed his idea nor drew the appropriate conclusions. The systematic education and training of the slaves would have been politically dangerous. The use of skilled workers would increasingly have required a smaller slave force, which would in turn have depended on expanding markets for surplus slaves and thus could not have been realized in the South as a whole. Other Southerners simply dropped the matter with the observation that the difference in productivity between free and slave labor only illustrated how well the Negroes were treated.

Ample evidence indicates that slaves worked well below their capabilities. In several instances in Mississippi, when cotton picking was carefully supervised in local experiments, slaves picked two or three times their normal output. The records of the Barrow plantation in Louisiana reveal that inefficiency and negligence resulted in two-thirds of the punishments inflicted on slaves, and other contemporary sources are full of corroborative data.

From Eugene D. Genovese, *The Political Economy of Slavery: Studies in the Economy and Society of the Slave South* (Vintage Books, 1965). Copyright © 1961, 1963, 1965 by Eugene D. Genovese. Reprinted by permission of Pantheon Books, a division of Random House, Inc. Notes omitted.

However much the slaves may have worked below their capacity, the limitations placed on that capacity were probably even more important in undermining productivity. In particular, the diet to which the slaves were subjected must be judged immensely damaging, despite assurances from contemporaries and later historians that the slave was well fed.

The slave usually got enough to eat, but the starchy, high-energy diet of cornmeal, pork, and molasses produced specific hungers, dangerous deficiencies, and that unidentified form of malnutrition to which the medical historian Richard H. Shryock draws attention. Occasional additions of sweet potatoes or beans could do little to supplement the narrow diet. Planters did try to provide vegetables and fruits, but not much land could be spared from the staples, and output remained minimal. Protein hunger alone—cereals in general and corn in particular cannot provide adequate protein—greatly reduces the ability of an organism to resist infectious diseases. Even increased consumption of vegetables probably would not have corrected the deficiency, for as a rule the indispensable amino acids are found only in such foods as lean meat, milk, and eggs. The abundant pork provided was largely fat. Since the slave economy did not and could not provide sufficient livestock, no solution presented itself.

In the 1890s a dietary study of Negro field laborers in Alabama revealed a total bacon intake of more than five pounds per week, or considerably more than the three and one-half pounds that probably prevailed in antebellum days. Yet, the total protein found in the Negroes' diet was only 60 per cent of that deemed adequate. Recent studies show that individuals with a high caloric but low protein intake will deviate from standard height-weight ratios by a disproportionate increase in weight. The slave's diet contained deficiencies other than protein; vitamins and minerals also were in short supply. Vitamin deficiencies produce xerophthalmia, beriberi, pellagra, and scurvy and create what one authority terms "states of vague indisposition [and] obscure and ill-defined disturbances."

There is nothing surprising in the slave's appearance of good health: his diet was well suited to guarantee the appearance of good health and to provide the fuel to keep him going in the fields, but it was not sufficient to ensure either sound bodies or the stamina necessary for sustained labor. We need not doubt the testimony of William Dosite Postell, who presents evidence of reasonably good medical attention to slaves and of adequate supply of food bulk. Rather, it is the finer questions of dietary balance that concern us. At that, Postell provides some astonishing statistics that reinforce the present argument: 7 per cent of a sample of more than 8,500 slaves from Georgia, Mississippi, Alabama, and Louisiana above the age of fifteen were either physically impaired or chronically ill. As W. Arthur Lewis writes of today's underdeveloped countries: "Malnutrition and chronic debilitating disease are probably the main reason why the inhabitants ... are easily exhausted. And this creates a chain which is hard to break, since malnutrition and disease cause low productivity, and low productivity, in turn, maintains conditions of malnutrition and disease."

The limited diet was by no means primarily a result of ignorance or viciousness on the part of masters, for many knew better and would have liked to do better. The problem was largely economic. Feeding costs formed a burdensome part of plantation expenses. Credit and market systems precluded the assignment of much land to crops other than cotton and corn. The land so assigned was generally the poorest available, and the quality of foodstuffs consequently suffered. For example, experiments have shown that the proportion of iron in lettuce may vary from one to fifty milligrams per hundred, according to soil conditions.

The slave's low productivity resulted directly from inadequate care, incentives, and training, and from such other well-known factors as the overseer system, but just how low was it? Can the productivity of slave labor, which nonstatistical evidence indicates to have been low, be measured? An examination of the most recent, and most impressive, attempt at measurement suggests that it cannot. Alfred H. Conrad and John R. Meyer have arranged the following data to demonstrate the movement of "crop value per hand per dollar of slave price" during the antebellum period: size of the cotton crop, average price, value of crop, number of slaves aged ten to fifty-four, crop value per slave, and price of prime field hands. Unfortunately, this method, like the much cruder one used by Algie M. Simons in 1911 and repeated by Lewis C. Gray, does not remove the principal difficulties.

First, the contribution of white farmers who owned no slaves or who worked in the fields beside the few slaves they did own, cannot be separated from that of the slaves. The output of slaveless farmers might be obtained by arduous digging in the manuscript census returns for 1850 and 1860, but the output of farmers working beside their slaves does not appear to lend itself to anything better than baseless guessing. There is also no reason to believe that slaves raised the same proportion of the cotton crop in any two years, and we have little knowledge of the factors determining fluctuations.

Second, we cannot assume that the same proportion of the slave force worked in the cotton fields in any two years. In periods of expected low prices slaveholders tried to deflect part of their force to food crops. We cannot measure the undoubted fluctuations in the man-hours applied to cotton. The Conrad-Meyer results, in particular, waver; they show a substantial increase in productivity before the Civil War, but the tendency to assign slaves to other crops in periods of falling prices builds an upward bias into their calculations for the prosperous 1850s. It might be possible to circumvent the problem by calculating for the total output instead of for cotton, but to do so would create even greater difficulties, such as how to value food grown for plantation use.

Not all bad effects of slavery on productivity were so direct. Critics of slaveholding have generally assumed that it created a contempt for manual labor, although others have countered with the assertion that the Southern yeoman was held in high esteem. True, the praises of the working farmer had to be sung in a society in which he had the vote, but an undercurrent of contempt was always there. Samuel Cartwright, an outspoken and socially minded Southern physician, referred scornfully to those whites "who make negroes of themselves" in the cotton and sugar fields. Indeed, to work hard was "to work like a nigger." If labor was not lightly held, why were there so many assurances from public figures that no one need be ashamed of it?

There were doubtless enough incentives and enough expressions of esteem to allow white farmers to work with some sense of pride; the full impact of the negative attitude toward labor fell on the landless. The brunt of the scorn was borne by those who had to work for others, much as the slave did. The proletarian, rural or urban, was free and white and therefore superior to one who was slave and black, but the difference was minimized when he worked alongside a Negro for another man. So demoralized was white labor that planters often preferred to hire slaves because they were better workers. How much was to be expected of white labor in a society that, in the words of one worried editor, considered manual labor "menial and revolting"?

The attitude toward labor was thus composed of two strains: an undercurrent of contempt for work in general and the more prevalent and probably more damaging contempt for labor performed for another, especially when considered "menial" labor. These notions undermined the productivity of those free workers who might have made important periodic contributions, and thus seriously lowered the level of productivity in the economy. Even today a tendency to eschew saving and to work only enough to meet essential needs has been observed in underdeveloped countries in which precapitalist social structure and ideology are strong.

Technological Retardation

Few now doubt that social structure has been an important factor in the history of science and technology or that capitalism has introduced the greatest advances in these fields. For American agriculture technology, the craftsman, the skilled worker, and the small producer—all anxious to conserve labor time and cut costs—may well have provided the most significant technological thrust. Specifically, the great advances of the modern era arose from a free-labor economy that gave actual producers the incentives to improve methods and techniques. In nineteenth-century America, writes one authority, "the farmers... directed and inspired the efforts of inventors, engineers, and manufacturers to solve their problems and supply their needs... [and] the early implements were in many cases invented or designed by the farmers themselves."

If workers are to contribute much to technology, the economy must permit and encourage an increasing division of labor, for skilled persons assigned to few tasks can best devise better methods and implements. Once an initial accumulation of capital takes place, the division of labor, if not impeded, will result in further accumulation and further division. Such extensive division cannot readily develop in slave economies. The heavy capitalization of labor, the high propensity to consume, and the weakness of the home market seriously impede the accumulation of capital. Technological progress and division of labor result in work for fewer hands, but slavery requires all hands to be occupied at all times. Capitalism has solved this problem by a tremendous economic expansion along varied lines (qualitative development), but slavery's obstacles to industrialization prevent this type of solution.

In part, the slave South offset its weakness by drawing upon the technology of more progressive areas. During the first half of the nineteenth century the North copied from Europe on a grand scale, but the South was limited even in the extent to which it could copy and was especially restricted in possibilities for improving techniques once they had been acquired. The regions in which transference of technical skills has always been most effective have been those with an abundance of trained craftsmen as well as of natural resources. In the North a shortage of unskilled labor and a preoccupation with labor-saving machinery stimulated the absorption of advanced techniques and the creation of new ones. In the South the importation of slaves remedied the labor shortage and simultaneously weakened nonslave productive units. The availability of a "routinized, poorly educated, and politically ineffectual rural labor force" of whites as well as Negroes rendered, and to some extent still renders, interest in labor-saving machinery pointless.

Negro slavery retarded technological progress in many ways: it prevented the growth of industrialism and urbanization; it retarded the division of labor, which might have spurred the creation of new technologies; it barred the labor force from that intelligent participation in production which has made possible the steady improvement of implements and machines; and it encouraged ways of thinking antithetical to the spirit of modern science. These impediments undoubtedly damaged Southern agriculture, for improved equipment largely accounted for the dramatic increases in crop yields per acre in the North during the nineteenth century....

Southern farmers suffered especially from technological backwardness, for the only way in which they might have compensated for the planters' advantage of large-scale operation would have been to attain a much higher technological level. The social pressure to invest in slaves and the high cost of machinery in a region that had to import much of its equipment made such an adjustment difficult.

Large-scale production gave the planter an advantage over his weaker competitors within the South, but the plantation was by no means more efficient than the family farm operating in the capitalist economy of the free states....

The Division of Labor

Although few scholars assert that the Southern slave plantations were self-sufficient units, most assume a fair degree of division of labor in their work force. The employment of skilled artisans usually receives scant attention. An examination of the plantation manuscripts and data in the manuscript census returns shows, however, considerable sums paid for the services of artisans and laborers and a low level of home manufactures.

As Tryon has shown, the Confederacy could not repeat the achievements of the colonies during the Revolutionary War, when family industry supplied the war effort and the home front. Although household manufacturing survived longer in the slave states than in other parts of the country, slave labor proved so inefficient in making cloth, for example, that planters preferred not to bother. In those areas of the South in which slavery predominated, household manufactures decreased rapidly after 1840, and the system never took hold in the newer slave states of Florida, Louisiana, and Texas. Whereas in the North its disappearance resulted from the development of much more advanced factory processes, in the South it formed part of a general decline in skill and technique.

An examination of the manuscript census returns for selected counties in 1860 bears out these generalizations. It also shows that the large plantations, although usually producing greater totals than the small farms, did poorly in the production of home manufactures. In Mississippi's cotton counties the big planters (thirty-one or more slaves) averaged only $76 worth of home manufactures during the year, whereas other groups of farmers and planters showed much less. In the Georgia cotton counties the small planters (twenty-one to thirty slaves) led other groups with $127, and the big planters produced only half as much. Fifty-eight per cent of the big planters in the Mississippi counties examined recorded no home manufactures at all, and most agriculturalists in the Georgia counties produced none. In Virginia the same results appeared: in tobacco counties the big planters led other groups with $56 worth of home manufactures, and in the tidewater and northern wheat counties the big planters led with only $35.

The Richmond *Dispatch* estimated in the 1850s that the South spent $5,000,000 annually for Northern shoes and boots. Although the figure cannot be verified, there is no doubt that Southerners bought most of their shoes in the North. One of the bigger planters, Judge Cameron of North Carolina, owner of five plantations and 267 slaves in 1834, had to purchase more than half the shoes needed for his Negroes despite his large establishment and a conscientious attempt to supply his own needs. Most planters apparently did not even try to produce shoes or clothing. When a planter with about thirty slaves in Scotland Neck, North Carolina, made arrangements to have clothing produced on his estate, he hired an outsider to do it. Yet, until 1830 shoes were produced in the United States by tools and methods not essentially different from those used by medieval serfs, and not much equipment would have been needed to continue those methods on the plantations. Even simple methods of production were not employed on the plantation because the low level of productivity made them too costly relative to available Northern shoes. At the same time, the latter were more expensive than they ought to have been, for transportation costs were high, and planters had little choice but to buy in the established New England shoe centers.

Plantation account books reveal surprisingly high expenditures for a variety of tasks requiring skilled and unskilled labor. A Mississippi planter with 130 slaves paid an artisan $320 for labor and supplies for a forty-one-day job in 1849. Other accounts show that Governor Hammond spent $452 to have a road built in 1850; another planter spent $108 for repair of a carriage and $900 for repair of a sloop in 1853, as well as $175 for repair of a bridge in 1857; a third spent $2,950 for the hire of artisans in 1856 on a plantation with more than 175 slaves.

The largest payments went to blacksmiths. A Panola, Mississippi, planter listed expenditures for the following in 1853: sharpening of plows, mending of shovels, and construction of plows, ox-chains, hooks, and other items. In 1847 a Greensboro, Alabama, planter, whose books indicate that he was business-like and efficient, spent about $140 for blacksmiths' services on his large plantation of seventy-five slaves. One South Carolina planter with forty-five slaves had an annual blacksmith's account of about $35, and expenditures by other planters were often higher.

Even simple tasks like the erection of door frames sometimes required the services of hired carpenters, as in the case of a Jefferson County, Mississippi, planter in 1851. If buildings, chimneys, or slave cabins had to be built, planters generally hired free laborers or slave artisans. Skilled slaves had unusual privileges and incentives, but there was not much for them to do on a single plantation. Rather than allow a slave to spend all his time acquiring a skill for which there was only a limited need, a planter would hire one for short periods. Even this type of slave specialization brought frowns from many planters, who considered the incentives and privileges subversive of general plantation discipline.

If it paid to keep all available slaves in the cotton fields during periods of high prices, the reverse was true during periods of low prices. At those times the factors forcing a one-crop agriculture and the low productivity of nonfield labor wrought devastating results. The South's trouble was not that it lacked sufficient shoe or clothing factories, or that it lacked a diversified agriculture, or that it lacked enough other industrial enterprises; the trouble was that it lacked all three at the same time. The slight division of labor on the plantations and the slight social division of labor in the region forced the planters into dependence on the Northern market. As a result, the cost of cotton production rose during periods of low as well as high cotton prices. Even during the extraordinary years of the Civil War, when Southerners struggled manfully to feed and clothe themselves, the attempt to produce home manufactures met with only indifferent results. These observations merely restate the problem of division of labor in the slave South: the low level of productivity, caused by the inefficiency of the slaves and the general backwardness of society, produced increasing specialization in staple-crop production under virtually colonial conditions.

Farm Implements and Machinery

"There is nothing in the progress of agriculture," the United States Agricultural Society proclaimed in 1853, "more encouraging than the rapid increase and extension of labor-saving machinery." The South did not profit much from these technological advances, nor did it contribute much to them.

The most obvious obstacle to the employment of better equipment was the slave himself. In 1843 a Southern editor sharply rebuked planters and overseers for complaining that Negroes could not handle tools. Such a complaint was, he said, merely a confession of poor management, for with proper supervision Negro slaves would provide proper care. The editor was unfair. Careful supervision of unwilling laborers would have entailed either more overseers than most planters could afford or a slave force too small to provide the advantages of large-scale operation. The harsh treatment that slaves gave equipment shocked travelers and other contemporaries, and neglect of tools figured prominently among the reasons given for punishing Negroes. In 1855 a South Carolina planter wrote in exasperation:

The wear and tear of plantation tools is harassing to every planter who does not have a good mechanic at his nod and beck every day in the year. Our plows are broken, our hoes are lost, our harnesses need repairing, and large demands are made on the blacksmith, the carpenter, the tanner, and the harnessmaker. [sic]

The implements used on the plantations were therefore generally much too heavy for efficient use. The "nigger hoe," often found in relatively advanced Virginia, weighed much more than the "Yankee hoe," which slaves broke easily. Those used in the Southwest weighed almost three times as much as those manufactured in the North for Northern use. Curiously, in many cases equipment was too light for adequate results. Whereas most planters bought extra-heavy implements in the hope that they would withstand rough handling, others resigned themselves and bought the cheapest possible. . . .

Most planters in Mississippi, wrote Philips, thought they could use one kind of plow for every possible purpose. The weakness was doubly serious, for the one kind was usually poor. The most popular plow in the Lower South—at least, well into the 1840s—was the shovel plow, which merely stirred the surface of the soil to a depth of two or three inches. Made of wrought iron, it was "a crude and inefficient instrument which, as commonly employed, underwent no essential improvement throughout its long career." It was light enough for a girl to carry and exemplified the "too light" type of implement used on the plantations.

In the 1850s the shovel plow slowly gave way in the South to a variety of light moldboard plows, which at least were of some help in killing and controlling weeds. Good moldboard plows should have offered other advantages, such as aid in burying manure, but those in the South were not nearly so efficient as those in the North. In 1830, Connecticut manufacturers began to produce large numbers of Cary plows, exclusively for the Southern market. These light wooden plows with wrought-iron shares were considered of good quality. Unfortunately, they required careful handling, for they broke easily, and they could not penetrate more than three or four inches below the surface. During the 1820s Northern farmers had been shifting to cast-iron plows that could cover 50 per cent more acreage with 50 per cent less animal- and man-power. When cast-iron plows did enter the South, they could not be used to the same advantage as in the North, for they needed the services of expert blacksmiths when, as frequently happened, they broke.

Twenty years after the introduction of the cultivator in 1820, Northern farmers considered it standard equipment, especially in the cornfields, but cultivators, despite their tremendous value, were so light that few planters would trust them to their slaves. Since little wheat was grown below Virginia, the absence of reapers did not hurt much, but the backwardness of cotton equipment did. A "cotton planter" (a modified grain drill) and one man could do as much work as two mules and four men, but it was rarely used. Similarly, corn planters, especially the one invented by George Brown in 1853, might have saved a good deal of labor time, but these were costly, needed careful handling, and would have rendered part of the slave force superfluous. Since slaveholding carried prestige and status, and since slaves were an economic necessity during the picking season, planters showed little interest.

The cotton picker presents special technical and economic problems. So long as a mechanical picker was not available a large labor force would have been needed for the harvest; but in 1850 Samuel S. Rembert and Jedediah Prescott of Memphis did patent a mule-drawn cotton picker that was a "simple prototype of the modern spindle picker." Virtually no progress followed upon the original design until forty years later, and then almost as long a span intervened before further advances were made. The reasons for these gaps were in part technical, and in part economic pressures arising from slavery and sharecropping. Although one can never be sure about such things, the evidence accumulated by historians of science and technology strongly suggests that the social and economic impediments to technological change are generally more powerful than the specifically technical ones. The introduction of a cotton picker would have entailed the full mechanization of farming processes, and such a development would have had to be accompanied by a radically different social order. Surely, it is not accidental that the mechanical picker has in recent decades taken hold in the Southwest, where sharecropping has been weak, and has moved east slowly as changes in the social organization of the countryside have proceeded. Even without a mechanical picker the plantations might have used good implements and a smaller labor force during most of the year and temporary help during the harvest. In California in 1951, for example, 50 per cent of the occasional workers needed in the cotton fields came from within the county and 90 per cent from within the state. Rural and town housewives, youths, and seasonal workers anxious to supplement their incomes provided the temporary employees. There is no reason to believe that this alternative would not have been open to the South in the 1850s if slavery had been eliminated.

A few examples, which could be multiplied many times, illustrate the weakness of plantation technology. A plantation in Stewart County, Georgia, with a fixed capital investment of $42,660 had only $300 invested in implements and machinery. The Tooke plantation, also in Georgia, had a total investment in implements and machinery of $195, of which a gin accounted for $110. Plantations had plows, perhaps a few harrows and colters, possibly a cultivator, and in a few cases a straw cutter or corn and cob crusher. Whenever possible, a farmer or planter acquired a gin, and all had small tools for various purposes.

The figures reported in the census tabulations of farm implements and machinery are of limited value and must be used carefully. We have little information on shifting price levels, and the valuations reported to the census takers did not conform to rigorous standards. The same type of plow worth five dollars in 1850 may have been recorded at ten dollars in 1860, and in view of the general rise in prices something of the kind probably occurred.

Even if we put aside these objections and examine investments in selected counties in 1860, the appalling state of plantation technology is evident.... If we assume that a cotton gin cost between $100 and $125, the figures for the cotton counties suggest that all except the planters (twenty or more slaves) either did without a gin or had little else. Note that an increase in the slave force did not entail significant expansion of technique. As the size of the slaveholdings increased in the cotton countries, the investments in implements increased also, but in small amounts. Only units of twenty slaves or more showed tolerably respectable amounts, and even these were poor when one considers the size of the estates.

Gray has suggested that the poor quality of Southern implements was due only in part to slave inefficiency. He lists as other contributing factors the lack of local marketplaces for equipment, the ignorance of the small farmers and overseers, prejudice against and even aversion to innovations, and a shortage of capital in the interior. Each of these contributing factors itself arose from the nature of slave society. The weakness of the market led to a lack of marketplaces. The social structure of the countryside hardly left room for anything but ignorance and cultural backwardness, even by the standards of nineteenth-century rural America. The social and economic pressures to invest in slaves and the high propensity to consume rendered adequate capital accumulation impossible. The psychological factor—hostility to innovation—transcended customary agrarian conservatism and grew out of the patriarchal social structure.

The attempts of reformers to improve methods of cultivation, diversify production, and raise more and better livestock were undermined at the outset by a labor force without versatility or the possibility of increasing its productivity substantially. Other factors must be examined in order to understand fully why the movement for agricultural reform had to be content with inadequate accomplishments, but consideration of the direct effects of slave labor alone tells us why so little could be done.

POSTSCRIPT

Was Slavery Profitable?

Since the mid-1950s, few issues in American history have generated more interest among scholars than the institution of slavery. Books and articles analyzing the treatment of slaves, comparative slave systems, the profitability of slavery, slave rebelliousness (or lack thereof), urban slavery, the slave family, and slave religion have abounded. This proliferation of scholarship, stimulated in part by the civil rights movement, contrasts sharply with slavery historiography between the two world wars, which was monopolized by a single book: Ulrich B. Phillips's apologetic and blatantly racist *American Negro Slavery: A Survey of the Supply, Employment and Control of Negro Labor as Determined by the Plantation System* (D. Appleton, 1918). Recognition of a "revisionist" interpretation of slavery was delayed until the post–World War II era, when Stampp published *The Peculiar Institution* (1956).

As the debate over the nature of slavery moved into the 1960s and 1970s, several scholars sought to provide a history of the institution "from the bottom up." They began to focus upon the slaves themselves as a contributing force in the slave system. Interviews with ex-slaves had been conducted in the 1920s and 1930s under the auspices of Southern University in Louisiana, Fisk University in Tennessee, and the Federal Writers Project of the Works Progress Administration. Drawing upon these interviews and previously ignored slave autobiographies, sociologist George Rawick and historians John Blassingame and Eugene D. Genovese, among others, portrayed a multifaceted community life over which slaves held a significant degree of influence. This community, operating beyond the view of the "Big House," was, in Genovese's phrase, "the world the slaves made." See George P. Rawick, *From Sundown to Sunup: The Making of the Black Community* (Greenwood Press, 1972); John W. Blassingame, *The Slave Community: Plantation Life in the Ante-Bellum South* (Oxford University Press, 1972); and Eugene D. Genovese, *Roll, Jordan, Roll: The World the Slaves Made* (Pantheon, 1974).

The debate over the profitability of slavery can be followed in a trio of journal articles: Harold D. Woodman, "The Profitability of Slavery: A Historical Perennial," *Journal of Southern History* (August 1963); Edward Saraydar, "A Note on the Profitability of Ante Bellum Slavery," *Southern Economic Journal* (April 1964); and Richard Sutch and Edward Saraydar, "The Profitability of Ante Bellum Slavery: Comment and Reply," *Southern Economic Journal* (April 1965). The issue is also taken up as part of Robert Fogel and Stanley Engerman's controversial econometric study *Time on the Cross: The Economics of American Negro Slavery*, 2 vols. (Little, Brown, 1974).

ISSUE 12

Was the Mexican War an Exercise in American Imperialism?

YES: Rodolfo Acuña, from *Occupied America: A History of Chicanos,* 3rd ed. (Harper & Row, 1988)

NO: Norman A. Graebner, from "The Mexican War: A Study in Causation," *Pacific Historical Review* (August 1980)

ISSUE SUMMARY

YES: Professor of history Rodolfo Acuña argues that Euroamericans took advantage of the young, independent, and unstable government of Mexico and waged unjust and aggressive wars against the Mexican government in the 1830s and 1840s in order to take away half of Mexico's original soil.

NO: Professor of diplomatic history Norman A. Graebner argues that President James Polk pursued an aggressive policy that he believed would force Mexico to sell New Mexico and California to the United States and to recognize the annexation of Texas without starting a war.

The American government in the early 1800s greatly benefited from the fact that European nations generally considered what was going on in North America of secondary importance to what was happening in their own countries. In 1801 President Thomas Jefferson became alarmed when he learned that France had acquired the Louisiana Territory from Spain. He realized that western states might revolt if the government did not control the city of New Orleans as a seaport for shipping their goods. Jefferson dispatched negotiators to buy the port. He pulled off the real estate coup of the nineteenth century when his diplomats caught Napoleon in a moment of despair. With a stroke of the pen and $15 million, the Louisiana Purchase of 1803 nearly doubled the size of the country. The exact northern, western, and southeastern boundaries were not clearly defined. "But," as diplomatic historian Thomas Bailey has pointed out, "the American negotiators knew that they had bought the western half of perhaps the most valuable river valley on the face of the globe, stretching between the Rockies and the Mississippi, and bounded somewhere on the north by British North America."

After England fought an indecisive war with the United States from 1812 to 1815, she realized that it was to her advantage to maintain peaceful relations with her former colony. In 1817 the Great Lakes, which border on the United States and Canada, were mutually disarmed. Over the next half century, the principle of demilitarization was extended to the land, resulting in an undefended frontier line that stretched for more that 3,000 miles. The Convention of 1818 clarified the northern boundary of the Louisiana Purchase and ran a line along the 49th parallel from Lake of the Woods in Minnesota to the Rocky Mountains. Beyond that point there was to be a 10-year joint occupancy in the Oregon Territory. In 1819 Spain sold Florida to the United States after Secretary of State John Quincy Adams sent a note telling the Spanish government to keep the Indians on their side of the border or else to get out of Florida. A few years later, the Spanish Empire crumbled in the New World and a series of Latin American republics emerged.

Afraid that the European powers might attack the newly independent Latin American republics and that Russia might expand south into the Oregon Territory, Adams convinced President James Monroe to reject a British suggestion for a joint declaration and to issue instead a unilateral policy statement. The Monroe Doctrine, as it was called by a later generation, had three parts. First, it closed the western hemisphere to any future colonization. Second, it forbade "any interposition" by the European monarchs that would "extend their system to any portion of this hemisphere as dangerous to our peace and safety." And third, the United States pledged to abstain from any involvement in the political affairs of Europe. Viewed in the context of 1823, it is clear that Monroe was merely restating the principles of unilateralism and nonintervention. Both of these were at the heart of American isolationism.

While Monroe renounced the possibility of American intervention in European affairs, he made no such disclaimer toward Latin America, as was originally suggested by Great Britain. It would be difficult to colonize in South America, but the transportation revolution, the hunger for land, and the need for ports on the Pacific to increase American trade in Asia encouraged the acquisition of new lands contiguous to the southwestern boundaries. In the 1840s journalists and politicians furnished an ideological rationale for this expansion and said it was to the Manifest Destiny of Americans to spread democracy, freedom, and white American settlers across the entire North American continent, excluding Canada because it was a possession of Great Britain. Blacks and Indians were not a part of this expansion.

In the first of the following selections, Rodolfo Acuña argues that Euroamericans took advantage of the young, independent, and unstable government of Mexico by waging an unjust and aggressive war against Mexico in the 1830s and 1840s for the purpose of taking away more than half of its original lands. In the second selection, Norman A. Graebner contends that President Polk pursued the aggressive policy of a stronger nation in order to force Mexico to sell New Mexico and California to the United States and to recognize America's annexation of Texas without causing a war.

Rodolfo Acuña

Legacy of Hate: The Conquest of Mexico's Northwest

An Overview

The United States invaded Mexico in the mid-nineteenth century during a period of dramatic change. Rapid technological breakthroughs transformed the North American nation, from a farm society into an industrial competitor. The process converted North America into a principal in the world marketplace. The wars with Mexico, symptoms of this transformation, stemmed from the need to accumulate more land, to celebrate heroes, and to prove the nation's power by military superiority.

This [selection] examines the link between the Texas (1836) and the Mexican (1845–1848) Wars. It analyzes North American aggression, showing how European peoples known as "Americans" acquired what is today the Southwest. The words "expansion" and "invasion" are used interchangeably. The North American invasions of Mexico are equated with the forging of European empires in Asia, Africa, and Latin America. The urge to expand, in the case of the United States, was not based on the need for land—the Louisiana Purchase, central Illinois, southern Georgia, and West Virginia lay vacant. Rather, the motive was profit—and the wars proved profitable, with the Euroamerican nation seizing over half of Mexico.

North Americans fought the Texas War—that is, U.S. dollars financed it, U.S. arms were used on Mexican soil, and Euroamericans almost exclusively profited from it. President Andrew Jackson approved of the war and ignored North American neutrality laws. The so-called Republic held Texas in trusteeship until 1844, when the United States annexed it. This act amounted to a declaration of war on Mexico. When Mexico responded by breaking diplomatic relations, the North Americans used this excuse to manufacture the war. Many North Americans questioned the morality of the war but supported their government because it was their country, right or wrong.

This [selection] does not focus on the wars' battles or heroes, but on how North Americans rationalized these invasions and have developed historical amnesia about its causes and results. War is neither romantic nor just, and the

Excerpted from Rodolfo Acuña, *Occupied America: A History of Chicanos,* 3rd ed. (Harper & Row, 1988). Copyright © 1988 by Rodolfo Acuña. Reprinted by permission of Addison-Wesley Educational Publishers, Inc. Notes omitted.

United States did not act benevolently toward Mexico. North Americans committed atrocities, and, when they could, Mexicans responded. Eventually, the Treaty of Guadalupe Hidalgo ended the Mexican-American War, and northern Mexico became part of the North American empire. The treaty, however, did not stop the bitterness or the violence between the two peoples. In fact, it gave birth to a legacy of hate.

Background to the Invasion of Texas

Anglo justifications for the conquest have ignored or distorted events that led up to the initial clash in 1836. To Anglo-Americans, the Texas War was caused by a tyrannical or, at best, an incompetent Mexican government that was antithetical to the ideals of democracy and justice. The roots of the conflict actually extended back to as early as 1767, when Benjamin Franklin marked Mexico and Cuba for future expansion. Anglo-American filibusters* planned expeditions into Texas in the 1790s. The Louisiana Purchase, in 1803, stimulated U.S. ambitions in the Southwest, and six years later Thomas Jefferson predicted that the Spanish borderlands "are ours the first moment war is forced upon us." The war with Great Britain in 1812 intensified Anglo-American designs on the Spanish territory.

Florida set the pattern for expansionist activities in Texas. In 1818 several posts in east Florida were seized in unauthorized, but never officially condemned, U.S. military expeditions. Negotiations then in progress with Spain finally terminated in the Adams-Onis, or Transcontinental, Treaty (1819), in which Spain ceded Florida to the United States and the United States, in turn, renounced its claim to Texas. Texas itself was part of Coahuila. Many North Americans still claimed that Texas belonged to the United States, repeating Jefferson's claim that Texas's boundary extended to the Río Grande and that it was part of the Louisiana Purchase. They condemned the Adams-Onis Treaty.

Anglo-Americans continued pretensions to Texas and made forays into Texas similar to those they had made into Florida. In 1819 James Long led an abortive invasion to establish the "Republic of Texas." Long, like many Anglos, believed that Texas belonged to the United States and that "Congress had no right or power to sell, exchange, or relinquish an 'American possession.' "

In spite of the hostility, the Mexican government opened Texas, provided that settlers agreed to certain conditions. Moses Austin was given permission to settle in Texas, but he died shortly afterwards, and his son continued his venture. In December 1821 Stephen Austin founded the settlement of San Félipe de Austin. Large numbers of Anglo-Americans entered Texas in the 1820s as refugees from the depression of 1819. In the 1830s entrepreneurs sought to profit from the availability of cheap land. By 1830 there were about 20,000 settlers, along with some 2,000 slaves.

Settlers agreed to obey the conditions set by the Mexican government— that all immigrants be Catholics and that they take an oath of allegiance to

---

* [A *filibuster* is an adventurer who engages in insurrectionist or revolutionary activity in a foreign country.]

Mexico. However, Anglo-Americans became resentful when Mexico tried to enforce the agreements. Mexico, in turn, became increasingly alarmed at the flood of immigrants from the U.S.

Many settlers considered the native Mexicans to be the intruders. In a dispute with Mexicans and Indians, as well as with Anglo-American settlers, Hayden Edwards arbitrarily attempted to evict settlers from the land before the conflicting claims could be sorted out by the Mexican authorities. As a result Mexican authorities nullified his settlement contract and ordered him to leave the territory. Edwards and his followers seized the town of Nacogdoches and on December 21, 1826, proclaimed the Republic of Fredonia. Mexican officials, supported by some Anglo-Americans (such as Stephen Austin), suffocated the Edwards revolt. However, many U.S. newspapers played up the rebellion as "200 Men Against a Nation!" and described Edwards and his followers as "apostles of democracy crushed by an alien civilization."

In 1824 President John Quincy Adams "began putting pressure on Mexico in the hope of persuading her to rectify the frontier. Any of the Texan rivers west of the Sabine—the Brazos, the Colorado, the Nueces—was preferable to the Sabine, though the Río Grande was the one desired." In 1826 Adams offered to buy Texas for the sum of $1 million. When Mexican authorities refused the offer, the United States launched an aggressive foreign policy, attempting to coerce Mexico into selling Texas.

Mexico could not consolidate its control over Texas: the number of Anglo-American settlers and the vastness of the territory made it an almost impossible task. Anglo-Americans had already created a privileged caste, which depended in great part on the economic advantage given to them by their slaves. When Mexico abolished slavery, on September 15, 1829, Euroamericans circumvented the law by "freeing" their slaves and then signing them to lifelong contracts as indentured servants. Anglos resented the Mexican order and considered it an infringement on their personal liberties. In 1830 Mexico prohibited further Anglo-American immigration. Meanwhile, Andrew Jackson increased tensions by attempting to purchase Texas for as much as $5 million.

Mexican authorities resented the Anglo-Americans' refusal to submit to Mexican laws. Mexico moved reinforcements into Coahuila, and readied them in case of trouble. Anglos viewed this move as an act of hostility.

Anglo colonists refused to pay customs and actively supported smuggling activities. When the "war party" rioted at Anahuac in December 1831, it had the popular support of Anglos. One of its leaders was Sam Houston, who "was a known protégé of Andrew Jackson, now president of the United States.... Houston's motivation was to bring Texas into the United States." ...

The Invasion of Texas

Not all the Anglo-Americans favored the conflict. Austin, at first, belonged to the peace party. Ultimately, this faction joined the "hawks." Eugene C. Barker states that the immediate cause of the war was "the overthrow of the nominal republic [by Santa Anna] and the substitution of centralized oligarchy," which allegedly would have centralized Mexican control. Barker admits that "earnest patriots like Benjamin Lundy, William Ellery Channing, and John Quincy Adams saw in the Texas revolution a disgraceful affair promoted by the sordid slaveholders and land speculators."

Barker parallels the Texas filibuster and the American Revolution, stating: "In each, the general cause of revolt was the same—a sudden effort to extend imperial authority at the expense of local privilege." According to Barker, in both instances the central governments attempted to enforce existing laws that conflicted with the illegal activities of some very articulate people. Barker further justified the Anglo-Americans' actions by observing: "At the close of summer in 1835 the Texans saw themselves in danger of becoming the alien subjects of a people to whom they deliberately believed themselves morally, intellectually, and politically superior. The racial feeling, indeed, underlay and colored Texan-Mexican relations from the establishment of the first Anglo-American colony in 1821." The conflict, according to Barker, was inevitable and, consequently, justified.

Texas history is a mixture of selected fact and generalized myth. Many historians admit that smugglers were upset with Mexico's enforcement of her import laws, that Euroamericans were angry about emancipation laws, and that an increasing number of the new arrivals from the United States actively agitated for independence. But despite these admissions, many historians like Barker refuse to blame the United States.

Austin gave the call to arms on September 19, 1835, stating, "War is our only recourse. There is no other remedy." Anglo-Americans enjoyed very real advantages in 1835. They were "defending" terrain with which they were familiar. The 5,000 Mexicans living in the territory did not join them, but the Anglo population had swelled to almost 30,000. The Mexican nation was divided, and the centers of power were thousands of miles from Texas. From the interior of Mexico, Santa Anna led an army of about 6,000 conscripts, many of whom had been forced into the army and then marched hundreds of miles over hot, arid desert land. Many were Mayan and did not speak Spanish. In February 1836 the majority arrived in Texas, sick and ill-prepared to fight.

In San Antonio the dissidents took refuge in a former mission, the Alamo. The siege began in the first week of March. In the days that followed, the defenders inflicted heavy casualties on the Mexican forces, but eventually the Mexicans won out. A score of popular books have been written about Mexican cruelty in relation to the Alamo and about the heroics of the doomed men. The result was the creation of the Alamo myth. Within the broad framework of what actually happened—187 filibusters barricading themselves in the Alamo in defiance of Santa Anna's force, which, according to Mexican sources, numbered 1,400, and the eventual triumph of the Mexicans—there has been major distortion.

Walter Lord, in an article entitled "Myths and Realities of the Alamo," sets the record straight. Texas mythology portrays the Alamo heroes as freedom-loving defenders of their homes; supposedly they were all good Texans. Actually, two-thirds of the defenders had recently arrived from the United States, and only a half dozen had been in Texas for more than six years. The men in the Alamo were adventurers. William Barret Travis had fled to Texas after killing a man, abandoning his wife and two children. James Bowie, an infamous brawler, made a fortune running slaves and had wandered into Texas searching for lost mines and more money. The fading Davey Crockett, a legend in his own time, fought for the sake of fighting. Many in the Alamo had come to Texas for riches and glory. These defenders were hardly the sort of men who could be classified as peaceful settlers fighting for their homes.

The folklore of the Alamo goes beyond the legendary names of the defenders. According to Lord, it is riddled with dramatic half-truths that have been accepted as history. Defenders are portrayed as selfless heroes who sacrificed their lives to buy more time for their comrades-in-arms. As the story goes, William Barret Travis told his men that they were doomed; he drew a line in the sand with his sword, saying that all who crossed it would elect to remain and fight to the last. Supposedly all the men there valiantly stepped across the line, with a man in a cot begging to be carried across it. Countless Hollywood movies have dramatized the bravery of the defenders.

In reality the Alamo had little strategic value, it was the best protected fort west of the Mississippi, and the men fully expected help. The defenders had 21 cannons to the Mexicans' 8 or 10. They were expert shooters equipped with rifles with a range of 200 yards, while the Mexicans were inadequately trained and armed with smooth-bore muskets with a range of only 70 yards. The Anglos were protected by the walls and had clear shots, while the Mexicans advanced in the open and fired at concealed targets. In short, ill-prepared, ill-equipped, and ill-fed Mexicans attacked well-armed and professional soldiers. In addition, from all reliable sources, it is doubtful whether Travis ever drew a line in the sand. San Antonio survivors, females and noncombatants, did not tell the story until many years later, when the tale had gained currency and the myth was legend. Probably the most widely circulated story was that of the last stand of the aging Davey Crockett, who fell "fighting like a tiger," killing Mexicans with his bare hands. This is a myth; seven of the defenders surrendered, and Crockett was among them. They were executed. And, finally, one man, Louis Rose, did escape.

Travis's stand delayed Santa Anna's timetable by only four days, as the Mexicans took San Antonio on March 6, 1836. At first, the stand at the Alamo did not even have propaganda value. Afterwards, Houston's army dwindled, with many volunteers rushing home to help their families flee from the advancing Mexican army. Most Anglo-Americans realized that they had been badly beaten. It did, nevertheless, result in massive aid from the United States in the form of volunteers, weapons and money. The cry of "Remember the Alamo" became a call to arms for Anglo-Americans in both Texas and the United States.

After the Alamo and the defeat of another garrison at Goliad, southeast of San Antonio, Santa Anna was in full control. He ran Sam Houston out of the territory northwest of the San Jacinto River and then camped an army of about 1,100 men near San Jacinto. There, he skirmished with Houston on April 20, 1836, but did not follow up his advantage. Predicting that Houston would attack on April 22, Santa Anna and his troops settled down and rested for the anticipated battle. The filibusters, however, attacked during the *siesta* hour on April 21. Santa Anna knew that Houston had an army of 1,000, yet he was lax in his precautionary defenses. The surprise attack caught him totally off guard. Shouts of "Remember the Alamo! Remember Goliad!" filled the air. Houston's successful surprise attack ended the war. He captured Santa Anna, who signed the territory away. Although the Mexican Congress repudiated the treaty, Houston was elected president of the Republic of Texas.

Few Mexican prisoners were taken at the battle of San Jacinto. Those who surrendered "were clubbed and stabbed, some on their knees. The slaughter . . . became methodical: the Texan riflemen knelt and poured a steady fire into the packed, jostling ranks." They shot the "Meskins" down as they fled. The final count showed 630 Mexicans dead versus 2 Texans.

Even Santa Anna was not let off lightly; according to Dr. Castañeda, Santa Anna "was mercilessly dragged from the ship he had boarded, subjected to more than six months' mental torture and indignities in Texas prison camps."

The Euroamerican victory paved the way for the Mexican-American War. Officially the United States had not taken sides, but men, money, and supplies poured in to aid fellow Anglo-Americans. U.S. citizens participated in the invasion of Texas with the open support of their government. Mexico's minister to the United States, Manuel Eduardo Gorostiza, protested the "arming and shipment of troops and supplies to territory which was part of Mexico, and the dispatch of United States troops into territory clearly defined by treaty as Mexican territory." General Edmund P. Gaines, Southwest commander, was sent into western Louisiana on January 23, 1836; shortly thereafter, he crossed into Texas in an action that was interpreted to be in support of the Anglo-American filibusters in Texas: "The Jackson Administration made it plain to the Mexican minister that it mattered little whether Mexico approved, that the important thing was to protect the border against Indians and Mexicans." U.S. citizens in and out of Texas loudly applauded Jackson's actions. The Mexican minister resigned his post in protest. "The success of the Texas Revolution thrust the Anglo-American frontier up against the Far Southwest, and the region came at once into the scope of Anglo ambition."

The Invasion of Mexico

In the mid-1840s, Mexico was again the target. Expansion and capitalist development moved together. The two Mexican wars gave U.S. commerce, industry, mining, agriculture, and stockraising a tremendous stimulus. "The truth is that [by the 1840s] the Pacific Coast belonged to the commercial empire that the United States was already building in that ocean."

The U.S. population of 17 million people of European extraction and 3 million slaves was considerably larger than Mexico's 7 million, of which 4 million were Indian and 3 million *mestizo* and European. The United States acted arrogantly in foreign affairs, partly because its citizens believed in their own cultural and racial superiority. Mexico was plagued with financial problems, internal ethnic conflicts, and poor leadership. General anarchy within the nation conspired against its cohesive development.

By 1844 war with Mexico over Texas and the Southwest was only a matter of time. James K. Polk, who strongly advocated the annexation of Texas and expansionism in general, won the presidency by only a small margin, but his election was interpreted as a mandate for national expansion. Outgoing President Tyler acted by calling upon Congress to annex Texas by joint resolution; the measure was passed a few days before the inauguration of Polk, who accepted the arrangement. In December 1845, Texas became a state.

Mexico promptly broke off diplomatic relations with the United States, and Polk ordered General Zachary Taylor into Texas to "protect" the border. The location of the border was in doubt. The North Americans claimed it was at the Río Grande, but based on historical precedent, Mexico insisted it was 150 miles farther north, at the Nueces River. Taylor marched his forces across the Nueces into the disputed territory, wanting to provoke an attack.

In November 1845, Polk sent John Slidell on a secret mission to Mexico to negotiate for the disputed area. The presence of Anglo-American troops between the Nueces and the Río Grande and the annexation of Texas made negotiations an absurdity. They refused to accept Polk's minister's credentials, although they did offer to give him an ad hoc status. Slidell declined anything less than full recognition and returned to Washington in March 1846, convinced that Mexico would have to be "chastised" before it would negotiate. By March 28, Taylor had advanced to the Río Grande with an army of 4,000.

Polk, incensed at Mexico's refusal to meet with Slidell on his terms and at General Mairano Paredes's reaffirmation of his country's claims to all of Texas, began to draft his declaration of war when he learned of the Mexican attack on U.S. troops in the disputed territory. Polk immediately declared that the United States had been provoked into war, that Mexico had "shed American blood upon the American soil." On May 13, 1846, Congress declared war and authorized the recruitment and supplying of 50,000 troops.

Years later, Ulysses S. Grant wrote that he believed that Polk provoked the war and that the annexation of Texas was, in fact, an act of aggression. He added: "I had a horror of the Mexican War . . . only I had not moral courage enough to resign. . . . I considered my supreme duty was to my flag."

The poorly equipped and poorly led Mexican army stood little chance against the expansion-minded Anglos. Even before the war Polk planned the campaign in stages: (1) Mexicans would be cleared out of Texas; (2) Anglos would occupy California and New Mexico; and (3) U.S. forces would march to Mexico City to force the beaten government to make peace on Polk's terms. And that was the way the campaign basically went. In the end, at a relatively small cost in men and money, the war netted the United States huge territorial gains. In all, the United States took over 1 million square miles from Mexico.

The Rationale for Conquest

In his *Origins of the War with Mexico: The Polk-Stockton Intrigue*, Glenn W. Price states: "Americans have found it rather more difficult than other peoples to deal rationally with their wars. We have thought of ourselves as unique, and of this society as specially planned and created to avoid the errors of all other nations." Many Anglo-American historians have attempted to dismiss it simply as a "bad war," which took place during the era of Manifest Destiny.

Manifest Destiny had its roots in Puritan ideas, which continue to influence Anglo-American thought to this day. According to the Puritan ethic, salvation is determined by God. The establishment of the City of God on earth is not only the duty of those chosen people predestined for salvation but is also the proof of their state of grace. Anglo-Americans believed that God had made them custodians of democracy and that they had a mission—that is, that they were predestined to spread its principles. As the young nation survived its infancy, established its power in the defeat of the British in the War of 1812, expanded westward, and enjoyed both commercial and industrial success, its sense of mission heightened. Many citizens believed that God had destined them to own and occupy all of the land from ocean to ocean and pole to pole. Their mission, their destiny made manifest, was to spread the principles of democracy and Christianity to the unfortunates of the hemisphere. By dismissing the war simply as part of the era of Manifest Destiny the apologists for the war ignore the consequences of the doctrine.

The Monroe Doctrine of the 1820s told the world that the Americas were no longer open for colonization or conquest; however, it did not say anything about that limitation applying to the United States. Uppermost in the minds of the U.S. government, the military, and much of the public was the acquisition of territory. No one ever intended to leave Mexico without extracting territory. Land was the main motive for the war.

This aggression was justified by a rhetoric of peace. Consider, for example, Polk's war message of May 11, 1846, in which he gave his reasons for going to war:

> The strong desire to establish peace with Mexico on liberal and honorable terms, and the readiness of this Government to regulate and adjust our boundary and other causes of difference with that power on such fair and equitable principles as would lead to permanent relations of the most friendly nature, induced me in September last to seek reopening of diplomatic relations between the two countries.

The United States, he continued, had made every effort not to provoke Mexico, but the Mexican government had refused to receive an Anglo-American minister. Polk reviewed the events leading to the war and concluded:

> As war exists, and notwithstanding all our efforts to avoid it, exists by the act of Mexico herself, we are called upon by every consideration of duty and patriotism to vindicate with decision the honor, the rights, and the interests of our country.

Historical distance from the war has not lessened the need to justify U.S. aggression. In 1920 Justin H. Smith received a Pulitzer prize in history for a work that blamed the war on Mexico. What is amazing is that Smith allegedly examined over 100,000 manuscripts, 120,000 books and pamphlets, and 200 or more periodicals to come to this conclusion. He was rewarded for relieving the Anglo-American conscience. His two-volume "study," entitled *The War with Mexico,* used analyses such as the following to support its thesis that the Mexicans were at fault for the war:

> At the beginning of her independent existence, our people felt earnestly and enthusiastically anxious to maintain cordial relations with our sister republic, and many crossed the line of absurd sentimentality in the cause. Friction was inevitable, however. The Americans were direct, positive, brusque, angular and pushing; and they would not understand their neighbors in the south. The Mexicans were equally unable to fathom our goodwill, sincerity, patriotism, resoluteness and courage; and certain features of their character and national condition made it far from easy to get on with them.

This attitude of self-righteousness on the part of government officials and historians toward U.S. aggressions spills over to the relationships between the majority society and minority groups. Anglo-Americans believe that the war was advantageous to the Southwest and to the Mexicans who remained or later migrated there. They now had the benefits of democracy and were liberated from their tyrannical past. In other words, Mexicans should be grateful to the Anglo-Americans. If Mexicans and the Anglo-Americans clash, the rationale runs, naturally it is because Mexicans cannot understand or appreciate the merits of a free society, which must be defended against ingrates. Therefore, domestic war, or repression, is justified by the same kind of rhetoric that justifies international aggression.

Professor Gene M. Brack questions historians who base their research on Justin Smith's outdated work: "American historians have consistently praised Justin Smith's influential and outrageously ethnocentric account."

The Myth of a Nonviolent Nation

Most studies on the Mexican-American War dwell on the causes and results of the war, sometimes dealing with war strategy. One must go beyond this point, since the war left bitterness, and since Anglo-American actions in Mexico are vividly remembered. Mexicans' attitude toward Anglo-Americans has been influenced by the war just as the easy victory of the United States conditioned Anglo-American behavior toward Mexicans. Fortunately, some Anglo-Americans condemned this aggression and flatly accused their leaders of being insolent and land-hungry, and of having manufactured the war. Abiel Abbott Livermore in *The War with Mexico Reviewed,* accused his country, writing:

> Again, the pride of race has swollen to still greater insolence the pride of country, always quite active enough for the due observance of the claims of universal brotherhood. The Anglo-Saxons have been apparently persuaded to think themselves the chosen people, annointed race of the Lord, commissioned to drive out the heathen, and plant their religion and institutions in every Canaan they could subjugate.... Our treatment both of the red man and the black man has habituated us to feel our power and forget right.... The passion for land, also, is a leading characteristic of the American people.... The god Terminus is an unknown deity in America. Like the hunger of the pauper boy of fiction, the cry had been, 'more, more, give us more.'

Livermore's work, published in 1850, was awarded the American Peace Society prize for "the best review of the Mexican War and the principles of Christianity, and an enlightened statesmanship."

In truth, the United States conducted a violent and brutal war. Zachary Taylor's artillery leveled the Mexican city of Matamoros, killing hundreds of innocent civilians with *la bomba* (the bomb). Many Mexicans jumped into the Río Grande, relieved of their pain by a watery grave. The occupation that followed was even more terrorizing. Taylor was unable to control his volunteers:

> The regulars regarded the volunteers, of whom about two thousand had reached Matamoros by the end of May, with impatience and contempt.... They robbed Mexicans of their cattle and corn, stole their fences for firewood, got drunk, and killed several inoffensive inhabitants of the town in the streets....

The Treaty of Guadalupe Hidalgo

By late August 1847 the war was almost at an end. Scott's defeat of Santa Anna in a hard-fought battle at Churubusco put Anglo-Americans at the gates of Mexico City. Santa Anna made overtures for an armistice that broke down after two weeks, and the war resumed. On September 13, 1847, Scott drove into the city. Although Mexicans fought valiantly, the battle left 4,000 dead, with another 3,000 prisoners. On September 13, before the occupation of Mexico City began, *Los Niños Héroes* (The Boy Heroes) leapt to their deaths rather than surrender. These teenage cadets were Francisco Márquez, Agustín Melgar, Juan Escutia, Fernando Montes de Oca, Vicente Suárez, and Juan de la Barrera. They became "a symbol and image of this unrighteous war."

The Mexicans continued fighting. The presiding justice of the Supreme Court, Manuel de la Peña, assumed the presidency. He knew that Mexico had lost and that he had to salvage as much as possible. Pressure increased, with U.S. troops in control of much of Mexico.

Nicholas Trist, sent to Mexico to act as peace commissioner, had arrived in Vera Cruz on May 6, 1847, but controversy with Scott over Trist's authority and illness delayed an armistice, and hostilities continued. After the fall of Mexico City, Secretary of State James Buchanan wanted to revise Trist's instructions. He ordered Trist to break off negotiations and return home. Polk wanted more land from Mexico. Trist, however, with the support of Winfield Scott, decided to ignore Polk's order, and began negotiations on January 2, 1848, on the original terms. Mexico, badly beaten, her government in a state of turmoil, had no choice but to agree to the Anglo-Americans' proposals.

On February 2, 1848, the Mexicans ratified the Treaty of Guadalupe Hidalgo, with Mexico accepting the Río Grande as the Texas border and ceding the Southwest (which incorporated the present-day states of California, New Mexico, Nevada, and parts of Colorado, Arizona, and Utah) to the United States in return for $15 million.

Polk, furious about the treaty, considered Trist "contemptibly base" for having ignored his orders. Yet he had no choice but to submit the treaty to the Senate. With the exception of Article X, which concerned the rights of Mexicans in the ceded territory, the Senate ratified the treaty on March 10, 1848, by a vote of 28 to 14. To insist on more territory would have meant more fighting, and both Polk and the Senate realized that the war was already unpopular in many circles. The treaty was sent to the Mexican Congress for ratification; although the Congress had difficulty forming a quorum, the treaty was ratified on May 19 by a 52 to 35 vote. Hostilities between the two nations officially ended. Trist, however, was branded as a "scoundrel," because Polk was disappointed in the settlement. There was considerable support in the United States for acquisition of all Mexico.

During the treaty talks Mexican negotiators, concerned about Mexicans left behind, expressed great reservations about these people being forced to "merge or blend" into Anglo-American culture. They protested the exclusion of provisions that protected Mexican citizens' rights, land titles, and religion. They wanted to protect their rights by treaty.

Articles VIII, IX, and X specifically referred to the rights of Mexicans. Under the treaty, Mexicans left behind had one year to choose whether to return to Mexico or remain in "occupied Mexico." About 2,000 elected to leave; most remained in what they considered *their* land.

Article IX of the treaty guaranteed Mexicans "the enjoyment of all the rights of citizens of the United States according to the principles of the Constitution; and in the meantime shall be maintained and protected in the free enjoyment of their liberty and property, and secured in the free exercise of their religion without restriction." Lynn I. Perrigo, in *The American Southwest,* summarizes the guarantees of Articles VIII and IX: "In other words, besides the rights and duties of American citizenship, they [the Mexicans] would have some special privileges derived from their previous customs in language, law, and religion."

The omitted Article X had comprehensive guarantees protecting "all prior and pending titles to property of every description." When Article X was deleted by the U.S. Senate, Mexican officials protested. Anglo-American emissaries reassured them by drafting a Statement of Protocol on May 26, 1848:

> The American government by suppressing the Xth article of the Treaty of Guadalupe Hidalgo did not in any way intend to annul the grants of lands made by Mexico in the ceded territories. These grants . . . preserve the legal value which they may possess, and the grantees may cause their legitimate (titles) to be acknowledged before the American tribunals.
>
> Conformable to the law of the United States, legitimate titles to every description of property, personal and real, existing in the ceded territories, are those which were legitimate titles under the Mexican law of California and New Mexico up to the 13th of May, 1846, and in Texas up to the 2nd of March, 1836.

Considering the Mexican opposition to the treaty, it is doubtful whether the Mexican Congress would have ratified the treaty without this clarification. The vote was close.

The Statement of Protocol was strengthened by Articles VIII and IX, which guaranteed Mexicans rights of property and protection under the law. In addition, court decisions have generally interpreted the treaty as protecting land titles and water rights. In practice, however, the treaty was ignored and during the nineteenth century most Mexicans in the United States were considered as a class apart from the dominant race. Nearly every one of the obligations discussed above was violated, confirming the prophecy of Mexican diplomat Manuel Crescion Rejón, who, at the time the treaty was signed, commented:

> Our race, our unfortunate people will have to wander in search of hospitality in a strange land, only to be ejected later. Descendants of the Indians that we are, the North Americans hate us, their spokesmen depreciate us, even if they recognize the justice of our cause, and they consider us unworthy to form with them one nation and one society, they clearly manifest that their future expansion begins with the territory that they take from us and pushing [sic] aside our citizens who inhabit the land.

As a result of the Texas War and the Anglo-American aggressions of 1845–1848, the occupation of conquered territory began. In material terms, in exchange for 12,000 lives and more than $100 million, the United States acquired a colony two and a half times as large as France, containing rich farmlands and natural resources such as gold, silver, zinc, copper, oil, and uranium, which would make possible its unprecedented industrial boom. It acquired ports on the Pacific that generated further economic expansion across that ocean. Mexico was left with its shrunken resources to face the continued advances of the United States.

Summary

The colonial experience of the United States differs from that of Third World nations. Its history resembles that of Australia and/or South Africa, where colonizers relegated indigenous populations to fourth-class citizenship or noncitizenship. North American independence came at the right time, slightly predating the industrialization of nineteenth-century Europe. Its merchants took over a lucrative trade network from the British; the new Republic established a government that supported trade, industry, and commercial agriculture. A North American ideology which presumed that Latin Americans had stolen the name "America" and that God, the realtor, had given them the land, encouraged colonial expansion.

Mexico, like most Third World nations after independence, needed a period of stability. North American penetration into Texas in the 1820s and 1830s threatened Mexico. The U.S. economic system encouraged expansion, and many of the first wave of migrants to Texas had lost their farms due to the depression of 1819. Land in Texas, generously cheap, provided room for the spread of slavery. Although many North Americans in all probability intended to obey Mexican laws and meet conditions for obtaining land grants, North American ethnocentricism and self-interest soon eroded those intentions. Clearly land values would zoom if Texas were part of the United States.

North American historians have frequently portrayed the Texas invasion as a second encounter in the "American War of Independence." Myths such as that of a tyrannical Mexican government have justified the war. In truth, the cause of the war was profit. Mexico did not invade Texas; it belonged to Mexico. Few if any of the North Americans in Texas had been born there or had lived in Texas for more than five years. Most had just recently arrived. Some rich Mexicans supported the North Americans for obvious reasons—it was in their economic self-interest. A stalemate resulted, with Euroamericans establishing the Texas Republic. In 1844, the United States broke the standoff and annexed Texas.

President James K. Polk manufactured the war with Mexico. Some North Americans opposed the war—not on grounds that it violated Mexico's territorial integrity, but because of the probability of the extension of slavery. Many North American military leaders admitted that the war was unjust, and that the United States had committed an act of aggression. However, patriotism and support for the war overwhelmed reason in the march "To the Halls of the Montezumas [sic]." North Americans, buoyant in their prosperity, wanted to prove that the United States was a world-class power.

The war became a Protestant Crusade. Texans made emotional pleas to avenge the Alamo. Both appeals were instrumental in arousing North Americans to the call to arms, to prove their valor and power of the young "American" democracy. North American soldiers committed atrocities against Mexican civilians; few were punished.

The Treaty of Guadalupe Hidalgo ended the war, and the United States grabbed over half of Mexico's soil. The war proved costly to Mexico and to Mexicans left behind. According to the treaty, Mexicans who elected to stay in the conquered territory would become U.S. citizens with all the rights of citizenship. However, the Treaty of Guadalupe Hidalgo, like those signed with the indigenous people of North American, depended on the good faith of the United States and its ability to keep its word.

NO

Norman A. Graebner

The Mexican War: A Study in Causation

On May 11, 1846, President James K. Polk presented his war message to Congress. After reviewing the skirmish between General Zachary Taylor's dragoons and a body of Mexican soldiers along the Rio Grande, the president asserted that Mexico "has passed the boundary of the United States, has invaded our territory and shed American blood upon the American soil.... War exists, and, notwithstanding all our efforts to avoid it, exists by act of Mexico." No country could have had a superior case for war. Democrats in large numbers (for it was largely a partisan matter) responded with the patriotic fervor which Polk expected of them. "Our government has permitted itself to be insulted long enough," wrote one Georgian. "The blood of her citizens has been spilt on her own soil. It appeals to us for vengeance." Still, some members of Congress, recalling more accurately than the president the circumstances of the conflict, soon rendered the Mexican War the most reviled in American history —at least until the Vietnam War of the 1960s. One outraged Whig termed the war "illegal, unrighteous, and damnable," and Whigs questioned both Polk's honesty and his sense of geography. Congressman Joshua R. Giddings of Ohio accused the president of "planting the standard of the United States on foreign soil, and using the military forces of the United States to violate every principle of international law and moral justice." To vote for the war, admitted Senator John C. Calhoun, was "to plunge a dagger into his own heart, and more so." Indeed, some critics in Congress openly wished the Mexicans well.

For over a century such profound differences in perception have pervaded American writings on the Mexican War. Even in the past decade, historians have reached conclusions on the question of war guilt as disparate as those which separated Polk from his wartime conservative and abolitionist critics....

In some measure the diversity of judgment on the Mexican War, as on other wars, is understandable. By basing their analyses on official rationalizations, historians often ignore the more universal causes of war which transcend individual conflicts and which can establish the bases for greater consensus. Neither the officials in Washington nor those in Mexico City ever acknowledged any alternatives to the actions which they took. But governments generally

From Norman A. Graebner, "The Mexican War: A Study in Causation," *Pacific Historical Review,* vol. 49, no. 3 (August 1980), pp. 405–426. Copyright © 1980 by The American Historical Association, Pacific Coast Branch. Reprinted by permission of The University of California Press Journals. Notes omitted.

have more choices in any controversy than they are prepared to admit. Circumstances determine their extent. The more powerful a nation, the more remote its dangers, the greater its options between action and inaction. Often for the weak, unfortunately, the alternative is capitulation or war.... Polk and his advisers developed their Mexican policies on the dual assumption that Mexico was weak and that the acquisition of certain Mexican territories would satisfy admirably the long-range interests of the United States. Within that context, Polk's policies were direct, timely, and successful. But the president had choices. Mexico, whatever its internal condition, was no direct threat to the United States. Polk, had he so desired, could have avoided war; indeed, he could have ignored Mexico in 1845 with absolute impunity.

࿊

In explaining the Mexican War historians have dwelled on the causes of friction in American-Mexican relations. In part these lay in the disparate qualities of the two populations, in part in the vast discrepancies between the two countries in energy, efficiency, power, and national wealth. Through two decades of independence Mexico had experienced a continuous rise and fall of governments; by the 1840s survival had become the primary concern of every regime. Conscious of their weakness, the successive governments in Mexico City resented the superior power and effectiveness of the United States and feared American notions of destiny that anticipated the annexation of Mexico's northern provinces. Having failed to prevent the formation of the Texas Republic, Mexico reacted to Andrew Jackson's recognition of Texan independence in March 1837 with deep indignation. Thereafter the Mexican raids into Texas, such as the one on San Antonio in 1842, aggravated the bitterness of Texans toward Mexico, for such forays had no purpose beyond terrorizing the frontier settlements.

Such mutual animosities, extensive as they were, do not account for the Mexican War. Governments as divided and chaotic as the Mexican regimes of the 1840s usually have difficulty in maintaining positive and profitable relations with their neighbors; their behavior often produces annoyance, but seldom armed conflict. Belligerence toward other countries had flowed through U.S. history like a torrent without, in itself, setting off a war. Nations do not fight over cultural differences or verbal recriminations; they fight over perceived threats to their interests created by the ambitions or demands of others.

What increased the animosity between Mexico City and Washington was a series of specific issues over which the two countries perennially quarreled—claims, boundaries, and the future of Texas. Nations have made claims a pretext for intervention, but never a pretext for war. Every nineteenth-century effort to collect debts through force assumed the absence of effective resistance, for no debt was worth the price of war. To collect its debt from Mexico in 1838, for example, France blockaded Mexico's gulf ports and bombarded Vera Cruz. The U.S. claims against Mexico created special problems which discounted their seriousness as a rationale for war. True, the Mexican government failed to protect the possessions and the safety of Americans in Mexico from robbery, theft, and other illegal actions, but U.S. citizens were under no obligation to do business in Mexico and should have understood the risk of transporting goods and money in that country. Minister Waddy Thompson wrote from Mexico City in 1842 that it would be "with somewhat of bad grace that we should war upon a country because it could not pay its debts when so many of our own states are in the same situation." Even as the United States after 1842 attempted futilely to collect the $2 million awarded its citizens by a claims commission, it was far more deeply in debt to Britain over speculative losses. Minister Wilson Shannon reported in the summer of 1844 that the claims issue defied settlement in Mexico City and recommended that Washington take the needed action to compel Mexico to pay. If Polk would take up the challenge and sacrifice American human and material resources in a war against Mexico, he would do so for reasons other than the enforcement of claims. The president knew well that Mexico could not pay, yet as late as May 9, 1846, he was ready to ask Congress for a declaration of war on the question of unpaid claims alone.

Congress's joint resolution for Texas annexation in February 1845 raised the specter of war among editors and politicians alike. As early as 1843 the Mexican government had warned the American minister in Mexico City that annexation would render war inevitable; Mexican officials in Washington repeated that warning. To Mexico, therefore, the move to annex Texas was an unbearable affront. Within one month after Polk's inauguration on March 4, General Juan Almonte, the Mexican minister in Washington, boarded a packet in New York and sailed for Vera Cruz to sever his country's diplomatic relations with the United States. Even before the Texas Convention could meet on July 4 to vote annexation, rumors of a possible Mexican invasion of Texas prompted Polk to advance Taylor's forces from Fort Jesup in Louisiana down the Texas coast. Polk instructed Taylor to extend his protection to the Rio Grande but to avoid any areas to the north of that river occupied by Mexican troops. Simultaneously the president reinforced the American squadron in the Gulf of Mexico. "The threatened invasion of Texas by a large Mexican army," Polk informed Andrew J. Donelson, the American chargé in Texas, on June 15, "is well calculated to excite great interest here and increases our solicitude concerning the final action by the Congress and the Convention of Texas." Polk assured Donelson that he intended to defend Texas to the limit of his constitutional power. Donelson resisted the pressure of those Texans who wanted Taylor to advance to the Rio Grande; instead, he placed the general at Corpus Christi on the Nueces River. Taylor agreed that the line from the mouth of the Nueces to San Antonio covered the Texas settlements and afforded a favorable base from which to defend the frontier.

Those who took the rumors of Mexican aggressiveness seriously lauded the president's action. With Texas virtually a part of the United States, argued the *Washington Union*, "We owe it to ourselves, to the proud and elevated character which America maintains among the nations of the earth, to guard our own territory from the invasion of the ruthless Mexicans." The *New York Morning News* observed that Polk's policy would, on the whole, "command a general concurrence of the public opinion of his country." Some Democratic leaders, fearful of a Mexican attack, urged the president to strengthen Taylor's forces and order them to take the offensive should Mexican soldiers cross the Rio Grande. Others believed the reports from Mexico exaggerated, for there was no apparent relationship between the country's expressions of belligerence and its capacity to act. Secretary of War William L. Marcy admitted that his information was no better than that of other commentators. "I have at no time," he wrote in July, "felt that war with Mexico was probable—and do not now believe it is, yet it is in the range of possible occurrences. I have officially acted on the hypothesis that our peace may be temporarily disturbed without however believing it will be." Still convinced that the administration had no grounds for alarm, Marcy wrote on August 12: "The presence of a considerable force in Texas will do no hurt and possibly may be of great use." In September William S. Parrott, Polk's special agent in Mexico, assured the president that there would be neither a Mexican declaration of war nor an invasion of Texas.

Polk insisted that the administration's show of force in Texas would prevent rather than provoke war. "I do not anticipate that Mexico will be mad enough to declare war," he wrote in July, but "I think she would have done so but for the appearance of a strong naval force in the Gulf and our army moving in the direction of her frontier on land." Polk restated this judgment on July 28 in a letter to General Robert Armstrong, the U.S. consul at Liverpool: "I think there need be but little apprehension of war with Mexico. If however she shall be mad enough to make war we are prepared to meet her." The president assured Senator William H. Haywood of North Carolina that the American forces in Texas would never aggress against Mexico; however, they would prevent any Mexican forces from crossing the Rio Grande. In conversation with Senator William S. Archer of Virginia on September 1, the president added confidently that "the appearance of our land and naval forces on the borders of Mexico & in the Gulf would probably deter and prevent Mexico from either declaring war or invading Texas." Polk's continuing conviction that Mexico would not attack suggests that his deployment of U.S. land and naval forces along Mexico's periphery was designed less to protect Texas than to support an aggressive diplomacy which might extract a satisfactory treaty from Mexico without war. For Anson Jones, the last president of the Texas Republic, Polk's deployments had precisely that purpose:

> Texas never actually needed the protection of the United States after I came into office.... There was no necessity for it after the 'preliminary Treaty,' as we were at peace with Mexico, and knew perfectly well that that Government, though she might bluster a little, had not the slightest idea of invading Texas either by land or water; and that nothing would provoke her to (active) hostilities, but the presence of troops in the immediate neighborhood of the Rio Grande, threatening her towns and settlements on the southwest side of that river.... But Donelson appeared so intent upon 'encumbering us with help,' that finally, to get rid of his annoyance, he was told he might give us as much protection as he pleased.... The protection asked for was only *prospective* and contingent; the *protection* he had in view was *immediate* and *aggressive.*

For Polk the exertion of military and diplomatic pressure on a disorganized Mexico was not a prelude to war. Whig critics of annexation had predicted war; this alone compelled the administration to avoid a conflict over Texas. In his memoirs Jones recalled that in 1845 Commodore Robert F. Stockton, with either the approval or the connivance of Polk, attempted to convince him that he should place Texas "in an attitude of active hostility toward Mexico, so that, when Texas was finally brought into the Union, *she might bring war with her.*" If Stockton engaged in such an intrigue, he apparently did so on his own initiative, for no evidence exists to implicate the administration. Polk not only preferred to achieve his purposes by means other than war but also assumed that his military measures in Texas, limited as they were, would convince the Mexican government that it could not escape the necessity of coming to terms with the United States. Washington's policy toward Mexico during 1845 achieved the broad national purpose of Texas annexation. Beyond that it brought U.S. power to bear on Mexico in a manner calculated to further the processes of negotiation. Whether the burgeoning tension would lead to a negotiated boundary settlement or to war hinged on two factors: the nature of Polk's demands and Mexico's response to them. The president announced his objectives to Mexico's troubled officialdom through his instructions to John Slidell, his special emissary who departed for Mexico in November 1845 with the assurance that the government there was prepared to reestablish formal diplomatic relations with the United States and negotiate a territorial settlement. . . .

Actually, Slidell's presence in Mexico inaugurated a diplomatic crisis not unlike those which precede most wars. Fundamentally the Polk administration, in dispatching Slidell, gave the Mexicans the same two choices that the dominant power in any confrontation gives to the weaker: the acceptance of a body of concrete diplomatic demands or eventual war. Slidell's instructions described U.S. territorial objectives with considerable clarity. If Mexico knew little of Polk's growing acquisitiveness toward California during the autumn of 1845, Slidell proclaimed the president's intentions with his proposals to purchase varying portions of California for as much as $25 million. Other countries such as England and Spain had consigned important areas of the New World through peaceful negotiations, but the United States, except in its Mexican relations, had never asked any country to part with a portion of its own territory. Yet Polk could not understand why Mexico should reveal any special reluctance to part with Texas, the Rio Grande, New Mexico, or California. What made the terms of Slidell's instructions appear fair to him was Mexico's military and financial helplessness. Polk's defenders noted that California was not a sine qua non of any settlement and that the president offered to settle the immediate controversy over the acquisition of the Rio Grande boundary alone in exchange for the cancellation of claims. Unfortunately, amid the passions of December 1845, such distinctions were lost. Furthermore, a settlement of the Texas boundary would not have resolved the California question at all.

Throughout the crisis months of 1845 and 1846, spokesmen of the Polk administration repeatedly warned the Mexican government that its choices were limited. In June 1845, Polk's mouthpiece, the *Washington Union*, had observed characteristically that, if Mexico resisted Washington's demands, "a corps of properly organized volunteers... would invade, overrun, and occupy Mexico. They would enable us not only to take California, but to keep it." American officials, in their contempt for Mexico, spoke privately of the need to chastize that country for its annoyances and insults. Parrott wrote to Secretary of State James Buchanan in October that he wished "to see this people well flogged by Uncle Sam's boys, ere we enter upon negotiations.... I know [the Mexicans] better, perhaps, than any other American citizen and I am fully persuaded, they can never love or respect us, as we should be loved and respected by them, until we shall have given them a positive proof of our superiority." Mexico's pretensions would continue, wrote Slidell in late December, "until the Mexican people shall be convinced by hostile demonstrations, that our differences must be settled promptly, either by negotiation or the sword." In January 1846 the *Union* publicly threatened Mexico with war if it rejected the just demands of the United States: "The result of such a course on her part may compel us to resort to more decisive measures.... to obtain the settlement of our legitimate claims." As Slidell prepared to leave Mexico in March 1846, he again reminded the administration: "Depend upon it, we can never get along well with them, until we have given them a good drubbing." In Washington on May 8, Slidell advised the president "to take the redress of the wrongs and injuries which we had so long borne from Mexico into our own hands, and to act with promptness and energy."

Mexico responded to Polk's challenge with an outward display of belligerence and an inward dread of war. Mexicans feared above all that the United States intended to overrun their country and seize much of their territory. Polk and his advisers assumed that Mexico, to avoid an American invasion, would give up its provinces peacefully. Obviously Mexico faced growing diplomatic and military pressures to negotiate away its territories; it faced no moral obligation to do so. Herrera and Paredes had the sovereign right to protect their regimes by avoiding any formal recognition of Slidell and by rejecting any of the boundary proposals embodied in his instructions, provided that in the process they did not endanger any legitimate interests of the American people. At least to some Mexicans, Slidell's terms demanded nothing less than Mexico's capitulation. By what standard was $2 million a proper payment for the Rio Grande boundary, or $25 million a fair price for California? No government would have accepted such terms. Having rejected negotiation in the face of superior force, Mexico would meet the challenge with a final gesture of defiance. In either case it was destined to lose, but historically nations have preferred to fight than to give away territory under diplomatic pressure alone. Gene M. Brack, in his long study of Mexico's deep-seated fear and resentment of the United States, explained Mexico's ultimate behavior in such terms:

> President Polk knew that Mexico could offer but feeble resistance militarily, and he knew that Mexico needed money. No proper American would exchange territory and the national honor for cash, but President Polk mistakenly believed that the application of military pressure would convince Mexicans to do so. They did not respond logically, but patriotically. Left

with the choice of war or territorial concessions, the former course, however dim the prospects of success, could be the only one.

⋘⊚⋙

Mexico, in its resistance, gave Polk the three choices which every nation gives another in an uncompromisable confrontation: to withdraw his demands and permit the issues to drift, unresolved; to reduce his goals in the interest of an immediate settlement; or to escalate the pressures in the hope of securing an eventual settlement on his own terms. Normally when the internal conditions of a country undermine its relations with others, a diplomatic corps simply removes itself from the hostile environment and awaits a better day. Mexico, despite its animosity, did not endanger the security interests of the United States; it had not invaded Texas and did not contemplate doing so. Mexico had refused to pay the claims, but those claims were not equal to the price of a one-week war. Whether Mexico negotiated a boundary for Texas in 1846 mattered little; the United States had lived with unsettled boundaries for decades without considering war. Settlers, in time, would have forced a decision, but in 1846 the region between the Nueces and the Rio Grande was a vast, generally unoccupied wilderness. Thus there was nothing, other than Polk's ambitions, to prevent the United States from withdrawing its diplomats from Mexico City and permitting its relations to drift. But Polk, whatever the language of his instructions, did not send Slidell to Mexico to normalize relations with that government. He expected Slidell to negotiate an immediate boundary settlement favorable to the United States, and nothing less.

Recognizing no need to reduce his demands on Mexico, Polk, without hesitation, took the third course which Mexico offered. Congress bound the president to the annexation of Texas; thereafter the Polk administration was free to formulate its own policies toward Mexico. With the Slidell mission Polk embarked upon a program of gradual coercion to achieve a settlement, preferably without war. That program led logically from his dispatching an army to Texas and his denunciation of Mexico in his annual message of December 1845 to his new instructions of January 1846, which ordered General Taylor to the Rio Grande. Colonel Atocha, spokesman for the deposed Mexican leader, Antonio López de Santa Anna, encouraged Polk to pursue his policy of escalation. The president recorded Atocha's advice:

> He said our army should be marched at once from Corpus Christi to the Del Norte, and a strong naval force assembled at Vera Cruz, that Mr. Slidell, the U.S. Minister, should withdraw from Jalappa, and go on board one of our ships of War at Vera Cruz, and in that position should demand the payment of [the] amount due our citizens; that it was well known the Mexican Government was unable to pay in money, and that when they saw a strong force ready to strike on their coasts and border, they would, he had no doubt, feel their danger and agree to the boundary suggested. He said that Paredes, Almonte, & Gen'l Santa Anna were all willing for such an arrangement, but that they dare not make it until it was made apparent to the Archbishop of Mexico & the people generally that it was necessary to save their country from a war with the U. States.

Thereafter Polk never questioned the efficacy of coercion. He asserted at a cabinet meeting on February 17 that "it would be necessary to take strong measures towards Mexico before our difficulties with that Government could be settled." Similarly on April 18 Polk told Calhoun that "our relations with Mexico had reached a point where we could not stand still but must treat all nations whether weak or strong alike, and that I saw no alternative but strong measures towards Mexico." A week later the president again brought the Mexican question before the cabinet. "I expressed my opinion," he noted in his diary, "that we must take redress for the injuries done us into our own hands, that we had attempted to conciliate Mexico in vain, and had forborne until forbearance was no longer either a virtue or patriotic." Convinced that Paredes needed money, Polk suggested to leading senators that Congress appropriate $1 million both to encourage Paredes to negotiate and to sustain him in power until the United States could ratify the treaty. The president failed to secure Calhoun's required support.

Polk's persistence led him and the country to war. Like all escalations in the exertion of force, his decision responded less to unwanted and unanticipated resistance than to the requirements of the clearly perceived and inflexible purposes which guided the administration. What perpetuated the president's escalation to the point of war was his determination to pursue goals to the end whose achievement lay outside the possibilities of successful negotiations. Senator Thomas Hart Benton of Missouri saw this situation when he wrote: "It is impossible to conceive of an administration less warlike, or more intriguing, than that of Mr. Polk. They were *men of peace, with objects to be accomplished by means of war*; so that war was a necessity and an indispensability to their purpose."

Polk understood fully the state of Mexican opinion. In placing General Taylor on the Rio Grande he revealed again his contempt for Mexico. Under no national obligation to expose the country's armed forces, he would not have advanced Taylor in the face of a superior military force. Mexico had been undiplomatic; its denunciations of the United States were insulting and provocative. But if Mexico's behavior antagonized Polk, it did not antagonize the Whigs, the abolitionists, or even much of the Democratic party. Such groups did not regard Mexico as a threat; they warned the administration repeatedly that Taylor's presence on the Rio Grande would provoke war. But in the balance against peace was the pressure of American expansionism. Much of the Democratic and expansionist press, having accepted without restraint both the purposes of the Polk administration and its charges of Mexican perfidy, urged the president on to more vigorous action....

Confronted with the prospect of further decline which they could neither accept nor prevent, [the Mexicans] lashed out with the intention of protecting their self-esteem and compelling the United States, if it was determined to have the Rio Grande, New Mexico, and California, to pay for its prizes with something other than money. On April 23, Paredes issued a proclamation declaring a defensive war against the United States. Predictably, one day later the Mexicans fired on a detachment of U.S. dragoons. Taylor's report of the attack reached Polk on Saturday evening, May 9. On Sunday the president drafted his war message and delivered it to Congress on the following day. Had Polk avoided the crisis, he might have gained the time required to permit the emigrants of 1845 and 1846 to settle the California issue without war.

What clouds the issue of the Mexican War's justification was the acquisition of New Mexico and California, for contemporaries and historians could not logically condemn the war and laud the Polk administration for its territorial achievements. Perhaps it is true that time would have permitted American pioneers to transform California into another Texas. But even then California's acquisition by the United States would have emanated from the use of force, for the elimination of Mexican sovereignty, whether through revolution or war, demanded the successful use of power. If the power employed in revolution would have been less obtrusive than that exerted in war, its role would have been no less essential. There simply was no way that the United States could acquire California peacefully. If the distraught Mexico of 1845 would not sell the distant province, no regime thereafter would have done so. Without forceful destruction of Mexico's sovereign power, California would have entered the twentieth century as an increasingly important region of another country.

Thus the Mexican War poses the dilemma of all international relations. Nations whose geographic and political status fails to coincide with their ambition and power can balance the two sets of factors in only one manner: through the employment of force. They succeed or fail according to circumstances; and for the United States, the conditions for achieving its empire in the Southwest and its desired frontage on the Pacific were so ideal that later generations could refer to the process as the mere fulfillment of destiny. "The Mexican Republic," lamented a Mexican writer in 1848, "... had among other misfortunes of less account, the great one of being in the vicinity of a strong and energetic people." What the Mexican War revealed in equal measure is the simple fact that only those countries which have achieved their destiny, whatever that may be, can afford to extol the virtues of peaceful change.

POSTSCRIPT

Was the Mexican War an Exercise in American Imperialism?

According to Graebner, President James Polk assumed that Mexico was weak and that acquiring certain Mexican territories would satisfy "the long-range interests" of the United States. But when Mexico refused Polk's attempts to purchase New Mexico and California, he was left with three options: withdraw his demands, modify and soften his proposals, or aggressively pursue his original goals. According to Graebner, the president chose the third option.

Graebner is one of the most prominent members of the "realist" school of diplomatic historians. His writings were influenced by the cold war realists, political scientists, diplomats, and journalists of the 1950s who believed that American foreign policy oscillated between heedless isolationism and crusading wars without developing coherent policies that suited the national interests of the United States.

Graebner's views on the Mexican War have not gone unchallenged. For example, both David M. Pletcher's *The Diplomacy of Annexation* (University of Missouri Press, 1973), which remains the definitive study of the Polk administration, and Charles Seller's biography *James K. Polk*, 2 vols. (Princeton University Press, 1957–1966) are critical of Polk's actions in pushing the Mexican government to assert its authority in the disputed territory.

Acuña offers a Mexican perspective on the war in the first chapter of his book *Occupied America: A History of Chicanos,* 3rd ed. (Harper & Row, 1988), from which his selection is taken. He rejects the cool, detached, realistic analysis of Graebner and argues in very passionate terms that the North Americans waged an unjust, aggressive war against their weaker neighbor to the south for the purpose of profit.

Acuña disagrees with older historians like Justin Smith and Eugene Barker, who justified the war as an inevitable conflict between a unique, nonviolent, capitalist, Protestant, democratic nation whose economic, religious, and political values were superior to a backward, feudal, Catholic, and authoritarian country.

Acuña also takes issue with Graebner, who considers Manifest Destiny to be mere political rhetoric with very limited goals. In Acuña's analysis, Manifest Destiny "had its roots in Puritan ideas, which continue to influence Anglo-American thought to this day. . . . Many citizens believed that God had destined them to own and occupy all of the land from ocean to ocean and pole to pole. Their mission, their destiny made manifest, was to spread the principles of democracy and Christianity to the unfortunates of the hemisphere."

Acuña receives support for his views from American historians like William Appleman Williams, who influenced an entire generation of diplomatic historians with his thesis on economic expansion, *The Tragedy of American Diplomacy* (Delta, 1962). Mexican historian Ramón Eduardo Ruiz, in his book *Triumphs and Tragedy: A History of the Mexican People* (W. W. Norton, 1992), is more balanced and nuanced than Acuña but is just as critical of the racist ideology behind the rhetoric of Manifest Destiny that justified taking land away from not only Mexican Americans but also the North American Indians. In his article "Manifest Destiny and the Mexican War," in Howard H. Quint et al., eds., *Main Problems in American History, vol. 1,* 5th ed. (Dorsey Press, 1988), Ruiz maintains that Mexico never recovered economically from the loss of its territories to the United States 150 years ago. In an interesting twist, Ruiz also contends that the United States did not absorb all of Mexico into the United States after the Mexican War because it did not want any further increase to its nonwhite population base.

Both Graebner and Acuña appear ethnocentric in their analysis of the origins of the war. Graebner neglects the emotionalism and instability of Mexican politics at the time, which may have precluded the rational analysis a realistic historian might have expected in the decision-making process. Acuña also oversimplifies the motives of the Euroamericans, and he appears blinded to the political divisions between slaveholders and nonslaveholders and between Whig and Democratic politicians over the wisdom of going to war with Mexico.

The best two collections of readings from the major writers on the Mexican War are old but essential: see Archie McDonald, ed., *The Mexican War: Crisis for American Democracy* (D. C. Heath, 1969) and Ramón Eduardo Ruiz, ed., *The Mexican War: Was It Manifest Destiny?* (Holt, Rinehart & Winston, 1963).

There are several nontraditional books that cover the Mexican War, including John H. Schroeder, *Mr. Polk's War: American Opposition and Dissent, 1846–1848* (University of Wisconsin Press, 1973). Robert W. Johannsen summarizes the ways in which contemporaries viewed the war in *To the Halls of the Montezumas: The Mexican War in the American Imagination* (Oxford University Press, 1985).

ISSUE 13

Did the Westward Movement Transform the Traditional Roles of Women in the Mid-Nineteenth Century?

YES: Sandra L. Myres, from *Westering Women and the Frontier Experience, 1800–1915* (University of New Mexico Press, 1982)

NO: John Mack Faragher, from *Women and Men on the Overland Trail* (Yale University Press, 1979)

ISSUE SUMMARY

YES: Professor of history Sandra L. Myres (1933–1991) argues that first- and second-generation American women often worked outside the home as teachers, missionaries, doctors, lawyers, ranchers, miners, and businesspeople instead of simply assuming the traditional roles of wife and mother.

NO: According to professor John Mack Faragher, women were reluctant pioneers because they were unwilling to break away from their close networks of female relatives and friends. However, nineteenth-century marital laws gave their husbands the sole authority to make the decision to move west.

In 1893 historian Frederick Jackson Turner (1861–1932) delivered an address before the American Historical Association entitled "The Significance of the Frontier in American History." According to Turner, American civilization was unique and different from European civilization because America contained an abundance of land that was settled in four major waves of migration from 1607 through 1890. During this migration European heritage was shed, and the American characteristics of individualism, mobility, nationalism, and democracy developed.

This frontier theory of American history did not go unchallenged. Other historians stated that Turner's definition of the frontier was too vague; that he underestimated the cultural forces that came to the West from Europe and the eastern states; that he neglected the forces of urbanization and industrialization in colonizing the West; that he placed an undue emphasis on sectional developments and neglected class struggles for power; and that his provincial view of

American history prolonged the isolationist views of a nation that had become involved in world affairs in the twentieth century. By the time Turner died, his thesis had been widely discredited. Historians continued to write about the West, but new fields and new theories were competing for attention.

Until recently, most historians did not consider women a part of western history. One scholar who searched 2,000 pages of Turner's work could find only one paragraph devoted to women. Men built railroads, drove cattle, led military expeditions, and governed territories. "Women," concluded one writer, "were invisible, few in number, and not important to the taming of the West."

When scholars did acknowledge the presence of women on the frontier, perceptions were usually based upon stereotypes that were created by male observers and had become prevalent in American literature. According to Sandra L. Myres, there were three main images. The first image was that of a frightened, tearful woman who lived in a hostile environment and who was overworked, overbirthed, depressed, lonely, and resigned to a hard life and an early death. The second image, in contrast, was that of a helpmate and a civilizer of the frontier who could fight Native Americans as well as take care of the cooking, the cleaning, and the rearing of children. A third image of the westering women was that of the "bad woman," who was more masculine than feminine in her behavior and who was "hefty, grotesque and mean with a pistol."

The proliferation of primary source materials found since the early 1970s —letters, diaries, and memoirs written by frontierswomen—has led to a reassessment of the role of westering women. They are no longer what Joan Hoff Wilson once referred to as the "orphans of women's history." There are disagreements in interpretation, but these disagreements are now based upon sound scholarship. One area where scholars disagree concerns the following issue: Were the traditional roles of women changed by their participation in the westward movements of the nineteenth century?

In the first selection, Sandra L. Myres applies the Turner thesis to women in a positive fashion. Myres states that first- and second-generation women often worked in various fields outside of the home. In the second selection, John Mack Faragher maintains that women were reluctant pioneers because the nineteenth-century marital laws gave their husbands the sole authority to make decisions to move west, thereby forcing their wives to break away from their close networks of female relatives and friends.

Sandra L. Myres

 **YES**

Women as Frontier Entrepreneurs

The West offered challenges to women's skills and provided opportunities for them to develop and test new talents and to broaden the scope of their home and community activities. It also offered, for whatever reason, a significant degree of political participation. But did the West offer economic opportunity as well? Frederick Jackson Turner maintained that the West was a liberating influence in American life and that the frontier setting offered westering Americans, at least westering males, both economic and political opportunity. "So long as free land exists," he wrote in his famous essay on the significance of the frontier, "the opportunity for a competency exists and economic power secures political power." In recent years, a number of historians have attacked portions of Turner's frontier hypothesis and especially its relevance to westering women. Indeed, several radical feminist authors have maintained that the West exerted a regressive rather than a progressive influence on women's lives. These authors contended that women on the frontiers were forced into unfamiliar, demeaning roles, and that although women in the Western settlements continued to try to reinstate a culture of domesticity, their work as virtual hired hands prevented them either from returning to older, more familiar roles in the social structure or from creating positive new roles. Unable to "appropriate their new work to their own ends and advantage," the authors of one article concluded, frontier women "remained estranged from their function as able bodies." ...

Writing from a somewhat different perspective, several historians questioned the application of Turner's thesis to women's frontier experiences and concluded that women did not share in the freedom and opportunities the West offered to men. The stereotype of American women as the "virtuous, religious, progenitor of democracy—the cornerstone of the family and society," one maintained, was a product of an agrarian mythology (and by implication a frontier mythology as well). He argued that it was not on the farm, or on the frontier, that women won political and legal rights, but rather in the city. "It was the city," he wrote, "which became the catalyst for all the aspirations of freedom and equality held by American women." The frontier influenced women as well as men, another historian agreed, but "If we accept Turner's own assumption that economic opportunity is what matters, and that the frontier was significant as the context within which economic opportunity occurred, then

From Sandra L. Myres, *Westering Women and the Frontier Experience 1800-1915* (University of New Mexico Press, 1982). Copyright © 1982 by University of New Mexico Press. Reprinted by permission. Notes omitted.

we must observe that for American women . . . opportunity began pretty much where the frontier left off." In a similar vein, another historian wrote that although there were independent Western women who may have been different from women in the urban East, industrialism and the city, not the Western farm, opened new avenues for women. The frontier, according to his interpretation, "strongly reinforced the traditional role of the sexes," and, he concluded, mill girls were likely to be "potentially far more 'revolutionary' than their rural, Western counterparts."

Yet despite arguments to the contrary, there is clear evidence that Western women did not confine themselves to purely traditional domestic and community concerns. It is true that most Western women were not revolutionary. Like Western men, they did not completely break with tradition nor, with very few exceptions, attempt radically to change women's lives and role in society. They did enlarge the scope of woman's place, however, and countered prevailing Eastern arguments about woman's sphere and the cult of true womanhood. Indeed, the ideals of true womanhood never really applied to a large number of women. As one historian has pointed out, at the very time that domesticity and true womanhood were being expounded as an American ideal, an increasing number of women were leaving their homes to become factory workers and wage earners. Factory work was obviously not available in frontier areas, but like many of their Eastern sisters, Western women were employed in a number of economic activities, and some of them engaged in new fields of endeavor outside what was considered their competency, skills, or proper sphere.

On the Western frontiers, as in other rural areas, much of women's work was tied to domestic manufacture. Historians have estimated that in the colonial period, when the United States was still predominantly rural, 60 to 75 percent of domestic manufacture, particularly in textiles, was carried out by women. . . .

Such domestic manufacture continued on the Western frontiers for many years after it had ceased in the East. Although by the nineteenth century, factories were beginning to produce foodstuffs, clothing, and other goods previously provided by home production, frontier women continued to manufacture such items themselves because "neither the goods, nor the cash to obtain them were readily available." Long, and often primitive, transportation made factory goods scarce and therefore expensive, and few frontier families, at least during the first years of settlement, had extra money to purchase what the women could, and did, produce at home. It was the women, as one Iowa man recalled, who saw that "the garden [was] tended, the turkeys dressed, the deer flesh cured and the fat prepared for candles or culinary use, the wild fruits were garnered and preserved or dried, that the spinning and knitting was done and the clothing made." Such production was not considered gainful employment, of course, and female home manufacturers were rarely, if ever, listed by census takers as employed or working women. Yet such employment was essential to the family economy. Women, as one historian wrote, were "to their families what the factory was to an industrialized society;" they were "the key link in turning unusable raw materials into consumable finished goods."

Not only did women provide needed goods and services for their families, which otherwise would have had to be purchased, but they often exchanged the produce of such work for needed goods or for cash. Margaret Murray recalled that her mother "sold Butter Eggs & Beeswax & anything we could spare off the farm, [and] in the summer and fall we gathered Black Berries wild grapes & anything we raised on the farm that would bring money or exchange for groceries." . . .

Through these contributions some women came to exert a good deal of influence on the family decision-making process. "The women were not unaware" of their contributions, one reported, and were "quite capable of scoring a point on occasion when masculine attitudes became too bumptious." Some women were openly aggressive or even contradictory in opposing male decisions, while others worked more subtly and were "careful to maintain the idea of male superiority." For example, one woman bought some milk cows and began a small dairy business while her husband was away doing carpenter work, but when he returned, he sold the cows since such work "did not appeal to him." The woman, however, without raising a fuss, simply took some inheritance money and reinvested in cows and "eventually the family acquired hogs to help consume the milk . . . [and] stock raising ended as the family's main economic activity."

Often women's domestic skills became the basis for a profitable business. Cooks, seamstresses, and washerwomen were in demand, especially in the mining camps and in other areas where the population included a number of single men. Although such work was laborious, it was usually well paid, particularly during the early frontier period. "I know girls that is ritch," one woman reported, "just working out bie the month," while another wrote that wages for women's work were high, "$50 to $75 a month." . . .

Most of this type of work could be done at home, and women thus provided a small income for their families while they continued to carry out their household chores and care for their children within a familiar setting. . . .

In frontier areas, women also served an important function as hotel and boardinghouse keepers. Women frequently boarded hired hands or seasonal workers. One California woman wrote that during the harvesting she had ten men in the family. "Washing and cooking for this crew," she reported, "takes me all the time. . . ." A Texas woman recorded that her husband owned a cotton gin for twenty-two years, and "I had my part to play in this business as we boarded the hands and I did the cooking." Other women opened their homes to boarders or operated small hotels to provide an income for themselves or their families. Shortly after her husband died, Amelia Barr wrote, "I have opened my house last week for boarders and intend to take about eight steady boarders," and a Texas woman recalled that her grandmother "kept a boarding house" to support her family when her Unionist husband left for Mexico.

Boardinghouses varied in size and type of services provided. Some boarding establishments furnished only meals while others supplied both meals and lodging. Others offered a combination of services. A Kansas woman recorded that she had two lodgers for whom she provided breakfast and supper and two others who "cook their own food and lodge in our little hut." Most boarding establishments were relatively small operations. With limited space and cooking facilities, most women could not accommodate more than eight to ten boarders at a time, but a few attempted to run fairly substantial operations....

On the frontier, women were actively sought not only as wives but as contributors to the local economy. Many community builders believed that a few good women would not only help in civilizing and taming the frontier but would add to its economic development as well. The Western agents for R. G. Dun and Company (the forerunner of Dun and Bradstreet) certainly were aware of women's potential economic contributions and recommended "equality of economic opportunity when it came to finding credit endorsements." Indeed, according to one analysis of Denver credit ratings for the period 1859 to 1877, "women without collateral could usually get recommendations for credit where men could not, even when everything was equal except their sex."

However remunerative, domestic work was often boring as well as laborious, and it kept women confined within their domestic spaces. "There is something dull in sitting here day by day, planning this garment and making that, but that seems to be my destiny just now," mourned a young Nebraska girl who made a good living as a seamstress. "There does not seem to be much that a girl can do here." Other women, equally bored by dull work, tried to find an outlet for their energies and creative urges in quiltmaking, fancy sewing, or by adding artistic touches to their home manufactures. Texas pioneer Ella Bird-Dumont longed to be a sculptress but, denied the opportunity to study in her Panhandle home, she settled instead for creating beauty in the gloves and vests she made and sold to neighboring ranch hands and cowmen....

Some frontier women refused to subvert their artistic talents to the tasks of sewing, butter making, and other home chores. A number of women were able to combine pioneering and domestic tasks and at the same time open new avenues into the "life of the mind." By the nineteenth century, writing was considered a fairly respectable occupation for women, and a number of them combined the pen with homemaking and child care. According to a recent study, between 1784 and 1860 at least one hundred magazines, most of which were devoted to women's interests, were founded in the United States and provided a market for articles by and for women. Many of these articles were about what women knew best—homemaking and the domestic arts—but the journals also published poetry, essays, and short stories by women. Women also became increasingly active in writing books as well as articles. Of the 1150 novels by American authors published in the United States between 1830 and 1850, a large proportion (perhaps as many as one-third) were written by women. So successful were some of these works that Nathaniel Hawthorne felt compelled to complain to his publisher that "America is wholly given over to a damned mob of scribbling women...." Although many of the "damned mob" admittedly produced third and fourth-rate works, their books were nonetheless popular and brought their authoresses a good deal of attention as well as a source of income....

Aside from the arts, teaching was about the only profession open to respectable women in the nineteenth century.... [E]ducation was considered an extension of women's traditional roles as child rearers and moral and cultural guardians, and American education became increasingly feminized during the nineteenth century. As Catherine Beecher pointed out, teaching young children not only provided an essential service to the community, but it helped women prepare themselves for "the great purpose of a woman's life—the happy superintendence of a family." Beecher's advice did not go unheeded: a number of women taught school at one time or another.

Although most women teachers were single, some women continued at least part-time teaching after their marriage. Especially in Western communities where men were engaged in the "multitudes of other employments that will... lead to wealth" (as Beecher so bluntly wrote), educated women, whatever their marital status, were frequently urged to help begin schools and teach for a term or two. The scarcity of teachers and the desire of frontier dwellers to provide an education for their children led to many attempts to recruit young women from the East. "We want good female teachers, who could obtain constant employment and the best of wages," a Kansas settler wrote home to a New England newspaper; "we want them immediately, and they would do much good." Various Eastern groups attempted to respond to the demand. Catherine Beecher began a campaign to send women teachers to the West, warning that "Western children were growing up without the benefit of either a practical or a moral education." Beecher, and the Board of National Popular Education, formed in 1847, did recruit some teachers. The Board served as an agency for single teachers and provided job training as well as placement services, but the number of Eastern teachers provided by the group never approached the 90,000 young women Beecher believed were needed "if the tides of barbarism were to be pushed back." Far more helpful in recruiting teachers in the West than the actions of Eastern groups and agencies were the more practical solutions found by frontier residents who relied on the resources available and found local women with at least a modicum of education to fulfill the communities' educational needs....

Despite poor working conditions, rowdy pupils, low salaries, and increasing educational requirements, some women chose full-time, lifetime careers in teaching and were able to advance themselves professionally. Many young women took advantage of the more liberal educational opportunities available to them in Western colleges and universities to improve their academic skills and qualify them for better-paying and more professionally fulfilling jobs in the educational system. When the franchise was opened to Western women, elective school offices were opened to them as well, and in most Western states, women held posts as principals, superintendents, and served on state boards of education....

A number of women combined a desire to teach with religious zeal and entered the mission field. Indeed, for some women the principal motivation for going West was not family desires or economic betterment but an answer to a religious calling to minister to the Indians....

During the 1790s, the Second Awakening "spawned a whole family of state, regional, and national societies." Thus, by the beginning of the nineteenth century most denominations sponsored both foreign and home missions, and several interdenominational societies had been formed to carry the gospel to both the Indians and the white inhabitants of new Western settlements.

The boards which organized and controlled Western missions were made up entirely of men, and decisions about the establishment and conduct of the missions were made in the East, not in the West. Nonetheless, it was the missionaries in the field who were crucial to the success of the missionary effort, and women, living and working in the West, made important and significant contributions to mission work. At first a number of mission boards refused to allow women to enter the field, fearing the frontier and Indian villages too dangerous and unseemly a place for delicate females. Women filled with missionary ardor had to content themselves with fund-raising activities and quiet support of the mission effort. Eventually, however, mission boards actively recruited both married and single women to wash, cook, and clean at the mission stations and to assist the male missionaries in teaching in the mission schools, in evangelizing among the Indian women, and in other aspects of mission work. Between 1820 and 1850, a growing number of women joined missions in the trans-Appalachian West and in Indian Territory. As the frontier moved further West, new mission fields opened, and women became increasingly prominent in missionary work. They broadened the scope of their activities, preached as well as taught, and occasionally had full responsibility for the establishment and operation of mission schools and churches. A few were ordained to the regular ministry, in order, as one put it, "to add in some ways to her power to serve." ...

Conservative and traditional in most of their views towards social progress and the role of women, the missionaries nonetheless helped broaden women's place within Western society and in the nation as a whole. Certainly they proved the ability of women to undertake successfully this strenuous and difficult calling. A number of them became strong advocates for improved education for women so that they could more effectively serve in the mission field, and their books about their mission life, their letters to newspapers and magazines, and their public speaking tours to raise funds provided a greater visibility for women as public rather than private participants in American life.

At the opposite end of the social scale from the missionaries were the practitioners of a very different, publically visible, but traditional and exclusively female occupation, the so-called soiled doves or ladies of the night. A great deal has been written about Western prostitutes; much of it, of a popular, and often sensational, nature, concentrated on such colorful characters as Poker Alice, Tit Bit, Big Nose Kate, and Rose of the Cimarron. These women were often portrayed as nice girls gone wrong, women of some character and experience who drank, gambled, and sold their favors but who still were of a basically honest nature and had "hearts of pure gold." Or they were pictured as women of "evil name and fame," depraved, vicious, and cruel "Cyprian sisters." Several recent and more scholarly studies have suggested that some girls entered the profession in order to advance themselves economically or to escape dull and dreary lives on isolated farms and ranches. Many were attracted by the bright lights and excitement of the mining camps and cattle towns and hoped to earn a little nest egg, meet a cowboy, farmer, or rancher, and eventually settle down to a respectable life. Others hoped to become economically independent and viewed prostitution as one of the few professions where women had some chance of financial success. As one Denver woman succinctly noted, "I went into the sporting life for business reasons and no other. It was a way for a woman in those days to make money and I made it." ...

Brothel owners and operators and girls who worked in the better establishments generally scorned the dance hall and saloon girls who rented upstairs rooms over the taverns and the "crib" girls who sold their wares from small two-room establishments with a bedroom with a window on the street and a kitchen in the rear. At the bottom of the scale were the women who walked the streets and who were often ill and frequently subjected to cruel and violent treatment at the hands of both customers and law enforcement officials. But whatever their social or economic level—madame, parlor girl, saloon or crib girl, or streetwalker, their life was a hard one. Many committed suicide, died of disease and alcoholism, drifted away into other occupations or, among the more fortunate, found a husband or protector. One survey of prostitutes in the Kansas cattle towns found that the average age of these women was 23.1 years, and very few were over the age of thirty. Despite the legendary success of a few women, prostitution was neither an attractive nor a rewarding occupation.

Prostitution was a town or city occupation as were other more respectable occupations such as domestic service, hotel and boardinghouse management, and teaching. The economic opportunities for rural women, especially in frontier areas, were more limited. Yet a surprising number of farm and ranch women were able to turn their knowledge of domestic production and farm and ranch management into prosperous business enterprises. In addition to their domestic occupations such as cloth production, and chicken, egg, dairy, and butter businesses, many rural women actually ran the family farm.... [W]omen often had to take over farm management when the men were ill or incapacitated or were gone from home prospecting, fighting Indians, working in town for cash, or just wandering. This was particularly true in Mormon settlements where the men were often required to be gone for one or two years on missions for the church or were involved in other church activities. Meanwhile, the women stayed at home to "milk the cows, plant the crops, and care for the children." In many instances, women (non-Mormon as well as Mormon) provided most of the support for themselves and their families. Even when their menfolk remained at home, most rural women worked with their husbands during especially busy times of the year, and they thus came to have a good understanding of the various farm operations. Wrote one young Iowa farm girl, "I can't describe a thrashing floor so you understand but some day I can show you just how it was done...." Such experience stood women in good stead when they were widowed or left alone and had to take over. In the East, single or widowed women probably would have relied on a father, brothers, or uncles to aid them, but in the West they had fewer of these support networks to draw on, hired help was scarce and expensive, and most simply took over and continued to operate the family farm until they remarried or retired and left the property to their children....

A surprising number of Western women, both single and married, took up land in their own name. In the former Mexican states and territories, where Spanish rather than English law prevailed, married women could hold separate property in their own name, and many took advantage of the opportunity to purchase and adminster their own land. Indeed, Jane McManus Storms Cazneau applied for, and received, an empresario grant from the Mexican government. During the Texas Revolution she offered to borrow money against her landholdings. "As a female, I cannot bear arms for my adopted country," she wrote in 1835, "but if the interest I possess in her soil, will be a guarantee for any money, I will with joy contribute my mite to purchase arms for her brave defenders." In other former Mexican states other women, both of Mexican and English ancestry, owned farm and ranch property which they administered themselves.

Between 1800 and 1850, many changes occurred in the social, economic, and legal position of women, and a number of states and territories outside the former Mexican provinces passed more liberal laws governing women's property rights. As one legal historian pointed out, the number of women with a stake in society increased rapidly during this period, and the English common law, primarily geared to the needs of the landed gentry, no longer was satisfactory for American needs. In fact, he wrote, "the tangle of rules and practices was potentially an impediment to the speed and efficiency of the land market. The statutes spoke of rights of husband and wife, as if the real issue was the intimate relations between the sexes. But the real point of the statutes was to rationalize more cold-blooded matters, such as the rights of a creditor to collect debts out of land owned by husbands and wives, or both." In 1839, Mississippi made the first tentative reforms in the laws relating to married women's property, and other states and territories soon followed suit. By 1850, seventeen states, many of them in the West, had granted married women legal control over their property, while in Oregon, the Donation Land Law of 1850 allowed wives of settlers to claim a half-section (320 acres) in their own right. Most Western states' legal codes made some provision for women to purchase homestead land and own and operate businesses in their own name. Husbands sometimes took advantage of these laws to escape debts or bankruptcy by transferring property to the wife's name, but this device often backfired, for women, once in legal possession of the property, frequently refused to return it, assisted in its administration, and used their legal ownership as a weapon to force their husbands to comply with their wishes....

Whether ranchwomen confined themselves to more traditional roles or actively participated in ranch operations, they tended to become increasingly self-reliant and independent. According to Nannie Alderson, "the new country offered greater personal liberty than an old and settled one," and although she admitted that her years of ranch life never taught her any business sense, she nonetheless believed that Western ranch life instilled a good deal of self-reliance in women and children. This opinion was shared by a number of outside observers. The English visitor Anthony Trollope wrote in 1862 that ranchwomen were "sharp as nails and just as hard." They were rarely obedient to their menfolk, he reported, and "they know much more than they ought to. If Eve had been a ranchwoman, she would never have tempted Adam with an apple. She would have ordered him to make his [own] meal." This was particularly true of girls who grew up on Western farms and ranches. They were even more likely than their mothers to learn riding and roping skills, participate in ranch work, and understand business operations. According to one such young woman, "it is as beneficial for a woman as for a man to be independent," and, she continued, she knew of no reasons "why the judgement of women should not be as good as that of men if they gave the subject attention." In later life, many of these ranch girls assisted their husbands in the ranching business, operated ranches of their own, or turned their talents into careers in rodeo and wild west shows. . . .

Some women turned their farm and ranch experience to the development of large-scale commercial agricultural enterprises, and others became very successful real estate investors. As early as 1742, a young frontiers-woman, Eliza Lucas, assumed management of her father's extensive Carolina estates and developed a profitable indigo market. Mention has already been made of Margaret Brent who managed not only her own lands but was executrix for Leonard Calvert's estate as well. These women established an early pattern for other women. By the late nineteenth century, a Western traveler commented on the number of "bright-minded women from other parts of the country" who were "engaged in real estate transactions in this country. . . . [I]t is not a rare thing," she continued, "for numbers of feminine speculators to attend the auction sales of land," and she estimated that of the sixty-five women teachers in the Los Angeles schools, "almost all own some land." . . .

In addition to real estate and commercial agriculture, Western women engaged in many other business and professional enterprises. A survey of the R. G. Dun and Company reports revealed a number of women in the Western states and territories owned and operated millinery shops, dressmaking establishments, grocery and dry goods stores, hotels and restaurants, and other similar establishments. For some, these enterprises served as a basis for other businesses or professions. For example, an Oregon woman, Bethenia Owens-Adair, opened a millinery shop in order to earn money for medical school, and other women reported that the income from their shops helped to underwrite real estate and mining investments. Two enterprising westering women purchased a supply of cloth and other dry goods which they sold from the back of their spring wagon to help pay their expenses to California.

Other women engaged in less-traditional businesses including manufacturing, mining, printing, and editing. Frontier women who had learned to "make-do" and who had devised various means to overcome shortages or unavailable goods applied for patents on various inventions, many of them developed out of their frontier experience. Most of these inventions were closely related to domestic and farm work—improvements for milk coolers, separators and churns, new types of wash tubs, quilting frames, beekeeping equipment, and new strains of farm and garden plants; but others, like Harriet Strong's patent for a "method and means for impounding debris and storing water," provided the basis for other businesses. Strong used her patents and her knowledge of engineering to develop an irrigation and water company in the San

Gabriel Valley and became an expert on underground water storage and flood control....

Women were also employed as reporters and contributors for many Western journals and newspapers. After 1850, Ladies' Department columns began to appear in newspapers, often run by the editor's wife or one of the paper's more notable female contributors. Talented women journalists, however, also wrote regular columns or contributed articles on topics of general interest....

By the end of the nineteenth century, according to a recent survey, 1,238 women were engaged in printing and publication and another 1,127 were employed as compositors, linotype operators, and typesetters in eleven far-Western states. A separate study identified twenty-five women newspaper owners and editors in Missouri in the same period.

Western women were also active in other professions including medicine and law. Although these women faced many of the same obstacles and discriminations as Eastern professional women, they had less difficulty in establishing themselves and gaining recognition of their professional status.... [F]rontier women often had to render medical assistance and treatment, and many were recognized as professional or near-professional practitioners of the healing arts. In Mexican-American communities and in many Indian societies, women were believed to have special gifts as healers, and *curanderas* and medicine women were valued for their skills in treating illness and reducing pain. A number of women assisted their physician-husbands and sometimes substituted for them in emergencies. Midwifery and nursing were common occupations for frontier women, although these services rarely earned them monetary remuneration, and they were not acknowledged as gainfully employed in the census or other official documents. After Elizabeth Blackwell's successful assault on male domination of medicine in 1847, an increasing number of women attended medical school and became licensed physicians. In Utah, the Mormon community actively supported women's work in all aspects of medicine and dentistry and produced one of "the most remarkable groups of women doctors in American history." In 1873 Church leader Brigham Young suggested that women's classes be formed in Salt Lake City to study physiology and obstetrics and that "the Bishops see that such women be supported." ...

Although Utah undoubtedly had the highest percentage of women doctors, other Western states and territories also had a fairly high percentage of professional women. By 1893, a number of coeducational medical schools had been established in the West and enrolled a number of women—19 percent at the University of Michigan, 20 percent at the University of Oregon, and 31 percent at Kansas Medical School.

Women had more difficulty in obtaining legal training because of statutory prohibitions based on English common law which prohibited women from being called to the bar. Nonetheless, after 1870, a few women succeeded in winning admission to legal practice, and those who did frequently vied with each other for the honor of being named the first woman admitted to practice before their state bar or the first woman to try a case before a state supreme court....

Everywhere in the West, by the end of the nineteenth century, women were entering new professions and businesses and were finding new roles outside the recognized scope of woman's place. Many of these Western female entrepreneurs first learned business skills by assisting their husbands, but others learned because of necessity and gained economic and technical expertise through hard work and often bitter experience.... Other women were forced to become independent because of the absence or death of their husbands. Certainly some were reluctant capitalists and businesswomen, but others, often to their own amazement, found that they enjoyed earning their own livelihood and controlling their own lives, and they became enthusiastic entrepreneurs. "I am a great believer in the independence of women," one wrote. "I think married women should be allowed to go on with their career if they wish...." Another, the very successful California businesswoman Harriet Strong, advocated business and economic education for all women so that they would be prepared to assume management of their property if necessary. She hoped to organize a Ladies Business League of America and establish a series of business colleges and training schools to teach women the basic principles of economics and business management. It was not easy for women to succeed in business, she cautioned. "Whatever vocation a woman would enter, she must give it the same scientific study and hard work that a man would in order to make a success." Moreover, she warned:

> A woman needs to have five times as much ability as a man in order to do the same thing. She may be permitted to conduct her own ranch and be a success in a small business enterprise—yes, but let her go into the business of incorporating a large enterprise and bonding it, as a man would... and then see if the word does not go forth, "This woman is going too far; she must be put down."...

Whether the frontier provided a liberating experience and economic as well as social and political opportunities for women is still a question of much debate. Certainly there is some evidence that it did not. As noted at the beginning of this [selection], some historians have concluded, based on women's reminiscences, diaries, and letters, that the frontier did not offer as many opportunities for women as it did for men and that women often failed to take advantage of the frontier experience as a means of liberating themselves from constricting and sexist patterns of behavior. Yet these same reminiscences, diaries, and letters also contain evidence to support the contention that women on the frontiers modified existing norms and adopted flexible attitudes and experimental behavior patterns. For some these changes were easily made and enthusiastically accepted; for others they were reluctantly made and strongly resisted. What has perhaps confused the various interpretations of woman's place and the westering experience is that the *reality* of women's lives changed dramatically as a result of adaptation to frontier conditions while the public *image* remained relatively static. Image, myth, and stereotype were contrary to what women were actually experiencing and doing. The ideal for women in the late nineteenth century moved more and more toward a romanticized view of the wife, mother, and lady, if not of leisure, at least of withdrawn and demure refinement. If frontier necessity, practice, and even law recognized female economic and political independence, social custom and tradition ignored it. Despite a growing emphasis on women's rights, nineteenth-century writers overlooked—or at least chose not to draw attention to—Western life models on which other women might pattern their own lives. Temperance and suffrage rather than economic education and independence for women dominated the feminist literature, often to the detriment of effective women's rights. Women who did not marry or who effectively ran businesses or professional enterprises were often viewed as being not quite respectable or at least unfeminine no matter how efficiently they also ran their homes or carried on family responsibilities in addition to challenging male domination of the marketplace.

Yet women who survived the first or even the second wave of adjustment to frontier conditions and changed roles for women tended to ignore, or at least not slavishly strive toward, Eastern-dictated models of femininity or the ideal of true womanhood. These hardy and self-sufficient women stepped out of woman's place with few regrets. If they did not glory in their new freedom, they did express pride in their newfound talents and accomplishments. It was the later generations of Western women, those who no longer lived on a frontier, who began to emulate Eastern models of propriety and sought to perpetuate the myths of woman's proper sphere. Yet even these later generations betrayed their frontier heritage in their personal values and attitudes. This heritage was reflected in a survey in 1943 which showed that Western women, as compared to those in the North and the South, were far better educated, held a wider variety of jobs, and were more likely to continue working, were less prone to adhere to traditional religious and denominational beliefs, were more excited and more optimistic about their lives, were more open to change, and were more likely to approve equal standards for men and women. Thus, the westering experience continued to influence Western women's values and attitudes long after the passing of the frontier.

John Mack Faragher  **NO**

The World of the Family

T he law of midwestern states provided official endorsement of notions of reciprocal marriage. Congress, in the Northwest Ordinance of 1787, and in the 1816 organization of the Missouri Territory, placed the areas that later became the states of Indiana, Illinois, Iowa, and Missouri under the protection of English common law; thus, in the Midwest, as in nearly all other areas of the United States, common-law definitions of marriage prevailed until amended by state statutes after mid-century. Through the common law the conventional roles of husband and wife were legally enshrined: a husband was obligated to provide a residence and household for his family, and to supply his wife with the means of feeding and clothing herself and her children; a wife was legally obligated to be her husband's helpmeet, to perform household and domestic duties freely and willingly without compensation. Both partners to the marriage contract had the exclusive legal right to the society, companionship, and conjugal affections of their spouse; there was a mutual obligation to love, to care for, and to labor faithfully to advance the interests of one's spouse.

But marriage legally obligated more than reciprocity. Legal marriage, like the marital relation in practice, gave the husband extraordinary power over the life and affairs of his wife. The law was the cultural capstone of the system of male privilege which extended from the uneven division of domestic labor through male control of the public world. Although each couple had ultimately to work out the relations of power and authority within their own marriage, the law represented the limits of the permissible and offered a sanctioned model of female subordination. The law, written by men and enforced by men, was a principal vehicle for furthering the ideological and social dominance of the patriarchy.

All women in nineteenth-century North American society, whether married or single, were without the benefits of the most basic civil rights: women could not vote, could not serve on juries, and in most places could not hold public office, all aspects of their general exclusion from the public world. Single women did enjoy almost equal legal status with men in contractual and property rights, but once married, women lost these rights as well, and very few women, of course, remained single. Married women were no longer responsible citizens but dependents, like children and idiots, relying for protection on the legal status of their husband-guardians. More than convention was operating when women dropped their maiden names and assumed the names of their husbands, since according to common-law doctrine, a man and a woman became a single legal person upon marriage, and, as Blackstone opined for every country lawyer in those hundreds of midwestern villages, that person was the husband.

The legal oppression of married women read like a bill of attainder. Since wives had no legal identity they could make no independent legal arrangements or contracts; they could neither sue nor be sued; they could not make an independent will; any contractual obligations undertaken before their marriages became the responsibility of husbands to fulfill. Wives forfeited to their husbands control and management of any and all real property they might have held before their marriage; husbands retained the rights to that property until their deaths, and indeed, if there were living issue of the marriage, the property previously owned by wives could then even be placed in trust for the children and kept out of women's hands. Husbands gained outright ownership of all the prenuptial personal property and chattels of their wives, and to husbands fell the right to proceed with any suits initiated by their wives and receive the settlements as their own. Husbands owned their wives' labor power; any wages wives received while married were legally owed to their husbands. Finally, since husbands and wives were legally one person, men could under no circumstances be charged with stealing from their wives, which gave men the widest possible leeway in their actions.

Husbands were recognized by law as the heads of their families; to them was delegated the obligation to control and discipline their wives. Hence husbands were permitted to physically punish their spouses within "reasonable limits," which by common law meant wives could be beaten as long as the instrument was no bigger around than the man's thumb. Wives were deprived of redress in the courts for injuries received at their husbands' hands. Husbands could legally confine their wives at home, refuse them visitors, even forcibly separate them from their parents. Divorce was difficult to obtain in most midwestern states; petition had to be made for a special legislative divorce. If there was a divorce, the legal assumption was that the custody of minor children went with the head of the family—the husband. For women, therefore, divorce usually meant giving up their children.

It is little wonder that the nascent women's rights movement took reform of the marriage law as one of its first objectives. Feminists supported the Married Women's Property Acts, which proposed to amend the law to allow married women to hold their prenuptial property in their own (married) names and reform women's contractual rights. Feminists had the powerful support, in most states, of legal reformers, wealthy families who wished to protect the dower property of their daughters from unscrupulous suitors, and impoverished farmers who hoped to save some of their estate from creditors by placing it in their wives' names. In the Midwest these reforms of the common law were in step with the rest of the nation, beginning during the 1850s. But the implementation of the intent of the laws was delayed many years by the determined rear guard of the exclusively male bench and bar which demonstrated real hostility to the acts. In any event, the general rule of common law continued to apply to relations between husband and wife, despite the fact that the Married Women's Acts logically renounced the legal fiction of two in one.

The property and contractual reforms would not have had much of a bearing upon the lives of most farm women in any case. Only rarely did any of these women enter a marriage with more than a modest personal dowry. The importance of the law lay rather in the considerable official authority it lent to the exercise of husbands' power. The common law sanctioned the existing power relations between midwestern men and women; it was patriarchal law.

It is interesting to look at the decision to emigrate to Oregon or California in the light of the legal model of husbands' power. In their diaries and recollections many women discussed the way in which the decision to move was made. Not one wife initiated the idea; it was always the husband. Less than a quarter of the women writers recorded agreeing with their restless husbands; most of them accepted it as a husband-made decision to which they could only acquiesce. But nearly a third wrote of their objections and how they moved only reluctantly. When John Jones informed his wife Mary of his plans, she remembered answering impulsively, "Oh, let us not go! But," she added, "it made no difference." One woman, writing of her own reluctance to move to Oregon, was reminded of the time her father had moved their family from Sangamon County to Missouri:

> I came in one evening to see a look on dear mother's face that I had never seen before. I walked away after the usual greeting and sat silent. After a time her voice strengthened and she said, "what do you think your father has done.... He has sold the farm and as soon as school closes we are to move to Missouri." ... What a shock these words gave me.

In her later years Lucy Deady wrote that her mother had known "nothing of this move until father had decided to go."

The decision to emigrate was the kind where husbands' patriarchal power made the difference: legally, after all, husbands had the right to enforce their own independent choice of domicile for the family; it was fully within a husband's prerogative to move his family without even consulting his wife....

We have no way of knowing, of course, how many wives were successful in either getting their restless husbands to take them along or in leashing them. But whatever power wives brought to bear was clearly defensive and responsive. Men held the customary authority to make these decisions, and they did so. Perhaps only when husbands proposed leaving alone, threatening the family unity upon which their authority was based, did wives most successfully challenge their dominance in worldly affairs. It is clear, at any rate, that many emigrating women had been given little if any opportunity to participate in the decision to emigrate. Enos Ellmaker described the process by which most couples probably decided to go: "After my fine [Iowa] farm had received so much improvements yet I was not satisfied with the country; *I finally got the consent of my wife to sell and move* to the far-distant Oregon." Their passive role necessarily meant that many women were reluctant participants in the crossing. "From Mrs Morrison's own lips I learned," wrote John Minto, "that the journey for which she was bending all her energies in preparation, was not in her judgement a wise business movement; but 'Wilson wished to go,' and that settled the question with her."

Women worked valiantly to preserve their domestic environment in transit, for if women had a power it was dependent upon their ability to meet their own, their husband's, and their children's domestic needs. It was in homemaking that women acquired their status, and homemaking, consequently, took up their time on the trail. For their task women demanded more equipment than men alone thought necessary. Sarah Royce remembered that family wagons "were easily distinguished by the greater number of conveniences, and household articles they carried." Some families came outfitted out of all proportion to the load limitations. Hugh Campbell remembered that their family traveled in a spring wagon built extrawide to accommodate a built-in stove, beds, and a rocking chair for his mother. The famous family wagon of the ill-fated Reed family—the Prairie Palace Car—also boasted a stove and even had a stovepipe sprouting from the canvas cover.

Most women made do with much less and yet were able, in the early stages at least, to create an air of homeyness about their camps. Sarah Royce noted the domestic articles of women—culinary equipment, food, boxes of clothing, tubs for washing—"disposed about the outside of the wagon in a home-like way," not simply strewn here and there as in the nearby male camps. "And where bushes, trees or logs formed partial enclosures, a kitchen or sitting room quite easily suggested itself to the feminine heart, yearning for home." Tents became living rooms where women held, as best they could, to the amenities they tried to teach at home. Ed Bryant was received by Nancy Thornton in her tent "as she would have done in her parlor at home." In these settings it was sometimes possible to pretend that home really did abide with the heart. "Mrs Fox and her daughter are with us and everything is so still and quiet we can almost imagine ourselves at home again. We took out our Daguerrotypes and tried to live over again some of the happy days of 'Auld Lang Syne.'" "In the evening the young ladies came over to our house and we had a concert with both guitars. Indeed it seemed almost like a pleasant evening at home. We could none of us realize that we were almost at the summit of the Rocky Mountains."

By this stage of the trip, ascending the foothills of the Rockies, most women had been badly frustrated in their domestic work and needed no reminding of where they were. Along the Platte, the easiest leg of the journey, the water supply was muddy and crowded with "wigglers"; "this unsanitary condition," Charles True remembered, "was difficult for mother, with her life-long habits of scrupulous cleanliness and neatness to reconcile." The animal and human excrement that littered the trail were a constant injury to women's habits. When the captain of their train selected an evening campsite filthy from earlier travelers, normally passive Lavinia Porter threatened her husband; "If you do not drive me to a cleaner place to camp and sleep tonight I will take my blankets and go alone." They moved on, and "the other women looked on my daring unsubordination with wondering eyes, and envious of my cleanly quarters, at last plucked up courage to follow my example, and with much profanity [on the part of the men] the camp was moved." But some conditions could not easily be overcome.

> Our tents stand in what we should style a barnyard at home and I am sure if I were there I should as soon think of setting a table there as in such a place. The stench is sometimes almost unendurable, it arises from a ravene that is resorted to for special purposes by all the Emigration, but such things we must put up with.

As the emigrants moved up the grade approaching the Rockies, it became obvious that the overloaded wagons had to be lightened, and gradually they discarded materials not essential for survival. Domestic goods, of course, were most easily excluded from the essential category, much to the dismay of the women. "We came across a heavy old fashioned cook stove which some emigrant had hauled all those weary miles of mountain and desert, only to discard it at last," wrote Lavinia Porter. "No doubt some poor forlorn woman was now compelled to do her cooking by the primitive camp fire, perhaps much against her will." True recalled that by the time his party reached the Great Basin all his mother's camping conveniences had been discarded, greatly adding to her labors and filling her days with anxiety. This anxiety was not only an effect of added work. Books, furniture, knickknacks, china, daguerreotypes, guitars— the very articles that most helped to establish a domestic feel about the camps were the first things to be discarded. Lightening the wagons, however necessary, was interpreted by women as a process operating against their interests. In one party a woman "exclaimed over an escritoire of rare workmanship" she had found along the trail "and pitied the poor woman who had to part with it."

The loss of a sense of home—the inability to "keep house" on the trail —was perhaps the hardest loss to bear, the thing that drove women closest to desperation. In their diary entries, women wished fervently for a return to the familiar routines of home and farm life. Those routines objectively required more than a fair share from women, but they were comforting in their conventionality and, perhaps more important, comforting in the way they reserved a unique position for women. "If I were in the states now I would be sitting in a comfortable house besides a fire; but our house now is in the open air," Esther Hanna wrote. Louisa Frizzell, a strong and determined woman, nonetheless echoed her younger and more delicate sister: "I feel tired and weary, O the luxury of a house, a house! . . . I would have given all my interest in California, to have been seated around my own fireside." Velina Williams added her lament: "Oh, for a little home to call my own!" The trip was so long, so extended, that women began to feel that the physical foundations of domesticity—their homes —had slipped irretrievably from them, that they were moving into a wild and savage land where, perhaps, they would discover that homes were nonexistent and women frightfully oppressed.

Women, then, clung to the things that belonged to them in the homestead marriage: clearly segregated work, a physical sphere for their activity, important work in reproducing the next generation and rearing healthy and happy young farmers and farm wives. They showed little inclination to trade these roles for the more socially active work that necessity demanded from them on the trail;

rather, they attempted to preserve at least the semblance of their traditional roles. Feminine farm roles had little to do with the fetishized domesticity that was a part of the womanly cult flowering in the East, for in most ways these pioneer wives and mothers were the very antithesis of that antiseptic and anesthetized version of femininity. These were working women who accepted, with their husbands, a view of marriage that was oppressive to women in practice but promised meaningful work and the rewards of achievement at tasks distinctively feminine and separate from men. For all the tensions and inadequacies of marriage, when placed under extraordinary stress women's vision could extend only far enough to wish themselves back on their well-ordered homesteads.

⌒⊚⌒

Denied the chance to participate in the decision to move, essentially because of the patriarchal bias of marital decision making, failing to accept as their own husbands' reasons for undertaking the move, women went not because they wanted to but because social expectations left them no choice. Understandably then, many women secretly blamed their husbands for their hardships on the trail. Lucy Rutledge Cook recorded in her letters home that her mother-in-law had vocally but privately complained to her, "Oh, I wish we never had started.... She looks so sorrowful and dejected," Lucy worried; "I think if Pa had not passengers to take through she would urge him to return; not that he would be so inclined, for returning is hopeless." The elder Mrs. Cook declared that "no argument used to induce her to leave there seems to have any weight now" and placed the blame for the move on those who had persuaded her against her better judgment—her husband and sons. A few days later Lucy herself was echoing her mother-in-law: "Oh, how I wish we never had started for the Golden Land," but she kept her own laments private too, secreted in her letters home.

A few nights into Indian territory the Hecox–Aram party was joined at their camp one evening by a small group of Indian men who sat up around their fire all night, drinking, dancing, and loudly boasting of war exploits. Margaret Hecox retreated with her four children to the cold, damp wagon where she spent the night "hugging my baby to my bosom, with three badly scared little girls crouched at my feet." A single question reverberated in her head: "What had possessed my husband, anyway, that he should have thought of bringing us away out through this God-forsaken country?" At about the same stage of their journey, Lucy Ide wrote in her diary, "Well, well, this is not so romantic; thoughts will stray back (in spite of all our attempts to the contrary) to the comfortable homes we left and the question arises in my mind—is this a good move—but echo answers not a word."

Women reluctantly agreed to the emigration because they were dependent upon their families for society and companionship and upon their husbands for livelihood and support. Husbands and families were crucial to women's identities; the options for women left behind were lonely ones at best and could be socially and psychologically disastrous. But women were not dragged screaming to the wagons; in this sense no one forced them to go. There were a few examples of resistance; occasional anxiety or bewilderment erupted into open revolt against going forward.

> This morning our company moved on, except one family. The woman got mad and wouldn't go or let the children go. He had the cattle hitched on for three hours and coaxed her to go, but she wouldn't stir. I told my husband the circumstances and he and Adam Polk and Mr Kimball went and each one took a young one and crammed them into the wagon, and the husband drove off and left her sitting. She got up, took the back track and traveled out of sight. Cut across, overtook her husband. Meantime he sent his boy back to camp after a horse that he had left and when she came up her husband says "Did you meet John?" "Yes," was the reply, "and I picked up a stone and knocked out his brains." Her husband went back to ascertain the truth, and when he was gone she set one of his wagons on fire, which was loaded with store goods. The cover burnt off and some valuable articles. He saw the flames and came running and put it out, and then mustered spunk enough to give her a good flogging.

Short of violent resistance, it was always possible that circumstances would force a family to reconsider and turn back. Mary Ellen Todd's family traveled in 1852, when cholera was a scourge along the trails. "There was great discouragement among the emigrants..., and everyday there were some who were going back.... Women cried, begging their menfolk to take them back. It is no wonder that stout hearts began to waver. Consequently, after many heated discussions and more tears," the reluctant men finally consented to return. Mary Ellen remembered that the men "did the hooking up of their oxen in a spiritless sort of way. Yet some of the girls and women were laughing." It would have been no surprise if some women had complained to their husbands as well as to their diaries. The carping woman was a standard image of overland folklore.

> The ladies have the hardest that emigrate by land,
> For when they cook with buffalo wood they often burn a hand;
> And when they jaw their husbands 'round, get mad and spill
>   the tea.
> Wish to the Lord they'd be taken down with a turn of the di-a-
>   ree.

Open resistance, constant complaining: these reactions would certainly have fit the disorder of women's powerlessness. But such stereotypical behavior rarely has an active existence; few women, if any, secretly plotted to sabotage the trip, and the wag who composed that verse about feminine emigrants was probably reflecting male fears of wifely resentment more than the abundance of shrews on the trail. Life is always richer and more complex than such reductionist images suggest. Women's leaving was determined by their social dependency, to be sure, and there was ample room for women to build and feel massive resentments; but their leaving was activated by the things women believed and expected of themselves. Their own social and personal values demanded that they be loving and obedient wives, faithful

and ever-present mothers. They struggled with their men about the fool-
ishness of going, but only until threatened with the loss of their wifely
status; then they capitulated and packed the trunks. Past this point resistance was hopeless, as Lucy Cook recognized, more important, it would be
destructive.

If we are to trust and respect their revelations in their diaries and recollections, the greatest struggle of women on the trail was the struggle to endure
the hardship and suffering without becoming bitter and resentful, without becoming the carping wife, without burdening their marital relationship with
the bad feelings that burned inside them. If we are to judge them not by our
standards but their own, we will not resurrect and applaud every little act
of womanly resistance and mean feminine spirit but examine and attempt
to understand the powers of endurance that permitted them to act out the
role of good wife through the whole hated experience. The women's materials give us a penetrating look at the feminine psychology of social dependency.

"Some there were, no doubt, who would have turned back," Sarah Royce
later wrote, in a description which applies well to women, "but they were
involved either in family or business relations with others more resolute—or
more rash—and, seeing the uselessness of resistance they took up their part of
the daily toil, in most cases, without complaining." Indeed, as we have seen,
women not only took up their part, but over the long haul they assumed more
than their 50 percent, often substituting for men, driving wagons and stock in
addition to doing their own wifely work. Wholehearted work may have been a
way of overcoming the inward resistance many women felt to working at all for
unwanted goals.

Fears and doubts too fearful to be spoken aloud to men were whispered
between mothers and daughters, sisters, or traveling female acquaintances.
Most women diarists used their daily entries as an opportunity to express their
feelings silently. Lavinia Porter recounted in the most melancholy terms her
"sad parting" from her sister on the plains of eastern Kansas but added, "Such
sorrows are to be endured not described." Endurance was the dominant emotional theme of Lavinia's overland account. "As the days wore on the irksome
monotony of the journey began to pall upon me, and I spent many unhappy
hours which I tried to conceal within my own breast, sometimes confiding to
my journal my woes and disappointments, but managed to keep up a cheerful
exterior before my husband and brother." Her resolve was to be "the courageous and valiant frontierswoman," but this outward appearance took a heavy
inward toll.

> I would make a brave effort to be cheerful and patient until the camp work
> was done. Then starting out ahead of the team and my men folks, when I
> thought I had gone beyond hearing distance, I would throw myself down
> on the unfriendly desert and give way like a child to sobs and tears, wishing
> myself back home with my friends and chiding myself for consenting to take
> this wild goose chase. . . .

Disquiet, anxiety, melancholy, and anger were repressed and hidden from husbands, brothers, and fathers, those most responsible for such feelings. I have previously drawn the inference that woman-to-woman relations encouraged articulation and expression. In their relationships with their menfolk, however, the dynamics of family psychology compelled women to adopt the contradictory emotional mode of inexpression and seeming passivity. Lavinia Porter ran ahead to hide her tears, and [others] struggled to "hold in" and "repress" their sadness, not wanting to reveal themselves to the men about them. The second day out of Council Bluffs, Catherine Haun had an attack of homesickness, but she composed herself. "Then wiping away my tears, lest they betray me to my husband, I prepared to continue my trip. I have often thought that had I confided in him he would have certainly turned back for he, as well as the other men of the party, was disheartened and was struggling not to betray it." Here she protected her husband from his own uncertainty and helped to uphold his manhood; but might she not also have been protecting herself against the later eventuality that she would be blamed as the *sole* cause of their joint failure of will?

There was, as well, a self-motivation to this enduring mode. Especially in the context of the man's world of the trail, it would have been strange had the standards of perseverance which men successfully demonstrated not been, in part, inwardly accepted by women as well. Women might well have despised their own doubts and fears and worked to overcome them, in spite of the detachment they felt from the emigration. Thus did Rebecca Ketcham characterize her anxieties as "wicked fears" and resolve to "try to be patient." Like Rebecca, . . . many women somehow felt that repression of feelings and patient endurance would reap a heavenly reward; they looked on the trail as a kind of cross for women to bear. Maria Belshaw comforted herself, "Thy will be done O God not mine, that I may receive a crown of righteousness at thy right hand." And Sarah Royce, after successfully "holding in" during the first of many late-night bouts of homesickness, wrote later that "in the morning there was a mildly exultant feeling which comes from having kept silent through a cowardly fit, and finding the fit gone off."

For men the trip West was an active test of competition, strength, and manliness. It meant measuring themselves against the already romanticized images of their heroic pioneer fathers and grandfathers traversing the Wilderness Road and the Cumberland Gap. For women the trip West was a test of their inner strength. They did their part and more; they were comforting wives and attentive mothers, to the many single men of the trail as well as their husbands. They did all this, because of, not in spite of, their not wanting to leave home in the first place.

The psychology of social dependency, with its costs and rewards, was the result of the systematic oppression of women, of which their marital relations were the key link. Their induction onto the trail, not as full and willing participants but more as reluctant draftees, was the cause not of rebellion and resistance, although there were occasional examples of those, but of self-denial, a kind of active passivity and endurance. The trail experience was, of course, an extreme case; daily life was more amiable to women, with smaller subjugations. But considering the weight of these small evidences of powerlessness over years of marriage, the lives of women had to be largely lives of endurance. On the trail women called up resources of courage and will which were stockpiled for just such emergencies.

POSTSCRIPT

Did the Westward Movement Transform the Traditional Roles of Women in the Mid-Nineteenth Century?

Faragher argues that frontier women were pioneers only because they were subordinate to their husbands. In spite of legal changes in the marriage laws made by many states in the mid-nineteenth century, husbands were still the controlling authority in the family. Most men made the decision to migrate west without consulting their wives.

Myres, on the other hand, gives a much more upbeat portrayal of westering women. Myres uses many diaries and letters of middle-class white women as sources, but she also includes materials on African American, Hispanic, and Native American women (but not immigrant women) and covers a broad time period. Myres sees frontier women as extremely active in business, manufacturing, agriculture, and the traditional teaching and nursing professions. Many of these jobs were located outside of the home.

A third study, Julie Roy Jeffrey's *Frontier Women: The Trans-Mississippi West 1840-1880* (Hill & Wang, 1979), emphasizes the conservative behavior of western women. Jeffrey states in her introduction, "I hoped to find that pioneer women used the frontier as a means of liberating themselves from stereotypes and behaviors which I found constricting and sexist. I discovered they did not. More important, I discovered why they did not."

The current scholarship on women has moved beyond literate white women who settled in the West and focuses upon minority women. Papers from the conferences held by the Coalition for Western Women's History and the Southwest Institute for Research on Women are published in Susan Armitage et al., eds., *The Women's West* (University of Oklahoma Press, 1987); Lillian Schlissel et al., eds., *Western Women: Their Land, Their Lives* (University of New Mexico Press, 1988); and Elizabeth Jameson and Susan Armitage, eds., *Writing the Range: Race, Class, and Culture in the Women's West* (University of Oklahoma Press, 1997).

The two best overviews of the new western history are Patricia Nelson Limerick, *The Legacy of Conquest: The Unbroken Part of the American West* (W. W. Norton, 1987) and Richard White, *It's Your Misfortune and None of My Own: A New History of the American West* (University of Oklahoma Press, 1992).

On the Internet . . .

Civil War Related Web Links

This site lists Civil War related links and was created by the United States Civil War Center. One section is devoted to causes of the Civil War, including the slavery issue, political turmoil, the socioeconomic structure of the South, tariffs and taxes, and more.

```
http://www.cwc.lsu.edu/cwc/links/links9.htm#Causes
```

The Battle of Antietam

This is a comprehensive site on the battle of Antietam. Read a copy of the orders issued by General Robert E. Lee to his army on the eve of the Maryland Campaign and the proclamation he issued to the people of Maryland.

```
http://www.civilwarhome.com/antietam.htm
```

Abraham Lincoln Online

Dedicated to the 16th president of the United States, Abraham Lincoln Online offers educational links, Lincoln's speeches and writings, historic places, and much more.

```
http://www.netins.net/showcase/creative/lincoln.html
```

Reconstruction Era Documents

This page includes links to various Reconstruction era documents by such authors as Booker T. Washington, W. E. B. Du Bois, and Frederick Douglass.

```
http://www.libraries.rutgers.edu/rul/rr_gateway/
research_guides/history/civwar.shtml
```

PART 4

Conflict and Resolution

*T*he changing nature of the United States and the demands of its own principles finally erupted into violent conflict. Perhaps it was an inevitable step in the process of building a coherent nation from a number of distinct and diverse groups. The leaders, attitudes, and resources that were available to the North and the South were to determine the course of the war itself, as well as the national healing process that followed.

- Have Historians Overemphasized the Slavery Issue as a Cause of the Civil War?

- Is Robert E. Lee Overrated as a General?

- Did Abraham Lincoln Free the Slaves?

- Was Reconstruction a "Splendid Failure"?

ISSUE 14

Have Historians Overemphasized the Slavery Issue as a Cause of the Civil War?

YES: Joel H. Silbey, from *The Partisan Imperative: The Dynamics of American Politics Before the Civil War* (Oxford University Press, 1985)

NO: Michael F. Holt, from *The Political Crisis of the 1850s* (John Wiley & Sons, 1978)

ISSUE SUMMARY

YES: Professor of history Joel H. Silbey argues that historians have overemphasized the sectional conflict over slavery and have neglected to analyze local enthnocultural issues among the events leading to the Civil War.

NO: Professor of history Michael F. Holt maintains that both Northern Republicans and Southern Democrats seized the slavery issue to sharply distinguish party differences and thus reinvigorate the loyalty of party voters.

In the 85 years between the start of the American Revolution and the coming of the Civil War, Americans made the necessary political compromises on the slavery issue in order not to split the nation apart. The Northwest Ordinance of 1787 forbade slavery from spreading into those designated territories under its control, and the new Constitution written in the same year prohibited the slave trade from Africa after 1808.

There was some hope in the early nineteenth century that slavery might die from natural causes. The Revolutionary generation was well aware of the contradiction between the values of an egalitarian society and the practices of a slave-holding aristocracy. Philosophically, slavery was viewed as a necessary evil, not a positive good. Several Northern states abolished slavery after 1800, and the erosion of the tobacco lands in Virginia and Maryland contributed to the lessening importance of a slave labor system.

Unfortunately, two factors—territorial expansion and the market economy —made slavery the key to the South's wealth in the 35 years before the Civil

War. First, new slave states were created out of a population expanding into lands ceded to the United States as a result of the Treaty of Paris of 1783 and the Louisiana Purchase of 1803. Second, slaves were sold from the upper to the lower regions of the South because the cotton gin (invented by Eli Whitney in 1793) made it possible to harvest large quantities of cotton, ship it to the textile mills of New England and the British Isles, and turn it into cloth and finished clothing as part of the new, specialized market economy.

The slavery issue came to the forefront in 1819 when some Northern congressmen proposed that slavery be banned from the states being carved out of the Louisiana Purchase. A heated debate ensued, but the Missouri Compromise of 1821 drew a line that preserved the balance between free and slave states and that (with the exception of Missouri) prohibited slavery north of the 36° 30′ latitude.

The annexation of Texas in 1845 and the acquisition of New Mexico, Utah, and California three years later reopened the slavery question. The question of whether or not to annex Texas to the Union, after she gained her independence from Mexico in 1836, scared politicians from all sections because they were afraid of upsetting the political balance between free and slave states. Attempts at compromises in 1850 and 1854 only accelerated the situation. The Kansas-Nebraska Act of 1854, which repealed the Missouri Compromise, allowed the citizens of those territories to decide whether or not they wanted slavery. Abolitionists were furious because Illinois senator Stephen A. Douglas's doctrine of "popular sovereignty" had the potential to allow slavery to spread to territories where it was previously forbidden by the Missouri Compromise. For the next three years, Kansas became a battleground between pro-slavery forces and "Free-soilers" who voted to keep slavery out of the territory.

The Kansas-Nebraska Act had major political implications. The second party system of Whigs versus Democrats fell apart, and a new realignment took place. The Whig Party disappeared. In the South the need to defend slavery caused pro-business and yeoman-farmer Whigs from the back country to join the Southern Democrats in a unified alliance against the North. Major and minor parties in the North joined to form the new Republican Party, whose unifying principle was to confine slavery to states where it already existed but not to allow it to spread to any new territories. Quickly the Republicans mounted a successful challenge against the Democrats.

The 1860 presidential election was won by the Republican Abraham Lincoln. However, the Southern states refused to accept the election of Lincoln. Seven states seceded from the Union before he was inaugurated on March 4, 1861. When Lincoln refused to abandon the federal forts off the coast of Charleston in April 1861, the governor of South Carolina fired on Fort Sumter. The Civil War had begun. Four more states then joined the Confederacy.

Have historians overemphasized the sectional conflict over the slavery question as a cause of the Civil War? In the following selection, Joel H. Silbey argues that historians have overemphasized the conflict over slavery and have neglected to analyze local ethnocultural issues among the events leading to the Civil War. In the second selection, Michael F. Holt contends that politicians in the 1850s used the slavery issue to sharply distinguish party differences.

Joel H. Silbey

The Civil War Synthesis in American Political History

The Civil War has dominated our studies of the period between the Age of Jackson and 1861. Most historians of the era have devoted their principal attention to investigating and analyzing the reasons for differences between the North and South, the resulting sectional conflict, and the degeneration of this strife into a complete breakdown of our political system in war. Because of this focus, most scholars have accepted, without question, that differences between the North and the South were the major political influences at work among the American people in the years between the mid-1840s and the war. Despite occasional warnings about the dangers of overemphasizing sectional influences, the sectional interpretation holds an honored and secure place in the historiography of the antebellum years. We now possess a formidable number of works which, in one way or another, center attention on the politics of sectionalism and clearly demonstrate how much the Civil War dominates our study of American political history before 1861.

Obviously nothing is wrong in such emphasis if sectionalism was indeed the dominant political influence in the antebellum era. However, there is the danger in such emphasis of claiming too much, that in centering attention on the war and its causes we may ignore or play down other contemporary political influences and fail to weigh adequately the importance of nonsectional forces in antebellum politics. And, in fact, several recent studies of American political behavior have raised serious doubts about the importance of sectional differences as far as most Americans were concerned. These have even suggested that the sectional emphasis has created a false synthesis in our study of history which increases the importance of one factor, ignores the significance of other factors, and ultimately distorts the reality of American political life between 1844 and 1861.

Scholars long have used the presidential election of 1844 as one of their major starting points for the sectional analysis of American political history. In a

From Joel H. Silbey, *The Partisan Imperative: The Dynamics of American Politics Before the Civil War* (Oxford University Press, 1985). Adapted from Joel H. Silbey, "The Civil War Synthesis in American Political History," *Civil War History*, vol. 10, no. 2 (June 1964). Copyright © 1964 by Kent State University Press. Reprinted by permission of Kent State University Press. Notes omitted.

general sense they have considered American expansion into Texas to be the most important issue of that campaign. The issue stemmed from the fact that Texas was a slave area and many articulate Northerners attacked the movement to annex Texas as a slave plot designed to enhance Southern influence within the Union. Allegedly because of these attacks, and the Southerners' defending themselves, many people in both North and South found themselves caught up in such sectional bitterness that the United States took a major step toward civil war. Part of this bitterness can be seen, it is pointed out, in the popular vote in New York State where the Whig candidate for the presidency, Henry Clay, lost votes to the abolitionist Liberty party because he was a slaveholder. The loss of these votes cost him New York and ultimately the election. As a result of Clay's defeat, historians have concluded that as early as 1844 the problem of slavery extension was important enough to arouse people to act primarily in sectional terms and thus for this episode to be a milestone on the road to war.

Recently Professor Lee Benson published a study of New York State politics in the Jacksonian era. Although Benson mainly concerned himself with other problems, some of his findings directly challenge the conception that slavery and sectional matters were of major importance in New York in 1844. In his analysis Benson utilized a more systematic statistical compilation of data than have previous workers in the field of political history. Observing that scholars traditionally have looked at what people said they did rather than at what they actually did, Benson compiled a great number of election returns for New York State in this period. His purpose was to see who actually voted for whom and to place the election in historical perspective by pinpointing changes in voting over time and thus identifying the basic trends of political behavior. Through such analysis Benson arrived at a major revision of the nature of New York State voting in 1844.

Benson pointed out, first of all, that the abolitionist, anti-Texas Liberty party whose vote total should have increased if the New York population wanted to strike against a slave plot in Texas, actually lost votes over what it had received in the most immediate previous election, that of 1843. Further analysis indicated that there was no widespread reaction to the Texas issue in New York State on the part of any large group of voters, although a high degree of anti-Texas feeling indeed existed among certain limited groups in the population. Such sentiment, however, did not affect voting margins in New York State. Finally, Benson concluded that mass voting in New York in 1844 pivoted not on the sectional issue but rather on more traditional divisions between ethnic and religious groups whose voting was a reaction to matters closer to home. These proved of a more personal and psychological nature than that of Texas and its related issue of slavery extension. Sectional bitterness, contrary to previous historical conceptions, neither dominated nor seriously influenced the 1844 vote in New York. Although Benson confined his study to one state, his conclusions introduce doubts about the influence of sectionalism in other supposedly less pivotal states.

Another aspect of the sectional interpretation of American politics in the pre–Civil War era involves Congress. Political historians have considered that body to be both a forum wherein leaders personally expressed attitudes that intensified sectional bitterness, as well as an arena which reflected the general pattern of influences operative in the country at large. Therefore, writers on the period have considered the behavior of congressmen to have been more and more dominated by sectionalism, particularly after David Wilmot introduced his antislavery extension proviso into the House of Representatives in 1846. Although there may have been other issues and influences present, it is accepted that these were almost completely overborne in the late 1840s and 1850s in favor of a widespread reaction to sectional differences.

In a recently completed study, I have analyzed congressional voting in the allegedly crucial pivotal decade 1841–52, the period which historians identify as embodying the transition from nationalism to sectionalism in congressional behavior. This examination indicates that a picture of the decade as one in which sectional influences steadily grew stronger, overwhelmed all other bases of divisions, and became a permanent feature of the voting behavior of a majority of congressmen, is grossly oversimplified and a distortion of reality. In brief, although sectional influences, issues, and voting did exist, particularly between 1846 and 1850, sectional matters were not the only problems confronting congressmen. In the period before the introduction of the Wilmot Proviso in 1846, national issues such as the tariff, financial policy, foreign affairs, and land policy divided congressmen along political, not sectional, lines. Furthermore, in this earlier period issues which many believed to have shown a high degree of sectional content, such as admittance of Texas and Oregon, reveal highly partisan national divisions and little sectional voting.

Even after the rise of the slavery-extension issue, other questions of a national character remained important. Slavery was but one of several issues before Congress and it was quite possible for congressmen to vote against one another as Northern and Southern sectionalists on an issue and then to join together, regardless of section, against other Northerners and Southerners on another matter. Certainly some men from both geographic areas were primarily influenced by sectional considerations at all times on all issues, but they were a minority of all congressmen in the period. The majority of congressmen were not so overwhelmingly influenced by their being Northerners or Southerners, but continued to think and act in national terms, and even resisted attempts by several sectionally minded congressmen to forge coalitions, regardless of party, against the other section.

A careful study of congressional voting in these years also demonstrates that another assumption of historians about the nature of politics is oversimplified: the period around 1846 did *not* begin the steady forward movement of congressional politics toward sectionalism and war. Rather, it was quite possible in the period between 1846 and 1852 for congressmen to assail one another bitterly in sectional terms, physically attack one another, and even threaten secession, and still for the majority of them to return in the following session to a different approach—that of nonsectional political differences with a concomitant restoration of nonsectional coalitions. For example, it was possible in 1850, after several years of sectional fighting, for a national coalition of Senators and Representatives to join together and settle in compromise terms the differences between North and South over expansion. And they were able to do this despite the simultaneous existence of a great deal of sectional maneuvering by some congressmen in an attempt to prevent any such compromise. Furthermore, during this same session Congress also dealt with matters of railroad land grants in a way that eschewed sectional biases. Obviously the usual picture of an inexorable growth of sectional partisanship after 1846 is quite overdone. And lest these examples appeared to be isolated phenomena, preliminary research both by Gerald Wolff and by myself demonstrates that as late as 1854 there was still no complete or overwhelming sectional voting even on such an issue as the Kansas-Nebraska Act.

Such analyses of congressional behavior in an alleged transition period reinforce what Lee Benson's work on New York politics demonstrated: many varieties and many complexities existed with respect to political behavior in the antebellum period, so that even slavery failed to be a dominating influence among all people at all times—or even among most people at most times—during the 1840s and early 1850s. Again, our previous image of American politics in this period must be reconsidered in light of this fact and despite the emergence of a Civil War in 1861.

Perhaps no aspect of antebellum politics should demonstrate more fully the overpowering importance of sectional influences than the presidential election of 1860. In the preliminaries to that contest the Democratic party split on the rock of slavery, the Republican party emerged as a power in the Northern states with a good chance of winning the presidency, and loud voices in the Southern states called for secession because of Northern attacks on their institutions. In dealing with these events, historians, as in their treatment of other aspects of antebellum politics, have devoted their primary attention to sectional bickering and maneuvering among party leaders, because they considered this activity to be the most important facet of the campaign and the key to explaining the election. Although such a focus obviously has merit if one is thinking in terms of the armed conflict which broke out only five months after the election, once again, as in the earlier cases considered here, recent research has raised pertinent questions about the political realities of the situation. We may indeed ask what were the issues of the campaign as seen by the majority of voters.

Earlier studies of the 1860 election, in concerning themselves primarily with the responses and activities of political leaders, have taken popular voting behavior for granted. This aspect has either been ignored or else characterized as reflecting the same influences and attitudes as that of the leadership. Therefore, the mass of men, it is alleged, voted in response to sectional influences in 1860. For instance, several scholars concerned with the Germans in the Middle

West in this period have characterized the attitudes of that group as overwhelmingly antislavery. Thus the Republican party attracted the mass of the German vote because the liberal "Forty-Eighters" saw casting a Lincoln vote as a way to strike a blow against slavery in the United States. Going beyond this, some historians have reached similar conclusions about other Middle Western immigrant groups. As a result, according to most historians, although narrowly divided, the area went for Lincoln thanks in large part to its newest citizens, who were Northern sectionalists in their political behavior. Such conclusions obviously reinforce the apparent importance of geographic partisanship in 1860.

Testing this hypothesis, two recent scholars systematically studied and analyzed election returns in Iowa during 1860. Such examinations are important because they should reveal, if the sectional theory is correct, preoccupation among Iowa voters—especially immigrants—with the slavery question and the increasingly bitter differences between North and South. Only one of these studies, that of Professor George H. Daniels of Northwestern University, has appeared in print. But Daniels's findings shatter earlier interpretations which pinpointed sectional concerns as the central theme of the 1860 election.

Briefly stated, Daniels isolated the predominantly German townships in Iowa and, following Lee Benson's methodological lead, analyzed their vote. He found that, far from being solidly Republican voters, or moved primarily by the slavery question, the Germans of Iowa voted overwhelmingly in favor of the Democratic party. And Daniels discovered that the primary issue motivating the Germans in 1860 was an ethnic one. They were conscious of the anti-alien Know-Nothing movement which had been so strong in the United States during the 1850s and they identified the Republican party as the heir and last refuge of Know-Nothingism. If the Germans of Iowa were attracted to the Republicans by the latter's antislavery attitudes, such attraction was more than overcome by the Republicans' aura of antiforeignism. Furthermore, the Republicans were also identified in the minds of the Iowa Germans as the party of prohibitionism, a social view strongly opposed by most Germans. Thus, as Daniels concludes, " . . . The rank and file Germans who did the bulk of the voting considered their own liberty to be of paramount importance. Apparently ignoring the advice of their leaders, they cast their ballots for the party which consistently promised them liberty from prohibition and native-American legislation." As a result, the Germans of Iowa voted Democratic, not Republican, in 1860.

Lest this appear to be an isolated case, the research of Robert Swierenga on Dutch voting behavior in Iowa in 1860 confirms Daniels's findings. Swierenga demonstrated that the Dutch also voted Democratic despite their vaunted antislavery attitudes; again, revulsion from certain Republican ideals overpowered any attraction toward that party on the slavery issue.

Such research into the election of 1860, as in the earlier cases of the election of 1844 and congressional voting behavior in the 1840s and early 1850s, suggests how far the sectional and slavery preconceptions of American historians have distorted reality. Many nonsectional issues were apparently more immediately important to the groups involved than any imminent concern with Northern-Southern differences. Once again, the Civil War synthesis appears to be historically inaccurate and in need of serious revision.

Several other provocative studies recently have appeared which, while dealing with nonpolitical subjects, support the conclusion that sectional problems,
the slavery issue, and increasing bitterness between North and South were
not always uppermost concerns to most Americans in the fifteen years before
the outbreak of the war. Building upon the work of Leon Litwack, which emphasizes the general Northern antagonism toward the Negro before 1860, and
that of Larry Gara demonstrating the fallacy of the idea that a well-organized
and widespread underground railroad existed in the North, Professor C. Vann
Woodward has cautioned students against an easy acceptance of a "North-Star"
image—a picture of a universally militant Northern population determined to
ease the burden of the slave in America. Rather, as Woodward points out, a great
many Northerners remained indifferent to the plight of the slave and hostile to
the would-be antislavery reformer in their midst.

In this same tenor, Milton Powell of Michigan State University has challenged long-held assumptions that the Northern Methodist church was a bulwark of antislavery sentiment after splitting with its Southern branch in 1844.
As Powell makes clear, Northern Methodists were concerned about many other
problems in which slavery played no part, as well as being beset by conditions
which served to tone down any antislavery attitudes they may have held. More
importantly, this led many of them to ignore slavery as an issue because of its
latent tendency to divide the organization to which they belonged. Thus, even
in areas outside of the political realm, the actual conditions of antebellum society challenge the validity of the sectional concept in its most general and
far-reaching form.

This review of recent research indicates that much of our previous work on
the prewar period should be reexamined free from the bias caused by looking first at the fact of the Civil War and then turning back to view the events
of the previous decade in relation only to that fact. Although it is true that
the studies discussed here are few in number and by no means include the entire realm of American politics in the antebellum era, their diversity in time
and their revisionist conclusions do strongly suggest the fallacy of many previous assumptions. No longer should any historian blithely accept the traditional
concept of a universal preoccupation with the sectional issue.

But a larger matter is also pointed up by this recent research and the destruction of this particular myth about political sectionalism. For a question
immediately arises as to how historians generally could have accepted so readily
and for so long such oversimplifications and inaccuracies. Fortunately for future
research, answers to this question have been implicitly given by the scholars
under review, and involve methodological problems concerning evidence and a
certain naïveté about the political process.

Historians generally have utilized as evidence the writings and commentaries of contemporary observers of, and participants in, the events being examined. But, as both Benson and Daniels emphasize, this can endanger our understanding of reality. For instance, not enough attention has been paid to who actually said what, or of the motives of a given reporter or the position he was in to know and understand what was going on around him. Most particularly, scholars have not always been properly skeptical about whether the observer's comments truly reflected actuality. As Daniels pointed out in his article on German voting behavior, "contemporary opinion, including that of newspapers, is a poor guide."

If such is true, and the evidence presented by these studies indicates that it is, a question is raised as to how a historian is to discover contemporary opinion if newspapers are not always reliable as sources. The work of Benson, Daniels, and myself suggests an answer: the wider use of statistics. When we talk of public opinion (that is, how the mass of men acted or thought) we are talking in terms of aggregate numbers, of majorities. One way of determining what the public thought is by measuring majority opinion in certain circumstances—elections, for example, or the voting of congressmen—and then analyzing the content and breakdown of the figures derived. If, for example, 80 percent of the Germans in Iowa voted Democratic in 1860, this tells us more about German public opinion in 1860 than does a sprightly quote from one of the Germans in the other 20 percent who voted Republican "to uphold freedom." Historians are making much more use of statistics than formerly and are utilizing more sophisticated techniques of quantitative analysis. And such usage seems to be prelude to, judging by the works discussed here, a fuller and more accurate understanding of our past.

There are also other ways of approaching the problems posed by the 1850s. Not enough attention has been paid, it seems to me, to the fact that there are many different levels of political behavior—mass voting, legislative activity, leadership manipulation, for example—and that what is influential and important on one level of politics may not be on another. Certainly the Germans and Dutch of Iowa in 1860 were not paying much attention to the desires of their leaders. They were responding to influences deemed more important than those influences shaping the responses of their leaders. As Swierenga pointed out in his analysis of Dutch voting:

> While Scholte [a leader of the Dutch community] fulminated against Democrats as slave mongers, as opponents of the Pacific Railroad and Homestead Bills, and as destroyers of the Constitution, the Dutch citizens blithely ignored him and the national issues he propounded and voted their personal prejudices against Republican nativists and prohibitionists.

Obviously, when historians generalize about the nature of political behavior they must also be sure which group and level of political activity they mean, and so identify it, and not confuse different levels or assume positive correlations between the actions of people on one level with those on another level. Such precision will contribute greatly to accuracy and overcome tendencies toward distortion.

Finally, based on the work under discussion here, it is clear that historians must become more aware of the complexities of human behavior. All people, even of the same stratum of society or living in the same geographic area, do not respond with the same intensity to the same social or political stimuli. Not everyone perceives his best interests in the same way, or considers the same things to be the most important problems confronting him. Depending upon time and circumstances, one man may respond primarily to economic influences; another one, at the same time and place, to religious influences; and so on. Sometimes most people in a given community will respond to the same influences equally, but we must be careful to observe *when* this is true and not generalize from it that this is *always* true. Single-factor explanations for human behavior do not seem to work, and we must remain aware of that fact.

With improved methodological tools and concepts historians may begin to engage in more systematic and complete analyses of popular voting, legislative voting, and the motivations and actions of political leaders. They will be able to weigh the relative influence of sectional problems against other items of interest and concern on all levels of political behavior. Until this is done, however, we do know on the basis of what already has been suggested that we cannot really accept glib explanations about the antebellum period. The Civil War has had a pernicious influence on the study of American political development that preceded it—pernicious because it has distorted the reality of political behavior in the era and has caused an overemphasis on sectionalism. It has led us to look not for what was occurring in American politics in those years, but rather for what was occurring in American politics that tended toward sectional breakdown and civil war—a quite different matter.

 **NO**

The Political Crisis of the 1850s

Historians have long looked to politics for the origins of the Civil War, and they have offered two major interpretations of political developments between 1845 and 1860. Both are primarily concerned with the breakdown of the old party system and the rise of the Republicans and not with the second aspect of the crisis—the loss of faith in politicians, the desire for reform, and their relationship to republican ideology. By spelling out my reservations about and disagreements with these interpretations, the assumptions behind and, I hope, the logic of my own approach to the political crisis of the 1850s will become clearer.

The standard interpretation maintains that intensifying sectional disagreements over slavery inevitably burst into the political arena, smashed the old national parties, and forced the formation of new, sectionally oriented ones. The Second Party System was artificial, some historians contend, since it could survive only by avoiding divisive sectional issues and by confining political debate to sectionally neutral economic questions on which the national parties had coherent stands. Once sectional pressure was reaggravated by the events of the late 1840s and early 1850s, those fragile structures shattered and were replaced. "On the level of politics," writes Eric Foner, "the coming of the Civil War is the intrusion of sectional ideology into the political system, despite the efforts of political leaders of both parties [Whigs and Democrats] to keep it out. Once this happened, political competition worked to exacerbate, rather than to solve, social and sectional conflicts."

There is much to be said for this interpretation. The Republican party did rise to dominance in the North largely because of an increase of Northern hostility toward the South, and its ascendance worsened relations between the sections. Attributing the political developments prior to its rise to the same sectional force that caused the rise has the virtue of simplicity. But that argument distorts a rapidly changing and very complex political situation between 1845 and 1860. There were three discrete, sequential political developments in those years that shaped the political crisis that led to war—the disappearance of the Whig party and with it of the old framework of two-party competition, a realignment of voters as they switched party affiliation, and a shift from a nationally balanced party system where both major parties competed on fairly

From Michael F. Holt, *The Political Crisis of the 1850s* (John Wiley & Sons, 1978). Copyright © 1978 by Michael F. Holt. Reprinted by permission of the author. Notes omitted.

even terms in all parts of the nation to a sectionally polarized one with Republicans dominant in the North and Democrats in the South. Although related, these were distinct phases, occurring with some exceptions in that order, and they were caused by different things. Although the inflammation of sectional antagonism between 1855 and 1860 helped to account for the new sectional alignment of parties, sectional conflict by itself caused neither the voter realignment of middecade nor the most crucial event of the period—the death of the Whig party, especially its death at the state level. It bears repeating that the demise of the Whig party, and with it of the traditional framework of two-party competition at the local, state, and national levels, was the most critical development in this sequence. Its disappearance helped foster popular doubts about the legitimacy of politics as usual, raised fears that powerful conspiracies were undermining republicanism, allowed the rise of the Republican party in the North, and created the situation in the lower South that produced secession there and not elsewhere.

The theory that the Second Party System was artificial and was shattered once the slavery issue arose, like the larger theory of the war's causation it reflects, founders on the problem of timing. There is considerable evidence that sectional conflict over slavery characterized the Second Party System throughout its history. Slavery was not swept under the rug; it was often the stuff of political debate. Proponents of the traditional interpretation, indeed, have often confused internal divisions within the national parties with their demise. Although they point to different dates when the rupture was fatal, they have assumed that once the national parties were split into Northern and Southern wings over slavery, the parties were finished. Yet the Whig and Jacksonian parties, like almost all political organizations at any time, had frequently been divided—over slavery as well as other issues. They functioned for years in that condition. To establish the existence of sectional splits within the national parties is not to answer the vexed question of why those divisions were fatal in the 1850s and not in the 1830s and 1840s. If it was the sectional conflict that destroyed the old party system, the crucial question is why the parties were able to manage that conflict at some times and not at others. For a number of reasons, the easy reply that the volatile slavery issue simply became more explosive in the 1850s than earlier is not an adequate answer to this question.

The second major interpretation of the politics of the 1850s also has its merits and liabilities. Arguing that traditional historians have viewed events in the 1850s with the hindsight knowledge that the Civil War occurred, a new group of political historians insist that the extent to which sectionalism affected political behavior, especially popular voting behavior at the grass-roots level, has been exaggerated. Local social tensions, especially ethnic and religious tensions, motivated voters in the 1850s, they contend, not national issues like slavery, which was of so much concern to national political elites. What applies to Congress and national leaders, these new political historians say in effect, does not apply to the local level of politics. Prohibitionism, nativism, and anti-Catholicism produced the voter realignment in which the Whigs disappeared and new parties emerged in the North.

By focusing on voting behavior, this ethnocultural interpretation presents a compelling analysis of why an anti-Democratic majority was created in many parts of the North. Explaining why Northern voters realigned between 1853 and 1856, however, does not answer why the Republican party appeared or why party politics were sectionally polarized at the end of the decade. Prophets of the ethnocultural thesis, moreover, have done little to explain Southern politics, yet developments in Dixie where Catholics and immigrants were few were just as important as events in the North in leading to war. Nor do voting studies really explain the crucial first phase—the death of the Whig party. Party reorganization accompanied voter realignment in the 1850s, and ethnocultural tensions alone do not explain why new parties were necessary. Why didn't anti-Democratic voters simply become Whigs? This question has a particular urgency when one realizes that in the 1840s ethnocultural issues had also been present and that the Whigs and Democrats had aligned on opposite sides of them. The problem with stressing ethnocultural issues, as with stressing sectionalism, is why those issues could be contained within, indeed could invigorate, old party lines at one time yet could help to destroy them at another.

The fundamental weakness of previous interpretations of why the old two-party system broke down is their misunderstanding of how and why it worked. They have not adequately explored either the relationship between political parties and issues or the impact of the federal system with its divided responsibilities among local, state, and national governments on the parties and the party system. Whether historians stress sectionalism or ethnocultural issues, their central assumption seems to be that issues arising from the society at large caused political events. The Second Party System functioned because it dealt with "safe" economic questions, but once those issues were replaced or displaced by new disruptive matters the parties broke down and realignment followed. Yet what made the Second Party System work in the end was not issues *per se* or the presence of safe issues and absence of dangerous ones. In the end what made the two-party system operate was its ability to allow political competition on a broad range of issues that varied from time to time and place to place. If the genius of the American political system has been the peaceful resolution of conflict, what has supported two-party systems has been the conflict itself, not its resolution. As long as parties fought with each other over issues or took opposing stands even when they failed to promote opposing programs, as long as they defined alternative ways to secure republican ideals, voters perceived them as different and maintained their loyalty to them. Party health and popular faith in the political process depended on the perception of party difference, which in turn depended on the reality—or at least the appearance—of interparty conflict. As long as parties seemed different from each other, voters viewed them as viable vehicles through which to influence government.

Politicians had long recognized that group conflict was endemic to American society and that the vitality of individual parties depended on the intensity of their competition with opposing parties. Thomas Jefferson had perceived in 1798 that "in every free and deliberating society, there must, from the nature of man, be opposite parties, and violent dissensions and discords." "Seeing that we must have somebody to quarrel with," he wrote John Taylor, "I had rather keep our New England associates for that purpose, than to see our bickerings transferred to others." Even more explicit in their recognition of what made parties work were the founders of New York's Albany Regency in the 1820s. They deplored the lack of internal discipline and cohesion in the Jeffersonian Republican party once the Federalists disappeared, and they moved quickly to remedy it. Although any party might suffer defeats, they realized, "it is certain to acquire additional strength... by the attacks of adverse parties." A political party, indeed, was "most in jeopardy when an opposition is not sufficiently defined." During "the contest between the great rival parties [Federalists and Jeffersonians] each found in the strength of the other a powerful motive of union and vigor." Significantly, those like Daniel Webster who deplored the emergence of mass parties in the 1820s and 1830s also recognized that strife was necessary to perpetuate party organization and that the best way to break it down was to cease opposition and work for consensus. Politicians in the 1840s and 1850s continued to believe that interparty conflict was needed to unify their own party and maintain their voting support. Thus an Alabama Democrat confessed that his party pushed a certain measure at the beginning of the 1840 legislative session explicitly as "the best means for drawing the party lines as soon as possible" while by 1852, when opposition to that state's Democracy appeared to disintegrate, another warned perceptively, "I think the only danger to the Democratic party is that it will become too much an omnibus in this State. We have nothing to fear from either the Union, or Whig party or both combined. From their friendship and adherence much." Many of the important decisions in the 1840s and 1850s reflected the search by political leaders for issues that would sharply define the lines between parties and thus reinvigorate the loyalty of party voters.

If conflict sustained the old two-party system, what destroyed it was the loss of the ability to provide interparty competition on *any* important issue at *any* level of the federal system. Because the political system's vitality and legitimacy with the voters depended on the clarity of the definition of the parties as opponents, the blurring of that definition undid the system. What destroyed the Second Party System was consensus, not conflict. The growing congruence between the parties on almost all issues by the early 1850s dulled the sense of party difference and thereby eroded voters' loyalty to the old parties. Once competing groups in society decided that the party system no longer provided them viable alternatives in which they could carry on conflict with each other, they repudiated the old system by dropping out, seeking third parties that would meet their needs, or turning to nonpartisan or extrapolitical action to achieve their goals. Because the collapse of the Second Party System was such a vital link in the war's causation, therefore, one arrives at a paradox. While the Civil War is normally viewed as the one time when conflict prevailed over consensus in American politics, the prevalence of consensus over conflict in crucial parts of the political system contributed in a very real way to the outbreak of war in the first place....

The sectionalization of American politics was emphatically *not* simply a reflection or product of basic popular disagreements over black slavery. Those had long existed without such a complete polarization developing. Even though a series of events beginning with the Kansas-Nebraska Act greatly increased sectional consciousness, it is a mistake to think of sectional antagonism as a spontaneous and self-perpetuating force that imposed itself on the political arena against the will of politicians and coerced parties to conform to the lines of sectional conflict. Popular grievances, no matter how intense, do not dictate party strategies. Political leaders do. Some one has to politicize events, to define their political relevance in terms of a choice between or among parties, before popular grievances can have political impact. It was not events alone that caused Northerners and Southerners to view each other as enemies of the basic rights they both cherished. Politicians who pursued very traditional partisan strategies were largely responsible for the ultimate breakdown of the political process. Much of the story of the coming of the Civil War is the story of the successful efforts of Democratic politicians in the South and Republican politicians in the North to keep the sectional conflict at the center of political debate and to defeat political rivals who hoped to exploit other issues to achieve election.

For at least thirty years political leaders had recognized that the way to build political parties, to create voter loyalty and mobilize support, and to win elections was to find issues or positions on issues that distinguished them from their opponents and that therefore could appeal to various groups who disliked their opponents by offering them an alternative for political action—in sociological terms, to make their party a vehicle for negative reference group behavior. Because of the American ethos, the most successful tactic had been to pose as a champion of republican values and to portray the opponent as antirepublican, as unlawful, tyrannical, or aristocratic. Jackson, Van Buren, and Polk, Antimasons and Whigs, had all followed this dynamic of the political system. Stephen A. Douglas and William H. Seward had pursued the same strategy in their unsuccessful attempt to rebuild the disintegrating Second Party System with the Kansas-Nebraska Act in 1854. After faith in the old parties had collapsed irreparably, when the shape of future political alignments was uncertain, Republican politicians quite consciously seized on the slavery and sectional issue in order to build a new party. Claiming to be the exclusive Northern Party that was necessary to halt slavery extension and defeat the Slave Power conspiracy was the way they chose to distinguish themselves from Democrats, whom they denounced as pro-Southern, and from the Know Nothings, who had chosen a different organizing principle—anti-Catholicism and nativism—to construct their new party.

To say that Republican politicians agitated and exploited sectional grievances in order to build a winning party is a simple description of fact. It is not meant to imply that winning was their only objective or to be a value judgment about the sincerity or insincerity of their personal hatred of black slavery. Some undoubtedly found slavery morally intolerable and hoped to use the national government to weaken it by preventing its expansion, abolishing it in federal enclaves like the District of Columbia, and undermining it within Southern states by whatever means were constitutionally possible, such as opening the mails to abolitionist literature and prohibiting the interstate slave trade. The antislavery pedigree of Republican leaders, however, was in a sense irrelevant to the triumph of the Republican party. The leaders were divided over the policies they might pursue if they won control of the national government, and leadership views were often far in advance of those held by their electorate. Much more important was the campaign they ran to obtain power, their skill in politicizing the issues at hand in such a way as to convince Northern voters that control of the national government by an exclusive Northern party was necessary to resist Slave Power aggressions. The Republicans won more because of what they were against than because of what they were for, because of what they wanted to stop, not what they hoped to do. . . .

The key to unraveling the paradoxes in Republican rhetoric, the juxtaposition of egalitarianism and racism, of pledges not to interfere with slavery in the South alongside calls to end slavery and join a great crusade for freedom, is to remember that the word "slavery" had long had a definite meaning aside from the institution of black slavery in the South. It was in this sense that many Republicans used the word. Slavery implied subordination to tyranny, the loss of liberty and equality, the absence of republicanism. Slavery resulted when republican government was overthrown or usurped, and that, charged Republicans, was exactly what the Slave Power was trying to do. Hence the slavery that many Republicans objected to most was not the bondage of blacks in the South but the subjugation of Northern whites to the despotism of a tiny oligarchy of slaveholders bent on destroying their rights, a minority who controlled the Democratic party and through it the machinery of the federal government. Thus one Republican complained privately in 1857, "The Slave power will not submit. The tyrants of the lash will not withhold until they have put padlocks on the lives of freemen. The Union which our fathers formed seventy years ago is not the Union today . . . the sons of the Revolutionary fathers are becoming *slaves* or *masters.*" Thus a Chicago Republican congressman, after reciting a litany of supposed Slave Power aggressions against the North, later recalled, "All these things followed the taking possession of the Government and lands by the slave power, until we [in the North] were the slaves of slaves, being chained to the car of this Slave Juggernaut." Thus the black abolitionist Frederick Douglass perceptively observed, "The cry of Free Men was raised, not for the extension of liberty to the black man, but for the protection of the liberty of the white."

The basic objective of Republican campaigns from 1856 to 1860, therefore, was to persuade Northerners that slaveholders meant to enslave them through their control of the national government and to enlist Northern voters behind the Republican party in a defensive phalanx to ward off *that* slavery, and not in an offensive crusade to end black slavery, by driving the Slave Power from its control of the national government. For such a tactic to succeed, the Republicans required two things. First, to make an asset and not a liability of their existence as an exclusive Northern party, they needed events to increase Northern antagonism toward the South so that men believed the South, and not foreigners and Catholics or the Republicans themselves, posed the chief threat to the republic. More important, they had successfully to identify the Democratic party as an agent or lackey of the South. Because the Republicans campaigned only in the North, because Northern voters chose among Northern candidates instead of between Northerners and Southerners, only by making

Northern Democrats surrogates for the Slave Power could they make their case that Republicans alone, and not simply any Northern politicians, were needed to resist and overthrow the slavocracy. Because they dared not promise overt action against slaveholders except for stopping slavery expansion, in other words, Republicans could not exploit Northern anger, no matter how intense it was, unless they could convince Northern voters that supporting the Republicans and defeating Northern Democrats was an efficacious and constitutional way to defeat the Slave Power itself.

By the summer of 1856 it was much easier to identify the Democracy with the South than it had been earlier. For one thing, the results of the congressional elections of 1854 and 1855 had dramatically shifted the balance of sectional power within the Democratic party, a result that was plainly evident when the 34th Congress met during 1856. From 1834 to 1854 the Democratic congressional delegation had usually been reasonably balanced between North and South. In the 33rd Congress, Northern Democrats had even outnumbered Southern Democrats in the House by a margin of 91 to 67. But in 1856 there were only 25 Northerners as compared to 63 Southerners, and even though Northern Democratic representation would increase after the 1856 elections, the sectional balance would never be restored before the Civil War. The South seemed to dominate the Democracy, and that fact was especially difficult to hide during a presidential election year. Because the Democrats, unlike the Republicans, met in a common national convention with Southerners and campaigned in both sections, Democrats could not deny their Southern connection. The democratic platform endorsing the Kansas-Nebraska Act strengthened that identification, thereby flushing out regular Northern Democrats who had tried to evade the Nebraska issue in 1854 and 1855 and infuriating anti-Nebraska Democrats who had clung to the party in hopes of reversing its policy but who now bolted to the Republicans. . . .

The Democratic party within the Deep South had, in fact, changed in significant ways. During the 1830s and 1840s, it had normally been controlled by and represented the interests of nonslaveholders from the hill country and piney woods regions. Even at that time slaveholders and their lawyer allies from the normally Whig black belt areas had contested for leadership of the Democracy. Sharing the same economic concerns as their Whig neighbors in those plantation regions, concerns that nonslaveholding Democrats generally opposed, Democrats from the black belt had bid for control of the party by trying to shift attention to national issues and asserting that the threat to Southern equality posed the greatest menace to the liberties of all Southern voters. During the 1850s, for a variety of reasons, those slaveholding elements took over the Democracy, and in state after state it became much less receptive at the state level to the wishes of the nonslaveholding majority who nonetheless remained Democrats because of traditional Jacksonian loyalties. For one thing, Franklin Pierce favored Southern Rights Democrats in the distribution of federal patronage. Second, as the Whig party dissolved, Democratic politicians from the slaveholding regions won over some of its former adherents by stressing the menace to slaveholders' interests, thereby increasing their own power within the Democratic party. Finally, during the 1850s, the cotton culture spread away from the old black belt to staunchly Democratic regions, thus enlarging the constituency that would respond to politicians riding the slavery issue.

As a result of this transformation, the economic priorities of the Democratic party changed. Democratic newspapers openly advised Democratic legislators not to offend their new Whig allies, and the new Democratic leaders wanted positive economic programs in any case. Occasionally the nonslaveholders found individual champions of the old Jacksonian orthodoxy like Governor George Winston of Alabama and Governor Joe Brown of Georgia who vetoed probusiness legislation, but Democratic legislatures invariably overrode those vetoes. To nonslaveholders, the Democratic party, as a party, and the political process as a whole no longer seemed as responsive as they once had been.

The shift of power within the dominant Democracy hastened the almost exclusive concentration of political rhetoric on the slavery and sectional issues. For one thing, slaveholders were more genuinely concerned about potential threats to black slavery than nonslaveholders. For another, the Democrats attributed their rise to dominance by 1852 to their ability to appear more pro-Southern than the Whigs, and they saw no reason to change a winning strategy. Third, the new leaders of the party continued to feel the need of holding the loyalty of the nonslaveholding backbone of the Democratic electorate. That support had always been won by identifying and crusading against antirepublican monsters. Because the new leaders did not want to attack the economic programs they were themselves promoting and because internal opposition was so weak from former Whigs who approved of those programs, they more and more portrayed the external Republican party as the chief danger to the liberty, equality, and self-esteem of all Southerners, slaveholders and nonslaveholders alike. Like the Republicans in the North, they translated the sectional conflict into the republican idiom in order to win the votes of men who were not primarily concerned with black slavery.

POSTSCRIPT

Have Historians Overemphasized the Slavery Issue as a Cause of the Civil War?

Silbey's selection represents the first sustained attack on the sectional interpretation of the events leading to the Civil War. Historians, he contends, have created a false "Civil War synthesis" that positions slavery as the major issue that divided America, thereby distorting "the reality of American political life between 1844 and 1861."

Silbey is one of the "new political historians" who have applied the techniques of modern-day political scientists in analyzing the election returns and voting patterns of Americans' nineteenth- and early-twentieth-century predecessors. These historians use computers and regression analysis of voting patterns, they favor a quantitative analysis of past behavior, and they reject the traditional sources of quotes from partisan newspapers and major politicians because these sources provide anecdotal and often misleading portraits of our past. Silbey and other new political historians maintain that all politics are local. Therefore, the primary issues in the 1860 election for voters and their politicians were ethnic and cultural, and party loyalty was more important than sectional considerations.

Holt is also interested in analyzing the struggles for power at the state and local levels by the major political parties, but he is critical of the ethnocultural school that Silbey represents. In Holt's view, Silbey's emphasis on voter analysis explains why an anti-Democratic bloc of voters developed in the North. But it does not explain why the Whig Party disappeared nor why the Republican Party became the majority party in the northern and western states by 1850. More important, since Silbey and other ethnoculturalists have little to say about Southern politics, reasons why secession and the subsequent Civil War took place are left unanswered.

Holt also rejects the more traditional view that the Civil War resulted from the "intensifying sectional disagreements over slavery." Instead, he promotes a more complicated picture of the events leading to the Civil War. Between 1845 and 1860, he maintains, three important things happened: the breakdown of the Whig Party; the realignment of voters; and "a shift from a nationally balanced party system where both major parties competed on fairly even terms in all parts of the nation to a sectionally polarized one with Republicans dominant in the North and Democrats in the South."

Holt builds his argument on the assumption that two-party competition at the state and local levels is healthy in resolving conflicts. With the demise of the Whig Party in the middle 1850s, the two-party system of competition broke down at the state and local levels. A national realignment was completed by 1860: Republicans controlled Northern states, while Democrats dominated the Southern ones. Holt maintains that the Whig and Democratic parties had argued over the slavery issue in the 1830s and 1840s but that they did not fragment into state and local parties. He implies that if the second-party system continued through the 1850s, the slavery issue might have been resolved in a more peaceful manner.

One criticism of both Silbey and Holt is that neither author interprets the political events leading up to the Civil War within the context of the socioeconomic changes taking place in the country. Both authors explain how many Americans manifested their hostility to the Irish Catholics who came here in the 1840s and 1850s by joining the Know-Nothing Party, which in turn caused a realignment of the political parties. But they make no mention of the reasons why the Irish and other immigrants came here: the market revolution and the need for workers to build and staff the canals, railroads, and factories.

The list of books about the Civil War is extensive. Two good starting points are John Niven, *The Coming of the Civil War, 1837–1861* (Harlan Davidson, 1990) and Bruce Levine, *Half Slave and Half Free* (Hill & Wang, 1992). An older, extensive work with a compelling narrative and sound interpretations is David Potter, *The Impending Crisis, 1848–1861* (Harper & Row, 1976). Michael Perman has updated the well-worn problems of American civilization in *The Coming of the American Civil War*, 3rd ed. (D. C. Heath, 1993).

Both Silbey and Holt have published numerous articles in scholarly journals. Silbey, who has extensive knowledge of the nineteenth-century Democratic Party, has collected his articles in *The American Political Nation 1838–1893* (Stanford University Press, 1991). A collection of Holt's articles can be found in *Political Parties and American Political Development From the Age of Jackson to the Age of Lincoln* (Louisiana State University Press, 1992).

Historians who reject the ethnocultural school, which minimizes the slavery issue as the cause of the Civil War, include Eric Foner and Kenneth M. Stampp. Foner's *Free Soil, Free Labor, Free Men* (Oxford University Press, 1970) is an excellent study of the bourgeois capitalism and conservative idealism that formed the ideological basis of the Republican Party before the Civil War. In *America in 1857: A Nation on the Brink* (Oxford University Press, 1990), Stampp argues that conflict became inevitable after the election of James Buchanan to the presidency, the firestorm in Kansas, and the Supreme Court's decision in *Dred Scott v. Sandford*. A summary of the traditional view is found in Richard H. Sewell's *House Divided: Sectionalism and Civil War, 1848–1865* (Johns Hopkins University Press, 1988).

ISSUE 15

Is Robert E. Lee Overrated as a General?

YES: Alan T. Nolan, from *"Rally, Once Again!" Selected Civil War Writings of Alan T. Nolan* (Madison House, 2000)

NO: Gary W. Gallagher, from "Another Look at the Generalship of R. E. Lee," in Gary W. Gallagher, ed., *Lee the Soldier* (University of Nebraska Press, 1996)

ISSUE SUMMARY

YES: Attorney Alan T. Nolan argues that General Robert E. Lee was a flawed grand strategist whose offensive operations produced heavy casualties in an unnecessarily prolonged war that the South could not win.

NO: According to professor of American history Gary W. Gallagher, General Lee was the most revered and unifying figure in the Confederacy, and he "formulated a national strategy predicated on the probability of success in Virginia and the value of battlefield victories."

O ver the past 125 years contemporaries and historians have advanced dozens of explanations for the defeat of the Confederacy in the Civil War. Most of these can be divided into two categories: internal and external.

According to a number of historians, internal divisions doomed the Confederacy. In his book *State Rights in the Confederacy* (Peter Smith, 1961), Frank Owsley maintains that the centrifugal forces of state rights killed the Confederacy. Owsley contends that governors in North Carolina and Georgia withheld men and equipment from the Confederate armies in order to build up their own state militias. On the Confederate tombstone, he said, should be inscribed: "Died of State Rights."

A second version of the internal conflict argument appeared in a 1960 essay in a symposium entitled *Why the North Won the Civil War* (Louisiana State University Press, 1960). In it, the editor, Pulitzer Prize–winning historian David Donald, argued that the resistance of Southerners to conscription, taxes, and limitations on speeches that were critical of the war effort fatally crippled the Confederacy's war effort. Instead of state rights, said Donald, the Confederate tombstone should read: "Died of Democracy."

A third variant of the internal conflict argument has recently been promoted by four Southern scholars: Richard E. Beringer, Herman Hattaway, Archer Jones, and William N. Still, Jr. Their main thesis is that the Confederacy lacked the will to win because of its inability to fashion a viable Southern nationalism, increasing religious doubts that God was on the Confederacy's side, and guilt over slavery.

Historians who emphasize external reasons for the Confederacy's failure stress two factors: The Union's overwhelming numbers and resources and the uneven quality of leadership between the two sides. The North possessed two-and-one-half times the South's population, three times its railroad capacity, and nine times its industrial production. The Unionists also appear to have had better leadership. Abraham Lincoln is ranked as America's greatest president because he united his political objectives of saving the Union and freeing the slaves with a military strategy designed to defeat the Confederacy. Lincoln's generals—Ulysses S. Grant, William T. Sherman, and Philip H. Sheridan—outsmarted the Confederate leadership. In 1864, for example, massive frontal attacks were made against the Confederates in the eastern and western theaters. At the same time, Sherman destroyed much of the agricultural base of the Southerners as he marched his troops through South Carolina and Georgia.

But what if the South had won the Civil War? Could the same external explanations that are attributed to the Union victory also be used to explain a Confederate win? Would one Confederate soldier be considered equal to four Union soldiers? Would a triumvirate of yeoman farmers, slaveholding planters, and small industrialists have proven the superiority of agrarian values over industrial ones? Would Jefferson Davis's leadership emerge as superior to Lincoln's? Would the great military leaders be Robert E. Lee, Thomas "Stonewall" Jackson, and Braxton Bragg instead of Grant, Sherman, and Sheridan?

No Civil War figure is more difficult to comprehend than General Lee. A product of the Virginia aristocracy, Lee ranked second in his class at West Point and distinguished himself as an army engineer, bridge builder, and scout during the Mexican War. While home in Virginia on an extended furlough to care for his invalid wife in October 1859, he took command of a detachment of marines to capture John Brown and his men inside the roundhouse during a raid on Harpers Ferry. Offered the command of all federal forces when the Civil War broke out, Lee made the fateful decision to resign his army commission and fight for the Confederacy.

In the first of the following selections, Alan T. Nolan challenges what he believes to be one of the biggest myths of the Civil War—the genius of Robert E. Lee. Written in the style of a lawyer's brief, Nolan portrays the "marble man" as a flawed grand strategist whose offensive operations produced heavy casualties in a war that was unnecessarily prolonged and that the South could not win.

In the second selection, Gary W. Gallagher contends that Lee was a truly revered and unifying figure in the Confederacy. According to Gallagher, most Southerners approved of Lee's offensive tactics, were appreciative of his battlefield victories, and believed that the Northern troops could not win the war unless they captured his army.

Alan T. Nolan

"Rally, Once Again!"

General Lee—A Different View

I believe that Lee's generalship hurt the Confederates' chances for victory. I do not fault his tactics or operational strategy. I do fault his sense of the South's *grand strategy.* Tactics, of course, refers to *how* a battle is fought. Operational strategy concerns the plan of a campaign or battle. *Grand strategy* pertains to the use of military forces in order to win the war.

I concede that Lee was an effective and sometimes brilliant field commander, but his towering reputation results from viewing his leadership a campaign or a battle at a time and disregarding considerations of grand strategy. I argue that in grand strategic terms Lee did not understand the war, an ultimate failure that his sometimes brilliant operational strategy and tactics simply do not overcome.

In order to evaluate my thesis, one has to identify his or her own opinion as to how the South could have won: with an offensive grand strategy that risked the depletion of its inferior numbers in an effort to defeat the North militarily, or the defensive, that is, fighting the war so as to prolong it and punish the North so that it would have decided that coercion was impossible or not worth the cost. Because of its relatively limited manpower and manufacturing base, the Confederacy was never in a position to defeat the North militarily. Its only chance was to make the war so costly to the North that the North would give it up. To do this, it was essential for Lee to observe a conserving, defensive grand strategy, the counterpart of Washington's grand strategy in the Revolution. The Americans could not and did not militarily defeat the British regulars, but within a grand defensive context they kept armies in the field and harassed the enemy until it gave up the contest.

In arguing for the defensive grand strategy, I am not advocating a perimeter war, a war of position or the exclusively defensive operational strategy and tactics of General Joseph E. Johnston in the Atlanta campaign. Nor do I believe that Lee could simply have remained idle. Within a defensive context he could have maneuvered and raided, as did Washington, and still avoided the expensive battles that his offensives induced. Occasional reasoned operationally strategic offensives and tactics could have been undertaken within the

From Alan T. Nolan, *"Rally, Once Again!" Selected Civil War Writings of Alan T. Nolan* (Madison House, 2000). Originally published in *The Color Bearer* (1995). Copyright © 1995 by The American Blue & Gray Association.

framework of the grand strategic defensive. Washington's leadership is again the model.

Lee's grand strategic view was set forth in a letter of July 6, 1864, to President Davis:

> If we can defeat or drive the armies of the enemy from the field, we shall have peace. All of our efforts and energies should be devoted to that object.

This is a statement of offensive grand strategy. Lee believed that to win the war the South had to overpower the North militarily, to decimate and disperse its armies. A reference to 1862–63 is appropriate. Having taken command of the Army of Northern Virginia on June 1, 1862, for two years Lee vigorously pursued the strategic offensive in an effort to defeat the North militarily: the Peninsula, the Second Bull Run Campaign, the Maryland Campaign, Chancellorsville, and the Pennsylvania Campaign. He either attacked or, in the case of Second Bull Run and the Maryland Campaign, maneuvered offensively so as to precipitate large and costly battles. He did this although he had predicted that a siege in the Richmond defenses would be fatal to his army. In order to avoid being fixed, to avoid a siege, an army must be mobile. And mobility, the capacity to maneuver, requires numbers in some reasonable relationship to the enemy's numbers. In the course of his offensives, Lee took disproportionate, irreplaceable and unaffordable losses that undermined the viability of his army, deprived it of mobility, and ultimately committed it to a siege. A comparison of Lee's and the Federals' losses is instructive [see Table 1].

Table 1

	Federals	Confederates
The Seven Days	9,796	19,739
	10.7%	20.7%
Second Bull Run	10,096	9,108
	13.3%	18.8%
Antietam	11,657	11,724
	15.5%	22.6%
Chancellorsville	11,116	10,746
	11.4%	18.7%
Gettysburg	17,684	22,638
	21.2%	30.2%

Fredericksburg. Lee's only 1862-3 genuinely defensive battle, provides a significant contrast: Burnside lost almost 11,000 killed and wounded (10.9%) as compared to Lee's 4,656 (6.4%).

Classic examples of Lee's mistaken offensive grand strategy are provided by his decisions that led to the battles at Antietam and Gettysburg. Having been victorious at Second Bull Run, Lee was in an ideal position in September 1862 to desist from a prompt offensive move. In spite of statements by some writers that he had no alternative to moving into Maryland, even Freeman concedes that after Second Bull Run he could have moved a "slight distance southward" from Manassas, "to Warrenton, for instance.... That would put the Army of Northern Virginia on the flank of any force advancing to Richmond, and would give it the advantage of direct rail communications with the capitaL" In spite of this alternative, Lee moved into Maryland, which forseeably drew the Federal army after him and resulted in the costly battle at Antietam. Lee knew that substantial casualties were inevitable in that battle whether he won or lost. The situation immediately after Chancellorsville is also illuminating. In that battle, Lee had demonstrated his offensive tactical brilliance—and he had taken heavy losses in the process. According to his aide, Col. Charles Marshall, and Lee's own comments, Lee then had three options: to attack Hooker across the Rappahannock, to position himself to defend against another Federal effort to attack him across the Rappahannock, and to raid into Maryland and Pennsylvania. Having wisely rejected attempting to attack Hooker across the river, Lee chose the Northern raid option. This choice ended at Gettysburg where, to quote Freeman, Lee's army was "wrecked." Surely Gettysburg, requiring a crossing and recrossing of the Potomac and with extended lines of communication, was the most risky of the options. As in the case of the 1862 move into Maryland, win, lose or draw, the Maryland-Pennsylvania move of 1863 was bound to result in substantial casualties.

Lee's offensive view of the war also appears in his dispatches after Gettysburg. On August 31, 1863, in a letter to Longstreet he said that "I can see nothing better to be done than to endeavor to bring General Meade out and use our efforts to crush his army." On October 11, 1863, he wrote the Secretary of War from near Madison Courthouse that, "Yesterday I moved the army to this position with the hope of getting an opportunity to strike a blow at the enemy." Less than a week later he informed President Davis from Bristoe Station as follows: "I have the honor to inform you that with the view of bringing on an engagement with the army of Gen. Meade ... this army ... arrived near Culpeper on the 11th." Later in 1863, he spoke of "preparations made to attack (Meade)," which were frustrated by Meade's retreat. In February of 1864 he wrote Davis of his desire to "drive him (the enemy) to the Potomac." Even after the Wilderness and Spotsylvania, Lee wrote Davis that "it seems to me our best policy to unite upon it (Grant's army) and endeavor to crush it." Also in 1864 he told General Jubal A. Early that "we must destroy this army of Grant's before he gets to the James River." Already reduced by his 1862-63 offensives, it was simply not possible for Lee to "crush" or "destroy" Grant's overwhelming force. He could injure or slow it down, but not destroy it. The point is that, as had been true from the beginning of his army command, even at this late date Lee thought strategically in Armageddon terms. Early's Shenandoah Valley campaign in 1864 is significant in another respect. Early was sent to the valley to draw Federal forces away from Petersburg and Richmond. To draw Federals into the valley and *keep them there,* Early's force had only to be present in the valley. But Lee's offensive spirit caused him to tell Early to attack the Federals' valley forces. Early pursued the offensive. His outnumbered army took heavy losses and was ultimately decimated and resoundingly defeated. This permitted the Federals to be returned to Grant before Richmond. The offensive urged by Lee countered Lee's purpose in sending Early to the valley.

Lee's 1862–63 costly offensive warfare defied his own concern about relative manpower. His correspondence with Davis and the Secretary of War is replete with statements of that concern. During the 1862–63 period, he wrote regularly of the "superior numbers of the enemy," the necessity to "husband our strength," "the falling off in (his army's) aggregate shows that its ranks are growing weaker and that its losses are not supplied by recruits and that the enemy "can be easily reinforced, while no addition can be made to our numbers." Some may contend that Lee's grand strategy was defensive, an offensive defensive. To make this claim, they must somehow exorcise Lee's own words, his consistent advocacy of the attack, and the way he used his army for two years, until its losses deprived him of mobility and the offensive option.

Forced to the strategic defensive by 1864, Lee demonstrated the value of that posture, exacting such a price from the North that it came close to abandoning the war. I contend that had he carried out his leadership in this way during the two costly offensive years, as he did only at Fredericksburg, he would have slowed the enemy's increase in numerical superiority to the extent that it arose from Lee's heavy, disproportionate, and irreplaceable losses. He would have saved a substantial portion of the approximately 100,000 soldiers that he lost on the offensive. With these additional numbers, he could have maintained mobility and avoided a siege. Maneuvers like Early's 1864 movement in the valley could have been undertaken with sufficient numbers to be effective. The Federals, on the offensive, could have suffered for an earlier or longer period the ceaseless Federal losses that began in May of 1864. The Northern people could have politically abandoned their support of the war.

Some who disagree with me argue that the defensive would not have punished the North more than the 1862–63 offensives did. That may be so, but, as indicated by Fredericksburg, the defensive would not have wasted Lee's own force, which was the principal defect with his offensives. My detractors further contend that traditional military doctrine advocates the offensive because it permits selection of the time and place of the battle. But the endemically outnumbered Lee was not in a traditional situation that afforded him a chance of winning the war militarily. It is also said that the Southern people would not have accepted the defensive. There is no evidence that Lee or the Confederate Administration relied on this factor in pursuing the 1862–3 offensives. Further, if Lee had believed that the offensive was destructive to his chances, his obligation, and that of the Administration, was to bring the public along with them.

Time, the duration of the war, was a problem for both sides, the South because of its relatively limited supply base and the North because of the risk that the public would abandon the contest as hopeless.

In short, I believe that Lee's offensive grand strategy was destructive to the South's chances. Lee's task was not to win great battles, to be spectacular, but to win the war The military historian Lt. Col. George A. Bruce states that "the art of war consists in using the forces of a nation to secure the end for which it is waged, and not in a succession of great battles that tend to defeat it." In 1862–63 Lee sought out the great battles. He went on the defensive in 1864 against his own strategic sense, only because his prior losses forced this posture. Maj. Gen. J. F. C. Fuller, the English military historian, seems to me to have fairly characterized Lee's leadership during the first two years of his command: Lee "rushed forth to find a battlefield, to challenge a contest between himself and the North." In this process, he unilaterally accomplished the attrition of his army that led to its being besieged and ultimately surrendered. His losses ultimately prevented his sustaining his army and punishing the North sufficiently to induce it to abandon the war—the only chance the South had to win. . . .

The Price of Honor: R. E. Lee and the Question of Confederate Surrender

. . . Robert E. Lee's belief in the inevitability of his final defeat, and the contrast between that belief and his combative persistence, together raise the question of his motivation. There are several worthwhile lines of inquiry regarding his motives, but before examining them it is necessary to consider briefly the question of his authority to surrender: did he have the authority to surrender his army and, if so, what circumstances permitted him to exercise that authority?

It is plain that Lee did have the right to surrender and was aware that he did. Between 7 April and 9 April 1865, as his correspondence with U.S. Grant proceeded, Lee consulted certain trusted aides and debated with himself the issue of surrender. But he insisted that, "if it is right, then *I* will take *all* the responsibility." On 9 April, the deed was done at Appomattox. On 12 April, Lee reported the surrender to Jefferson Davis, explaining that maintaining the battle "one day longer . . . would have been at a great sacrifice of life, and at its end I did not see how a surrender could have been avoided." In short, on 9 April 1865, believing that ultimate surrender was inevitable, he could not justify the sacrifice of life that further prolonging the combat would entail.

The situation at Appomattox was surely grim, but as has been noted, Lee had viewed the South's situation in the same grim terms for anywhere from twenty to five months prior to 9 April 1865. He had the same authority then to surrender as he had on 9 April. As the casualties and other losses—physical, financial, and emotional—mounted, what interest did Lee believe he was serving in continuing the hopeless struggle? His own statements suggest four possible answers to this question: he believed that the North was such a monstrous tyrant that defeat and death were the only moral responses; God willed his continuing to fight in spite of the inevitability of defeat; he was bound to persist because he was subject to Confederate civilian control, which did not want him to surrender; or his personal sense of duty demanded it.

The first answer suggests the philosophical proposition that there are worse fates than defeat and death. Americans in Lee's day, as well as today, were the heirs of a liberty-or-death tradition. Lee identified with this tradition. Despite his personal opposition to secession, he is quoted as having said, "We had, I was satisfied, sacred principles to maintain and rights to defend, for which we were in duty bound to do our best, even if we perished in the endeavor." On 7 April or 8 April, sometime within two days of the surrender, General William N. Pendleton, representing a group of officers, suggested surrender to Lee. Lee rejected the idea, stating that rather than surrender "we must all determine to die at our posts." But the liberty-or-death motive does not adequately explain Lee's prolonging the war after he adopted a belief in its futility, bearing in mind that he did in fact surrender, despite his prior rhetorical flourishes. Furthermore, he flatly rejected General Edward Porter Alexander's suggestion of guerrilla warfare as an alternative means of continuing the war because of its deleterious effect on the country as a whole. His 20 April 1865 letter to President Davis also discouraged Alexander's guerrilla warfare suggestion and urged Davis to seek a general peace. And on 13 June 1865, Lee applied for amnesty and the "benefits and full restoration of all rights and privileges" as a citizen of the United States. Each of these facts contradicts the notion that Lee was motivated by the belief that ultimate resistance to the Federals was the appropriate moral position.

Untroubled by any questions concerning the correctness of Lee's conduct, his biographer Douglas Southall Freeman comes close to suggesting that Lee persisted in the war because he believed that, regardless of the odds and the inevitability of defeat, God wanted him to keep fighting. Thus, Freeman stated that "nothing of his serenity during the war or of his silent labor in defeat can be understood unless one realizes that he submitted himself in all things faithfully to the will of a Divinity which, in his simple faith, was directing wisely the fate of nations and the daily life of His children." It is certainly true that Lee had a strong personal sense of the presence of God and God's responsibility for human events. But given the general's Herculean efforts, and his reliance on God to give him victories, it seems unreasonable to suggest that he persisted in futile combat because of some sense that God intended him to do so. Had this been his conviction, he presumably would not have surrendered on 9 April 1865.

Freeman was at pains to point out that Lee accepted wholeheartedly the American constitutional premise of military subordination to the civil government: "Lee ... applied literally and loyally his conviction that the President was the commander-in-chief." This constitutional principle was consistent with one of the general's life principles described by Freeman as "respect for constituted authority" and "his creed of obedience to constituted authority." Biographer Clifford Dowdey's description of certain events in February and March 1865 provides an interesting insight into the question of Lee's deference to authority. Referring to the period following the Hampton Roads meeting of 3 February

1865, between Confederate representatives and Abraham Lincoln and his aides, Dowdey wrote:

> Lee had held a private conversation with Virginia's Senator R. M. T. Hunter.... Lee urged him to offer a resolution in the Senate that would obtain better terms than, as Hunter reported Lee as saying, "were likely to be given after a surrender." Hunter claimed that Davis had already impugned his motives for seeking peace terms, and told Lee, "if he thought the chances of success desperate, thought he ought to say so to the President." Though Lee held frequent conversations with Davis during February, it is unlikely that he ever brought himself to introduce a subject which would be so distasteful to the President.

Dowdey then recounted the views of Secretary of War James A. Seddon, his successor in that office, John C. Breckenridge, and James Longstreet, all of whom shared Lee's recognition of the fact the war was lost and peace was needed. Dowdey concluded by observing, "The crux of the matter was that men in a position to know recognized that the South was defeated, *but no one was willing to assume the responsibility of trying to convince Davis of this*"! (emphasis added). Lee had by this time become general-in-chief of the Confederate armies. Considering Dowdey's unflinching admiration for Lee, his attributing Lee's position and that of the others mentioned to an unwillingness to take responsibility is surely an unintended indictment. In any event, although it is evident that Lee accepted subordination to civilian authority, he ultimately took responsibility for the surrender and simply announced it to Davis. It cannot, therefore, be said that civilian control was the reason for Lee's persistence.

Finally, can Lee's resolve to fight on in the face of certain defeat be explained by his sense of duty and honor? Historian Gaines M. Foster has described the South as "a culture based on honor," and Bertram Wyatt-Brown has detailed the entire complex white culture of the South in terms of a code called "Honor." The authors of *Why the South Lost the Civil War* have attempted to give a short definition of the concept: "When Confederates talked of honor they did not mean pride so much as moral integrity, personal bravery, Christian graciousness, deference to and respect for others, and self-worth, recognized by their peers."

In Lee, honor and its companion, duty, were, to be sure, highly and self-consciously developed; so too was their consequence, the self-regard that Wyatt-Brown describes. All biographies of Lee quote at length his many aphorisms about these values. He said, for example, that the Confederates were "duty bound to do our best, even if we perished." On 22 February 1865, in a letter to his wife, he stated, "I shall... endeavour to do my duty & fight to the last." In a March 1865 interview with General John B. Gordon, he spoke of "what duty to the army and our people required of us." Preparing to evacuate the Petersburg-Richmond line and move west toward Appomattox, "he acted," Lieutenant Colonel Walter H. Taylor noted, "as one who was conscious of having accomplished all that was possible in the line of duty, and who was undisturbed by the adverse conditions in which he found himself."

In regard to the effort to escape the pursuing Federals between Richmond and Appomattox, Freeman observed: "So long as this chance was open to him, his sense of duty did not permit him to consider any alternative" and "as long as there was a prospect of escape Lee felt it was his duty to fight on. He would not yield one hour before he must." Freeman also noted approvingly Lee's memorandum to himself: "There is a true glory and a true honor: the glory of duty done—the honor of the integrity of principle." Commenting on "the dominance of a sense of duty in [Lee's] actions," Dowdey stated that "this is not so much a sense of duty in the abstract as a duty to do the best he could. The point can clearly be seen when duty, *as a sense of the pride of a professional in his craft*, caused him to practice meticulously the techniques of command *long after any military purpose could be achieved*" (emphasis added).

Such a narrow definition of Lee's sense of honor and duty seems to be another unintended indictment by Dowdey. However defined, this sense of honor appears, after all, to have been an essentially personal emotional commitment that compelled Lee to fight on, regardless of the cost and long after he believed that it was futile to continue the contest. Referring to the Confederacy's hopeless situation during the winter of 1864–1865 and sympathetic to his personal commitment, Dowdey recognized "the moral obligation that required [Lee] to act as though defeat could be held off."

In a chapter entitled "The Sword of Robert E. Lee," Freeman set forth "an accounting of his service to the state." Having noted Lee's mobilization of Virginia, the Seven Days, the repulse of Federal offensives against Richmond, and his victories in six of ten major battles from Gaines's Mill through Spotsylvania, Freeman proceeded,

> During the twenty-four months when he had been free to employ open manoeuvre, a period that had ended with Cold Harbor, he had sustained approximately 103,000 casualties and had inflicted 145,000. Holding, as he usually had, to the offensive, his combat losses had been greater in proportion to his numbers than those of the Federals, but he had demonstrated how strategy may increase an opponent's casualties, for his losses included only 16,000 prisoners, whereas he had taken 38,000. Chained at length to the Richmond defenses, he had saved the capital from capture for ten months. All this he had done in the face of repeated defeats for the Southern troops in nearly every other part of the Confederacy.... These difficulties of the South would have been even worse had not the Army of Northern Virginia occupied so much of the thought and armed strength of the North. Lee is to be judged, in fact, not merely by what he accomplished with his own troops but by what he prevented the hosts of the Union from doing sooner elsewhere.

In reciting what Lee had accomplished, Freeman did not allude to the fact that for perhaps the last twenty months of these efforts, and surely for a substantial lesser period, Lee was proceeding in a cause that he personally believed was lost.

James M. McPherson has summarized the ultimate consequences of the prolonging of the war, to which Lee's accomplishments made a significant contribution:

> the South was not only invaded and conquered, it was utterly destroyed. By 1865 the Union forces had ... destroyed two-thirds of the assessed value of

Southern wealth, two-fifths of the South's livestock, and one-quarter of her white men between the ages of twenty and forty. More than half the farm machinery was ruined, and the damage to railroads and industries was incalculable.... Southern wealth decreased by 60 percent (or 30 percent if the slaves are not counted as wealth). These figures provide eloquent testimony to the tragic irony of the South's counterrevolution of 1861 to preserve its way of life.

In conjunction, the statements of Freeman and McPherson raise reasonable questions regarding Lee and history and Lee's role as an American idol. On the one hand, the Lee tradition projects a tragic hero, a man who courageously pursued a cause that he believed to be doomed. On the other hand, this heroic tradition must be balanced against the consequences of Lee's heroism. There is, of course, a nobility and poignancy, a romance, in the tragic and relentless pursuit of a hopeless cause. But in practical terms such pursuit is subject to a very different interpretation.

In reality, military leadership is not just a private or personal activity. Nor is a military leader's sense of honor and duty simply a private and personal impulse. Military leadership and the leader's sense of duty are of concern not only to the leader, but also to the followers and to the enemy, ordinary people, many of whom die, are maimed, or otherwise suffer. In short, military leadership involves responsibility for what happens to other persons. There is, therefore, no matter how sincerely a leader may believe in the justice of a cause, a difference between undertaking or continuing military leadership in a cause that the leader feels can succeed and undertaking or continuing such leadership in a cause that the leader feels is hopeless. In the latter circumstance, the leader knows that his order "once more into the breach" will kill or injure many of his soldiers as well as the enemy's and also realizes that his order and these deaths and injuries are without, in Dowdey's phrase, "any military purpose." Lacking a military purpose, they also have no political purpose. Thus they are without any rational purpose.

The absence of any rational purpose behind Lee's persistence is suggested by his sense of the meaning of the deaths of his men as revealed by his early advocate, the Reverend J. William Jones. Among the general's wartime papers that Jones found after his death were "maxims, proverbs, quotations from the Psalms, selections from standard authors, and reflections of his own." One of these, in Lee's own hand, read, "The warmest instincts of every man's soul declare the glory of the soldier's death. It is more appropriate to the Christian than to the Greek to sing: 'Glorious his fate, and envied is his lot, Who for his country fights and for it dies.' "

As suggested earlier by McPherson's description of the war's impact on the South, the conflict involved catastrophic consequences for the people of the United States both North and South. During the war as a whole more than half a million soldiers died. Untold thousands were maimed. The families of all of these men also suffered grievously. Whatever portion of the catastrophe occurred after the time when Lee had become convinced that the war was lost—whether Lee came to believe this twenty, fifteen, ten, or only five months before the end—significant harm took place, in the West as well as the East, before Lee finally called a halt to the fighting. For the plain people who suffered, Lincoln's "him who shall have borne the battle, and... his widow, and his orphan," the consequences of the war were dire in the extreme.

Freeman wrote bitterly about Southerners who were fearful or doubtful or who wished for peace, comparing them unfavorably to the dauntless Lee and to President Davis. But the authors of *Why the South Lost the Civil War* made a different observation: "By late 1864, very likely earlier, those Confederates who argued for an end of war, even if that meant returning to the Union, did not include only the war-weary defeatists. Many among those who took that statesman-like position may have lost their will, but they weigh more on the scales of humanity than those who would have fought to the last man."

The Lee orthodoxy insists that the Confederate officers and soldiers at Appomattox were tearful and heartbroken at their surrender—they wanted to keep fighting. But even purveyors of the orthodoxy occasionally, perhaps unwittingly, contradict the tradition. Thus, quoting Lieutenant Colonel Charles Venable, Dowdey wrote that soldiers who learned of Lee's intent to surrender were "convulsed with passionate grief." But Dowdey also reported that "Lee was aware that many of his soldiers, officers and men, were ready to end 'the long agony'.... He could sense the attitude." He also described enlisted men who, en route to Appomattox, "overcome by exhaustion... were lying stretched out flat or sitting with their heads on their knees, waiting to be gathered up by the enemy." A suggestive Federal account by an eyewitness agreed with Dowdey's report. "Billy," an enlisted man in the 1st Michigan Volunteers, wrote to his family from Appomattox on the day of the surrender. He described the pursuit to Appomattox and then added, "The best of it is the Rebs are as pleased over the surrender as we are, and when the surrender was made known to them cheer after cheer went up along their whole line." ...

On 9 April 1865, Lee apparently felt that he had fully and finally served his personal sense of duty. He had fulfilled, at last, what Dowdey described as his personal sense of "duty to do the best he could, ... a sense of the pride of a professional in his craft." He was prepared, at last, again quoting Dowdey, "to assume the responsibility" for introducing a subject "distasteful" to Jefferson Davis. The awful human cost of his persistence had, of course, been paid by countless other people, including his own soldiers.

Giving Lee full credit for good faith and high personal character, the historian must nonetheless—as a practitioner of a discipline regarded as one of the humanities—take into account the human and social consequences of his continuing to lead others in a war that he believed was lost. It is fair to observe that Virginia, reputedly the focus of Lee's primary interest, suffered especially devastating losses of life and property because it was the scene of almost constant warfare. The facts cast serious doubt on the traditional assumption that Lee's persistence was wholly admirable.

 **NO**

Another Look at the Generalship of R. E. Lee

Americans have embraced Abraham Lincoln and R. E. Lee as the two great figures of the Civil War. In one of the many ironies associated with the conflict, the principal rebel chieftain overshadows Ulysses S. Grant, William Tecumseh Sherman, and all other Federal generals who helped to save the Union. Although Lee's transcendent reputation as a great captain remains firmly ensconced in the popular mind and virtually no one challenges his brilliance as a field commander, scholars increasingly have questioned his larger contribution to the Confederate war effort. Did he fail to see beyond his beloved Virginia, crippling Confederate strategic planning through a stubborn refusal to release troops badly needed elsewhere? Did his strategic and tactical choices lengthen the conflict, thereby increasing the odds that Northern civilian morale would falter? Or did his penchant for the offensive unnecessarily bleed Confederate manpower when a defensive strategy punctuated by limited counteroffensives would have conserved Southern resources? Did his celebrated victories improve the odds for Confederate nationhood, or were they nothing but gaudy sideshows that diverted attention from more significant military events elsewhere? In short, what was Lee's impact on the outcome of the war?

One of the most common criticisms of Lee alleges a lack of appreciation for the problems and importance of the trans-Appalachian Confederacy. J. F. C. Fuller frequently alluded to Lee's inability to see the war as a whole. The British author stated in one characteristic passage that Lee "was so obsessed by Virginia that he considered it the most important area of the Confederacy.... To him the Confederacy was but the base of Virginia." A number of subsequent historians expanded upon the idea that Lee failed to take in the entire strategic situation. Especially strident in this regard was Thomas L. Connelly, who wondered "whether Lee possessed a sufficiently broad military mind to deal with over-all Confederate matters." Connelly saw Lee as intensely parochial, blinded by a desire to protect Richmond. and unwilling, or unable, to look beyond each immediate threat to his native state and its capital. When Lee did turn his attention to the West, averred Connelly, he invariably made suggestions "in the context of his strategy for Virginia." Connelly and Archer Jones reiterated many of these points in their study of Confederate command and strategy. They questioned Lee's knowledge about the geography of the West and deplored his habit of requesting reinforcements for the Army of Northern Virginia at the expense of other Confederate armies. Even Lee's grudging deployment of two-thirds of James Longstreet's First Corps to Georgia in September 1863 had a Virginia twist—he hoped that the movement might save Knoxville and shield Virginia's western flank.

Connelly and Jones admitted that all theater commanders tended to see their own region as most important but asserted that Lee's viewing Virginia in this way proved especially harmful. He had been Jefferson Davis's military adviser in the early days of the war and remained close to the president throughout the conflict; moreover, his reputation exceeded that of any other Confederate army commander. The result was as predictable as it was pernicious for the Confederacy: "His prestige as a winner and his unusual opportunity to advise undoubtedly to some degree influenced the government to take a narrower view on strategy and to go for the short gain in Virginia where victory seemed more possible." In the opinion of Connelly and Jones, Lee's influence was such that a powerful "Western Concentration Bloc," the roster of which included Joseph E. Johnston, P. G. T. Beauregard, James Longstreet, and John C. Breckinridge, could not counter his lone voice. The consequent failure to shift forces to threatened areas west of Virginia hindered the Southern cause.

Lee's aggressive style of generalship, with its attendant high casualties, also has generated much criticism. Grady McWhiney and Perry D. Jamieson propounded the thesis that a reckless devotion to offensive tactics bled the South "nearly to death in the first three years of the war" and sealed the fate of the Confederacy. Lee fit this pattern perfectly, they observed, sustaining losses approaching 20 percent in his first half-dozen battles compared to fewer than 15 percent for the Federals. A controversial aspect of McWhiney and Jamieson's book ascribed the South's love of direct assaults to a common Celtic ancestry. Whether or not readers accept the proposition that a cultural imperative prompted Lee to order attacks, McWhiney and Jamieson succeeded in accentuating his heavy losses throughout the war. Elsewhere, McWhiney bluntly claimed that the "aggressiveness of Robert E. Lee, the greatest Yankee killer of all time, cost the Confederacy dearly."

A number of other historians agreed with McWhiney. The Army of Northern Virginia suffered more than fifty thousand casualties in the three months after Lee assumed command, claimed Thomas L. Connelly, and overall "the South's largest field army, contained in the smallest war theater, was bled to death by Lee's offensive tactics." Russell F. Weigley asserted that Lee shared Napoleon's "passion for the strategy of annihilation and the climactic, decisive battle" and "destroyed in the end not the enemy armies) but his own." J. F. C. Fuller believed that Lee's only hope for success lay in emulating "the great Fabius," who often retreated to avoid costly battles. Instead, time and again Lee "rushed forth to find a battlefield" and "by his restless audacity, he mined such strategy as his government created." Alan T. Nolan's reasoned analysis of Lee explored the question of "whether the general's actions related positively or negatively to the war objectives and national policy of his government." Nolan thought that Lee came up far short when measured against this standard. His strategy and tactics won specific contests and made headlines but traded irreplaceable manpower for only fleeting advantage. "If one covets the haunting romance of the Lost Cause," wrote Nolan, "then the inflicting of casualties on the enemy, tactical victory in great battles, and audacity are enough." But such accomplishments did not bring the Confederacy closer to independence. Lee's relentless pursuit of the offensive contravened the strategy best calculated to win Southern independence and thus "contributed to the loss of the Lost Cause."

One last piece of testimony on this point typifies a common tension between admiration for Lee's generalship and a sense that his aggressive actions might have hurt the Confederacy. In a lecture delivered at a symposium on Lee in 1984, Frank E. Vandiver commented that his subject "lost a lot of men by attacking and attacking and attacking" and "may have been too addicted to the offensive, even against outstanding firepower." Vandiver then quickly hedged his conclusion:" "I think that you have to balance the fact that he lost a lot of men and stuck to the offensive against what he considered to be the strategic necessities of attack. So I would level the charge that he might have been too addicted to the offensive with some trepidation."

These historians raise serious questions about the relationship between Lee's generalship and Confederate chances for independence. A different reading of the evidence, however, suggests that Lee pursued a strategy attuned to the expectations of most Confederate citizens and calculated to exert maximum influence on those who made policy in the North and in Europe. Far from being innocent of the importance of the West and the psychological dimension of his operations, he might have seen more clearly than any of his peers the best road to Confederate independence. His victories buoyed Southern hopes when defeat lay in all other directions, dampened spirits in the North, and impressed European political leaders. They also propelled him to a position where, long before the end of the war, he stood unchallenged as a military hero and his Army of Northern Virginia had become synonymous with the Confederacy in the minds of many Southern whites. While his army remained in the field there was hope for victory; his capitulation extinguished such hope and in effect ended the war. Lee had selected a strategy that paradoxically enabled the Confederacy to resist for four years *and* guaranteed that it would not survive the surrender of his army at Appomattox.

Modern historians usually attribute Confederate military defeat to failure in the West, where vast chunks of territory and crucial cities fell to the Federals. They often add that Lee's unwillingness to send part of his own army to bolster forces beyond the Appalachians may have hastened Confederate defeat. Is this belief in the primacy of western campaigns a modern misreading of the actual situation? Certainly it was the Virginia theater that captivated foreign observers. For example, Lee's victories at the Seven Days and Second Manassas in the summer of 1862 conveyed to London and Paris a sense of impending Confederate success. Apparently unimpressed by the string of Union triumphs in the West that extended from Fort Henry through the fall of New Orleans, Prime Minister Viscount Palmerston and Emperor Napoleon III leaned toward some type of intervention by the first week in September. Northern public opinion also seemed to give greater weight to the Seven Days than to events in Tennessee, prompting Lincoln's famous complaint to French Count Agénor-Etienne de Gasparin in early August: "Yet it seems unreasonable that a series of successes, extending through half-a-year, and clearing more than a hundred thousand square miles of country, should help us so little, while a single half-defeat should hurt us so much."

Other evidence of a Northern preoccupation with the East abounds. Albert Castel has noted that Lincoln himself, who beyond doubt believed the West to be more important, visited the Army of the Potomac several times but never favored a western army with his presence. (Jefferson Davis joined his western armies on three occasions.) Senator Charles Sumner revealed a good deal about attitudes among powerful Northern politicians when he wrote during the winter of 1865 that Secretary of War Edwin M. Stanton thought "peace can be had only when Lee's army is beaten, captured or dispersed." Sumner had "for a long time been sanguine that, when Lee's army is out of the way, the whole rebellion will disappear." So long as Lee remained active, "there is still hope for the rebels, & the unionists of the South are afraid to show themselves." Among the most telling indications of the public mood was a demand that Grant go east when he became general-in-chief of the Union armies in March 1864. He could have run the war as efficiently from Tennessee or Georgia, but the North wanted its best general to bring his talents to bear on the frustrating Virginia theater.

If anything, the South exhibited a more pronounced interest in the East. Following reverses in Tennessee and along the Mississippi River during the winter and spring of 1862, Confederates looked increasingly to Virginia for good news from the battlefield. Stonewall Jackson supplied it in the spring of 1862 with his Shenandoah Valley campaign—after that, Lee and the Army of Northern Virginia provided the only reliable counterpoint to Northern gains in other theaters and consequently earned a special position in the minds of their fellow Confederates. William M. Blackford of Lynchburg, an antislavery man who nonetheless supported the Confederacy and sent five sons into Southern service, applauded the cumulative effect of Lee's 1862 campaigns: "The defeats of the enemy in the Valley, in the Peninsular, in the Piedmont, the invasion of Maryland, the capture of Harper's Ferry and lastly the victory at Fredericksburg," he remarked. "taken all together, are achievements which do not often crown one year." Lamenting the fall of Vicksburg in late July 1863, Kate Stone, a young refugee in Texas, added that "[o]ur only hope is in Lee the Invincible." Ten months and the reverse at Gettysburg did not alter Stone's thinking about Lee. "A great battle is rumored in Virginia," she wrote in May 1864. "Grant's first fight in his 'On to Richmond.' He is opposed by the Invincible Lee and so we are satisfied we won the victory." A Louisiana officer serving in the West echoed Stone's opinion on 27 May 1864, dismissing talk of a setback in Virginia with an expression of "complete faith in General Lee, who has never been known to suffer defeat, and probably never will."

No one better illustrated the tendency to focus on Lee than Catherine Ann Devereux Edmondston of North Carolina. "What a position does he occupy," she recorded in her diary on 11 June 1864, "the idol, the point of trust, of confidence & repose of thousands! How nobly has he won the confidence, the admiration of the nation." Shifting to a comparison between Lee and officers who had failed in other theaters, Edmondston remarked: "God grant that he may long be spared to us. He nullifies Bragg, Ransom. & a host of other incapables." The *Charleston Daily Courier* implicitly contrasted Lee with Confederate generals in the West when it noted that "Grant is now opposed to a General who stands in the foremost rank of Captains, and his army is confronted with men accustomed to victory." More explicit was a Georgian who after the fall of Atlanta gazed longingly at the commander in Virginia: "Oh, for a General Lee at the head of every *corps d'armee!*"

Well before the close of the war, Lee's position in the Confederacy approximated that held by Washington during the American Revolution. "It is impossible for me to describe the emotions of my heart.... I felt proud that the Southern Confederacy could boast of such a man," a North Carolina lieutenant wrote after Lee had reviewed his unit in May 1863. "In fact, I was almost too proud for the occasion for I could not open my mouth to give vent to the emotions that were struggling within." The *Lynchburg Virginian* affirmed after Chancellorsville that the "central figure of this war is, beyond all question, that of Robert E. Lee." Alluding to the phenomenon of Lee's offsetting Confederate reverses in the West, the Virginian admired his "calm, broad military intellect that reduced the chaos after Donelson to form and order." "He should certainly have entire control of all military operations through-out the Confederate States," stated one of the generals artillerists in mid-1864. "In fact I should like to see him as King or Dictator. He is one of the few great men who ever lived, who could be trusted." Lee's belated elevation to general-in-chief of the Confederate armies in February 1865 prompted Edward O. Guerrant, an officer serving in southwest Virginia, to observe that "[this] has inspired our country with more hope, courage, & confidence than it has had for a year or two.... It puts us all in good humor, & good spirits, and for myself—I feel more confident of our final triumph than for several months past." Gen. Henry A. Wise told Lee on 6 April 1865 that there "has been no country, general, for a year or more. You are the country to these men. They have fought for you."

Testimony from soldiers lends powerful support to Wise's statements. A Georgian in the Army of Northern Virginia wrote shortly after Gettysburg that "[i]t looks like it does not do any good to whip them here in this state, and out West they are tearing everything to pieces.... But I am willing to fight them as long as General Lee says fight." When Lee reviewed the First Corps after its return to Virginia from East Tennessee in April 1864, a South Carolinian described an emotional scene: "[T]he men caught sight of his well known figure, [and] a wild and prolonged cheer... ran along the lines and rose to the heavens. Hats were thrown high, and many persons became almost frantic with emotion.... One heard on all sides such expressions as: 'What a splendid figure!' 'What a noble face and head!' 'Our destiny is in his hands!' 'He is the best and greatest man on this continent!' " A perceptive foreign observer picked up on this attitude when he described Lee in March 1865 as the "idol of his soldiers & the Hope of His country" and spoke of "the prestige which surrounds his person & the almost fanatical belief in his judgment & capacity wh[ich] is the one idea of an entire people."

Many Confederates tied Lee directly to the sainted Washington. During the fall of 1862, the *Columbus* (Georgia) *Times* spoke of his winning everybody's confidence" and noted that he "has much of the Washingtonian dignity about him, and is much respected by all with whom he is thrown." Peter W. Alexander, perhaps the most widely read Confederate war correspondent, assessed Lee just before the battle of Fredericksburg in December 1862: "Like Washington, he is a wise man, and a good man, and possesses in an eminent degree those qualities which are indispensable in the great leader and champion upon whom the country rests its hope." Alexander added that the Confederacy "should feel grateful that Heaven has raised up one in our midst so worthy of our confidence and so capable to lead"—the "grand-son of Washington, so to speak . . . the wise and modest chief who commands the Army of Northern Virginia." In the wake of Lee's triumph at Fredericksburg in December 1862, Georgian Mary Jones expressed thanks "that in this great struggle the head of our army is a noble son of Virginia, and worthy of the intimate relation in which he stands connected with our immortal Washington. What confidence his wisdom, integrity, and valor and undoubted piety inspire!" Eliza Frances Andrews, another resident of Georgia, called Lee simply "that star of light before which even Washington's glory pales."

In line with such sentiment inside and outside his army, Lee's surrender understandably signaled the end of the war to most Confederates (as it did to most Northerners). President Davis might speak bravely of the war's simply moving into a new phase after Appomattox, but a trio of women voiced far more common sentiments. "How can I write it?" asked Catherine Edmondston. "How find words to tell what has befallen us? *Gen Lee has surrendered!* . . . We stand appalled at our disaster! . . . [That] *Lee,* Lee upon whom hung the hopes of the whole country, should be a prisoner seems almost too dreadful to be realized!" The first report of Lee's capitulation reached Eliza Andrews on 18 April 1865: "No one seems to doubt it," she wrote sadly, "and everybody feels ready to give up hope. 'It is useless to struggle longer,' seems to be the common cry, and the poor wounded men go hobbling about the streets with despair on their faces." From Florida, a young woman reacted with the "wish we were all dead. It is as if the very earth had crumbled beneath our feet." A North Carolinian in the Army of Northern Virginia spoke for many soldiers and civilians in a single succinct sentence written the day Lee agreed to Grant's terms: "The life of the 'C.S.' is gon' when Gen Lee and his army surrendered."

The foregoing testimony indicates a widespread tendency *during the war* to concentrate attention on Lee and Virginia. Lee himself discerned the centrality of his military operations to Confederate morale (after Gettysburg he commented on the "unreasonable expectations of the public" concerning the Army of Northern Virginia), as well as to perceptions in the North and Europe. A man of far more than ordinary intelligence, he read Northern and Southern newspapers assiduously, corresponded widely, and discussed the political and civilian dimensions of the conflict with a broad range of persons. He appreciated the incalculable industrial and emotional value of Richmond as well as the profound concern for Washington among Northern leaders. He knew the records and personalities of officers who led Confederate armies in the West. He watched the dreary procession of defeats from Fort Donelson and Pea Ridge through Shiloh, Perryville, Stones River, Vicksburg, and Chattanooga. Robustly aware of his own ability and the superior quality of his army, he faced successive opponents with high expectations of success. A combination of these factors likely persuaded him that victories in Virginia were both more probable and calculated to yield larger results than whatever might transpire in the West.

Within this context, it followed that the Confederacy should augment his army to the greatest degree possible. Lee's official restraint prevented his questioning overtly the competence of fellow army commanders; however, in opposing the transfer of George E. Pickett's division to the West in May 1863, he mentioned the "uncertainty of its application" under John C. Pemberton. That guarded phrase came from the pen of a man who quite simply believed he was the best the Confederacy had and thus should be given adequate resources to do his job. Braxton Bragg's sheer waste of two divisions under James Longstreet in the fall of 1863 demonstrated the soundness of Lee's reluctance to reinforce western armies at the expense of the Army of Northern Virginia. As Richard M. McMurry has suggested, the "Rebels' dilemma was that they did not have either the leadership or the manpower and materiel" to hang on to both Virginia and the West. That being the case, perhaps they should have sent available resources to Virginia: "Such a strategy would have employed their best army under their best general at the point where conditions were most favorable to them.. If the Confederates could not have won their independence under such circumstances, they could not have won it anywhere under any possible circumstances." To put it another way, the Confederacy could lose the war in either the West or the East, but it could win the war only in the East.

What about Lee's supposed overreliance on the offensive? His periodic use of highly questionable and costly assaults is beyond debate. Natural audacity overcame the dictates of reason when he ordered frontal attacks at Malvern Hill, on the third day at Gettysburg, and elsewhere, and when he elected to give battle north of the Potomac after 15 September 1862. But these unfortunate decisions should not unduly influence interpretations of his larger military record. After all, Grant and Sherman also resorted to unimaginative direct attacks at various times in their careers. Many critics fail to give Lee credit for what he accomplished through aggressive generalship. At the Seven Days he blunted a Federal offensive that seemed destined to pin defending Confederates in Richmond; his counterpunch in the campaign of Second Manassas pushed the eastern military frontier back to the Potomac and confronted Lincoln with a major crisis at home and abroad. The tactical masterpiece at Chancellorsville, coming as it did on the heels of a defensive win at Fredericksburg, again sent tremors through the North. Lee failed to follow up either pair of victories with a third win at Antietam or Gettysburg; however, in September 1862 and June 1863 it was not at all clear that the Army of Northern Virginia would suffer defeat in Maryland and Pennsylvania. A victory in either circumstance might have altered the course of the conflict.

Too many critics of Lee's offensive movements neglect to place them within the context of what the Confederate people would tolerate. It is easy from a late-twentieth-century perspective to study maps, point to the defensive power of the rifle-musket, speculate about the potential of wide-scale guerrilla warfare, and reach a conclusion that Lee's aggressive strategic and tactical decisions shortened the life of the Confederacy. From the opening of the war, however, Southern civilians, newspaper editors, and political leaders clamored for decisive action on the battlefield and berated generals who shunned confrontations with the Federals.

As early as the winter of 1861–62, the Richmond Dispatch described a "public mind... restless and anxious to be relieved by some decisive action that shall have a positive influence in the progress of the war." In mid-June 1862, shortly after Lee assumed command of the Army of Northern Virginia, the *Richmond Enquirer* conceded the value of entrenchments but stressed the need for offensive moves. "To attack the enemy at every opportunity. to harass him, cut him up, and draw him into general engagements," insisted the *Enquirer,* "is the policy of every commander who has confidence in the strength and spirit of his army.... [L]et activity, aggression. attack, stand recorded and declared as our line of policy." Three months later the Macon (Georgia) *Journal & Messenger* greeted news of Lee's raid into Maryland in typically bellicose fashion: "Having in this war exercised Christian forbearance to its utmost extent, by acting on the defensive, it will now be gratifying to all to see... the war carried upon the soil of those barbarians who have so long been robbing and murdering our quiet and unoffending citizens." Confederate writings, both public and private, bristle with innumerable sentiments of this type.

Although Confederates often linked Lee and George Washington, they really craved a type of generalship different from that of their Revolutionary hero. Joseph E. Johnston retreated often, fought only when absolutely necessary, and otherwise fit Washington's military mold quite closely. Such behavior created an impression in the Confederacy that he gave up too much territory far too easily. A young lieutenant in Savannah complained to his father on 12 May 1862 about the Peninsula campaign: "General Joseph Johnston, from whom we were led to expect so much, has done little else than *evacuate,* until the very mention of the word sickens one *usque ad nauseam.*" Twelve days later Virginia planter William Bulware excoriated Johnston in a conversation with Edmund Ruffin. The general had avoided battle for days and given up twenty miles of ground, facts that demonstrated his "incompetency and mismanagement." Bulware predicted that Johnston would continue to withdraw, causing the "surrender of Richmond, & evacuation of all lower Virginia." Criticism intensified during Johnston's retreat toward Atlanta in 1864. "I don't think he will suit the emergency," complained Josiah Gorgas long before Johnston reached Atlanta. "He is falling back just as fast as his legs can carry him.... Where he will stop Heaven only knows." Long since disenchanted with Johnston's tendency to retreat (together with many other facets of his behavior), Jefferson Davis finally replaced him with John Bell Hood, an officer who understood Southern expectations and immediately went on the offensive.

Lee's style of generalship suited the temperament of his people—though many fellow Confederates initially harbored doubts about his competency to succeed Joseph Johnston in field command. Known as "Granny Lee" or the "King of Spades" early in the war, he seemed more devoted to fortifications than to smiting the enemy. Edward Porter Alexander recalled that John M. Daniel, editor of the Richmond Examiner, bitterly attacked Lee in June 1862 as one who would misuse the army: "It would only be allowed to dig, that being the West Point idea of war, & West Point now being in command; that guns & ammunition would now only be in the way, spades & shovels being the only implements Gen. Lee knew anything about, &c., &c." The correspondent for the Enquirer remarked at this same time that "you have only to go into the army, amongst the men in the ranks, to hear curses heaped upon West Point and the spade."

Questions about Lee's aggressiveness disappeared rapidly after his victory in the Seven Days. His admittedly bloody battles in 1862–63 created an aura of invincibility that offset gloomy events in the West, and that aura clung to him and his army through the defensive struggles of 1864–65. Lee's initial eighteen months as commander of the Army of Northern Virginia built credibility on which he drew for the rest of the war to sustain civilian morale. Confidence in his army as it lay pinned in the trenches at Petersburg during the summer of 1864 remained high, while Northerners experienced their darkest period of doubt. Far from hastening the demise of the Confederacy, Lee's generalship provided hope that probably carried the South beyond the point at which its citizens otherwise would have abandoned their quest for nationhood.

Nor was Lee's generalship hopelessly "old-fashioned." The simplistic notion that Grant was among the first modern generals and Lee one of the last of the old school withers under the slightest scrutiny. Lee differed in many respects from Grant and Sherman—most notably in his rejection of war against civilians—but had come to terms with many facets of a modern struggle between societies. He predicted from the beginning a long war that would demand tremendous sacrifice in the Confederacy. A member of the Virginia secession convention recounted how Lee warned the delegates shortly after Fort Sumter fell that "they were just on the threshold of a long and bloody war." He knew the Northern people well and believed "they never would yield . . . except at the conclusion of a long and desperate struggle." "The war may last 10 years," he predicted to his wife on 30 April 1861, and no part of Virginia would offer safe refuge from the armies. Clear eyed about the chances for European intervention at the time of the *Trent* affair, Lee insisted that Confederates "must make up our minds to fight our battles & win our independence alone. No one will help us." He believed in the subordination of "every other consideration . . . to the great end of the public safety," testified Colonel Charles Marshall of his staff, "and that since the whole duty of the nation would be war until independence should be secured, the whole nation should for the time be converted into an army, the producers to feed and the soldiers to fight."

Lee's actions underscored this attitude. Although wearing the uniform of a republic fond of rhetoric praising state and individual rights, he demanded that the national interest come first. He issued an order in March 1862, for example, calling for more unified control of Southern railroad traffic to better satisfy the "exigencies of the service." As early as December 1861, he urged extending the terms of service for soldiers then under arms who originally had signed on for just twelve months: "The troops, in my opinion, should be organized for the war," he wrote. "We cannot stop short of its termination, be it long or short." A staunch supporter of national conscription, Lee played a key role in the process that resulted in the Confederate conscription law of April 1862. Beyond coercing military service, Lee supported the concentration of manpower in the principal Southern field armies, the central government's right to procure needed war material through impressment, and other measures strikingly at odds with the doctrine of state rights.

Late in the war Lee publicly endorsed arming black men and granting them freedom in return for Confederate service. He thus undercut the institution of slavery (with state rights one of the twin pillars on which the Confederacy had been founded), proclaiming openly what he long had urged confidentially. Loath to disagree with his government or intrude in the political sphere during the conflict, Lee had waited to express himself officially on this question until too late to affect Confederate fortunes. He later spoke privately of telling Jefferson Davis "often and early in the war that the slaves should be emancipated, that it was the only way to remove a weakness at home and to get sympathy abroad." A presidential "proclamation of gradual emancipation and the use of the negroes as soldiers" would have furthered the Confederate cause, but Davis resisted taking this step because of the political firestorm it would ignite.

Contrary to what critics such as John Keegan say, Lee was not a man of "limited imagination" whose "essentially conventional outlook" helped undo the Confederacy. He formulated a national strategy predicated on the probability of success in Virginia and the value of battlefield victories. The ultimate failure of his strategy neither proves that it was wrongheaded nor diminishes Lee's pivotal part in keeping Confederate resistance alive through four brutally destructive years. That continued resistance held the key to potential victory—Southern armies almost certainly lacked the capacity to defeat decisively their Northern counterparts, but a protracted conflict marked by periodic Confederate successes on the battlefield more than once threatened to destroy the North's will to continue the war. Indeed, the greatest single obstacle to Northern victory after June 1862 was R. E. Lee and his Army of Northern Virginia. Without Lee and that famous field command, the Confederate experiment in rebellion almost certainly would have ended much sooner.

POSTSCRIPT

Is Robert E. Lee Overrated as a General?

Most of the biographers and military historians who write about Robert E. Lee treat him with awe and reverence. Lost-cause ex-Confederate warriors created Lee's image as a noble warrior and as a soldier of unparalleled skill. He died in 1870 while still president of Washington College in Lexington, Virginia (later renamed Washington and Lee College). After his death, monuments to the general appeared across the South, and in the twentieth century his birthday came to be celebrated as a holiday in many states below the Mason-Dixon line.

Typical were the remarks of a Virginia congressman who, in the House of Representatives on Lee's 123rd birthday, commented on the "beautiful and perfect symmetry of character" of "the matchless soldier... [whose] genius for war at once placed him in the front ranks of the soldier of all ages." The hagiographical treatment of Lee culminated in 1935, when Virginia newsman Douglas Southall Freeman won the Pulitzer Prize for his massively detailed and worshipful *R. E. Lee: A Biography,* 4 vols. (Scribner's, 1937–1940), a work that is still in print today and that has influenced most writings about the general.

Only a handful of books have dared to criticize this idolatrous portrait of Lee. In 1933 J. F. C. Fuller's *Grant and Lee: A Study in Personality and Generalship* (Indiana University Press, 1957) foreshadowed later criticisms of Lee's strategic vision and offensive tactics. It took almost 50 years for a second critical work to appear: Thomas L. Connelly's *The Marble Man: Robert E. Lee and His Image in American Society* (Louisiana State University Press, 1978). In it, Connelly attacked Lee's obsession with Virginia, psychoanalyzed the man probably beyond the historical evidence, and argued that the Lee image was the creation primarily of the lost-cause, post–Civil War South.

Nolan's selection is a summary of his book *Lee Considered: General Robert E. Lee and Civil War History* (University of North Carolina Press, 1991), a frank reevaluation of the traditional uncritical image of Lee. Nolan charges that Lee sustained an excessive number of casualties because his grand strategy was flawed. Although he was a brilliant tactician, says Nolan, Lee might have won the war had he resorted primarily to a defensive war and not an offensive grand strategy, which Nolan maintains caused Lee to sustain heavy casualties of irreplaceable troops to an enemy that easily outnumbered the Confederacy three to one in potential manpower.

Nolan also argues that Lee unnecessarily prolonged the war even though he knew it was lost a year before he surrendered. Nolan states that Lee's "sense of honor appears... to have been an essentially personal emotional commitment that compelled Lee to fight on, regardless of the cost and long after he believed that it was futile to continue the contest." Finally, Nolan denies that Lee fought on because he was subject to civilian control over the military.

Gallagher is the leader of the younger generation of historians who have been reevaluating the events of the Civil War in the 1990s. While not as worshipful as Douglas Southall Freeman about the general, Gallagher feels that critics like Nolan have gone too far. He defends Lee for his brilliance as both a tactician and a grand strategist. He defends Lee's Virginia strategy, arguing that many Western confederate generals wasted the troops that were sent them in flawed campaigns. Although he lost the war, Gallagher asserts that Lee's "style of generalship suited the temperament of his people" and that Lee was beloved during the war by both his troops and the Confederate population as a whole. Gallagher argues that Lee's only hope was to take to the offensive yet hold onto Virginia. He maintains that Lincoln, Grant, and other Northern politicians knew that if they wanted to win the war they would have to defeat Lee's army.

The starting point for this issue is Gallagher's edited book *Lee the Soldier* (University of Nebraska Press, 1996), which contains a sample of almost every important book and article written about Lee's military career. Anything written by Gallagher is worth reading. See his collection of articles on Civil War battlefields, Ken Burns's prize-winning 11-hour PBS television series *The Civil War,* and other related topics in *Lee and His Generals in War and Memory* (Louisiana State University Press, 1998). For Gallagher's assessment of the dozen books and articles to have come out on Lee since 1995, see "An Old-Fashioned Soldier in a Modern War? Robert E. Lee as Confederate General," *Civil War History* (December 1999).

A peripheral but important question pertaining to this issue is addressed in "Why the South Lost the Civil War: Ten Experts Explain the Fall of Dixie," *American History* (October 1995). The Spring 1993 issue of the *Maryland Historical Magazine* contains a collection of articles written in the late 1980s as well as a review essay by David Osher and Peter Wallenstein of *Why the Confederacy Lost* edited by Gabor S. Boritt (Oxford University Press, 1992). These articles should be compared with those written by the historians of the previous generation who met at Gettysburg College in 1958 to discuss the reasons for the Confederate loss, which can be found in David Donald, ed., *Why the North Won the Civil War* (Louisiana State University Press, 1960). The controversial view that the South "lost its will" to win the Civil War is argued in Richard E. Beringer et al., *Why the South Lost the Civil War* (University of Georgia Press, 1986).

Two great bibliographical starting points that reconcile the military history of the battles with the new social history are Joseph T. Glatthar, "The 'New' Civil War History: An Overview," *The Pennsylvania Magazine of History and Biography* (July 1991) and Marvin R. Cain, "A 'Face of Battle' Needed: An Assessment of Motives and Men in Civil War Historiography," *Civil War History* (March 1982). Of the many military books, start with the following three: James M. McPherson's Pulitzer Prize–winning *Battle Cry of Freedom: The Civil War Era* (Oxford University Press, 1988), which reconciles political and military events; Thomas L. Connelly and Archer Jones, *The Politics of Command: Factions and Ideas in Confederate Strategy* (Louisiana State University Press, 1973); and military historian Russell F. Weigley's *A Great Civil War: A Military and Political History, 1861–1865* (Indiana University Press, 2000).

ISSUE 16

Did Abraham Lincoln Free the Slaves?

YES: James M. McPherson, from *Drawn With the Sword: Reflections on the American Civil War* (Oxford University Press, 1996)

NO: Vincent Harding, from *There Is a River: The Black Struggle for Freedom in America* (Vintage Books, 1981)

ISSUE SUMMARY

YES: Historian James M. McPherson maintains that Abraham Lincoln was the indispensable agent in emancipating the slaves through his condemnation of slavery as a moral evil, his refusal to compromise on the question of slavery's expansion, his skillful political leadership, and his implementation and direction of Union troops as an army of liberation.

NO: Professor of religion and social transformation Vincent Harding credits slaves themselves for engaging in a dramatic movement of self-liberation. He argues that Lincoln initially refused to declare the destruction of slavery as a war aim and then issued the Emancipation Proclamation, which failed to free any slaves in areas over which he had any authority.

Numerous explanations have been offered for the Civil War. Some historians see the conflict as the product of a conspiracy housed either in the North or South, depending upon one's regional perspective. For many in the Northern states, the chief culprits were the planters and their political allies who were willing to defend Southern institutions at all costs. South of the Mason-Dixon line, blame was given to the abolitionists and the Free-soil architects of the Republican Party. Some viewed secession and war as the consequence of a constitutional struggle between states' rights advocates and defenders of the federal government, while others focused upon the economic rivalries or the cultural differences between North and South. Embedded in each of these interpretations, however, is the powerful influence of the institution of slavery.

Abraham Lincoln fully understood the role that slavery had played in the outbreak of the Civil War. In March 1865, as the war was nearing its end, he presented the following analysis: "One eighth of the whole population [in 1861] was colored slaves, not distributed generally over the Union, but localized in the Southern part of it. These slaves constituted a peculiar and powerful interest. All knew that this interest was somehow the cause of the war. To strengthen, perpetuate, and extend this interest was the object [of the South] . . . , while the [North] . . . claimed no right to do more than to restrict the territorial enlargement of it."

In light of Lincoln's recognition of the role that slavery played in the clash between North and South, none should find it surprising that the Emancipation Proclamation that he issued in September 1862 established a policy to end slavery. Hence, the demise of slavery became a war aim, and Lincoln seemed to have earned his place in history as "the Great Emancipator." Upon learning of the President's announcement, the fugitive slave and abolitionist Frederick Douglass was ecstatic. "We shout for joy," he declared, "that we live to record this righteous decree."

But Douglass had not always been so encouraged by Lincoln's commitment to freedom. Lincoln was not an abolitionist by any stretch of the imagination, but Douglass was convinced that the Republican victory in the presidential election of 1860 had brought to the White House a leader with a deserved reputation as an antislavery man. That confidence declined, however, in the early months of Lincoln's presidency as Douglass and other abolitionists lobbied for emancipation during the secession crisis only to have their demands fall on deaf ears. Lincoln consistently avoided any public pronouncements that would suggest his desire to end slavery as a war aim. The priority was preserving the Union, and Lincoln did not view emancipation as essential to that goal.

Until Lincoln changed his course in 1862, it appeared that the slaves would have to free themselves. This is precisely what some scholars insist happened. Southern slaves, they argue, became the key agents for liberation by abandoning their masters, undermining the plantation routine, serving as spies for Union troops, and taking up arms against the Confederacy. Black Northerners pitched in as well by enlisting in the United States Army and risking their lives to defeat the Confederacy and end slavery.

The question "Who freed the slaves?" is the focus of the following selections. James M. McPherson reinforces the conclusion that Lincoln freed the slaves. McPherson recognizes the limited nature of the Emancipation Proclamation, but he insists that Lincoln's commitment to an antislavery philosophy, exercise of skillful political leadership, and direction of the Union armies made him perhaps the only person who could have brought an end to the institution of slavery by 1865.

For Vincent Harding, credit for the end of slavery belongs not to the alleged "Great Emancipator," who took only halting steps toward eliminating slavery, but to the masses of slaves who sought self-liberation by running away from their masters, undermining plantation operations, engaging in local insurrections, and offering their services to the Union army and navy.

James M. McPherson

Who Freed the Slaves?

If we were to go out on the streets of almost any town in America and ask the question posed by the title of this [selection], probably nine out of ten respondents would answer unhesitatingly, "Abraham Lincoln." Most of them would cite the Emancipation Proclamation as the key document. Some of the more reflective and better informed respondents would add the Thirteenth Amendment and point to Lincoln's important role in its adoption. And a few might qualify their answer by noting that without Union military victory the Emancipation Proclamation and Thirteenth Amendment would never have gone into effect, or at least would not have applied to the states where most of the slaves lived. But, of course, Lincoln was commander in chief of Union armies, so the credit for their victories would belong mainly to him. The answer would still be the same: Lincoln freed the slaves.

In recent years, though, this answer has been challenged as another example of elitist history, of focusing only on the actions of great white males and ignoring the actions of the overwhelming majority of the people, who also make history. If we were to ask our question of professional historians, the reply would be quite different. For one thing, it would not be simple or clearcut. Many of them would answer along the lines of "On the one hand ... but on the other. . . ." They would speak of ambivalence, ambiguity, nuances, paradox, irony. They would point to Lincoln's gradualism, his slow and apparently reluctant decision for emancipation, his revocation of emancipation orders by Generals John C. Frémont and David Hunter, his exemption of border states and parts of the Confederacy from the Emancipation Proclamation, his statements seemingly endorsing white supremacy. They would say that the whole issue is more complex than it appears—in other words many historians, as is their wont, would not give a straight answer to the question.

But of those who did, a growing number would reply, as did a historian speaking to the Civil War Institute at Gettysburg College in 1991: "THE SLAVES FREED THEMSELVES." They saw the Civil War as a potential war for abolition well before Lincoln did. By flooding into Union military camps in the South, they forced the issue of emancipation on the Lincoln administration. By creating a situation in which Northern officials would either have to return them to slavery or acknowledge their freedom, these "contrabands," as they came to

From James M. McPherson, *Drawn With the Sword: Reflections on the American Civil War* (Oxford University Press, 1996). Copyright © 1996 by James M. McPherson. Reprinted by permission of Oxford University Press, Inc. Notes omitted.

be called, "acted resolutely to place their freedom—and that of their posterity —on the wartime agenda." Union officers, then Congress, and finally Lincoln decided to confiscate this human property belonging to the enemy and put it to work for the Union in the form of servants, teamsters, laborers, and eventually soldiers in Northern armies. Weighed in the scale of war, these 190,000 black soldiers and sailors (and probably a larger number of black army laborers) tipped the balance in favor of Union victory. Even deep in the Confederate interior remote from the fighting fronts, with the departure of masters and overseers to the army, "leaving women and old men in charge, the balance of power gradually shifted in favor of slaves, undermining slavery on farms and plantations far from the line of battle."

One of the leading exponents of the black self-emancipation thesis is the historian and theologian Vincent Harding, whose book *There Is a River: The Black Struggle for Freedom in America* has become almost a Bible for the argument. "While Lincoln continued to hesitate about the legal, constitutional, moral, and military aspects of the matter," Harding writes, "the relentless movement of the self-liberated fugitives into the Union lines" soon "approached and surpassed every level of force previously known.... Making themselves an unavoidable military and political issue... this overwhelming human movement... of self-freed men and women... took their freedom into their own hands." The Emancipation Proclamation, when it finally and belatedly came, merely "confirmed and gave ambiguous legal standing to the freedom which black people had already claimed through their own surging, living proclamations."

During the 1980s this self-emancipation theme achieved the status of orthodoxy among social historians. The largest scholarly enterprise on the history of emancipation and the transition from a slave to a free society during the Civil War era, the Freedmen and Southern Society project at the University of Maryland, stamped its imprimatur on the interpretation. The slaves, wrote the editors of this project, were "the prime movers in securing their own liberty." The Columbia University historian Barbara J. Fields gave wide publicity to this thesis. On camera in the PBS television documentary *The Civil War* and in an essay in the lavishly illustrated volume accompanying the series, she insisted that "freedom did not come to the slaves from words on paper, either the words of Congress or those of the President," but "from the initiative of the slaves" themselves. "It was they who taught the nation that it must place the abolition of slavery at the head of its agenda.... The slaves themselves had to make their freedom real."

Two important corollaries of the self-emancipation thesis are the arguments, first, that Lincoln hindered more than he helped the cause, and second, that the image of him as the Great Emancipator is a myth created by whites to deprive blacks of credit for achieving their own freedom. This "reluctant ally of black freedom," wrote Vincent Harding, "played an actively conservative role in a situation which... needed to be pushed toward its most profound revolutionary implications." Lincoln repeatedly "placed the preservation of the white Union above the death of black slavery"; even as late as August 1862, when he wrote his famous letter to Horace Greeley stating that "if I could save the Union without freeing *any* slave, I would do it," he was "still trapped in his own obsession with saving the white Union at all costs, even the cost of continued black slavery." By exempting one-third of the South from the Emancipation Proclamation, wrote Barbara Fields, "Lincoln was more determined to retain the goodwill of the slaveowners than to secure the liberty of the slaves." Despite Lincoln, though, "no human being alive could have held back the tide that swept toward freedom" by 1863.

Nevertheless, lamented Vincent Harding, "while the concrete historical realities of the time testified to the costly, daring, courageous activities of hundreds of thousands of black people breaking loose from slavery and setting themselves free, the myth gave the credit for this freedom to a white Republican president." University of Pennsylvania historian Robert Engs goes even farther; he thinks the "fiction" that " 'Massa Lincoln' freed the slaves" was a sort of tacit conspiracy among whites to convince blacks that "white America, personified by Abraham Lincoln, had *given* them their freedom [rather] than allow them to realize the *empowerment* that their taking of it implied. The poor, uneducated freedman fell for that masterful propaganda stroke. But so have most of the rest of us, black and white, for over a century!"

How valid are these statements? First, we must recognize the considerable degree of truth in the main thesis. By coming into Union lines, by withdrawing their labor from Confederate owners, by working for the Union army and fighting as soldiers in it, slaves did play an active part in achieving their own freedom and, for that matter, in preserving the Union. Like workers, immigrants, women, and other nonelites, slaves were neither passive victims nor pawns of powerful white males who loom so large in our traditional image of American history. They too played a part in determining their own destiny; they too made a history that historians have finally discovered. That is all to the good. But by challenging the "myth" that Lincoln freed the slaves, proponents of the self-emancipation thesis are in danger of creating another myth—that he had little to do with it. It may turn out, upon close examination, that the traditional answer to the question "Who Freed the Slaves?" is closer to being the right answer than is the new and currently more fashionable answer.

First, one must ask what was the sine qua non of emancipation in the 1860s—the essential condition, the one thing without which it would not have happened. The clear answer is the war. Without the Civil War there would have been no confiscation act, no Emancipation Proclamation, no Thirteenth Amendment (not to mention the Fourteenth and Fifteenth), certainly no self-emancipation, and almost certainly no end of slavery for several more decades at least. Slavery had existed in North America for more than two centuries before 1861, but except for a tiny fraction of slaves who fought in the Revolution, or escaped, or bought their freedom, there had been no self-emancipation during that time. Every slave insurrection or insurrection conspiracy failed in the end. On the eve of the Civil War, plantation agriculture was more profitable, slavery more entrenched, slave owners more prosperous, and the "slave power" more dominant within the South if not in the nation at large than it had ever been. Without the war, the door to freedom would have remained closed for an indeterminate length of time.

What brought the war and opened that door? The answer, of course, is complex as well as controversial. A short and simplified summary is that secession and the refusal of the United States government to recognize the legitimacy of secession brought on the war. In both of these matters Abraham Lincoln moves to center stage. Seven states seceded and formed the Confederacy because he won election to the presidency on an antislavery platform; four more seceded after shooting broke out when he refused to evacuate Fort Sumter; the shooting escalated to full-scale war because he called out the troops to suppress rebellion. The common denominator in all of the steps that opened the door to freedom was the active agency of Abraham Lincoln as antislavery political leader, president-elect, president, and commander in chief.

The statement quoted above, that Lincoln "placed the preservation of the white Union above the death of black slavery," while true in a narrow sense, is highly misleading when shorn of its context. From 1854, when he returned to politics, until nominated for president in 1860, the dominant, unifying theme of Lincoln's career was opposition to the expansion of slavery as the vital first step toward placing it in the course of ultimate extinction. A student of Lincoln's oratory has estimated that he gave 175 political speeches during those six years. The "central message" of these speeches showed Lincoln to be a "one-issue" man—the issue being slavery. Over and over again, Lincoln denounced slavery as a "monstrous injustice," "an unqualified evil to the negro, to the white man, to the soil, and to the State." He attacked his main political rival, Stephen A. Douglas, for his "*declared* indifference" to the moral wrong of slavery. Douglas "*looks to no end of the institution of slavery*," said Lincoln.

> That is the real issue. That is the issue that will continue in this country when these poor tongues of Judge Douglas and myself shall be silent. It is the eternal struggle between these two principles—right and wrong—throughout the world.... One is the common right of humanity and the other the divine right of kings.... No matter in what shape it comes, whether from the mouth of a king who seeks to bestride the people of his own nation and live by the fruit of their labor, or from one race of men as an apology for enslaving another race, it is the same tyrannical principle.

Southerners read Lincoln's speeches; they knew by heart his words about the house divided and the ultimate extinction of slavery. Lincoln's election in 1860 was a sign that they had lost control of the national government; if they remained in the Union, they feared that ultimate extinction of their way of life would be their destiny. That is why they seceded. It was not merely Lincoln's election but his election as a *principled opponent of slavery on moral grounds* that precipitated secession. Militant abolitionists critical of Lincoln for falling short of their own standard nevertheless recognized this truth. No longer would the slave power rule the nation, said Frederick Douglass. "Lincoln's election has vitiated their authority, and broken their power." Without Lincoln's election, Southern states would not have seceded in 1861, the war would not have come when and as it did, the door of emancipation would not have been opened as it was. Here was an event that qualifies as a sine qua non, and it proceeded more from the ideas and agency of Abraham Lincoln than from any other single cause.

But, we must ask, would not the election of *any* Republican in 1860 have provoked secession? Probably not, if the candidate had been Edward Bates—who might conceivably have won the election but had no chance of winning the nomination. Yes, almost certainly, if William H. Seward had been the nominee. Seward's earlier talk of a "higher law" and an "irrepressible conflict" had given him a more radical reputation than Lincoln. But Seward might not have won the election. More to the point, if he had won, seven states would undoubtedly have seceded but Seward would have favored compromises and concessions to keep others from going out and perhaps to lure those seven back in. Most important of all, he would have evacuated Fort Sumter and thereby extinguished the spark that threatened to flame into war.

As it was, Seward did his best to compel Lincoln into concessions and evacuation of the fort. But Lincoln stood firm. When Seward flirted with the notion of supporting the Crittenden Compromise, which would have repudiated the Republican platform by permitting the expansion of slavery, Lincoln stiffened the backbones of Seward and other key Republican leaders. "Entertain no proposition for a compromise in regard to the *extension* of slavery," he wrote to them. "The tug has to come, & better now, than any time hereafter." Crittenden's compromise "would lose us everything we gained by the election." It "acknowledges that slavery has equal rights with liberty, and surrenders all we have contended for.... We have just carried an election on principles fairly stated to the people. Now we are told in advance, the government shall be broken up, unless we surrender to those we have beaten.... If we surrender, it is the end of us. They will repeat the experiment upon us *ad libitum*. A year will not pass, till we shall have to take Cuba as a condition upon which they will stay in the Union."

It is worth emphasizing here that the common denominator in these letters from Lincoln to Republican leaders was slavery. To be sure, on the matters of slavery where it already existed and enforcement of the fugitive slave provision of the Constitution, Lincoln was willing to reassure the South. But on the crucial issue of 1860, slavery in the territories, he refused to compromise, and this refusal kept his party in line. Seward, or any other person who might conceivably have been elected president in 1860, would have pursued a different course. This sheds a different light on the assertion that Lincoln "placed the preservation of the white Union above the death of black slavery." The Crittenden Compromise did indeed place preservation of the Union above the death of slavery. So did Seward; so did most white Americans during the secession crisis. But that assertion does *not* describe Lincoln. He refused to yield the core of his antislavery position to stay the breakup of the Union. As Lincoln expressed it in a private letter to his old friend Alexander Stephens, "You think slavery is *right* and ought to be extended; while we think it is *wrong* and ought to be restricted. That I suppose is the rub."

It was indeed the rub. Even more than in his election to the presidency, Lincoln's refusal to compromise on the expansion of slavery or on Fort Sumter proved decisive. If another person had been in his place, the course of history

—and of emancipation—would have been different. Here again we have without question a sine qua non.

It is quite true that once the war started, Lincoln moved more slowly and apparently more reluctantly toward making it a war for emancipation than black leaders, abolitionists, radical Republicans, and the slaves themselves wanted him to move. He did reassure Southern whites that he had no intention and no constitutional power to interfere with slavery in the states. In September 1861 and May 1862 he revoked orders by Generals Frémont and Hunter freeing the slaves of Confederates in their military districts. In December 1861 he forced Secretary of War Simon Cameron to delete from his annual report a paragraph recommending the freeing and arming of slaves. And though Lincoln signed the confiscation acts of August 1861 and July 1862 that freed some slaves owned by Confederates, this legislation did not come from his initiative. Out in the field it was the slaves who escaped to Union lines and officers like General Benjamin Butler who accepted them as "contraband of war" that took the initiative.

All of this appears to support the thesis that slaves emancipated themselves and that Lincoln's image as emancipator is a myth. But let us take a closer look. It seems clear today, as it did in 1861, that no matter how many thousands of slaves came into Union lines, the ultimate fate of the millions who did not, as well as the fate of the institution of slavery itself, depended on the outcome of the war. If the North won, slavery would be weakened if not destroyed; if the Confederacy won, slavery would survive and perhaps grow stronger from the postwar territorial expansion of an independent and confident slave power. Thus Lincoln's emphasis on the priority of Union had positive implications for emancipation, while precipitate or premature actions against slavery might jeopardize the cause of Union and therefore boomerang in favor of slavery.

Lincoln's chief concern in 1861 was to maintain a united coalition of War Democrats and border-state Unionists as well as Republicans in support of the war effort. To do this he considered it essential to define the war as being waged solely for Union, which united this coalition, and not a war against slavery, which would fragment it. When General Frémont issued his emancipation edict in Missouri on August 30, 1861, the political and military efforts to prevent Kentucky, Maryland, and Missouri from seceding and to cultivate Unionists in western Virginia and eastern Tennessee were at a crucial stage, balancing on a knife edge. To keep his fragile coalition from falling apart, therefore, Lincoln rescinded Frémont's order.

Almost certainly this was the right decision at the time. Lincoln's greatest skills as a political leader were his sensitivity to public opinion and his sense of timing. Within six months of his revocation of Frémont's order, he began moving toward a stronger antislavery position. During the spring and early summer of 1862 he alternately coaxed and prodded border-state Unionists toward recognition of the inevitable escalation of the conflict into a war against slavery and toward acceptance of his plan for compensated emancipation in their states. He warned them that the "friction and abrasion" of a war that had by this time swept every institution into its maelstrom could not leave slavery untouched. But the border states remained deaf to Lincoln's warnings and refused to consider his offer of federally compensated emancipation.

By July 1862, Lincoln turned a decisive corner toward abolition. He made up his mind to issue an emancipation proclamation. Whereas a year earlier, even three months earlier, Lincoln had believed that avoidance of such a drastic step was necessary to maintain that knife-edge balance in the Union coalition, things had now changed. The escalation of the war in scope and fury had mobilized all the resources of both sides, including the slave labor force of the Confederacy. The imminent prospect of Union victory in the spring had been shredded by Robert E. Lee's successful counteroffensives in the Seven Days. The risks of alienating the border states and Northern Democrats, Lincoln now believed, were outweighed by the opportunity to energize the Republican majority and to mobilize part of the slave population for the cause of Union— and freedom. When Lincoln told his cabinet on July 22, 1862, that he had decided to issue an emancipation proclamation, Montgomery Blair, speaking for the forces of conservatism in the North and border states, warned of the consequences among these groups if he did so. But Lincoln was done conciliating them. He had tried to make the border states see reason; now "we must make the forward movement" without them. "They [will] acquiesce, if not immediately, soon." As for the Northern Democrats, "their clubs would be used against us take what course we might."

Two years later, speaking to a visiting delegation of abolitionists, Lincoln explained why he had moved more slowly against slavery than they had urged. Having taken an oath to preserve and defend the Constitution, which protected slavery, "I did not consider that I had a *right* to touch the 'State' institution of 'Slavery' until all other measures for restoring the Union had failed.... The moment came when I felt that slavery must die that the nation might live!... Many of my strongest supporters urged *Emancipation* before I thought it indispensable, and, I may say, before I thought the country ready for it. It is my conviction that, had the proclamation been issued even six months earlier than it was, public sentiment would not have sustained it."

Lincoln actually could have made a case that the country had not been ready for the Emancipation Proclamation in September 1862, even in January 1863. Democratic gains in the Northern congressional elections of 1862 resulted in part from a voter backlash against the preliminary Emancipation Proclamation. The morale crisis in Union armies and swelling Copperhead strength during the winter of 1863 grew in part from a resentful conviction that Lincoln had unconstitutionally transformed the purpose of the war from restoring the Union to freeing the slaves. Without question, this issue bitterly divided the Northern people and threatened fatally to erode support for the war effort—the very consequence Lincoln had feared in 1861 and Montgomery Blair had warned against in 1862. Not until after the twin military victories at Gettysburg and Vicksburg did this divisiveness diminish and emancipation gain a clear mandate in the off-year elections of 1863. In his annual message of December 1863, Lincoln conceded that the Emancipation Proclamation a year earlier had been "followed by dark and doubtful days." But now, he added, "the crisis which threatened to divide the friends of the Union is past."

Even that statement turned out to be premature and overoptimistic. In the summer of 1864, Northern morale again plummeted and the emancipation issue once more threatened to undermine the war effort. By August, Grant's campaign in Virginia had bogged down in the trenches after enormous casualties. Sherman seemed similarly thwarted before Atlanta and smaller Union armies elsewhere appeared to be accomplishing nothing. War weariness and defeatism corroded the will of Northerners as they contemplated the staggering cost of this conflict in the lives of their young men. Lincoln came under enormous pressure to open peace negotiations to end the slaughter. Even though Jefferson Davis insisted that Confederate independence was his essential condition for peace, Northern Democrats managed to convince many Northern people that only Lincoln's insistence on emancipation blocked peace. A typical Democratic newspaper editorial declared that "tens of thousands of white men must yet bite the dust to allay the negro mania of the President."

Even Republicans like Horace Greeley, who had criticized Lincoln two years earlier for slowness to embrace emancipation, now criticized him for refusing to abandon it as a precondition for negotiations. The Democratic national convention adopted a platform for the 1864 presidential election calling for peace negotiations to restore the Union with slavery. Every political observer, including Lincoln himself, believed in August that the Republicans would lose the election. The *New York Times* editor and Republican national chairman Henry Raymond told Lincoln that "two special causes are assigned [for] this great reaction in public sentiment,—the want of military success, and the impression... that we *can* have peace with Union if we would... [but that you are] fighting not for Union but for the abolition of slavery."

The pressure on Lincoln to back down on emancipation caused him to waver temporarily but not to buckle. Instead, he told weak-kneed Republicans that "no human power can subdue this rebellion without using the Emancipation lever as I have done." More than one hundred thousand black soldiers and sailors were fighting for the Union, said Lincoln. They would not do so if they thought the North intended to "betray them.... If they stake their lives for us they must be prompted by the strongest motive... There have been men who proposed to me to return to slavery the black warriors" who had fought for the Union. "I should be damned in time & in eternity for so doing. The world shall know that I will keep my faith to friends and enemies, come what will."

When Lincoln said this, he fully expected to lose the election. In effect, he was saying that he would rather be right than president. In many ways this was his finest hour. As matters turned out, of course, he was both right and president. Sherman's capture of Atlanta, Sheridan's victories in the Shenandoah Valley, and military success elsewhere transformed the Northern mood from deepest despair in August 1864 to determined confidence by November, and Lincoln was triumphantly reelected. He won without compromising one inch on the emancipation question.

It is instructive to consider two possible alternatives to this outcome. If the Democrats had won, at best the Union would have been restored without a Thirteenth Amendment; at worst the Confederacy would have achieved its independence. In either case the institution of slavery would have survived.

That this did not happen was owing more to the steadfast purpose of Abraham Lincoln than to any other single factor.

The proponents of the self-emancipation thesis, however, would avow that all of this is irrelevant. If it is true, as Barbara Fields maintains, that by the time of the Emancipation Proclamation "no human being alive could have held back the tide that swept toward freedom," that tide must have been even stronger by the fall of 1864. But I disagree. The tide of freedom could have been swept back. On numerous occasions during the war, it was. When Union forces moved through or were compelled to retreat from areas of the Confederacy where their presence had attracted and liberated contrabands, the tide of slavery closed in behind them and reenslaved those who could not keep up with the advancing or retreating armies. Many of the thousands who did keep up with the Army of the Ohio when it was forced out of Alabama and Tennessee by the Confederate invasion of Kentucky in the fall of 1862 were seized and sold as slaves by Kentuckians. Lee's army captured dozens of black people in Pennsylvania in June 1863 and sent them back South into slavery. Hundreds of black Union soldiers captured by Confederate forces were reenslaved. Lincoln took note of this phenomenon when he warned that if "the pressure of the war should call off our forces from New Orleans to defend some other point, what is to prevent the masters from reducing the blacks to slavery again; for I am told that whenever the rebels take any black prisoners, free or slave, they immediately auction them off!" The editors of the Freedmen's and Southern Society project, the most scholarly advocates of the self-emancipation thesis, acknowledge that "Southern armies could recapture black people who had already reached Union lines.... Indeed, any Union retreat could reverse the process of liberation and throw men and women who had tasted freedom back into bondage.... Their travail testified to the link between the military success of the Northern armies and the liberty of Southern slaves."

Precisely. That is the crucial point. Slaves did not emancipate themselves; they were liberated by Union armies. Freedom quite literally came from the barrel of a gun. And who was the commander in chief that called these armies into being, appointed their generals, and gave them direction and purpose? There, indubitably, is our sine qua non.

But let us grant that once the war was carried into slave territory, no matter how it came out the ensuring "friction and abrasion" would have enabled thousands of slaves to escape to freedom. In that respect, a degree of self-emancipation did occur. But even on a large scale, such emancipation was very different from *the abolition of the institution of slavery.* During the American Revolution almost as large a percentage of the slaves won freedom by coming within British lines as achieved liberation by coming within Union lines during the Civil War. Yet slavery survived the Revolution. Ending the institution of bondage required Union victory; it required Lincoln's reelection in 1864; it required the Thirteenth Amendment. Lincoln played a vital role, indeed the central role, in all of these achievements. It was also his policies and his skillful political leadership that set in motion the processes by which the reconstructed or Unionist states of Louisiana, Arkansas, Tennessee, Maryland, and Missouri abolished the institution in those states during the war itself.

Regrettably, Lincoln did not live to see the final ratification of the Thirteenth Amendment. But if he had never lived, it seems safe to say that we would not have had a Thirteenth Amendment in 1865. In that sense, the traditional answer to the question "Who Freed the Slaves?" is the right answer. Lincoln did not accomplish this in the manner sometimes symbolically portrayed, breaking the chains of helpless and passive bondsmen with the stroke of a pen by signing the Emancipation Proclamation. But by pronouncing slavery a moral evil that must come to an end and then winning the presidency in 1860, provoking the South to secede, by refusing to compromise on the issue of slavery's expansion or on Fort Sumter, by careful leadership and timing that kept a fragile Unionist coalition together in the first year of war and committed it to emancipation in the second, by refusing to compromise this policy once he had adopted it, and by prosecuting the war to unconditional victory as commander in chief of an army of liberation, Abraham Lincoln freed the slaves.

Vincent Harding  **NO**

The Blood-Red Ironies of God

Although the destruction of the oppressors God may not effect by the oppressed, yet the Lord our God will surely bring other destructions upon them—for not infrequently will he cause them to rise up against one another, to be split and divided, and to oppress each other, and sometimes to open hostilities with sword in hand.

— David Walker, 1829

On certain stark and bloody levels, a terrible irony seemed to be at work. For those who interpreted the events of their own times through the wisdom and anguish of the past, the guns of Charleston certainly sounded like the signal for the fulfillment of David Walker's radical prophecies. Here at last was the coming of the righteous God in judgment, preparing to bring "destructions" upon America. Here was the divine culmination of the struggle toward freedom and justice long waged by the oppressed black people. From such a vantage point, the conflict now bursting out was the ultimate justification of the costly freedom movement, a welcome vindication of the trust in Providence. And yet the war was not simply an ally. Like all wars, it brought with it a train of demoralizing, destructive elements, deeply affecting even those persons and causes which seemed to be its chief beneficiaries. In the case of black people, the guns broke in upon their freedom struggle at many levels, diverted and diffused certain of its significant radical elements, and became a source of profound confusion and disarray among its most committed forces. This was especially the case where independent radical black struggle for justice and self-determination was concerned....

When the war broke out, black men and women were convinced that it had to destroy slavery. Especially in the North, this inner certainty flooded their consciousness, buoyed up their hopes. Now it appeared that God was providing a way out of the darkness of slavery and degradation, a way which would release some of the frightening tension of the previous decade. Because they wanted a way out so desperately, because it was hard to be driven by a fierce urgency, fearsome to experience the personal honing in spite of one's own softer and blunter ways, the children of Africa in America clutched at a solution which would not cause them to be driven into the depths of radicalism. For they must

From Vincent Harding, *There Is a River: The Black Struggle for Freedom in America* (Vintage Books, 1981). Copyright © 1981 by Vincent Harding. Reprinted by permission of Harcourt Brace & Company. Notes omitted.

have realized that the chances were good that they might not survive without being seriously, unpredictably transformed. Therefore, when the guns began, black people shunted aside the knowledge of certain fierce realities.

In that mood their men surged forward to volunteer for service in the Union cause, repressing bitter memories. In spite of their misgivings, disregarding the fact that it was not the North which had initiated this righteous war, they offered their bodies for the Northern cause, believing that it was—or would be—the cause of black freedom. If the excited, forgetful young volunteers sought justification, they could find it in the *Anglo-African*: "Talk as we may, we are concerned in this fight and our fate hangs upon its issues. The South must be subjugated, or we shall be enslaved. In aiding the Federal government in whatever way we can, we are aiding to secure our own liberty; for this war can end only in the subjugation of the North or the South." When hard pressed, the journal, like the young men it encouraged, knew very well the nature of the "liberty" they had found so far in the unsubjugated North, and the writer admitted that the North was not consciously fighting for black rights. However, the *Anglo-African* chose to see a power beyond the councils of the North: "Circumstances have been so arranged by the decrees of Providence, that in struggling for their own nationality they are forced to defend our rights." ...

And what of the South? What of those sometimes God-obsessed black believers who had long lifted their cries for deliverance in songs and shouts, in poetry filled with rich and vibrant images? Did they sense the coming of Moses now? Was this finally the day of the delivering God, when he would set his people free? Did they hear Nat Turner's spirit speaking in the guns? Did they believe he was calling them to freedom through all the lines of skirmishers who left their blood upon the leaves? Did they have any difficulty knowing which of the white armies was Pharaoh's?

The answers were as complex as life itself. In many parts of the nation and the world there had been predictions that secession, disunion, and war would lead to a massive black insurrection which would finally vindicate Turner and Walker, and drown the South in blood. Such predictions were made without knowledge of the profound racism and fear which pervaded the white North, and certainly without awareness of the keen perceptions of black people in the South. For most of the enslaved people knew their oppressors, and certainly realized that such a black uprising would expose the presence of Pharaoh's armies everywhere. To choose that path to freedom would surely unite the white North and South more quickly than any other single development, making black men, women, and children the enemy—the isolated, unprepared enemy. For anyone who needed concrete evidence, Gen. George B. McClellan, the commander of the Union's Army of the Ohio, had supplied it in his "Proclamation to the people of Western Virginia" on May 26, 1861: "Not only will we abstain from all interferences with your slaves, but we will, with an iron hand, crush any attempt at insurrection on their part."

So, heeding their own intuitive political wisdom, the black masses confirmed in their actions certain words which had recently appeared in the *Anglo-African*. Thomas Hamilton, the editor, had heard of Lincoln's decision to countermand an emancipation order issued by one of his most fervent Republican generals, John C. Fremont, in Missouri. Hamilton predicted: "The forlorn hope of insurrection among the slaves may as well be abandoned. They are too well informed and too *wise* to court destruction at the hands of the combined Northern and Southern armies—for the man who had reduced back to slavery the slaves of rebels in Missouri would order the army of the United States to put down a slave insurrection in Virginia or Georgia." He was right, of course, and the enslaved population was also right. Therefore, instead of mass insurrection, the Civil War created the context for a vast broadening and intensifying of the self-liberating black movement which had developed prior to the war. Central to this black freedom action, as always, was the continuing series of breaks with the system of slavery, the denials of the system's power, the self-emancipation of steadily increasing thousands of fugitives. Thus, wherever possible, black people avoided the deadly prospects of massive, sustained confrontation, for their ultimate objective was freedom, not martyrdom.

As the guns resounded across the Southern lands, the movement of black folk out of slavery began to build. Quickly it approached and surpassed every level of force previously known. Eventually the flood of fugitives amazed all observers and dismayed not a few, as it sent waves of men, women, and children rushing into the camps of the Northern armies. In this overwhelming human movement, black people of the South offered their own responses to the war, to its conundrums and mysteries. Their action testified to their belief that deliverance was indeed coming through the war, but for thousands of them it was not a deliverance to be bestowed by others. Rather it was to be independently seized and transformed through all the courage, wisdom, and strength of their waiting black lives.

This rapidly increasing movement of black runaways had been noted as soon as the reality of Southern secession had been clearly established. Shortly after the guns of April began to sound in Charleston harbor, large companies of fugitives broke loose from Virginia and the Carolinas and moved toward Richmond. Again, one day in Virginia in the spring of 1861, a black fugitive appeared at the Union-held Fortress Monroe. Two days later eight more arrived, the next day more than fifty, soon hundreds. The word spread throughout the area: there was a "freedom fort," as the fugitives called it, and within a short time thousands were flooding toward it. Similarly, in Louisiana two families waded six miles across a swamp, "spending two days and nights in mud and water to their waists, their children clinging to their backs, and with nothing to eat." In Georgia, a woman with her twenty-two children and grandchildren floated down the river on "a dilapidated flatboat" until she made contact with the Union armies. In South Carolina, black folk floated to freedom on "basket boats made out of reeds," thus reviving an ancient African craft. A contemporary source said of the black surge toward freedom in those first two years of the war: "Many thousands of blacks of all ages, ragged, with no possessions, except the bundles which they carried, had assembled at Norfolk, Hampton, Alexandria and Washington. Others... in multitudes... flocked north from Tennessee, Kentucky, Arkansas, and Missouri."

This was black struggle in the South as the guns roared, coming out of loyal and disloyal states, creating their own liberty. This was the black movement toward a new history, a new life, a new beginning. W. E. B. Du Bois later said, "The whole move was not dramatic or hysterical, rather it was like the great unbroken swell of the ocean before it dashes on the reefs." Yet there was great drama as that flowing movement of courageous black men and women and children sensed the movement of history, heard the voice of God, created and signed their own emancipation proclamations, and seized the time. Their God was moving and they moved with him.

And wherever this moving army of self-free men and women and children went, wherever they stopped to wait and rest and eat and work, and watch the movement of the armies in the fields and forests—in all these unlikely sanctuaries, they sent up their poetry of freedom. Some of them were old songs, taking on new meaning:

> Thus said the Lord, Bold Moses said
> Let my people go
> If not I'll smite your first-born dead
> Let my people go.
> No more shall they in bondage toil
> Let my people go.

But now there was no need to hide behind the stories of thousands of years gone by, now it was clearly a song of black struggle, of deliverance for their own time of need. Now the singers themselves understood more fully what they meant when they sang again:

> One of dese mornings, five o'clock
> Dis ole world gonna reel and rock,
> Pharaoh's Army got drownded
> Oh, Mary, don't you weep.

They were part of the drowning river. Out there, overlooking the battlefields of the South, they were the witnesses to the terrible truth of their own sons, to the this-worldliness of their prayers and aspirations. Remembering that morning in Charleston harbor, who could say they were wrong? "Dis ole world gonna reel and rock..."

Every day they came into the Northern lines, in every condition, in every season of the year, in every state of health. Children came wandering, set in the right direction by falling, dying parents who finally knew why they had lived until then. Women came, stumbling and screaming, their wombs bursting with the promise of new and free black life. Old folks who had lost all track of their age, who knew only that they had once heard of a war against "the Redcoats," also came, some blind, some deaf, yet no less eager to taste a bit of that long-anticipated freedom of their dreams. No more auction block, no more driver's lash, many thousands gone.

This was the river of black struggle in the South, waiting for no one to declare freedom for them, hearing only the declarations of God in the sound of the guns, and moving.

By land, by river, creating their own pilgrim armies and their own modes of travel, they moved south as well as north, heading down to the captured areas of the coast of South Carolina. *Frederick Douglass's Monthly* of February 1862 quoted the report of a *New York Times* correspondent in Port Royal: "Everywhere I find the same state of things existing; everywhere the blacks hurry in droves to our lines; they crowd in small boats around our ships; they swarm upon our decks; they hurry to our officers from the cotton houses of their masters, in an hour or two after our guns are fired.... I mean each statement I make to be taken literally; it is not garnished for rhetorical effect." As usual, black people were prepared to take advantage of every disruption in the life of the oppressing white community. When they heard the guns, they were ready, grasping freedom with their own hands, walking to it, swimming to it, sailing to it—determined that it should be theirs. By all these ways, defying masters, patrols, Confederate soldiers, slowly, surely, they pressed themselves into the central reality of the war.

... By the end of the spring of 1862, tens of thousands [of self-liberated fugitives] were camped out in whatever areas the Northern armies had occupied, thereby making themselves an unavoidable military and political issue. In Washington, D.C., the commander-in-chief of the Union armies had developed no serious plans for the channeling of the black river. Consequently, in the confusion which all war engenders, his generals in the field made and carried out their own plans. They were badly strapped for manpower, and the black fugitives provided some answers to whatever prayers generals pray. The blacks could relieve white fighting men from garrison duties. They could serve as spies, scouts, and couriers in the countryside they knew so well. They could work the familiar land, growing crops for the food and profit of the Union armies. But as the war dragged on and Northern whites lost some of their early enthusiasm, many Union commanders saw the black men among them primarily as potential soldiers. Many of the black men were eager to fight, but Lincoln was still not prepared to go that far.

Nevertheless, some Union commanders like Gen. David Hunter in South Carolina were again issuing their own emancipation proclamations and beginning to recruit black soldiers. In places like occupied New Orleans it was the unmanageable and threatening movement of the blacks themselves which placed additional pressures on the Union's leader. Reports were pouring into Washington which told not only of the flood of fugitives, but of black unrest everywhere. Black men were literally fighting their way past the local police forces to get themselves and their families into the Union encampments. There was word of agricultural workers killing or otherwise getting rid of their overseers, and taking over entire plantations. Commanders like Gen. Ben Butler warned that only Union bayonets prevented widespread black insurrection. (In August 1862, to preserve order and satisfy his need for manpower, Butler himself had begun to recruit black troups in New Orleans, beginning with the well-known Louisiana Native Guards.) The dark presence at the center of the national conflict could no longer be denied. Lincoln's armies were in the midst of a surging movement of black people who were in effect freeing themselves from slavery. His generals were at once desperate for the military resources represented by the so-called contrabands, and convinced that only through military discipline could this volatile, potentially revolutionary black element be contained. As a result, before 1862 was over, black troops were being enlisted to fight for their own freedom in both South Carolina and Louisiana.

In Washington, Congress was discussing its own plans for emancipation, primarily as a weapon against the South, hoping to deprive the Confederacy of a major source of human power and transfer it into Union hands. Their debates and imminent action represented another critical focus of pressure on the President. While Lincoln continued to hesitate about the legal, constitutional, moral, and military aspects of the matter, he was also being constantly attacked in the North for his conduct of the war. The whites were weary and wanted far better news from the fronts. The blacks were angry about his continued refusal to speak clearly to the issue of their people's freedom and the black right to military service. In the summer of 1862 Frederick Douglass declared in his newspaper: "Abraham Lincoln is no more fit for the place he holds than was James Buchanan.... The country is destined to become sick of both [Gen. George B.] McClellan and Lincoln, and the sooner the better. The one plays lawyer for the benefit of the rebels, and the other handles the army for the benefit of the traitors. We should not be surprised if both should be hurled from their places before this rebellion is ended.... The signs of the times indicate that the people will have to take this war into their own hands." But Frederick Douglass was not one to dwell on such revolutionary options. (Besides, had he considered what would happen to the black cause, if the white "people" really did take the war into their own hands?) Fortunately, by the time Douglass's words were published, he had seen new and far more hopeful signs of the times.

In September 1862 Abraham Lincoln, in a double-minded attempt both to bargain with and weaken the South while replying to the pressures of the North, finally made public his proposed Emancipation Proclamation. Under its ambiguous terms, the states in rebellion would be given until the close of the year to end their rebellious action. If any did so, their captive black people would not be affected; otherwise, the Emancipation Proclamation would go into effect on January 1, 1863, theoretically freeing all the enslaved population of the Confederate states and promising federal power to maintain that freedom.

What actually was involved was quite another matter. Of great import was the fact that the proclamation excluded from its provisions the "loyal" slave states of Missouri, Kentucky, Delaware, and Maryland, the anti-Confederate West Virginia Territory, and loyal areas in certain other Confederate states. Legally, then, nearly one million black people whose masters were "loyal" to the Union had no part of the emancipation offered. In effect, Lincoln was announcing freedom to the captives over whom he had least control, while allowing those in states clearly under the rule of his government to remain in slavery. However, on another more legalistic level, Lincoln was justifying his armies' use of the Confederates' black "property," and preparing the way for an even more extensive use of black power by the military forces of the Union. Here, the logic of his move was clear, providing an executive confirmation and extension of Congress's Second Confiscation Act of 1862: once the Emancipation Proclamation went into effect, the tens of thousands of black people who were creating their own freedom, and making themselves available as workers in the Union camps, could be used by the North without legal qualms. Technically, they would no longer be private property, no longer cause problems for a President concerned about property rights.

It was indeed a strange vessel that the Lord had chosen, but black folk in the South were not waiting on such legal niceties. Not long after the preliminary proclamation, an insurrectionary plot was uncovered among a group of blacks in Culpepper County, Virginia. Some were slaves and some free, and the message of their action carried a special resonance for South and North alike, and perhaps for the President himself. For a copy of Lincoln's preliminary proclamation was reportedly found among the possessions of one of the conspirators. Though at least seventeen of the group were executed, their death could not expunge the fact that they had attempted to seize the time, to wrest their emancipation out of the hands of an uncertain President. On Nat's old "gaining ground" they had perhaps heard the voice of his God and, forming their own small army, were once again searching for Jerusalem.

Such action symbolized a major difference in the movement of the Southern and Northern branches of the struggle. In the South, though most of the self-liberating black people eventually entered the camps, or came otherwise under the aegis of the Northern armies, they were undoubtedly acting on significant, independent initiatives. During the first years of the war, the mainstream of the struggle in the South continued to bear this independent, self-authenticating character, refusing to wait for an official emancipation.

In such settings black hope blossomed, fed by its own activity. Even in the ambiguous context of the contraband communities the signs were there. In 1862–63, in Corinth, Mississippi, newly free blacks in one of the best of the contraband camps organized themselves under federal oversight, and created the beginnings of an impressive, cohesive community of work, education, family life, and worship. They built their own modest homes, planted and grew their crops (creating thousands of dollars of profit for the Union), supported their own schools, and eventually developed their own military company to fight with the Union armies. It was not surprising, then, that black fugitives flocked there from as far away as Georgia. Nor was it unexpected that, in 1863, federal military plans demanded the dismantling of the model facility. Nevertheless, the self-reliant black thrust toward the future had been initiated, and Corinth was only one among many hopeful contraband communities.

Such movement, and the vision which impelled it, were integral aspects of the freedom struggle in the South. Meanwhile, to aid that struggle, by 1863 Harriet Tubman had entered the South Carolina war zone. Working on behalf of the Union forces, she organized a corps of black contrabands and traveled with them through the countryside to collect information for army raids, and to urge the still-enslaved blacks to leave their masters. Apparently the intrepid leader and her scouts were successful at both tasks, though Tubman complained that her long dresses sometimes impeded her radical activities.

In the North the situation was somewhat different. Word of Lincoln's anticipated proclamation had an electrifying effect on the black community there, but at the same time further removed the focus from the black freedom-seizing movement in the South. The promised proclamation now gave the Northerners more reason than ever to look to others for release, to invest their hope in the Union cause. Now it seemed as if they would not need to be isolated opponents of an antagonistic federal government. Again, because they wanted to believe, needed to hope, yearned to prove themselves worthy, they thought they saw ever more clearly the glory of the coming; before long, in their eyes the proclamation was clothed in what appeared to be almost angelic light. As such, it became an essentially religious rallying point for the development of a new, confusing mainstream struggle: one which, nervous and excited, approached and embraced the central government and the Republican Party as agents of deliverance. Doubts from the past were now cast aside, for their struggle was unquestionably in the hands of Providence and the Grand Army of the Republic. The voice of God was joined to that of Abraham Lincoln.

. . . [F]rom a certain legal point of view it could be argued that the Emancipation Proclamation set free no enslaved black people at all. Since by December 31, 1862, no Confederate state had accepted Lincoln's invitation to return to the fold with their slaves unthreatened, and since Lincoln acknowledged that he had no real way of enforcing such a proclamation within the rebellious states, the proclamation's power to set anyone free was dubious at best. (Rather, it confirmed and gave ambiguous legal standing to the freedom which black people had already claimed through their own surging, living proclamations.)

Indeed, in his annual address to Congress on December 1, 1862, Lincoln had not seemed primarily concerned with the proclamation. Instead, he had taken that crucial opportunity to propose three constitutional amendments which reaffirmed his long-standing approach to national slavery. The proposed amendments included provisions for gradual emancipation (with a deadline as late as 1900), financial compensation to the owners, and colonization for the freed people. In other words, given the opportunity to place his impending proclamation of limited, immediate emancipation into the firmer context of a constitutional amendment demanding freedom for all enslaved blacks, Lincoln chose another path, one far more in keeping with his own history.

But none of this could dampen the joy of the black North. Within that community, it was the Emancipation Proclamation of January 1, 1863, which especially symbolized all that the people so deeply longed to experience, and its formal announcement sent a storm of long-pent-up emotion surging through the churches and meeting halls. It was almost as if the Northern and Southern struggles had again been joined, this time not through wilderness flights, armed resistance, and civil disobedience, but by a nationwide, centuries-long cord of boundless ecstasy. In spite of its limitations, the proclamation was taken as the greatest sign yet provided by the hand of Providence. The river had burst its boundaries, had shattered slavery's dam. It appeared as if the theodicy of the Northern black experience was finally prevailing. For the freedom struggle, especially in the South, had begun to overwhelm the white man's war, and had forced the President and the nation officially to turn their faces toward the moving black masses. Wherever black people could assemble, by themselves or with whites, they came together to lift joyful voices of thanksgiving, to sing songs of faith, to proclaim, "Jehovah hath triumphed, his people are free." For them, a new year and a new era had been joined in one.

On the evening of December 31, 1862, Frederick Douglass was in Boston attending one of the hundreds of freedom-watch-night services being held across the North in anticipation of the proclamation. That night, a line of messengers had been set up between the telegraph office and the platform of the Tremont Temple, where the Boston meeting was being held. After waiting more than two hours in agonized hope, the crowd was finally rewarded as word of the official proclamation reached them. Douglass said: "The effect of this announcement was startling beyond description, and the scene was wild and grand. Joy and gladness exhausted all forms of expression, from shouts of praise to sobs and tears... a Negro preacher, a man of wonderful vocal power, expressed the heartfelt emotion of the hour, when he led all voice in the anthem, 'Sound the loud timbrel o'er Egypt's dark sea, Jehovah hath triumphed, his people are free.' "

Such rapture was understandable, but like all ecstatic experiences, it carried its own enigmatic penalties. Out of it was born the mythology of Abraham Lincoln as Emancipator, a myth less important in its detail than in its larger meaning and consequences for black struggle. The heart of the matter was this: while the concrete historical realities of the time testified to the costly, daring, courageous activities of hundreds of thousands of black people breaking loose from slavery and setting themselves free, the myth gave the credit for this freedom to a white Republican president. In those same times when black men and women saw visions of a new society of equals, and heard voices pressing them against the American Union of white supremacy, Abraham Lincoln was unable to see beyond the limits of his own race, class, and time, and dreamed of a Haitian island and of Central American colonies to rid the country of the constantly accusing, constantly challenging black presence. Yet in the mythology of blacks and whites alike, it was the independent, radical action of the black movement toward freedom which was diminished, and the coerced, ambiguous role of a white deliverer which gained pre-eminence.

POSTSCRIPT

Did Abraham Lincoln Free the Slaves?

Abraham Lincoln's reputation as "the Great Emancipator" traditionally has been based upon his decision in 1862 to issue the Emancipation Proclamation. While Harding stresses that Lincoln was forced to act by the large number of slaves who already had engaged in a process of self-liberation, he and other scholars point out the limited impact of Lincoln's emancipation policy.

Critics of Lincoln's uncertain approach to ending slavery also cite a number of other examples that draw Lincoln's commitment to freedom into question. During the presidential election campaign of 1860, candidate Lincoln had insisted that he had no desire to abolish slavery where the institution already existed. As president he stated that he would be willing to keep slavery intact if that was the best means of preserving the Union. Lincoln initially opposed arming black citizens for military service, he countermanded several of his field generals' emancipation orders, and he consistently expressed doubts that blacks and whites would be able to live in the United States as equal citizens.

In assessing Lincoln's racial attitudes and policies, care should be taken not to read this historical record solely from a late-twentieth-century perspective. Lincoln may not have been the embodiment of the unblemished racial egalitarian that some might hope for, but few whites were, including most of the abolitionists. Still, as historian Benjamin Quarles has written, Lincoln "treated Negroes as they wanted to be treated—as human beings." Unlike most white Americans of his day, Lincoln opposed slavery, developed a policy that held out hope for emancipation, and supported the Thirteenth Amendment.

Lincoln is the most written-about president. Students should consult *With Malice Toward None: The Life of Abraham Lincoln* (Harper & Row, 1977) and Philip Shaw Paludan, *The Presidency of Abraham Lincoln* (University Press of Kansas, 1994). Gabor S. Boritt, ed., *The Historian's Lincoln: Pseudohistory, Psychohistory, and History* (University of Illinois Press, 1988) is a valuable collection. John Hope Franklin's *The Emancipation Proclamation* (Harlan Davidson, 1995) is the best study of this presidential policy.

In addition to the work of Harding, the self-emancipation thesis is developed in Ira Berlin, Barbara J. Fields, Thavolia Glymph, Joseph P. Reidy, and Leslie S. Rowland, eds., *Freedom: A Documentary History of Emancipation, 1861–1867*, 3 vols. (Cambridge University Press, 1986–1991). The role of African Americans in the Civil War is the subject of James G. Hollandsworth, Jr., *The Louisiana Native Guards: The Black Military Experience During the Civil War* (Louisiana State University Press, 1995).

ISSUE 17

Was Reconstruction a "Splendid Failure"?

YES: Eric Foner, from "The New View of Reconstruction," *American Heritage* (October/November 1983)

NO: Thomas Holt, from *Black Over White: Negro Political Leadership in South Carolina During Reconstruction* (University of Illinois Press, 1977)

ISSUE SUMMARY

YES: Professor of history Eric Foner asserts that although Reconstruction did not achieve radical goals, it was a "splendid failure" because it offered African Americans in the South a temporary vision of a free society.

NO: Thomas Holt, a professor of American and African American history, contends that in South Carolina, where African Americans wielded significant political clout, Reconstruction failed to produce critical economic reforms for working-class blacks because of social and cultural divisions within the black community.

Given the complex political, economic, and social issues that America's leaders were forced to address in the post–Civil War years, it is not surprising that the era of Reconstruction (1865–1877) is shrouded in controversy. For the better part of a century following the war, historians typically characterized Reconstruction as a total failure that had proved detrimental to all Americans— northerners and southerners, whites and blacks. According to this traditional interpretation, a vengeful Congress, dominated by radical Republicans, imposed military rule upon the southern states. Carpetbaggers from the North, along with traitorous white scalawags and their black accomplices in the South, established coalition governments that rewrote state constitutions, raised taxes, looted state treasuries, and disenfranchised former Confederates while extending the ballot to the freedmen. This era finally ended in 1877 when courageous southern white Democrats successfully "redeemed" their region from "Negro rule" by toppling the Republican state governments.

This portrait of Reconstruction dominated the historical profession until the 1960s. One reason for this is that white historians (both northerners and southerners) who wrote about this period operated from two basic assumptions: (1) the South was capable of solving its own problems without federal government interference; and (2) the former slaves were intellectually inferior to whites and incapable of running a government (much less one in which some whites would be their subordinates). African American historians, such as W. E. B. Du Bois, wrote several essays and books that challenged this negative portrayal of Reconstruction, but their works were seldom taken seriously in the academic world and were rarely read by the general public. Still, these black historians foreshadowed the acceptance of revisionist interpretations of Reconstruction, which coincided with the successes of the civil rights movement (or "Second Reconstruction") in the 1960s.

Without ignoring obvious problems and limitations connected with this period, revisionist historians identified a number of accomplishments of the Republican state governments in the South and their supporters in Washington, D.C. For example, revisionists argued that the state constitutions that were written during Reconstruction were the most democratic documents that the South had seen up to that time. Also, while taxes increased in the southern states, the revenues generated by these levies financed the rebuilding and expansion of the South's railroad network, the creation of a number of social service institutions (including hospitals, orphanages, and mental institutions), and the establishment of a public school system that benefited African Americans as well as whites. At the federal level, Reconstruction achieved the ratification of the Fourteenth and Fifteenth Amendments, which extended significant privileges of citizenship (including the right to vote) to African Americans, both North and South. Revisionists also placed the charges of corruption leveled by traditionalists against the Republican regimes in the South in a more appropriate context by insisting that political corruption was a national malady in the second half of the nineteenth century. Finally, revisionist historians sharply attacked the notion that African Americans dominated the reconstructed governments of the South. They pointed out that there were no black governors, only 2 black senators, and 15 black congressmen during this period. Furthermore, in no southern state did blacks control both houses of the legislature.

More recently, a third group of historians, the postrevisionists, have challenged the validity of the term *radical* as it has been applied to the Reconstruction era by both traditionalists and revisionists. The following selections represent two variations of this postrevisionist approach. In the first selection, Eric Foner concedes that Reconstruction was not very radical, much less revolutionary. Nevertheless, he argues, it was a "splendid failure" (a phrase coined by Du Bois) because it offered African Americans a vision of how a free society could look. Thomas Holt, however, maintains that there was nothing splendid at all about the failure of the Reconstruction government in South Carolina to provide necessary economic reforms for black laborers and that proposals to benefit working-class blacks fell victim to the opposition of free-born, mulatto Republican politicians, whose social and cultural origins distanced them from the black proletariat.

Eric Foner  **YES**

The New View of Reconstruction

In the past twenty years, no period of American history has been the subject of a more thoroughgoing reevaluation than Reconstruction—the violent, dramatic, and still controversial era following the Civil War. Race relations, politics, social life, and economic change during Reconstruction have all been reinterpreted in the light of changed attitudes toward the place of blacks within American society. If historians have not yet forged a fully satisfying portrait of Reconstruction as a whole, the traditional interpretation that dominated historical writing for much of this century has irrevocably been laid to rest.

Anyone who attended high school before 1960 learned that Reconstruction was an era of unrelieved sordidness in American political and social life. The martyred Lincoln, according to this view, had planned a quick and painless readmission of the Southern states as equal members of the national family. President Andrew Johnson, his successor, attempted to carry out Lincoln's policies but was foiled by the Radical Republicans (also known as Vindictives or Jacobins). Motivated by an irrational hatred of Rebels or by ties with Northern capitalists out to plunder the South, the Radicals swept aside Johnson's lenient program and fastened black supremacy upon the defeated Confederacy. An orgy of corruption followed, presided over by unscrupulous carpet-baggers (Northerners who ventured south to reap the spoils of office), traitorous scalawags (Southern whites who cooperated with the new governments for personal gain), and the ignorant and childlike freedmen, who were incapable of properly exercising the political power that had been thrust upon them. After much needless suffering, the white community of the South banded together to overthrow these "black" governments and restore home rule (their euphemism for white supremacy). All told, Reconstruction was just about the darkest page in the American saga.

Originating in anti-Reconstruction propaganda of Southern Democrats during the 1870s, this traditional interpretation achieved scholarly legitimacy around the turn of the century through the work of William Dunning and his students at Columbia University. It reached the larger public through films like *Birth of a Nation* and *Gone With the Wind* and that best-selling work of myth-making masquerading as history, *The Tragic Era* by Claude G. Bowers. In language as exaggerated as it was colorful, Bowers told how Andrew Johnson

From Eric Foner, "The New View of Reconstruction," *American Heritage*, vol. 34, no. 6 (October/November 1983). Copyright © 1983 by *American Heritage*. Reprinted by permission.

"fought the bravest battle for constitutional liberty and for the preservation of our institutions ever waged by an Executive" but was overwhelmed by the "poisonous propaganda" of the Radicals. Southern whites, as a result, "literally were put to the torture" by "emissaries of hate" who manipulated the "simple-minded" freedmen, "inflaming the negroes' egotism" and even inspiring "lustful assaults" by blacks upon white womanhood.

In a discipline that sometimes seems to pride itself on the rapid rise and fall of historical interpretations, this traditional portrait of Reconstruction enjoyed remarkable staying power. The long reign of the old interpretation is not difficult to explain. It presented a set of easily identifiable heroes and villains. It enjoyed the imprimatur of the nation's leading scholars. And it accorded with the political and social realities of the first half of this century. This image of Reconstruction helped freeze the mind of the white South in unalterable opposition to any movement for breaching the ascendancy of the Democratic party, eliminating segregation, or readmitting disfranchised blacks to the vote.

Nevertheless, the demise of the traditional interpretation was inevitable, for it ignored the testimony of the central participant in the drama of Reconstruction—the black freedman. Furthermore, it was grounded in the conviction that blacks were unfit to share in political power. As Dunning's Columbia colleague John W. Burgess put it, "A black skin means membership in a race of men which has never of itself succeeded in subjecting passion to reason, has never, therefore, created any civilization of any kind." Once objective scholarship and modern experience rendered that assumption untenable, the entire edifice was bound to fall.

The work of "revising" the history of Reconstruction began with the writings of a handful of survivors of the era, such as John R. Lynch, who had served as a black congressman from Mississippi after the Civil War. In the 1930s white scholars like Francis Simkins and Robert Woody carried the task forward. Then, in 1935, the black historian and activist W. E. B. Du Bois produced *Black Reconstruction in America,* a monumental reevaluation that closed with an irrefutable indictment of a historical profession that had sacrificed scholarly objectivity on the altar of racial bias. "One fact and one alone," he wrote, "explains the attitude of most recent writers toward Reconstruction; they cannot conceive of Negroes as men." Du Bois's work, however, was ignored by most historians.

It was not until the 1960s that the full force of the revisionist wave broke over the field. Then, in rapid succession, virtually every assumption of the traditional viewpoint was systematically dismantled. A drastically different portrait emerged to take its place. President Lincoln did not have a coherent "plan" for Reconstruction, but at the time of his assassination he had been cautiously contemplating black suffrage. Andrew Johnson was a stubborn, racist politician who lacked the ability to compromise. By isolating himself from the broad currents of public opinion that had nourished Lincoln's career, Johnson created an impasse with Congress that Lincoln would certainly have avoided, thus throwing away his political power and destroying his own plans for reconstructing the South.

The Radicals in Congress were acquitted of both vindictive motives and the charge of serving as the stalking-horses of Northern capitalism. They emerged instead as idealists in the best nineteenth-century reform tradition. Radical leaders like Charles Sumner and Thaddeus Stevens had worked for the rights of blacks long before any conceivable political advantage flowed from such a commitment. Stevens refused to sign the Pennsylvania Constitution of 1838 because it disfranchised the state's black citizens; Sumner led a fight in the 1850s to integrate Boston's public schools. Their Reconstruction policies were based on principle, not petty political advantage, for the central issue dividing Johnson and these Radical Republicans was the civil rights of freedmen. Studies of congressional policy-making such as Eric L. McKitrick's *Andrew Johnson and Reconstruction*, also revealed that Reconstruction legislation, ranging from the Civil Rights Act of 1866 to the Fourteenth and Fifteenth Amendments, enjoyed broad support from moderate and conservative Republicans. It was not simply the work of a narrow radical faction.

◦◦◉◦◦

Even more startling was the revised portrait of Reconstruction in the South itself. Imbued with the spirit of the civil rights movement and rejecting entirely the racial assumptions that had underpinned the traditional interpretation, these historians evaluated Reconstruction from the black point of view. Works like Joel Williamson's *After Slavery* portrayed the period as a time of extraordinary political, social, and economic progress for blacks. The establishment of public school systems, the granting of equal citizenship to blacks, the effort to restore the devastated Southern economy, the attempt to construct an interracial political democracy from the ashes of slavery, all these were commendable achievements, not the elements of Bowers's "tragic era."

Unlike earlier writers, the revisionists stressed the active role of the freedmen in shaping Reconstruction. Black initiative established as many schools as did Northern religious societies and the Freedmen's Bureau. The right to vote was not simply thrust upon them by meddling outsiders, since blacks began agitating for the suffrage as soon as they were freed. In 1865 black conventions throughout the South issued eloquent, though unheeded, appeals for equal civil and political rights.

With the advent of Radical Reconstruction in 1867, the freedmen did enjoy a real measure of political power. But black supremacy never existed. In most states blacks held only a small fraction of political offices, and even in South Carolina, where they comprised a majority of the state legislature's lower house, effective power remained in white hands. As for corruption, moral standards in both government and private enterprise were at low ebb throughout the nation in the postwar years—the era of Boss Tweed, the Credit Mobilier scandal, and the Whiskey Ring. Southern corruption could hardly be blamed on former slaves.

Other actors in the Reconstruction drama also came in for reevaluation. Most carpetbaggers were former Union soldiers seeking economic opportunity in the postwar South, not unscrupulous adventurers. Their motives, a typically American amalgam of humanitarianism and the pursuit of profit, were no more insidious than those of Western pioneers. Scalawags, previously seen as traitors to the white race, now emerged as "Old Line" Whig Unionists who had opposed secession in the first place or as poor whites who had long resented planters' domination of Southern life and who saw in Reconstruction a chance to recast Southern society along more democratic lines. Strongholds of Southern white Republicanism like east Tennessee and western North Carolina had been the scene of resistance to Confederate rule throughout the Civil War; now, as one scalawag newspaper put it, the choice was "between salvation at the hand of the Negro or destruction at the hand of the rebels."

At the same time, the Ku Klux Klan and kindred groups, whose campaign of violence against black and white Republicans had been minimized or excused in older writings, were portrayed as they really were. Earlier scholars had conveyed the impression that the Klan intimidated blacks mainly by dressing as ghosts and playing on the freedmen's superstitions. In fact, black fears were all too real: the Klan was a terrorist organization that beat and killed its political opponents to deprive blacks of their newly won rights. The complicity of the Democratic party and the silence of prominent whites in the face of such outrages stood as an indictment of the moral code the South had inherited from the days of slavery.

By the end of the 1960s, then, the old interpretation had been completely reversed. Southern freedmen were the heroes, the "Redeemers" who overthrew Reconstruction were the villains, and if the era was "tragic," it was because change did not go far enough. Reconstruction had been a time of real progress and its failure a lost opportunity for the South and the nation. But the legacy of Reconstruction—the Fourteenth and Fifteenth Amendments—endured to inspire future efforts for civil rights. As Kenneth Stampp wrote in *The Era of Reconstruction,* a superb summary of revisionist findings published in 1965, "If it was worth four years of civil war to save the Union, it was worth a few years of radical reconstruction to give the American Negro the ultimate promise of equal civil and political rights."

As Stampp's statement suggests, the reevaluation of the first Reconstruction was inspired in large measure by the impact of the second—the modern civil rights movement. And with the waning of that movement in recent years, writing on Reconstruction has undergone still another transformation. Instead of seeing the Civil War and its aftermath as a second American Revolution (as Charles Beard had), a regression into barbarism (as Bowers argued), or a golden opportunity squandered (as the revisionists saw it), recent writers argue that Radical Reconstruction was not really very radical. Since land was not distributed to the former slaves, they remained economically dependent upon their former owners. The planter class survived both the war and Reconstruction with its property (apart from slaves) and prestige more or less intact.

Not only changing times but also the changing concerns of historians have contributed to this latest reassessment of Reconstruction. The hallmark of the past decade's historical writing has been an emphasis upon "social history" —the evocation of the past lives of ordinary Americans—and the downplaying of strictly political events. When applied to Reconstruction, this concern with the "social" suggested that black suffrage and officeholding, once seen as the most radical departures of the Reconstruction era, were relatively insignificant.

•◦❦◦•

Recent historians have focused their investigations not upon the politics of Reconstruction but upon the social and economic aspects of the transition from slavery to freedom. Herbert Gutman's influential study of the black family during and after slavery found little change in family structure or relations between men and women resulting from emancipation. Under slavery most blacks had lived in nuclear family units, although they faced the constant threat of separation from loved ones by sale. Reconstruction provided the opportunity for blacks to solidify their preexisting family ties. Conflicts over whether black women should work in the cotton fields (planters said yes, many black families said no) and over white attempts to "apprentice" black children revealed that the autonomy of family life was a major preoccupation of the freedmen. Indeed, whether manifested in their withdrawal from churches controlled by whites, in the blossoming of black fraternal, benevolent, and self-improvement organizations, or in the demise of the slave quarters and their replacement by small tenant farms occupied by individual families, the quest for independence from white authority and control over their own day-to-day lives shaped the black response to emancipation.

In the post–Civil War South the surest guarantee of economic autonomy, blacks believed, was land. To the freedmen the justice of a claim to land based on their years of unrequited labor appeared self-evident. As an Alabama black convention put it, "The property which they [the planters] hold was nearly all earned by the sweat of *our* brows." As Leon Litwack showed in *Been in the Storm So Long,* a Pulitzer Prize–winning account of the black response to emancipation, many freedmen in 1865 and 1866 refused to sign labor contracts, expecting the federal government to give them land. In some localities, as one Alabama overseer reported, they "set up claims to the plantation and all on it."

In the end, of course, the vast majority of Southern blacks remained propertyless and poor. But exactly why the South, and especially its black population, suffered from dire poverty and economic retardation in the decades following the Civil War is a matter of much dispute. In *One Kind of Freedom,* economists Roger Ransom and Richard Sutch indicted country merchants for monopolizing credit and charging usurious interest rates, forcing black tenants into debt and locking the South into a dependence on cotton production that impoverished the entire region. But Jonathan Wiener, in his study of postwar Alabama, argued that planters used their political power to compel blacks to remain on the plantations. Planters succeeded in stabilizing the plantation system, but only by blocking the growth of alternative enterprises, like factories, that might draw off black laborers, thus locking the region into a pattern of economic backwardness.

If the thrust of recent writing has emphasized the social and economic aspects of Reconstruction, politics has not been entirely neglected. But political studies have also reflected the postrevisionist mood summarized by C. Vann Woodward when he observed "how essentially nonrevolutionary and conservative Reconstruction really was." Recent writers, unlike their revisionist predecessors, have found little to praise in federal policy toward the emancipated blacks.

A new sensitivity to the strength of prejudice and laissez-faire ideas in the nineteenth-century North has led many historians to doubt whether the Republican party ever made a genuine commitment to racial justice in the South. The granting of black suffrage was an alternative to a long-term federal responsibility for protecting the rights of the former slaves. Once enfranchised, blacks could be left to fend for themselves. With the exception of a few Radicals like Thaddeus Stevens, nearly all Northern policy-makers and educators are criticized today for assuming that, so long as the unfettered operations of the marketplace afforded blacks the opportunity to advance through diligent labor, federal efforts to assist them in acquiring land were unnecessary.

Probably the most innovative recent writing on Reconstruction politics has centered on a broad reassessment of black Republicanism, largely undertaken by a new generation of black historians. Scholars like Thomas Holt and Nell Painter insist that Reconstruction was not simply a matter of black and white. Conflicts within the black community, no less than divisions among whites, shaped Reconstruction politics. Where revisionist scholars, both black and white, had celebrated the accomplishments of black political leaders, Holt, Painter, and others charge that they failed to address the economic plight of the black masses. Painter criticized "representative colored men," as national black leaders were called, for failing to provide ordinary freedmen with effective political leadership. Holt found that black officeholders in South Carolina mostly emerged from the old free mulatto class of Charleston, which shared many assumptions with prominent whites. "Basically bourgeois in their origins and orientation," he wrote, they "failed to act in the interest of black peasants."

In emphasizing the persistence from slavery of divisions between free blacks and slaves, these writers reflect the increasing concern with continuity and conservatism in Reconstruction. Their work reflects a startling extension of revisionist premises. If, as has been argued for the past twenty years, blacks were active agents rather than mere victims of manipulation, then they could not be absolved of blame for the ultimate failure of Reconstruction.

Despite the excellence of recent writing and the continual expansion of our knowledge of the period, historians of Reconstruction today face a unique dilemma. An old interpretation has been overthrown, but a coherent new synthesis has yet to take its place. The revisionists of the 1960s effectively established a series of negative points: the Reconstruction governments were not as bad as had been portrayed, black supremacy was a myth, the Radicals were not cynical manipulators of the freedmen. Yet no convincing overall portrait of the quality of political and social life emerged from their writings. More recent historians have rightly pointed to elements of continuity that spanned the nineteenth-century Southern experience, especially the survival, in modified form, of the plantation system. Nevertheless, by denying the real changes that did occur, they have failed to provide a convincing portrait of an era characterized above all by drama, turmoil, and social change.

Building upon the findings of the past twenty years of scholarship, a new portrait of Reconstruction ought to begin by viewing it not as a specific time period, bounded by the years 1865 and 1877, but as an episode in a prolonged historical process—American society's adjustment to the consequences of the Civil War and emancipation. The Civil War, of course, raised the decisive questions of America's national existence: the relations between local and national authority, the definition of citizenship, the balance between force and consent in generating obedience to authority. The war and Reconstruction, as Allan Nevins observed over fifty years ago, marked the "emergence of modern America." This was the era of the completion of the national railroad network, the creation of the modern steel industry, the conquest of the West and final subduing of the Indians, and the expansion of the mining frontier. Lincoln's America —the world of the small farm and artisan shop—gave way to a rapidly industrializing economy. The issues that galvanized postwar Northern politics—from the question of the greenback currency to the mode of paying holders of the national debt—arose from the economic changes unleashed by the Civil War.

Above all, the war irrevocably abolished slavery. Since 1619, when "twenty negars" disembarked from a Dutch ship in Virginia, racial injustice had haunted American life, mocking its professed ideals even as tobacco and cotton, the products of slave labor, helped finance the nation's economic development. Now the implications of the black presence could no longer be ignored. The Civil War resolved the problem of slavery but, as the Philadelphia diarist Sydney George Fisher observed in June 1865, it opened an even more intractable problem: "What shall we do with the Negro?" Indeed, he went on, this was a problem *"incapable* of any solution that will satisfy both North and South."

As Fisher realized, the focal point of Reconstruction was the social revolution known as emancipation. Plantation slavery was simultaneously a system of labor, a form of racial domination, and the foundation upon which arose a distinctive ruling class within the South. Its demise threw open the most fundamental questions of economy, society, and politics. A new system of labor, social, racial, and political relations had to be created to replace slavery.

The United States was not the only nation to experience emancipation in the nineteenth century. Neither plantation slavery nor abolition were unique to the United States. But Reconstruction was. In a comparative perspective Radical Reconstruction stands as a remarkable experiment, the only effort of a society experiencing abolition to bring the former slaves within the umbrella of equal citizenship. Because the Radicals did not achieve everything they wanted, historians have lately tended to play down the stunning departure represented by black suffrage and officeholding. Former slaves, most fewer than two years removed from bondage, debated the fundamental questions of the polity: What is a republican form of government? Should the state provide equal education for all? How could political equality be reconciled with a society in which property was so unequally distributed? There was something inspiring in the way such men met the challenge of Reconstruction. "I knew nothing more than to obey my master," James K. Greene, an Alabama black politician later recalled. "But the tocsin of freedom sounded and knocked at the door and we walked out like free men and we met the exigencies as they grew up, and shouldered the responsibilities."

⋯❀⋯

You never saw a people more excited on the subject of politics than are the negroes of the south," one planter observed in 1867. And there were more than a few Southern whites as well who in these years shook off the prejudices of the past to embrace the vision of a new South dedicated to the principles of equal citizenship and social justice. One ordinary South Carolinian expressed the new sense of possibility in 1868 to the Republican governor of the state: "I am sorry that I cannot write an elegant stiled letter to your excellency. But I rejoice to think that God almighty has given to the poor of S. C. a Gov. to hear to feel to protect the humble poor without distinction to race or color.... I am a native borned S. C. a poor man never owned a Negro in my life nor my father before me.... Remember the true and loyal are the poor of the whites and blacks, outside of these you can find none loyal."

Few modern scholars believe the Reconstruction governments established in the South in 1867 and 1868 fulfilled the aspirations of their humble constituents. While their achievements in such realms as education, civil rights, and the economic rebuilding of the South are now widely appreciated, historians today believe they failed to affect either the economic plight of the emancipated slave or the ongoing transformation of independent white farmers into cotton tenants. Yet their opponents did perceive the Reconstruction governments in precisely this way—as representatives of a revolution that had put the bottom rail, both racial and economic, on top. This perception helps explain the ferocity of the attacks leveled against them and the pervasiveness of violence in the postmancipation South.

The spectacle of black men voting and holding office was anathema to large numbers of Southern whites. Even more disturbing, at least in the view of those who still controlled the plantation regions of the South, was the emergence of local officials, black and white, who sympathized with the plight of the black laborer. Alabama's vagrancy law was a "dead letter" in 1870, "because those who are charged with its enforcement are indebted to the vagrant vote for their offices and emoluments." Political debates over the level and incidence of taxation, the control of crops, and the resolution of contract disputes revealed that a primary issue of Reconstruction was the role of government in a plantation society. During presidential Reconstruction, and after "Redemption," with planters and their allies in control of politics, the law emerged as a means of stabilizing and promoting the plantation system. If Radical Reconstruction failed to redistribute the land of the South, the ouster of the planter class from control of politics at least ensured that the sanctions of the criminal law would not be employed to discipline the black labor force.

An understanding of this fundamental conflict over the relation between government and society helps explain the pervasive complaints concerning corruption and "extravagance" during Radical Reconstruction. Corruption there was aplenty; tax rates did rise sharply. More significant than the rate of taxation, however, was the change in its incidence. For the first time, planters and white farmers had to pay a significant portion of their income to the government, while propertyless blacks often escaped scot-free. Several states, moreover, enacted heavy taxes on uncultivated land to discourage land speculation and force land onto the market, benefiting, it was hoped, the freedmen.

As time passed, complaints about the "extravagance" and corruption of Southern governments found a sympathetic audience among influential Northerners. The Democratic charge that universal suffrage in the South was responsible for high taxes and governmental extravagance coincided with a rising conviction among the urban middle classes of the North that city government had to be taken out of the hands of the immigrant poor and returned to the "best men"—the educated, professional, financially independent citizens unable to exert much political influence at a time of mass parties and machine politics. Increasingly the "respectable" middle classes began to retreat from the very notion of universal suffrage. The poor were no longer perceived as honest producers, the backbone of the social order; now they became the "dangerous classes," the "mob." As the historian Francis Parkman put it, too much power rested with "masses of imported ignorance and hereditary ineptitude." To Parkman the Irish of the Northern cities and the blacks of the South were equally incapable of utilizing the ballot: "Witness the municipal corruptions of New York, and the monstrosities of negro rule in South Carolina." Such attitudes helped to justify Northern inaction as, one by one, the Reconstruction regimes of the South were overthrown by political violence.

In the end, then, neither the abolition of slavery nor Reconstruction succeeded in resolving the debate over the meaning of freedom in American life. Twenty years before the American Civil War, writing about the prospect of abolition in France's colonies, Alexis de Tocqueville had written, "If the Negroes have the right to become free, the [planters] have the incontestable right not to be ruined by the Negroes' freedom." And in the United States, as in nearly every plantation society that experienced the end of slavery, a rigid social and political dichotomy between former master and former slave, an ideology of racism, and a dependent labor force with limited economic opportunities all survived abolition. Unless one means by freedom the simple fact of not being a slave, emancipation thrust blacks into a kind of no-man's land, a partial freedom that made a mockery of the American ideal of equal citizenship.

Yet by the same token the ultimate outcome underscores the uniqueness of Reconstruction itself. Alone among the societies that abolished slavery in the nineteenth century, the United States, for a moment, offered the freedmen a measure of political control over their own destinies. However brief its sway, Reconstruction allowed scope for a remarkable political and social mobilization of the black community. It opened doors of opportunity that could never be completely closed. Reconstruction transformed the lives of Southern blacks in ways unmeasurable by statistics and unreachable by law. It raised their expectations and aspirations, redefined their status in relation to the larger society, and allowed space for the creation of institutions that enabled them to survive the repression that followed. And it established constitutional principles of civil and political equality that, while flagrantly violated after Reconstruction, planted the seeds of future struggle.

Certainly, in terms of the sense of possibility with which it opened, Reconstruction failed. But as Du Bois observed, it was a "splendid failure." For its animating vision—a society in which social advancement would be open to all on the basis of individual merit, not inherited caste distinctions—is as old as America itself and remains relevant to a nation still grappling with the unresolved legacy of emancipation.

Black Leaders and Black Labor:
An Unexpected Failure

Reconstruction in South Carolina was a political failure. Of course, there were some notable successes: the establishment of a public education system, and the general process of democratizing a state which had been infamous for the lack of popular participation were significant achievements. Most significant of all, perhaps, was the fact that Reconstruction postponed, if not entirely forestalled, the development of an apartheid system of racial and economic relationships of the dimensions prefigured in the Black Codes.

Nevertheless, Republican government ultimately failed in its two most important tasks—the task of staying in power, and the task of using that power to solve the most critical problems of its constituents. After a fleeting moment of experimentation, blacks were consigned to a special caste in America's class society. Politically they were gradually reduced to a nonentity. Economically they were bound by new and insidious devices, such as debts, poverty, and convict lease, to sell their labor in a buyer's market. Socially they became America's untouchables.

Of course, black South Carolinians did not bear this oppression alone; the bright promise of emancipation had soured in other reconstructed states as well. But South Carolina was unique, because if political Reconstruction should have succeeded anywhere, ostensibly it should have succeeded in the Palmetto State. South Carolina had a black majority from 1820 to 1930, and in the middle of the Reconstruction period (1875) that majority rose to over 60 percent. This state placed more black leaders in elective office than any other southern state. Yet the legislative accomplishments of this brief interregnum do not match the actual or potential power of that leadership. Various explanations are offered to explain the political disaster in the election of 1876, but few have explained the failure of the Republican leadership to use its full power for the social and economic advancement of the black masses during the years preceding 1876. Indeed, if anything the party seemed to be retrogressing during the last two years of Republican rule. Rather than advancing measures to further social change in

South Carolina, Negro leaders found themselves struggling, sometimes unsuccessfully, to defeat the socially reactionary legislative initiatives of their own Governor Chamberlain.

But what did black leaders accomplish during the pre-Chamberlain years of 1868 through 1874 to promote the welfare of their constituents? Their work in establishing a modern, generally progressive and comparatively democratic constitution has been highlighted and commended by most scholars, but considerably less attention has been given to the legislative program after that date, except for the railroads, bond issues, and related activities. The fact is that the major legislative conflicts among Republicans developed around the latter issues, and not around the social or economic legislation most relevant to the poor blacks who were their constituents. Even the few modest programs launched to assist those constituents either were unsuccessful, or were so compromised as to become ineffective. The land commission, for example, was designed to purchase and subdivide the surplus property of debt-ridden planters for landless blacks and whites. But it was placed in the charge of an arrogant, corrupt, and inept administrator who perpetrated several fraudulent and costly transactions. The effort to replace this director involved the commission in new frauds which left its resources further depleted and its capacity to make significant land-reform initiatives severely limited. A public school system was established, but again it was so badly administered that its impact on illiteracy never reached its potential. Of course, there was success in the establishment of a state normal school and a scholarship program which opened up the state university to impecunious blacks. There was also progress in opening public accommodations to blacks, though the custom of segregation in many other aspects of social life remained largely unchanged and unchallenged.

On the whole, one is left with the impression that black freedmen, armed with an overwhelming electoral advantage, had a tremendous opportunity but failed to act to satisfy their most critical needs. Given this very uneven performance of the Republican government, how does one characterize the Republican leadership's performance during Reconstruction? Indeed, how does one characterize the Negroes who constituted the single most numerous group within that leadership? The most persistent image of the latter is that of a largely poor, working-class group, or representatives of the working class. In a sense, the crystallization of this image is represented in the work of W. E. B. Du Bois, who characterized the Reconstruction as "a vast labor movement" and marvelled that "poverty was so well represented," seeing in this "certain tendencies toward a dictatorship of the proletariat." Indeed, this attempt to impose a not entirely crystallized Marxian interpretation of Reconstruction politics brought Du Bois a great deal of criticism; consequently, many of his other insights have been ignored.

In one such insight he qualified his description of the black leadership class as representatives of the black proletariat; he observed that the group was intelligent, but "not at all clear in its economic thought." He recognized that "on the whole, it believed in the accumulation of wealth and exploitation of labor as the normal method of economic development." It failed to unite black and white labor "because black leadership still tended toward the ideas of the petty bourgeois." He believed, nevertheless, that their participation and leadership in the incipient national black labor movement was proof that this orientation was undergoing a change as a result of pressure from the legislators' poor working-class constituents.

And indeed, pressure there was from constituents—but the pressure groups never effectively harnessed the political process to serve their ends. At least twenty bills purporting to govern the relationship between planters and laborers were introduced during the period of Republican rule, yet very few of these measures ever became law, and none seemed to have protected farm laborers satisfactorily. Their legislative histories are tangled; often there were no roll calls, and extant reports of the legislative progress of the proposals are filled with unaccountable gaps at critical junctures. But a pattern is apparent from the information that does survive. Black legislators introduced legislation designed to surround the laborer with a variety of legal protections against capricious eviction, fraud in the division of the crop, and the accustomed dictation by planters of many non-economic aspects of his life. These legislative initiatives were bottled up in hostile committees in many instances, compromised through drastic amendments in others, and killed outright on not a few occasions. Those few offered little protection to the laborers, and in some cases merely legalized their oppression.

Within days of the inauguration of Republican rule in South Carolina and the convening of the special session of the 1868 legislature, State Senator Benjamin F. Randolph introduced a "Bill to enable laborers who work under contract or otherwise to recover pay for their labor when said contract is not complied with." The judiciary committee, chaired by D. T. Corbin (who was also U. S. district attorney for South Carolina), reported unfavorably on this bill on July 22; this report was adopted, thereby defeating the bill. But a short time later a second bill was introduced by William Beverly Nash under the title, "A Bill to define the law of contract for hire." Supporters of this measure sought to bypass the hostile judiciary committee by referring it to a special three-man committee, but were defeated. Senator Randolph then moved to force the judiciary committee to report within a specified period. This effort was also unsuccessful, and no bill reached the floor of the Senate during the special session. Among this stalled legislation was a "Bill to protect laborers and persons working under contracts on shares of the crops" which had passed the House, but was postponed in the Senate until the session beginning the following November.

The latter bill, or at least one bearing its title, did pass during the regular session of the legislature and was approved by Governor Scott on March 19, 1869. That this new law intended no radical changes in the legal status of farmworkers vis-à-vis the planters is clear, however, from the action taken on it during the session. At the end of February Alonzo J. Ransier, chairman of the special committee in the House to which it was referred, reported "A bill to establish an agent to supervise contracts, and to provide for the protection of laborers working on shares of the crop," which had originally been introduced by William H. Jones. In committee the bill had been drastically altered, and all references to the appointment of contract agents were dropped in the revised text. A new title was appended which read simply "A bill to protect laborers and persons working under contract on shares of crops." When this revised bill was taken up on March 3, Thaddeus K. Sasportas offered the following substitute for the first two sections.

> Section 1. That any person or persons entering into contracts as laborers, consideration for which labor is a portion of the crop, are hereby declared to be co-partners, with all rights, privileges and emoluments guaranteed to corporations by existing law, in said crop, and no further.
>
> Section 2. That a claim for labor, whenever performed, shall constitute a lien having a priority over all other liens. All Acts and parts of Acts inconsist [*sic*] with this Act be, and the same are hereby, repealed.

Claude Turner, a Democratic member, moved to postpone the whole matter indefinitely. Robert B. Elliott moved that the bill and the substitute be tabled in order to take up out of its regular order a "Bill to define contracts for laborers, and for other purposes." Elliott's motion was approved 33 to 10, but action on the second bill was postponed to take up the Port Royal Railroad Bill.

The bill to define contracts for laborers was evidently the same proposal Senator Nash had introduced during the special session which had been continued to the regular session. However, Nash's bill had been altered in Whipper's judiciary committee with the following very critical substitute for section five of the original measure:

> Section 5. Employees absenting themselves from labor without the consent of their employers, except in case of sickness, or on public days, or the usual holidays, shall forfeit his or her pay *for the week or month*, as the case may be, for which he or she was hired; Provided, however, That any persons attending public meetings shall forfeit only at the rate of their wages for the time lost.

This substitute, by which a laborer could be docked for up to a month's wages for one day's unexcused absence, was adopted on March 11 when consideration of the labor bill resumed. It was passed and sent to the Senate on March 16. Subsequent actions on the bill are unclear, but it was postponed until the following session and, apparently, allowed to die quietly.

Meanwhile, the bill written by Ransier's special committee had passed the House and Senate and had been approved by the governor in March, 1869. Judging from the content of the new law, however, the title—"To protect laborers" —was a misnomer, since in its practical application the planters would receive more "protection" than the farmworkers. . . .

[T]he distinctive voting patterns on the two roll calls on the labor issue suggest the legislators' motives and, given other evidence, might permit some inferences to be drawn from their performance on this issue.

The first roll call was ordered on February 5, when the labor committee's substitute passed its second reading by a vote of 57 to 9. The second occurred when George Lee's motion to kill the Henderson bill was approved, 43 to 20. Therefore, 86 percent of those voting favored the substitute, with only five Democrats, three white Republicans, and one Negro voting against it. On the

Henderson bill, however, only 60 percent of the Negroes (as compared with 90 percent of the white Republicans) voted against the proposal—i.e., for Lee's motion to strike the resolving clause. However, the opposition included many House leaders, such as Robert B. Elliott and Robert C. De Large, along with more conservative Negroes like Henry W. Purvis, Philip Ezekiel, and Charles M. Wilder. The voting patterns of the Negroes by prewar origin and color indicate that those representatives closer to working-class blacks—that is, the black ex-slaves—tended to favor Henderson's bill, which promised direct assistance to resolve labor problems, rather than the legalistic and complex procedures favored by their freeborn and mulatto colleagues. With 50 and 60 percent of those voting on the bill identified by color and origins, respectively, only 11 percent of the freeborn compared to 48 percent of the slave-born, and 18 percent of the mulattoes compared to 35 percent of the blacks voted for Henderson's bill. When the categories of origins and color are combined, it is evident that black ex-slaves gave the bill its heaviest support and freeborn mulattoes its stiffest opposition. Thus, the voting behavior of the legislators on these two roll calls on the labor issue follow the pattern discerned in other roll calls during the early sessions of the legislature, when free mulattoes and black ex-slaves were found at the opposite ends of a conservative-to-radical continuum. Such opposition suggests that social class influenced political behavior.

Of course, a division along lines of prewar status and color does not prove that open class antagonism was reflected in this vote. Indeed, one would not expect such class conflict to be openly expressed, or possibly even honestly perceived by the participants. After all, these legislators, whatever their origins, color, or class, depended upon the poor black farmworkers to keep them in office. But the failure of the legislature to enact meaningful labor laws certainly suggests an underlying failure of purposefulness, a failure of perception, a lack of urgency in acting on the critical needs of those constituents. Legislation involving other economic issues, such as banks, bond issues, and railroads, had experienced much less frustration, being pushed along with more tenacity and skill than those relating to the common laborers. One is forced to the conclusion that while it did not cause this failure to legislate successfully for the working class, the considerable social and cultural distance between many of these legislators and their constituents must have contributed to that failure.

The forty-seven Negro legislators who were either elected from or resided in Charleston County are admittedly not a *random* sampling of the Negro leadership cadre for this period, but Charleston County offers the distinct advantage of extant and well-maintained tax records for the 1870's, in which the property holdings of two-thirds of these forty-seven men are recorded. In addition to this convenience, it is also evident that the twenty votes of the Charleston delegation were critical to the success of any legislation in the General Assembly. The median value of property of the legislators in this sample was $1,000: five men were listed as owning neither personal nor real property; ten others paid taxes on property valued at less than $1,000, and eleven on property valued at between $1,000 and $5,000, four on property worth $5,001 to $10,000, and one was taxed for property worth $14,000.

Twenty-one of these men were paying taxes on real estate, and while some of them were legitimate farmers, others appear to have been land speculators. Some had properties in the country, a significant proportion of which was arable soil and under cultivation. For example, William R. Jervay's 136 acres in the Stephens district included 30 acres under cultivation, housed six buildings and several farm animals. A similar situation could be found with William H. W. Gray's 25 acres in St. John's.

On the other hand, a fair number of them appear to have been real estate speculators. This can be inferred from the fact that they held large sections, often in scattered sites in country districts, which were largely undeveloped, having much of the land covered with woods and few or no buildings or farm animals listed. This appears to have been the case with the 100 acres in the possession of Aaron Logan in St. Thomas, Samuel E. Gaillard's property at St. James Goose Creek, and George Lee's wooded lot in Summerville.

The practice of investing accumulated capital in land had roots in the prewar period, when this was one of the few capital ventures open to the mulatto bourgeoisie. The McKinlays, *père* and *fils*, were the wealthiest Negro politicians; much of their wealth, aggregating to $40,000 for the collective family estate and consisting primarily of investments in rental properties around Charleston's Fourth Ward, came from real estate purchased before the war. The McKinlays also invested heavily in the stocks and bonds of their city and state and in the new, largely black-owned Enterprise Railroad. Bosemon, Louisa Ransier (wife of Congressman Alonzo J. Ransier), George Lee, and Florian Henry Frost also invested substantially in these same issues, especially the Enterprise Railroad. Frost had a part interest in a sloop, the *Martha Raven*, in addition to his other investments.

One suspects then that these people were, or aspired to become, a part of the emerging capitalist class of postwar Charleston. The economic temper was optimistic, boomed by various schemes for an east-west rail link which would usher that port city into a new era of prosperity. While their capitalist allies in the Republican party built railroads across the continent, some of the Negro leaders launched kindred ventures on a smaller scale in Charleston. A few weeks after they failed to get a labor bill through the General Assembly, a group of prominent Negro politicians succeeded in their effort to launch the Enterprise Railroad, a horse-drawn freight streetcar line which was set up to move goods in and out of Charleston harbor. All but one of the officers and directors were Negro. Richard H. Cain was president of the company; William James Whipper, vice-president; Alonzo J. Ransier, secretary; William R. Jervay, corresponding secretary; and William McKinlay, treasurer. The twelve-man board of directors included Joseph H. Rainey, Benjamin A. Bosemon, William J. Brodie, Charles Hayne, Thaddeus K. Sasportas, John B. Wright, Henry J. Maxwell, Lucius Wimbush, Robert Smalls, William E. Johnston, and Samuel Johnson. The incorporators were to subscribe $13,000 of the capital stock of the company. Some of the incorporators were publicly attacked because their rail line would throw the black draymen out of work. The road was established, however, and paid a handsome profit to its investors; it was still in use in the 1880's.

Other ventures of a similar nature were not so entirely black-controlled as the Enterprise Railroad. William J. McKinlay, Samuel E. Gaillard, William R. Jervay, and others incorporated the Charleston and Sullivan's Island Railroad in 1874 to run from Christ Church Parish to Moultrieville and connect Charleston with some of the outlying islands. And in the spring of 1870 William McKinlay and Charles M. Wilder were elected to the board of directors of the South Carolina Bank and Trust Company.

Others factors—more suggestive than demonstrative—point to the class consciousness of these men. Personal possessions are identified in the tax ledgers, and they often hint at a lifestyle that is clearly more middle than working-class. There appear in these ledgers the carriages, pianos, organs, and jewelry of people that have or seek a cultivated ease, charm, and elegance suggestive of an emerging bourgeoisie. Of course, the nouveau (as distinct from the traditional) bourgeoisie often reflected a certain lack of polish, the gaucheness expected of those who were only recently ushered to a new social level. The relish of ostentatious display evident in State Representative Sammy Green as he sped through the sandy streets of Beaufort with his thousand-dollar barouche and team exemplifies not only the cruder side of these aspirations, but the growing distance between Green and his constituents as well. In this case, as in many others, the social distance was not reflected in a concurrent political distance, for Green was generally identified with the extreme radical bloc in the legislature throughout his career. It merely points up the fact that what one expects to find here is not an iron law for the prediction of political behavior from social class, but something more subtle.

Certainly, the subtleties of the situation were not lost on some of the more perceptive observers of South Carolina society and politics. In a lengthy article in a Beaufort paper, a native white Southerner, obviously from the planter class, surprisingly favored the Civil Rights Bill of 1875 which was then being debated in Congress. The writer, who signed himself "W," declared that whites need not concern themselves with the Civil Rights Bill, for it would only benefit the educated class among the blacks and would serve to ally them even closer to the upper-class whites. He lectured his readers on emerging class and racial patterns in the state which would operate to maintain that status quo.

> Among them will be found two classes whose conditions will be so distinctive that their own lines of demarkation will be as wide and as well defined as that which exists between the more cultivated and refined of the white race and those less trained and cultured of either. The one will consist of such as are as highly intelligent and educated as they are capable of; the other of such as are untutored and degraded as the need of such advantages makes them. In proportion to the advantages embraced by the first will their pride and conservatism be increased.

"W" went on to conclude that the Civil Rights Bill could never reconcile these two antagonistic classes among the Negroes, and thus the various constitutional amendments and civil rights laws would never be pushed beyond the "naturally constituted barriers of taste and prejudice." The Negro bourgeoisie would prevent such eventualities, because it would seek to maintain its own social distance from the black masses. The writer felt that the experience of the past few years in Beaufort had certainly established that point, for there "where the colored element predominates there have been the fewest demonstrations of a desire upon their parts to assume any unwarranted position...." Thus the whites could expect to find allies among the Negro bourgeoisie.

> From the educated and intelligent of the colored race whose home is to be amongst us we confidently predict so much conservatism and so much exclusivism among themselves that any effort to make use of them to entertain ill-blood among the races will prove futile. From the ignorant and vicious of the same race there need be no fear of other than an enforced obedience to the natural order which society is constituted according to organic law which man neither made nor can alter.

The radical and economic prejudices of "W" are clear, and his interpretation of the postwar social scene was with respect to his class self-congratulatory, if not self-serving. But his comments cannot be dismissed as mere wishful thinking, for they might have been based on observable phenomena. At least one of his Beaufort neighbors was a perfect example of the nexus between the solidification of class interests and an evolving political ideology. Thomas Hamilton was a Republican, although he was often a maverick on partisan issues. During the 1875–76 session Hamilton had a fairly radical voting record on fiscal issues but was clearly conservative on those relative to political and social reform that came to a roll call vote. His views are expressed more clearly and directly, though, in a speech to striking rice workers in 1876.

> My friends, the longer I live and pursue my avocation as a planter the more am I impressed with the knowledge that our interests are identical with the owners of these plantations. Surely, if they are not prosperous, how can they pay you wages? You complain now that you don't get enough for your labor, but would you not have greater cause of complaint if you destroy entirely their ability to pay you at all? I am a rice planter, and employ a certain number of hands. Now, if my work is not permitted to go on, how can I gather my crops and pay my laborers, and how can my laborers support their families? They are dependent upon their labor for support; they are not calculated for anything else; they can't get situations in stores as clerks; they can't all write, nor are they fitted for anything else. There is but one course for you to pursue, and that is to labor industriously and live honestly.

In the critical election of 1876, Hamilton, whose comments prefigured the anti-labor, capitalistic, accommodationist philosophy of Booker T. Washington, abandoned the Republicans for Wade Hampton to complete the overthrow of Republican government, the last hope of justice—though perhaps a misplaced one—for those rice workers whom he addressed in the summer of 1876.

The rhetoric of some of Hamilton's colleagues was more pro-labor, but their accomplishments were no less pro-planter. That the 1869 labor law was not operating satisfactorily for farmworkers can be surmised from the fact that proposals were introduced in practically every subsequent session to remedy its defects. Most of the new laws that were passed, however, actually aided the planter much more than the worker.

Not that there were no legislative victories for the farmworker, but the practical effect of these victories was often quite different from the apparent intent. For instance, the cash-poor planters had instituted a system in some areas whereby they paid wage laborers in scrip or checks redeemable with certain local merchants. Sometimes the planter was also the merchant; in effect, he simply bartered high-priced merchandise for low-paid labor. In either case, the mark-up on prices at the company store was astronomical, and the workers got the short end of a line of credit that ultimately reached banking institutions beyond the state.

In 1872 the South Carolina legislature outlawed the issuance of checks except where it was specifically provided for in the labor contract beforehand. Of course, it is difficult to judge how much the loophole exempting cases where scrip was a prior contractual arrangement vitiated the effects of the law, since planters could make such arrangements a standard item in their contracts. But it is clear that the practice was continued, because it was directly responsible for the strike of rice workers in the summer of 1876. The law had been amended in March, 1875, so that scrips or checks would be prohibited only in those cases where they had to be redeemed "at some future time, or in the shops or stores of the employers." Thus the key features of the system were preserved—that is, workers could be paid in scrip instead of currency, and this scrip was only redeemable for goods available at the local store at exorbitant prices.

The workers in the lowland rice areas were mostly wage laborers, and therefore the primary victims of the scrip system. They rebelled in July, 1876, with a massive and violent strike. The workers abandoned the fields and generally coerced their less resolute colleagues to do likewise. The whites declared that it was insurrection and called upon Governor Chamberlain to send in the state militia. But, facing a gubernatorial election in the fall, Chamberlain also sent "the King of Beaufort," Congressman Robert Smalls, to investigate. Smalls, who was also a commander in the state militia, reported that the militia was no longer needed, that the ringleaders had been arrested, and that the workers had just grievances against the checks system. His position (which Chamberlain also adopted) was that the workers had a right to strike, but not to prevent others from working. This principle of "the right to work" was respectable enough, and certainly in keeping with the prevalent free enterprise philosophy of many Republican contemporaries. Smalls reported that the workers also agreed with his position, but evidently they were not so deluded as to believe they could win the strike following such a policy. They continued successfully to use might where right had failed to induce potential strikebreakers to adopt the better part of valor. Convinced that the state government would not protect them from the violent and illegal actions of the strikers, the planters decided to settle and to abandon the checks system.

One rice planter who deplored the government's vacillating course was State Representative Hamilton, who instructed the rice workers on the dangers inherent in such action. "I consider it a great misfortune that an example was not made of those persons who were tried a few days ago for whipping and otherwise maltreating laborers who were disposed to work, for it emboldens others to repeat that which may be repeated too often, and until all patience and sympathy is exhausted."

While the legislators' efforts to regulate the use of checks failed to prevent the strike or protect the workers, their accomplishments on another labor-related issue were more successful. In 1872 a bill was passed which regulated the leasing of convicts by merely providing that their labor could not be sold at rates less than those current for comparable labor, and that the proceeds must go to the state. Two years later the leasing of convicts to private parties was outlawed altogether, and such use of inmates was restricted to state projects. During the 1875–76 session Governor Chamberlain's attempt to revive the practice of leasing to private concerns was defeated. Thus, although the system of convict lease was instituted under Republican government, it was also terminated by that government.

Unfortunately, this was one of the few entirely pro-labor accomplishments in nine years of Republican rule. On March 19, 1874, an "Act for the better protection of landowners and persons renting land to others for agricultural purposes" was passed. This law established for planters a preferential lien on one-third of the crop against the rental of the land or advances to farmworkers during the season. In December, 1876, after an election which brought an end to Republican hegemony in South Carolina, two legislatures convened in Columbia, one Democratic and one Republican, both claiming to be the legitimate representatives of the people. In the course of this heated dispute over the political future of the state, the economic future of black laborers received a fatal blow. Almost as an afterthought, the laws which had given laborers a lien on the crop of the planter were quietly repealed. This was done not by the Democratic Wallace House, but by the Republican Mackey House. It was not, in the end, such a splendid failure after all.

POSTSCRIPT

Was Reconstruction a "Splendid Failure"?

Both the traditional and revisionist writers of Reconstruction history have treated African Americans in a passive manner. Traditionalists like James G. Randall and E. Merton Coulter, who assumed that African Americans were intellectually inferior to whites, argued that black politicians were the junior partners of the white carpetbaggers and scalawags in robbing the Reconstruction governments. Revisionists like Kenneth M. Stampp, who believed in the biological equality of all humans, maintained that the African American politicians did not constitute a majority in the Reconstruction governments, were not totally corrupt, and did not want to disenfranchise whites. African Americans, Stampp insisted, only deserved their civil and political constitutional rights. Writing at the peak of the civil rights movement in 1965, Stampp was trying to assure his readers that black Americans only wanted to become good Americans and obtain (in this "second Reconstruction") what had been denied them a century earlier.

Foner's conclusions are more upbeat than those of most postrevisionists. However brief, he argues, "the United States . . . offered the freedmen a measure of political control over their own destinies. . . . [It] transformed the lives of Southern blacks in ways unmeasurable by statistics. . . . It raised their expectations and aspirations . . . [and] established constitutional principles of civil and political equality that . . . planted the seeds of future struggle."

In *Nothing But Freedom: Emancipation and Its Legacy* (Louisiana State University Press, 1984), Foner advances his interpretation by comparing the treatment of American ex-slaves with that of newly emancipated slaves in Haiti and the British West Indies. Only in the United States, he contends, were the freedmen given voting and economic rights. Although these rights had been stripped away from the majority of black southerners by 1900, Reconstruction had, nevertheless, created a legacy of freedom that inspired succeeding generations of African Americans.

C. Vann Woodward, in *The Future of the Past* (Oxford University Press, 1988), is more pessimistic about the outcome of Reconstruction than Foner. For all the successes listed by the revisionists, he argues that the experiment failed. Woodward makes use of both counterfactual ("what if") history and comparative history to counter the optimistic assumption of some of the earlier revisionists that if the national government had engaged in extensive land reforms and enforced laws protecting the civil rights of African Americans, Reconstruction would have worked. In contrast to Foner, Woodward argues that former slaves were as poorly treated in the United States as they were in other countries. He also maintains that the confiscation of former plantations and the redistribution of land to the former slaves would have failed in the same way that the Homestead Act of 1862 failed to generate equal distribution of government lands to poor, white settlers. Finally, Woodward contends that reformers who worked with African Americans during Reconstruction and with Native Americans a decade or two later were often the same people and that they failed in both instances because their goals were out of touch with the realities of the late nineteenth century.

The study of the Reconstruction period benefits from an extensive bibliography. Traditional accounts of the period can be sampled in William Archibald Dunning's *Reconstruction, Political and Economic, 1865–1877* (Harper & Brothers, 1907); Claude Bowers's *Tragic Era: The Revolution After Lincoln* (Riverside Press, 1929); and E. Merton Coulter's *South During Reconstruction, 1865–1877* (Louisiana State University Press, 1947), the last major work written from the Dunning (or traditional) point of view. Early revisionist views are presented in W. E. B. Du Bois, *Black Reconstruction in America: An Essay Toward a History of the Part Which Black Folk Played in the Attempt to Reconstruct Democracy in America, 1860–1880* (Harcourt, Brace, 1935), a Marxist analysis; John Hope Franklin, *Reconstruction: After the Civil War* (University of Chicago Press, 1961); and Kenneth M. Stampp, *The Era of Reconstruction, 1865–1877* (Alfred A. Knopf, 1965). Foner's *Reconstruction: America's Unfinished Revolution, 1863–1877* (Harper & Row, 1988) includes one of the most complete bibliographies on the subject. Briefer overviews are available in Forrest G. Wood, *The Era of Reconstruction, 1863–1877* (Harlan Davidson, 1975) and Michael Perman, *Emancipation and Reconstruction, 1862–1879* (Harlan Davidson, 1987). One of the best-written studies of a specific episode during the Reconstruction years is Willie Lee Rose's *Rehearsal for Reconstruction: The Port Royal Experiment* (Bobbs-Merrill, 1964), which describes the failed effort at land reform in the sea islands of South Carolina. Richard Nelson Current's *Those Terrible Carpetbaggers: A Reinterpretation* (Oxford University Press, 1988) is a superb challenge to the traditional view of these much-maligned Reconstruction participants. Finally, for collections of interpretive essays on various aspects of the Reconstruction experience, see Staughton Lynd, ed., *Reconstruction* (Harper & Row, 1967); Seth M. Scheiner, ed., *Reconstruction: A Tragic Era?* (Holt, Rinehart & Winston, 1968); and Edwin C. Rozwenc, ed., *Reconstruction in the South*, 2d ed. (D. C. Heath, 1972).

Contributors to This Volume

EDITORS

LARRY MADARAS is a professor of history and political science at Howard Community College in Columbia, Maryland. He received a B.A. from the College of the Holy Cross in 1959 and an M.A. and a Ph.D. from New York University in 1961 and 1964, respectively. He has also taught at Spring Hill College, the University of South Alabama, and the University of Maryland at College Park. He has been a Fulbright Fellow and has held two fellowships from the National Endowment for the Humanities. He is the author of dozens of journal articles and book reviews.

JAMES M. SoRELLE is chair and a professor of history at Baylor University in Waco, Texas. He received a B.A. and an M.A. from the University of Houston in 1972 and 1974, respectively, and a Ph.D. from Kent State University in 1980. In addition to introductory courses in American history, he teaches upper-level sections in African American, urban, and late-nineteenth- and twentieth-century U.S. history. His scholarly articles have appeared in *Houston Review, Southwestern Historical Quarterly,* and *Black Dixie: Essays in Afro-Texan History and Culture in Houston,* edited by Howard Beeth and Cary D. Wintz (Texas A&M University Press, 1992). He has also contributed entries to *The Handbook of Texas, The Oxford Companion to Politics of the World,* and *Encyclopedia of the Confederacy.*

STAFF

Theodore Knight   List Manager
David Brackley   Senior Developmental Editor
Juliana Gribbins   Developmental Editor
Rose Gleich   Administrative Assistant
Brenda S. Filley   Director of Production/Design
Juliana Arbo   Typesetting Supervisor
Diane Barker   Proofreader
Richard Tietjen   Publishing Systems Manager
Larry Killian   Copier Coordinator

AUTHORS

RODOLFO ACUÑA is a professor of Chicano studies at California State University, Northridge. He is credited with being active in the efforts to establish Chicano studies curricula at several universities. He is the author of *Anything but Mexican: Chicanos in Contemporary Los Angeles* (Verso, 1996).

IRVING H. BARTLETT is the John F. Kennedy Professor Emeritus of American Civilization at the University of Massachusetts, Boston. His publications include *The American Mind in the Mid-Nineteenth Century* (Harlan Davidson, 1982) and *John C. Calhoun: A Biography* (W. W. Norton, 1993).

PATRICIA U. BONOMI is a professor in the Department of History at New York University in New York City. She is the author of *Colonial Dutch Studies: An Interdisciplinary Approach* (New York University Press, 1988) and *The Lord Cornbury Scandal: The Politics of Reputation in British America* (University of North Carolina Press, 1998).

PAUL BOYER is a professor in the Department of History at the University of Wisconsin–Madison. He earned his Ph.D. at Harvard University, and his research and teaching interests include American intellectual and cultural history and American religious history.

JON BUTLER is the William Robertson Coe Professor of American History at Yale University in New Haven, Connecticut. He is the author of *Becoming America: The Revolution Before 1776* (Harvard University Press, 2000) and *Religion in Colonial America* (Oxford University Press, 2000).

LAURIE WINN CARLSON, a historian, is the author of 13 books—11 of which are children's books—including *On Sidesaddles to Heaven: The Women of the Rocky Mountain Mission* (Caxton Press, 1998). She has an M.A. in history and teaches history part-time.

LOIS GREEN CARR is an adjunct professor at the University of Maryland at College Park, and she is also associated with St. Mary's City Historic Commission. She is the author of *County Government in Maryland, 1689–1709* (Garland, 1987).

WILLIAM COHEN is a professor in the Department of History at Hope College in Holland, Michigan, where he has been teaching since 1971. He specializes in early American and nineteenth-century U.S. history, and he is particularly interested in the subject of race in American life. He is the author of *At Freedom's Edge: Black Mobility and the Southern White Quest for Racial Control, 1861–1915* (Louisiana State University Press, 1991).

AVERY CRAVEN is a noted historian who served as chairman of the history department at the University of Chicago. He is the author of *Repressible Conflict, 1830–1861* (AMS Press, 1989) and *Rachel of Old Louisiana* (Louisiana State University Press, 1995).

CARL N. DEGLER is the Margaret Byrne Professor Emeritus of American History at Stanford University in Stanford, California. He is a member of the editorial board for the Plantation Society as well as a member and former president of the American History Society and the Organization of American Historians. His book *Neither Black nor White: Slavery and Race Relations in Brazil and the United States* (University of Wisconsin Press, 1972) won the 1972 Pulitzer Prize for history. He is also the author of *In Search of Human Nature: The Decline and Revival of Darwinism in American Social Thought* (Oxford University Press, 1992).

JOHN MACK FARAGHER is the Arthur Unobskey Professor of American History at Yale University in New Haven, Connecticut. He is the editor of *The American Heritage Encyclopedia of American History* (Henry Holt, 1998) and the author of *Women and Men on the Overland Trail* (Yale University Press, 1980), which won the Frederick Jackson Turner Award of the Organization of American Historians.

ERIC FONER is the DeWitt Clinton Professor of History at Columbia University in New York City. He earned his B.A. and his Ph.D. from Columbia in 1963 and 1969, respectively, and he was elected president of the American Historical Association in 2000. His many publications include *A Short History of Reconstruction, 1863–1877* (Harper & Row, 1990) and *America's Reconstruction: People and Politics After the Civil War,* coauthored with Olivia Mahoney (HarperPerennial, 1995).

GARY W. GALLAGHER is a professor of American history at Pennsylvania State University in University Park, Pennsylvania. He earned his Ph.D. from the University of Texas at Austin in 1982, and he specializes in the U.S. Civil War and Reconstruction. He is the author of *Fighting for the Confederacy: The Personal Recollections of General Edward Porter Alexander* (University of North Carolina Press, 1989), which won the 1990 Douglas Southall Freeman Award, and the editor of *The Antietam Campaign* (University of North Carolina Press, 1999).

EUGENE D. GENOVESE, a prominent Marxist historian and Civil War scholar, is president of the Historical Society, a professional organization of historians, and a former president of the Organization of American Historians. His many publications include *A Consuming Fire: The Fall of the Confederacy in the Mind of the White Christian South* (University of Georgia Press, 1998) and *The Southern Front: History and Politics in the Cultural War* (University of Missouri Press, 1995).

NORMAN A. GRAEBNER is the Randolph P. Compton Professor Emeritus of History at the University of Virginia in Charlottesville, Virginia. He has held a number of other academic appointments and has received distinguished teacher awards at every campus at which he has taught. He has edited and written numerous books, articles, and texts on American history, including *Foundations of American Foreign Policy: A Realist Appraisal From Franklin to McKinley* (Scholarly Resources Press, 1985) and *Empire on the Pacific: A Study in American Continental Expansion,* 2d ed. (Regina Books, 1983).

VINCENT HARDING is a professor of religion and social transformation at the Iliff School of Theology and has long been involved in domestic and international movements for peace and justice. He is the author of *Hope and History: Why We Must Share the Story of the Movement* (Orbis Books, 1990) and coauthor, with Robin D. G. Kelley and Earl Lewis, of *We Changed the World: African Americans, 1945–1970* (Oxford University Press, 1997).

JAMES A. HENRETTA is a professor of history at the University of Maryland in College Park, Maryland. He received his M.A. and Ph.D. from Harvard University in 1963 and 1968, respectively. He is coauthor, with Jürgen Heideking, of *Republicans and Liberalism in America and the German States, 1750–1850* (Cambridge University Press, 2001).

MICHAEL F. HOLT is the Langbourne M. Williams Professor of American History at the University of Virginia in Charlottesville, Virginia. He has published a collection of his many journal articles in *Political Parties and American Political Development From the Age of Jackson to the Age of Lincoln* (Louisiana State University Press, 1992), and he is the author of *The Rise and Fall of the American Whig Party: Jacksonian Politics and the Onset of the Civil War* (Oxford University Press, 1999).

THOMAS HOLT is the James Westfall Thompson Professor of American and African American History at the University of Chicago in Chicago, Illinois. He has also taught at Howard University, Harvard University, and the University of Michigan. He earned his Ph.D. from Yale University in 1973, and he was president of the American Historical Association in 1994–1995. He is the author of the award-winning *Problem of Freedom: Race, Labor, and Politics in Jamaica and Britain, 1832–1938* (Johns Hopkins University Press, 1992).

JAMES T. LEMON was a professor of geography at the University of Toronto in Ontario, Canada, before his retirement. He has also been a professor of history at the University of California, Los Angeles, and his research interests include historical urban planning, colonial America, and American and Canadian culture. He is the author of *Liberal Dreams and Nature's Limits: Great Cities of North America Since 1600* (Oxford University Press, 1996).

DUMAS MALONE (1892–1986) was an American historian, an editor, and a professor of history at Columbia University. He also served as editor in chief of *The Dictionary of American Biography* and as managing editor of *Political Science Quarterly*. His many publications include *American and World Leadership, 1940–1965* (Appleton-Century-Crofts, 1965) and *Malone and Jefferson: The Biographer and the Sage* (University of Virginia Library, 1981).

JAMES M. McPHERSON is the Edwards Professor of American History at Princeton University in Princeton, New Jersey. His publications include *Abraham Lincoln and the Second American Revolution* (Oxford University Press, 1990) and *The Atlas of the Civil War* (Macmillan, 1994).

SANDRA L. MYRES (1933–1991), a specialist in western history and women's history, was a professor at the University of Texas at Arlington. She is the editor of *Ho for California! Women's Overland Diaries From the Huntington Library* (Huntington Library, 1980) and the author of *One Man, One Vote: Gerrymandering vs. Reapportionment* (Steck-Vaughn, 1970).

STEPHEN NISSENBAUM is a professor in the Department of History at the University of Massachusetts, Amherst. He earned his Ph.D. from the University of Wisconsin in 1968, and he has served as president of the Massachusetts Foundation for the Humanities and as historical adviser to a number of films. He is the author of *The Battle for Christmas* (Alfred A. Knopf, 1996).

ALAN T. NOLAN has been with the law firm of Ice Miller Donadio & Ryan in Indianapolis, Indiana, since 1948. He has also been chairman of the board of trustees of the Indiana Historical Society since 1986. He has written extensively on Civil War history, including the book *The Iron Brigade: A Military History*, 2d ed. (State Historical Society of Wisconsin, 1975), and he is coeditor, with Gary W. Gallagher, of *The Myth of the Lost Cause and Civil War History* (Indiana University Press, 2000).

MARY BETH NORTON is the Mary Donlon Alger Professor of American History at Cornell University. She is the author of *Founding Mothers and Fathers: Gendered Power and the Forming of American Society* (Alfred A. Knopf, 1996) and *Liberty's Daughters: The Revolutionary Experience of American Women, 1750–1800* (Cornell University Press, 1996).

ROBERT V. REMINI is a professor emeritus of history at the University of Illinois at Chicago. He won the D. B. Hardeman Prize for *Daniel Webster: The Man and His Time* (W. W. Norton, 1997), and he has written biographies on Andrew Jackson, Henry Clay, and Martin Van Buren.

JOHN P. ROCHE (1923–1993) was the Olin Distinguished Professor of American Civilization and Foreign Affairs at the Fletcher School of Law and Diplomacy in Medford, Massachusetts, and director of the Fletcher Media Institute. His many publications include *Shadow and Substance: Essays on the Theory and Structure of Politics* (Macmillan, 1964).

ROBERT ROYAL is vice president and the Olin Fellow in Religion and Society at the Ethics and Public Policy Center in Washington, D.C. He is the author of *The Catholic Martyrs of the Twentieth Century: A Comprehensive World History* (Crossroad, 2000) and *The Virgin and the Dynamo: Use and Abuse of Religion in Environmental Debates* (W. B. Eerdmans, 1999).

KIRKPATRICK SALE is a contributing editor to *The Nation* and the author of *Rebels Against the Future: The Luddites and Their War on the Industrial Revolution: Lessons for the Computer Age* (Perseus Press, 1996).

JOEL H. SILBEY is the President White Professor of History at Cornell University in Ithaca, New York. He has written several books and many important articles on the political parties during the Civil War. Among his publications are *The American Political Nation, 1838–1893* (Stanford University Press, 1991) and his edited book *Russian-American Dialogue on the History of U.S. Political Parties* (University of Missouri Press, 2000).

KENNETH M. STAMPP is the Morrison Professor Emeritus of History at the University of California, Berkeley. He has written numerous books on southern history, slavery, and the Civil War, including *And the War Came: The North and the Secession Crisis, 1860–1861* (Louisiana University Press, 1970) and *America in 1857: A Nation on the Brink* (Oxford University Press,

1990). He is also the general editor of *Records of Ante-Bellum Southern Plantations From the Revolution Through the Civil War* (University Publications of America, 1985).

ANTHONY F. C. WALLACE is an anthropologist whose published works include *King of the Delawares: Teedyuscung, 1700–1763* (Syracuse University Press, 1990) and *St. Clair: A Nineteenth-Century Coal Town's Experience With a Disaster-Prone Industry* (Cornell University Press, 1988).

LORENA S. WALSH is a fellow with the Colonial Williamsburg Foundation and the author of several key articles on seventeenth-century Maryland. She is the author of *From Calabar to Carter's Grove: The History of a Virginia Slave Community* (University Press of Virginia, 1997).

GORDON S. WOOD is the Alva O. Way University Professor at Brown University in Providence, Rhode Island, where he has been teaching since 1969. He has also taught at Harvard University, the University of Michigan, and Cambridge University. He received his M.A. and his Ph.D. from Harvard University in 1959 and 1964, respectively, and he is a member of the National Council of History Education's Board of Trustees. His publications include *Russian-American Dialogue on the American Revolution,* coedited with Louise G. Wood (University of Missouri Press, 1995).

ALFRED F. YOUNG was a professor at Northern Illinois University in De Kalb, Illinois, before retiring. He is the author of *Dissent: Explorations in the History of American Radicalism* (Northern Illinois University Press, 1992) and coeditor, with Lawrence W. Towner and Robert W. Karrow, of *Past Imperfect: Essays on History, Libraries, and the Humanities* (University of Chicago Press, 1993).

Index

abolitionists, controversy over, 208–229
Acuña, Rodolfo, on the Mexican War, 256–268
Adams, John, 131, 132, 142, 154, 185, 211, 220, 224, 258
Adams-Onis Treaty, 257
African Americans: colonization of, 170–171, 176, 178–179; Reconstruction and, 376–395. *See also* slavery
agriculture: of colonial Pennsylvania, 68–77, 78, 80, 82–83; Reconstruction and, 394–395; slavery and, 234–252; of the Taino people, 8
Alamo, 259–261
American Revolution, 93, 259; controversy over, as a conservative movement, 118–135; controversy over the Great Awakening and, 103, 104, 112
Anglican Church: American Revolution and, 118; controversy over the Great Awakening and, 93
Anthony, Susan B., 210
Antietam, Battle of, 331, 332
Appomattox, 339
Arawak people, 7
Arminianism, 95, 105, 106, 111, 112
Articles of Confederation, 141–142, 143, 144, 156
Austin, Moses, 257
Austin, Stephen, 257, 258, 259

Bartlett, Irving H., on the abolitionists, 218–229
Benson, Lee, 311, 312, 316
Berkeley, George, 92
Bill of Rights, 158
Birney, James, 215
Bonomi, Patricia U., on the Great Awakening, 92–102
Bowie, James, 260
Boyer, Paul, on the Salem witch trials, 46–54
Brearley Committee on Postponed Matters, 148
Britain, 127, 152, 153, 167
Bureau of Indian Affairs, 192
Butler, Jon, on the Great Awakening, 103–112

Cairnes, John Elliott, 236, 238, 243
Calhoun, John, 194, 197, 201, 276
Calvin, John, 105, 106
Calvinism, 92, 105–106, 111, 112
capitalism, controversy over American colonists and, 68–87
Carib people, 7; cannibalism of, 18, 19

Carlson, Laurie Winn, on the Salem witch trials, 55–64
carpetbaggers, 376, 379
Carr, Lois Green, on women in the colonial period, 26–33
Cass, Lewis, 199–200
Chancellorsville, Battle of, 331, 332
Cherokee Nation v. Georgia, 189
Cherokee people, 185, 189–191, 194, 200, 201
Chickasaw people, 188–189
childbirth, hazards of, in the colonial period, 29, 39–40
children, antislavery literature and, 212–214
Chittenden Compromise, 358
Choctaw people, 187–189, 200
citizenship, 150; property requirements for, 131–132
Civil Rights Act of 1866, 378
Civil Rights Bill of 1875, 392–393
Civil War: and controversy over Abraham Lincoln and slavery, 354–372; controversy over General Robert E. Lee and, 330–349; controversy over Reconstruction and, 376–395; controversy over slavery as the cause of, 310–325
class structure, 81, 99, 110, 130; in colonial Pennsylvania, 71–75; in post-Revolutionary society, 120–124, 133–134
Clay, Henry, 185, 221, 311
Coffee, John, 188–189, 199
Cohen, William, on Thomas Jefferson and slavery, 172–180
Coles, Edward, 167–169, 171
Colón, Christóbal. *See* Columbus
colonization, of African Americans, 170–171, 176, 178–179
Columbus, Christopher, controversy over, 4–21
Common Sense (Paine), 154
Confederacy. *See* Civil War
Confiscation Acts, 123
Congregational Church: disestablishment and, 124–125; and the Great Awakening, 93, 100, 109
Congress, Civil War and, 312–313
Connecticut Compromise, 147
conservatism, of the American Revolution, controversy over, 118–135
constitution: British, 152, 154; Rhodesian, 124; Vietnamese, 124; of Virginia, 131–132
Constitution, U.S.: controversy over the Founding Fathers and, 140–159; separation of church and state and, 118–120

Constitutional Convention, 140–159
Cornwallis, Charles, 172, 173
Crandall, Prudence, 224
Craven, Avery, on the abolitionists, 208–217
Creek people, 189
"Critical Period" thesis, 142
Crockett, Davey, 260

Danger of an Unconverted Ministry, The
    (Tennent), 101
Daniels, George H., 314, 316
Davenport, James, 101, 105
Davis, Jefferson, 332, 333, 345, 347, 349, 361
Declaration of Independence, American, 119,
    120, 122, 124, 220
Degler, Carl N., on the American Revolution,
    118–125
Democratic Party, 313–314, 320, 324–325, 360;
    anti-Reconstruction propaganda of,
    376–377
Dexter, Elisabeth Anthony, 36
disestablishment, 118–120, 124–125
divorce, 41, 295
Douglas, Stephen A., 357
Douglass, Frederick, 215, 323, 357, 369, 372
Dresser, Amos, 224
Du Bois, W. E. B., 367, 377, 387
Dutch Reformed Church, and the Great
    Awakening, 93

Early, Jubal A., 332–333
Eaton, John, 199–200
economic role of women: in the colonial period,
    28, 32, 34–35, 36–37, 38; in the West,
    282–303
economy: of colonial America, 75, 86;
    post-Revolutionary, 123–124;
    Reconstruction and, 379, 380, 391;
    slavery and, 234–252; and Washington,
    Booker T., 393
Edwards, Jonathan, 104, 105, 106, 107
electoral college, 148–149
emancipation. See slavery
Emancipation Proclamation, 354, 355, 356,
    360, 362, 369–371
encephalitis lethargica, and controversy over
    witchcraft in Salem, 56–57, 62–63
English Common Law, 294–296
enlightenment rationalism, 92
entail, 123, 133
entrepreneurs, frontier women as, 282–293
ergot poisoning, witchcraft in Salem and, 61
Eurocentrism, 5
executive branch, of government, 148

factionalism, in Salem, 52–54

family: African American, and Reconstruction,
    380; as an economic unit in colonial
    America, 84–87; frontier women and,
    282–303
Faragher, John Mack, on the westward
    movement and the roles of women,
    294–303
federalism, controversy over, at the
    Constitutional Convention, 140–159
Federalist, The (Madison), 144, 148, 157
feminism, 295–296
Fernandez de Oviedo, Gonzalo, 19
Fernández-Armesto, Felipe, 18, 19
Fifteenth Amendment, 356, 378, 379
Florida, 257
Foner, Eric, on Reconstruction, 376–385
Forsyth, John, 197
Founding Fathers, 121–122, 126; controversy
    over, as democratic reformers, 140–159;
    Native Americans and, 184
Fourteenth Amendment, 356, 378, 379
France, 176–177; revolution in, 122, 126, 129,
    175–176
Franklin, Benjamin, 107, 121, 151, 154, 257
Freedmen's Bureau, 378
Frelinghuysen, Theodore, 92, 185, 191,
    196–198
Frémont, John C., 354, 359
Fugitive Slave Law, 228
Fuson, Robert H., 15–16

Gallagher, Gary W., on General Robert E. Lee,
    340–349
Gardner, Henry, 226
Garrison, William Lloyd, 208–210, 219, 224,
    228
Genovese, Eugene D., on the profitability of
    slavery, 243–252
George III, England's king, 154
Georgia, 189–191, 194–195, 198
Gettysburg, Battle of, 331, 344, 345, 346
Giddings, Joshua R., 269
gold, Columbus's search for, 17, 18
Graebner, Norman A., on the Mexican War,
    269–277
Grant, Ulysses S., 262, 334, 335, 340, 343, 361
Great Awakening, 82; controversy over, 92–112
Guacanagarí, 12, 15, 16–17

Hamilton, Alexander, 144, 152, 153, 155–156
Hancock, John, 155
Harding, Vincent, on Abraham Lincoln and
    slavery, 364–372; reaction to the views of,
    355–356
Henretta, James A., on the motivations of
    American colonists, 78–87
Henry, Patrick, 141
Hispaniola, 17, 18, 19

Holt, Michael F., on the cause of the Civil War, 318–325
Holt, Thomas, on Reconstruction, 386–395; reaction to the views of, 381
housekeeping: and the role of women in the colonial period, 28, 32, 34–35, 36–37, 38, 40; and the role of women in the West, 282, 283–285, 297–299
Houston, Sam, 258, 260–261
Hunter, David, 354, 359
hysteria, mass, and witchcraft in Salem, 58–59

immigration, of colonial women, 26–33
imperialism, controversy over Christopher Columbus and, 4–21; controversy over the Mexican War and, 256–277
indentured servants, 71, 82, 134; women as, in seventeenth-century Maryland, 26–28
Indian Removal Act of 1830, 185–201
individualism, 69–77, 78–80
industrialization, 184; slavery and, 246–247
infant mortality, in colonial Maryland, 29
inheritance, of women: in seventeenth-century Maryland, 30–33; in the West, 289. See also entail; primogeniture

Jackson, Andrew: controversy over Indian removel policy of, 184–201; Texas War and, 256, 258, 261, 270
Jefferson, Thomas, 132, 141, 142, 257, 320; and controversy over slavery, 164–180; policy of, toward Native Americans, 184–185
Johnson, Andrew, 377–378
judiciary, Constitutional Convention and, 150

Kansas-Nebraska Act, 322, 324
Know-Nothings, 226, 322
Koning, Hans, 16
Ku Klux Klan, 228, 379

Las Casas, Bartolomé de, 14, 18
Lee, Robert E., controversy over, 330–349
Lemon, James T., on the motivations of American colonists, 68–77; reaction to the views of, 78–82
liberalism, in colonial Pennsylvania, 77
Lincoln, Abraham, 226, 340, 343, 376, 377–378; controversy over slavery and, 354–372
literature, antislavery, 212–214
Livingston, Robert R., Jr., 155
Log College, 96–97
Louisiana Territory, 176–177, 178
Lovejoy, Elijah, 220, 224, 225
Lundy, Benjamin, 209, 210

Madison, James, 143–145, 147–148, 153, 154–157, 158
Malone, Dumas, on Thomas Jefferson and slavery, 164–171
Manifest Destiny, 262–263
manufacturing, in colonial Pennsylvania, 76
marriage: and controversy over the role of colonial women, 26, 27–31, 37; and the roles of women in the West, 294–303
Married Women's Property Acts, 295
Marshall, John, 189–190, 201
Martin, Luther, 143, 144, 147
Maryland, the role of white women in seventeenth-century, 26–33
Mason, George, 149, 151
Mass Psychogenic Illness (MPI), witchcraft in Salem and, 59
Massachusetts, 48–49, 50–54
Mather, Cotton, 47, 49, 53, 54
McKenney, Thomas, 199–200
McPherson, James M., on Abraham Lincoln and slavery, 354–363
Memorable Providences Relating to Witchcrafts and Possessions (Mather), 53
Mennonites, 74, 77
Mercer, Charles F., 170, 171
Mexican War, controversy over, 256–277
migration, westward, in colonial America, 77, 81–82
misogyny, witchcraft in Salem and, 58
Missouri, 177, 178
monarchy, 154
Monroe Doctrine, 263
Morris, Gouverneur, 147, 151, 152, 153–154, 155–156
mortality, in colonial Maryland, 26, 27, 29–31
Myres, Sandra L., on the westward movement and the roles of women, 282–293

Napoleon (Bonaparte), 176–177
Native Americans, 35; controversy over Andrew Jackson's policy toward, 184–201; controversy over Christopher Columbus and, 4–21
New Jersey plan, 145–146
Nissenbaum, Stephen, on the Salem witch trials, 46–54
Nolan, Alan T., on General Robert E. Lee, 330–339; reaction to the views of, 341–342
Norton, Mary Beth, on women in the colonial period, 34–41
Notes on Virginia (Jefferson), 164, 165
nullification, doctrine of, 194, 197, 201

oral culture, in the colonial period, 35–36

Paine, Thomas, 154, 156, 157, 158
Parris, Samuel, 47, 50, 51, 52–53
Penn, William, 74
Pennsylvania, 68–77, 106–107
Peters, Thomas, 155, 156
Phillips, Wendell, 218–229
pietism, 92, 106, 111, 112
Pinckney, Charles, 146, 150
politics: abolitionists and, 225, 226, 227;
    antebellum, 310–325; Reconstruction and,
    380–395
Polk, James K., 261–262, 263, 265–266, 268,
    269–275
poverty: as a cause of revolution, 127; in
    colonial Pennsylvania, 71
Presbyterian Church, and the Great Awakening,
    93–112
primogeniture, 123, 133
prostitution, frontier women and, 288
psychoanalysis, witchcraft in Salem and, 59–61
Puritans, Salem witch trials and, 46–64
Putnam, Thomas, Jr., 50, 51

Quakers, 73–74, 77, 187, 210

radicalism, of the American Revolution,
    controversy over, 126–135, 140
Randolph, Edmund, 147, 150
Randolph Plan, 143, 150
Reconstruction, controversy over, 376–395
religion: antislavery movement and, 219–220,
    223; in colonial Pennsylvania, 73–74, 79;
    frontier women and, 286–288; Great
    Awakening and, 92–112; Native
    Americans and, 5, 12, 21, 197–198;
    separation of church and state and,
    118–120, 124–125
Remini, Robert V., on Andrew Jackson's Indian
    removal policy, 184–193
Republican Party, 358, 361; African Americans
    and, 381–395; Reconstruction and,
    376–379, 386–395; rise of, 313–314,
    318–325
revival, religious, and controversy over the
    Great Awakening, 92–112
Rhodesia, constitution of, 124
Roche, John P., on the Founding Fathers,
    140–151
Roosevelt, Theodore, 223
Rowland, John, 97
Royal, Robert, on Christopher Columbus,
    13–21

Sale, Kirkpatrick, on Christopher Columbus,
    4–12, 20

Salem witch trials, controversy over
    socioeconomic tensions as the cause of,
    46–64
Salem Witchcraft Papers, The (Boyer and
    Nissenbaum), 56
San Salvador, 5–6
Santa Anna, Antonio López de, 259–261, 265,
    275
Sauer, Carl, 8, 10
scalawags, 376, 379
Second Awakening, 286–287
Second Bull Run Campaign, 331, 332
sectionalism, controversy over, as the cause of
    the Civil War, 310–325
self-emancipation, of slaves, 354–356, 359,
    362, 366–368
Seminole people, 189
separation of church and state, American
    Revolution and, 118–120, 124–125
Seven Days Campaign, 331, 337, 342–343,
    346, 348, 360
Seward, William H., 358
sex ratio, in the colonial period, 26, 27, 28, 31,
    36–37
sex roles, in the colonial period, 38; of slaves,
    39
Shays, Daniel, 155–156
Sherman, William Tecumseh, 340, 361
Silbey, Joel H., on the cause of the Civil War,
    310–317
Slave Power, 323–324
slavery, 39, 82; American Revolution and, 120,
    129, 132, 134; Christopher Columbus and,
    7, 11, 17, 18; in the colonial period, 39;
    controversy over abolitionists and,
    208–229; controversy over Abraham
    Lincoln and, 354–372; controversy over,
    as the cause of the Civil War, 310–325;
    controversy over, and the Constitutional
    Convention, 149, 155, 156; controversy
    over profitability of, 234–252; controversy
    over Thomas Jefferson and, 164–180;
    Robert E. Lee and, 349; Reconstruction
    and, 376, 380
Slidell, John, 262, 273, 274, 275
social class. See class structure
social dependency, of women, and controversy
    over the roles of women in the West,
    294–303
social movement, American Revolution as,
    126–135
socioeconomic tensions, and controversy over
    witchcraft in Salem, 46–64
South Carolina, 381, 386–395
Spain, Christopher Columbus and, 4–6, 7, 14,
    15, 19
Stampp, Kenneth M., on the profitability of
    slavery, 234–242
states' rights, controversy over, at the
    Constitutional Convention, 140–159
statistics, historians and the use of, 316
Stevens, Thaddeus, 378

subsistence farming, in colonial Pennsylvania, 68–77, 78, 83
suffrage, 153–154; African American, 378, 380, 381, 383–384; women's, 210
Sumner, Charles, 224, 225, 343, 378

Virginia Plan, 143, 144–147
Von Economo, Constantin, 62–63, 64
voting behavior: of African Americans during Reconstruction, 389–390; antebellum, 312–314, 320

Taino people, and controversy over Christopher Columbus, 7–10, 12, 15–17, 19
Taviani, Paolo Emilio, 14–15
Taylor, Zachary, 262, 269, 275, 276
teachers, women as, in the West, 285–286
technology, slavery and, 246–247, 249–252
Tennent, Charles, 95, 97
Tennent, Gilbert, 95, 96, 97–98, 100
Tennent, William, Sr., 95–97
Texas, 310–311; and controversy over the Mexican War, 256–277
Thirteenth Amendment, 354, 356, 363
Three-Fifths Compromise, 149
Tocqueville, Alexis de, 384
Toland, John, 132
trade, in colonial Pennsylvania, 70, 75–76
"Trail of Tears," 187, 199
Treaty of Dancing Rabbit Creek, 187–188
Treaty of Guadalupe Hidalgo, 265–267, 268
Turner, Frederick Jackson, 80, 81, 282–283
two-party system, 319–321

Wallace, Anthony F. C., on Andrew Jackson's Indian removal policy, 194–201
Walsh, Lorena S., on women in the colonial period, 26–33
Washington, George, 142, 148, 175, 184, 344, 345, 347
Watt, David, 8
Webster, Daniel, 218, 221, 222, 321
Weld, Theodore, 210–211, 216
Westminster Confession, 95
westward movement, and controversy over the roles of women, 282–303
Whig party, 318–319, 320, 324–325, 379
Whiskey Rebellion, 156
Whitefield, George, 93, 97, 98, 100–101, 105, 106, 107, 112
Wilson, James, 147, 153, 155–156
witchcraft, Salem witch trials and, 46–64
women, 129; African American, and Reconstruction, 380; controversy over the role of, in the colonial period, 26–41; controversy over the roles of, in the West, 282–303; Salem witch trials and, 46–64; suffrage and, 210
Wood, Gordon S., on the American Revolution, 126–135
Worcester v. Georgia, 189, 191

Uncle Tom's Cabin (Stowe), 213, 214

Vietnam, constitution of, 124
violence, Christopher Columbus and, 12, 13, 19–20
Virginia: constitution of, 131–132; Robert E. Lee and, 330–349; slavery in, 164–169, 170, 171, 172–176, 179–180

Yates, Abraham, 154–155, 156, 158
Young, Alfred F., on the Founding Fathers, 152–159